Social
and Political
Philosophy

Social
and Political
Philosophy

*Classic and
Contemporary
Readings*

Edited by

Andrea Veltman

OXFORD
UNIVERSITY PRESS

OXFORD
UNIVERSITY PRESS

8 Sampson Mews, Suite 204, Don Mills, Ontario M3C 0H5
www.oupcanada.com

Oxford University Press is a department of the University of Oxford.
It furthers the University's objective of excellence in research, scholarship,
and education by publishing worldwide in

Oxford New York

Auckland   Cape Town   Dar es Salaam   Hong Kong   Karachi
Kuala Lumpur   Madrid   Melbourne   Mexico City   Nairobi
New Delhi   Shanghai   Taipei   Toronto
With offices in
Argentina   Austria   Brazil   Chile   Czech Republic   France   Greece
Guatemala   Hungary   Italy   Japan   Poland   Portugal   Singapore
South Korea   Switzerland   Thailand   Turkey   Ukraine   Vietnam

Oxford is a trade mark of Oxford University Press
in the UK and in certain other countries

Published in Canada
by Oxford University Press

Copyright © Oxford University Press Canada 2008

The moral rights of the author have been asserted

Database right Oxford University Press (maker)

First published 2008

Library and Archives Canada Cataloguing in Publication

Social and political philosophy : classic and contemporary readings /
edited by Andrea Veltman.

Includes bibliographical references and index.
ISBN 978-0-19-542429-4

1. Sociology—Philosophy. 2. Political science—Philosophy. 3. Multiculturalism—
Philosophy. 4. Feminist theory. I. Veltman, Andrea II. Title.

JA71.S612 2008   301.01   C2007-905967-8

Cover image: James Endicott/Veer

5 6 7– 15 14 13

This book is printed on permanent (acid-free) paper ∞.

Printed in the United States

Contents

IV. Twentieth-Century Philosophers

Preface

Social and political institutions are not elements in an unchangeable natural order but variable human constructions subject to critical scrutiny and normative evaluation. The development of principles for assessing, justifying, or changing social and political orders is the central task of social and political philosophy. Political philosophy encompasses such issues as the justification of the state, the legitimate limits of the coercive force of the state (or, conversely, the proper scope of individual liberty), the foundation of political communities, the best forms of government, and the nature of civic obligation. Social philosophers examine social ideals like justice, utility, liberty, and equality, as well as distributions of social goods like wealth, power, and opportunity. The disciplines of social and political philosophy overlap extensively and, for this reason, are often discussed and studied in tandem.

This collection brings together classical and contemporary readings in social and political philosophy with an emphasis on multicultural and feminist perspectives in the contemporary era. The initial chapters include substantial excerpts from canonical texts in the classical and modern periods of Western philosophy; the latter include representative selections from nineteenth- and twentieth-century social and political thought. Contemporary social and political philosophy is a burgeoning field, and the multiplicity of new themes and directions is difficult to capture in an anthology like this one. The contemporary selections included here represent several influential perspectives in twentieth-century social and political thought, including not only Arendtian, Habermasian, and Rawlsian political thought but also libertarianism, egalitarianism, feminism, communitarianism, and liberalism. The post-Rawlsian theorists carry forward several classical themes (such as rights, liberties, justice, and democracy) in addition to introducing a range of new themes, including gender and race, political violence and terrorism, multiculturalism and social identity, justice within the family, and the accommodation of cultural and religious differences in liberal democratic societies.

I would like to thank my editors at Oxford University Press Canada—Lisa Meschino, Roberta Osborne, Rachael Cayley, and Jennifer Charlton—for their continued support and advice throughout my work on this collection. Special thanks also to Oxford associates Janna Green and Raquel Goldberg for their fine work in handling permissions correspondence. I am grateful to John Hospers, Carole Pateman, Charles Mills, Michael Walzer, Charles Taylor, and Will Kymlicka for granting permission to reprint their work; I am particularly grateful to Charles Mills for editing an excerpt of *The Racial Contract* for this collection. I would also like to thank many of my colleagues in the profession for helpful advice regarding selections and translations, and many of my students at James Madison University and York University for their sustained dialogues with me on issues in social and political philosophy. I dedicate this collection to my students, past and future, whose engagement with philosophy constitutes one of my most valuable intellectual collaborations.

PART I

Ancient Greek Philosophers

Plato

A student of Socrates and a teacher of Aristotle, Plato (428–347 BC) was the first philosopher to write systematically on philosophical subjects ranging from metaphysics and epistemology to ethics and social and political philosophy. Born of an aristocratic family in the Greek city-state Athens, he received the finest education available for Athenian youth, and from a young age felt himself destined for political participation and leadership. But Plato witnessed the rise and fall of Athenian political regimes, became disillusioned with politics, and left Athens in his twenties to travel to Egypt, Greece, Italy, and Sicily. After studying abroad for over a decade, he returned to Athens and founded the Academy, an institution of higher education that lasted for over 900 years. He wrote over 25 dialogues, among which are the *Republic*, the *Symposium*, the *Theaetetus*, and the *Laws*.

Socrates (470–399 BC) did not write dialogues or treatises himself, for he aimed not to preach any positive doctrine but to search for wisdom through ongoing questioning and reflection. He lived under the democratic rule of Pericles in Athens and spent much of his time in the *agora* or marketplace, conversing with ordinary citizens, rhetoricians, and public men about the nature of virtue and the good life. Socrates saw himself as an intellectual gadfly whose divine mission was to prod others into reflecting on unexamined beliefs. His public philosophical scrutiny of prominent Athenian citizens made him enemies in high places, and in 399 BC three Athenian citizens—Meletus, Anytus, and Lycon—brought charges of impiety against him. Socrates was convicted of corrupting the youth and disbelieving in the gods of the state and was executed by the state of Athens.

The trial, imprisonment, and execution of Socrates are chronicled in a trilogy of dialogues, the *Apology*, the *Crito,* and the *Phaedo*. The *Crito* is the penultimate dialogue in this series. When the dialogue opens, Socrates' friend Crito has come to visit to him while he awaits execution in jail. Nearly a month elapsed between the time of Socrates' trial and his execution, owing to an Athenian custom that allowed no political executions while state vessels sailed on pilgrimage. When Crito comes bearing news that the return of the ship is imminent, he urges Socrates to take a final opportunity to escape and flee to a neighbouring Greek island. Socrates' jailors can be bribed for a moderate amount of money, and Crito and other of Socrates' friends have brought a sufficient sum.

Socrates' opportunity to escape from prison provides occasion for a discussion of civil disobedience: Should citizens disobey unjust laws or unjust applications of the law? Socrates considers himself innocent of the charges of corrupting the youth and disbelieving in the gods of the state (see *Apology* 24b–28b), but he nevertheless defends an obligation to obey the law, noting that the state is like a benefactor and a parent to its citizens. At 51c–53d, he also suggests that a social contract generates an obligation to obey the law: living in a city as an adult, while having opportunity to leave if one pleases, creates an implicit agreement on the part of a citizen to obey the laws of a city. If Socrates were to flee Athens upon his nearing execution after living agreeably in the city for 70 years, he would effectively break his agreement with the city and attempting to undermine its laws. Rather than depart shamefully and return a wrong for a wrong, Socrates chooses to stay in prison and be executed by the city he loves.

Whereas the *Crito* is an early Socratic dialogue in which Plato represents the views of the historical Socrates, the *Republic* is a later Platonic dialogue in which Plato uses Socrates as a mouthpiece in developing his own views. The *Republic* is among the finest, longest, and most widely read of all the Platonic dialogues. Its primary subject matter is the nature of justice and the structure of an ideal city, but it also sets out Plato's mature views on knowledge, belief, ultimate reality, art, education, and the social roles of men and women. Our selection of the *Republic* opens with Book II, after Socrates has flustered the sophist Thrasymachus, who argues that injustice is generally more profitable for an individual than justice. At the beginning of Book II, Plato's brothers Glaucon and Adeimantus restate Thrasymachus' charge that justice is 'another's good' and challenge Socrates to show that justice always pays.

Crito

SOCRATES. Why have you come at this hour, Crito? It's still very early, isn't it?   43a
CRITO. Yes, very.
SOCRATES. About what time?
CRITO. Just before daybreak.
SOCRATES. I'm surprised the prison-warder was willing to answer the door.
CRITO. He knows me by now, Socrates, because I come and go here so often; and besides, I've done him a small favour.
SOCRATES. Have you just arrived, or have you been here for a while?

CRITO. For quite a while.

b   SOCRATES. Then why didn't you wake me up right away instead of sitting by me in silence?

CRITO. Well *of course* I didn't wake you, Socrates! I only wish I weren't so sleepless and wretched myself. I've been marvelling all this time as I saw how peacefully you were sleeping, and I deliberately kept from waking you, so that you could pass the time as peacefully as possible. I've often admired your disposition in the past, in fact all your life; but more than ever in your present plight, you bear it so easily and patiently.

SOCRATES. Well, Crito, it really would be tiresome for a man of my age to get upset if the time has come when he must end his life.

c. CRITO. And yet others of your age, Socrates, are overtaken by similar troubles, but their age brings them no relief from being upset at the fate which faces them.

SOCRATES. That's true. But tell me, why *have* you come so early?

CRITO. I bring painful news, Socrates—not painful for you, I suppose, but painful and hard for me and all your friends—and hardest of all for me to bear, I think.

SOCRATES. What news is that? Is it that the ship has come back from Delos, the one on

d   whose return I must die?

CRITO. Well no, it hasn't arrived yet, but I think it will get here today, judging from reports of people who've come from Sunium, where they disembarked. That makes it obvious that it will get here today; and so tomorrow, Socrates, you will have to end your life.

SOCRATES. Well, may that be for the best, Crito. If it so please the gods, so be it. All the same, I don't think it will get here today.

44a CRITO. What makes you think that?

SOCRATES. I'll tell you. You see, I am to die on the day after the ship arrives, am I not?

CRITO. At least that's what the authorities say.

SOCRATES. Then I don't think it will get here on the day that is just dawning, but on the next one. I infer that from a certain dream I had in the night—a short time ago, so it may be just as well that you didn't wake me.

CRITO. And what was your dream?

SOCRATES. I dreamt that a lovely, handsome woman approached me, robed in white. She

b   called me and said: 'Socrates,

Thou shalt reach fertile Phthia upon the third day.'

CRITO. What a curious dream, Socrates.

SOCRATES. Yet its meaning is clear, I think, Crito.

CRITO. All too clear, it would seem. But please, Socrates, my dear friend, there is still time to take my advice, and make your escape—because if you die, I shall suffer more than one misfortune: not only shall I lose such a friend as I'll never find again, but it will look to many people, who hardly know you or me, as if I'd abandoned you—since I could have rescued you if I'd been willing to put up the money. And yet what could be   c more shameful than a reputation for valuing money more highly than friends? Most people won't believe that it was you who refused to leave this place yourself, despite our urging you to do so.

SOCRATES. But why should we care so much, my good Crito, about what most people believe? All the most capable people, whom we should take more seriously, will think the matter has been handled exactly as it has been.

CRITO. Yet surely, Socrates, you can see that one must heed popular opinion too. Your   d present plight shows by itself that the populace can inflict not the least of evils, but just about the worst, if someone has been slandered in their presence.

SOCRATES. Ah Crito, if only the populace *could* inflict the worst of evils! Then they would also be capable of providing the greatest of goods, and a fine thing that would be. But the fact is that they can do neither: they are unable to give anyone understanding or lack of it, no matter what they do.

CRITO. Well, if you say so. But tell me this, Socrates: can it be that you are worried for   e me and your other friends, in case the blackmailers give us trouble, if you escape, for having smuggled you out of here? Are you worried that we might be forced to forfeit all our property as well, or pay heavy fines, or even incur some further penalty? If you're afraid of anything like that, put it out of your mind. In rescuing you we are surely justified   45a in taking that risk, or even worse if need be. Come on, listen to me and do as I say.

SOCRATES. Yes, those risks do worry me, Crito—amongst many others.

CRITO. Then put those fears aside—because no great sum is needed to pay people who are willing to rescue you and get you out of here. Besides, you can surely see that those blackmailers are cheap, and it wouldn't take much to buy them off. My own means are   b available to you and would be ample, I'm sure. Then again, even if—out of concern on my behalf—you think you shouldn't be spending my money, there are visitors here who are ready to spend theirs. One of them, Simmias from Thebes, has actually brought enough money for this very purpose, while Cebes and quite a number of others are also prepared to contribute. So, as I say, you shouldn't hesitate to save yourself on account of those fears.

And don't let it trouble you, as you were saying in court, that you wouldn't know what

c	to do with yourself if you went into exile. There will be people to welcome you anywhere else you may go: if you want to go to Thessaly, I have friends there who will make much of you and give you safe refuge, so that no one from anywhere in Thessaly will trouble you.

Next, Socrates, I don't think that what you propose—giving yourself up, when you could be rescued—is even just. You are actually hastening to bring upon yourself just the sorts of thing which your enemies would hasten to bring upon you—indeed, they have done so—in their wish to destroy you.

What's more, I think you're betraying those sons of yours. You will be deserting them,

d	if you go off when you could be raising and educating them: as far as you're concerned, they will fare as best they may. In all likelihood, they'll meet the sort of fate which usually befalls orphans once they've lost their parents. Surely, one should either not have children at all, or else see the toil and trouble of their upbringing and education through to the end; yet you seem to me to prefer the easiest path. One should rather choose the path that a good and resolute man would choose, particularly if one professes to cultivate

e	goodness all one's life. Frankly, I'm ashamed for you and for us, your friends: it may appear that this whole predicament of yours has been handled with a certain feebleness on our part. What with the bringing of your case to court when that could have been avoided, the actual conduct of the trial, and now, to crown it all, this absurd outcome of the business, it may seem that the problem has eluded us through some fault or

46a	feebleness on our part—in that we failed to save you, and you failed to save yourself, when that was quite possible and feasible, if we had been any use at all.

Make sure, Socrates, that all this doesn't turn out badly, and a disgrace to you as well as us. Come now, form a plan—or rather, don't even plan, because the time for that is past, and only a single plan remains. Everything needs to be carried out during the coming night; and if we go on waiting around, it won't be possible or feasible any longer. Come on, Socrates, do all you can to take my advice, and do exactly what I say.

b	SOCRATES. My dear Crito, your zeal will be invaluable if it should have right on its side; but otherwise, the greater it is, the harder it makes matters. We must therefore consider whether or not the course you urge should be followed—because it is in my nature, not just now for the first time but always, to follow nothing within me but the principle which appears to me, upon reflection, to be best.

I cannot now reject the very principles that I previously adopted, just because this fate has overtaken me; rather, they appear to me much the same as ever, and I respect and

adult status, and has observed the conduct of city business and ourselves, the Laws, may—if he is dissatisfied with us—go wherever he pleases and take his property. Not one of us Laws hinders or forbids that: whether any of you wishes to emigrate to a colony, or to go and live as an alien elsewhere, he may go wherever he pleases and keep his property, e if we and the city fail to satisfy him.

'We do say, however, that if any of you remains here after he has observed the system by which we dispense justice and otherwise manage our city, then he has agreed with us by his conduct to obey whatever orders we give him. And thus we claim that anyone who fails to obey is guilty on three counts: he disobeys us as his parents; he disobeys those who nurtured him; and after agreeing to obey us he neither obeys nor persuades us if we are doing anything amiss, even though we offer him a choice, and do not harshly insist that he must do whatever we command. Instead, we give him two options: he must 52a either persuade us or else do as we say; yet he does neither. Those are the charges, Socrates, to which we say you too will be liable if you carry out your intention; and among Athenians, you will be not the least liable, but one of the most.'

And if I were to say, 'How so?' perhaps they could fairly reproach me, observing that I am actually among those Athenians who have made that agreement with them most emphatically.

'Socrates,' they would say, 'we have every indication that you were content with us, b as well as with our city, because you would never have stayed home here, more than is normal for all other Athenians, unless you were abnormally content. You never left our city for a festival—except once to go to the Isthmus—nor did you go elsewhere for other purposes, apart from military service. You never travelled abroad, as other people do; nor were you eager for acquaintance with a different city or different laws: we and our city sufficed for you. Thus, you emphatically opted for us, and agreed to be a citizen on our c terms. In particular, you fathered children in our city, which would suggest that you were content with it.

'Moreover, during your actual trial it was open to you, had you wished, to propose exile as your penalty; thus, what you are now attempting to do without the city's consent, you could then have done with it. On that occasion, you kept priding yourself that it would not trouble you if you had to die: you would choose death ahead of exile, so you said. Yet now you dishonour those words, and show no regard for us, the Laws, in your effort to destroy us. You are acting as the meanest slave would act, by trying to run away d in spite of those compacts and agreements you made with us, whereby you agreed to be a citizen on our terms.

'First, then, answer us this question: Are we right in claiming that you agreed, by your conduct if not verbally, that you would be a citizen on our terms? Or is that untrue?'

What shall we say in reply to that, Crito? Mustn't we agree?

CRITO. We must, Socrates.

SOCRATES. 'Then what does your action amount to,' they would say, 'except breaking the
e   compacts and agreements you made with us? By your own admission, you were not coerced or tricked into making them, or forced to reach a decision in a short time: you had 70 years in which it was open to you to leave if you were not happy with us, or if you thought those agreements unfair. Yet you preferred neither Lacedaemon nor Crete—
53a places you often say are well governed—nor any other Greek or foreign city: in fact, you went abroad less often than the lame and the blind or other cripples. Obviously, then, amongst Athenians you were exceptionally content with our city and with us, its Laws— because who would care for a city apart from its laws? Won't you, then, abide by your agreements now? Yes you will, if you listen to us, Socrates; and then at least you won't make yourself an object of derision by leaving the city.

'Just consider: if you break those agreements, and commit any of those offences, what
b   good will you do yourself or those friends of yours? Your friends, pretty obviously, will risk being exiled themselves, as well as being disenfranchised or losing their property. As for you, first of all, if you go to one of the nearest cities, Thebes or Megara—they are both well governed—you will arrive as an enemy of their political systems, Socrates: all who are concerned for their own cities will look askance at you, regarding you as a subverter of laws. You will also confirm your jurors in their judgment, making them think they
c   decided your case correctly: any subverter of laws, presumably, might well be thought to be a corrupter of young, unthinking people.

'Will you, then, avoid the best-governed cities and the most respectable of men? And if so, will your life be worth living? Or will you associate with those people, and be shameless enough to converse with them? And what will you say to them, Socrates? The things you used to say here, that goodness and justice are most precious to mankind, along with institutions and laws? Don't you think that the predicament of Socrates will
d   cut an ugly figure? Surely you must.

'Or will you take leave of those spots, and go to stay with those friends of Crito's up in Thessaly? That, of course, is a region of the utmost disorder and licence; so perhaps they would enjoy hearing from you about your comical escape from gaol, when you dressed up in some outfit, wore a leather jerkin or some other runaway's garb, and altered your appearance. Will no one observe that you, an old man with probably only a short

time left to live, had the nerve to cling so greedily to life by violating the most important e
laws? Perhaps not, so long as you don't trouble anyone. Otherwise, Socrates, you will hear
a great deal to your own discredit. You will live as every person's toady and lackey; and
what will you be doing—apart from living it up in Thessaly, as if you had travelled all the
way to Thessaly to have dinner? As for those principles of yours about justice and 54a
goodness in general—tell us, where will they be then?

'Well then, is it for your children's sake that you wish to live, in order to bring them
up and give them an education? How so? Will you bring them up and educate them by
taking them off to Thessaly and making foreigners of them, so that they may gain that
advantage too? Or if, instead of that, they are brought up here, will they be better brought
up and educated just because you are alive, if you are not with them? Yes, you may say,
because those friends of yours will take care of them. Then will they take care of them if
you travel to Thessaly, but not take care of them if you travel to Hades? Surely if those
professing to be your friends are of any use at all, you must believe that they will. b

'No, Socrates, listen to us, your own nurturers: do not place a higher value upon
children, upon life, or upon anything else, than upon what is just, so that when you
leave for Hades, this may be your whole defence before the authorities there: to take that
course seems neither better nor more just or holy, for you or for any of your friends here
in this world. Nor will it be better for you when you reach the next. As things stand, you
will leave this world (if you do) as one who has been treated unjustly not by us Laws, c
but by human beings; whereas if you go into exile, thereby shamefully returning injustice
for injustice and ill-treatment for ill-treatment, breaking the agreements and compacts
you made with us, and inflicting harm upon the people you should least harm—yourself,
your friends, your fatherland, and ourselves—then we shall be angry with you in your
lifetime; and our brother Laws in Hades will not receive you kindly there, knowing that
you tried, to the best of your ability, to destroy us too. Come then, do not let Crito d
persuade you to take his advice rather than ours.'

That, Crito, my dear comrade, is what I seem to hear them saying, I do assure you. I
am like the Corybantic revellers who think they are still hearing the music of pipes: the
sound of those arguments is ringing loudly in my head, and makes me unable to hear the
others. As far as these present thoughts of mine go, then, you may be sure that if you object
to them, you will plead in vain. Nonetheless, if you think you will do any good, speak up.

CRITO. No, Socrates, I've nothing to say.

SOCRATES. Then let it be, Crito, and let us act accordingly, because that is the direction e
in which God is guiding us.

Republic

Book II (357–360d)

I thought that, with these words, I was quit of the discussion; but it seems this was only a prelude. Glaucon, undaunted as ever, was not content to let Thrasymachus abandon the field.

Socrates, he broke out, you have made a show of proving that justice is better than injustice in every way. Is that enough, or do you want us to be really convinced?

Certainly I do, if it rests with me.

Then you are not going the right way about it. I want to know how you classify the things we call good. Are there not some which we should wish to have, not for their consequences, but just for their own sake, such as harmless pleasures and enjoyments that have no further result beyond the satisfaction of the moment?

Yes, I think there are good things of that description.

And also some that we value both for their own sake and for their consequences—things like knowledge and health and the use of our eyes?

Yes.

And a third class which would include physical training, medical treatment, earning one's bread as a doctor or otherwise—useful, but burdensome things, which we want only for the sake of the profit or other benefit they bring.

Yes, there is that third class. What then?

In which class do you place justice?

I should say, in the highest, as a thing which anyone who is to gain happiness must value both for itself and for its results.

Well, that is not the common opinion. Most people would say it was one of those things, tiresome and disagreeable in themselves, which we cannot avoid practising for the sake of reward or a good reputation.

I know, said I; that is why Thrasymachus has been finding fault with it all this time and praising injustice. But I seem to be slow in seeing his point.

Listen to me, then, and see if you agree with mine. There was no need, I think, for Thrasymachus to yield so readily, like a snake you had charmed into submission; and nothing so far said about justice and injustice has been established to my satisfaction. I want to be told what each of them really is, and what effect each has, in itself, on the soul that harbours it, when all rewards and consequences are left out of account. So here is my plan, if you approve. I shall revive Thrasymachus' theory. First, I will state what is commonly held about the nature of justice and its origin; secondly, I shall maintain that it is always practised with reluctance, not as good in itself, but as a thing one cannot do without; and thirdly, that this reluctance is reasonable, because the life of injustice is much the better life of the two—so people say. That is not what I think myself, Socrates; only I am bewildered by all that Thrasymachus and ever so many others have dinned into my ears; and I have never yet heard the case for justice stated as I wish to hear it. You, I believe, if anyone, can tell me what is to be said in praise of justice in and for itself; that is what I want. Accordingly, I shall set you an example by glorifying the life of injustice with all the energy that I hope you will show later in denouncing it and exalting justice in its stead. Will that plan suit you?

Nothing could be better, I replied. Of all subjects this is one on which a sensible man must always be glad to exchange ideas.

Good, said Glaucon. Listen then, and I will begin with my first point: the nature and origin of justice.

What people say is that to do wrong is, in itself, a desirable thing; on the other hand, it is not at all desirable to suffer wrong, and the harm to the sufferer outweighs the advantage to the doer. Consequently, when men have had a taste of both, those who have not the power to seize the advantage and escape the harm decide that they would be better off if they made a compact neither to do wrong nor to suffer it. Hence they began to make laws and covenants with one another; and whatever the law prescribed they called lawful and right. That is what right or justice is and how it came into existence; it stands half-way between the best thing of all—to do wrong with impunity —and the worst, which is to suffer wrong without the power to retaliate. So justice is accepted as a compromise, and valued, not as good in itself, but for lack of power to do wrong; no man worthy of the name, who had that power, would ever enter into such a compact with anyone; he would be mad if he did. That, Socrates, is the nature of justice according to this account, and such the circumstances in which it arose.

The next point is that men practise it against the grain, for lack of power to do wrong. How true that is, we shall best see if we imagine two men, one just, the other unjust, given full licence to do whatever they like, and then follow them to observe where each will be led by his desires. We shall catch the just man taking the same road as the unjust; he will be moved by self-interest, the end which it is natural to every creature to pursue as good, until forcibly turned aside by law and custom to respect the principle of equality.

Now, the easiest way to give them that complete liberty of action would be to imagine them possessed of the talisman found by Gyges, the ancestor of the famous Lydian. The story tells how he was a shepherd in the King's service. One day there was a great storm, and the ground where his flock was feeding was rent by an earthquake. Astonished at the sight, he went down into the chasm and saw, among other wonders of which the story tells, a brazen horse, hollow, with windows in its sides. Peering in, he saw a dead body, which seemed to be of more than human size. It was naked save for a gold ring, which he took from the finger and made his way out. When the shepherds met, as they did every month, to send an account to the King of the state of his flocks, Gyges came wearing the ring. As he was sitting with the others, he happened to turn the bezel of the ring inside his hand. At once he became invisible, and his companions, to his surprise, began to speak of him as if he had left them. Then, as he was fingering the ring, he turned the bezel outwards and became visible again. With that, he set about testing the ring to see if it really had this power, and always with the same result: according as he turned the bezel inside or out he vanished and reappeared. After this discovery he contrived to be one of the messengers sent to the court. There he seduced the Queen, and with her help murdered the King and seized the throne.

Now suppose there were two such magic rings, and one were given to the just man, the other to the unjust. No one, it is commonly believed, would have such iron strength of mind as to stand fast in doing right or keep his hands off other men's goods, when he could go to the marketplace and fearlessly help himself to anything he wanted, enter houses and sleep with any woman he chose, set prisoners free and kill men at his pleasure, and in a word go about among men with the powers of a god. He would behave no better than the other; both would take the same course. Surely this would be strong proof that men do right only under compulsion; no individual thinks of it as good for him personally, since he does wrong whenever he finds he has the power. Every man believes that wrongdoing pays him personally much better, and, according to this theory, that is the truth. Granted full licence to do as he liked, people would think him a miserable fool if they found him refusing to wrong his neighbours or to touch their belongings, though in public they would keep up a pretence of praising his conduct, for fear of being wronged themselves. So much for that. . . .

(368c–370c)

Glaucon and the others begged me to step into the breach and carry through our inquiry into the real nature of justice and injustice, and the truth about their respective advantages. So I told them what I thought. This is a very obscure question, I said, and we shall need keen sight to see our way. Now, as we are not remarkably clever, I will make a suggestion as to how we should proceed. Imagine a rather short-sighted person told to read an inscription in small letters from some way off. He would think it a godsend if someone pointed out that the same inscription was written up elsewhere on a bigger scale, so that he could first read the larger characters and then make out whether the smaller ones were the same.

No doubt, said Adeimantus; but what analogy do you see in that to our inquiry?

I will tell you. We think of justice as a quality that may exist in a whole community as well as in an individual, and the community is the bigger of the two. Possibly, then, we may find justice there in larger proportions, easier to make out. So I suggest that we should begin by inquiring what justice means in a state. Then we can go on to look for its counterpart on a smaller scale in the individual.

That seems a good plan, he agreed.

Well then, I continued, suppose we imagine a state coming into being before our eyes.

We might then be able to watch the growth of justice or of injustice within it. When that is done, we may hope it will be easier to find what we are looking for.

Much easier.

Shall we try, then, to carry out this scheme? I fancy it will be no light undertaking; so you had better think twice.

No need for that, said Adeimantus. Don't waste any more time.

My notion is, said I, that a state comes into existence because no individual is self-sufficing; we all have many needs. But perhaps you can suggest some different origin for the foundation of a community?

No, I agree with you.

So, having all these needs, we call in one another's help to satisfy our various requirements; and when we have collected a number of helpers and associates to live together in one place, we call that settlement a state.

Yes.

So if one man gives another what he has to give in exchange for what he can get, it is because each finds that to do so is for his own advantage.

Certainly.

Very well, said I. Now let us build up our imaginary state from the beginning. Apparently, it will owe its existence to our needs, the first and greatest need being the provision of food to keep us alive. Next we shall want a house; and thirdly, such things as clothing.

True.

How will our state be able to supply all these demands? We shall need at least one man to be a farmer, another a builder, and a third a weaver. Will that do, or shall we add a shoemaker and one or two more to provide for our personal wants?

By all means.

The minimum state, then, will consist of four or five men.

Apparently.

Now here is a further point. Is each one of them to bring the product of his work into a common stock? Should our one farmer, for example, provide food enough for four people and spend the whole of his working time in producing corn, so as to share with the rest; or should he take no notice of them and spend only a quarter of his time on growing just enough corn for himself, and divide the other three-quarters between building his house, weaving his clothes, and making his shoes, so as to save the trouble of sharing with others and attend himself to all his own concerns?

The first plan might be the easier, replied Adeimantus.

That may very well be so, said I; for, as you spoke, it occurred to me, for one thing, that no two people are born exactly alike. There are innate differences which fit them for different occupations.

I agree.

And will a man do better working at many trades, or keeping to one only?

Keeping to one.

And there is another point: obviously work may be ruined, if you let the right time go by. The workman must wait upon the work; it will not wait upon his leisure and allow itself to be done in a spare moment. So the conclusion is that more things will be produced and the work be more easily and better done, when every man is set free from all other occupations to do, at the right time, the one thing for which he is naturally fitted.

That is certainly true.

(372e–374e)

. . . The community I have described seems to me the ideal one, in sound health as it were: but if you want to see one suffering from inflammation, there is nothing to hinder us.

So some people, it seems, will not be satisfied to live in this simple way; they must have couches and tables and furniture of all sorts; and delicacies too, perfumes, unguents, courtesans, sweetmeats, all in plentiful variety. And besides, we must not limit ourselves now to those bare necessaries of house and clothes and shoes; we shall have to set going the arts of embroidery and painting, and collect rich materials, like gold and ivory.

Yes.

Then we must once more enlarge our community. The healthy one will not be big enough now; it must be swollen up with a whole multitude of callings not ministering to any bare necessity: hunters and fishermen, for instance; artists in sculpture, painting, and music; poets with their attendant train of professional reciters, actors, dancers, producers; and makers of all sorts of household gear, including everything for women's adornment. And we shall want more servants: children's nurses and attendants, lady's maids, barbers, cooks, and confectioners. And then swineherds—there was no need for them in our original state, but we shall want them now; and a great quantity of sheep and cattle too, if people are going to live on meat.

Of course.

And with this manner of life physicians will be in much greater request.

No doubt.

The country, too, which was large enough to support the original inhabitants, will now be too small. If we are to have enough pasture and plough land, we shall have to cut off a slice of our neighbours' territory; and if they too are not content with necessaries, but give themselves up to getting unlimited wealth, they will want a slice of ours.

That is inevitable, Socrates.

So the next thing will be, Glaucon, that we shall be at war.

No doubt.

We need not say yet whether war does good or harm, but only that we have discovered its origin in desires which are the most fruitful source of evils both to individuals and to states.

Quite true.

This will mean a considerable addition to our community—a whole army, to go out to battle with any invader, in defence of all this property and of the citizens we have been describing.

Why so? Can't they defend themselves?

Not if the principle was right, which we all accepted in framing our society. You remember we agreed that no one man can practise many trades or arts satisfactorily.

True.

Well, is not the conduct of war an art, quite as important as shoemaking?

Yes.

But we would not allow our shoemaker to try to be also a farmer or weaver or builder, because we wanted our shoes well made. We gave each man one trade, for which he was naturally fitted; he would do good work, if he confined himself to that all his life, never letting the right moment slip by. Now in no form of work is efficiency so important as in war; and fighting is not so easy a business that a man can follow another trade, such as farming or shoemaking, and also be an efficient soldier. Why, even a game like draughts or dice must be studied from childhood; no one can become a fine player in his spare moments. Just taking up a shield or other weapon will not make a man capable of fighting that very day in any sort of warfare, any more than taking up a tool or implement of some kind will make a man a craftsman or an athlete, if he does not understand its use and has never been properly trained to handle it.

No; if that were so, tools would indeed be worth having.

These guardians of our state, then, inasmuch as their work is the most important of all, will need the most complete freedom from other occupations and the greatest amount of skill and practice.

I quite agree.

And also a native aptitude for their calling.

Certainly.

So it is our business to define, if we can, the natural gifts that fit men to be guardians of a commonwealth, and to select them accordingly. It will certainly be a formidable task; but we must grapple with it to the best of our power.

Yes. . . .

Book III (412b–415d)

Good, said I; and what is the next point to be settled? Is it not the question, which of these guardians are to be rulers and which are to obey?

No doubt.

Well, it is obvious that the elder must have authority over the young, and that the rulers must be the best.

Yes.

And as among farmers the best are those with a natural turn for farming, so, if we want the best among our guardians, we must take those naturally fitted to watch over a commonwealth. They must have the right sort of intelligence and ability; and also they must look upon the commonwealth as their special concern—the sort of concern that is felt for something so closely bound up with oneself that its interests and fortunes, for good or ill, are held to be identical with one's own.

Exactly.

So the kind of men we must choose from among the Guardians will be those who, when we look at the whole course of their lives, are found to be full of zeal to do whatever they believe is for the good of the commonwealth and never willing to act against its interest.

Yes, they will be the men we want. . . .

As I said just now, then, we must find out who are the best guardians of this inward conviction that they must always do what they believe to be best for the commonwealth. We shall have to watch them from earliest childhood and set them tasks in which they would be most likely to forget or to be beguiled out of this duty. We shall then choose only those whose memory holds firm and who are proof against delusion.

Yes.

We must also subject them to ordeals of toil and pain and watch for the same qualities there. And we must observe them when exposed to the test of yet a third kind of bewitchment. As people lead colts up to alarming noises to see whether they are timid, so these young men must be brought into terrifying situations and then into scenes of pleasure, which will put them to severer proof than gold tried in the furnace. If we find one bearing himself well in all these trials and resisting every enchantment, a true guardian of himself, preserving always that perfect rhythm and harmony of being which he has acquired from his training in music and poetry, such a one will be of the greatest service to the commonwealth as well as to himself. Whenever we find one who has come unscathed through every test in childhood, youth, and manhood, we shall set him as a Ruler to watch over the commonwealth; he will be honoured in life, and after death receive the highest tribute of funeral rites and other memorials. All who do not reach this standard we must reject. And that, I think, my dear Glaucon, may be taken as an outline of the way in which we shall select Guardians to be set in authority as Rulers.

I am very much of your mind.

These, then, may properly be called Guardians in the fullest sense, who will ensure that neither foes without shall have the power, nor friends within the wish, to do harm. Those young men whom up to now we have been speaking of as Guardians, will be better described as Auxiliaries, who will enforce the decisions of the Rulers.

I agree.

Now, said I, can we devise something in the way of those convenient fictions we spoke of earlier, a single bold flight of invention, which we may induce the community in general, and if possible the Rulers themselves, to accept?

What kind of fiction?

Nothing new; something like an Eastern tale of what, according to the poets, has happened before now in more than one part of the world. The poets have been believed; but the thing has not happened in our day, and it would be hard to persuade anyone that it could ever happen again.

You seem rather shy of telling this story of yours.

With good reason, as you will see when I have told it.

Out with it; don't be afraid.

Well, here it is; though I hardly know how to find the courage or the words to express it. I shall try to convince, first the Rulers and the soldiers, and then the whole community, that all that nurture and education which we gave them was only something they seemed to experience as it were in a dream. In reality they were the whole time down inside the earth, being moulded and fostered while their arms and all their equipment were being fashioned also; and at last, when they were complete, the earth sent them up from her womb into the light of day. So now they must think of the land they dwell in as a mother and nurse, whom they must take thought for and defend against any attack, and of their fellow citizens as brothers born of the same soil.

You might well be bashful about coming out with your fiction.

No doubt; but still you must hear the rest of the story. It is true, we shall tell our people in this fable, that all of you in this land are brothers; but the god who fashioned you mixed gold in the composition of those among you who are fit to rule, so that they are of the most precious quality; and he put his silver in the Auxiliaries, and iron and brass in the farmers and craftsmen. Now, since you are all of one stock, although your children will generally be like their parents, sometimes a golden parent may have a silver child or a silver parent a golden one, and so on with all the other combinations. So the first and chief injunction laid by heaven upon the Rulers is that, among all the things of which they must show themselves good guardians, there is none that needs to be so carefully watched as the mixture of metals in the souls of children. If a child of their own is born with an alloy of iron or brass, they must, without the smallest pity, assign him the station proper to his nature and thrust him out among the craftsmen or the farmers. If, on the contrary, these classes produce a child with gold or silver in his composition, they will promote him, according to his value, to be a Guardian or an Auxiliary. They will appeal to a prophecy that ruin will come upon the state when it passes into the keeping of a man of iron or brass. Such is the story; can you think of any device to make them believe it?

Not in the first generation; but their sons and descendants might believe it, and finally the rest of mankind.

Well, said I, even so it might have a good effect in making them care more for the commonwealth and for one another; for I think I see what you mean. . . .

Book IV (419–421d)

Here Adeimantus interposed. Socrates, he said, how would you meet the objection that you are not making these people particularly happy? It is their own fault too, if they are not; for they are really masters of the state, and yet they get no good out of it as other rulers do, who own lands, build themselves fine houses with handsome furniture, offer private sacrifices to the gods, and entertain visitors from abroad; who possess, in fact, that gold and silver you spoke of, with everything else that is usually thought necessary for happiness. These people seem like nothing so much as a garrison of mercenaries posted in the city and perpetually mounting guard.

Yes, I said, and what is more they will serve for their food only without getting a mercenary's pay, so that they will not be able to travel on their own account or to make presents to a mistress or to spend as they please in other ways, like the people who are commonly thought happy. You have forgotten to include these counts in your indictment, and many more to the same effect.

Well, take them as included now.

And you want to hear the answer?

Yes.

We shall find one, I think, by keeping to the line we have followed so far. We shall say that, though it would not be surprising if even these people were perfectly happy under such conditions, our aim in founding the commonwealth was not to make any one class specially happy, but to secure the greatest possible happiness for the community as a whole. We thought we should have the best chance of finding justice in a state so constituted, just as we should find injustice where the constitution was of the worst possible type; we could then decide the question which has been before us all this time. For the moment, we are constructing, as we believe, the state which will be happy as a whole, not trying to secure the well-being of a select few; we shall study a state of the opposite kind presently. It is as if we were colouring a statue and someone came up and blamed us for not putting the most beautiful colours on the noblest parts of the figure; the eyes, for instance, should be painted crimson, but we had made them black. We should think it a fair answer to say: Really, you must not expect us to paint eyes so handsome as not to look like eyes at all. This applies to all the parts: the question is whether, by giving each its proper colour, we make the whole beautiful. So too, in the present case, you must not press us to endow our Guardians with a happiness that will make them anything rather than guardians. We could quite easily clothe our farmers in gorgeous robes, crown them with gold, and invite them to till the soil at their pleasure; or we might set our potters to lie on couches by their fire, passing round the wine and making merry, with their wheel at hand to work at whenever they felt so inclined. We could make all the rest happy in the same sort of way, and so spread this well-being through the whole community. But you must not put that idea into our heads; if we take your advice, the farmer will be no farmer, the potter no longer a potter; none of the elements that make up the community will keep its character. In many cases this does not matter so much: if a cobbler goes to the bad and pretends to be what he is not, he is not a danger to the state; but, as you must surely see, men who make only a vain show of being guardians of the laws and of the commonwealth bring the whole state to utter ruin, just as, on the other hand, its good government and well-being depend entirely on them. We, in fact, are making genuine Guardians who will be the last to bring harm upon the commonwealth; if our critic aims rather at producing a happiness like

that of a party of peasants feasting at a fair, what he has in mind is something other than a civic community. So we must consider whether our aim in establishing Guardians is to secure the greatest possible happiness for them, or happiness is something of which we should watch the development in the whole commonwealth. If so, we must compel these Guardians and Auxiliaries of ours to second our efforts; and they, and all the rest with them, must be induced to make themselves perfect masters each of his own craft. In that way, as the community grows into a well-ordered whole, the several classes may be allowed such measure of happiness as their nature will compass.

I think that is an admirable reply. . . .

(427d–434d)

So now at last, son of Ariston, said I, your commonwealth is established. The next thing is to bring to bear upon it all the light you can get from any quarter, with the help of your brother and Polemarchus and all the rest, in the hope that we may see where justice is to be found in it and where injustice, how they differ, and which of the two will bring happiness to its possessor, no matter whether gods and men see that he has it or not.

Nonsense, said Glaucon; you promised to conduct the search yourself, because it would be a sin not to uphold justice by every means in your power.

That is true; I must do as you say, but you must all help.

We will.

I suspect, then, we may find what we are looking for in this way. I take it that our state, having been founded and built up on the right lines, is good in the complete sense of the word.

It must be.

Obviously, then, it is wise, brave, temperate, and just.

Obviously.

Then if we find some of these qualities in it, the remainder will be the one we have not found. It is as if we were looking somewhere for one of any four things: if we detected that one immediately, we should be satisfied; whereas if we recognized the other three first, that would be enough to indicate the thing we wanted; it could only be the remaining one. So here we have four qualities. Had we not better follow that method in looking for the one we want?

Surely.

To begin then: the first quality to come into view in our state seems to be its wisdom; and there appears to be something odd about this quality.

What is there odd about it?

I think the state we have described really has wisdom; for it will be prudent in counsel, won't it?

Yes.

And prudence in counsel is clearly a form of knowledge; good counsel cannot be due to ignorance and stupidity.

Clearly.

But there are many and various kinds of knowledge in our commonwealth. There is the knowledge possessed by the carpenters or the smiths, and the knowledge how to raise crops. Are we to call the state wise and prudent on the strength of these forms of skill?

No; they would only make it good at furniture-making or working in copper or agriculture.

Well then, is there any form of knowledge, possessed by some among the citizens of our new-founded commonwealth, which will enable it to take thought, not for some particular interest, but for the best possible conduct of the state as a whole in its internal and external relations?

Yes, there is.

What is it, and where does it reside?

It is precisely that art of guardianship which resides in those Rulers whom we just now called Guardians in the full sense.

And what would you call the state on the strength of that knowledge?

Prudent and truly wise.

And do you think there will be more or fewer of these genuine Guardians in our state than there will be smiths?

Far fewer.

Fewer, in fact, than any of those other groups who are called after the kind of skill they possess?

Much fewer.

So, if a state is constituted on natural principles, the wisdom it possesses as a whole will be due to the knowledge residing in the smallest part, the one which takes the lead and governs the rest. Such knowledge is the only kind that deserves the name of wisdom, and it appears to be ordained by nature that the class privileged to possess it should be the smallest of all.

Quite true.

Here then we have more or less made out one of our four qualities and its seat in the structure of the commonwealth.

To my satisfaction, at any rate.

Next there is courage. It is not hard to discern that quality or the part of the community in which it resides so as to entitle the whole to be called brave.

Why do you say so?

Because anyone who speaks of a state as either brave or cowardly can only be thinking of that part of it which takes the field and fights in its defence; the reason being, I imagine, that the character of the state is not determined by the bravery or cowardice of the other parts.

No.

Courage, then, is another quality which a community owes to a certain part of itself. And its being brave will mean that, in this part, it possesses the power of preserving, in all circumstances, a conviction about the sort of things that it is right to be afraid of—the conviction implanted by the education which the lawgiver has established. Is not that what you mean by courage?

I do not quite understand. Will you say it again?

I am saying that courage means preserving something.

Yes, but what?

The conviction, inculcated by lawfully established education, about the sort of things which may rightly be feared. When I added 'in all circumstances', I meant preserving it always and never abandoning it, whether under the influence of pain or of pleasure, of desire or of fear. If you like, I will give an illustration.

Please do.

You know how dyers who want wool to take a purple dye, first select the white wool from among all the other colours, next treat it very carefully to make it take the dye in its full brilliance, and only then dip it in the vat. Dyed in that way, wool gets a fast colour, which no washing, even with soap, will rob of its brilliance; whereas if they choose wool of any colour but white, or if they neglect to prepare it, you know what happens.

Yes, it looks washed-out and ridiculous.

That illustrates the result we were doing our best to achieve when we were choosing our fighting men and training their minds and bodies. Our only purpose was to contrive influences whereby they might take the colour of our institutions like a dye, so that, in virtue of having both the right temperament and the

right education, their convictions about what ought to be feared and on all other subjects might be indelibly fixed, never to be washed out by pleasure and pain, desire and fear, solvents more terribly effective than all the soap and fuller's earth in the world. Such a power of constantly preserving, in accordance with our institutions, the right conviction about the things which ought, or ought not, to be feared, is what I call courage. That is my position, unless you have some objection to make.

None at all, he replied; if the belief were such as might be found in a slave or an animal—correct, but not produced by education—you would hardly describe it as in accordance with our institutions, and you would give it some other name than courage.

Quite true.

Then I accept your account of courage.

You will do well to accept it, at any rate as applying to the courage of the ordinary citizen; if you like we will go into it more fully some other time. At present we are in search of justice, rather than of courage; and for that purpose we have said enough.

I quite agree.

Two qualities, I went on, still remain to be made out in our state, temperance and the object of our whole inquiry, justice. Can we discover justice without troubling ourselves further about temperance?

I do not know, and I would rather not have justice come to light first, if that means that we should not go on to consider temperance. So if you want to please me, take temperance first.

Of course I have every wish to please you. Do go on then.

I will. At first sight, temperance seems more like some sort of concord or harmony than the other qualities did.

How so?

Temperance surely means a kind of order-liness, a control of certain pleasures and appetites. People use the expression, 'master of oneself', whatever that means, and various other phrases that point the same way.

Quite true.

Is not 'master of oneself' an absurd expression? A man who was master of himself would presumably be also subject to himself, and the subject would be master; for all these terms apply to the same person.

No doubt.

I think, however, the phrase means that within the man himself, in his soul, there is a better part and a worse; and that he is his own master when the part which is better by nature has the worse under its control. It is certainly a term of praise; whereas it is considered a disgrace, when, through bad breeding or bad company, the better part is overwhelmed by the worse, like a small force outnumbered by a multitude. A man in that condition is called a slave to himself and intemperate.

Probably that is what is meant.

Then now look at our newly founded state and you will find one of these two conditions realized there. You will agree that it deserves to be called master of itself, if temperance and self-mastery exist where the better part rules the worse.

Yes, I can see that is true.

It is also true that the great mass of multi-farious appetites and pleasures and pains will be found to occur chiefly in children and women and slaves, and, among free men so called, in the inferior multitude; whereas the simple and moderate desires which, with the aid of reason and right belief, are guided by reflection, you will find only in a few, and those with the best inborn dispositions and the best educated.

Yes, certainly.

Do you see that this state of things will exist in your commonwealth, where the desires of the inferior multitude will be controlled by the desires and wisdom of the superior few? Hence, if any society can be called master of itself and in control of pleasures and desires, it will be ours.

Quite so.

On all these grounds, then, we may describe it as temperate. Furthermore, in our state, if anywhere, the governors and the governed will share the same conviction on the question who ought to rule. Don't you think so?

I am quite sure of it.

Then, if that is their state of mind, in which of the two classes of citizens will temperance reside—in the governors or in the governed?

In both, I suppose.

So we were not wrong in divining a resemblance between temperance and some kind of harmony. Temperance is not like courage and wisdom, which made the state wise and brave by residing each in one particular part. Temperance works in a different way; it extends throughout the whole gamut of the state, producing a consonance of all its elements from the weakest to the strongest as measured by any standard you like to take—wisdom, bodily strength, numbers, or wealth. So we are entirely justified in identifying with temperance this unanimity or harmonious agreement between the naturally superior and inferior elements on the question which of the two should govern, whether in the state or in the individual.

I fully agree.

Good, said I. We have discovered in our commonwealth three out of our four qualities, to the best of our present judgment. What is the remaining one, required to make up its full complement of goodness? For clearly this will be justice.

Clearly.

if we can reach the shore, hoping for some Arion's dolphin or other miraculous deliverance to bring us safe to land.

I suppose so.

Come then, let us see if we can find the way out. We did agree that different natures should have different occupations, and that the natures of man and woman are different; and yet we are now saying that these different natures are to have the same occupations. Is that the charge against us?

Exactly.

It is extraordinary, Glaucon, what an effect the practice of debating has upon people.

Why do you say that?

Because they often seem to fall unconsciously into mere disputes which they mistake for reasonable argument, through being unable to draw the distinctions proper to their subject; and so, instead of a philosophical exchange of ideas, they go off in chase of contradictions which are purely verbal.

I know that happens to many people; but does it apply to us at this moment?

Absolutely. At least I am afraid we are slipping unconsciously into a dispute about words. We have been strenuously insisting on the letter of our principle that different natures should not have the same occupations, as if we were scoring a point in a debate; but we have altogether neglected to consider what sort of sameness or difference we meant and in what respect these natures and occupations were to be defined as different or the same. Consequently, we might very well be asking one another whether there is not an opposition in nature between bald and long-haired men, and, when that was admitted, forbid one set to be shoemakers, if the other were following that trade.

That would be absurd.

Yes, but only because we never meant any and every sort of sameness or difference in nature, but the sort that was relevant to the occupations in question. We meant, for instance, that a man and a woman have the same nature if both have a talent for medicine; whereas two men have different natures if one is a born physician, the other a born carpenter.

Yes, of course.

If, then, we find that either the male sex or the female is specially qualified for any particular form of occupation, then that occupation, we shall say, ought to be assigned to one sex or the other. But if the only difference appears to be that the male begets and the female brings forth, we shall conclude that no difference between man and woman has yet been produced that is relevant to our purpose. We shall continue to think it proper for our Guardians and their wives to share in the same pursuits.

And quite rightly.

The next thing will be to ask our opponent to name any profession or occupation in civic life for the purposes of which woman's nature is different from man's.

That is a fair question.

He might reply, as you did just now, that it is not easy to find a satisfactory answer on the spur of the moment, but that there would be no difficulty after a little reflection.

Perhaps.

Suppose, then, we, invite him to follow us and see if we can convince him that there is no occupation concerned with the management of social affairs that is peculiar to women. We will confront him with a question: When you speak of a man having a natural talent for something, do you mean that he finds it easy to learn, and after a little instruction can find out much more for himself; whereas a man who is not so gifted learns with difficulty and no amount of instruction and practice will make him even remember what he has been taught? Is the talented man one whose bodily powers are readily at the service of his mind, instead of being a hindrance? Are not these the marks by which you distinguish the presence of a natural gift for any pursuit?

Yes, precisely.

Now do you know of any human occupation in which the male sex is not superior to the female in all these respects? Need I waste time over exceptions like weaving and watching over saucepans and batches of cakes, though women are supposed to be good at such things and get laughed at when a man does them better?

It is true, he replied, in almost everything one sex is easily beaten by the other. No doubt many women are better at many things than many men; but taking the sexes as a whole, it is as you say.

To conclude, then, there is no occupation concerned with the management of social affairs which belongs either to woman or to man, as such. Natural gifts are to be found here and there in both creatures alike; and every occupation is open to both, so far as their natures are concerned, though woman is for all purposes the weaker.

Certainly.

Is that a reason for making over all occupations to men only?

Of course not.

No, because one woman may have a natural gift for medicine or for music, another may not.

Surely.

Is it not also true that a woman may, or may not, be warlike or athletic?

I think so.

And again, one may love knowledge, another hate it; one may be high-spirited, another spiritless?

True again.

It follows that one woman will be fitted by nature to be a Guardian, another will not; because these were the qualities for which we selected our men Guardians. So for the pur-

pose of keeping watch over the commonwealth, woman has the same nature as man, save insofar as she is weaker.

So it appears.

It follows that women of this type must be selected to share the life and duties of Guardians with men of the same type, since they are competent and of a like nature, and the same natures must be allowed the same pursuits.

Yes.

We come round, then, to our former position, that there is nothing contrary to nature in giving our Guardians' wives the same training for mind and body. The practice we proposed to establish was not impossible or visionary, since it was in accordance with nature. Rather, the contrary practice which now prevails turns out to be unnatural.

So it appears.

Well, we set out to inquire whether the plan we proposed was feasible and also the best. That it is feasible is now agreed; we must next settle whether it is the best.

Obviously.

Now, for the purpose of producing a woman fit to be a Guardian, we shall not have one education for men and another for women, precisely because the nature to be taken in hand is the same.

True.

What is your opinion on the question of one man being better than another? Do you think there is no such difference?

Certainly I do not.

And in this commonwealth of ours, which will prove the better men—the Guardians who have received the education we described, or the shoemakers who have been trained to make shoes?

It is absurd to ask such a question.

Very well. So these Guardians will be the best of all the citizens?

By far.

And these women the best of all the women?

Yes.

Can anything be better for a commonwealth than to produce in it men and women of the best possible type?

No.

And that result will be brought about by such a system of mental and bodily training as we have described?

Surely.

We may conclude that the institution we proposed was not only practicable, but also the best for the commonwealth.

Yes.

The wives of our Guardians, then, must strip for exercise, since they will be clothed with virtue, and they must take their share in war and in the other social duties of guardianship. They are to have no other occupation; and in these duties the lighter part must fall to the women, because of the weakness of their sex. The man who laughs at naked women, exercising their bodies for the best of reasons, is like one that 'gathers fruit unripe, ' for he does not know what it is that he is laughing at or what he is doing. There will never be a finer saying than the one which declares that whatever does good should be held in honour, and the only shame is in doing harm.

That is perfectly true. . . .

(457b–473e)

So far, then, in regulating the position of women, we may claim to have come safely through with one hazardous proposal, that male and female Guardians shall have all occupations in common. The consistency of the argument is an assurance that the plan is a good one and also feasible. We are like swimmers who have breasted the first wave without being swallowed up.

Not such a small wave either.

You will not call it large when you see the next.

Let me have a look at the next one, then.

Here it is: a law which follows from that principle and all that has gone before, namely that, of these Guardians, no one man and one woman are to set up house together privately: wives are to be held in common by all; so too are the children, and no parent is to know his own child, nor any child his parent.

It will be much harder to convince people that that is either a feasible plan or a good one.

As to its being a good plan, I imagine no one would deny the immense advantage of wives and children being held in common, provided it can be done. I should expect dispute to arise chiefly over the question whether it is possible.

There may well be a good deal of dispute over both points.

You mean, I must meet attacks on two fronts. I was hoping to escape one by running away: if you agreed it was a good plan, then I should only have had to inquire whether it was feasible.

No, we have seen through that manoeuvre. You will have to defend both positions.

Well, I must pay the penalty for my cowardice. But grant me one favour. Let me indulge my fancy, like one who entertains himself with idle daydreams on a solitary walk. Before he has any notion how his desires can be realized, he will set aside that question, to save himself the trouble of reckoning what may or may not be possible. He will assume that his wish has come true, and amuse himself with settling all the details of what he means to do then. So a lazy mind encourages itself to be lazier than ever; and I am giving way to the same weakness myself. I want to put off till later that question, how the thing can be done. For the moment, with your leave,

I shall assume it to be possible, and ask how the Rulers will work out the details in practice; and I shall argue that the plan, once carried into effect, would be the best thing in the world for our commonwealth and for its Guardians. That is what I shall now try to make out with your help, if you will allow me to postpone the other question.

Very good; I have no objection.

Well, if our Rulers are worthy of the name, and their Auxiliaries likewise, these latter will be ready to do what they are told, and the Rulers, in giving their commands, will themselves obey our laws and will be faithful to their spirit in any details we leave to their discretion.

No doubt.

It is for you, then, as their lawgiver, who have already selected the men, to select for association with them women who are so far as possible of the same natural capacity. Now since none of them will have any private home of his own, but they will share the same dwelling and eat at common tables, the two sexes will be together; and meeting without restriction for exercise and all through their upbringing, they will surely be drawn towards union with one another by a necessity of their nature—necessity is not too strong a word, I think?

Not too strong for the constraint of love, which for the mass of mankind is more persuasive and compelling than even the necessity of mathematical proof.

Exactly. But in the next place, Glaucon, anything like unregulated unions would be a profanation in a state whose citizens lead the good life. The Rulers will not allow such a thing.

No, it would not be right.

Clearly, then, we must have marriages, as sacred as we can make them; and this sanctity will attach to those which yield the best results.

Certainly.

How are we to get the best results? You must tell me, Glaucon, because I see you keep sporting dogs and a great many game birds at your house; and there is something about their mating and breeding that you must have noticed.

What is that?

In the first place, though they may all be of good stock, are there not some that turn out to be better than the rest?

There are.

And do you breed from all indiscriminately? Are you not careful to breed from the best so far as you can?

Yes.

And from those in their prime, rather than the very young or the very old?

Yes.

Otherwise, the stock of your birds or dogs would deteriorate very much, wouldn't it?

It would.

And the same is true of horses or of any animal?

It would be very strange if it were not.

Dear me, said I; we shall need consummate skill in our Rulers, if it is also true of the human race.

Well, it is true. But why must they be so skilful?

Because they will have to administer a large dose of that medicine we spoke of earlier. An ordinary doctor is thought good enough for a patient who will submit to be dieted and can do without medicine; but he must be much more of a man if drugs are required.

True, but how does that apply?

It applies to our Rulers: it seems they will have to give their subjects a considerable dose of imposition and deception for their good. We said, if you remember, that such expedients would be useful as a sort of medicine.

Yes, a very sound principle.

Well, it looks as if this sound principle will play no small part in this matter of marriage and child-bearing.

How so?

It follows from what we have just said that, if we are to keep our flock at the highest pitch of excellence, there should be as many unions of the best of both sexes, and as few of the inferior, as possible, and that only the offspring of the better unions should be kept. And again, no one but the Rulers must know how all this is being effected; otherwise our herd of Guardians may become rebellious.

Quite true.

We must, then, institute certain festivals at which we shall bring together the brides and the bridegrooms. There will be sacrifices, and our poets will write songs befitting the occasion. The number of marriages we shall leave to the Rulers' discretion. They will aim at keeping the number of the citizens as constant as possible, having regard to losses caused by war, epidemics, and so on; and they must do their best to see that our state does not become either great or small.

Very good. . . .

This, then, Glaucon, is the manner in which the Guardians of your commonwealth are to hold their wives and children in common. Must we not next find arguments to establish that it is consistent with our other institutions and also by far the best plan?

Yes, surely.

We had better begin by asking what is the greatest good at which the lawgiver should aim in laying down the constitution of a state, and what is the worst evil. We can then consider whether our proposals are in keeping with that good and irreconcilable with the evil.

By all means.

Does not the worst evil for a state arise from anything that tends to rend it asunder and destroy its unity, while nothing does it

more good than whatever tends to bind it together and make it one?

That is true.

And are not citizens bound together by sharing in the same pleasures and pains, all feeling glad or grieved on the same occasions of gain or loss; whereas the bond is broken when such feelings are no longer universal, but any event of public or personal concern fills some with joy and others with distress?

Certainly.

And this disunion comes about when the words 'mine' and 'not mine', 'another's' and 'not another's' are not applied to the same things throughout the community. The best-ordered state will be the one in which the largest number of persons use these terms in the same sense, and which accordingly most nearly resembles a single person. When one of us hurts his finger, the whole extent of those bodily connections which are gathered up in the soul and unified by its ruling element is made aware and it all shares as a whole in the pain of the suffering part; hence we say that the man has a pain in his finger. The same thing is true of the pain or pleasure felt when any other part of the person suffers or is relieved.

Yes; I agree that the best-organized community comes nearest to that condition. . . .

Very good; but here is a further point. Will you not require them, not merely to use these family terms, but to behave as a real family? Must they not show towards all whom they call 'father' the customary reverence, care, and obedience due to a parent, if they look for any favour from gods or men, since to act otherwise is contrary to divine and human law? Should not all the citizens constantly reiterate in the hearing of the children from their earliest years such traditional maxims of conduct towards those whom they are taught to call father and their other kindred?

They should. It would be absurd that terms of kinship should be on their lips without any action to correspond.

In our community, then, above all others, when things go well or ill with any individual, everyone will use that word 'mine' in the same sense and say that all is going well or ill with him and his.

Quite true.

And, as we said, this way of speaking and thinking goes with fellow-feeling; so that our citizens, sharing as they do in a common interest which each will call his own, will have all their feelings of pleasure or pain in common.

Assuredly.

A result that will be due to our institutions, and in particular to our Guardians' holding their wives and children in common.

Very much so.

But you will remember how, when we compared a well-ordered community to the body which shares in the pleasures and pains of any member, we saw in this unity the greatest good that a state can enjoy. So the conclusion is that our commonwealth owes to this sharing of wives and children by its protectors its enjoyment of the greatest of all goods.

Yes, that follows.

Moreover, this agrees with our principle that they were not to have houses or lands or any property of their own, but to receive sustenance from the other citizens, as wages for their guardianship, and to consume it in common. Only so will they keep to their true character; and our present proposals will do still more to make them genuine Guardians. They will not rend the community asunder by each applying that word 'mine' to different things and dragging off whatever he can get for himself into a private home, where he will have his separate family, forming a centre of exclusive joys and sorrows. Rather they will all, so far as may be, feel together and aim at the same

ends, because they are convinced that all their interests are identical.

Quite so.

Again, if a man's person is his only private possession, lawsuits and prosecutions will all but vanish, and they will be free of those quarrels that arise from ownership of property and from having family ties. Nor would they be justified even in bringing actions for assault and outrage; for we shall pronounce it right and honourable for a man to defend himself against an assailant of his own age, and in that way they will be compelled to keep themselves fit.

That would be a sound law. . . .

But really, Socrates, Glaucon continued, if you are allowed to go on like this, I am afraid you will forget all about the question you thrust aside some time ago: whether a society so constituted can ever come into existence, and if so, how. No doubt, if it did exist, all manner of good things would come about. I can even add some that you have passed over. Men who acknowledged one another as fathers, sons, or brothers and always used those names among themselves would never desert one another; so they would fight with unequalled bravery. And if their womenfolk went out with them to war, either in the ranks or drawn up in the rear to intimidate the enemy and act as a reserve in case of need, I am sure all this would make them invincible. At home, too, I can see many advantages you have not mentioned. But, since I admit that our commonwealth would have all these merits and any number more, if once it came into existence, you need not describe it in further detail. All we have now to do is to convince ourselves that it can be brought into being and how.

This is a very sudden onslaught, said I; you have no mercy on my shilly-shallying. Perhaps you do not realize that, after I have barely escaped the first two waves, the third, which

3. In Book IV, Plato discovers the real nature of justice and provides a defence of justice as an intrinsic good for the one who possesses it. What is justice for Plato? How does Plato's discovery of justice work to provide a defence of the virtue against Thrasymachus?

4. In Book V, what reasons does Plato provide for his proposal that women and men receive the same education and share the responsibilities of running the city? Why does Plato recommend communal living among men and women of the guardian class?

5. In Book IX, Plato juxtaposes descriptions of the just and unjust types of individuals in order to show that justice is more profitable than injustice. Explain Plato's argument. Has he succeeded in demonstrating that justice always pays?

Recommended Readings

Annas, Julia, 'Plato's *Republic* and Feminism,' *Philosophy* 51 (1976): 307–21.

———— *An Introduction to Plato's* Republic (Oxford University Press, 1981).

Brickhouse, Thomas, and Nicholas Smith, *Plato's Socrates* (Oxford University Press, 1994).

King, Martin Luther, 'Letter from a Birmingham City Jail,' in *A Testament of Hope: The Essential Writings and Speeches of Martin Luther King, Jr.* (Harper, 1990).

Nathanson, Steven, 'Super Patriotism' and 'Political Cynicism,' in *Should We Consent to Be Governed? A Short Introduction to Political Philosophy*, 2nd edn (Wadsworth, 2001).

Kraut, Richard, *Socrates and the State* (Princeton University Press, 1984).

———— ed., *Plato's* Republic: *Critical Essays* (Rowman and Littlefield, 1997).

Santas, Gerasimos, ed., *The Blackwell Guide to Plato's* Republic (Blackwell, 2006).

Vlastos, Gregory, *Socrates, Plato and Their Tradition*, edited by Daniel Graham (Princeton University Press, 1996).

Weiss, Roslyn, *Socrates Dissatisfied: An Analysis of Plato's* Crito (Oxford University Press, 1998).

Aristotle

Aristotle (384–322 BC) was born in the Macedonian city of Stagira in northern Greece. Raised in a royal residence in which his father served as a medical doctor, Aristotle was sent to Athens at 17 to study with Plato at the Academy. He remained at the Academy for 20 years as a student and, eventually, as a research and teaching associate; he left when Plato died in 347 BC. Aristotle travelled widely and pursued research in many locations: he was a member of a philosophical circle in Asia Minor, conducted extensive biological research on the island of Lesbos, and served as tutor to Alexander the Great. In 335, he returned to Athens and established his own institution of higher education, the Lyceum, where he taught and wrote most of his works that survive today. In 323, Aristotle faced charges of impiety, and remarking that he would 'not allow Athens to sin twice against philosophy,' he fled to the city of Chalcis in Macedonia, where he lived in relative isolation until his death the following year.

Over his lifetime, Aristotle developed a comprehensive system of scientific and philosophical thought spanning theoretical, practical, and productive knowledge. In his view, his treatises on ethics and politics were contributions to practical knowledge concerned with human action, and his work on poetics and rhetoric was part of productive knowledge concerned with the making of things. His prodigious body of work in metaphysics, epistemology, logic, mathematics, biology, and physics belonged to the theoretical sciences, in which knowledge is pursued for its own sake. Approximately three-fourths of Aristotle's writings—including all of his dialogues and his polished works intended for publication—were lost after the decline of the Roman Empire; only his terse and compressed lecture notes have survived.

A later Aristotelian work in practical knowledge, the *Politics* is primarily a discourse on the organization and governance of human societies. In Greece in fourth century BC, the basic unit of political organization was not the nation-state but the smaller and self-sufficient *polis* or city-state. In the city-state, citizens know one another, speak face to face, and can convene in a single political assembly to discuss law, morality, lawsuits, and candidates for political office. In the *Politics*, Aristotle argues that the city-state is the proper highest association among human beings. He is aware of larger nation-states like the Persian Empire, but he sees the city-state as best suited for the political nature of human beings. Unlike smaller villages, a city-state is large enough to meet varied human social needs, but unlike larger nations, it is not so large that individuals have little or no effect upon the formation of laws and institutions.

One of the primary arguments of the *Politics* is that the city-state exists for the sake of promoting the good life for human beings. A well-constituted city provides not only the background structures necessary for good living but also the education and leisure that enable citizens to flourish and live virtuously. The Aristotelian ideal of promoting human flourishing contrasts with ancient and modern contractarian social theory, in which a city arises as a mechanism for mutual self-preservation or commercial alliance among citizens. Aristotle notes that a state should provide peace and security, but he argues further that a city should be directed at the overall good of its citizens. For Aristotle, the human good requires virtuous activity, intellectual contemplation, and political participation, in which human beings exercise their distinctive capacities for language and rational thought.

Unlike Plato, Aristotle upholds the commonplace assumptions of his day regarding the social place of women and slaves. In the *Politics*, he argues that slavery is essential to the city and that women possess limited rational faculties, which makes them fit for only a domestic role. The labour necessary for trade, commerce, and the maintenance of life is endlessly time-consuming, draining, and inconsistent with a good life in which one has time for education and reflection (1328b33–1329a32). Since the good life is incompatible with manual labour, and since the purpose of the city is to promote the good life for its citizens, people who are not citizens must perform the labour necessary to maintain life and therein make the good life possible for citizens. For Aristotle, nature makes possible this opportune fit between citizens and labourers, for some human beings innately lack the capacity to reason well and guide themselves. Those who are natural slaves—born with inferior intellectual abilities—are by nature suited to serve the virtuous and rational, enabling the latter to have the leisure necessary for good living.

Politics

BOOK I

THE HOUSEHOLD AND THE CITY

A: The Political Association and Its Relation to Other Associations

Chapter 1

All associations have ends: the political association has the highest; but the principle of association expresses itself in different forms, and through different modes of government.

1252ª1 Observation shows us, first, that every city [*polis*] is a species of association, and, secondly, that all associations come into being for the sake of some good—for all men do all their acts with a view to achieving something which is, in their view, a good. It is clear therefore that all associations aim at some good, and that the particular association which is the most sovereign of all, and includes all the rest, will pursue this aim most, and will thus be directed to the most sovereign of all goods. This most sovereign and inclusive association is the city [or *polis*], as it is called, or the political association.

1252ᵃ7 It is a mistake to believe that the statesman is the same as the monarch of a kingdom, or the manager of a household, or the master of a number of slaves. Those who hold this view consider that each one of these differs from the others not with a difference of kind, but according to the number, large or small, of those with whom he deals. On this view someone who is concerned with few people is a master, someone who is concerned with more is the manager of a household, and someone who is concerned with still more is a statesman, or a monarch. This view abolishes any real difference between a large household and a small city; and it also reduces the difference between the 'statesman' and the monarch to the one fact that the latter has an uncontrolled and sole authority, while the former exercises his authority in conformity with the rules imposed by the art of statesmanship and as one who rules and is ruled in turn. But this is a view which cannot be accepted as correct.

1252ᵃ18 Our point will be made clear if we proceed to consider the matter according to our normal method of analysis. Just as, in all other fields, a compound should be analysed until we reach its simple elements (or, in other words, the smallest parts of the whole which it constitutes), so we must also consider analytically the elements of which a city is composed. We shall then gain a better insight into the way in which these differ from one another; and we shall also be in a position to discover whether there is any kind of expertise to be acquired in connection with the matters under discussion.

Chapter 2

To distinguish the different forms of association we must trace the development successively of the association of the household, that of the village, and that of the city or polis. The polis, or political

association, is the crown: it completes and fulfils the nature of man: it is thus natural to him, and he is himself 'naturally a polis-animal'; it is also prior to him, in the sense that it is the presupposition of his true and full life.

1252ᵃ24 In this, as in other fields, we shall be able to study our subject best if we begin at the beginning and consider things in the process of their growth. First of all, there must necessarily be a union or pairing of those who cannot exist without one another. Male and female must unite for the reproduction of the species—not from deliberate intention, but from the natural impulse, which exists in animals generally as it also exists in plants, to leave behind them something of the same nature as themselves. Next, there must necessarily be a union of the naturally ruling element with the element which is naturally ruled, for the preservation of both. The element which is able, by virtue of its intelligence, to exercise forethought, is naturally a ruling and master element; the element which is able, by virtue of its bodily power, to do the physical work, is a ruled element, which is naturally in a state of slavery; and master and slave have accordingly a common interest.

1252ᵇ2 The female and the slave are naturally distinguished from one another. Nature makes nothing in a miserly spirit, as smiths do when they make the Delphic knife to serve a number of purposes: she makes each separate thing for a separate end; and she does so because the instrument is most perfectly made when it serves a single purpose and not a variety of purposes. Among barbarians, however, the female and the slave occupy the same position—the reason being that no naturally ruling element exists among them, and conjugal union thus comes to be a union of a female who is a slave with a male who is also a slave. This is why our poets have said,

Meet it is that barbarous peoples should be
governed by the Greeks

the assumption being that barbarian and slave
are by nature one and the same.

The first result of these two elementary
associations is the household or family. Hes-
iod spoke truly in the verse,

First house, and wife, and ox
to draw the plough,

for oxen serve the poor in lieu of household
slaves. The first form of association naturally
instituted for the satisfaction of daily recurrent
needs is thus the family; and the members of
the family are accordingly termed by Charon-
das 'associates of the breadchest', as they are
also termed by Epimenides the Cretan 'associates of the manger'.

1252ᵇ17 The next form of association—
which is also the first to be formed from more
households than one, and for the satisfaction
of something more than daily recurrent
needs—is the village. The most natural form
of the village appears to be that of a colony [or
offshoot] from a family; and some have thus
called the members of the village by the name
of 'sucklings of the same milk', or, again, of
'sons and the sons of sons'. This, it may be
noted, is the reason why cities were originally
ruled, as the peoples of the barbarian world
still are, by kings. They were formed of people
who were already monarchically governed, for
every household is monarchically governed by
the eldest of the kin, just as villages, when they
are offshoots from the household, are similarly
governed in virtue of the kinship between
their members. This is what Homer describes:

Each of them ruleth
Over his children and wives,

a passage which shows that they lived in scattered groups, as indeed men generally did in
ancient times. The fact that men generally
were governed by kings in ancient times, and
that some still continue to be governed in that
way, is the reason that leads everyone to say
that the gods are also governed by a king. People make the lives of the gods in the likeness
of their own—as they also make their shapes.

1252ᵇ27 When we come to the final and
perfect association, formed from a number of
villages, we have already reached the city [or
polis]. This may be said to have reached the
height of full self-sufficiency; or rather we may
say that while it comes into existence for the
sake of mere life, it exists for the sake of a good
life. For this reason every city exists by nature,
just as did the earlier associations [from which
it grew]. It is the end or consummation to
which those associations move, and the 'nature'
of things consists in their end or consummation; for what each thing is when its growth is
completed we call the nature of that thing,
whether it be a man or a horse or a family.
Again the end, or final cause, is the best and
self-sufficiency is both the end, and the best.

1253ᵃ2 From these considerations it is
evident that the city belongs to the class of
things that exist by nature, and that man is by
nature a political animal. He who is without a
city, by reason of his own nature and not of
some accident, is either a poor sort of being, or
a being higher than man: he is like the man of
whom Homer wrote in denunciation:

Clanless and lawless and heartless is he.

The man who is such by nature at once
plunges into a passion of war; he is in the position of a solitary advanced piece in a game of
draughts.

1253ᵃ7 It is thus clear that man is a political animal, in a higher degree than bees or
other gregarious animals. Nature, according to
our theory, makes nothing in vain; and man
alone of the animals is furnished with the

faculty of language. The mere making of sounds serves to indicate pleasure and pain, and is thus a faculty that belongs to animals in general: their nature enables them to attain the point at which they have perceptions of pleasure and pain, and can signify those perceptions to one another. But language serves to declare what is advantageous and what is the reverse, and it is the peculiarity of man, in comparison with other animals, that he alone possesses a perception of good and evil, of the just and the unjust, and other similar qualities; and it is association in these things which makes a family and a city.

1253ª18 We may now proceed to add that the city is prior in the order of nature to the family and the individual. The reason for this is that the whole is necessarily prior to the part. If the whole body is destroyed, there will not be a foot or a hand, except in that ambiguous sense in which one uses the same word to indicate a different thing, as when one speaks of a 'hand' made of stone; for a hand, when destroyed [by the destruction of the whole body], will be no better than a stone 'hand'. All things derive their essential character from their function and their capacity; and it follows that if they are no longer fit to discharge their function, we ought not to say that they are still the same things, but only that, by an ambiguity, they still have the same names.

1253ª25 We thus see that the city exists by nature and that it is prior to the individual. For if the individual is not self-sufficient when he is isolated he will stand in the same relation to the whole as other parts do to their wholes. The man who is isolated, who is unable to share in the benefits of political association, or has no need to share because he is already self-sufficient, is no part of the city, and must therefore be either a beast or a god. There is therefore a natural impulse in all men towards an association of this sort. But the man who

first constructed such an association was nonetheless the greatest of benefactors. Man, when perfected, is the best of animals; but if he be isolated from law and justice he is the worst of all. Injustice is all the graver when it is armed injustice; and man is furnished from birth with weapons which are intended to serve the purposes of wisdom and goodness, but which may be used in preference for opposite ends. That is why, if he be without goodness [of mind and character], he is a most unholy and savage being, and worse than all others in the indulgence of lust and gluttony. The virtue of justice belongs to the city; for justice is an ordering of the political association, and the virtue of justice consists in the determination of what is just.

B: The Association of the Household and Its Different Factors

Chapter 3

1. The constituent elements of the household. The three relations of master and slave, husband and wife, parent and child. The fourth element of 'acquisition'.

1253ᵇ1 Having ascertained, from the previous analysis, what are the elements of which the city is constituted, we must first consider the management of the household; for every city is composed of households. The parts of household management will correspond to the parts of which the household itself is constituted. A complete household consists of slaves and free men. But every subject of inquiry should first be examined in its simplest elements; and the primary and simplest elements of the household are the connection of master and slave, that of the husband and wife, and that of parents and children. We must accordingly consider each of these connections, examining the nature of each and the qualities it ought to possess. The factors to be examined are therefore three: first, the relationship of master and slave; next, what may be called the marital relationship (for there is no word in our language which exactly describes the union of husband and wife); and lastly, what may be called the parental relationship, which again has no single word in our language peculiar to itself. But besides the three factors which thus present themselves for examination there is also a fourth, which some regard as identical with the whole of household management, and others as its principal part. This is the element called 'the art of acquisition'; and we shall have to consider its nature.

1253ᵇ14 We may first speak of master and slave, partly in order to gather lessons bearing on the necessities of practical life, and partly in order to discover whether we can attain any view, superior to those now generally held, which is likely to promote an understanding of the subject. There are some who hold that the exercise of authority over slaves is a kind of knowledge. They believe (as we said in the beginning) that household management, slave ownership, statesmanship, and kingship are all the same. There are others, however, who regard the control of slaves by a master as contrary to nature. In their view the distinction of master and slave is due to law or convention; there is no natural difference between them: the relation of master and slave is based on force, and so has no warrant in justice.

Chapter 4

2. Slavery. The instruments of the household form its stock of property: they are animate and inanimate: the slave is an animate instrument, intended (like all the instruments of the household) for action, and not for production.

1253ᵇ23 Property is part of the household and the art of acquiring property is part of household management, for it is impossible to live well, or indeed at all, unless the necessary conditions are present. Thus the same holds true in the sphere of household management as in the specialized arts: each must be furnished with its appropriate instruments if its function is to be fulfilled. Instruments are partly inanimate and partly animate: the steersman of a ship, for instance, has an inanimate instrument in the rudder, and an animate instrument in the look-out man (for in the arts a subordinate is of the nature of an instrument). Each article of property is thus an instrument for the purpose of life, property in general is a quantity of such instruments, the slave is an animate article of property, and subordinates, or servants, in general may be described as instruments which are prior to other instruments. We can imagine a situation in which each instrument could do its own work, at the word of command or by intelligent anticipation, like the statues of Daedalus or the tripods made by Hephaestus, of which the poet relates that

> Of their own motion they entered the
> conclave of Gods on Olympus.

A shuttle would then weave of itself, and a plectrum would do its own harp-playing. In this situation managers would not need subordinates and masters would not need slaves.

1254ᵃ1 The instruments of which we have just been speaking are instruments of production; but property is an instrument of action. From the shuttle there issues something which is different, and exists apart, from the immediate act of its use; but from garments or beds there comes only the one fact of their use. We may add that, since production and action are different in kind, and both of them need instruments, those instruments must also show a corresponding difference. Life is action and not production; and therefore the slave is a servant in the sphere of action.

1254ª8 The term 'article of property' is used in the same way in which the term 'part' is also used. A part is not only a part of something other than itself: it also belongs entirely to that other thing. It is the same with an article of property. Accordingly, while the master is merely the master of the slave, and does not belong to him, the slave is not only the slave of his master; he also belongs entirely to him.

1254ª13 From these considerations we can see clearly what is the nature of the slave and what is his capacity: anybody who by his nature is not his own man, but another's, is by his nature a slave; anybody who, being a man, is an article of property is another's man; an article of property is an instrument intended for the purpose of action and separable from its possessor.

Chapter 5

There is a principle of rule and subordination in nature at large: it appears especially in the realm of animate creation. By virtue of that principle, the soul rules the body; and by virtue of it the master, who possesses the rational faculty of the soul, rules the slave, who possesses only bodily powers and the faculty of understanding the directions given by another's reason. But nature, though she intends, does not always succeed in achieving a clear distinction between men born to be masters and men born to be slaves.

1254ª17 We have next to consider whether there are, or are not, some people who are by nature such as are here defined; whether, in other words, there are some people for whom slavery is the better and just condition, or whether the reverse is the case and all slavery

is contrary to nature. The issue is not difficult, whether we study it philosophically in the light of reason, or consider it empirically on the basis of the actual facts. The relation of ruler and ruled is one of those things which are not only necessary, but also beneficial; and there are species in which a distinction is already marked, immediately at birth, between those of its members who are intended for being ruled and those who are intended to rule. There are also many kinds both of ruling and ruled elements. (Moreover the rule which is exercised over the better sort of subjects is a better sort of rule—as, for example, rule exercised over a man is better than rule over an animal. The reason is that the value of something which is produced increases with the value of those contributing to it; and where one element rules and the other is ruled, there is something which they jointly produce.) In all cases where there is a compound, constituted of more than one part but forming one common entity, whether the parts be continuous or discrete, a ruling element and a ruled can always be traced. This characteristic is present in animate beings by virtue of the whole constitution of nature; for even in things which are inanimate there is a sort of ruling principle, such as is to be found, for example, in a musical harmony. But such considerations perhaps belong to a more popular method of inquiry; and we may content ourselves here with saying that animate beings are composed, in the first place, of soul and body, with the former naturally ruling and the latter naturally ruled. When investigating the natural state of things, we must fix our attention, not on those which are in a corrupt, but on those which are in a natural condition. It follows that we must consider the man who is in the best state both of body and soul, and in whom the rule of soul over body is accordingly evident; for with vicious people or those in a vicious condition, the reverse would often appear to be true—the body ruling the soul as the result of their evil and unnatural condition.

1254ᵇ2 It is possible, as we have said, to observe first in animate beings the presence of a ruling authority, both of the sort exercised by a master over slaves and of the sort exercised by a statesman over fellow citizens. The soul rules the body with the authority of a master: reason rules the appetite with the authority of a statesman or a monarch. In this sphere it is clearly natural and beneficial to the body that it should be ruled by the soul, and again it is natural and beneficial to the affective part of the soul that it should be ruled by the reason and the rational part; whereas the equality of the two elements, or their reverse relation, is always detrimental. The same principle is true of the relation of man to other animals. Tame animals have a better nature than wild, and it is better for all such animals that they should be ruled by man because they then get the benefit of preservation. Again, the relation of male to female is naturally that of the superior to the inferior, of the ruling to the ruled. This general principle must similarly hold good of all human beings generally.

1254ᵇ16 We may thus conclude that all men who differ from others as much as the body differs from the soul, or an animal from a man (and this is the case with all whose function is bodily service, and who produce their best when they supply such service)— all such are by nature slaves. In their case, as in the other cases just mentioned, it is better to be ruled by a master. Someone is thus a slave by nature if he is capable of becoming the property of another (and for this reason does actually become another's property) and if he participates in reason to the extent of apprehending it in another, though destitute of it himself. Other animals do not apprehend reason but obey their instincts. Even so there is

little divergence in the way they are used; both of them (slaves and tame animals) provide bodily assistance in satisfying essential needs.

1254ᵇ27 It is nature's intention also to erect a physical difference between the bodies of free men and those of the slaves, giving the latter strength for the menial duties of life, but making the former upright in carriage and (though useless for physical labour) useful for the various purposes of civic life—a life which tends, as it develops, to be divided into military service and the occupations of peace. The contrary of nature's intention, however, often happens: there are some slaves who have the bodies of free men, as there are others who have a free man's soul. But, if there were men who were as distinguished in their bodies alone as are the statues of the gods, all would agree that the others should be their slaves. And if this is true when the difference is one of the body, it may be affirmed with still greater justice when the difference is one of the soul; though it is not as easy to see the beauty of the soul as it is to see that of the body.

1254ᵇ39 It is thus clear that, just as some are by nature free, so others are by nature slaves, and for these latter the condition of slavery is both beneficial and just.

Chapter 6

Legal or conventional slavery: the divergence of views about its justice, and the reason for this divergence. In spite of the divergence, there is a general consensus—though it is not clearly formulated—that superiority in goodness justifies the owning and controlling of slaves. Granted such superiority in the master, slavery is a beneficial and just system.

1255ᵃ3 But it is easy to see that those who hold an opposite view are also in a way correct. 'Slavery' and 'slave' are terms which are used in two different senses; for there is also a kind of slave, and of slavery, which owes its existence to law. (The law in question is a kind of understanding that those vanquished in war are held to belong to the victors.) That slavery can be justified by such a convention is a principle against which a number of jurists bring an 'indictment of illegality', as one might against an orator. They regard it as a detestable notion that someone who is subjugated by force should become the slave and subject of one who has the capacity to subjugate him, and is his superior in power. Even among men of judgment there are some who accept this and some who do not. The cause of this divergence of view, and the reason why the opposing contentions overlap one another, is to be found in the following consideration. There is a sense in which good qualities, when they are furnished with the right resources, have the greatest power to subjugate; and a victor is always pre-eminent in respect of some sort of good. It thus appears that 'power never goes without good qualities'; and the dispute between the two sides thus comes to turn exclusively on the point of justice. (In this matter some think that being just consists in goodwill while others hold that the rule of the stronger is in itself justice.) If these different positions are distinguished from one another, no other argument has any cogency, or even plausibility, against the view that one who is superior in goodness ought to rule over, and be the master of, his inferiors.

1255ª21 There are some who, clinging, as they think, to a sort of justice (for law is a sort of justice), assume that slavery in war is just. Simultaneously, however, they contradict that assumption; for in the first place it is possible that the original cause of a war may not be just, and in the second place no one would ever say that someone who does not deserve to be in a condition of slavery is really a slave. If

such a view were accepted, the result would be that men reputed to be of the highest rank would be turned into slaves or the children of slaves, if they [or their parents] happened to be captured and sold into slavery. This is the reason why they do not like to call such people slaves, but prefer to confine the term to barbarians. But by this use of terms they are, in reality, only seeking to express that same idea of the natural slave which we began by mentioning. They are driven, in effect, to admit that there are some who are everywhere slaves, and others who are everywhere free. The same line of thought is followed in regard to good birth. Greeks regard themselves as well born not only in their own country, but absolutely and in all places; but they regard barbarians as well born only in their own country—thus assuming that there is one sort of good birth and freedom which is absolute, and another which is only relative. We are reminded of what Helen says in the play of Theodectes:

> Scion of Gods, by both descents alike,
> Who would presume to call me serving-maid?

When they use such terms as these, men are using the one criterion of the presence, or absence, of goodness for the purpose of distinguishing between slave and free man, or again, between the well-born and the low-born. They are claiming that just as man is born of man, and animal of animal, so a good man is born of good men. It is often the case, however, that nature wishes but fails to achieve this result.

1255ᵇ4 It is thus clear that there is some reason for the divergence of view which has been discussed—it is not true that the one group are natural slaves and the other natural free men. It is also clear that there are cases where such a distinction exists, and that here it is beneficial and just that the former should actually be a slave and the latter a master—the one being ruled, and the other exercising the kind of rule for which he is naturally intended and therefore acting as master. But a wrong exercise of his rule by a master is a thing which is disadvantageous for both master and slave. The part and the whole, like the body and the soul, have an identical interest; and the slave is a part of the master, in the sense of being a living but separate part of his body. There is thus a community of interest, and a relation of friendship, between master and slave, when both of them naturally merit the position in which they stand. But the reverse is true, when matters are otherwise and slavery rests merely on legal sanction and superior power. . . .

BOOK II

REVIEW OF CONSTITUTIONS

A: Constitutions in Theory

Chapter 1

1. Plato's Republic. Before describing our own conception of the best constitution we must consider both those constitutions that are in force in cities considered to be well governed and those constitutions that have been proposed by our predecessors. In doing so we should note that political association is a sharing: so we may ask 'How much should be shared?' In Plato's Republic *it is proposed that women, children, and property should be held in common.*

1260ᵇ27 Our purpose is to consider what form of political association is best for people able so far as possible to live as they would wish. We must therefore consider not only constitutions actually in force in cities that are said to be well governed, but also other forms of constitution which people have proposed if

these are thought to have merit. In this way we will be able to see in what respects these constitutions are properly designed and useful. What is more, when we proceed to look for something different from them, we shall not seem to be the sort of people who desire at all costs to show their own ingenuity, but rather to have adopted our method in consequence of the defects we have found in existing forms.

1260ᵇ36 Our starting-point must be the one that is natural for such a discussion. It is necessary either that the citizens have all things in common, or that they have nothing in common, or that they have some things in common, and others not. It is clearly impossible that they should have nothing in common: the constitution of a city involves in itself some sort of association, and its members must in the first place share a common locality. Just as a single city [*polis*] must have a single locality, so citizens are those who share in a single city. But is it better that a city which is to be well conducted should share in all the things in which it is possible for it to share, or that it should share in some things and not in others? It is certainly possible that the citizens should share children and women and property with one another. This is the plan proposed in the *Republic* of Plato, where 'Socrates' argues that children and women and property should be held in common. We are thus faced by the question whether it is better to remain in our present condition or to follow the rule of life laid down in the *Republic*.

Chapter 2

Community of women and children. Criticisms of the end or object (unity) which Plato proposes to attain by it: (a) carried to its logical extreme, that object would produce a one-man city; (b) it neglects the social differentiation necessary in a city (a differentiation which, even in a city of 'equals and likes', produces the distinction of rulers and ruled); (c) it thus makes self-sufficiency impossible, because self-sufficiency involves different elements making different contributions.

1261ᵃ10 A system in which women are common to all involves, among many others, the following difficulties. The *object* for which Socrates states that it ought to be instituted is evidently not established by the arguments which he uses. Moreover, the end which he states as necessary for the city [*polis*] is impracticable; and yet he gives no account of the lines on which it ought to be interpreted. I have in mind here the idea, which Socrates takes as his premise, that the greatest possible unity of the whole city is the supreme good. Yet it is obvious that a city which goes on becoming more and more of a unit, will eventually cease to be a city at all. A city, by its nature, is some sort of plurality. If it becomes more of a unit, it will first become a household instead of a city, and then an individual instead of a household; for we should all call the household more of a unit than the city, and the individual more of a unit than the household. It follows that, even if we could, we ought not to achieve this object: it would be the destruction of the city.

1261ᵃ22 Not only is the city composed of a *number* of people: it is also composed of different *kinds* of people, for a city cannot be composed of those who are like one another. There is a difference between a city and a military alliance. An alliance, formed by its very nature for the sake of the mutual help which its members can render to one another, possesses utility purely in virtue of its quantity, even if there is no difference of kind among its members. It is like a weight which depresses the scales more heavily in the balance. In this respect a *city* will also differ from a tribe, assuming that the members of the tribe are not scattered in separate villages, but [are united

in a confederacy] like the Arcadians. A real unity must be made up of elements which differ in kind. It follows that the stability of every city depends on each of its elements rendering to the others an amount equivalent to what it receives from them—a principle already laid down in the *Ethics*. This has to be the case even among free and equal citizens. They cannot all rule simultaneously; they must therefore each hold office for a year, unless they adopt some other arrangement or some other period of time. In this way it comes about that all are rulers, just as it would if shoemakers and carpenters changed their occupations so that the same people were not always following these professions. Since the arrangement [followed in the arts and crafts] is also better when applied to the affairs of the political association, it would clearly be better for the same people always to be rulers wherever possible. But where this is impossible, through the natural equality of all the citizens—and also because justice requires the participation of all in office (whether office be a good thing or a bad)—there is an imitation of it, if equals retire from office in turn and are all, apart from their period of office, in the same position. This means that some rule, and others are ruled, in turn, as if they had become, for the time being, different people. We may add that even those who are rulers differ from one another, some holding one kind of office and some another.

1261ᵇ6 These considerations are sufficient to show, first, that it is not the nature of the city to be a unit in the sense in which some thinkers say that it is, and secondly, that what is said to be the supreme good of a city is really its ruin. But surely the 'good' of each thing is what preserves it in being.

1261ᵇ10 There is still another consideration which may be used to prove that the policy of attempting an extreme unification of the city is not a good policy. A household is something which attains a greater degree of self-sufficiency than an individual; and a city, in turn, is something which attains self-sufficiency to a greater degree than a household. But it becomes fully a city, only when the association which forms it is large enough to be self-sufficing. On the assumption, therefore, that the higher degree of self-sufficiency is the more desirable thing, the lesser degree of unity is more desirable than the greater.

Chapter 3

Community of women and children (continued). Criticisms of such community considered as a means for producing the end of unity: (a) as all collectively, and not each individually, are parents, there will be no real feeling, but rather a general apathy; (b) kinship will be fractional kinship (when 1,000 are father to the same child, each father is only 1/1,000 father); (c) nature will 'recur', and spoil the scheme.

1261ᵇ16 Even if it were the supreme good of a political association that it should have the greatest possible unity, this unity does not appear to follow from the formula of 'All men saying "Mine" and "Not mine" at the same time,' which, in the view of 'Socrates', is the index of the perfect unity of a city. The word 'all' has a double sense: if it means 'each separately', the object which 'Socrates' desires to realize may perhaps be realized in a greater degree: each and all separately will then say 'My wife' (or 'My son') of one and the same person; and each and all separately will speak in the same way of property, and of every other concern. But it is not in the sense of 'each separately' that all who have children and women in common will actually speak of them. They will all call them 'Mine'; but they will do so collectively, and not individually. The same is true of property also; [all will call it 'Mine'] but

they will do so in the sense of 'all collectively', and not in the sense of 'each separately'. It is therefore clear that there is a certain fallacy in the use of the term 'all'. 'All' and 'both' and 'odd' and 'even' are liable by their ambiguity to produce captious arguments even in reasoned discussions. We may therefore conclude that the formula of 'all men saying "Mine" of the same object' is in one sense something fine but impracticable, and in another sense does nothing to promote harmony.

1261ᵇ32 In addition to these problems the formula also involves another disadvantage. What is common to the greatest number gets the least amount of care. People pay most attention to what is their own: they care less for what is common; or, at any rate, they care for it only to the extent to which each is individually concerned. Even where there is no other cause for inattention, people are more prone to neglect their duty when they think that another is attending to it: this is what happens in domestic service, where many attendants are sometimes of less assistance than a few. [The scheme proposed in the *Republic* means that] each citizen will have a thousand sons: they will not be the sons of each citizen individually: any son whatever will be equally the son of any father whatever. The result will be that all will equally neglect them.

1262ª1 Furthermore each person, when he says 'Mine' of any citizen who is prosperous or the reverse, is speaking fractionally. He means only that he is 'Mine' to the extent of a fraction determined by the total number of citizens. When he says 'He is mine' or 'He is so-and-so's,' the term 'Mine' or 'So-and-so's' is used with reference to the whole body concerned—the whole 1,000, or whatever may be the total number of citizens. Even so he cannot be sure; for there is no evidence who had a child born to him, or whether, if one was born, it managed to survive. Which is the better system—that each of 2,000, or 10,000, people should say 'Mine' of a child in this fractional sense, or that each should say 'Mine' in the sense in which the word is now used in ordinary cities? As things are, one man calls by the name of 'My son' the same person whom a second man calls by the name of 'My brother': a third calls him 'My cousin' or 'My relative', because he is somehow related to him, either by blood or by connection through marriage; while besides these different modes of address someone else may use still another, and call him 'My clansman' or 'My tribesman'. It is better to be someone's own cousin than to be his son after this fashion. Even on Plato's system it is impossible to avoid the chance that some of the citizens might guess who are their brothers, or children, or fathers, or mothers. The resemblances between children and parents must inevitably lead to their drawing conclusions about one another. That this actually happens in real life is stated as fact by some of the writers on descriptive geography. They tell us that some of the inhabitants of upper Libya have their women in common; but the children born of such unions can still be distinguished by their resemblance to their fathers. Indeed there are some women, and some females in the animal world (mares, for instance, and cows), that show a strong natural tendency to produce offspring resembling the male parent: the Pharsalian mare which was called the 'Just Return' is a good example.

Chapter 4

Community of women and children (continued). Problems arise when parents do not know their children, or children their parents. At best such a community produces a watery sort of friendship. The addition to it of a scheme of transposition of ranks raises further difficulties.

1262ª25 There are also other difficulties which those who construct such a community will not find it easy to avoid. We may take as examples cases of assault, homicide, whether unintentional or intentional, fighting, and slander. All these offences, when they are committed against father or mother or a near relative, differ from offences against people who are not so related, in being breaches of natural piety. Such offences must happen more frequently when men are ignorant of their relatives than when they know who they are; and when they do happen, the customary penance can be made if people know their relatives, but none can be made if they are ignorant of them. It is also surprising that, after having made sons common to all, [Plato] should simply forbid lovers from engaging in carnal intercourse. Nor does he forbid other familiarities which, if practised between son and father, or brother and brother, are the very height of indecency, all the more as this form of love [even if it is not expressed] is in itself indecent. It is surprising, too, that he should debar male lovers from carnal intercourse on the one ground of the excessive violence of the pleasure, and that he should think it a matter of indifference that the lovers may be father and son, or again that they may be brothers.

1262ª40 Community of women and children would seem to be more useful if it were practised among the farmers rather than among the guardians. The spirit of friendship is likely to exist to a lesser degree where women and children are common; and the governed class ought to have little of that spirit if it is to obey and not to attempt revolution. Generally, such a system must produce results directly opposed to those which a system of properly constituted laws should produce, and equally opposed to the very object for which, in the view of 'Socrates', this community of women and children ought to be instituted.

Friendship, we believe, is the chief good of cities, because it is the best safeguard against the danger of factional disputes. 'Socrates' himself particularly commends the ideal of the unity of the city; and that unity is commonly held, and expressly stated by him, to be the result of friendship. We may cite the argument of the discourses on love, where 'Aristophanes', as we know, speaks of lovers desiring out of friendship to grow together into a unity, and to be one instead of two. Now in that case it would be inevitable that both or at least one of them should cease to exist. But in the case of the political association there would be merely a watery sort of friendship: a father would be very little disposed to say 'Mine' of a son, and a son would be as little disposed to say 'Mine' of a father. Just as a little sweet wine, mixed with a great deal of water, produces a tasteless mixture, so family feeling is diluted and tasteless when family names have as little meaning as they have in a constitution of this sort, and when there is so little reason for a father treating his sons as sons, or a son treating his father as a father, or brothers one another as brothers. There are two things which particularly move people to care for and love an object. One of these is that the object should belong to yourself: the other is that you should like it. Neither of these motives can exist among those who live under a constitution such as this.

1262ᵇ24 There is still a further difficulty. It concerns the way in which children born among the farmers and craftsmen are to be transferred to the guardian class, and vice versa. How such transposition is actually to be effected is a matter of great perplexity; and in any case those who transfer such children, and assign them their new place, will be bound to know who are the children so placed and with whom they are being placed. In addition, those problems of assault, unnatural affection, and

homicide, which have already been mentioned, will occur even more in the case of these people. Those transferred from the guardian class to that of the other citizens will cease for the future to address the guardians as brothers, or children, or fathers, or mothers, as the case may be; and it will have the same effect for those who have been transferred from among the other citizens to the guardians. Such people will no longer avoid committing these offences on account of their kinship.

1262ᵇ35 This may serve as a determination of the issues raised by the idea of community of women and children.

Chapter 5

Community of property. Three possible systems of property. The difficulties of a system under which ownership and use are both common: the merits of a system under which ownership is private and use is common—it gives more pleasure, and it encourages goodness more. Communism cannot remedy evils which really spring from the defects of human nature: it is also based on a false conception of unity, and neglects the true unity which comes from education; finally, it is contradicted by experience. Plato's particular scheme of community of property leaves the position of the farming class obscure. The system of government which he connects with his scheme is too absolute, and is likely to cause discontent: it also deprives the ruling class of any happiness.

1262ᵇ39 The next subject for consideration is property. What is the proper system of property for citizens who are to live under the best form of constitution? Should property be held in common or not? This is an issue which may be considered in itself, and apart from any proposals for community of women and children. Even if women and children are held separately, as is now universally the case, questions relating to property still remain for discussion. Should use and ownership both be common? For example, there may be a system under which plots of land are owned separately, but the crops (as actually happens among some tribal peoples) are brought into a common stock for the purpose of consumption. Secondly, and conversely, the land may be held in common ownership, and may also be cultivated in common, but the crops may be divided among individuals for their private use: some of the barbarian peoples are also said to practise this second method of sharing. Thirdly, the plots and the crops may both be common.

1263ᵃ8 When the cultivators of the soil are a different body from the citizens who own it, the position will be different and easier to handle; but when the citizens who own the soil do the work themselves, the problems of property will cause a good deal of trouble. If they do not share equally in the work and in the enjoyment of the produce, those who do more work and get less of the produce will be bound to raise complaints against those who get a large reward and do little work. In general it is a difficult business to live together and to share in any form of human activity, but it is specially difficult in such matters. Fellow-travellers who merely share in a journey furnish an illustration: they generally quarrel about ordinary matters and take offence on petty occasions. So, again, the servants with whom we are most prone to take offence are those who are particularly employed in ordinary everyday services.

1263ᵃ21 Difficulties such as these, and many others, are involved in a system of community of property. The present system would be far preferable, if it were embellished with social customs and the enactment of proper laws. It would possess the advantages of both systems, and would combine the merits of a system of community of property with those of the system of private property. For, although there is a sense in which property *ought* to be common, it should in general be private. When everyone has his own separate sphere of interest, there will not be the same ground for quarrels; and they will make more effort, because each man will feel that he is applying himself to what is his own.

1263ᵃ30 On such a scheme, too, moral goodness will ensure that the property of each is made to serve the use of all, in the spirit of the proverb which says 'Friends' goods are goods in common.' Even now there are some cities in which the outlines of such a scheme are so far apparent, as to suggest that it is not impossible; in well-ordered cities, more particularly, there are some elements of it already existing, and others which might be added. [In these cities] each citizen has his own property; part of which he makes available to his friends, and part of which he uses as though it was common property. In Sparta, for example, men use one another's slaves, and one another's horses and dogs, as if they were their own; and they take provisions on a journey, if they happen to be in need, from the farms in the countryside. It is clear from what has been said that the better system is that under which property is privately owned but is put to common use; and the function proper to the legislator is to make men so disposed that they will treat property in this way.

1263ᵃ40 In addition, to think of a thing as your own makes an inexpressible difference, so far as pleasure is concerned. It may well be that regard for oneself is a feeling implanted by nature, and not a mere random impulse. Self-love is rightly censured, but that is not so much loving oneself as loving oneself in excess. It is the same with one who loves money; after all, virtually everyone loves things of this kind. We may add that a very

Carthage, where a number of official bodies are entitled to decide cases of all kinds.

1275ᵇ13 But our definition of citizenship can be amended. In other kinds of constitution members of the assembly and the courts do not hold that office for an indeterminate period. They hold it for a limited term; and it is to some or all of these that the citizen's function of deliberating and judging (whether on all issues or only a few) is assigned. From these considerations it emerges clearly who a citizen is. We say that one who is entitled to share in deliberative or judicial office is thereby a citizen of that city, and a city, in its simplest terms, is a body of such people adequate in number for achieving a self-sufficient existence. . . .

Chapter 5

There is a further question relating to citizenship, 'Can mechanics and labourers be citizens, and if they cannot be citizens, how are they to be described?' They should not be citizens, because they cannot achieve the excellence of the good citizen, though they are necessary to the existence of the city. But the answer varies from one kind of constitution to another: in an aristocratic constitution, mechanics and labourers cannot be citizens; in an oligarchy, a rich mechanic may.

1277ᵇ33 There is still a question which remains to be considered in regard to the citizen. Is the citizen in the true sense one who is entitled to share in office, or must mechanics be also included in the ranks of citizens? If we hold that those, who have no share in public offices, are also to be included, we shall have some citizens who can never achieve the excellence of the good citizen (for this man will also be a citizen). If, on the other hand, someone of this sort is not a citizen, in what class is he to be placed? He is not a resident alien, neither is he a foreigner. Or shall we say that this point

does not involve us in any absurdity? For the same is true of slaves and freed men. The truth is that we cannot include as citizens all who are necessary to the city's existence. Similarly, too, children are not citizens in the same sense as adult males. Adults are citizens absolutely; children are citizens only in a qualified sense—they are citizens but undeveloped ones. There were some places, in ancient times, where the class of mechanics was actually composed of slaves or foreigners only, and this explains why a great number of mechanics are slaves or foreigners even today.

1278ᵃ8 The best form of city will not make the mechanic a citizen. Where mechanics are admitted to citizenship we shall have to say that the citizen excellence of which we have spoken cannot be attained by every citizen, by all who are simply free men, but can only be achieved by those who are free from the necessary tasks of life. Those who do the necessary tasks may be divided into two classes, slaves, who do them for individuals, and mechanics and labourers, who do them for the community.

1278ᵃ13 If we start from this basis, and carry our inquiry a little further, the position of these mechanics and labourers will soon become evident; in fact, enough has already been said to make it clear, once the bearing of the argument is grasped. Constitutions are various: there must thus be various kinds of citizens; more especially, there must be various kinds of citizens who are subjects. In one variety of constitution it will be necessary that mechanics and labourers should be citizens: in other varieties it will be impossible. It will be impossible, for example, where there is a constitution of the type termed 'aristocratic', with offices distributed on the basis of worth and excellence; for one who lives the life of a mechanic or labourer cannot pursue the things which belong to excellence. The case is different in oligarchies. Even there, it is true, a labourer cannot be a citizen (participation in office depending on a high property qualification); but a mechanic may, for the simple reason that craftsmen often become rich. Yet in Thebes there was a law that no one could share in office who had not abstained from selling in the market for a period of ten years. On the other hand, there are many constitutions where the law goes to the length of admitting aliens to citizenship. There are, for example, some democracies where someone who has only a citizen mother is admitted; and there are many cities where the same privilege is given to those of illegitimate birth. But the policy of extending citizenship so widely is [generally] due to a dearth of genuine citizens; and it is only shortage of population which produces such legislation. When they have sufficient numbers they gradually disqualify such people: first sons of a slave father or slave mother are disqualified; then those who are born of a citizen mother but an alien father; and finally citizenship is confined to those who are of citizen parentage on both sides.

1278ᵃ34 These considerations prove two things: that there are several different kinds of citizens, and that the name of citizen is particularly applicable to those who share in the offices and honours of the city. Homer accordingly speaks in the *Iliad* of a man being treated

like an alien man, without honour;

and it is true that those who do not share in positions of honour in the city are just like resident aliens. When restrictions are imposed by subterfuge their only object is to hoodwink those inhabitants who are not citizens.

1278ᵃ40 Two conclusions also emerge from our discussion of the question, 'Is the excellence of the good man identical with that of the good citizen, or different from it?' The first is that there are some cities in which the

good man and the good citizen are identical, and some in which they are different. The second is that, in cities of the former type, it is not all good citizens who are also good men, but only those among them who hold the position of statesmen—in other words, those who direct or are capable of directing, either alone or in conjunction with others, the conduct of public affairs. . . .

B: Constitutions and Their Classification

Chapter 6

The definition of a constitution. The classification of constitutions depends on (1) the ends pursued by cities, and (2) the kind of rule exercised by their governments. The true end of a city is a good life, and it is the common interest to achieve this: the right kind of rule is authority exercised in the common interest. We may thus distinguish 'right' constitutions, which are directed to the common interest, and 'wrong' or 'perverted' constitutions directed to the selfish interest of the ruling body.

1278ᵇ6 Having determined these matters we have next to consider whether there is a single type of constitution, or whether there are a number of types. If there are a number of types, what are these types; how many of them are there; and how do they differ? A constitution [or *politeia*] may be defined as 'the organization of a city [or *polis*], in respect of its offices generally, but especially in respect of that particular office which is sovereign in all issues.' The civic body is everywhere the sovereign of the city; in fact the civic body is the constitution itself. In democratic cities, for example, the people [*dēmos*] is sovereign: in oligarchies, on the other hand, the few [or *oligoi*] have that position; and this difference in the sovereign bodies is the reason why we say that the two types of constitution differ—as we may equally apply the same reasoning to other types besides these.

1278ᵇ15 We must first ascertain two things: the nature of the end for which a city exists, and the various kinds of rule to which mankind and its associations are subject. It has already been stated, in our first book (where we were concerned with the management of the household and the control of slaves), that 'man is a political animal.' For this reason people desire to live a social life even when they stand in no need of mutual succour; but they are also drawn together by a common interest, in proportion as each attains a share in the good life. The good life is the chief end, both for the community as a whole and for each of us individually. But people also come together, and form and maintain political associations, merely for the sake of life; for perhaps there is some element of the good even in the simple fact of living, so long as the evils of existence do not preponderate too heavily. It is an evident fact that most people cling hard enough to life to be willing to endure a good deal of suffering, which implies that life has in it a sort of healthy happiness and a natural quality of pleasure.

1278ᵇ30 It is easy enough to distinguish the various kinds of rule of which people commonly speak; and indeed we have often had occasion to define them ourselves in works intended for the general public. The rule of a master is one kind; and here, though there is really a common interest which unites the natural master and the natural slave, the fact remains that the rule is primarily exercised with a view to the master's interest, and only incidentally with a view to that of the slave, who must be preserved in existence if the rule is to remain. Rule over wife and children, and over the household generally, is a second kind of rule, which we have called by the name of household management. Here the rule is either exercised in the interest of the ruled or for the attainment of some advantage common to both ruler and ruled. Essentially it is exercised in the interest of the ruled, as is also plainly the case with other arts besides that of ruling, such as medicine and gymnastics—though an art may incidentally be exercised for the benefit of its practitioner, and there is nothing to prevent (say) a trainer from becoming occasionally a member of the class he instructs, in the same sort of way as a steersman is always one of the crew. Thus a trainer or steersman primarily considers the good of those who are subject to his authority; but when he becomes one of them personally, he incidentally shares in the benefit of that good—the steersman thus being also a member of the crew, and the trainer (though still a trainer) becoming also a member of the class which he instructs.

1279ᵃ8 For this reason, when the constitution of a city is constructed on the principle that its members are equals and peers, the citizens think it proper that they should hold office by turns. At any rate this is the natural system, and the system which used to be followed in the days when people believed that they ought to serve by turns, and each assumed that others would take over the duty of considering his benefit, just as he himself, during his term of office, had considered their interest. Today because of the profits to be derived from office and the handling of public property, people want to hold office continuously. It is as if they were invalids, who got the benefit of being healthy by being permanently in office: at any rate their ardour for office is just what it would be if that were the case. The conclusion which follows is clear: those constitutions which consider the common interest are right constitutions, judged by the standard of absolute justice. Those constitutions which consider only the personal interest of the rulers are all wrong constitutions, or perversions of the right forms. Such perverted forms are despotic; whereas the city is an association of free men.

Chapter 7

These two types of constitution each fall into three subdivisions on the basis of number, i.e. according as the One, or the Few, or the Many are the ruling authority in each type. We have thus, as the three subdivisions of the 'right' type, Kingship, Aristocracy, and 'Constitutional Government' or 'Polity'; as the three subdivisions of the 'wrong' type, Tyranny, Oligarchy, and Democracy.

1279ª22 Now that these matters have been determined, the next subject for consideration is the number and nature of the different constitutions. We may first examine those constitutions that are rightly formed, since, when these have been determined, the different perversions will at once be apparent.

1279ª25 The term 'constitution' [*politeia*] signifies the same thing as the term 'civic body' [*politeuma*]. The civic body in every city [*polis*] is the sovereign [*to kurion*]; and the sovereign must necessarily be either One, or Few, or Many. On this basis we may say that when the One, or the Few, or the Many rule with a view to the common interest, the constitutions under which they do so must necessarily be right constitutions. On the other hand, the constitutions directed to the personal interests of the One, or the Few, or the Masses, must necessarily be perversions. Either we should say that those who do not share in the constitution are not citizens, or they ought to have their share of the benefits. According to customary usage, among monarchical forms of government the type which looks to the common interest is called Kingship; among forms of government by a few people (but more than

one) it is called Aristocracy—that name being given to this species either because the best [*aristoi*] are the rulers, or because its object is what is best [*ariston*] for the city and its members. Finally, when the masses govern the city with a view to the common interest, the form of government is called by the generic name common to all constitutions (or polities)—the name of 'Constitutional Government'. There is a good reason for this usage: it is possible for one man, or a few, to be of outstanding excellence; but when it comes to a large number, we can hardly expect precision in all the varieties of excellence. What we can expect particularly is the military kind of excellence, which is the kind that shows itself in a mass. This is the reason why the defence forces are the most sovereign body under this constitution, and those who possess arms are the ones who participate in it.

1279ᵇ4 The perversions that correspond to the constitutions just mentioned are: Tyranny, [the perversion of] Kingship; Oligarchy, [the perversion of] Aristocracy; and Democracy, [the perversion of] 'Constitutional Government' [or polity]. Tyranny is a government by a single person directed to the interest of that person; Oligarchy is directed to the interest of the well-to-do; Democracy is directed to the interest of the poor. None of these benefits the common interest.

Chapter 8

The basis of number is not, however, adequate. The real basis, at any rate so far as oligarchy and democracy are concerned, is social class: what makes an oligarchy is the rule of the rich (rather than the few), and what makes a democracy is the rule of the poor (rather than the many). Number is an accidental, and not an essential, attribute; but the accidental generally accompanies the essential.

1279ᵇ11 We must consider at somewhat greater length what each of these constitutions is. There are certain difficulties involved; and when one is pursuing a philosophical method of inquiry in any branch of study, and not merely looking to practical considerations, the proper course is to set out the truth about every particular with no neglect or omission.

1279ᵇ16 Tyranny, as has just been said, is single-person government of the political association on the lines of despotism; oligarchy exists where those who have property are the sovereign authority of the constitution; and, conversely, democracy exists where sovereign authority is composed of the poorer classes, who are without much property.

1279ᵇ20 The first difficulty which arises is a matter of definition. It could be that the majority are well-to-do and that these hold the sovereignty in a city; but when the majority is sovereign there is [said to be] democracy. Similarly it could happen that the poorer classes were fewer in number than the well-to-do, and yet were stronger and had sovereign authority in the constitution; but where a small number has sovereignty there is said to be oligarchy. Thus it may seem that the definitions we have given of these constitutions cannot be correct.

1279ᵇ26 We might attempt to overcome the difficulty by combining both of the factors: wealth with paucity of numbers, and poverty with mass. On this basis oligarchy might be defined as the constitution under which the rich, being also few in number, hold the public offices; and similarly democracy might be defined as the constitution under which the poor, being also many in number, are in control. But this involves us in another difficulty. If there are no forms of oligarchy and democracy other than those enumerated, what names are we to give to the constitutions just suggested as conceivable—those where the wealthy form a majority and the poor a minority, and where

the wealthy majority in the one case, and the poor minority in the other, are the sovereign authority of the constitution? The course of the argument thus appears to show that whether the sovereign body is small or large in number (as it is respectively in oligarchies or in democracies) is an accidental attribute, due to the simple fact that the wealthy are generally few and the poor are generally numerous. Therefore the causes originally mentioned are not in fact the real causes of the difference between oligarchies and democracies. The real ground of the difference between oligarchy and democracy is poverty and riches. It is inevitable that there should be an oligarchy where the rulers, whether they are few or many, owe their position to riches; and it is equally inevitable that there should be democracy where the poor rule.

1280ᵃ2 It happens, however, as we have just remarked, that the former [i.e. the wealthy] are few and the latter [i.e. the poor] are numerous. It is only a few who have riches, but all alike share in free status; and it is on these grounds that the two parties dispute the control of the constitution.

C: The Principles of Oligarchy and Democracy and the Nature of Distributive Justice

Chapter 9

The principle of a constitution is its conception of justice; and this is the fundamental ground of difference between oligarchy and democracy. Democrats hold that if men are equal by birth, they should in justice have an equal share in office and honours: oligarchs hold that if they are unequal in wealth, they should in justice have unequal shares in these things. True justice means that those who have contributed to the end of the city should have privileges in proportion to their contribution to that end. The end of the city is not mere life, nor an alliance for mutual defence; it is the common promotion of a good quality of life. This although the citizens of a city must always inhabit a single territory, engage in intermarriage, and co-operate with each other in economic matters, the operative aim is always the promotion of a good quality of life. Those who contribute most to the realization of that aim should in justice have the largest share of office and honour.

1280ª7 We must next ascertain what are said to be the distinctive principles of oligarchy and democracy, and what are the oligarchical and the democratic conceptions of justice. All parties have a hold on a sort of conception of justice; but they both fail to carry it far enough, and do not express the true conception of justice in the whole of its range. For example, justice is considered to mean equality. It does mean equality—but equality for those who are equal, and not for all. Again, inequality is considered to be just; and indeed it is—but only for those who are unequal, and not for all. These people fail to consider for whom there should be equality or inequality and thus make erroneous judgments. The reason is that they are judging in their own case; and most people, as a rule, are bad judges where their own interests are involved. Justice is concerned with people; and a just distribution is one in which there is proportion between the things distributed and those to whom they are distributed, a point which has already been made in the *Ethics*. There is general agreement about what constitutes equality in the thing, but disagreement about what constitutes it in people. The main reason for this is the reason just stated, they are judging, and judging erroneously, in their own case; but there is also another reason, they are misled by the fact that they are professing a sort of conception of justice, and professing it up to a point, into thinking that

they profess one which is absolute and complete. Some think that if they are superior in one point, for example in wealth, they are superior in all: others believe that if they are equal in one respect, for instance in free birth, they are equal all round.

1280ª25 Both sides, however, fail to mention the really cardinal factor. If property is the end for which people come together and form an association, one's share of the city would be proportionate to one's share of the property; and in that case the argument of the oligarchical side would appear to be strong: they say that is not just for someone who has contributed one mina to share in a sum of a hundred minae on equal terms with one who has contributed all the rest and that this applies both to the original sum and to the interest accruing upon it. But the end of the city is not mere life; it is, rather, a good quality of life. Otherwise, there might be a city of slaves, or even a city of animals; but in the world as we know it any such city is impossible, because slaves and animals do not share in happiness nor in living according to their own choice. Similarly, it is not the end of the city to provide an alliance for mutual defence against all injury, nor does it exist for the purpose of exchange or [commercial] dealing. If that had been the end, the Etruscans and the Carthaginians would be in the position of belonging to a single city; and the same would be true to all peoples who have commercial treaties with one another. It is true that such peoples have agreements about imports; treaties to ensure just conduct; and written terms of alliance for mutual defence. On the other hand, they have no common offices to deal with these matters: each, on the contrary, has its own offices, confined to itself. Neither party concerns itself to ensure a proper quality of character among the members of the other; neither of them seeks to ensure that all who are included in the scope of the treaties are just and free from any form of vice; and they do not go beyond the aim of preventing their own members from committing injustice against one another. But it is the goodness or badness in the life of the city which engages the attention of those who are concerned to secure good government.

1280ᵇ6 The conclusion which clearly follows is that any city which is truly so called, and is not merely one in name, must devote itself to the end of encouraging goodness. Otherwise, a political association sinks into a mere alliance, which only differs in space [i.e. in the contiguity of its members] from other forms of alliance where the members live at a distance from one another. Otherwise, too, law becomes a mere covenant—or (in the phrase of the sophist Lycophron) 'a guarantor of just claims'—but lacks the capacity to make the citizens good and just.

1280ᵇ12 That this is the case may be readily proved. If two different sites could be united in one, so that the city [i.e. the *polis*] of Megara and that of Corinth were embraced by a single wall, that would not make a single city. If the citizens of two cities intermarried with one another, that would not make a single city, even though intermarriage is one of the forms of social life which are characteristic of a city. Nor would it make a city if a number of people, living at a distance from one another, but not at so great a distance but they could still associate, had a common system of laws to prevent their injuring one another in the course of exchange. We can imagine, for instance, one being a carpenter, another a farmer, a third a shoemaker, and others producing other goods; and we can imagine a total number of as many as 10,000. But if these people were associated in nothing further than matters such as exchange and alliance, they would still have failed to reach

the stage of a city. Why should this be the case? It cannot be ascribed to any lack of contiguity in such an association. The members of a group so constituted might come together on a single site; but if that were all—if each still treated his private house as if it were a city, and all of them still confined their mutual assistance to action against aggressors (as if it were only a question of a defensive alliance)—if, in a word, they associated with each other in the same fashion after coming together as they did when they were living apart—their association, even on its new basis, could not be deemed by any accurate thinker to be a city.

1280ᵇ29 It is clear, therefore, that a city is not an association for residence on a common site, or for the sake of preventing mutual injustice and easing exchange. These are indeed conditions which must be present before a city can exist; but the presence of all these conditions is not enough, in itself, to constitute a city. What constitutes a city is an association of households and clans in a good life, for the sake of attaining a perfect and self-sufficing existence. This, however, will not come about unless the members inhabit one and the self-same place and practise intermarriage. It was for this reason that the various institutions of a common social life—marriage-connections, kin-groups, religious gatherings, and social pastimes generally—arose in cities. This sort of thing is the business of friendship, for the pursuit of a common social life is friendship. Thus the purpose of a city is the good life, and these institutions are a means to that end. A city is constituted by the association of families and villages in a perfect and self-sufficing existence; and such an existence, on our definition, consists in living a happy and truly valuable life.

1281ᵃ2 It is therefore for the sake of actions valuable in themselves, and not for the sake of social life, that political associations must be considered to exist. Those who contribute most to this association have a greater share in the city than those who are equal to them (or even greater) in free birth and descent, but unequal in civic excellence, or than those who surpass them in wealth but are surpassed by them in excellence. From what has been said it is plain that all sides in the dispute about constitutions profess only a partial conception of justice.

Chapter 10

What person or body of people should be sovereign in a city: the people, the rich, the better sort of citizens, the one best, or the tyrant? All these alternatives present difficulties; and there is a difficulty even in a further alternative, that no person or body of people, but law, should be sovereign.

1281ª11 A difficulty arises when we turn to consider what body should be sovereign in a city. The people at large, the wealthy, the better sort, the one who is best of all, the tyrant. But all these alternatives appear to involve unpleasant results: indeed, how can it be otherwise? What if the poor, on the ground of their being a majority, proceed to divide among themselves the possessions of the wealthy—will not this be unjust? 'No, by heaven' (someone may reply); 'it has been justly decreed so by the sovereign body.' But if this is not the extreme of injustice, what is? Whenever a majority takes everything and divides among its members the possessions of a minority, that majority is obviously ruining the city. But goodness does not ruin whatever possesses it, nor can justice be such as to ruin a city. It is therefore clear that a law of this kind cannot possibly be just. The tyrant's acts too would necessarily be just; for he too uses coercion by virtue of superior power in just the same sort of way as the people coerce the wealthy. Is it just that a minority

composed of the wealthy should rule? Then if they too behave like the others—if they plunder and confiscate the property of the people—their action is just. If it is, then this behaviour would also be just in the former case. It is clear that all these acts of oppression are mean and unjust. But should the better sort have authority and be sovereign in all matters? In that case, the rest of the citizens would necessarily be deprived of honour, since they will not enjoy the honour of holding civic office. We speak of offices as honours; and when the same people hold office all the time, the rest of the community must necessarily be deprived of honour. Is it better that the one best man should rule? This is still more oligarchical because the number of those deprived of honour is even greater. It may perhaps be urged that it is a poor sort of policy to vest sovereignty in a human being, rather than in law; for human beings are subject to the passions that beset their souls. But the law itself may incline either towards oligarchy or towards democracy; and what difference will the sovereignty of law then make in the problems which have just been raised? The consequences already stated will follow just the same.

Chapter 11

It is possible, however, to defend the alternative, that the people should be sovereign. The people, when they are assembled, have a combination of qualities which enables them to deliberate wisely and to judge soundly. This suggests that they have a claim to be the sovereign body; it also suggests the scope of affairs in which they should be sovereign, or the powers which they should exercise. They should exercise deliberative and judicial functions; in particular, they should elect the magistrates and examine their conduct at the end of their tenure. Two objections may be raised. (1) It may be argued that experts are better judges than the non-expert; but this objection may be met by reference to (a) the combination of qualities in the assembled people (which makes them collectively better judges than the expert), and (b) the fact that in some cases laymen are in as good a position to judge as experts (which enables them to pass judgment on the behaviour of magistrates). (2) It may be urged that the people, if they have such powers, have more authority than the better sort of citizens who hold office as magistrates, though they are not of so good a quality; but we may answer to this that the people as a whole may well be of a high quality. We have always, however, to remember that rightly constituted laws should be the final sovereign, and that personal authority of any sort should only act in the particular cases which cannot be covered by a general law.

1281ª39 The other alternatives may be reserved for later inquiry; but the suggestion that the people at large should be sovereign rather than the few best men would [seem to present problems which] need resolution, and while it presents some difficulty it perhaps also contains some truth. There is this to be said for the many: each of them by himself may not be of a good quality; but when they all come together it is possible that they may surpass—collectively and as a body, although not individually—the quality of the few best, in much the same way that feasts to which many contribute may excel those provided at one person's expense. For when there are many, each has his share of goodness and practical wisdom; and, when all meet together, the people may thus become something like a single person, who, as he has many feet, many hands, and many senses, may also have many qualities of character and intelligence. This is the reason why many are also better judges of music and the writings of poets: some appreciate one part, some another, and all together appreciate all. The thing which makes a good

man differ from a unit in the crowd—as it is also the thing which is generally said to make a beautiful person differ from one who is not beautiful, or an artistic representation differ from ordinary reality—is that elements which are elsewhere scattered and separate are here combined in a unity. If the elements are taken separately, one may say of an artistic representation that it is surpassed by the eye of this person and by some other feature of that [person].

1281ᵇ15 It is not clear, however, that this contrast between the many, on the one hand, and the few good men, on the other, can apply to every people and to every large group. Perhaps, by heaven, there are some of which it clearly cannot be true; for otherwise the same argument would apply to the beasts. Yet what difference, one may ask, is there between some men and the beasts? All the same, there is nothing to prevent the view we have stated from being true of a particular group.

1281ᵇ21 It would thus seem possible to solve, by the considerations we have advanced, both the problem raised in the previous chapter ['Which people should be sovereign?'] and the further problem which follows upon it, 'What are the matters over which free men, or the general body of citizens—the sort of people who neither have wealth nor can make any claim on the ground of goodness—should properly exercise sovereignty?' Of course there is a danger in people of this sort sharing in the highest offices, as injustice may lead them into wrongdoing, and thoughtlessness into error. But there is also a serious risk in not letting them have some share of power; for a city with a body of disfranchised citizens who are numerous and poor must necessarily be a city which is full of enemies. The alternative left is to let them share in the deliberative and judicial functions. This is why Solon, and some of the other legislators, allow the people to elect officials and to call them to account at the end of their tenure of office, but not to hold office themselves in their individual capacity. When they all meet together, the people display a good enough gift of perception, and combined with the better class they are of service to the city (just as impure food, when it is mixed with pure, makes the whole concoction more nutritious than a small amount of pure would be); but each of them is imperfect in the judgments he forms by himself.

1281ᵇ38 But this arrangement of the constitution presents some difficulties. The first difficulty is that it may well be held that the function of judging when medical attendance has been properly given should belong to those whose profession it is to attend patients and cure the complaints from which they suffer—in a word, to members of the medical profession. The same may be held to be true of all other professions and arts; and just as medical men should have their conduct examined before a body of medics, so, too, should those who follow other professions have theirs examined before a body of members of their own profession. But the term 'medic' is applied to the ordinary practitioner, to the specialist who directs the course of treatment, and to someone who has some general knowledge of the art of medicine. (There are people of this last type to be found in connection with nearly all the arts.) We credit those who have a general knowledge with the power of judging as much as we do the experts. When we turn to consider the matter of election, the same principles would appear to apply. To make a proper election is equally the work of experts. It is the work of those who are versed in geometry to choose a geometrician, or again, of those who are acquainted with steering to choose a steersman; and even if, in some occupations and arts, there are some non-experts who also share in the ability to choose, they do not share in a higher degree than the experts. It would thus appear, on this line of argument, that the people should not be made sovereign, either in the matter of election of magistrates or in that of their examination.

1282ᵃ14 It may be, however, that these arguments are not altogether well founded for the reason given above—provided, that is to say, that the people is not too debased in character. Each individual may indeed be a worse judge than the experts; but all, when they meet together, are either better than experts or at any rate no worse. In the second place, there are a number of arts in which the craftsman is not the only, or even the best, judge. These are the arts whose products can be understood even by those who do not possess any skill in the art. A house, for instance, is something which can be understood by others besides the builder: indeed the user of a house, or in other words the householder, will judge it even better than he does. In the same way a steersman will judge a rudder better than a shipwright does; and the diner, not the cook, will be the best judge of a feast.

1282ᵃ23 The first difficulty would appear to be answered sufficiently by these considerations. But there is a second difficulty still to be faced, which is connected with the first. It would seem to be absurd that people of poor character should be sovereign on issues which are more important than those assigned to the better sort of citizens. The election of officials, and their examination at the end of their tenure, are the most important of issues; and yet there are constitutions, as we have seen, under which these issues are assigned to the people, since the assembly is sovereign in all such matters. To add to the difficulty, membership of the assembly, which carries deliberative and judicial functions, is vested in people of little property and of any age; but a high property qualification is demanded from those who serve as treasurers or generals, or hold any of the highest offices.

1282ᵃ32 This difficulty too may, however, be met in the same way as the first; and the practice followed in these constitutions is perhaps, after all, correct. It is not the individual juryman, councillor, or assemblyman, who is vested with office, but the court, the council, or the popular assembly; and in these bodies each member, whether he be a councillor, an assemblyman, or a juryman, is simply a part of the whole. It is therefore just that the people should be sovereign on the more important issues, since the assembly, the council, and the court consist of many people. Moreover, the property owned by all these people is greater than that of those who either as individuals or as members of small bodies hold the highest offices.

1282ᵃ41 This may serve as a settlement of the difficulties which have been discussed. But the discussion of the first of these difficulties leads to one conclusion above all others. Rightly constituted laws should be [the final] sovereign; but rulers, whether one or many, should be sovereign in those matters on which law is unable, owing to the difficulty of framing general rules for all contingencies, to make an exact pronouncement. But what rightly constituted laws ought to be is a matter that is not yet clear; and here we are still confronted by the difficulty stated at the end of the previous chapter. Laws must be good or bad, just or unjust in the same way as the constitutions to which they belong. The one clear fact is that laws must be laid down in accordance with constitutions; and if this is the case, it follows that laws which are in accordance with right constitutions must necessarily be just, and laws which are in accordance with perverted constitutions must be unjust.

Chapter 12

Justice is the political good. It involves equality, or the distribution of equal amounts to those who are equal. But who are equals, and by what criterion are they to be reckoned as equals? Many criteria can be applied; but the only proper criterion, in a political society, is that of contribution to the function of that society. Those who are equal in that respect should receive equal amounts: those who are superior or inferior should receive superior or inferior amounts, in proportion to the degree of their superiority or inferiority. If all are thus treated proportionately to the contribution they make, all are really receiving equal treatment; for the proportion between contribution and reward is the same in every case. The sort of equality which justice involves is thus proportionate equality; and this is the essence of distributive justice.

1282ᵇ14 In all branches of knowledge and in every kind of craft the end in view is some good. In the most sovereign of these, the capacity for [leadership in] political matters, the end in view is the greatest good and the good which is most to be pursued. The good in the sphere of politics is justice; and justice consists in what tends to promote the common interest. General opinion makes it consist in some sort of equality. Up to a point this agrees with the philosophical inquiries which contain our conclusions on ethics. In other words, it holds that justice involves two factors—things, and those to whom things are assigned—and it considers that those who are equal should have assigned to them equal things. But here there arises a question which must not be overlooked. Equals and unequals —yes; but equals and unequals in what? This is a question which raises difficulties, and involves us in philosophical speculation on politics. It is possible to argue that offices and honours ought to be distributed unequally on the basis of superiority in any kind of goodness whatsoever—even if those concerned are similar, and do not differ, in any other respect. The reason is that where people differ from one another there must be a difference in what is just and proportionate to their merits. If this argument were right, the mere fact of a better complexion, or greater height, or any other such advantage, would establish a claim for a greater share of political rights to be given to its possessor. But is not the argument obviously wrong? To be clear that it is, we have only to consider other kinds of knowledge and ability. In dealing with a number of equally skilled flute-players, you should not assign a better supply of flutes to those who are better born. Rather those who are better at the job should be given the better supply of tools. If our point is not yet plain, it can be made so if we push it still further. Let us suppose someone who is superior to others in flute-playing, but far inferior in birth and beauty. Even if birth and beauty are greater goods than ability to play the flute, and even if those who possess them may surpass the flute-player proportionately more in these qualities than he surpasses them in his flute-playing, the fact remains that he is the one who ought to get the superior flutes. Superiority, whether in birth or in wealth, ought to contribute something to the performance of that function; and here these qualities contribute nothing to such performance.

1283ª3 There is a further objection. If we accept this argument, every quality will have to be commensurable with every other. You will begin by reckoning a given degree of (say) height as superior to a given degree of some other quality, and you will thus be driven to pit height in general against (say) wealth and birth in general. But on this basis—i.e., that, *in a given case*, A is counted as excelling in height to a greater degree than B does in goodness, and that, *in general*, height is counted as excelling to a greater degree than goodness does—qualities are made commensurable. [We are involved in mere arithmetic]; for if amount X of some quality is 'better' than amount Y of some other, some amount which is other than X must clearly be equal to it [i.e., must be *equally* good]. This is impossible. It is therefore clear that in matters political there is no good reason for basing a claim to the exercise of authority on any and every kind of superiority. (Some may be swift and others slow; but this is no reason why the one should have more, and the other less—it is in athletic contests that the superiority of the swift receives its reward.) Claims must be based on the elements which constitute the being of the city. There are thus good grounds for the claims to honour which are made by people of good descent, free birth, or wealth, since those who hold office must necessarily be free men and pay the property assessment. (A city could not be composed entirely of those without means, any more than it could be composed entirely of slaves.) But we must add that if wealth and free birth are necessary elements, the qualities of being just and being a good soldier are also necessary. These too are elements which must be present if people are to live together in a city. The one difference is that the first two elements are necessary for the simple existence of a city, and the last two for its good life.

Study Questions for *Politics*

1. Why is the city-state the highest association among human beings, according to Aristotle?
2. What does Aristotle mean in saying 'man is a political animal'? What evidence does he provide for this claim?
3. What justifications does Aristotle supply for slavery? What distinction in types of slavery does Aristotle make? In your view, is Aristotle's defence of slavery essential to his political theory?
4. What criticisms does Aristotle make of Plato's proposals for communism and communal living among the guardian class of the ideal city?
5. Describe Aristotle's account of citizenship in Book III. Why should a well-governed city exclude mechanics and manual labourers from citizenship?
6. How does Aristotle define and classify constitutions in chapters 6–8 of Book III? Why is democracy a perversion of constitutional government, according to Aristotle?
7. What is the fundamental difference between oligarchy and democracy, according to Aristotle? What does he identify as the aim of a properly constituted city?
8. What does Aristotle conclude regarding political sovereignty? Should a person, a body of people, or the law be sovereign? Explain Aristotle's reasoning.

Recommended Readings

Ackrill, J.L., *Aristotle the Philosopher* (Oxford University Press, 1981).

Cooper, John, *Reason and Human Good in Aristotle* (Harvard University Press, 1975; Hackett, 1986).

Fortenbaugh, William, 'Aristotle on Slaves and Women,' in *Articles on Aristotle*, edited by Jonathan Barnes et al. (St Martin's Press, 1977).

George, Robert, 'Government and Character,' in *Making Men Moral* (Oxford University Press, 1993).

Keyt, David, and Fred Miller, eds, *A Companion to Aristotle's* Politics (Oxford University Press, 1991).

Kraut, Richard. *Aristotle on the Human Good* (Princeton University Press, 1989).

Miller, Fred. *Nature, Justice and Rights in Aristotle's* Politics (Oxford University Press, 1997).

Spelman, Elizabeth, 'Aristotle and the Politicization of the Soul,' in *Discovering Reality*, edited by Sandra Harding (Kluwer Academic Publishers, 2003).

Yack, Bernard, *The Problems of a Political Animal* (University of California Press, 1993).

PART II

Modern Philosophers

Thomas Hobbes

Thomas Hobbes (1588–1679) was born in Wiltshire, England, to a family of no great means. He excelled in his early studies of Greek and Latin and rose from his lowly familial position to attend Oxford University in the early seventeenth century. Upon graduating from Oxford, Hobbes served as tutor to William Cavendish, a future earl of Devonshire, and worked for the Cavendish family for most of his life. He travelled widely and never married, taking advantage of his position as tutor to meet prominent Enlightenment thinkers such as Galileo, Descartes, Bacon, and Gassendi. In November of 1640, Hobbes fled England for France to avoid the English civil war and escape persecution for his political ideas. In 1640, England had a volatile political climate and a strong anti-royalist sentiment, and Hobbes's first philosophical manuscript, *The Elements of Laws, Natural and Politic* (circulated in 1640), had a royalist sympathy that perturbed members of the English Parliament. When the *Leviathan* was published in 1651 and Oliver Cromwell came to power, Hobbes was allowed to return to England. Ironically, Hobbes's recommendations should have favoured the English monarch Charles II, but Cromwell liked the *Leviathan* and welcomed its justification of political powers established through rebellion or revolution. Hobbes remained a controversial figure in seventeenth-century England, and in 1683 copies of his *Leviathan* were burned by his alma mater, Oxford University, for being heretical and blasphemous. Hobbes died at the impressively old age of 91.

The *Leviathan* is among the most important political treatises in the history of Western philosophy. The work supplies an answer to one of the basic questions in modern political philosophy: What is the foundation of the authority of the state? Hobbes employs the idea of a social contract in all his political writings in justifying the right of the state to govern its citizens. In the *Leviathan*, he invites his reader to imagine a state of nature prior to the formation of any government, in which there is no law and no sovereign power to maintain peace and security. In a state of nature, human instincts for self-preservation would lead us into a perpetual state of war, for self-preservation requires material goods that are always limited in number. When individuals desire the same limited resources—or when appetites for power collide—the result is a state of conflict and mutual fear, a state in which there can be neither security and stability nor any knowledge, arts, scientific progress, or cultural flourishing. To escape this perpetual state of war, in which life would be 'solitary, nasty, brutish, and short,' prudent individuals contract to create a governing power, a sovereign, in whom they invest their natural rights and liberties.

Unlike other social contract theorists in the modern era, Hobbes argues that a sovereign state power should have absolute authority over its citizens, for a sovereign with limited authority cannot resolve all conflicts among individuals. Viable forms of sovereignty include oligarchy or aristocracy, in which a few individuals have ruling power; democracy, in which power derives from a collective of people; and monarchy, in which power resides in a single individual. For Hobbes, monarchy is the best form of government, for monarchies are stable, consistent in their policies, and can be supported by the council of privately selected experts. Unlike John Locke, Hobbes also opposes diffusing power into different branches of government, because 'mixed' governments, in which power resides in various hands, lead to conflicts among self-interested individuals. Citizens are free to do anything the law does not forbid, but the sovereign may enact laws regarding any area of human life, and the power of the sovereign is not to be divided.

Part of the timeless appeal of the *Leviathan* is Hobbes's rigorous philosophical methodology. Hobbes was heavily influenced by Euclid and intended to bring clear argumentation and a geometrical form of reasoning to political philosophy. Thus, the *Leviathan* proceeds by laying out a series of interconnected propositions and ideas that build in logical succession. In the beginning of the treatise, Hobbes establishes a materialistic and mechanistic view of human beings as bodies guided by complex physical motions, in like manner as the rest of the physical universe. As the *Leviathan* progresses, Hobbes eschews scholastic philosophical jargon and makes no appeals to authority, using only reason and science to convince potentially skeptical readers. Our selection of the *Leviathan* begins with Chapter XIII, following Hobbes's argument that our natural drives for honour, worthiness, and dignity are all facets of a more basic drive for power.

Leviathan

PART I
OF MAN

Chapter XIII

Of the Natural Condition of Mankind As Concerning Their Felicity, and Misery

Men by nature equal. 1. NATURE hath made men so equal, in the faculties of the body, and mind; as that though there be found one man sometimes manifestly stronger in body, or of quicker mind than another; yet when all is reckoned together, the difference between man, and man, is not so considerable, as that one man can thereupon claim to himself any benefit, to which another may not pretend, as well as he. For as to the strength of body, the weakest has strength enough to kill the strongest, either by secret machination, or by confederacy with others, that are in the same danger with himself.

2. And as to the faculties of the mind, (setting aside the arts grounded upon words, and especially that skill of proceeding upon general, and infallible rules, called science; which very few have, and but in few things; as being not a native faculty, born with us; nor attained (as prudence,) while we look after somewhat else,) I find yet a greater equality amongst men, than that of strength. For prudence, is but experience; which equal time, equally bestows on all men, in those things they equally apply themselves unto. That which may perhaps make such equality incredible, is but a vain conceit of one's own wisdom, which almost all men think they have in a greater degree, than the vulgar; that is, than all men but themselves, and a few others, whom by fame, or for concurring with themselves, they approve. For such is the nature of men, that howsoever they may acknowledge many others to be more witty, or more eloquent, or more learned; yet they will hardly believe there be many so wise as themselves; for they see their own wit at hand, and other men's at a distance. But this proveth rather that men are in that point equal, than unequal. For there is not ordinarily a greater sign of the equal distribution of anything, than that every man is contented with his share.

From equality proceeds diffidence. 3. From this equality of ability, ariseth equality of hope in the attaining of our ends. And therefore if any two men desire the same thing, which nevertheless they cannot both enjoy, they become enemies; and in the way to their end, (which is principally their own conservation, and sometimes their delectation only,) endeavour to destroy, or subdue one another. And from hence it comes to pass, that where an invader hath no more to fear, than another man's single power; if one plant, sow, build, or possess a convenient seat, others may probably be expected to come prepared with forces united, to dispossess, and deprive him, 'not only of the fruit of his labour, but also of his life, or liberty. And the invader again is in the like danger of another.

From diffidence war. 4. And from this diffidence of one another, there is no way for any man to secure himself, so reasonable, as anticipation; that is, by force, or wiles, to master the persons of all men he can, so long, till he see no other power great enough to endanger him: and this is no more than his own conservation requireth, and is generally allowed. Also because there be some, that taking pleasure in contemplating their own power in the acts of conquest, which they pursue farther than their security requires; if others, that otherwise would be glad to be at ease within modest bounds, should not by invasion increase their power, they would not be able, long time, by standing only on their defence, to subsist. And by consequence, such augmentation of dominion over men, being necessary to a man's conservation, it ought to be allowed him.

5. Again, men have no pleasure, (but on the contrary a great deal of grief) in keeping company, where there is no power able to over-awe them all. For every man looketh that his companion should value him, at the same rate he sets upon himself: and upon all signs of contempt, or undervaluing, naturally endeavours, as far as he dares (which amongst them that have no common power to keep them in quiet, is far enough to make them destroy each other,) to extort a greater value from his contemners, by damage; and from others, by the example.

6. So that in the nature of man, we find three principal causes of quarrel. First, competition; secondly, diffidence; thirdly, glory.

7. The first, maketh men invade for gain; the second, for safety; and the third, for reputation. The first use violence, to make themselves masters of other men's persons, wives, children, and cattle; the second, to defend them; the third, for trifles, as a word, a smile, a different opinion, and any other sign of undervalue, either direct in their persons, or by reflection in their kindred, their friends, their nation, their profession, or their name.

Out of civil states, there is always war of every one against every one.

8. Hereby it is manifest, that during the time men live without common power to keep them all in awe, they are in that condition which is called war; and such a war, as is of every man, against every man. For WAR, consisteth not in battle only, or the act of fighting; but in a tract of time, wherein the will to contend by battle is sufficiently known: and therefore the notion of *time*, is to be considered in the nature of war; as it is in the nature of weather. For as the nature of foul weather, lieth not in a shower or two of rain; but in an inclination thereto of many days together: so the nature of war, consisteth not in actual fighting; but in the known disposition thereto, during all the time there is no assurance to the contrary. All other time is PEACE.

The incommodities of such a war.

9. Whatsoever therefore is consequent to a time of war, where every man is enemy to every man; the same is consequent to the time, wherein men live without other security, than what their own strength, and their own invention shall furnish them withal. In such condition, there is no place for industry; because the fruit thereof is uncertain: and consequently no culture of the earth; no navigation, nor use of the commodities that may be imported by sea; no commodious building; no instruments of moving, and removing such things as require much force; no knowledge of the face of the earth; no account of time; no arts, no letters; no society; and which is worst of all, continual fear, and danger of violent death; and the life of man, solitary, poor, nasty, brutish, and short.

10. It may seem strange to some man, that has not well weighed these things; that nature should thus dissociate, and render men apt to invade, and destroy one another: and he may therefore, not trusting to this inference, made from the passions, desire perhaps to have the same confirmed by experience. Let him therefore consider with himself, when taking a journey, he arms himself, and seeks to go well accompanied; when going to sleep, he locks his doors; when even in his house he locks his chests; and this when he knows there be laws, and public officers, armed, to revenge all injuries shall be done him; what opinion he has of his fellow-subjects, when he rides arms; of his fellow citizens, when he locks his doors; and of his children, and servants, when he locks his chests. Does he not there as much accuse mankind by his actions, as I do by my words? But neither of us accuse man's nature in it. The desires, and other passions of man, are in themselves no sin. No more are the actions, that proceed from those passions, till they know a law that forbids them: which till laws be made they cannot know: nor can any law be made, till they have agreed upon the person that shall make it.

11. It may peradventure be thought, there was never such a time, nor condition of war as this; and I believe it was never

generally so, over all the world: but there are many places, where they live so now. For the savage people in many places of America, except the government of small families, the concord whereof dependeth on natural lust, have no government at all; and live at this day in that brutish manner, as I said before. Howsoever, it may be perceived what manner of life there would be, where there were no common power to fear; by the manner of life, which men that have formerly lived under a peaceful government, use to degenerate into, in a civil war.

12. But though there had never been any time, wherein particular men were in a condition of war one against another; yet in all times, kings and persons of sovereign authority, because of their independency, are in continual jealousies, and in the state and posture of gladiators; having their weapons pointing, and their eyes fixed on one another; that is, their forts, garrisons, and guns upon the frontiers of their kingdoms; and continual spies upon their neighbours; which is a posture of war. But because they uphold thereby, the industry of their subjects; there does not follow from it, that misery, which accompanies the liberty of particular men.

In such a war nothing is unjust.

13. To this war of every man against every man, this also is consequent; that nothing can be unjust. The notions of right and wrong, justice and injustice have there no place. Where there is no common power, there is no law: where no law, no injustice. Force, and fraud, are in war the two cardinal virtues. Justice, and injustice are none of the faculties neither of the body, nor mind. If they were, they might be in a man that were alone in the world, as well as his senses, and passions. They are qualities, that relate to men in society,

not in solitude. It is consequent also to the same conditions, that there be no propriety, no dominion, no *mine* and *thine* distinct; but only that to be every man's, that he can get; and for so long, as he can keep it. And thus much for the ill condition, which man by mere nature is actually placed in; though with a possibility to come out of it, consisting partly in the passions, partly in his reason.

14. The passions that incline men to peace, are fear of death; desire of such things as are necessary to commodious living; and a hope by their industry to obtain them. And reason suggesteth convenient articles of peace, upon which men may be drawn to agreement. These articles, are they, which otherwise are called the Laws of Nature: whereof I shall speak more particularly, in the two following chapters.

The passions that incline men to peace.

Chapter XIV

Of the First and Second Natural Laws, and of Contracts

1. The RIGHT OF NATURE, which writers commonly call *jus naturale*, is the liberty each man hath, to use his own power, as he will himself, for the preservation of his own nature; that is to say, of his own life; and consequently, of doing anything, which in his own judgment, and reason, he shall conceive to be the aptest means thereunto.

Right of nature what.

2. By LIBERTY, is understood, according to the proper signification of the word, the absence of external impediments: which impediments, may oft take away part of a man's power to do what he would; but cannot hinder him from using the power left him, according as his judgment, and reason shall dictate to him.

Liberty what.

A law of nature what.

3. A LAW OF NATURE, (*lex naturalis,*) is a precept, or general rule, found out by reason, by which a man is forbidden to do, that, which is destructive of his life, or taketh away the means of preserving the same; and to omit, that, by which he thinketh it may be best preserved. For though they that speak of this subject, use to confound *jus,* and *lex, right* and *law;* yet they ought to be distinguished; because RIGHT, consisteth in liberty to do, or to forbear: whereas LAW, determineth, and bindeth to one of them: so that law, and right, differ as much, as obligation, and liberty; which in one and the same matter are inconsistent.

Difference of right and law.

4. And because the condition of man, (as hath been declared in the precedent chapter) is a condition of war of every one against every one; in which case everyone is governed by his own reason; and there is nothing he can make use of, that may not be a help unto him, in preserving his life against his enemies; it followeth, that in such a condition, every man has a right to every thing; even to one another's body. And therefore, as long as this natural right of every man to every thing endureth, there can be no security to any man, (how strong or wise soever he be,) of living out the time, which nature ordinarily alloweth men to live. And consequently it is a precept, or general rule of reason, *that every man, ought to endeavour peace, as far as he has hope of obtaining it; and when he cannot obtain it, that he may seek, and use, all helps, and advantages of war.* The first branch of which rule, containeth the first, and fundamental law of nature; which is, *to seek peace, and follow it.* The second, the sum of the right of nature; which is, *by all means we can, to defend ourselves.*

Naturally every man has right to every thing.

The fundamental law of nature.

5. From this fundamental law of nature, by which men are commanded to endeavour peace, is derived this second law; *that a man be willing, when others are so too, as far-forth, as for peace, and defence of himself he shall think it necessary, to lay down this right to all things; and be contented with so much liberty against other men, as he would allow other men against himself.* For as long as every man holdeth this right, of doing anything he liketh; so long are all men in the condition of war. But if other men will not lay down their right, as well as he; then there is no reason for anyone, to divest himself of his: for that were to expose himself to prey, (which no man is bound to) rather than to dispose himself to peace. This is that law of the Gospel; *whatsoever you require that others should do to you, that do ye to them.* And that law of all men, *quod tibi fieri non vis, alteri ne feceris.*

The second law of nature.

6. To *lay down* a man's *right* to anything, is to *divest* himself of the *liberty,* of hindering another of the benefit of his own right to the same. For he that renounceth, or passeth away his right, giveth not to any other man a right which he had not before; because there is nothing to which every man had not right by nature: but only standeth out of his way, that he may enjoy his own original right, without hindrance from him; not without hindrance from another. So that the effect which redoundeth to one man, by another man's defect of right, is but so much diminution of impediments to the use of his own right original.

What it is to lay down a right.

7. Right is laid aside, either by simply renouncing it; or by transferring it to another. By *simply* RENOUNCING; when he cares not to whom the benefit thereof redoundeth. By TRANSFERRING; when he intendeth the benefit thereof to some certain person, or persons. And when a man hath in either manner abandoned, or granted away his right; then he is said to

Renouncing a right what it is.

Transferring right what.

Obligation. be OBLIGED, or BOUND, not to hinder those, to whom such right is granted or abandoned, from the benefit of it: and that *Duty.* he *ought*, and it is his DUTY, not to make void that voluntary act of his own: and *Injustice.* that such hindrance is INJUSTICE, and INJURY, as being *sine jure*; the right being before renounced, or transferred. So that *injury*, or *injustice*, in the controversies of the world, is somewhat like to that, which in the disputations of scholars is called absurdity. For as it is there called an *absurdity*, to contradict what one maintained in the beginning: so in the world, it is called injustice, and injury, voluntarily to undo that, which from the beginning he had voluntarily done. The way by which a man either simply renounceth, or transferreth his right, is a declaration, or signification, by some voluntary and sufficient sign, or signs, that he doth so renounce, or transfer; or hath so renounced, or transferred the same, to him that accepteth it. And these signs are either words only, or actions only; or (as it happeneth most often) both words, and actions. And the same are the BONDS, by which men are bound, and obliged: bonds, that have their strength, not from their own nature, (for nothing is more easily broken than a man's word,) but from fear of some evil consequence upon the rupture.

8. Whensoever a man transferreth his right, or renounceth it; it is either in consideration of some right reciprocally transferred to himself; or for some other good he hopeth for thereby. For it is a voluntary act: and of the voluntary acts of every man, the object is some *good to himself*. And *Not all rights* therefore there be some rights, which no *are alienable.* man can be understood by any words, or other signs, to have abandoned, or transferred. As first a man cannot lay down the right of resisting them, that assault him by force, to take away his life; because he cannot be understood to aim thereby, at any good to himself. The same may be said of wounds, and chains, and imprisonment; both because there is no benefit consequent to such patience; as there is to the patience of suffering another to be wounded, or imprisoned: as also because a man cannot tell, when he seeth men proceed against him by violence, whether they intend his death or not. And lastly the motive, and end for which this renouncing, and transferring of right is introduced, is nothing else but the security of a man's person, in his life, and in the means of so preserving life, as not to be weary of it. And therefore if a man by words, or other signs, seem to despoil himself of the end, for which those signs were intended; he is not to be understood as if he meant it, or that it was his will; but that he was ignorant to how such words and actions were to be interpreted.

9. The mutual transferring of right, is *Contract* that which men call CONTRACT. *what.*

10. There is difference, between transferring of right to the thing; and transferring, or tradition, that is, delivery of the thing itself. For the thing may be delivered together with the translation of the right; as in buying and selling with ready money; or exchange of goods, or lands: and it may be delivered some time after.

11. Again, one of the contractors, may deliver the thing contracted for on his part, and leave the other to perform his part at some determinate time after, and in the meantime be trusted; and then the contract on his part, is called PACT, or COVENANT: or both parts may contract *Covenant* now, to perform hereafter: in which cases, *what.* he that is to perform in time to come,

being trusted, his performance is called *keeping of promise,* or faith; and the failing of performance (if it be voluntary) *violation of faith.*

12. When the transferring of right, is not mutual; but one of the parties transferreth, in hope to gain thereby friendship, or service from another, or from his friends; or in hope to gain the reputation of charity, or magnanimity; or to deliver his mind from the pain of compassion; or in hope of reward in heaven; this is not contract, but GIFT, FREE GIFT, GRACE: which words signify one and the same thing.

Free gift.

13. Signs of contract, are either *express,* or *by inference.* Express, are words spoken with understanding of what they signify: and such words are either of the time *present,* or *past;* as *I give, I grant, I have given, I have granted, I will that this be yours;* or of the future; as, *I will give, I will grant:* which words of the future are called PROMISE.

Signs of contract express.

Promise.

14. Signs by inference, are sometimes the consequence of words; sometimes the consequence of silence; sometimes the consequence of actions; sometimes the consequence of forbearing an action: and generally a sign by inference, of any contract, is whatsoever sufficiently argues the will of the contractor.

Signs of contract by inference.

15. Words alone, if they be of the time to come, and contain a bare promise, are an insufficient sign of a free gift, and therefore not obligatory. For if they be of the time to come, as, *tomorrow I will give,* they are a sign I have not given yet, and consequently that my right is not transferred, but remaineth till I transfer it by some other act. But if the words be of the time present, or past, as, *I have given,* or *do give to be delivered tomorrow,* then is my morrow's right given away today; and that by

Free gift passeth by word of the present or past.

the virtue of the words, though there were no other argument of my will. And there is a great difference in the signification of these words, *volo hoc tuum esse cras,* and *cras dabo;* that is, between *I will that this be thine tomorrow,* and, *I will give it thee tomorrow:* for the word *I will,* in the former manner of speech, signifies an act of the will present; but in the latter, it signifies a promise of an act of the will to come: and therefore the former words, being of the present, transfer a future right; the latter, that be of the future, transfer nothing. But if there be other signs of the will to transfer a right, besides words; then, though the gift be free, yet may the right be understood to pass by words of the future: as if a man propound a prize to him that comes first to the end of a race, the gift is free; and though the words be of the future, yet the right passeth: for if he would not have his words so be understood, he should not have let them run.

16. In contracts, the right passeth, not only where the words are of the time present, or past; but also where they are of the future: because all contract is mutual translation, or change of right; and therefore he that promiseth only, because he hath already received the benefit for which he promiseth, is to be understood as if he intended the right should pass: for unless he had been content to have his words so understood, the other would not have performed his part first. And for that cause, in buying, and selling, and other acts of contract, a promise is equivalent to a covenant; and therefore obligatory.

Signs of contract are words both of the past, present, and future.

17. He that performeth first in the case of a contract, is said to MERIT that which he is to receive by the performance of the other; and he hath it as *due.* Also when a prize is propounded to many, which is to

Merit what.

be given to him only that winneth; or money is thrown amongst many, to be enjoyed by them that catch it; though this be a free gift; yet so to win, or so to catch, is to *merit*, and to have it as DUE. For the right is transferred in the propounding of the prize, and in throwing down the money; though it be not determined to whom, but by the event of the contention. But there is between these two sorts of merit, this difference, that in contract, I merit by virtue of my own power, and the contractor's need; but in this case of free gift, I am enabled to merit only by the benignity of the giver: in contract, I merit at the contractor's hand that he should depart with his right; in this case of gift, I merit not that the giver should part with his right; but that when he has parted with it, it should be mine, rather than another's. And this I think to be the meaning of that distinction of the Schools, between *meritum congrui*, and *meritum condigni*. For God Almighty, having promised Paradise to those men (hoodwinked with carnal desires,) that can walk through this world according to the precepts, and limits prescribed by him; they say, he that shall so walk, shall merit Paradise *ex congruo*. But because no man can demand a right to it, by his own righteousness, or any other power in himself, but by the free grace of God only; they say, no man can merit Paradise *ex condigno*. This I say, I think is the meaning of that distinction; but because disputers do not agree upon the signification of their own terms of art, longer than it serves their turn; I will not affirm anything of their meaning: only this I say; when a gift is given indefinitely, as a prize to be contended for, he that winneth meriteth, and may claim the prize as due.

18. If a covenant be made, wherein neither of the parties perform presently, but trust one another; in the condition of mere nature, (which is a condition of war of every man against every man,) upon any reasonable suspicion, it is void: but if there be a common power set over them both, with right and force sufficient to compel performance, it is not void. For he that performeth first, had no assurance the other will perform after; because the bonds of words are too weak to bridle men's ambition, avarice, anger, and other passions, without the fear of some coercive power; which in the condition of mere nature, where all men are equal, and judges of the justness of their own fears, cannot possibly be supposed. And therefore he which performeth first, does but betray himself to his enemy; contrary to the right (he can never abandon) of defending his life, and means of living. *Covenants of mutual trust, when invalid.*

19. But in a civil estate, where there is a power set up to constrain those that would otherwise violate their faith, that fear is no more reasonable; and for that cause, he which by the covenant is to perform first, is obliged so to do.

20. The cause of fear, which maketh such a covenant invalid, must be always something arising after the covenant made; as some new fact, or other sign of the will not to perform: else it cannot make the covenant void. For that which could not hinder a man from promising, ought not to be admitted as a hindrance of performing.

21. He that transferreth any right, transferreth the means of enjoying it, as far as lieth in his power. As he that selleth land, is understood to transfer the herbage, and whatsoever grows upon it; nor can he that sells a mill turn away the stream that drives it. And they that give to a man the *Right to the end, containeth right to the means.*

right of government in sovereignty, are understood to give him the right of levying money to maintain soldiers; and of appointing magistrates for the administration of justice.

22. To make covenants with brute beasts, is impossible; because not understanding our speech, they understand not, nor accept of any translation of right; nor can translate any right to another: and without mutual acceptation, there is no covenant.

23. To make covenant with God, is impossible, but by mediation of such as God speaketh to, either by revelation supernatural, or by his lieutenants that govern under him, and in this name: for otherwise we know not whether our covenants be accepted, or not. And therefore they that vow anything contrary to any law of nature, vow in vain; as being a thing unjust to pay such vow. And if it be a thing commanded by the law of nature, it is not the vow, but the law that binds them.

24. The matter, or subject of a covenant, is always something that falleth under deliberation; (for to covenant, is an act of the will; that is to say an act, and the last act, of deliberation;) and is therefore always understood to be something to come; and which is judged possible for him that covenanteth, to perform.

25. And therefore, to promise that which is known to be impossible, is no covenant. But if that prove impossible afterwards, which before was thought possible, the covenant is valid, and bindeth, (though not to the thing itself,) yet to the value; or, if that also be impossible, to the unfeigned endeavour of performing as much as is possible: for to more no man can be obliged.

26. Men are freed of their covenants two ways; by performing; or by being forgiven. For performance, is the natural end of obligation; and forgiveness, the restitution of liberty; as being a retransferring of that of that right, in which the obligation consisted.

27. Covenants entered into by fear, in the condition of mere nature, are obligatory. For example, if I covenant to pay a ransom, or service for my life, to an enemy; I am bound by it. For it is a contract, wherein one receiveth the benefit of life; the other is to receive money, or service for it; and consequently, where no other law (as in the condition, of mere nature) forbiddeth the performance, the covenant is valid. Therefore prisoners of war, if trusted with the payment of their ransom, are obliged to pay it: and if a weaker prince, make a disadvantageous peace with a stronger, for fear; he is bound to keep it; unless (as hath been said before) there ariseth some new, and just cause of fear, to renew the war. And even in commonwealths, if I be forced to redeem myself from a thief by promising him money, I am bound to pay it, till the civil law discharge me. For whatsoever I may lawfully do without obligation, the same I may lawfully covenant to do through fear: and what I lawfully covenant, I cannot lawfully break.

28. A former covenant, makes void a later. For a man that hath passed away his right to one today, hath it not to pass tomorrow to another: and therefore the later promise passeth no right, but is null.

29. A covenant not to defend myself from force, by force, is always void. For (as I have showed before) no man can transfer, or lay down his right to save himself from death, wounds, and imprisonment, (the

avoiding whereof is the only end of the laying down any right;) and therefore the promise of not resisting force, in no covenant transferreth any right; nor is obliging. For though a man may covenant thus, *unless I do so, or so, kill me*; he cannot covenant thus, *unless I do so, I will not resist you, when you come to kill me.* For man by nature chooseth the lesser evil, which is danger of death in resisting, rather than the greater, which is certain and present death in not resisting. And this is granted to be true by all men, in that they lead criminals to execution, and prison, with armed men, notwithstanding that such criminals have consented to the law, by which they are condemned.

No man obliged to accuse himself.

30. A covenant to accuse oneself, without assurance of pardon, is likewise invalid. For in the condition of nature, where every man is judge, there is no place for accusation: and in the civil state, the accusation is followed with punishment; which being force, a man is not obliged not to resist. The same is also true, of the accusation of those, by whose condemnation a man falls into misery; as of a father, wife, or benefactor. For the testimony of such an accuser, if it be not willingly given, is presumed to be corrupted by nature: and therefore not to be received: and where a man's testimony is not to be credited, he is not bound to give it. Also accusations upon torture, are not to be reputed as testimonies. For torture is to be used but as means of conjecture, and light, in the further examination, and search of truth: and what is in that case confessed, tendeth to the ease of him that is tortured; not to the informing of the torturers: and therefore ought not to have the credit of a sufficient testimony: for whether he deliver himself by true, or false accusation, he does it by the right of preserving his own life.

31. The force of words, being (as I have formerly noted) too weak to hold men to the performance of their covenants: there are in man's nature, but two imaginable helps to strengthen it. And those are either a fear of the consequence of breaking their word; or a glory, or pride in appearing not to need to break it. This latter is a generosity too rarely found to be presumed on, especially in the pursuers of wealth, command, or sensual pleasure; which are the greatest part of mankind. The passion to be reckoned upon, is fear; whereof there be two very general objects: one, the power of spirits invisible; the other, the power of those men they shall therein offend. Of these two, though the former be the greater power, yet the fear of the latter is commonly the greater fear. The fear of the former is in every man, his own religion: which hath place in the nature of man before civil society. The latter hath not so; at least not place enough, to keep men to their promises; because in the condition of mere nature, the inequality of power is not discerned, but by the event of battle. So that before the time of civil society, or in the interruption thereof by war, there is nothing can strengthen a covenant of peace agreed on, against the temptations of avarice, ambition, lust, or other strong desire, but the fear of that invisible power, which they every one worship as God; and fear as a revenger of their perfidy. All therefore that can be done between two men not subject to civil power, is to put one another to swear by the God he feareth: which *swearing*, or OATH, is a *form of speech, added to a promise; by which he that promiseth, signifieth, that unless he perform, he renounceth the mercy of his God, or calleth to him for vengeance on himself.* Such was the heathen form, *Let* Jupiter *kill me else,*

The end of an oath.

The form of an oath.

as I kill this beast. So is our form, *I shall do thus, and thus, so help me God.* And this, with the rites and ceremonies, which everyone useth in his own religion, that the fear of breaking faith might be the greater.

32. By this it appears, that an oath taken according to any other form, or rite, than his, that sweareth, is in vain; and no oath: and that there is no swearing by any- *No oath but* thing which the swearer thinks not God. *by God.* For though men have sometimes used to swear by their kings, for fear, or flattery; yet they would have it thereby understood, they attributed to them divine honour. And that swearing unnecessarily by God, is but profaning of his name: and swearing by other things, as men do in common dis- course, is not swearing, but an impious custom, gotten by too much vehemence of talking.

An oath adds 33. It appears also, that the oath adds *nothing to the* nothing to the obligation. For a covenant, *obligation.* if lawful, binds in the sight of God, with- out the oath, as much as with it: if unlaw- ful, bindeth not at all; though it be confirmed with an oath. . . .

PART 2
OF COMMONWEALTH

Chapter XVII

Of the Causes, Generation, and Definition of a Commonwealth

The end of 1. The final cause, end, or design of men, *commonwealth,* (who naturally love liberty, and dominion *particular* over others,) in the introduction of that *security:* restraint upon themselves, (in which we see them live in commonwealths,) is the foresight of their own preservation, and of a more contented life thereby; that is to say, of getting themselves out from that miserable condition of war, which is nec- essarily consequent (as hath been shown, chapter XIII) to the natural passions of men, when there is no visible power to keep them in awe, and tie them by fear of punishment to the performance of their covenants, and observation of those laws of nature set down in the fourteenth and fifteenth chapter.

2. For the laws of nature (as *justice,* *Which is not* *equity, modesty, mercy,* and (in sum) *doing to* *to be had* *others, as we would be done to,*) of them- *from the law* selves, without the terror of some power, *of nature:* to cause them to be observed, are contrary to our natural passions, that carry us to partiality, pride, revenge, and the like. And covenants, without the sword, are but words, and of no strength to secure a man at all. Therefore notwithstanding the laws of nature (which everyone hath then kept, when he has the will to keep them, when he can do it safely) if there be no power erected, or not great enough for our secu- rity; every man will, and may lawfully rely on his own strength and art, for caution against all other men. And in all places, where men have lived by small families, to rob and spoil one another, has been a trade, and so far from being reputed against the law of nature, that the greater spoils they gained, the greater was their honour; and men observed no other laws therein, but the laws of honour; that is, to abstain from cruelty, leaving to men their lives, and instruments of husbandry. And as small families did then; so now do cities and kingdoms which are but greater fam- ilies (for their own security) enlarge their dominions, upon all pretences of danger, and fear of invasion, or assistance that may be given to invaders, and endeavour as

much as they can, to subdue, or weaken their neighbours, by open force, and secret arts, for want of other caution, justly; and are remembered for it in after ages with honour.

Nor from the conjunction of a few men or families:

3. Nor is it the joining together of a small number of men, that gives them this security; because in small numbers, small additions on the one side or the other, make the advantage of strength so great, as is sufficient to carry the victory; and therefore gives encouragement to an invasion. The multitude sufficient to confide in for our security, is not determined by any certain number, but by comparison with the enemy we fear; and is then sufficient, when the odds of the enemy is not of so visible and conspicuous moment, to determine the event of war, as to move him to attempt.

Nor from a great multitude, unless directed by one judgment.

4. And be there never so great a multitude; yet if their actions be directed according to their particular judgments, and particular appetites, they can expect thereby no defence, nor protection, neither against a common enemy, nor against the injuries of one another. For being distracted in opinions concerning the best use and application of their strength, they do not help, but hinder one another; and reduce their strength by mutual opposition to nothing: whereby they are easily, not only subdued by a very few that agree together; but also when there is no common enemy, they make war upon each other, for their particular interests. For if we could suppose a great multitude of men to consent in the observation of justice, and other laws of nature, without a common power to keep them all in awe; we might as well suppose all mankind to do the same; and then there neither would be, nor need to be any civil government, or commonwealth at all; because there would be peace without subjection.

5. Nor is it enough for the security, which men desire should last all the time of their life, that they be governed, and directed by one judgment, for a limited time; as in one battle, or one war. For though they obtain a victory by their unanimous endeavour against a foreign enemy; yet afterwards, when either they have no common enemy, or he that by one part is held for an enemy, is by another part held for a friend, they must needs by the difference of their interests dissolve, and fall again into a war amongst themselves.

And that continually.

6. It is true, that certain living creatures, as bees, and ants, live sociably one with another, (which are therefore by Aristotle numbered amongst political creatures;) and yet have no other direction, than their particular judgments and appetites; nor speech, whereby one of them can signify to another, what he thinks expedient for the common benefit: and therefore some man may perhaps desire to know, why mankind cannot do the same. To which I answer,

Why certain creatures without reason, or speech, do nevertheless live in society, without any coercive power.

7. First, that men are continually in competition for honour and dignity, which these creatures are not; and consequently amongst men there ariseth on that ground, envy and hatred, and finally war; but amongst these not so.

8. Secondly, that amongst these creatures, the common good differeth not from the private; and being by nature inclined to their private, they procure thereby the common benefit. But man, whose joy consisteth in comparing himself with other men, can relish nothing but what is eminent.

9. Thirdly, that these creatures, having not (as man) the use of reason, do not see, nor think they see any fault, in the

therefore to him that hath the sovereign power, to be judge, or constitute all judges of opinions and doctrines, as a thing necessary to peace; thereby to prevent discord and civil war.

10. Seventhly, is annexed to the sovereignty, the whole power of prescribing the rules, whereby every man may know, what goods he may enjoy, and what actions he may do, without being molested by any of his fellow-subjects: and this is it men call *propriety*. For before constitution of sovereign power (as hath already been shown) all men had right to all things; which necessarily causeth war: and therefore this propriety, being necessary to peace, and depending on sovereign power, is the act of that power, in order to the public peace. These rules of propriety (or *meum* and *tuum*) and of *good, evil, lawful,* and *unlawful* in the actions of subjects, are the civil laws; that is to say, the laws of each commonwealth in particular; though the name of civil law be now restrained to the ancient civil laws of the city of Rome; which being the head of a great part of the world, her laws at that time were in these parts the civil law.

11. Eighthly, is annexed to the sovereignty, the right of judicature; that is to say, of hearing and deciding all controversies, which may arise concerning law, either civil, or natural; or concerning fact. For without the decision of controversies, there is no protection of one subject, against the injuries of another; the laws concerning *meum* and *tuum* are in vain; and to every man remaineth, from the natural and necessary appetite of his own conservation, the right of protecting himself by his private strength, which is the condition of war, and contrary to the end for which every commonwealth is instituted.

12. Ninthly, is annexed to the sovereignty, the right of making war, and peace with other nations, and commonwealths; that is to say, of judging when it is for the public good, and how great forces are to be assembled, armed, and paid for that end; and to levy money upon the subjects, to defray the expenses thereof. For the power by which the people are to be defended, consisteth in their armies; and the strength of an army, in the union of their strength under one command; which command the sovereign instituted, therefore hath; because the command of the *militia*, without other institution, maketh him that hath it sovereign. And therefore whosoever is made general of an army, he that hath the sovereign power is always generalissimo [commander-in-chief].

13. Tenthly, is annexed to the sovereignty, the choosing of all counsellors, ministers, magistrates, and officers, both in peace, and war. For seeing the sovereign is charged with the end, which is the common peace and defence; he is understood to have power to use such means, as he shall think most fit for his discharge.

14. Eleventhly, to the sovereign is committed the power of rewarding with riches, or honour; and of punishing with corporal, or pecuniary punishment, or with ignominy every subject according to the law he hath formerly made; or if there be no law made, according as he shall judge most to conduce to the encouraging of men to serve the commonwealth, or deterring of them from doing disservice to the same.

15. Lastly, considering what value men are naturally apt to set upon themselves; what respect they look for from others; and how little they value other men; from whence continually arise amongst them,

emulation, quarrels, factions, and at last war, to the destroying of one another, and diminution of their strength against a common enemy; it is necessary that there be laws of honour, and a public rate of the worth of such men as have deserved, or are able to deserve well of the commonwealth; and that there be force in the hands of some or other, to put those laws in execution. But it hath already been shown, that not only the whole militia, or forces of the commonwealth; but also the judicature of all controversies, is annexed to the sovereignty. To the sovereign therefore it belongeth also to give titles of honour; and to appoint what order of place, and dignity, each man shall hold; and what signs of respect, in public or private meetings, they shall give to one another.

These rights are indivisible. 16. These are the rights, which make the essence of sovereignty; and which are the marks, whereby a man may discern in what man, or assembly of men, the sovereign power is placed, and resideth. For these are incommunicable, and inseparable. The power to coin money; to dispose of the estate and persons of infant heirs; to have praeemption in markets; and all other statute prerogatives, may be transferred by the sovereign; any yet the power to protect his subjects be retained. But if he transfer the militia, he retains the judicature in vain, for want of execution of the laws: or if he grant away the power of raising money; the militia is in vain: or if he give away the government of doctrines, men will be frighted into rebellion with the fear of spirits. And so if we consider anyone of the said rights, we shall presently see, that the holding of all the rest, will produce no effect, in the conservation of peace and justice, the end for which all commonwealths are instituted. And this division is it,

whereof it is said, *a kingdom divided in itself cannot stand*: for unless this division precede, division into opposite armies can never happen. If there had not first been an opinion received of the greatest part of England, that these powers were divided between the King, and the Lords, and the House of Commons, the people had never been divided and fallen into this civil war; first between those that disagreed in politics; and after between the dissenters about the liberty of religion; which have so instructed men in this point of sovereign right, that there be few now (in England,) that do not see, that these rights are inseparable, and will be so generally acknowledged at the next return of peace; and so continue, till their miseries are forgotten; and no longer, except the vulgar be better taught than they have hitherto been.

17. And because they are essential and inseparable rights, it follows necessarily, that in whatsoever words any of them seem to be granted away, yet if the sovereign power itself be not in direct terms renounced, and the name of sovereign no more given by the grantees to him that grants them, the grant is void: for when he has granted all he can, if we grant back the sovereignty, all is restored, as inseparably annexed thereunto. *And can by no grant pass away without direct renouncing of the sovereign power.*

18. This great authority being indivisible, and inseparably annexed to the sovereignty, there is little ground for the opinion of them, that say of sovereign kings, though they be *singulis majores*, of greater power than every one of their subjects, yet they be *universis minores*, of less power than them all together. For if by *all together*, they mean not the collective body as one person, then *all together* and *every one*, signify the same; and the speech is absurd. But if by *all together*, they understand them as one *The power and honour of subjects vanisheth in the presence of the power of the sovereign.*

person (which person the sovereign bears,) then the power of all together, is the same with the sovereign's power; and so again the speech is absurd: which absurdity they see well enough, when the sovereignty is in an assembly of the people; but in a monarch they see it not; and yet the power of sovereignty is the same in whomsoever it be placed.

19. And as the power, so also the honour of the sovereign, ought to be greater, than that of any, or all the subjects. For in the sovereignty is the fountain of honour. The dignities of lord, earl, duke, and prince are his creatures. As in the presence of the master, the servants are equal, and without any honour at all; so are the subjects, in the presence of the sovereign. And though they shine some more, some less, when they are out of his sight; yet in his presence, they shine no more than the stars in the presence of the sun.

Sovereign power not so hurtful as the want of it, and the hurt proceeds for the greatest part from not submitting readily to a less.

20. But a man may here object, that the condition of subjects is very miserable; as being obnoxious to the lusts, and other irregular passions of him, or them that have so unlimited a power in their hands. And commonly they that live under a monarch, think it the fault of monarchy; and they that live under the government of democracy, or other sovereign assembly, attribute all the inconvenience to that form of commonwealth; whereas the power in all forms, if they be perfect enough to protect them, is the same; not considering that the state of man can never be without some incommodity or other; and that the greatest, that in any form of government can possibly happen to the people in general, is scarce sensible, in respect of the miseries, and horrible calamities, that accompany a civil war; or that dissolute condition of masterless men, without subjection to laws,

and a coercive power to tie their hands from rapine and revenge: nor considering that the greatest pressure of sovereign governors, proceedeth not from any delight, or profit they can expect in the damage, or weakening of their subjects, in whose vigour, consisteth their own strength and glory; but in the restiveness of themselves, that unwillingly contributing to their own defence, make it necessary for their governors to draw from them what they can in time of peace, that they may have means on any emergent occasion, or sudden need, to resist, or take advantage on their enemies. For all men are by nature provided of notable multiplying glasses (that is their passions and self-love,) through which, every little payment appeareth a great grievance; but are destitute of those prospective glasses, (namely moral and civil science,) to see afar off the miseries that hang over them, and cannot without such payments be avoided.

Chapter XIX

Of the Several Kinds of Commonwealth by Institution, and of Succession to the Sovereign Power

1. The difference of commonwealths, consisteth in the difference of the sovereign, or the person representative of all and every one of the multitude. And because the sovereignty is either in one man, or in an assembly of more than one; and into that assembly either every man hath right to enter, or not everyone, but certain men distinguished from the rest; it is manifest, there can be but three kinds of commonwealth. For the representative must needs

The different forms of commonwealths but three.

be one man, or more: and if more, then it is the assembly of all, or but of a part. When the representative is one man, then is the commonwealth a MONARCHY: when an assembly of all that will come together, then it is a DEMOCRACY, or popular commonwealth: when an assembly of a part only, then it is called an ARISTOCRACY. Other kind of commonwealth there can be none: for either one, or more, or all, must have the sovereign power (which I have shown to be indivisible) entire.

Tyranny and oligarchy, but different names of monarchy, and aristocracy.

2. There be other names of government, in the histories, and books of policy; as *tyranny*, and *oligarchy*: but they are not the names of other forms of government, but of the same forms misliked. For they that are discontented under *monarchy*, call it *tyranny*; and they that are displeased with *aristocracy*, call it *oligarchy*: so also, they which find themselves grieved under a *democracy*, call it *anarchy*, (which signifies want of government;) and yet I think no man believes, that want of government, is any new kind of government: nor by the same reason ought they to believe, that the government is of one kind, when they like it, and another, when they mislike it, or are oppressed by the governors.

Subordinate representatives dangerous.

3. It is manifest, that men who are in absolute liberty, may, if they please, give authority to one man, to represent them every one; as well as give such authority to any assembly of men whatsoever; and consequently may subject themselves, if they think good, to a monarch, as absolutely, as to any other representative. Therefore, where there is already erected a sovereign power, there can be no other representative of the same people, but only to certain particular ends, by the sovereign limited. For that were to erect two sovereigns; and every man to have his person represented by two actors, that by opposing one another, must needs divide that power, which (if men will live in peace) is indivisible; and thereby reduce the multitude into the condition of war, contrary to the end for which all sovereignty is instituted. And therefore as it is absurd, to think that a sovereign assembly, inviting the people of their dominion, to send up their deputies, with power to make known their advice, or desires, should therefore hold such deputies, rather than themselves, for the absolute representatives of the people: so it is absurd also, to think the same in a monarchy. And I know not how this so manifest a truth, should of late be so little observed; that in a monarchy, he that had the sovereignty from a descent of six hundred years, was alone called sovereign, had the title of Majesty from every one of his subjects, and was unquestionably taken by them for their king, was notwithstanding never considered as their representative; that name without contradiction passing for the title of those men, which at his command were sent up by the people to carry their petitions, and give him (if he permitted it) their advice. Which may serve as an admonition, for those that are the true, and absolute representative of a people, to instruct men in the nature of that office, and to take heed how they admit of any other general representation upon any occasion whatsoever, if they mean to discharge the trust committed to them.

4. The difference between these three kinds of commonwealth, consisteth not in the difference of power; but in the difference of convenience, or aptitude to produce the peace, and security of the people; for which end they were instituted. And to compare monarchy with the other two, we

Comparison of monarchy, with sovereign assemblies.

may observe; first, that whosoever beareth the person of the people, or is one of that assembly that bears it, beareth also his own natural person. And though he be careful in his politic person to procure the common interest; yet he is more, or no less careful to procure the private good of himself, his family, kindred, and friends; and for the most part, if the public interest chance to cross the private, he prefers the private: for the passions of men, are commonly more potent than their reason. From whence it follows, that where the public and private interest are most closely united, there is the public most advanced. Now in monarchy, the private interest is the same with the public. The riches, power, and honour of a monarch arise only from the riches, strength, and reputation of his subjects. For no king can be rich, nor glorious, nor secure; whose subjects are either poor, or contemptible, or too weak through want, or dissension, to maintain a war against their enemies: whereas in a democracy, or aristocracy, the public prosperity confers not so much to the private fortune of one that is corrupt, or ambitious, as doth many times a perfidious advice, a treacherous action, or a civil war.

5. Secondly, that a monarch receiveth counsel of whom, when, and where he pleaseth; and consequently may hear the opinion of men versed in the matter about which he deliberates, of what rank or quality soever, and as long before the time of action, and with as much secrecy, as he will. But when a sovereign assembly has need of counsel, none are admitted but such as have a right thereto from the beginning; which for the most part are of those who have been versed more in the acquisition of wealth than of knowledge; and are

to give their advice in long discourses, which may, and do commonly excite men to action, but not govern them in it. For the *understanding* is by the flame of the passions, never enlightened, but dazzled. Nor is there any place, or time, wherein an assembly can receive counsel with secrecy, because of their own multitude.

6. Thirdly, that the resolutions of a monarch, are subject to no other inconstancy, than that of human nature; but in assemblies, besides that of nature, there ariseth an inconstancy from the number. For the absence of a few, that would have the resolution once taken, continue firm, (which may happen by security, negligence, or private impediments,) or the diligent appearance of a few of the contrary opinion, undoes today, all that was concluded yesterday.

7. Fourthly, that a monarch cannot disagree with himself, out of envy, or interest; but an assembly may; and that to such a height, as may produce a civil war.

8. Fifthly, that in monarchy there is this inconvenience; that any subject, by the power of one man, for the enriching of a favourite or flatterer, may be deprived of all he possesseth; which I confess is a great and inevitable inconvenience. But the same may as well happen, where the sovereign power is in an assembly: for their power is the same; and they are as subject to evil counsel, and to be seduced by orators, as a monarch by flatterers; and becoming one another's flatterers, serve one another's covetousness and ambition by turns. And whereas the favourites of monarchs, are few, and they have none else to advance but their own kindred; the favourites of an assembly, are many; and the kindred much more numerous, than of any monarch. Besides, there is no

favourite of a monarch, which cannot as well succour his friends, as hurt his enemies: but orators, that is to say, favourites of sovereign assemblies, though they have great power to hurt, have little to save. For to accuse, requires less eloquence (such is man's nature) than to excuse; and condemnation, than absolution more resembles justice.

9. Sixthly, that it is an inconvenience in monarchy, that the sovereignty may descend upon an infant, or one that cannot discern between good and evil: and consisteth in this, that the use of his power, must be in the hand of another man, or of some assembly of men, which are to govern by his right, and in his name; as curators, and protectors of his person, and authority. But to say there is inconvenience, in putting the use of the sovereign power, into the hand of a man, or an assembly of men; is to say that all government is more inconvenient, than confusion, and civil war. And therefore all the danger that can be pretended, must arise from the contention of those, that for an office of so great honour, and profit, may become competitors. To make it appear, that this inconvenience, proceedeth not from that form of government we call monarchy, we are to consider, that the precedent monarch, hath appointed who shall have the tuition of his infant successor, either expressly by testament, or tacitly, by not controlling the custom in that case received: and then such inconvenience (if it happen) is to be attributed, not to the monarchy, but to the ambition, and injustice of the subjects; which in all kinds of government, where the people are not well instructed in their duty, and the rights of sovereignty, is the same. Or else the precedent monarch hath not at all taken order for such tuition; and then the law of nature hath provided this sufficient rule, that the tuition shall be in him, that hath by nature most interest in the preservation of the authority of the infant, and to whom least benefit can accrue by his death, or diminution. For seeing every man by nature seeketh his own benefit, and promotion; to put an infant into the power of those, that can promote themselves by his destruction, or damage, is not tuition, but treachery. So that sufficient provision being taken, against all just quarrel, about the government under a child, if any contention arise to the disturbance of the public peace, it is not to be attributed to the form of monarchy, but to the ambition of subjects, and ignorance of their duty. On the other side, there is no great commonwealth, the sovereignty whereof is in a great assembly, which is not, as to consultations of peace, and war, and making of laws, in the same condition, as if the government were in a child. For as a child wants the judgment to dissent from counsel given him, and is thereby necessitated to take the advice of them, or him, to whom he is committed: so an assembly wanteth the liberty, to dissent from the counsel of the major part, be it good, or bad. And as a child has need of a tutor, or protector, to preserve his person, and authority: so also (in great commonwealths,) the sovereign assembly, in all great dangers and troubles, have need of *custodes libertatis*; that is of dictators, or protectors of their authority; which are as much as temporary monarchs; to whom for a time, they may commit the entire exercise of their power; and have (at the end of that time) been oftener deprived thereof, than infant kings, by their protectors, regents, or any other tutors.

10. Though the kinds of sovereignty be, as I have now shown, but three; that is to say, monarchy, where one man has it; or democracy, where the general assembly of subjects hath it; or aristocracy, where it is in an assembly of certain persons nominated, or otherwise distinguished from the rest: yet he that shall consider the particular commonwealths that have been, and are in the world, will not perhaps easily reduce them to three, and may thereby be inclined to think there be other forms, arising from these mingled together. As for example, elective kingdoms; where kings have the sovereign power put into their hands for a time; or kingdoms, wherein the king hath a power limited: which governments, are nevertheless by most writers called monarchy. Likewise if a popular, or aristocratical commonwealth, subdue an enemy's country, and govern the same, by a president, procurator, or other magistrate; this may seem perhaps at first sight, to be a democratical, or aristocratical government. But it is not so. For elective kings, are not sovereigns, but ministers of the sovereign; nor limited kings sovereigns, but ministers of them that have the sovereign power: nor are those provinces which are in subjection to a democracy, or aristocracy of another commonwealth, democratically or aristocratically governed, but monarchically. . . .

Chapter XXI

Of the Liberty of Subjects

Liberty, what. 1. LIBERTY, or FREEDOM, signifieth (properly) the absence of opposition; (by opposition, I mean external impediments of motion;) and may be applied no less to irrational, and inanimate creatures, than to rational. For whatsoever is so tied, or environed, as it cannot move, but within a certain space, which space is determined by the opposition of some external body, we say it hath not liberty to go further. And so of all living creatures, whilst they are imprisoned, or restrained, with walls, or chains; and of the water whilst it is kept in by banks, or vessels, that otherwise would spread itself into a larger space, we use to say, they are not at liberty, to move in such manner, as without those external impediments they would. But when the impediment of motion, is in the constitution of the thing itself, we use not to say, it wants the liberty; but the power to move; as when a stone lieth still, or a man is fastened to his bed by sickness.

2. And according to this proper, and generally received meaning of the word, a FREEMAN, *is he, that in those things, which by his strength and wit he is able to do, is not hindered to do what he has a will to.* But when the words *free*, and *liberty*, are applied to anything but *bodies*, they are abused; for that which is not subject to motion, is not subject to impediment: and therefore, when 'tis said (for example) the way is free, no liberty of the way is signified, but of those that walk in it without stop. And when we say a gift is free, there is not meant any liberty of the gift, but of the giver, that was not bound by any law, or covenant to give it. So when we *speak freely*, it is not the liberty of voice, or pronunciation, but of the man, whom no law hath obliged to speak otherwise than he did. Lastly, from the use of the word *free-will*, no liberty can be inferred of the will, desire, or inclination, but the liberty of the man; which consisteth in this, that he finds no stop, in doing what he has the will, desire, or inclination to do.

What it is to be free.

3. Fear and liberty are consistent; as when a man throweth his goods into the sea for *fear* the ship should sink, he doth it nevertheless very willingly, and may refuse to do it if he will: it is therefore the action, of one that was *free*: so a man sometimes pays his debt, only for *fear* of imprisonment, which because nobody hindered him from detaining, was the action of a man at *liberty*. And generally all actions which men do in commonwealths, for *fear* of the law, are actions, which the doers had *liberty* to omit.

4. *Liberty*, and *necessity* are consistent: as in the water, that hath not only *liberty*, but a *necessity* of descending by the channel; so likewise in the actions which men voluntarily do: which, because they proceed from their will, proceed from *liberty*; and yet, because every act of man's will, and every desire, and inclination proceedeth from some cause, and that from another cause, in a continual chain, (whose first link is in the hand of God the first of all causes,) they proceed from *necessity*. So that to him that could see the connection of those causes, the *necessity* of all men's voluntary actions, would appear manifest. And therefore God, that seeth, and disposeth all things, seeth also that the *liberty* of man in doing what he will, is accompanied with the *necessity* of doing that which God will, and no more, nor less. For though men may do many things, which God does not command, nor is therefore author of them; yet they can have no passion, nor appetite to anything, of which appetite God's will is not the cause. And did not his will assure the *necessity* of man's will, and consequently of all that on man's will dependeth, the *liberty* of men would be a contradiction, and impediment to the omnipotence and *liberty* of God.

And this shall suffice, (as to the matter in hand) of that natural *liberty*, which only is properly called *liberty*.

5. But as men, for the attaining of peace, and conservation of themselves thereby, have made an artificial man, which we call a commonwealth; so also have they made artificial chains, called *civil laws*, which they themselves, by mutual covenants, have fastened at one end, to the lips of that man, or assembly, to whom they have given the sovereign power; and at the other end to their own ears. These bonds in their own nature but weak, may nevertheless be made to hold, by the danger, though not by the difficulty of breaking them.

6. In relation to these bonds only it is, that I am to speak now, of the *liberty of subjects*. For seeing there is no commonwealth in the world, wherein there be rules enough set down, for the regulating of all actions, and words of men; (as being a thing impossible:) it followeth necessarily, that in all kinds of actions, by the laws praetermitted [passed over], men have the liberty, of doing what their own reasons shall suggest, for the most profitable to themselves. For if we take liberty in the proper sense, for corporal liberty; that is to say, freedom from chains, and prison, it were very absurd for men to clamour as they do, for the liberty they so manifestly enjoy. Again, if we take liberty, for an exemption from laws, it is no less absurd, for men to demand as they do, that liberty, by which all other men may be masters of their lives. And yet as absurd as it is, this is it they demand; not knowing that the laws are of no power to protect them, without a sword in the hands of a man, or men, to cause those laws to be put in execution. The liberty of a subject, lieth therefore only

in those things, which in regulating their actions, the sovereign hath praetermitted: such as is the liberty to buy, and sell, and otherwise contract with one another; to choose their own abode, their own diet, their own trade of life, and institute their children as they themselves think fit; and the like.

7. Nevertheless we are not to understand, that by such liberty, the sovereign power of life, an death, is either abolished, or limited. For it has been already shown, that nothing the sovereign representative can do to a subject, on what pretence soever, can properly be called injustice, or injury; because every subject is author of every act the sovereign doth; so that he never wanteth right to anything, otherwise, than as he himself is the subject of God, and bound thereby to observe the laws of nature. And therefore it may, and doth often happen in commonwealths, that a subject may be put to death, by the command of the sovereign power; and yet neither do the other wrong: as when Jeptha caused his daughter to be sacrificed: in which, and the like cases, he that so dieth, had liberty to do the action, for which he is nevertheless, without injury put to death. And the same holdeth also in a sovereign prince, that putteth to death an innocent subject. For though the action be against the law of nature, as being contrary to equity, (as was the killing of Uriah, by David;) yet it was not an injury to Uriah, but to God. Not to Uriah, because the right to do what he pleased, was given him by Uriah himself: and yet to God, because David was God's subject; and prohibited all iniquity by the law of nature. Which distinction, David himself, when he repented the fact, evidently confirmed, saying, *To thee only have I sinned.* In the same manner, the people of Athens, when they banished the most potent of their commonwealth for ten years, thought they committed no injustice; and yet they never questioned what crime he had done; but what hurt he would do: nay they commanded the banishment of they knew not whom; and every citizen bringing his oyster shell into the marketplace, written with the name of him he desired should be banished, without actually accusing him, sometimes banished an Aristides, for his reputation of justice; and sometimes a scurrilous jester, as Hyperbolus, to make a jest of it. And yet a man cannot say, the sovereign people of Athens wanted right to banish them; or an Athenian the liberty to jest, or to be just.

8. The liberty, whereof there is so frequent, and honourable mention, in the histories, and philosophy of the ancient Greeks, and Romans, and in the writings, and discourse of those that from them have received all their learning in the politics, is not the liberty of particular men; but the liberty of the commonwealth: which is the same with that, which every man then should have, if there were no civil laws, nor commonwealth at all. And the effects of it also be the same. For as amongst masterless men, there is perpetual war, of every man against his neighbour; no inheritance, to transmit to the son, nor to expect from the father; no propriety of goods, or lands; no security; but a full and absolute liberty in every particular man: so in states, and commonwealths not dependent on one another, every commonwealth, (not every man) has an absolute liberty, to do what it shall judge (that is to say, what that man, or assembly that representeth it, shall judge) most conducing to their benefit. But

withal, they live in the condition of a perpetual war, and upon the confines of battle, with their frontiers armed, and cannons planted against their neighbours round about. The Athenians, and Romans were free; that is, free commonwealths: not that any particular men had the liberty to resist their own representative; but that their representative had the liberty to resist, or invade other people. There is written on the turrets of the city of Lucca in great characters at this day, the word LIBERTAS; yet no man can thence infer, that a particular man has more liberty, or immunity from the service of the commonwealth there, than in Constantinople. Whether a commonwealth be monarchical, or popular, the freedom is still the same.

9. But it is an easy thing, for men to be deceived, by the specious name of liberty; and for want of judgment to distinguish, mistake that for their private inheritance, and birthright, which is the right of the public only. And when the same error is confirmed by the authority of men in reputation for their writings on this subject, it is no wonder if it produce sedition, and change of government. In these western parts of the world, we are made to receive our opinions concerning the institution, and rights of commonwealths, from Aristotle, Cicero, and other men, Greeks and Romans, that living under popular states, derived those rights, not from the principles of nature, but transcribed them into their books, out of the practice of their own commonwealths, which were popular; as the grammarians describe the rules of language, out of the practice of the time; or the rules of poetry, out of the poems of Homer and Virgil. And because the Athenians were taught, (to keep them from desire of changing their government,) that

they were freemen, and all that lived under monarchy were slaves; therefore Aristotle puts it down in his *Politics*, (lib. 6. cap. 2.) *In democracy,* LIBERTY *is to be supposed: for it is commonly held, that no man is* FREE *in any other government.* And as Aristotle; so Cicero, and other writers have grounded their civil doctrine, on the opinions of the Romans, who were taught to hate monarchy, at first, by them that having deposed their sovereign, shared amongst them the sovereignty of Rome; and afterwards by their successors. And by reading of these Greek, and Latin authors, men from their childhood have gotten a habit (under a false show of liberty,) of favouring tumults, and of licentious controlling the actions of their sovereigns; and again of controlling those controllers; with the effusion of so much blood; as I think I may truly say, there was never anything so dearly bought, as these western parts have bought the learning of the Greek and Latin tongues.

10. To come now to the particulars of the true liberty of a subject; that is to say, what are the things, which though commanded by the sovereign, he may nevertheless, without injustice, refuse to do; we are to consider, what rights we pass away, when we make a commonwealth; or (which is all one) what liberty we deny ourselves, by owning all the actions (without exception) of the man, or assembly we make our sovereign. For in the act of our *submission,* consisteth both our *obligation,* and our *liberty;* which must therefore be inferred by arguments taken from thence; there being no obligation on any man, which ariseth not from some act of his own; for all men equally, are by nature free. And because such arguments, must either be drawn from the express words, *I authorize all his actions,* or from

Liberty of subjects how to be measured.

John Locke

John Locke (1632–1704) is the foremost liberal political philosopher of the modern era. His *Two Treatises on Government* promote the values of individual rights, liberty, privacy, and toleration in arguing against aristocratic privilege and absolutist forms of government. For Locke, government should be an instrument for securing the life, liberty, and well-being of a people, a set of institutions that promote a stable society in which citizens are free to choose their own individual pursuits of happiness. Since human beings share a fundamental moral equality, governing powers should be seen not as sovereign fathers but as public servants elected to carry out collective tasks. When a government fails to uphold the trust of its citizens—by tending toward tyranny and oppression, invading the private property rights of citizens, or corrupting representatives—the people can rightly rebel and reclaim their original political authority in revolution.

Locke was born in Somerset, England, and received an Oxford education in medicine and philosophy. His interest in medicine and science continued throughout his life, and as an adult he became a fellow of the Royal Society (the first scientific society of England) and a friend to several prominent scientific figures, including Sir Isaac Newton, Robert Boyle, and Thomas Sydenham. He was also a close friend of the first earl of Shaftsbury, Lord Ashley, serving as his physician, research associate, co-author, and political secretary. As a supporter of Ashley, Locke wrote anonymously published treatises against existing political powers and participated in radical political movements intended to prevent James II, the Catholic duke of York, from succeeding to the throne. In a climate of growing political unrest in 1683, Locke fled England to Holland, where he participated actively in an international community of exiled revolutionaries. Several years later, he returned to England and published his major work in epistemology, *An Essay Concerning Human Understanding* (1689), in which he argued for an empirical foundation of all knowledge. For his remaining active years, Locke enjoyed status as an intellectual celebrity, held minor political offices, and wrote widely on issues ranging from education to religion to finance. For nearly all of his life, it was not known by his contemporaries that he wrote the *Two Treatises on Government*. The *Treatises* were published anonymously in 1689, and Locke revealed his authorship of the texts in his will upon his death.

The first treatise of the *Two Treatises on Government* aims to refute the theory that kings possess divinely ordained political rights. In the seventeenth century, Sir Robert Filmer and other theological-political theorists had argued that kingly power was inherited from Adam, who possessed divine natural rights over Eve, their children, and the entire created world. Locke spends the majority of the *First Treatise* demonstrating that Filmer proves neither the original absolute sovereignty of Adam nor any historical lineage between Adam and English kings. He also argues in opposition to Filmer that the authority of kings is not akin to the authority of fathers over their children, for citizens are not like children and parental authority ceases when children reach adulthood. The first chapter of the *Second Treatise* summarizes the arguments of the *First Treatise* against paternalistic and divinely ordained kingly power.

The *Second Treatise on Government* puts forward Locke's own positive account of the origin and purpose of government. Like Hobbes, Locke not only stands against theocratic political power but also offers a social contract theory of political obligation, beginning with an account of the state of nature that human beings inhabit prior to living in civil societies backed by governments. Unlike Hobbes, Locke appeals to natural moral laws accessible to humanity in the hypothetical state of nature by the use of their reason, arguing that the state of nature need not become a state of war. Without a sovereign power, human beings could live peacefully, following their natural duties of self-preservation and respectfulness toward others. However, as greed and irrationality lead some individuals to violate natural moral laws, people living in a state of nature still face the need to punish and restrain wrongdoers. Our natural rights to punish wrongdoers— along with our other natural rights—are best entrusted to a sovereign power in a state, which can impartially enact just punishments and secure rights to life, liberty, and property.

A Letter Concerning Toleration, published anonymously by Locke in 1689, complements the arguments of *The Second Treatise of Government*. In the latter, we find the argument that the proper scope of the authority of the state extends only to securing individuals' natural rights to life, liberty, and property. Although Locke does not mention religious toleration in the *Second Treatise*, his arguments for limitations upon social and political power in the treatise are extended to diverse religious practices in the *Letter*. Locke argues that societies and states must tolerate all harmless religious practices, for controlling religious belief is not necessary to securing rights to life, liberty, and property; moreover, individual salvation cannot be secured by means of the coercive force of the state. *A Letter Concerning Toleration* was radical in its time. Its proposals for religious toleration and freedom of religious belief were attractive to only a small minority of political liberals, and the *Letter* was widely attacked as atheistic and heretical.

The Second Treatise of Government:
An Essay concerning the True Original Extent and End of Civil Government

I

1. It having been shown in the foregoing discourse,

    1. That Adam had not, either by natural right of fatherhood, nor by positive donation from God, any such authority over his children, or dominion over the world, as is pretended.
    2. That if he had, his heirs yet had no right to it.
    3. That if his heirs had, there being no law of nature nor positive law of God that determines which is the right heir in all cases that may arise, the right of succession, and consequently of bearing rule, could not have been certainly determined.
    4. That if even that had been determined, yet the knowledge of which is the eldest line of Adam's posterity being so long since utterly lost, that in the races of mankind and families of the world, there remains not to one above another, the least pretence to be the eldest house, and to have the right of inheritance.

All these premises having, as I think, been clearly made out, it is impossible that the rulers now on earth should make any benefit, or derive any the least shadow of authority from that, which is held to be the fountain of all power, *Adam's private dominion and paternal jurisdiction*; so that he that will not give just occasion to think that all government in the world is the product only of force and violence, and that men live together by no other rules but that of beasts, where the strongest carries it, and so lay a foundation for perpetual disorder and mischief, tumult, sedition, and rebellion (things that the followers of that hypothesis so loudly cry out against), must of necessity find out another rise of government, another original of political power, and another way of designing and knowing the persons that have it, than what Sir Robert Filmer hath taught us.

2. To this purpose, I think it may not be amiss, to set down what I take to be political power; that the power of a magistrate over a subject may be distinguished from that of a father over his children, a master over his servant, a husband over his wife, and a lord over his slave. All which distinct powers happening sometimes together in the same man, if he be considered under these different relations, it may help us to distinguish these powers one from another, and show the difference betwixt a ruler of a commonwealth, a father of a family, and a captain of a galley.

3. Political power, then, I take to be a right of making laws with penalties of death, and consequently all less penalties, for the regulating and preserving of property, and of employing the force of the community, in the execution of such laws, and in the defence of the commonwealth from foreign injury; and all this only for the public good.

II

Of the State of Nature

4. To understand political power aright, and derive it from its original, we must consider, what state all men are naturally in, and that is, a state of perfect freedom to order their actions, and dispose of their possessions and persons, as they think fit, within the bounds of the law of nature, without asking leave, or depending upon the will of any other man.

A state also of equality, wherein all the power and jurisdiction is reciprocal, no one having more than another; there being nothing more evident, than that creatures of the same species and rank, promiscuously born to all the same advantages of nature, and the use of the same faculties, should also be equal one amongst another without subordination or subjection, unless the lord and master of them all should, by any manifest declaration of his will, set one above another, and confer on him, by an evident and clear appointment, an undoubted right to dominion and sovereignty. . . .

6. But though this be a state of liberty, yet it is not a state of licence: though man in that state have an uncontrollable liberty to dispose of his person or possessions, yet he has not liberty to destroy himself, or so much as any creature in his possession, but where some nobler use than its bare preservation calls for it. The state of nature has a law of nature to govern it, which obliges everyone, and reason, which is that law, teachers all mankind, who will but consult it, that being all equal and independent, no one ought to harm another in his life, health, liberty, or possessions: for men being all the workmanship of one omnipotent, and infinitely wise maker; all the servants of one sovereign master, sent into the world by his order, and about his business; they are his property, whose workmanship they are, made to last during his, not one another's pleasure: and being furnished with like faculties, sharing all in one community of nature, there cannot be supposed any such subordination among us, that may authorize us to destroy one another, as if we were made for one another's uses, as the inferior ranks of creatures are for ours. Everyone, as he is bound to preserve himself, and not to quit his station wilfully, so by the like reason, when his own preservation comes not in competition, ought he as much as he can to preserve the rest of mankind, and not unless it be to do justice on an offender, take away, or impair the life, or what tends to the preservation of the life, the liberty, health, limb, or goods of another.

7. And that all men may be restrained from invading others rights, and from doing hurt to one another, and the law of nature be observed, which willeth the peace and preservation of all mankind, the execution of the law of nature is, in that state, put into every man's hands, whereby everyone has a right to punish the transgressors of that law to such a degree, as may hinder its violation. For the law of nature would, as all other laws that concern men in this world, be in vain, if there were nobody that in the state of nature had a power to execute that law, and thereby preserve the innocent and restrain offenders. And if anyone in the state of nature may punish another for any evil he has done, everyone may do so: for in that state of perfect equality where naturally there is no superiority or jurisdiction of one over another, what any may do in prosecution of that law, everyone must needs have a right to do.

8. And thus, in the state of nature, one man comes by a power over another; but yet no absolute or arbitrary power, to use a criminal, when he has got him in his hands, according to the passionate heats, or boundless extravagancy

of his own will; but only to retribute to him, so far as calm reason and conscience dictates, what is proportionate to his transgression, which is so much as may serve for reparation and restraint: for these two are the only reasons why one man may lawfully do harm to another, which is that we call punishment. In transgressing the law of nature, the offender declares himself to live by another rule than that of reason and common equity, which is that measure God has set to the actions of men for their mutual security, and so he becomes dangerous to mankind, the tie, which is to secure them from injury and violence, being slighted and broken by him, which being a trespass against the whole species, and the peace and safety of it, provided for by the law of nature, every man upon this score, by the right he hath to preserve mankind in general, may restrain, or where it is necessary, destroy things noxious to them, and so may bring such evil on anyone, who hath transgressed that law, as may make him repent the doing of it, and thereby deter him, and, by his example others, from doing the like mischief. And in this case, and upon this ground, every man hath a right to punish the offender, and be executioner of the law of nature. . . .

10. Besides the crime which consists in violating the law, and varying from the right rule of reason, whereby a man so far becomes degenerate, and declares himself to quit the principles of human nature and to be a noxious creature, there is commonly injury done, and some person or other, some other man receives damage by his transgression; in which case he who hath received any damage, has, besides the right of punishment common to him with other men, a particular right to seek reparation from him that has done it: and any other person, who finds it just, may also join with him that is injured, and assist him in recovering from the offender so much as may make satisfaction for the harm he has suffered.

11. From these two distinct rights, the one of punishing the crime for restraint, and preventing the like offence, which right of punishing is in everybody; the other of taking reparation, which belongs only to the injured party, comes it to pass that the magistrate, who by being magistrate hath the common right of punishing put into his hands, can often, where the public good demands not the execution of the law, remit the punishment of criminal offences by his own authority, but yet cannot remit the satisfaction due to any private man for the damage he has received. That, he who has suffered the damage has a right to demand in his own name, and he alone can remit: the damnified person has this power of appropriating to himself the goods or service of the offender, by right of self-preservation, as every man has a power to punish the crime, to prevent its being committed again, by the right he has of preserving all mankind, and doing all reasonable things he can in order to that end: and thus it is, that every man, in the state of nature, has a power to kill a murderer, both to deter others from doing the like injury, which no reparation can compensate, by the example of the punishment that attends it from every body, and also to secure men from the attempts of a criminal, who having renounced reason, the common rule and measure God hath given to mankind, hath, by the unjust violence and slaughter he hath committed upon one, declared war against all mankind, and therefore may be destroyed as a lion or a tiger, one of those wild savage beasts, with whom men can have no society nor security: and upon this is grounded that great law of nature, *Whoso sheddeth man's blood, by man shall his blood be shed.* And Cain was so fully convinced, that everyone had a right to destroy such a criminal, that after the murder of his brother, he cries out, *Everyone that findeth me shall slay me*; so plain was it writ in the hearts of all mankind.

12. By the same reason may a man in the state of nature punish the lesser breaches of that law. It will perhaps be demanded, with death? I answer, each transgression may be punished to that degree, and with so much severity, as will suffice to make it an ill bargain to the offender, give him cause to repent, and terrify others from doing the like. Every offence, that can be committed in the state of nature, may in the state of nature be also punished equally, and as far forth as it may, in a commonwealth: for though it would be besides my present purpose, to enter here into the particulars of the law of nature, or its measures of punishment; yet, it is certain there is such a law, and that too as intelligible and plain to a rational creature, and a studier of that law, as the positive laws of commonwealths: nay, possibly plainer; as much as reason is easier to be understood, than the fancies and intricate contrivances of men, following contrary and hidden interests put into words; for so truly are a great part of the municipal laws of countries, which are only so far right, as they are founded on the law of nature, by which they are to be regulated and interpreted.

13. To this strange doctrine, *viz.* That in the state of nature everyone has the executive power of the law of nature, I doubt not but it will be objected, that it is unreasonable for men to be judges in their own cases, that self-love will make men partial to themselves and their friends: and on the other side, ill-nature, passion, and revenge will carry them too far in punishing others; and hence nothing but confusion and disorder will follow; and that therefore God hath certainly appointed government to restrain the partiality and violence of men. I easily grant that civil government is the proper remedy for the inconveniences of the state of nature, which must certainly be great where men may be judges in their own case, since 'tis easy to be imagined, that he who was so unjust as to do his brother an injury, will scarce be so just as to condemn himself for it; but I shall desire those who make this objection, to remember, that absolute monarchs are but men; and if government is to be the remedy of those evils, which necessarily follow from men's being judges in their own cases, and the state of nature is therefore not to be endured, I desire to know what kind of government that is, and how much better it is than the state of nature, where one man commanding a multitude, has the liberty to be judge in his own case, and may do to all his subjects whatever he pleases, without the least question or control of those who execute his pleasure? and in whatsoever he doth, whether led by reason, mistake, or passion, must be submitted to? which men in the state of nature are not bound to do one to another. And if he that judges, judges amiss in his own, or any other case, he is answerable for it to the rest of mankind.

14. 'Tis often asked as a mighty objection, where are, or ever were there any men in such a state of nature? To which it may suffice as an answer at present, that since all princes and rulers of *independent* governments all through the world, are in a state of nature, 'tis plain the world never was, nor never will be, without numbers of men in that state. I have named all governors of *independent* communities, whether they are, or are not, in league with others: for 'tis not every compact that puts an end to the state of nature between men, but only this one of agreeing together mutually to enter into one community, and make one body politic; other promises, and compacts, men may make one with another, and yet still be in the state of nature. The promises and bargains for truck, etc. between the two men in the desert island, mentioned by Garcilasso de la Vega, in his history of Peru; or between a Swiss and an Indian, in the woods of America, are

provisions there was a long time in the world, and the few spenders, and to how small a part of that provision the industry of one man could extend itself and engross it to the prejudice of others, especially keeping within the bonds set by reason of what might serve for his use, there could be then little room for quarrels or contentions about property so established.

32. But the chief matter of property being now not the fruits of the earth and the beasts that subsist on it, but the earth itself, as that which takes in and carries with it all the rest, I think it is plain that property in that too is acquired as the former. As much land as a man tills, plants, improves, cultivates, and can use the product of, so much is his property. He by his labour does, as it were, enclose it from the common. Nor will it invalidate his right to say, Every body else has an equal title to it, and therefore he cannot appropriate, he cannot enclose, without the consent of all his fellow-commoners, all mankind. God, when he gave the world in common to all mankind, commanded man also to labour, and the penury of his condition required it of him. God and his reason commanded him to subdue the earth—i.e., improve it for the benefit of life and therein lay out something upon it that was his own; his labour. He that, in obedience to this command of God, subdued, tilled, and sowed any part of it, thereby annexed to it something that was his property, which another had no title to, nor could without injury take from him.

33. Nor was this appropriation of any parcel of land, by improving it, any prejudice to any other man, since there was still enough and as good left, and more than the yet unprovided could use. So that, in effect, there was never the less left for others because of his enclosure for himself. For he that leaves as much as another can make use of does as good

as take nothing at all. Nobody could think himself injured by the drinking of another man, though he took a good draught, who had a whole river of the same water left him to quench his thirst. And the case of land and water, where there is enough of both, is perfectly the same.

34. God gave the world to men in common, but since he gave it them for their benefit and the greatest conveniences of life they were capable to draw from it, it cannot be supposed he meant it should always remain common and uncultivated. He gave it to the use of the industrious and rational (and labour was to be his title to it); not to the fancy or covetousness of the quarrelsome and contentious. He that had as good left for his improvement as was already taken up needed not complain, ought not to meddle with what was already improved by another's labour; if he did 'tis plain he desired the benefit of another's pains, which he had no right to, and not the ground which God had given him, in common with others, to labour on, and whereof there was as good left as that already possessed, and more than he knew what to do with, or his industry could reach to.

35. 'Tis true, in land that is common in England or any other country, where there are plenty of people under government who have money and commerce, no one can enclose or appropriate any part without the consent of all his fellow-commoners; because this is left common by compact, i.e., by the law of the land, which is not to be violated. And, though it be common in respect of some men, it is not so to all mankind, but is the joint property of this country, or this parish. Besides, the remainder, after such enclosure, would not be as good to the rest of the commoners as the whole was, when they could all make use of the whole; whereas in the beginning and first peopling of the great common of the world it

was quite otherwise. The law man was under was rather for appropriating. God commanded, and his wants forced him to labour. That was his property, which could not be taken from him wherever he had fixed it. And hence subduing or cultivating the earth and having dominion, we see, are joined together. The one gave title to the other. So that God, by commanding to subdue, gave authority so far to appropriate. And the condition of human life, which requires labour and materials to work on, necessarily introduce private possessions.

36. The measure of property nature has well set by the extent of men's labour and the conveniency of life. No man's labour could subdue or appropriate all, nor could his enjoyment consume more than a small part; so that it was impossible for any man, this way, to entrench upon the right of another or acquire to himself a property to the prejudice of his neighbour, who would still have room for as good and as large a possession (after the other had taken out his) as before it was appropriated. Which measure did confine every man's possession to a very moderate proportion, and such as he might appropriate to himself without injury to anybody in the first ages of the world, when men were more in danger to be lost, by wandering from their company, in the then vast wilderness of the earth, than to be straitened for want of room to plant in. And the same measure may be allowed still, without prejudice to anybody, as full as the world seems. For, supposing a man or family, in the state they were at first, peopling of the world by the children of Adam or Noah; let him plant in some inland vacant places of America, we shall find that the possessions he could make himself, upon the measures we have given, would not be very large, nor, even to this day, prejudice the rest of mankind or give them reason to complain or think themselves

injured by this man's encroachment, though the race of men have now spread themselves to all corners of the world, and do infinitely exceed the small number [there] was at the beginning. Nay, the extent of ground is of so little value without labour that I have heard it affirmed that in Spain itself a man may be permitted to plough, sow, and reap, without being disturbed, upon land· he has no other title to, but only his making use of it. But, on the contrary, the inhabitants think themselves beholden to him who, by his industry on neglected, and consequently waste land, has increased the stock of corn, which they wanted. But be this as it will, which I lay no stress on, this I dare boldly affirm, that the same rule of propriety (viz.), that every man should have as much as he could make use of, would hold still in the world, without straitening anybody, since there is land enough in the world to suffice double the inhabitants, had not the invention of money, and the tacit agreement of men to put a value on it, introduced (by consent) larger possessions and a right to them; which, how it has done, I shall by and by show more at large.

37. This is certain, that in the beginning, before the desire of having more than man needed had altered the intrinsic value of things, which depends only on their usefulness to the life of man, or had agreed that a little piece of yellow metal, which would keep without wasting or decay, should be worth a great piece of flesh or a whole heap of corn, though men had a right to appropriate by their labour, each one to himself, as much of the things of nature as he could use, yet this could not be much, nor to the prejudice of others, where the same plenty was still left, to those who would use the same industry.

Before the appropriation of land, he who gathered as much of the wild fruit, killed, caught, or tamed as many of the beasts as he could—he that so employed his pains about any of the spontaneous products of nature as any way to alter them from the state nature put them in, by placing any of his labour on them, did thereby acquire a propriety in them; but if they perished in his possession without their due use—if the fruits rotted or the venison putrified before he could spend it, he offended against the common law of nature, and was liable to be punished: he invaded his neighbour's share for he had no right farther than his use called for any of them, and they might serve to afford him conveniences of life.

38. The same measures governed the possession of land, too. Whatsoever he tilled and reaped, laid up and made use of before it spoiled, that was his peculiar right; whatsoever he enclosed, and could feed and make use of, the cattle and product was also his. But if either the grass of his enclosure rotted on the ground, or the fruit of his planting perished without gathering and laying up, this part of the earth, notwithstanding his enclosure, was still to be looked on as waste, and might be the possession of any other. Thus, at the beginning, Cain might take as much ground as he could till and make it his own land, and yet leave enough to Abel's sheep to feed on: a few acres would serve for both their possessions. But as families increased and industry enlarged their stocks, their possessions enlarged with the need of them; but yet it was commonly without any fixed property in the ground they made use of till they incorporated, settled themselves together, and built cities, and then, by consent, they came in time to set out the bounds of their distinct territories and agree on limits between them and their neighbours, and by laws within themselves settled the properties of those of the same society. For we see that in that part of the world which was first inhabited, and therefore like to be best peopled, even as low down as Abraham's time,

they wandered with their flocks and their herds, which was their substance, freely up and down—and this Abraham did in a country where he was a stranger. Whence it is plain that, at least, a great part of the land lay in common, that the inhabitants valued it not, nor claimed property in any more than they made use of; but when there was not room enough in the same place for their herds to feed together, they, by consent, as Abraham and Lot did, *Gen.* xiii. 5, separated and enlarged their pasture where it best liked them. And for the same reason, Esau went from his father and his brother, and planted in Mount Seir, *Gen.* xxxvi. 6.

39. And thus, without supposing any private dominion and property in Adam over all the world, exclusive of all other men, which can no way be proved, nor anyone's property be made out from it, but supposing the world, given as it was to the children of men in common, we see how labour could make men distinct titles to several parcels of it for their private uses, wherein there could be no doubt of right, no room for quarrel.

40. Nor is it so strange as perhaps before consideration, it may appear, that the property of labour should be able to overbalance the community of land, for 'tis labour indeed that puts the difference of value on everything; and let anyone consider what the difference is between an acre of land planted with tobacco or sugar, sown with wheat or barley, and an acre of the same land lying in common without any husbandry upon it, and he will find that the improvement of labour makes the far greater part of the value. I think it will be but a very modest computation to say, that of the products of the earth useful to the life of man, nine-tenths are the effects of labour: nay, if we will rightly estimate things as they come to our use, and cast up the several expenses about them, what in them is purely owing to nature

and what to labour, we shall find that in most of them ninety-nine hundredths are wholly to be put on the account of labour.

41. There cannot be a clearer demonstration of anything than several nations of the Americans are of this, who are rich in land and poor in all the comforts of life; whom nature, having furnished as liberally as any other people with the materials of plenty, i.e., a fruitful soil, apt to produce in abundance what might serve for food, raiment, and delight; yet, for want of improving it by labour, have not one hundredth part of the conveniences we enjoy. And a king of a large and fruitful territory there feeds, lodges, and is clad worse than a day labourer in England. . . .

45. Thus labour, in the beginning, gave a right of property, wherever anyone was pleased to employ it, upon what was common, which remained a long while, the far greater part, and is yet more than mankind makes use of. Men at first, for the most part, contented themselves with what unassisted nature offered to their necessities; and though afterwards, in some parts of the world, where the increase of people and stock, with the use of money, had made land scarce, and so of some value, the several communities settled the bounds of their distinct territories, and, by laws, within themselves, regulated the properties of the private men of their society, and so, by compact and agreement, settled the property which labour and industry began; and the leagues that have been made between several states and kingdoms, either expressly or tacitly disowning all claim and right to the land in the other's possession, have, by common concept, given up their pretences to their natural common right, which originally they had to those countries; and so have, by positive agreement, settled a property amongst themselves, in distinct parts of the world; yet there are still great tracts of ground to be found, which the inhabitants thereof, not having joined with the rest of mankind in the consent of the use of their common money, lie waste, and are more than the people who dwell on it, do, or can make use of, and so still lie in common; though this can scarce happen amongst that part of mankind that have consented to the use of money.

46. The greatest part of things really useful to the life of man, and such as the necessity of subsisting made the first commoners of the world look after, as it doth the Americans now, are generally things of short duration, such as, if they are not consumed by use, will decay and perish of themselves. Gold, silver, and diamonds are things that fancy or agreement hath put the value on, more than real use and the necessary support of life. Now of those good things which nature hath provided in common, everyone had a right (as hath been said) to as much as he could use, and had a property in all that he could effect with his labour; all that his industry could extend to, to alter from the state nature had put it in, was his. He that gathered a hundred bushels of acorns or apples had thereby a property in them, they were his goods as soon as gathered. He was only to look that he used them before they spoiled, else he took more than his share, and robbed others. And, indeed, it was a foolish thing, as well as dishonest, to hoard up more than he could make use of. If he gave away a part to anybody else, so that it perished not uselessly in his possession, these he also made use of. And if he also bartered away plums that would have rotted in a week, for nuts that would last good for his eating a whole year, he did no injury; he wasted not the common stock; destroyed no part of the portion of goods that belonged to others, so long as nothing perished uselessly in his hands. Again, if he would give his nuts for a piece of metal, pleased with its colour, or exchange his sheep

for shells, or wool for a sparkling pebble or a diamond, and keep those by him all his life, he invaded not the right of others; he might heap up as much of these durable things as he pleased; the exceeding of the bounds of his just property not lying in the largeness of his possession, but the perishing of anything uselessly in it.

47. And thus came in the use of money, some lasting thing that men might keep without spoiling, and that, by mutual consent, men would take in exchange for the truly useful but perishable supports of life. . . .

50. But since gold and silver, being little useful to the life of man, in proportion to food, raiment, and carriage, has its value only from the consent of men, whereof labour yet makes in great part the measure, it is plain that the consent of men have agreed to a disproportionate and unequal possession of the earth, I mean out of the bounds of society and compact; for in governments the laws regulate it; they having, by consent, found out and agreed in a way how a man may rightfully, and without injury, possess more than he himself can make use of by receiving gold and silver, which may continue long in a man's possession without decaying for the overplus, and agreeing those metals should have a value. . . .

51. And thus, I think, it is very easy to conceive, without any difficulty, how labour could at first begin a title of property in the common things of nature, and how the spending it upon our uses bounded it; so that there could then be no reason of quarrelling about title, nor any doubt about the largeness of possession it gave. Right and conveniency went together. For as a man had a right to all he could employ his labour upon, so he had no temptation to labour for more than he could make use of. This left no room for controversy about the title, nor for encroachment on the right of others. What portion a man carved to

himself was easily seen; and it was useless as well as dishonest to carve himself too much, or take more than he needed. . . .

VII

Of Political or Civil Society

77. God, having made man such a creature that, in his own judgment, it was not good for him to be alone, put him under strong obligations of necessity, convenience, and inclination, to drive him into society, as well as fitted him with understanding and language to continue and enjoy it. The first society was between man and wife, which gave beginning to that between parents and children, to which, in time, that between master and servant came to be added. And though all these might, and commonly did, meet together, and make up but one family, wherein the master or mistress of it had some sort of rule proper to a family, each of these, or all together, came short of *political society*, as we shall see if we consider the different ends, ties, and bounds of each of these. . . .

89. Wherever therefore any number of men are so united into one society as to quit everyone his executive power of the law of nature, and to resign it to the public, there and there only is a political or civil society. And this is done wherever any number of men, in the state of nature, enter into society to make one people, one body politic under one supreme government: or else when anyone joins himself to and incorporates with any government already made. For hereby he authorizes the society, or which is all one, the legislative thereof, to make laws for him as the public good of the society shall require, to the execution whereof his own assistance (as to his own decrees) is due. And this puts men out of a state of nature into that of a commonwealth,

by setting up a judge on earth with authority to determine all the controversies and redress the injuries that may happen to any member of the commonwealth; which judge is the legislative or magistrates appointed by it. And wherever there are any number of men, however associated, that have no such decisive power to appeal to, there they are still in the state of nature.

90. And hence it is evident that absolute monarchy, which by some men is counted for the only government in the world, is indeed inconsistent with civil society, and so can be no form of civil government at all. For the end of the civil society being to avoid and remedy those inconveniences of the state of nature which necessarily follow from every man's being judge in his own case, by setting up a known authority, to which everyone of that society may appeal upon any injury received, or controversy that may arise, and which everyone of the society ought to obey; wherever any persons are who have not such an authority to appeal to, for the decision of any difference between them there, those persons are still in the state of nature. And so is every absolute prince in respect of those who are under his *dominion*. . . .

VIII

Of the Beginning of Political Societies

95. Men being, as has been said, by nature all free, equal, and independent, no one can be put out of his estate and subjected to the political power of another without his own consent, which is done by agreeing with other men, to join and unite into a community for their comfortable, safe, and peaceable living, one amongst another, in a secure enjoyment of their properties, and a greater security against any that are not of it. This any number

of men may do, because it injures not the freedom of the rest; they are left, as they were, in the liberty of the state of nature. When any number of men have so consented to make one community or government, they are thereby presently incorporated, and make one body politic, wherein the majority have a right to act and conclude the rest.

96. For, when any number of men have, by the consent of every individual, made a community, they have thereby made that community one body, with a power to act as one body, which is only by the will and determination of the majority. For [any acting] community, being only the consent of the individuals of it, and it being one body, must move one way, it is necessary the body should move that way whither the greater force carries it, which is the consent of the majority, or else it is impossible it should act or continue one body, one community, which the consent of every individual that united into it agreed that it should; and so everyone is bound by that consent to be concluded by the majority. And therefore we see that in assemblies empowered to act by positive laws where no number is set by that positive law which empowers them, the act of the majority passes for the act of the whole, and of course determines as having, by the law of nature and reason, the power of the whole.

97. And thus every man, by consenting with others to make one body politic under one government, puts himself under an obligation to everyone of that society to submit to the determination of the majority, and to be concluded by it; or else this original compact, whereby he with others incorporates into one society, would signify nothing, and be no compact if he be left free and under no other ties than he was in before in the state of nature. For what appearance would there be of any compact? What new engagement if he were no

farther tied by any decrees of the society than he himself thought fit and did actually consent to? This would be still as great a liberty as he himself had before his compact, or anyone else in the state of nature hath, who may submit himself and consent to any acts of it if he thinks fit.

98. For if the consent of the majority shall not in reason be received as the act of the whole, and conclude every individual, nothing but the consent of every individual can make anything to be the act of the whole, which, considering the infirmities of health and avocations of business, which in a number though much less than that of a commonwealth, will necessarily keep many away from the public assembly; and the variety of opinions and contrariety of interests which unavoidably happen in all collections of men, 'tis next impossible ever to be had. And, therefore, if coming into society be upon such terms, it will be only like Cato's coming into the theatre, *tantum ut exiret.* Such a constitution as this would make the mighty *Leviathan* of a shorter duration than the feeblest creatures, and not let it outlast the day it was born in, which cannot be supposed till we can think that rational creatures should desire and constitute societies only to be dissolved. For where the majority cannot conclude the rest, there they cannot act as one body, and consequently will be immediately dissolved again.

99. Whosoever therefore out of a state of nature unite into a community, must be understood to give up all the power necessary to the ends for which they unite into society to the majority of the community, unless they expressly agreed in any number greater than the majority. And this is done by barely agreeing to unite into one political society, which is all the compact that is, or needs be, between the individuals that enter into or make up a commonwealth. And thus, that which begins

and actually constitutes any political society is nothing but the consent of any number of freemen capable of a majority, to unite and incorporate into such a society. And this is that, and that only, which did or could give beginning to any lawful government in the world.

100. To this I find two objections made:

First, *That there are no instances to be found in history of a company of men, independent and equal one amongst another, that met together, and in this way began and set up a government.*

Secondly, *'Tis impossible of right that men should do so, because all men, being born under government, they are to submit to that, and are not at liberty to begin a new one.*

101. To the first there is this to answer: That it is not at all to be wondered that history gives us but a very little account of men that lived together in the state of nature. The inconveniencies of that condition, and the love and want of society, no sooner brought any number of them together, but they presently united and incorporated if they designed to continue together. And if we may not suppose men ever to have been in the state of nature, because we hear not much of them in such a state, we may as well suppose the armies of Salmanasser or Xerxes were never children, because we hear little of them till they were men and embodied in armies. Government is everywhere antecedent to records, and letters seldom come in amongst a people till a long continuation of civil society has, by other more necessary arts, provided for their safety, ease, and plenty. And then they begin to look after the history of their founders, and search into their original when they have outlived the memory of it. For 'tis with commonwealths as with particular persons, they are commonly ignorant of their own births and infancies; and if they know anything of their original, they are beholding for it to the accidental records that others have

kept of it. And those that we have of the beginning of any polities in the world, excepting that of the Jews, where God himself immediately interposed, and which favours not at all paternal dominion, are all either plain instances of such a beginning as I have mentioned, or at least have manifest footsteps of it.

102. He must show a strange inclination to deny evident matter of fact, when it agrees not with his hypothesis, who will not allow that the beginning of Rome and Venice were by the uniting together of several men, free and independent one of another, amongst whom there was no natural superiority or subjection. And if Josephus Acosta's word may be taken, he tells us that in many parts of America there was no government at all. *There are great and apparent conjectures*, says he, *that these men*, speaking of those of Peru, *for a long time had neither kings nor commonwealths, but lived in troops, as they do this day in* Florida—*the* Cheriquanas, *those of* Brazil, *and many other nations, which have no certain kings, but, as occasion is offered in peace or war, they choose their captains as they please*, I. i. c. 25. If it be said that every man there was born subject to his father, or the head of his family, that the subjection due from a child to a father took not away his freedom of uniting into what political society he thought fit, has been already proved; but be that as it will, these men, 'tis evident, were actually free; and whatever superiority some politicians now would place in any of them, they themselves claimed it not; but, by consent, were all equal, till, by the same consent, they set rulers over themselves. So that their politic societies all began from a voluntary union, and the mutual agreement of men freely acting in the choice of their governors and forms of government. . . .

The other objection, I find, urged against the beginning of polities, in the way I have mentioned, is this, viz.:

113. *That all men being born under government, some or other, it is impossible any of them should ever be free and at liberty to unite together and begin a new one, or ever be able to erect a lawful government.*

If this argument be good, I ask, How came so many lawful monarchies into the world? For if anybody, upon this supposition, can show me any one man, in any age of the world, free to begin a lawful monarchy, I will be bound to show him ten other free men at liberty, at the same time, to unite and begin a new government under a regal or any other form. It being demonstration, that if anyone born under the domination of another may be so free as to have a right to command others in a new and distinct empire, everyone that is born under the dominion of another may be so free too, and may become a ruler or subject of a distinct separate government. And so, by this their own principle, either all men, however born, are free, or else there is but one lawful prince, one lawful government in the world; and then they have nothing to do but barely to show us which that is, which, when they have done, I doubt not but all mankind will easily agree to pay obedience to him.

114. Though it be a sufficient answer to their objection to show that it involves them in the same difficulties that it doth those they use it against, yet I shall endeavour to discover the weakness of this argument a little farther.

All men, say they, *are born under government, and therefore they cannot be at liberty to begin a new one. Everyone is born a subject to his father or his prince, and is therefore under the perpetual tie of subjection and allegiance.* 'Tis plain mankind never owned nor considered any such natural subjection that they were born in, to one or to the other, that tied them, without their own consents, to a subjection to them and their heirs.

115. For there are no examples so frequent in history, both sacred and profane, as those of men withdrawing themselves and their obedience from the jurisdiction they were born under, and the family or community they were bred up in, and setting up new governments in other places, from whence sprang all that number of petty commonwealths in the beginning of ages, and which always multiplied as long as there was room enough, till the stronger or more fortunate swallowed the weaker; and those great ones, again breaking to pieces, dissolved into lesser dominions; all which are so many testimonies against paternal sovereignty, and plainly prove that it was not the natural right of the father descending to his heirs that made governments in the beginning; since it was impossible, upon that ground, there should have been so many little kingdoms but only one universal monarchy if men had not been at liberty to separate themselves from their families and the government, be it what it will that was set up in it, and go and make distinct commonwealths and other governments as they thought fit. . . .

119. Every man being, as has been showed, naturally free, and nothing being able to put him into subjection to any earthly power, but only his own consent, it is to be considered what shall be understood to be a sufficient declaration of a man's consent to make him subject to the laws of any government. There is a common distinction of an express and a tacit consent, which will concern our present case. Nobody doubts but an express consent of any man, entering into any society, makes him a perfect member of that society, a subject of that government. The difficulty is, what ought to be looked upon as a tacit consent, and how far it binds, i.e., how far anyone shall be looked on to have consented, and thereby submitted to any government, where he has made no expressions of it at all. And to this I say, that every man that hath any possession or enjoyment of any part of the dominions of any government doth thereby give his tacit consent, and is as far forth obliged to obedience to the laws of that government, during such enjoyment, as anyone under it, whether this his possession be of land to him and his heirs forever, or a lodging only for a week; or whether it be barely travelling freely on the highway; and, in effect, it reaches as far as the very being of anyone within the territories of that government.

120. To understand this the better, it is fit to consider that every man when he at first incorporates himself into any commonwealth, he, by his uniting himself thereunto, annexes also, and submits to the community those possessions which he has, or shall acquire, that do not already belong to any other government. For it would be a direct contradiction for anyone to enter into society with others for the securing and regulating of property, and yet to suppose his land, whose property is to be regulated by the laws of the society, should be exempt from the jurisdiction of that government to which he himself, the proprietor of the land, is a subject. By the same act, therefore, whereby anyone unites his person, which was before free, to any commonwealth, by the same he unites his possessions, which were before free, to it also; and they become, both of them, person and possession, subject to the government and dominion of that commonwealth as long as it hath a being. Whoever therefore, from thenceforth, by inheritance, purchase, permission, or otherwise enjoys any part of the land so annexed to, and under the government of that commonwealth, must take it with the condition it is under; that is, of submitting to the government of the commonwealth, under whose jurisdiction it is, as far forth as any subject of it.

121. But since the government has a direct jurisdiction only over the land and reaches the possessor of it (before he has actually incorporated himself in the society) only as he dwells upon and enjoys that, the obligation anyone is under by virtue of such enjoyment to submit to the government begins and ends with the enjoyment; so that whenever the owner, who has given nothing but such a tacit consent to the government, will, by donation, sale or otherwise, quit the said possession, he is at liberty to go and incorporate himself into any other commonwealth, or agree with others to begin a new one in *vacuis locis*, in any part of the world they can find free and unpossessed; whereas he that has once, by actual agreement and any express declaration, given his consent to be of any commonweal, is perpetually and indispensably obliged to be, and remain unalterably a subject to it, and can never be again in the liberty of the state of nature, unless by any calamity the government he was under comes to be dissolved; or else by some public act cuts him off from being any longer a member of it.

122. But submitting to the laws of any country, living quietly, and enjoying privileges and protection under them, makes not a man a member of that society; this is only a local protection and homage due to and from all those who, not being in a state of war, come within the territories belonging to any government, to all parts whereof the force of its law extends. But this no more makes a man a member of that society, a perpetual subject of that commonwealth, than it would make a man a subject to another in whose family he found it convenient to abide for some time, though, whilst he continued in it, he were obliged to comply with the laws and submit to the government he found there. And thus we see that foreigners, by living all their lives under another government, and enjoying the privileges and protection of it, though they are bound, even in conscience, to submit to its administration as far forth as any denizen, yet do not thereby come to be subjects or members of that commonwealth. Nothing can make any man so but his actually entering into it by positive engagement and express promise and compact. This is that which I think, concerning the beginning of political societies, and that consent which makes anyone a member of any commonwealth.

IX

Of the Ends of Political Society and Government

123. If man in the state of nature be so free as has been said; if he be absolute lord of his own person and possessions; equal to the greatest and subject to nobody, why will he part with his freedom? Why will he give up this empire, and subject himself to the dominion and control of any other power? To which 'tis obvious to answer, that though in the state of nature he hath such a right, yet the enjoyment of it is very uncertain and constantly exposed to the invasion of others; for all being kings as much as he, every man his equal, and the greater part no strict observers of equity and justice, the enjoyment of the property he has in this state is very unsafe, very unsecure. This makes him willing to quit this condition which, however free, is full of fears and continual dangers; and 'tis not without reason that he seeks out and is willing to join in society with others who are already united, or have a mind to unite for the mutual preservation of their lives, liberties, and estates, which I call by the general name, property.

124. The great and chief end therefore, of men's uniting into commonwealths, and putting themselves under government, is the

preservation of their property; to which in the state of nature there are many things wanting.

First, There wants an established, settled, known law, received and allowed by common consent to be the standard of right and wrong, and the common measure to decide all controversies between them. For though the law of nature be plain and intelligible to all rational creatures, yet men, being biased by their interest, as well as ignorant for want of study of it, are not apt to allow of it as a law binding to them in the application of it to their particular cases.

125. *Secondly,* In the state of nature there wants a known and indifferent judge, with authority to determine all differences according to the established law. For everyone in that state being both judge and executioner of the law of nature, men being partial to themselves, passion and revenge is very apt to carry them too far, and with too much heat in their own cases, as well as negligence and unconcernedness, make them too remiss in other men's.

126. *Thirdly*, In the state of nature there often wants power to back and support the sentence when right, and to give it due execution. They who by any injustice offended, will seldom fail where they are able by force to make good their injustice. Such resistance many times makes the punishment dangerous, and frequently destructive to those who attempt it.

127. Thus mankind, notwithstanding all the privileges of the state of nature, being but in an ill condition while they remain in it, are quickly driven into society. Hence it comes to pass, that we seldom find any number of men live any time together in this state. The inconveniences that they are therein exposed to by the irregular and uncertain exercise of the power every man has of punishing the transgressions of others, make them take sanctuary under the established laws of government, and therein seek the preservation of their property. 'Tis this makes them so willingly give up everyone his single power of punishing to be exercised by such alone as shall be appointed to it amongst them, and by such rules as the community, or those authorized by them to that purpose, shall agree on. And in this we have the original right and rise of both the legislative and executive power as well as of the governments and societies themselves.

128. For in the state of nature to omit the liberty he has of innocent delights, a man has two powers.

The first is to do whatsoever he thinks fit for the preservation of himself and others within the permission of the law of nature; by which law, common to them all, he and all the rest of mankind are one community, make up one society distinct from all other creatures and were it not for the corruption and viciousness of degenerate men, there would be no need of any other, no necessity that men should separate from this great and natural community, and associate into less combinations.

The other power a man has in the state of nature is the power to punish the crimes committed against that law. Both these he gives up when he joins in a private, if I may so call it, or particular political society, and incorporates into any commonwealth separate from the rest of mankind.

129. The first power, *viz.* of doing whatsoever he thought fit for the preservation of himself and the rest of mankind, he gives up to be regulated by laws made by the society, so far forth as the preservation of himself and the rest of that society shall require; which laws of the society in many things confine the liberty he had by the law of nature.

130. *Secondly,* The power of punishing he wholly gives up, and engages his natural force (which he might before employ in the

execution of the law of nature, by his own single authority, as he thought fit) to assist the executive power of the society as the law thereof shall require. For being now in a new state, wherein he is to enjoy many conveniences from the labour, assistance, and society of others in the same community, as well as protection from its whole strength, he is to part also with as much of his natural liberty, in providing for himself, as the good, prosperity, and safety of the society shall require, which is not only necessary but just, since the other members of the society do the like.

131. But though men when they enter into society give up the equality, liberty, and executive power they had in the state of nature into the hands of the society, to be so far disposed of by the legislative as the good of the society shall require, yet it being only with an intention in everyone the better to preserve himself, his liberty, and property (for no rational creature can be supposed to change his condition with an intention to be worse), the power of the society or legislative constituted by them can never be supposed to extend farther than the common good, but is obliged to secure everyone's property by providing against those three defects above-mentioned that made the state of nature so unsafe and uneasy. And so, whoever has the legislative or supreme power of any commonwealth, is bound to govern by established standing laws, promulgated and known to the people, and not by extemporary decrees, by indifferent and upright judges, who are to decide controversies by those laws; and to employ the force of the community at home only in the execution of such laws, or abroad to prevent or redress foreign injuries and secure the community from inroads and invasion. And all this to be directed to no other end but the peace, safety, and public good of the people. . . .

XI

Of the Extent of the Legislative Power

134. The great end of men's entering into society being the enjoyment of their properties in peace and safety, and the great instrument and means of that being the laws established in that society, the first and fundamental positive law of all commonwealths is the establishing of the legislative power; as the first and fundamental natural law, which is to govern even the legislative itself, is the preservation of the society, and (as far as will consist with the public good) of every person in it. This legislative is not only the supreme power of the commonwealth, but sacred and unalterable in the hands where the community have once placed it; nor can any edict of anybody else, in what form soever conceived, or by what power soever backed, have the force and obligation of a law which has not its sanction from that legislative which the public has chosen and appointed; for without this the law could not have that which is absolutely necessary to its being a law, the consent of the society, over whom nobody can have a power to make laws but by their own consent and by authority received from them; and therefore all the obedience, which by the most solemn ties anyone can be obliged to pay, ultimately terminates in this supreme power, and is directed by those laws which it enacts. Nor can any oaths to any foreign power whatsoever, or any domestic subordinate power, discharge any member of the society from his obedience to the legislative, acting pursuant to their trust, nor oblige him to any obedience contrary to the laws so enacted or farther than they do allow, it being ridiculous to imagine one can be tied ultimately to obey any power in the society which is not the supreme.

135. Though the legislative, whether placed in one or more, whether it be always in being or only by intervals, though it be the supreme power in every commonwealth, yet

First, It is not, nor can possibly be, absolutely arbitrary over the lives and fortunes of the people. For it being but the joint power of every member of the society given up to that person or assembly which is legislator, it can be no more than those persons had in a state of nature before they entered into society, and gave it up to the community. For nobody can transfer to another more power than he has in himself, and nobody has an absolute arbitrary power over himself, or over any other, to destroy his own life, or take away the life or property of another. A man, as has been proved, cannot subject himself to the arbitrary power of another; and having, in the state of nature, no arbitrary power over the life, liberty, or possession of another, but only so much as the law of nature gave him for the preservation of himself and the rest of mankind, this is all he doth, or can give up to the commonwealth, and by it to the legislative power, so that the legislative can have no more than this. Their power in the utmost bounds of it is limited to the public good of the society. It is a power that hath no other end but preservation, and therefore can never have a right to destroy, enslave, or designedly to impoverish the subjects; the obligations of the law of nature cease not in society, but only in many cases are drawn closer, and have, by human laws, known penalties annexed to them to enforce their observation. Thus the law of nature stands as an eternal rule to all men, legislators as well as others. The rules that they make for other men's actions must, as well as their own and other men's actions, be conformable to the law of nature, i.e., to the will of God, of which that is a declaration, and the fundamental law of nature being the preservation of mankind, no human sanction can be good or valid against it.

136. *Secondly,* The legislative or supreme authority cannot assume to itself a power to rule by extemporary arbitrary decrees, but is bound to dispense justice and decide the rights of the subject by promulgated standing laws, and known authorized judges. For the law of nature being unwritten, and so nowhere to be found but in the minds of men, they who, through passion or interest, shall miscite or misapply it, cannot so easily be convinced of their mistake where there is no established judge; and so it serves not as it ought, to determine the rights and fence the properties of those that live under it, especially where everyone is judge, interpreter, and executioner of it too, and that in his own case; and he that has right on his side, having ordinarily but his own single strength, hath not force enough to defend himself from injuries or to punish delinquents. To avoid these inconveniencies which disorder men's properties in the state of nature, men unite into societies that they may have the united strength of the whole society to secure and defend their properties, and may have standing rules to bound it by which everyone may know what is his. To this end it is that men give up all their natural power to the society they enter into, and the community put the legislative power into such hands as they think fit, with this trust, that they shall be governed by declared laws, or else their peace, quiet, and property will still be at the same uncertainty as it was in the state of nature. . . .

138. *Thirdly,* The supreme power cannot take from any man any part of his property without his own consent. For the preservation of property being the end of government, and that for which men enter into society, it necessarily supposes and requires that the people

should have property, without which they must be supposed to lose that by entering into society which was the end for which they entered into it; too gross an absurdity for any man to own. Men therefore in society having property, they have such a right to the goods, which by the law of the community are theirs, that nobody hath a right to their substance, or any part of it, from them without their own consent; without this they have no property at all. For I have truly no property in that which another can by right take from me when he pleases against my consent. Hence it is a mistake to think that the supreme or legislative power of any commonwealth can do what it will, and dispose of the estates of the subject arbitrarily, or take any part of them at pleasure. This is not much to be feared in governments where the legislative consists wholly or in part in assemblies which are variable, whose members upon the dissolution of the assembly are subjects under the common laws of their country, equally with the rest. But in governments where the legislative is in one lasting assembly, always in being, or in one man as in absolute monarchies, there is danger still, that they will think themselves to have a distinct interest from the rest of the community, and so will be apt to increase their own riches and power by taking what they think fit from the people. For a man's property is not at all secure, though there be good and equitable laws to set the bounds of it between him and his fellow-subjects, if he who commands those subjects have power to take from any private man what part he pleases of his property, and use and dispose of it as he thinks good. . . .

141. *Fourthly,* The legislative cannot transfer the power of making laws to any other hands, for it being but a delegated power from the people, they who have it cannot pass it over to others. The people alone can appoint the form of the commonwealth, which is by constituting the legislative, and appointing in whose hands that shall be. And when the people have said, We will submit, and be governed by laws made by such men, and in such forms, nobody else can say other men shall make laws for them; nor can they be bound by any laws but such as are enacted by those whom they have chosen and authorized to make laws for them. The power of the legislative being derived from the people by a positive voluntary grant and institution, can be no other than what that positive grant conveyed, which being only to make laws, and not to make legislators, the legislative can have no power to transfer their authority of making laws, and place it in other hands.

142. These are the bounds which the trust that is put in them by the society and the law of God and nature have set to the legislative power of every commonwealth, in all forms of government.

First, They are to govern by promulgated established laws, not to be varied in particular cases, but to have one rule for rich and poor, for the favourite at court, and the countryman at plough.

Secondly, These laws also ought to be designed for no other end ultimately but the good of the people.

Thirdly, They must not raise taxes on the property of the people without the consent of the people given by themselves or their deputies. And this properly concerns only such governments where the legislative is always in being, or at least where the people have not reserved any part of the legislative to deputies, to be from time to time chosen by themselves.

Fourthly, The legislative neither must nor can transfer the power of making laws to anybody else, or place it anywhere but where the people have.

XII

Of the Legislative, Executive, and Federative Power of the Commonwealth

143. The legislative power is that which has a right to direct how the force of the commonwealth shall be employed for preserving the community and the members of it. But because those laws which are constantly to be executed, and whose force is always to continue, may be made in a little time; therefore there is no need that the legislative should be always in being, not having always business to do. And because it may be too great temptation to human frailty, apt to grasp at power, for the same persons who have the power of making laws, to have also in their hands the power to execute them, whereby they may exempt themselves from obedience to the laws they make, and suit the law, both in its making and execution, to their own private advantage, and thereby come to have a distinct interest from the rest of the community, contrary to the end of society and government. Therefore in well-ordered commonwealths, where the good of the whole is so considered as it ought, the legislative power is put into the hands of divers persons who, duly assembled, have by themselves, or jointly with others, a power to make laws, which when they have done, being separated again, they are themselves subject to the laws they have made; which is a new and near tie upon them to take care that they make them for the public good.

144. But because the laws that are at once, and in a short time made, have a constant and lasting force, and need a perpetual execution, or an attendance thereunto, therefore 'tis necessary there should be a power always in being, which should see to the execution of the laws that are made, and remain in force.

And thus the legislative and executive power come often to be separated.

145. There is another power in every commonwealth which one may call natural, because it is that which answers to the power every man naturally had before he entered into society. For though in a commonwealth the members of it are distinct persons, still, in reference to one another, and, as such, are governed by the laws of the society; yet, in reference to the rest of mankind, they make one body, which is, as every member of it before was, still in the state of nature with the rest of mankind. Hence it is that the controversies that happen between any man of the society with those that are out of it are managed by the public, and an injury done to a member of their body engages the whole in the reparation of it. So that under this consideration the whole community is one body in the state of nature in respect of all other states or persons out of its community.

146. This, therefore, contains the power of war and peace, leagues and alliances, and all the transactions with all persons and communities without the commonwealth, and may be called federative if anyone pleases. So the thing be understood, I am indifferent as to the name.

147. These two powers, executive and federative, though they be really distinct in themselves, yet one comprehending the execution of the municipal laws of the society within itself upon all that are parts of it; the other the management of the security and interest of the public without, with all those that it may receive benefit or damage from, yet they are always almost united. And though this federative power in the well or ill management of it be of great moment to the commonwealth, yet it is much less capable to be directed by antecedent, standing, positive laws than the executive, and so must necessarily be left to the prudence and wisdom of those whose

hands it is in, to be managed for the public good. For the laws that concern subjects one amongst another, being to direct their actions, may well enough precede them. But what is to be done in reference to foreigners, depending much upon their actions, and the variation of designs and interests, must be left in great part to the prudence of those who have this power committed to them, to be managed by the best of their skill for the advantage of the commonwealth.

148. Though, as I said, the executive and federative power of every community be really distinct in themselves, yet they are hardly to be separated and placed at the same time in the hands of distinct persons. For both of them requiring the force of the society for their exercise, it is almost impracticable to place the force of the commonwealth in distinct and not subordinate hands; or that the executive and federative power should be placed in persons that might act separately, whereby the force of the public would be under different commands, which would be apt sometime or other to cause disorder and ruin. . . .

XIX

Of the Dissolution of Government

211. He that will with any clearness speak of the dissolution of government, ought in the first place to distinguish between the dissolution of the society and the dissolution of the government. That which makes the community, and brings men out of the loose state of nature into one politic society, is the agreement which everyone has with the rest to incorporate and act as one body, and so be one distinct commonwealth. The usual, and almost only way whereby this union is dissolved, is the inroad of foreign force making a conquest upon them. For in that case (not being able to

maintain and support themselves as one entire and independent body) the union belonging to that body which consisted therein, must necessarily cease, and so everyone return to the state he was in before, with a liberty to shift for himself and provide for his own safety, as he thinks fit, in some other society. Whenever the society is dissolved, 'tis certain the government of that society cannot remain. Thus conquerors' swords often cut up governments by the roots, and mangle societies to pieces, separating the subdued or scattered multitude from the protection of and dependence on that society which ought to have preserved them from violence. The world is too well instructed in, and too forward to allow of this way of dissolving of governments, to need any more to be said of it; and there wants not much argument to prove that where the society is dissolved, the government cannot remain; that being as impossible as for the frame of a house to subsist when the materials of it are scattered and dissipated by a whirlwind, or jumbled into a confused heap by an earthquake.

212. Besides this overturning from without, governments are dissolved from within,

First, When the legislative is altered, civil society being a state of peace amongst those who are of it, from whom the state of war is excluded by the umpirage which they have provided in their legislative for the ending all differences that may arise amongst any of them. 'Tis in their legislative that the members of a commonwealth are united and combined together into one coherent living body. This is the soul that gives form, life, and unity to the commonwealth. From hence the several members have their mutual influence, sympathy, and connexion. And therefore when the legislative is broken, or dissolved, dissolution and death follows. For the essence and union of the society consisting in having one will, the legislative, when once established by the majority, has the declaring and, as it were, keeping of that will. The constitution of the legislative is the first and fundamental act of society, whereby provision is made for the continuation of their union under the direction of persons and bonds of laws, made by persons authorized thereunto, by the consent and appointment of the people, without which no one man, or number of men, amongst them can have authority of making laws that shall be binding to the rest. When anyone, or more, shall take upon them to make laws whom the people have not appointed so to do, they make laws without authority, which the people are not therefore bound to obey; by which means they come again to be out of subjection, and may constitute to themselves a new legislative, as they think best, being in full liberty to resist the force of those who, without authority, would impose anything upon them. Everyone is at the disposure of his own will, when those who had, by the delegation of the society, the declaring of the public will, are excluded from it, and others usurp the place who have no such authority or delegation.

213. This being usually brought about by such in the commonwealth who misuse the power they have, it is hard to consider it aright, and know at whose door to lay it, without knowing the form of government in which it happens. Let us suppose then the legislative placed in the concurrence of three distinct persons.

1. A single hereditary person having the constant, supreme, executive power, and with it the power of convoking and dissolving the other two within certain periods of time.
2. An assembly of hereditary nobility.
3. An assembly of representatives chosen *pro tempore*, by the people. Such a form of government supposed, it is evident:

214. *First*, That when such a single person or prince sets up his own arbitrary will in place of the laws, which are the will of the society, declared by the legislative, then the legislative is changed. For that being in effect the legislative whose rules and laws are put in execution, and required to be obeyed, when other laws are set up, and other rules pretended and enforced than what the legislative constituted by the society have enacted, it is plain that the legislative is changed. Whoever introduces new laws, not being thereunto authorized by the fundamental appointment of the society, or subverts the old, disowns and overturns the power by which they were made, and so sets up a new legislative.

215. *Secondly*, When the prince hinders the legislative from assembling in its due time, or from acting freely, pursuant to those ends for which it was constituted, the legislative is altered. For 'tis not a certain number of men, no, nor their meeting, unless they have also freedom of debating and leisure of perfecting what is for the good of the society, wherein the legislative consists; when these are taken away, or altered, so as to deprive the society of the due exercise of their power, the legislative is truly altered. For it is not names that constitute governments, but the use and exercise of those powers that were intended to accompany them; so that he who takes away the freedom, or hinders the acting of the legislative in its due seasons, in effect takes away the legislative, and puts an end to the government.

216. *Thirdly*, When, by the arbitrary power of the prince, the electors or ways of election are altered, without the consent, and contrary to the common interest of the people, there also the legislative is altered. For if others than those whom the society hath authorized thereunto do choose, or in another way than what the society hath prescribed, those chosen are not the legislative appointed by the people.

217. *Fourthly*, The delivery also of the people into the subjection of a foreign power, either by the prince or by the legislative, is certainly a change of the legislative, and so a dissolution of the government. For the end why people entered into society being to be preserved one entire, free, independent society, to be governed by its own laws, this is lost whenever they are given up into the power of another.

218. Why, in such a constitution as this, the dissolution of the government in these cases is to be imputed to the prince is evident, because he, having the force, treasure, and offices of the State to employ, and often persuading himself, or being flattered by others, that, as supreme magistrate, he is uncapable of control; he alone is in a condition to make great advances toward such changes under pretence of lawful authority, and has it in his hands to terrify or suppress opposers as factious, seditious, and enemies to the government; whereas no other part of the legislative, or people, is capable by themselves to attempt any alteration of the legislative without open and visible rebellion, apt enough to be taken notice of; which, when it prevails, produces effects very little different from foreign conquest. Besides, the prince, in such a form of government, having the power of dissolving the other parts of the legislative, and thereby rendering them private persons, they can never, in opposition to him, or without his concurrence, alter the legislative by a law, his consent. being necessary to give any of their decrees that sanction. But yet so far as the other parts of the legislative any way contribute to any attempt upon the government, and do either promote, or not, what lies in them hinder such designs, they are guilty, and partake in this, which is certainly the greatest crime men can be guilty of one towards another.

219. There is one way more whereby such a government may be dissolved, and that is: When he who has the supreme executive power neglects and abandons that charge, so that the laws already made can no longer be put in execution. This is demonstratively to reduce all to anarchy, and so effectively to dissolve the government. For laws not being made for themselves, but to be, by their execution, the bonds of the society to keep every part of the body politic in its due place and function, when that totally ceases, the government visibly ceases, and the people become a confused multitude without order or connexion. Where there is no longer the administration of justice for the securing of men's rights, nor any remaining power within the community to direct the force, or provide for the necessities of the public, there is no government left. Where the laws cannot be executed it is all one as if there were no laws, and a government without laws is, I suppose, a mystery in politics unconceivable to human capacity, and inconsistent with human society.

220. In these, and the like cases, when the government is dissolved, the people are at liberty to provide for themselves by erecting a new legislative, differing from the other by the change of persons, or form, or both, as they shall find it most for their safety and good. For the society can never, by the fault of another, lose the native and original right it has to preserve itself, which can only be done by a settled legislative and a fair impartial execution of the laws made by it. But the state of mankind is not so miserable that they are not capable of using this remedy till it be too late to look for any. To tell people they may provide for themselves by erecting a new legislative, when, by oppression, artifice, or being delivered over to a foreign power, their old one is gone, is only to tell them they may expect relief when it is too late, and the evil is past

cure. This is in effect no more than to bid them first be slaves, and then to take care of their liberty, and, when their chains are on, tell them they may act like freemen. This, if barely so, is rather mockery than relief, and men can never be secure from tyranny if there be no means to escape it till they are perfectly under it. And therefore it is, that they have not only a right to get out of it, but to prevent it.

221. There is therefore *Secondly* another way whereby governments are dissolved, and that is, when the legislative, or the prince, either of them act contrary to their trust.

First, The legislative acts against the trust reposed in them when they endeavour to invade the property of the subject, and to make themselves, or any part of the community, masters or arbitrary disposers of the lives, liberties, or fortunes of the people.

222. The reason why men enter into society is the preservation of their property; and the end why they choose and authorize a legislative is that there may be laws made, and rules set, as guards and fences to the properties of all the members of the society, to limit the power and moderate the dominion of every part and member of the society. For since it can never be supposed to be the will of the society that the legislative should have a power to destroy that which everyone designs to secure by entering into society, and for which the people submitted themselves to legislators of their own making: whenever the legislators endeavour to take away and destroy the property of the people, or to reduce them to slavery under arbitrary power, they put themselves into a state of war with the people, who are thereupon absolved from any farther obedience, and are left to the common refuge which God hath provided for all men against force and violence. Whensoever therefore the leg-

islative shall transgress this fundamental rule of society, and either by ambition, fear, folly, or corruption, endeavour to grasp themselves, or put into the hands of any other, an absolute power over the lives, liberties, and estates of the people, by this breach of trust they forfeit the power the people had put into their hands for quite contrary ends, and it devolves to the people; who have a right to resume their original liberty, and by the establishment of a new legislative (such as they shall think fit), provide for their own safety and security, which is the end for which they are in society. . . .

243. To conclude, The power that every individual gave the society when he entered into it, can never revert to the individuals again, as long as the society lasts, but will always remain in the community; because without this there can be no community, no commonwealth, which is contrary to the original agreement; so also when the society hath placed the legislative in any assembly of men, to continue in them and their successors, with direction and authority for providing such successors, the legislative can never revert to the people whilst that government lasts; because, having provided a legislative with power to continue forever, they have given up their political power to the legislative, and cannot resume it. But if they have set limits to the duration of their legislative, and made this supreme power in any person or assembly only temporary; or else when, by the miscarriages of those in authority, it is forfeited; upon the forfeiture of their rulers, or at the determination of the time set, it reverts to the society, and the people have a right to act as supreme, and continue the legislative in themselves or place it in a new form, or new hands, as they think good.

A Letter concerning Toleration

Honoured Sir,

Since you are pleased to inquire what are my thoughts about the mutual toleration of Christians in their different professions of religion, I must needs answer you freely, that I esteem that toleration to be the chief characteristic mark of the true Church. For whatsoëver some people boast of the antiquity of places and names, or of the pomp of their outward worship; others, of the reformation of their discipline; all, of the orthodoxy of their faith—for everyone is orthodox to himself—these things, and all others of this nature, are much rather marks of men striving for power and empire over one another, than of the Church of Christ. Let anyone have never so true a claim to all these things, yet if he be destitute of charity, meekness, and goodwill in general towards all mankind, even to those that are not Christians, he is certainly yet short of being a true Christian himself. "The kings of the Gentiles exercise lordship over them," said our Saviour to His disciples, "but ye shall not be so." [Luke 22:25] The business of true religions is quite another thing. It is not instituted in order to the erecting of an external pomp, nor to the obtaining of ecclesiastical dominion, nor to the exercising of compulsive force, but to the regulating of men's lives, according to the rules of virtue and piety. . . .

The toleration of those that differ from others in matters of religion, is so agreeable to the Gospel of Jesus Christ, and to the genuine reason of mankind, that it seems monstrous for men to be so blind as not to perceive the necessity and advantage of it in so clear a light. I will not here tax the pride and ambition of some, the passion and uncharitable zeal of others. These are faults from which human

affairs can perhaps scarce ever be perfectly freed; but yet such as nobody will bear the plain imputation of, without covering them with some specious colour; and so pretend to commendation, whilst they are carried away by their own irregular passions. But, however, that some may not colour their spirit of persecution and unchristian cruelty with a pretence of care of the public weal and observation of the laws; and that others, under pretence of religion, may not seek impunity for their libertinism and licentiousness; in a word, that none may impose either upon himself or others, by the pretences of loyalty and obedience to the prince, or of tenderness and sincerity in the worship of God; I esteem it above all things necessary to distinguish exactly the business of civil government from that of religion, and to settle the just bounds that lie between the one and the other. If this be not done, there can be no end put to the controversies that will be always arising between those that have, or at least pretend to have, on the one side, a concernment for the interest of men's souls, and, on the other side, a care of the commonwealth.

The commonwealth seems to me to be a society of men constituted only for the procuring, preserving, and advancing their own civil interests.

Civil interests I call life, liberty, health, and indolency of body; and the possession of outward things, such as money, lands, houses, furniture, and the like.

It is the duty of the civil magistrate, by the impartial execution of equal laws, to secure unto all the people in general, and to everyone of his subjects in particular the just possession of these things belonging to this life. If anyone presume to violate the laws of public justice and equity, established for the preservation of those things, his presumption is to be checked by the fear of punishment, consisting of the deprivation or diminution of those civil interests, or goods, which otherwise he might and ought to enjoy. But seeing no man does willingly suffer himself to be punished by the deprivation of any part of his goods, and much less of his liberty or life, therefore, is the magistrate armed with the force and strength of all his subjects, in order to [execute] the punishment of those that violate any other man's rights.

Now that the whole jurisdiction of the magistrate reaches only to these civil concernments, and that all civil power, right and dominion, is bounded and confined [only to the] care of promoting these things; and that it neither can nor ought in any manner to be extended to the salvation of souls, these following considerations seem unto me abundantly to demonstrate.

First, because the care of souls is not committed to the civil magistrate, any more than to other men. It is not committed unto him, I say, by God; because it appears not that God has ever given any such authority to one man over another, as to compel anyone to his religion. Nor can any such power be vested in the magistrate by the consent of the people, because no man can so far abandon the care of his own salvation as blindly to leave to the choice of any other, whether prince or subject, to prescribe to him what faith or worship he shall embrace. For no man can, if he would, conform his faith to the dictates of another. All the life and power of true religion consist in the inward and full persuasion of the mind; and faith is not faith without believing. Whatever profession we make, to whatever outward worship we conform, if we are not fully satisfied in our own mind that the one is true, and the other well pleasing unto

God, such profession and such practice, far from being any furtherance, are indeed great obstacles to our salvation. For in this manner, instead of expiating other sins by the exercise of religion, I say, in offering thus unto God Almighty such a worship as we esteem to be displeasing unto Him, we add unto the number of our other sins those also of hypocrisy, and contempt of His Divine Majesty.

In the second place, the care of souls cannot belong to the civil magistrate, because his power consists only in outward force; but true and saving religion consists in the inward persuasion of the mind, without which nothing can be acceptable to God. And such is the nature of the understanding, that it cannot be compelled to the belief of anything by outward force. Confiscation of estate, imprisonment, torments, nothing of that nature can have any such efficacy as to make men change the inward judgment that they have framed of things.

It may indeed be alleged that the magistrate may make use of arguments, and thereby draw the heterodox into the way of truth, and procure their salvation. I grant it; but this is common to him with other men. In teaching, instructing, and redressing the erroneous by reason, he may certainly do what becomes any good man to do. Magistracy does not oblige him to put off either humanity or Christianity; but it is one thing to persuade, another to command; one thing to press with arguments, another with penalties. This civil power alone has a right to do; to the other goodwill is authority enough. Every man has commission to admonish, exhort, convince another of error, and, by reasoning, to draw him into truth; but to give laws, receive obedience, and compel with the sword, belongs to none but the magistrate. And upon this ground, I affirm that the magistrate's power extends not to the establishing of any articles of faith, or forms of worship, by the force of his laws. For laws are of no force at all without penalties, and penalties in this case are absolutely impertinent, because they are not proper to convince the mind. Neither the profession of any articles of faith, nor the conformity to any outward form of worship (as has been already said), can be available to the salvation of souls, unless the truth of the one, and the acceptableness of the other unto God, be thoroughly believed by those that so profess and practise. But penalties are no way capable to produce such belief. It is only light and evidence that can work a change in men's opinions; which light can in no manner proceed from corporal sufferings, or any other outward penalties.

In the third place, the care of the salvation of men's souls cannot belong to the magistrate, because, though the rigour of laws and the force of penalties were capable to convince and change men's minds, yet would not that help at all to the salvation of their souls. For there being but one truth, one way to heaven, what hope is there that more men would be led into it if they had no rule but the religion of the court, and were put under the necessity to quit the light of their own reason, and oppose the dictates of their own consciences, and blindly to resign themselves up to the will of their governors, and to the religion which either ignorance, ambition, or superstition had chanced to establish in the countries where they were born? In the variety and contradiction of opinions in religion, wherein the princes of the world are as much divided as in their secular interests, the narrow way would be much straitened; one country alone would be in the right, and all the rest of the world put under an obligation of following their princes in the ways that lead to destruction; and that which heightens the absurdity, and very ill suits the notion of a Deity, men would owe their eternal happiness or misery to the places of their nativity.

These considerations, to omit many others that might have been urged to the same purpose, seem unto me sufficient to conclude that all the power of civil government relates only to men's civil interests, is confined to the care of the things of this world, and hath nothing to do with the world to come. . . .

The end of a religious society (as has already been said) is the public worship of God, and, by means thereof, the acquisition of eternal life. All discipline ought therefore to tend to that end, and all ecclesiastical laws to be thereunto confined. Nothing ought nor can be transacted in this society relating to the possession of civil and worldly goods. No force is here to be made use of upon any occasion whatsoever. For force belongs wholly to the civil magistrate, and the possession of all outward goods is subject to his jurisdiction.

But, it may be asked, by what means then shall ecclesiastical laws be established, if they must be thus destitute of all compulsive power? I answer: They must be established by means suitable to the nature of such things, whereof the external profession and observation—if not proceeding from a thorough conviction and approbation of the mind—is altogether useless and unprofitable. The arms by which the members of this society are to be kept within their duty are exhortations, admonitions, and advices. If by these means the offenders will not be reclaimed, and the erroneous convinced, there remains nothing further to be done but that such stubborn and obstinate persons, who give no ground to hope for their reformation, should be cast out and separated from the society. This is the last and utmost force of ecclesiastical authority. No other punishment can thereby be inflicted than that, the relation ceasing between the body and the member which is cut off. The person so condemned ceases to be a part of that church.

These things being thus determined, let us inquire, in the next place: How far the duty of toleration extends, and what is required from everyone by it?

And, first, I hold that no church is bound, by the duty of toleration, to retain any such person in her bosom as, after admonition, continues obstinately to offend against the laws of the society. For these being the condition of communion and the bond of the society, if the breach of them were permitted without any animadversion the society would immediately be thereby dissolved. But, nevertheless, in all such cases care is to be taken that the sentence of excommunication, and the execution thereof, carry with it no rough usage of word or action whereby the ejected person may any wise be damnified in body or estate. For all force (as has often been said) belongs only to the magistrate, nor ought any private persons at any time to use force, unless it be in self-defence against unjust violence. Excommunication neither does, nor can, deprive the excommunicated person of any of those civil goods that he formerly possessed. All those things belong to the civil government, and are under the magistrate's protection. The whole force of excommunication consists only in this: that the resolution of the society in that respect being declared, the union that was between the body and some member comes thereby to be dissolved; and that relation ceasing, the participation of some certain things which the society communicated to its members, and unto which no man has any civil right, comes also to cease. For there is no civil injury done unto the excommunicated person by the church minister's refusing him that bread and wine, in the celebration of the Lord's Supper, which was not bought with his but other men's money.

Secondly, no private person has any right in any manner to prejudice another person in his civil enjoyments because he is of another church or religion. All the rights and franchises that belong to him as a man, or as a denizen, are inviolably to be preserved to him. These are not the business of religion. No violence nor injury is to be offered him, whether he be Christian or Pagan. Nay, we must not content ourselves with the narrow measures of bare justice; charity, bounty, and liberality must be added to it. This the Gospel enjoins, this reason directs, and this that natural fellowship we are born into requires of us. If any man err from the right way, it is his own misfortune, no injury to thee; nor therefore art thou to punish him in the things of this life because thou supposest he will be miserable in that which is to come.

What I say concerning the mutual toleration of private persons differing from one another in religion, I understand also of particular churches which stand, as it were, in the same relation to each other as private persons among themselves: nor has any one of them any manner of jurisdiction over any other; no, not even when the civil magistrate (as it sometimes happens) comes to be of this or the other communion. For the civil government can give no new right to the church, nor the church to the civil government. So that whether the magistrate join himself to any church, or separate from it, the church remains always as it was before—a free and voluntary society. It neither requires the power of the sword by the magistrate's coming to it, nor does it lose the right of instruction and excommunication by his going from it. This is the fundamental and immutable right of a spontaneous society—that it has power to remove any of its members who transgress the rules of its institution; but it cannot, by the accession of any new members, acquire any right of jurisdiction over those that are not joined with it. And therefore peace, equity, and friendship are always mutually to be observed by particular churches, in the same manner as by private persons, without any pretence of superiority or jurisdiction over one another.

That the thing may be made clearer by an example, let us suppose two churches—the one of Arminians, the other of Calvinists—residing in the city of Constantinople. Will anyone say that either of these churches has right to deprive the members of the other of their estates and liberty (as we see practised elsewhere), because of their differing from it in some doctrines and ceremonies, whilst the Turks in the meanwhile silently stand by, and laugh to see with what inhuman cruelty Christians thus rage against Christians? But if one of these churches hath this power of treating the other ill, I ask which of them it is to whom that power belongs, and by what right? It will be answered, undoubtedly, that it is the orthodox church which has the right of authority over the erroneous or heretical. This is, in great and specious words, to say just nothing at all. For every church is orthodox to itself; to others, erroneous or heretical. For whatsoever any church believes, it believes to be true; and the contrary unto those things, it pronounces to be error. So that the controversy between these churches about the truth of their doctrines, and the purity of their worship, is on both sides equal; nor is there any judge, either at Constantinople or elsewhere upon earth, by whose sentence it can be determined. The decision of that question belongs only to the Supreme Judge of all men, to whom also alone belongs the punishment of the erroneous. In the meanwhile, let those men consider how heinously they sin, who, adding injustice, if not to their error, yet certainly to their pride, do rashly and arrogantly take upon them to misuse the servants of another master, who are not at all accountable to them.

Nay, further: if it could be manifest which of these two dissenting churches were in the right, there would not accrue thereby unto the orthodox any right of destroying the other. For churches have neither any jurisdiction in worldly matters, nor are fire and sword any proper instruments wherewith to convince men's minds of error, and inform them of the truth. Let us suppose, nevertheless, that the civil magistrate inclined to favour one of them, and to put his sword into their hands, that (by his consent) they might chastise the dissenters as they pleased. Will any man say that any right can be derived unto a Christian church over its brethren from a Turkish emperor? An infidel, who has himself no authority to punish Christians for the articles of their faith, cannot confer such an authority upon any society of Christians, nor give unto them a right which he has not himself. This would be the case at Constantinople; and the reason of the thing is the same in any Christian kingdom. The civil power is the same in every place. Nor can that power, in the hands of a Christian prince, confer any greater authority upon the Church than in the hands of a heathen; which is to say, just none at all.

Nevertheless, it is worthy to be observed and lamented that the most violent of these defenders of the truth, the opposers of errors, the exclaimers against schism do hardly ever let loose this their zeal for God, with which they are so warmed and inflamed, unless where they have the civil magistrate on their side. But so soon as ever court favour has given them the better end of the staff, and they begin to feel themselves the stronger, then presently peace and charity are to be laid aside. Otherwise they are religiously to be observed. Where they have not the power to carry on persecution and to become masters, there they desire to live upon fair terms, and preach up toleration. When they are not strengthened with the civil power, then they can bear most patiently and unmovedly the contagion of idolatry, superstition, and heresy in their neighbourhood; of which on other occasions the interest of religion makes them to be extremely apprehensive. They do not forwardly attack those errors which are in fashion at court or are countenanced by the government. Here they can be content to spare their arguments; which yet (with their leave) is the only right method of propagating truth, which has no such way of prevailing as when strong arguments and good reason are joined with the softness of civility and good usage.

Nobody, therefore, in fine, neither single persons nor churches, nay, nor even commonwealths, have any just title to invade the civil rights and worldly goods of each other upon pretence of religion. Those that are of another opinion would do well to consider with themselves how pernicious a seed of discord and war, how powerful a provocation to endless hatreds, rapines, and slaughters they thereby furnish unto mankind. No peace and security, no, not so much as common friendship, can ever be established or preserved amongst men so long as this opinion prevails, that dominion is founded in grace and that religion is to be propagated by force of arms. . . .

In the last place, let us now consider what is the magistrate's duty in the business of toleration, which certainly is very considerable.

We have already proved that the care of souls does not belong to the magistrate. Not a magisterial care, I mean (if I may so call it), which consists in prescribing by laws and compelling by punishments. But a charitable care, which consists in teaching, admonishing, and persuading, cannot be denied unto any man. The care, therefore, of every man's soul belongs unto himself, and is to be left unto himself. But what if he neglect the care of his soul? I answer: What if he neglect the care

of his health or of his estate, which things are nearlier related to the government of the magistrate than the other? Will the magistrate provide by an express law that such a one shall not become poor or sick? Laws provide, as much as is possible, that the goods and health of subjects be not injured by the fraud and violence of others; they do not guard them from the negligence or ill-husbandry of the possessors themselves. No man can be forced to be rich or healthful whether he will or no. Nay, God Himself will not save men against their wills. Let us suppose, however, that some prince were desirous to force his subjects to accumulate riches, or to preserve the health and strength of their bodies. Shall it be provided by law that they must consult none but Roman physicians, and shall everyone be bound to live according to their prescriptions? What, shall no potion, no broth, be taken, but what is prepared either in the Vatican, suppose, or in a Geneva shop? Or, to make these subjects rich, shall they all be obliged by law to become merchants or musicians? Or, shall everyone turn victualler, or smith, because there are some that maintain their families plentifully and grow rich in those professions? But, it may be said, there are a thousand ways to wealth, but one only way to heaven. It is well said, indeed, especially by those that plead for compelling men into this or the other way. For if there were several ways that led thither, there would not be so much as a pretence left for compulsion. But now if I be marching on with my utmost vigour in that way which, according to the sacred geography, leads straight to Jerusalem, why am I beaten and ill-used by others because, perhaps, I wear not buskins; because my hair is not of the right cut; because, perhaps, I have not been dipped in the right fashion; because I eat flesh upon the road, or some other food which agrees with my stomach; because I avoid certain by-ways, which seem unto me to lead into briars or precipices; because, amongst the several paths that are in the same road, I choose that to walk in which seems to be the straightest and cleanest; because I avoid to keep company with some travellers that are less grave, and others that are more sour than they ought to be; or, in fine, because I follow a guide that either is, or is not, clothed in white, or crowned with a mitre? Certainly, if we consider right, we shall find that, for the most part, they are such frivolous things as these that (without any prejudice to religion or the salvation of souls, if not accompanied with superstition or hypocrisy) might either be observed or omitted. I say, they are such-like things as these which breed implacable enmities amongst Christian brethren, who are all agreed in the substantial and truly fundamental part of religion.

But let us grant unto these zealots, who condemn all things that are not of their mode, that from these circumstances are different ends. What shall we conclude from thence? There is only one of these which is the true way to eternal happiness: but in this great variety of ways that men follow, it is still doubted which is the right one. Now, neither the care of the commonwealth, nor the right enacting of laws, does discover this way that leads to heaven more certainly to the magistrate than every private man's search and study discovers it unto himself. I have a weak body, sunk under a languishing disease, for which (I suppose) there is one only remedy, but that unknown. Does it therefore belong unto the magistrate to prescribe me a remedy, because there is but one, and because it is unknown? Because there is but one way for me to escape death, will it therefore be safe for me to do whatsoever the magistrate ordains? Those things that every man ought sincerely to inquire into himself, and by meditation, study,

search, and his own endeavours, attain the knowledge of, cannot be looked upon as the peculiar possession of any sort of men. Princes, indeed, are born superior unto other men in power, but in nature equal. Neither the right nor the art of ruling does necessarily carry along with it the certain knowledge of other things, and least of all of true religion. For if it were so, how could it come to pass that the lords of the earth should differ so vastly as they do in religious matters? But let us grant that it is probable the way to eternal life may be better known by a prince than by his subjects, or at least that in this incertitude of things the safest and most commodious way for private persons is to follow his dictates. You will say, what then? If he should bid you follow merchandise for your livelihood, would you decline that course for fear it should not succeed? I answer: I would turn merchant upon the prince's command, because in case I should have ill-success in trade, he is abundantly able to make up my loss some other way. If it be true, as he pretends, that he desires I should thrive and grow rich, he can set me up again when unsuccessful voyages have broken me. But this is not the case in the things that regard the life to come; if there I take a wrong course, if in that respect I am once undone, it is not in the magistrate's power to repair my loss, to ease my suffering, nor to restore me in any measure, much less entirely to a good estate. What security can be given for the Kingdom of Heaven?

Perhaps some will say that they do not suppose this infallible judgment, that all men are bound to follow in the affairs of religion, to be in the civil magistrate, but in the Church. What the Church has determined, that the civil magistrate orders to be observed; and he provides by his authority that nobody shall either act or believe in the business of religion otherwise than the Church teaches. So that the judgment of those things is in the Church; the magistrate himself yields obedience thereunto, and requires the like obedience from others. I answer: Who sees not how frequently the name of the Church, which was venerable in time of the apostles, has been made use of to throw dust in the people's eyes, in the following ages? But, however, in the present case it helps us not. The one only narrow way which leads to heaven is not better known to the magistrate than to private persons, and therefore I cannot safely take him for my guide, who may probably be as ignorant of the way as myself, and who certainly is less concerned for my salvation than I myself am. Amongst so many kings of the Jews, how many of them were there whom any Israelite, thus blindly following, had not fallen into idolatry, and thereby into destruction? Yet nevertheless, you bid me be of good courage, and tell me that all is now safe and secure, because the magistrate does not now enjoin the observance of his own decrees in matters of religion, but only the decrees of the Church. Of what church, I beseech you? of that, certainly, which likes him best. As if he that compels me by laws and penalties to enter into this or the other church, did not interpose his own judgment in the matter. What difference is there whether he lead me himself, or deliver me over to be led by others? I depend both ways upon his will, and it is he that determines both ways of my eternal state. Would an Israelite, that had worshipped Baal upon the command of his king, have been in any better condition, because somebody had told him that the king ordered nothing in religion upon his own head, nor commanded anything to be done by his subjects in divine worship but what was approved by the counsel of priests, and declared to be of divine right by the doctors of their church? If the religion of any church become therefore true and saving, because the head of that sect, the prelates and priests, and those of that tribe, do all of them, with all their might, extol and praise it, what religion can ever be accounted erroneous, false, and destructive? I am doubtful concerning the doctrine of the Socinians, I am suspicious of the way of worship practised by the Papists, or Lutherans; will it be ever a jot safer for me to join either unto the one or the other of those churches, upon the magistrate's command, because he commands nothing in religion but by the authority and counsel of the doctors of that church?

But, to speak the truth, we must acknowledge that the Church (if a convention of clergymen, making canons, must be called by that name) is for the most part more apt to be influenced by the court than the court by the Church. How the Church was under the vicissitude of orthodox and Arian emperors is very well known. Or if those things be too remote, our modern English history affords us fresh examples in the reigns of Henry VIII, Edward VI, Mary, and Elizabeth, how easily and smoothly the clergy changed their decrees, their articles of faith, their form of worship, everything according to the inclination of those kings and queens. Yet were those kings and queens of such different minds in point of religion, and enjoined thereupon such different things, that no man in his wits (I had almost said none but an atheist) will presume to say that any sincere and upright worshipper of God could, with a safe conscience, obey their several decrees. To conclude, it is the same thing whether a king that prescribes laws to another man's religion, pretend to do it by his own judgment, or by the ecclesiastical authority and advice of others. The decisions of churchmen, whose differences and disputes are sufficiently known, cannot be any sounder or safer than his; nor can all their suffrages joined together add a new strength to the civil power. Though this also must be taken notice of—that princes seldom have any regard to the suffrages of ecclesiastics that are not favourers of their own faith and way of worship.

But, after all, the principal consideration, and which absolutely determines this controversy, is this: Although the magistrate's opinion in religion be sound, and the way that he appoints be truly Evangelical, yet, if I be not thoroughly persuaded thereof in my own mind, there will be no safety for me in following it. No way whatsoever that I shall walk in against the dictates of my conscience will ever bring me to the mansions of the blessed. I may grow rich by an art that I take not delight in, I may be cured of some disease by remedies that I have not faith in; but I cannot be saved by a religion that I distrust, and by a worship that I abhor. It is in vain for an unbeliever to take up the outward show of another man's profession. Faith only, and inward sincerity, are the things that procure acceptance with God. The most likely and most approved remedy can have no effect upon the patient if his stomach reject it as soon as taken; and you will in vain cram a medicine down a sick man's throat, which his particular constitution will be sure to turn into poison. In a word, whatsoever may be doubtful in religion, yet this at least is certain, that no religion which I believe not to be true can be either true or profitable unto me. In vain, therefore, do princes compel their subjects to come into their church communion, under pretence of saving their souls. If they believe, they will come of their own accord; if they believe not, their coming will nothing avail them. How great soever, in fine, may be the pretence of goodwill and charity, and concern for the salvation of men's souls, men cannot be forced to be saved whether they will or no. And therefore, when all is done, they must be left to their own consciences.

Study Questions for *The Second Treatise of Government*

1. In what respect is the state of nature a state of perfect freedom and equality? What natural rights and duties do human beings possess in the state of nature?
2. How does Locke differentiate the state of nature from a state of war? Why is the state of nature not necessarily a state of war?
3. How does Locke define natural and social liberty in his discussion of slavery in chapter IV? Describe the argument Locke provides for his claim that no one can voluntarily enter into a condition of slavery.
4. Describe the origin of private property in the state of nature. By what means do individuals rightly acquire property? What clause or proviso does Locke add to his account of our natural right to hold private property?
5. What is the purpose of political society and government according to Locke? What motivates individuals living peacefully in a state of nature to form a social contract and create a commonwealth?
6. How does Locke define the legislative power of the state in chapter XI? What is the proper extent of the legislative power of the state?
7. What are the executive and federative powers of the commonwealth? Why does Locke recommend subordinating executive and federative power to legislative power?
8. Under what conditions does power rightly revert to the people in revolution?

Study Questions for *A Letter concerning Toleration*

1. How does the basic purpose of the commonwealth support a proposal for religious toleration?
2. Identify and describe the three reasons Locke provides for his thesis that the care of the soul does not properly belong to political magistrates.

Recommended Readings

Ashcraft, Richard, *Revolutionary Politics and Locke's* Two Treatises of Government (Princeton University Press, 1986).

Brown, Wendy, *Regulating Aversion: Tolerance in the Age of Identity and Empire* (Princeton University Press, 2006).

Clark, Lorenne, 'Women and John Locke; or, Who Owns the Apples in the Garden of Eden?' in *Canadian Journal of Philosophy* 7 (1977): 699–724.

Cranston, Maurice, *John Locke* (Oxford University Press, 1985).

Dunn, John, *The Political Thought of John Locke* (Cambridge University Press, 1969).

Locke, John, *Second Treatise of Government*, as presented by Jonathan Bennett at www.earlymoderntexts.com.

Mack, E., 'The Self-Ownership Proviso: A New and Improved Lockean Proviso,' in *Social Philosophy and Policy* 12 (1995): 186–218.

Macpherson, C.B., *The Political Theory of Possessive Individualism* (Oxford University Press, 1962).

Narveson, Jan, 'Original Appropriation and Lockean Provisos,' *Public Affairs Quarterly* 13 (1999): 205–27.

Simmons, A.J., *The Lockean Theory of Rights* (Princeton University Press, 1992).

——— *On the Edge of Anarchy* (Princeton University Press, 1993).

Strauss, Leo, *Natural Right and History* (Cambridge University Press, 1979).

Thomas, D.A. Lloyd, *Locke on Government* (Routledge, 1995).

Jean-Jacques Rousseau

Born in the francophone city of Geneva in Switzerland, Jean-Jacques Rousseau (1712–1778) had a tumultuous childhood and did not receive a formal academic education as a young man. Raised by his extended family following the death of his mother and the exile of his father, Rousseau held a series of apprenticeships in his early teens and was beaten by an engraver to whom he was apprenticed. He wandered around western Europe on his own in his late teens and, having no means of subsistence, converted from Protestantism to Catholicism in order to receive 20 francs and temporary housing. As an adult, Rousseau held positions as a tutor and a secretary, and while living in France, he was an active participant in the literary salons of Paris. Upon publication of his most famous works, *Emile* (1762) and *Of the Social Contract* (1762), Rousseau made himself an enemy of the French government and was forced to flee France to avoid arrest. After living in seclusion for a year, he accepted an offer of asylum from the philosopher David Hume, with whom he would live in England while he wrote part of his autobiographical *Confessions* (1782). Suffering from persecution paranoia, Rousseau suspected Hume of plotting against his life and fled to Paris, where he lived out his remaining years in poverty. His tombstone stands isolated on a small island in the middle of a lake in France.

A self-educated intellectual of diverse talents, Rousseau not only wrote political philosophy but also composed operas and dramas, invented a new system of musical notation, and wrote social and cultural criticism. He was known in the intellectual circles of Paris for his passionate defence of freedom and for his view that human beings are by nature good but are corrupted by modern social intuitions, which promote inequalities, greed, and misery. Rousseau was propelled into intellectual fame upon winning an essay contest sponsored by the Academy of Dijon, which invited papers on the question 'Has the progress of the sciences and the arts contributed to the purification of manners and morals?' Rousseau argued to the surprise of the Academy that advancements in sciences and arts have not improved human moral life; the ancient Spartans, he thought, exhibited greater virtue than modern individuals, who are often weak, effeminate, and lacking in self-discipline. The theory of innate human goodness developed in this prize-winning essay (entitled *Discourse on the Arts and Sciences*) was later published in his *Discourse on the Origin of Inequality* (1755).

In the *Discourse on the Origin of Inequality*, Rousseau argues that modern society has destroyed the natural freedom of human beings and secured the domination of the poor by the rich. In a state of nature without government or private property, human beings would be ignorant but compassionate, less concerned with personal material gain, and free to pursue their natural instincts without quarrelling over property and money. For Rousseau, the basic social and political problem is remedying the selfishness and greed bred into modern individuals without eliminating the protections and security afforded by a modern political society. In *Of the Social Contract* and *Emile*, he presents schemes of political organization and civic education that would help to restore virtue, freedom, and equality. In a democracy in which all citizens are educated and participate directly in political decision making, sovereignty is expressed in the general will of citizens, who exercise freedom in indirect self-governance. Rousseau's *Social Contract*—and its call for 'liberty, fraternity, and equality' among all citizens—was the foremost ideological influence behind the French Revolution.

Discourse on the Origin of Inequality

I shall be speaking of man, and the issue I discuss tells me that I shall be speaking to men, for such questions are not raised by persons who are afraid to acknowledge the truth. Thus, I confidently defend humanity's cause before the men of wisdom who have invited me to do so, and I would not be displeased with myself if I prove worthy of my subject and my critics.

The human species has, I think, two sorts of inequality: the one I call natural or physical because it is established by nature, and consists of differences in age, health, physical strength, and traits of the mind or soul; the other kind we can call moral or political inequality, for it depends on a sort of convention and is established, or at least sanctioned, by the consent of men. This inequality consists of the various privileges that some persons enjoy at the expense of others—such as being wealthier, more honoured, and more powerful than others, and even getting themselves obeyed by others.

One cannot ask what the source of natural inequality is because the answer is expressed by the very definition of the word. Still less can one enquire whether there is not some essential connection between the two kinds of inequality, for that would be to ask, in other words, whether those who command are necessarily worthier than those who obey, and whether bodily or intellectual vigour, wisdom, and virtue are always to be found in individuals in proportion to their power or wealth—possibly a good question to raise among slaves in the hearing of their masters, but one not applicable to free and reasonable men in search of the truth.

So what, precisely, is the subject of this discourse? To pinpoint the moment in the development of events when right replaced violence and nature was subjected to law, and to explain by what sequence of marvellous events the strong could resolve to serve the weak and the people to purchase a semblance of peace at the price of true felicity.

Philosophers examining the foundations of society have all felt the need to go back to the state of nature, but not one of them has managed to reach it. Some have not hesitated to assume that man in that state possessed a notion of the just and the unjust, without bothering to show that he must have had such a concept or that he would even find it useful. Others have spoken of the natural right of each person to keep what belongs to him without saying what they mean by 'belong'. Still others begin by giving the strongest persons authority over the weaker ones, and straightaway introduced government without thinking of the time that had to elapse before the words 'authority' and 'government' could have any meaning among men. All these philosophers, in short, constantly talking of need, greed, oppression, desires, and pride have imported into the state of nature ideas they had taken from society. They talk of savage man and they depict civilized man. Doubts about the quondam existence of a state of nature have never entered most philosophers' heads, yet a reading of the Scriptures plainly reveals that the first man, immediately on receiving the light of reason and the commandments of God, was not himself in this state and that giving the writings of Moses the credence that every Christian philosopher owes them, it must be denied that men were in the pure state of nature even before the Flood, unless through some extraordinary circumstance they reverted to it—a paradox that would be scarcely defensible and quite impossible to prove.

Let us begin by setting aside all the facts, for they have no bearing on this question. This kind of enquiry is not like the pursuit of historical truth, but depends solely on hypothetical and conditional reasoning, better suited to illuminate the nature of things than to show their actual origin, reasoning similar to that done every day by physicists to explain the formation of the world. Religion commands us to believe that because God took men out of the state of nature, it was his will that they be unequal, but this does not forbid us to make conjectures based solely on the nature of man and the beings around him, concerning what the human race might have become if it had been left to itself. That, then, is what has been

asked of me and what I propose to examine in this discourse. Because my subject concerns man in general, I shall try to use terms intelligible to every nation or rather, forgetting time and place in order to think only of the men I am addressing, I shall imagine myself in the Lyceum of Athens, repeating the lessons of my teachers, with a Plato and Xenocrates as my judges and the human race as my audience.

O Man listen, whatever be your country and your opinions: here, as I have read it, is your history, not in the books of your fellow men, who lie, but in nature which never lies. Everything issuing from nature is true; nothing in it is false except what I myself have inadvertently put in of my own. The times of which I speak are very remote—how much you have changed from what you once were! I shall, as it were, describe the life of your species, in light of the characteristics you once received which your education and habits could corrupt but not entirely destroy. There is, I think, an age at which the individual would like to go on unchanged; you are going to seek the age at which you would wish your whole species had remained. Dissatisfied with your present condition for reasons that presage even greater unhappiness for your unfortunate posterity, you might wish you could go back in time—and this sentiment must elicit the eulogy of your earliest ancestors, the censure of your contemporaries, and the fright of those who have the misfortune to live after you.

Part I

. . . I see in every animal merely an ingenious machine to which nature has given senses to keep it going by itself and to protect itself, up to a certain point, from everything likely to distress or annihilate it. I see precisely the same things in the human machine, with the difference that nature alone does everything in the activities of a beast while man contributes to his own, in his capacity as a free agent. The beast chooses or rejects by instinct, man by free action, meaning that the beast cannot deviate from the rule prescribed for it, even when it might benefit from doing so, whereas man often deviates from such laws to his own detriment. That is why a pigeon would die of hunger next to a dish filled with choice meats and a cat next to a heap of fruit or grain, even though either of them could get nourishment from the foods it disdains if it only had thought of trying them. Thus, dissolute men give themselves over the excesses that bring on fevers and death, because the mind perverts the senses and the will continues to speak when nature is silent.

Every animal has ideas because it has senses, and even combines these ideas up to a certain point; in this respect man differs from the beast only in degree. Some philosophers have suggested that there is a greater difference between one man and another than between a given man and a given beast. Thus it is not his understanding that constitutes the distinctive characteristic of man among all other animals, but his capacity as a free agent. Nature commands every animal, and the beast obeys. Man experiences the same impulsion, but he recognizes that he is free to comply or resist; and it is above all the awareness of this freedom that reveals the spirituality of his soul, for physics in some way explains the mechanism of the senses and the formation of ideas, but in the power of willing, or rather choosing, and in our sense of this power, we find purely mental acts wholly inexplicable by the laws of mechanics.

Although the difficulties surrounding all these questions leave some room for disagreement about this difference between man and beast, there is one further highly specific, distinctive, and indisputable feature of man, and

that is his faculty of self-improvement—a faculty that, with the help of circumstances, successively develops all the others and that in man inheres as much in the species as in the individual, whereas an animal at the end of a few months already is what it will remain all its life, and its species will be at the end of a thousand years what it was in the first of those thousand years. Why is only man prone to turn senile? Is it not the case that he thus returns to his primitive state and that, while the beast that has acquired nothing and hence has nothing to lose is always left with its instincts, man, losing through old age or some accident all that his *perfectibility* has enabled him to acquire, thus sinks lower than the beast? It would be sad for us to be forced to admit that this distinctive and nearly unlimited faculty was the source of all man's unhappiness and, in time, draws him out of that primordial condition in which he would savour peaceful and innocent days; and that it was this faculty, causing over the centuries his acumen and his errors, his vices and virtues to flourish, which eventually makes man a tyrant over himself and nature. It would be appalling to be obliged to praise as a beneficent creature the man who first suggested to the inhabitants of the banks of the Orinoco the practice of flattening their infants' temples with boards and so ensuring them of at least a part both of their imbecility and original happiness.

The savage man, consigned by nature to instinct alone—or rather compensated for the instinct he may lack by faculties that can replace it at first and later raise him far above nature—begins with purely animal functions; his earliest state will be perception and feeling, experiences shared by every other animal. Willing and unwilling, desiring and fearing, will be his soul's first and just about only operations until new circumstances cause it to undergo new developments.

Whatever moralists say about it, the human understanding owes a great deal to the passions, which, by common consent, also owe a great deal to the understanding. Reason develops through the activity of the passions; we seek to know only because we wish to enjoy, and it is inconceivable that a man who had neither fears nor desires would bother to reason. The passions, in turn, originate in our needs and owe their progress to our knowledge, for we can desire or fear things only if we can form some ideas of them in our mind or through a simple impulse of nature. The savage, lacking any sort of enlightenment, experiences passions only of the latter kind; his desires do not go beyond his physical needs; the only goods in the world he knows are food, a female, and repose, and the only evils he fears are pain and hunger. I say pain and not death, for an animal will never know what it is to die, and a knowledge of death and its terrors is one of man's first acquisitions upon leaving the animal condition.

... For myself, daunted by the myriad difficulties and convinced of the nearly certain impossibility that languages could have been created and established by purely human means, I leave to anyone who will undertake it the discussion of the following difficult problem: Which was more necessary, a previously established society for the invention of language, or a previously invented language for the establishment of society?

Whatever the origins of language may be, it is easy to see at least from the lack of care taken by nature to bring men together through mutual needs, or to make the use of speech easier, how little it prepared them to be sociable or contributed to all they have done to establish their social bonds. Indeed, it is unimaginable why in that primitive state one man would need a fellow man any more than a monkey or a wolf needs its fellow creature,

or, assuming he did, what reason could induce the other man to minister to it, or in the latter case, how the two could agree among themselves on the conditions. I know we are repeatedly told that nothing was so miserable as man in the state of nature; and if it is true, as I believe I have proved, that man could have either the desire or the chance to leave that state only after many centuries, this is an accusation to lodge against nature and not against him whom nature so fashioned. If, however, I understand the term 'miserable' correctly, it is a word that means nothing or merely a painful deprivation and suffering in body or soul. Now I would like to have it explained to me what kind of misery could exist in a free being whose heart is at peace and whose body is healthy: I ask which kind of life—civilized or natural—is more apt to become unbearable to those who experience it? Around us we see people almost all of whom complain of their existence and even several of whom renounce it as much as possible; and divine and human law together do little to arrest this disorder. I wonder whether anyone has ever heard of a free savage who ever dreamt of complaining about his life or killing himself? Let it be judged with less vanity on which side true misery lies. On the contrary, nothing would be as miserable as a savage man dumbfounded by knowledge, tormented by passions, and reasoning about state different from his own. Thanks to a very wise providence, his potential faculties developed only with the opportunities to use them, so that they were neither superfluous nor prematurely onerous, nor belated and unavailing when they were needed. In instinct alone man had everything he needed to live in the state of nature, and in cultivated reason, he has everything he needs to live in society.

At first glance, it would seem that because in the state of nature men have no kind of moral relationships to each other, nor any recognized duties, they would be neither good nor evil, and could have neither vices nor virtues; unless we took those word in a physical sense and could call an individual's 'vices' those attributes that might be deleterious to his own survival and 'virtues' those that might be propitious for it, in which case we should have to call most virtuous the person who least resisted the simple impulses of nature. But without diverging from ordinary usage, we would do well to suspend judgment on this situation and guard against our own biases until we have observed, with the scales of impartiality in our hands, more virtues than vices among civilized men, whether those men's virtues are more beneficial than their vices are pernicious; or whether the advancement of their knowledge adequately compensates for the harm they do each other, as they learn of the good they should do each other; or whether, all things considered, they would not be in a happier situation, having neither harm to fear from anyone nor good to hope from anyone, rather than subjecting themselves to a universal dependence and obligating themselves to accept everything from those who do not obligate themselves to give them anything.

Above all, let us not conclude with Hobbes that man is naturally wicked because he has no idea of goodness or vice-ridden because he has no knowledge of virtue, that he always withholds from his fellow men services that he does not believe he owes them, or on the strength of his properly claimed right to the things he needs, he madly imagines himself to be the sole owner of the universe. Hobbes clearly saw the flaw in all modern definitions of natural right, but the conclusions he drew from his own definition show that his own concept of natural right is no less false. Reasoning according to his own principles, that writer should have said instead that because

the state of nature is the one in which man's concern for his survival least encroaches on that of others, it is the one most conducive to peace and befitting of mankind. He said precisely the opposite as a result of improperly introducing into savage man's concern for his own survival the need to satisfy a host of passions that are the handiwork of society and that have made laws necessary. The wicked man, he said, is a robust child; it remains to be seen whether savage man is this robust child. Even if we conceded this point to Hobbes, what would he conclude from it? That if this man were as dependent on others when he is robust as when he is weak, there is no kind of excess he would not commit: that he would assault his mother when she delayed nursing him at her breast, that he would strangle one younger brother who annoyed him, or bite the leg of another when struck or otherwise bothered by him. But Hobbes is here making two conflicting suppositions about man in the state of nature: that he is robust and that he is dependent. Man is weak when he is dependent, and becomes emancipated before he is robust. Hobbes did not see that the same cause preventing savages from using their reason (as our jurists claim) also prevents them from abusing their faculties (as Hobbes himself claims), so that it could be said that savages are not wicked precisely because they do not know what it is to be good, for it is neither the development of knowledge nor the restraint of law, but the calm of the passions, and ignorance of vice that keeps them from doing wrong. 'Tanto plus in illis proficit vitiorum ignoratio, quam in his cognitio virtutis.' There is, moreover, another principle that Hobbes failed to see and that—having been given to man to temper the fierceness of his vanity or his desire for self-preservation before the birth of this vanity— moderates his zeal for his own well-being by an innate aversion to the sight of a fellow creature's suffering. I believe I need have no fear of contradiction when I credit man with the one natural virtue that the most intemperate detractor of human virtues has been forced to recognize. I speak of pity, a fitting predisposition for creatures as weak and subject to as many ills as we, a virtue all the more universal and useful to man because it precedes any kind of reflection in him, and so natural that even the beasts themselves sometimes show discernible signs of it. Without speaking of the tenderness of mother for their young and the dangers they brave in order to protect them, we observe every day the aversion of horses to trampling any living body underfoot; an animal never passes a dead creature from its own species without uneasiness; there are even some that give their dead a sort of burial; and the sorrowful lowing of cattle entering a slaughterhouse bespeaks their feelings about the horrible spectacle facing them. One sees with pleasure how the author of *The Fable of the Bess*, forced to recognize man as a sensitive and compassionate creature, departs from his cold and brittle style in the example he gives of this, presenting us with the heart-rending image of a man compelled to behold, from a place of confinement, a wild beast tear a child from his mother's breast, crushing the child's fragile limbs with its murderous fangs and ripping out the quivering entrails with its claws. What terrible agitation must be felt by this witness of an event in which he has no personal stake! What agony he must suffer at seeing this sight, and being unable to do anything to help the fainting mother or the dying child! . . .

Part II

The true founder of civil society was the first man who, having enclosed a piece of land, thought of saying 'This is mine,' and came across people simple enough to believe him. How many crimes, wars, murders and how much misery and horror the human race might have been spared if someone had pulled up the stakes or filled in the ditch, and cried out to his fellows: 'Beware of listening to this charlatan. You are lost if you forget that the fruits of the earth belong to all and that the earth itself belongs to no one!' Quite evidently, however, things had by this time reached a point at which they could not continue as they had been, for since the idea of property depends on many anterior ideas that could only have arisen in sequential stages, it was not produced in the human mind all at once. Before arriving at this final stage of the state of nature, men had to make a good deal of progress, acquire considerable ingenuity and knowledge, and transmit and increase them from age to age. So let us go further back into the matter, and try to look from a single viewpoint at the slow chain of events and learning in their most natural order.

Man's first sentiment was that of his existence, and his first concern was that of his own preservation. The products of the earth furnished all the necessary support and prompted him to make use to them by instinct. Hunger and other cravings made him in turn experience various ways of living, but one particular craving goaded him to perpetuate his own species: and this blind inclination, devoid of any sentiment of the heart, occasioned only a purely animal act. Once the need was satisfied, · the two sexes no long recognized each other, and even the child meant nothing to the mother once he could do without her.

Such was the condition of nascent man; such was the life of an animal initially limited to pure sensations, scarcely profiting from the gifts supplied him by nature, much less imagining he could wrest anything from it. Difficulties soon cropped up, however, and man had to learn to overcome them—the height of trees, which prevented him from reaching their fruits; competition from animals seeking to feed on these fruits; the ferocity of animals that were after his life—all this obliged man to engage in physical exercise; he had to make himself agile, fleet of foot, and spirited in combat. He soon found natural weapons at hand, such as stones and tree branches. He learned to surmount nature's obstacles, to battle against other animals if need be, to fight with other men for his subsistence, or to offset what he was forced to cede to the stronger.

As the human race increased, so did its problems. Differences in terrain, soils, climates, and seasons might have forced men to adopt different ways of living. Barren years, long hard winters, and scorching summers that despoiled everything called for a new industriousness. Along the seashores and riverbanks men invented the hook and line, becoming fishermen and eaters of fish. In the forests they made bows and arrows, becoming hunters and warriors. In cold countries they clothed themselves with the hides of the beasts they had slain. Lightning, a volcano, or some happy accident introduced them to fire—a fresh resource against the severity of winter. They learned to preserve this element, then to reproduce it, and eventually to use it to prepare the meats they had once eaten raw. . . .

Although his fellow men were not for him what they are for us and he had little more dealings with them than he had with other animals, they did not go unnoticed. The similarities that he could in time behold between them, his female, and himself, led him to think of those he did not perceive; and, seeing that they all behaved the same way he did in similar circumstances, he concluded that their manner of thinking and feeling was entirely consistent with his own; and once this important truth was well implanted in his mind, he

was led to follow, by an intuition as certain as and more immediate than logic, the best rules of conduct he found suitable to observe toward them for his own advantage and safety.

Taught by experience that the lone motive of human action is love of well-being, he was ready to identify the rare circumstances in which the common interest justified his counting on the aid of his fellows, and the even rarer occasions in which competition should make him distrust them. In the former case, he joined them in a flock, or at most in a sort of free association that was binding to no one and lasted only as long as the transient need responsible for it. In the latter case, each person sought his own advantage, either by overt force, if he believed he was strong enough, or by his wits and cunning if he believed he was the weaker.

In this way, men were able gradually to acquire some rough idea of mutual commitments and the benefits of keeping them, but only as much as clear and present interests might require, for men had no foresight, and far from concerning themselves with a distant future, they hardly thought of the next day. When it came to tracking down a deer, everyone realized that he should remain dependably at his post; but if a hare happened to pass within reach of one of them, he undoubtedly would not have hesitated to run off after it and, catching his prey, he would have troubled himself little about causing his companions to lose theirs. . . .

As ideas and feelings succeeded one another, and hearts and minds were cultivated, the human race became more sociable, contacts increased, and bonds grew tighter. People developed the habit of gathering together in front of their huts or around a large tree; song and dance, true children of love and leisure, became the entertainment, or rather the occupation, of the idle men and women thus flocked together. Each person began to gaze on the others and to want to be gazed upon himself, and what came to be prized was public esteem. Anyone who best sang or danced; he who was the most handsome, the strongest, the most skilful, or the most eloquent came to be the most highly regarded, and this was the first step toward inequality and also toward vice. These first preferences gave rise, on the one side, to vanity and scorn, and on the other, to shame and envy; and the ferment produced by these new leavens eventually led to concoctions ruinous to happiness and innocence.

Once men learned to appraise one another and formed the idea of esteem, everyone claimed a right to it, and no one could then be denied it without taking affront. This was the source of the first duties of courtesy, even among savages; and henceforth every intentional wrong became a grave offence, for along with the harm resulting from the affront, the offended party often saw an insult to his person as more intolerable than the harm itself. Thus, because the attack of one person scorned by another was commensurate with the value he placed on himself, revenge became terrible, and men bloodthirsty and cruel. This is precisely the stage reached by most of the savage peoples known to us, and because so many writers have not sufficiently distinguished between ideas and seen how far those peoples already are from the first state of nature, these thinkers have hastened to conclude that man is naturally cruel and needs civil government to make him gentler, although in truth nothing is gentler than man in his primitive state where, placed by nature midway between the stupidity of brutes and the fatal enlightenment of civilized man and limited equally by reason and instinct to ward off the evils threatening him, his natural pity deters him from doing harm to anyone, even when he has encountered harm himself. For

according to the wise Locke: 'Where there is no property, there is no injury.'

It should be noted, however, that once society came into existence and relations between individuals were established, different traits of men were required from those they owed to their primitive constitution; that since morality began to be introduced into human actions and since prior to the existence of laws each man was the sole judge and avenger of the offences committed against him, the goodness suitable to the pure state of nature was no longer suitable to the nascent society; that punishments had to be more severe as the occasions for giving offence became more common and the terror of revenge had to stand in for the check of laws. Thus, although men had come to be less patient and their natural pity had been somewhat attenuated, this period in the development of human faculties, striking a good balance between the indolence of the primitive state and the fervid activity of our own vanity, must have been the happiest and most enduring age. The more we reflect on it, the more we realize that this state was the best for man and the least subject to revolutions; and that man can have left it only as the result of some fatal accident that, for the common good, ought never to have happened. The example of savages, almost always found to be at this stage, appears to confirm that the human race was made to remain there forever, that this state was the true youth of the world, and that all subsequent advances appear to be so many steps toward improvement of the individual but, in fact, toward the enfeeblement of the species.

As long as men were content with their rustic huts, as long as they confined themselves to stitching their garments of hides with thorns or fishbones, and adorning themselves with feathers or shells, to painting their bodies with various colours, to improving or decorating their bows and arrows, and to carving fishing-boats or a few crude musical instruments; in short, so long as they applied themselves only to work that one person alone could accomplish and to arts that did not require the collaboration of several hands, they lived as free, healthy, good, and happy lives as their nature permitted and continued to enjoy among themselves the delights of independent activity. But from the moment one man needed help from another, and as soon as they found it useful for one man to have provisions enough for two, equality evaporated, property was introduced, and work became mandatory; vast forests were transformed into sunny open country that had to be watered with the sweat of man, and where slavery and adversity were soon seen to germinate and ripen with the crops.

This great revolution followed from the invention of the arts of agriculture and metallurgy. For the poet it is gold and silver, but for the philosopher it is iron and wheat that first civilized and ruined the human race. Neither of these arts were known to the savages of America who thus have remained savages; the other peoples seem to have remained barbarians as long as they practised one of these arts and not the other, and one of the best reasons why Europe, if not the earliest to be civilized, has been at least more continuously and better civilized than other parts of the world, may be that it is the richest in iron and the most productive of wheat.

It is very difficult to envision how men came first to know and use iron, for it is unlikely they would think on their own of drawing ore from the mine and giving it the needed preparations for smelting before knowing what the results would be. On the other hand, we can even less readily credit this discovery to some accidental fire, for mines are formed only in dry areas devoid of trees and plants, so one might say that nature had taken pains to hide this fatal secret from us. Hence there remains only the phenomenal event of some volcano disgorging molten metallic substances and thereby giving those who witnessed it the idea of duplicating this natural process. We would also have to assume those men had enough drive to undertake such onerous labour and enough foresight to project far into the future the benefits they might derive from it, which is scarcely creditable even to minds more developed than theirs.

As for agriculture, its principle was known long before the practice of it was launched, and it is indeed highly unlikely that men who perpetually lived off trees and plants would not rather quickly get an idea of the means nature uses to reproduce vegetation. But men's activity probably took that turn only very late—because trees, which together with hunting and fishing supplied their food, needed no care, or because men had no knowledge of the use of wheat or no tools for farming it, or because of lack of foresight concerning future needs, or because of a lack of a way to prevent others from seizing the fruits of their labour. As men became more skilled, we can believe that they began using sharp stones and pointed sticks to grow a few vegetables or roots around their huts; although it took a long time before they knew how to process wheat or had the tools needed for large-scale growing; they also had to learn that in order to devote oneself to this activity and sow the land, one must accept an initial loss for the sake of a greater gain in the future—a prescience quite alien to the savage's turn of mind since, as I have said, he is hard pressed to imagine in the morning the needs he will have that evening.

The invention of the other arts must thus have been necessary to compel the human race to take up agriculture. When some men were needed to smelt and forge iron, others were needed to supply them with food. The more the number of labourers grew, the fewer hands were engaged in providing for the common subsistence, without there being any fewer mouths to consume it; and because some men needed foodstuffs in return for their iron, others finally discovered the secret of using iron to increase the supply of food. From this arose, on the one hand, ploughing and agriculture, and, on the other, the art of working metals and extending their uses.

The cultivation of the land necessarily led to its division, and the recognition of property led to the first rules of justice: for in order to render to each his own, each must be able to own something; moreover, as men began to direct their gaze into the future and all saw that they had some goods to lose, there was no one who did not fear reprisals against himself for the wrongs he might do to others. This origin is all the more natural because the idea of property could not conceivably have arisen from anything other than manual labour, for it is not apparent what else besides his own labour a man can add to things he has not made, in order to make them his property. Labour alone gives the grower the right to the crops from the land he has tilled and this consequently gives him the right to the produce of the land and hence to the land itself, at least until the harvest, and hence from year to year, that which constitutes uninterrupted possession is easily transformed into property. Grotius says that when the ancients gave Ceres the title of Legislatrix, and the name Thesmaphoria to the festival celebrated in her honour, they implied that the division of land had produced a new sort of right, that is, the right to property, which is different from the right derived from natural law.

Things in this state might have remained equal if abilities had been equal and if, for example, the use of iron and the consumption of foodstuffs had always exactly matched each other; because, however, this equilibrium was protected by nothing, it was soon upset: the stronger produced more work, the more skilled did better work, and the cleverer found ways to shorten their labour. The farmer had greater need of iron or the blacksmith greater need of wheat and, with both working the same amount, the one earned a great deal while the other had scarcely enough to live on. Thus, natural inequality gradually leads to inequality of rank, and the differences between men, augmented by differences of circumstance, become more conspicuous and lasting in their effects and begin to exert a correspondingly powerful influence over the fate of individuals.

Once things reached this point, we can readily imagine the rest. I shall not dwell on a description of the successive invention of the other arts, the development of languages, the testing and use of abilities, the inequality of fortunes, the use and misuse of wealth, and all the consequent details that can easily be given by any of us. I shall simply confine myself to casting a glance over the human race as it fitted into this new order of things.

Behold, then, all our faculties trained, our memory and imagination in play, our pride engaged, our reason activated, and our minds as near-perfect as possible. Behold all the natural characteristics called into action, every man's rank and fate settled, not only as to the amount of his possessions and power to help or to harm, but also as to his intelligence, good looks, strength or skill, merit or abilities; and because only these traits could elicit esteem, it soon became necessary to have them or purport to have them. It was soon to one's advantage to be other than one actually was. Being and appearing became two quite different things, and from this distinction emerged striking ostentation, deceitful cunning, and all the vices that follow in their wake. From another point of view, behold man, once free and independent, now subject, so to speak, through a multitude of new needs, to all of nature and above all to his fellow men, whose slave he has in a sense become, even when he becomes their master. For if he is rich, he needs their services; if he is poor, he needs their aid; and even a position in between does not enable him to do without them. Thus, he must constantly seek to involve others in his lot, and get them to see an advantage, either real or apparent, in working for his benefit: all of which makes him deceitful and crafty with some people, harsh and domineering with others, and forces him to hoodwink all those he needs if he cannot make them fear him and when he does not consider it to his advantage to be of service to them. Finally, in all men a consuming ambition, the burning passion to increase one's relative fortune, less out to real need than to make oneself superior to others, inspires a dark propensity to harm each other, a secret jealousy that is all the more dangerous because, to strike out from a more secure position, it often assumes the mask of benevolence; in short, we have competition and rivalry on the one hand, and antagonistic interests on the other, and always the hidden desire to gain some advantage at other people's expense. All these evils are the first effects of property and the inseparable escort of nascent inequality.

Before the invention of symbols to represent it, wealth could hardly consist of anything except land and livestock, the only real goods that men could possess. When, however, inheritances so increased in number and extent that they covered all the land and every estate bordered on another one, none could be enlarged except at the expense of some neighbouring one, and the landless supernumer-

aries whom frailty or indolence barred from acquiring anything for themselves, became poor without having lost anything, because, with everything changing around them, they alone remained unchanged and so were obliged to receive—or steal—their subsistence from the hands of the rich. Out of this situation arose either domination and servitude, or plunder and violence, depending on the different characters of the rich and the poor. The rich, for their part, had hardly learned the joys of domination before they disdained all other ones, and using their current slaves to subdue new ones, they dreamed only of subjugating and enslaving their neighbours, like those ravenous wolves that, having once tasted human flesh, reject all other nourishment and thenceforth desire only to feed on man.

Thus, with the mightiest or the poorest regarding their powers or their needs as a kind of right to the belongings of others, equivalent, according to them, to the right of property, the loss of equality was succeeded by the most appalling disorder. Thus, the encroachments of the rich, the thievery of the poor, and the unbridled passions of everyone, stifling natural pity and the still-hushed voice of justice, made men greedy, ambitious, and wicked. Between the right of the strongest and the right of the first occupant there arose a perpetual conflict that ended only in fights and murders. Nascent society made way for the most horrible state of war: the human race, degraded and ravaged, could not then retrace its path or renounce its unfortunate acquisitions, but working only toward its shame through the misuse of faculties that should be its honour, brought itself to the brink of ruin.

> Attonitus novitate mali, diverque miserque,
> Effugere optat opes, et quae modo voverat, odit.

It was at last impossible for men not to devote some thought to this awful situation and the calamities that had befallen them. The rich in particular must have realized the great disadvantages to them of a perpetual war in which they bore all the costs and in which the risk of life was universal but the risk of property theirs alone. Furthermore, whatever disguise they might put upon their usurpations, they were well aware that these were based solely on precarious and sham rights, and that force could divest them of what force alone had procured and they would thus have no grounds for complaint. Even those who had been enriched by their own industry could not base their right to their property on better credentials. They might well have said: 'I built this wall: I earned the right to this field by my own labour.' They might be answered with 'Who gave you the boundary lines? And on what basis do you demand payment from us for work we never requested of you? Are you unaware that vast numbers of your fellow men suffer or perish from need of the things that you have to excess, and that you required the explicit and unanimous consent of the whole human race for you to appropriate from the common subsistence anything besides that required for your own?' Lacking valid reasons to justify himself and sufficient strength to defend himself; handily overpowering an individual but overpowered himself by bandits; alone against all and, owing to mutual jealousies, unable to form alliances with his peers against enemies banded together in the shared hope of plunder, the rich man, goaded by necessity, eventually conceived of the shrewdest scheme ever to enter the human mind: to employ on his behalf the very forces of his attackers, to make his opponents his defenders, to inspire them with new slogans, and give them new institutions as favourable to him as natural right was detrimental.

To this end, after showing his neighbours the horror of a situation that pitted all against the others, made their possessions as burdensome as their needs, and that yielded no safety to those in poverty or in prosperity, he readily concocted specious reasons to guide men to his goal. 'Let us unite,' he said to them, 'to protect the weak from oppression, hold the overdesirous in check, and ensure for each the possession of what belongs to him. Let us establish rules of justice and peace that everyone is obligated to conform to without favouring any one person, and that will make amends, as it were, for the caprices of fortune by subjecting the powerful and the weak equally to reciprocal duties. In short, rather than train our forces against each other, let us unite them together in one supreme power that will govern us all according to wise laws, protect and defend all the members of the association, fend off common enemies, and preserve us in everlasting concord.'

Much less than the equivalent of this speech was needed to win over men so uncultivated and gullible, especially as they had too many scores to settle among themselves to do without arbiters, and too much greed and ambition to do for long without masters. All ran headlong for their chains in the belief that they were securing their liberty; for although they had enough reason to see the advantages of political institutions, they did not have enough experience to foresee their dangers. Those most capable of predicting the abuses were precisely the ones who counted on profiting from them; and the wise ones saw that men must resolve to sacrifice one part of their freedom in order to preserve the other, just as a wounded man has his arm cut off to save the rest of his body.

Such was, or must have been, the origin of society and of law, which put new shackles on the weak and gave new powers to the rich, which destroyed natural freedom irretrievably, laid down for all time the law of property and inequality, made clever usurpation into an irrevocable right, and henceforth subjected, for the benefit of a few ambitious men, the human race to labour, servitude, and misery. We can easily see how the founding of one society made that of all the rest inevitable, and how, in order to hold their own against united forces, others in turn had to unite. Societies, as they proliferated and spread, soon covered the whole surface of the earth, and it was no longer possible to find a single corner on the globe where one might free oneself from the yoke and shield one's head from the often precariously held sword that every man saw perpetually dangling over him. Because civil law thus became the common rule over citizens, the law of nature obtained only between the various societies where, under the name of law of nations, it was moderated by certain tacit conventions designed to allow for relations and to stand in for the natural commiseration that, from society to society, having lost nearly all the force it had from man to man, lives on only in a few great cosmopolitan souls, who break through the imaginary barriers between peoples and, following the example of their sovereign creator, include the whole human race in their benevolence.

The bodies politic, thus remaining in the state of nature in relation to each other, soon experienced the same disadvantages that had forced individuals to leave it; the state of nature proved even more catastrophic to these large bodies than it had once been for individuals of whom they were composed. From this there arose wars between nations, battles, killings, reprisals that make nature shudder and offend reason, and all those horrible preconceived ideas that make a virtue out of the shedding of human blood. Perfectly decent men learned to count among their duties the killing of their fellows; an in time men came to massacre one another by the thousands without knowing why, committing more murders in a single day's battle and more atrocities in a single city's capture than had been committed in the state of nature for whole centuries over the entire face of the earth. Such are the first observed effects of the division of the human race into different societies. But let us return to their beginnings.

I know that many have suggested other origins for political societies, such as conquest by the most powerful or the union of the weak, but the choice between these causes is immaterial to what I wish to establish. The one I have just sketched, however, seems to me the most natural for the following reasons: (1) Because in the first place, the right of conquest is not a right at all and so could not have been the basis of any other; the conqueror and the people conquered will always remain in a state of war toward each other, unless the conquered nation, with its freedom fully restored, voluntarily chooses its conqueror for its ruler. Up to that point, whatever capitulations were made were based solely on violence and are thereby invalid, so there cannot on this hypothesis be any authentic society or body politic or any law but the law of the strongest. (2) Because in the latter case, the words 'strong' and 'weak' are equivocal; for during the period between the establishment of the right to property or the right of the first occupant and the establishment of political governments, the meaning of these terms is better expressed by the words 'poor' and 'rich', since before the introduction of laws a man's only means of subjugating his peers was to raid their goods or make them a part of his own. (3) Because, with nothing to lose but their freedom, it would have been an act of lunacy for the poor voluntarily to divest themselves of the only good that still remained to them and get nothing in return. It was much easier, however, to harm the rich, who were vulnerable, so to speak, in every part of their wealth and thus had to take more steps for their own protection; and lastly it is reasonable to believe that a thing was invented by those to whom it was advantageous rather than by those to whom it was detrimental.

The nascent government had no durable and regular form. The lack of experience and wisdom made only current troubles salient, and men thought of remedies for others ills only when they became clearly evident. Despite the efforts of the wisest legislators, the political state remained ever flawed, because it was almost entirely the handiwork of chance, and, because this state got off to a poor start, time, though revealing defects and suggesting remedies, could never repair the defects of the constitution. Constitutions were constantly patched up, even though it was really necessary to begin by clearing the ground and scrapping the old materials, as Lycurgus did in Sparta, in order to build a solid edifice. At first, society consisted only of a few general conventions which all individuals committed themselves to observe and which the community guaranteed for each one of them. Experience was bound to expose the weakness of such a constitution and the ease with which offenders could escape conviction or punishment for crimes of which only the public was witness and judge. The laws were bound to be circumvented in a thousand ways; troubles and disorders were ever bound to multiply until men at last thought of handing over the dangerous trust of public authority to certain individuals and assigning to magistrates the task of securing compliance to the deliberations of the people, for to say that the leaders were chosen before the confederation was created, and that ministers responsible for the laws existed before the laws themselves is a suggestion unworthy of serious debate.

It would be no more reasonable to believe that men first flung themselves unconditionally and irrevocably into the arms of an absolute master, and that first means that occurred to proud and spirited men for providing for their common security was to rush headlong into slavery. Indeed, why did they give themselves overseers if not as a defence against oppression, and a means of safeguarding their possessions, their freedoms, and their lives, which are, so to speak, the constitutive elements of their being? Since the worst thing that can happen to someone in the relations between one man and another is to find oneself at the other's mercy, would it not be contrary to common sense to hand over to a superior the only things one needs his help to preserve? What thing of equivalent value could he offer them in return for the surrender of so precious a right? And if he dared to demand this surrender on the pretext of defending them, would he not promptly have been given the answer from the fable: 'What more will the enemy do to us?' Thus, it is undeniable—and indeed the fundamental principle of all political right—that people have instituted leaders in order to defend their freedom and not to enslave themselves. 'If we have a prince,' said Pliny to Trajan, 'it is in order that he may preserve us from having a master.'. . .

Just as an unbroken horse tosses its mane, stamps the ground with its hoof, and rears up furiously at the mere approach of the bit, while a broken-in horse patiently suffers even the whip and spurs, savage man will not bend his neck to the yoke that civilized man wears without a whimper; savage man prefers the most tempestuous freedom to the most tranquil subservience. Hence it is not to the degradation of enslaved peoples that we should look in judging man's natural disposition toward or against servitude, but rather to the wonders worked by all free peoples in saving themselves from oppression. I know that enslaved peoples do nothing but boast of the peace and repose they enjoy in their chains, and that *miserrimam servitutem pacem appellant*. When, however, I see free peoples sacrificing pleasure, repose, wealth, power, and even life itself for the sake of preserving the lone good that is so scorned by those who have lost it; when I see animals, born free and abhorring captivity, smashing their heads against the bars of their prison; when I see multitudes of naked savages scorn European pleasures and brave hunger, fire, the sword, and death just to safeguard their independence, I feel that it is not for slaves to deliberate about freedom.

Of the Social Contract

BOOK I

Note

It is my wish to inquire whether it be possible, within the civil order, to discover a legitimate and stable basis of government. This I shall do by considering human beings as they are and laws as they might be. I shall attempt, throughout my investigations, to maintain a constant connection between what right permits and interest demands, in order that no separation may be made between justice and utility. I intend to begin without first proving the importance of my subject. Am I, it will be asked, either prince or legislator that I take it upon me to write of politics? My answer is—No; and it is for that very reason that I have chosen politics as the matter of my book. Were I either the one or the other I should not waste my time in laying down what has to be done. I should do it, or else hold my peace.

I was born into a free state and am a member of its sovereign body. My influence on public affairs may be small, but because I have a right to exercise my vote, it is my duty to learn their nature, and it has been for me a matter of constant delight, while meditating on problems of government in general, to find ever fresh reasons for regarding with true affection the way in which these things are ordered in my native land.

I

The Subject of the First Book

Man is born free, and everywhere he is in chains. Many a man believes himself to be the master of others who is, no less than they, a slave. How did this change take place? I do not know. What can make it legitimate? To this question I hope to be able to furnish an answer.

Were I considering only force and the effects of force, I should say: 'So long as a people is constrained to obey, and does, in fact, obey, it does well. So soon as it can shake off its yoke, and succeeds in doing so, it does better. The fact that it has recovered its liberty by virtue of that same right by which it was stolen, means either that it is entitled to resume it, or that its theft by others was, in the first place, without justification.' But the social order is a sacred right which serves as a foundation for all other rights. This right, however, since it comes not by nature, must have been built upon conventions. To discover what these conventions are is the matter of our inquiry. But, before proceeding further, I must establish the truth of what I have so far advanced.

II

Of Primitive Societies

The oldest form of society—and the only natural one—is the family. Children remain bound to their father for only just so long as they feel the need of him for their self-preservation. Once that need ceases the natural bond is dissolved. From then on, the children, freed from the obedience which they formerly owed, and the father, cleared of his debt of responsibility to them, return to a condition of equal independence. If the bond remain operative it is no longer something imposed by nature, but has become a matter of deliberate choice. The family is a family still, but by reason of convention only.

This shared liberty is a consequence of man's nature. Its first law is that of self-preservation: its first concern is for what it owes itself. As soon as a man attains the age of reason he becomes his own master, because he alone can judge of what will best assure his continued existence.

We may, therefore, if we will, regard the family as the basic model of all political associations. The ruler is the father writ large: the people are, by analogy, his children, and all, ruler and people alike, alienate their freedom only so far as it is to their advantage to do so. The only difference is that, whereas in the family the father's love for his children is sufficient reward to him for the care he has lavished on them, in the state, the pleasure of commanding others takes its place, since the ruler is not in a relation of love to his people.

Grotius denies that political power is ever exercised in the interests of the governed, and quotes the institution of slavery in support of his contention. His invariable method of arguing is to derive right from fact. It might be possible to adopt a more logical system of reasoning, but none which would be more favourable to tyrants.

According to Grotius, therefore, it is doubtful whether the term 'human race' belongs to only a few hundred men, or whether those few hundred men belong to the human race. From the evidence of his book it seems clear that he holds by the first of these alternatives, and on this point Hobbes is in agreement with him. If this is so, then humanity is divided into herds of livestock, each with its 'guardian' who watches over his charges only that he may ultimately devour them.

Just as the shepherd is superior in kind to his sheep, so, too, the shepherds of men, or, in other words, their rulers, are superior in kind to their peoples. This, according to Philo, was the argument advanced by Caligula, the emperor, who drew from the analogy the perfectly true conclusion that either kings are gods or their subjects brute beasts.

The reasoning of Caligula, of Hobbes, and of Grotius is fundamentally the same. Far earlier, Aristotle, too, had maintained that men are not by nature equal, but that some are born to be slaves, others to be masters.

Aristotle was right: but he mistook the effect for the cause. Nothing is more certain than that a man born into a condition of slavery is a slave by nature. A slave in fetters loses everything—even the desire to be freed from them. He grows to love his slavery, as the companions of Ulysses grew to love their state of brutish transformation.

If some men are by nature slaves, the reason is that they have been made slaves *against* nature. Force made the first slaves: cowardice has perpetuated the species.

I have made no mention of King Adam or of the Emperor Noah, the father of three great monarchs who divided up the universe between them, as did the children of Saturn, whom some have been tempted to identify with them. I trust that I may be given credit for my moderation, since, being descended in a direct line from one of these princes, and quite possibly belonging to the elder branch, I may, for all I know, were my claims supported in law, be even now the legitimate sovereign of the human race. However that may be, all will concur in the view that Adam was king of the world, as was Robinson Crusoe of his island, only so long as he was its only inhabitant, and that the great advantage of empire held on such terms was that the monarch, firmly seated on his throne, had no need to fear rebellions, conspiracy, or war.

III

Of the Right of the Strongest

However strong a man, he is never strong enough to remain master always, unless he transform his might into right, and obedience into duty. Hence we have come to speak of the right of the strongest, a right which, seemingly assumed in irony, has, in fact, become established in principle. But the meaning of the phrase has never been adequately explained. Strength is a physical attribute, and I fail to see how any moral sanction can attach to its effects. To yield to the strong is an act of necessity, not of will. At most it is the result of a dictate of prudence. How, then, can it become a duty?

Let us assume of a moment that some such right does really exist. The only deduction from this premise is inexplicable gibberish. For the admit that might makes right is to reverse the process of effect and cause. The mighty man who defeats his rival becomes heir to his right. So soon as we can disobey with impunity, disobedience becomes legitimate. And, since the mightiest is always right, it merely remains for us to become possessed of might. But what validity can there be in a right which ceases to exist when might changes hands? If a man be constrained by might to obey, what need has he to obey by duty? And if he is not constrained to obey, there is no further obligation on him to do so. It follows, therefore, that the word right adds nothing to the idea of might. It becomes, in this connection, completely meaningless.

Obey the powers that be. If that means yield to force, the precept is admirable but redundant. My reply to those who advance it is that no case will ever be found of its violation. All power comes from God. Certainly, but so do all ailments. Are we to conclude from such an argument that we are never to call in the doctor? If I am waylaid by a footpad at the corner of a wood, I am constrained by force to give him my purse. But if I can manage to keep it from him, is it my duty to hand it over? His pistol is also a symbol of power. It must, then, be admitted that might does not create right, and that no man is under an obligation to obey any but the legitimate powers of the state. And so I continually come back to the question I first asked.

V

Of Slavery

Since no man has natural authority over his fellows, and since might can produce no right, the only foundation left for legitimate authority in human societies is agreement.

If a private citizen, says Grotius, can alienate his liberty and make himself another man's slave, why should not a whole people do the same, and subject themselves to the will of a king? The argument contains a number of ambiguous word s which stand in need of explanation. But let us confine our attention to one only—*alienate*. To alienate means to give or to sell. Now a man who becomes the slave of another does not give himself. He sells himself in return for bare subsistence, if for nothing more. But why should a whole people sell themselves? So far from furnishing subsistence to his subjects, a king draws his own from them, and from them alone. According to Rabelais, it takes a lot to keep a king. Do we, then, maintain that a subject surrenders his person on condition that his property be taken too? It is difficult to see what he will have left.

It will be said that the despot guarantees civil peace to his subjects. So be it. But how are they the gainers if the wars to which his ambition may expose them, his insatiable greed, and the vexatious demands of his ministers cause them more lose than would any outbreak of internal dissension? How do they benefit if that very condition of civil peace be one of the causes of their wretchedness? One can live peacefully enough in a dungeon, but such peace will hardly, of itself, ensure one's happiness. The Greeks imprisoned in the cave of Cyclops lived peacefully while awaiting their turn to be devoured.

To say that a man gives himself for nothing is to commit oneself to an absurd and inconceivable statement. Such an act of surrender is illegitimate, null, and void by the mere fact that he who makes it is not in his right mind. To say the same thing of a whole people is tantamount to admitting that the people in question are a nation of imbeciles. Imbecility does not produce right.

Even if a man can alienate himself, he cannot alienate his children. They are born free, their liberty belongs to them, and no one but themselves has a right to dispose of it. Before they have attained the age of reason their father may make, on their behalf, certain rules with a view to ensuring their preservation and well-being. But any such limitation of their freedom of choice must be regarded as neither irrevocable nor unconditional, for to alienate another's liberty is contrary to the natural order, and is an abuse of the father's rights. It follows that an arbitrary government can be legitimate only on condition that each successive generation of subjects is free either to accept or to reject it, and if this is so, then the government will no longer be arbitrary.

When a man renounces his liberty he renounces his essential manhood, his rights, and even his duty as a human being. There is no compensation possible for such complete renunciation. It is incompatible with man's nature, and to deprive him of his free will is to deprive his actions of all moral sanction. The convention, in short, which sets up on one side an absolute authority, and on the other an obligation to obey without question, is vain and meaningless. Is it not obvious that where we can demand everything we owe nothing? Where there is no mutual obligation, no interchange of duties, it must, surely, be clear that the actions of the commanded cease to have any moral value? For how can it be maintained that my slave has any 'right' against me when everything that he has is my property? His right being *my* right, it is absurd to speak of it as ever operating to my disadvantage.

Grotius, and those who think like him, have found in the fact of war another justification for the so-called 'right' of slavery. They argue that since the victor has a *right* to kill his defeated enemy, the latter may, if he so wish, ransom his life at the expense of his liberty, and that this compact is the more legitimate in that it benefits both parties.

But it is evident that this alleged *right* of a man to kill his enemies is not in any way a derivative of the state of war, if only because men, in their primitive condition of independence, are not bound to one another by any relationship sufficiently stable to produce a state either of war or of peace. They are not *naturally* enemies. It is the link between *things* rather than between *men* that constitutes war, and since a state of war cannot originate in simple personal relations, but only in relations between things, private hostility between man and man cannot obtain either in a state of nature where there is no generally accepted system of private property, or in a state of society where law is the supreme authority.

Single combats, duels, personal encounters are incidents which do not constitute a 'state' of anything. As to those private wars which were authorized by the ordinances of King Louis IX and suspended by the peace of God, they were merely an abuse of feudalism—that most absurd of all systems of government, so contrary was it to the principles of natural right and of all good polity.

War, therefore, is something that occurs not between man and man, but between states. The individuals who become involved in it are enemies only by accident. They fight not as men or even as citizens, but as soldiers: not as members of this or that national group, but as its defenders. A state can have as its enemies only other states, not men at all, seeing that there can be no true relationship between things of a different nature.

This principle is in harmony with that of all periods, and with the constant practice of every civilized society. A declaration of war is a warning, not so much to governments as to their subjects. The foreigner—whether king, private person, or nation as a whole—who steals, murders, or holds in durance the subjects of another country without first declaring war on that country's prince, acts not as an enemy but as a brigand. Even when war has been joined, the just prince, though he may seize all public property in enemy territory, yet respects the property and possessions of individuals, and, in so doing, shows his concern for those rights on which his own laws are

based. The object of war being the destruction of the enemy state, a commander has a perfect right to kill its defenders so long as their arms are in their hands: but once they have laid them down and have submitted, they cease to be enemies, or instruments employed by an enemy, and revert to the condition of men, pure and simple, over whose lives no one can any longer exercise a rightful claim. Sometimes it is possible to destroy a state without killing any of its subjects, and nothing in war can be claimed as a right save what may be necessary for the accomplishment of the victor's end. These principles are not those of Grotius, nor are they based on the authority of poets, but derive from the nature of things, and are founded upon reason.

The right of conquest finds its sole sanction in the law of the strongest. If war does not give to the victor the right to massacre his defeated enemies, he cannot base upon a non-existent right any claim to the further one of enslaving them. We have the right to kill our enemies only when we cannot enslave them. It follows, therefore, that the right to enslave cannot be deduced from the right to kill, and that we are guilty of enforcing an iniquitous exchange if we make a vanquished foeman purchase with his liberty that life over which we have no right. Is it not obvious that once we begin basing the right of life and death on the right to enslave, and the right to enslave on the right of life and death, we are caught in a vicious circle? Even if we assume the existence of this terrible right to kill all and sundry, I still maintain that a man enslaved, or a people conquered, in war is under no obligation to obey beyond the point at which force ceases to be operative. If the victor spares the life of his defeated opponent in return for an equivalent, he cannot be said to have shown him mercy. In either case he destroys him, but in the latter case he derives value from his act, while in the former he gains nothing. His authority, however, rests on no basis but that of force. There is still a state of war between the two men, and it conditions the whole relationship in which they stand to one another. The enjoyment of the rights of war presupposes that there has been no treaty of peace. Conqueror and conquered have, to be sure, entered into a compact, but such a compact, far from liquidating the state of war, assumes its continuance.

Thus, in whatever way we look at the matter, the 'right' to enslave has no existence, not only because it is without legal validity, but because the very term is absurd and meaningless. The word *slavery* and *right* are contradictory and mutually exclusive. Whether we be considering the relation of one man to another man, or of an individual to a whole people, it is equally idiotic to say—'You and I have made a compact which represents nothing but loss to you and gain to me. I shall observe it so long as it pleases me to do so—and so shall you, until I cease to find it convenient.'

V

That We Must Always Go Back to an Original Compact

Even were I to grant all that I have so far refuted, the champions of despotism would not be one whit the better off. There will always be a vast difference between subduing a mob and governing a social group. No matter how many isolated individuals may submit to the enforced control of a single conqueror, the resulting relationship will ever be that of master and slave, never of people and ruler. The body of men so controlled may be an agglomeration; it is not an association. It implies neither public welfare nor a body politic. An individual may conquer half the world, but he is still only an individual. His interests, wholly different from those of his subjects, are private to himself. When he dies his empire is left scattered and disintegrated. He is like an oak which crumbles and collapses in ashes so soon as the fire consumes it.

'A people', says Grotius, 'may give themselves to a king.' His argument implies that the said people were already a people before this act of surrender. The very act of gift was that of a political group and presupposed public deliberation. Before, therefore, we consider the act by which a people chooses their king, it were well if we considered the act by which a people is constituted as such. For it necessarily precedes the other, and is the true foundation on which all societies rest.

Had there been no original compact, why, unless the choice were unanimous, should the minority ever have agreed to accept the decision of the majority? What right have the hundred who desire a master to vote for the ten who do not? The institution of the franchise is, in itself, a form of compact, and assumes that, at least once in its operation, complete unanimity existed.

VI

Of the Social Pact

I assume, for the sake of argument, that a point was reached in this history of mankind when the obstacles to continuing in a state of nature were stronger than the forces which each individual could employ to the end of continuing in it. The original state of nature, therefore, could no longer endure, and the human race would have perished had it not changed its manner of existence.

Now, since men can by no means engender new powers, but can only unite and control those of which they are already possessed, there is no way in which they can maintain themselves save by coming together and pooling their strength in a way that will enable them to withstand any resistance exerted upon them from without. They must develop some sort of central direction and learn to act in concert.

Such a concentration of powers can be brought about only as the consequence of an agreement reached between individuals. But the self-preservation of each single man derives primarily from his own strength and from his own freedom. How, then, can he limit these without, at the same time, doing himself an injury and neglecting that care which it is his duty to devote to his own concerns? This difficulty, insofar as it is relevant to my subject, can be expressed as follows:

'Some form of association must be found as a result of which the whole strength of the community will be enlisted for the protection of the person and property of each constituent member, in such a way that each, when united to his fellows, renders obedience to his own will, and remains as free as he was before.' That is the basic problem of which the social contract provides the solution.

The clauses of this contract are determined by the act of association in such a way that the least modification must render them null and void. Even though they may never have been formally enunciated, they must be everywhere the same, and everywhere tacitly admitted and recognized. So completely must this be the case that, should the social compact be violated, each associated individual would at once resume all the rights which once were his, and regain his natural liberty, by the mere fact of losing the agreed liberty for which he renounced it.

It must be clearly understood that the clauses in question can be reduced, in the last analysis, to one only, to wit, the complete alienation by each associate member to the community of *all his rights*. For, in the first

place, since each has made surrender of himself without reservation, the resultant conditions are the same for all: and, because they are the same of all, it is in the interest of none to make them onerous to his fellows.

Furthermore, this alienation having been made unreservedly, the union of individuals is as perfect as it well can be, none of the associated members having any claim against the community. For should there be any rights left to individuals, and no common authority be empowered to pronounce as between them and the public, then each, being in some things his own judge, would soon claim to be so in all. Were that so, a state of nature would still remain in being, the conditions of association becoming either despotic or ineffective.

In short, whoso gives himself to all gives himself to none. And, since there is no member of the social group over whom we do not acquire precisely the same rights as those over ourselves which we have surrendered to him, it follows that we gain the exact equivalent of what we lose, as well as an added power to conserve what we already have.

If, then, we take from the social pact everything which is not essential to it, we shall find it to be reduced to the following terms: 'each of us contributes to the group his person and the powers which he wields as a person under the supreme direction of the general will, and we received into the body politic each individual as forming an indivisible part of the whole.'

As soon as the act of association becomes a reality, it substitutes for the person of each of the contracting parties a moral and collective body made up of as many members as the constituting assembly has votes, which body receives from this very act of constitution its unity, its dispersed *self*, and its will. The public person thus formed by the union of individuals was known in the old days as a *city*, but now as the *republic* or *body politic*. This, when it fulfils a passive role, is known by its members as *the state*, when an active one, as *the sovereign people*, and, in contrast to other similar bodies, as a *power*. In respect of the constituents associates, it enjoys the collective name of *the people*, the individuals who compose it being known as *citizens* insofar as they share in the sovereign authority, as *subjects* insofar as they owe obedience to the laws of the state. But these different terms frequently overlap, and are used indiscriminately one for the other. It is enough that we should realize the difference between them when they are employed in a precise sense.

VII

Of the Sovereign

It is clear from the above formula that the act of association implies a mutual undertaking between the body politic and its constituent members. Each individual comprising the former contracts, so the speak, with himself and has a twofold function. As a member of the sovereign people he owes a duty to each of his neighbours, and, as a citizen, to the sovereign people as a whole. But we cannot here apply that maxim of civil law according to which no man can be held to an undertaking entered into with himself, because there is a great difference between a man's duty to himself and to a whole of which he forms a part.

Here it should be pointed out that a public decision which can enjoin obedience on all subjects to their sovereign, by reason of the double aspect under which each is seen, cannot, on the contrary, bind the sovereign in his dealings with himself. Consequently, it is against the nature of the body politic that the sovereign should impose upon himself a law which he cannot infringe. For, since he can regard himself under one aspect only, he is in the position of an individual entering into a contract with himself. Whence it follows that there is not, nor can be, any fundamental law which is obligatory for the whole body of the people, not even the social contract itself. This does not mean that the body politic is unable to enter into engagements with some other power, provided always that such engagements do not derogate from the nature of the contract; for the relation of the body politic to a foreign power is that of a simple individual.

But the body politic, or sovereign, in that it derives its being simply and solely from the sanctity of the said contract, can never bind itself, even in its relations with a foreign power, by any decision which might derogate from the validity of the original act. It may not, for instance, alienate any portion of itself, nor make submission to any other sovereign. To violate the act by reason of which it exists would be tantamount to destroying itself, and that which is nothing can produce nothing.

As soon as a mob has become united into a body politic, any attack upon one of its members is an attack upon itself. Still more important is the fact that, should any offence be committed against the body politic as a whole, the effect must be felt by each of its members. Both duty and interest, therefore, oblige the two contracting parties to render one another mutual assistance. The same individuals should seek to unite under this double aspect all the advantages which flow from it.

Now, the sovereign people, having no existence outside that of the individuals who compose it, has, and can have, no interest at variance with theirs. Consequently, the sovereign power need give no guarantee to its subjects, since it is impossible that the body should wish to injure all its members, nor, as we shall see later, can it injure any single individual. The sovereign, by merely existing, is always what it should be.

But the same does not hold true of the relation of subject to sovereign. In spite of common interest, there can be no guarantee that the subject will observe his duty to the sovereign unless means are found to ensure his loyalty.

Each individual, indeed, may, as a man, exercise a will at variance with, or different from, that general will to which, as citizen, he contributes. His personal interest may dictate a line of action quite other than that demanded by the interest of all. The fact that his own existence as an individual has an absolute value, and that he is, by nature, an independent being, may lead him to conclude that what he owes to the common cause is something that he renders of his own free will; and he may decide that by leaving the debt unpaid he does less harm to his fellows than he would to himself should be make the necessary surrender. Regarding the moral entity constituting the state as a rational abstraction because it is not a man, he might enjoy his rights as a citizen without, at the same time, fulfilling his duties as a subject, and the resultant injustice might grow until it brought ruin upon the whole body politic.

In order, then, that the social compact may not be but a vain formula, it must contain, though unexpressed, the single undertaking which can alone give force to the whole, namely, that whoever shall refuse to obey the general will must be constrained by the whole body of his fellow citizens to do so: which is no more than to say that it may be necessary to compel a man to be free—freedom being that condition which, by giving each citizen to his country, guarantees him from all personal dependence and is the foundation upon which the whole political machine rests, and supplies the power which works it. Only the recognition by the individual of the rights of the community can give legal force to undertakings entered into between citizens, which, otherwise, would become absurd, tyrannical, and exposed to vast abuses.

VIII

Of the Civil State

The passage from the state of nature to the civil state produces a truly remarkable change in the individual. It substitutes justice for instinct in his behaviour, and gives to his actions a moral basis which formerly was lacking. Only when the voice of duty replaces physical impulse and when right replaces the cravings of appetite does the man who, till then, was concerned solely with himself, realize that he is under compulsion to obey quite different principles, and that he must now consult his reason and not merely respond to the promptings of desire. Although he may find himself deprived of many advantages which were his in a state of nature, he will recognize that he has gained others which are of far greater value. By dint of being exercised, his faculties will develop, his ideas take on a wider scope, his sentiments become ennobled, and his whole soul be so elevated, that, but for the fact that misuse of the new conditions still, at times, degrades him to a point below that from which he has emerged, he would unceasingly bless the day which freed him forever from his ancient state, and turned him from a limited and stupid animal into an intelligent being and a man.

Let us reduce all this to terms which can be easily compared. What a man loses as a result of the social contract is his natural liberty and his unqualified right to lay hands on all that tempts him, provided only that he can compass its possession. What he gains is civil liberty and the ownership of what belongs to him. That we may labour under no illusion concerning these compensations, it is well that we distinguish between natural liberty which the individual enjoys so long as he is strong enough to maintain it, and civil liberty which is curtailed by the general will; and between possessions which derive from physical strength and the right of the first-comer, and ownership which can be based only on a positive title.

To the benefits conferred by the status of citizenship might be added that of moral freedom, which alone makes a man his own master. For to be subject to appetite is to be a slave, while to obey the laws laid down by society is to be free. But I have already said enough on this point, and am not concerned here with the philosophical meaning of the word *liberty*.

IX

Of Real Property

Each individual member of the community gives himself to it at the moment of its formation. What he gives is the whole man as he then is, with all his qualities of strength and power, and everything of which he stands possessed. Not that, as a result of this act of gift, such possessions, by changing hands and becoming the property of the sovereign, change their nature. Just as the resources of strength upon which the city can draw are incomparably greater than those at the disposition of any single individual, so, too, is public possession when backed by a greater power. It is made more irrevocable, though not, so far, at least, as regards foreigners, more legitimate. For the state, by reason of the social contract which, within it, is the basis of all rights, is the master of all its members' goods, though, in its dealings with other powers, it is so only by virtue of its rights as first occupier, which come to it from the individuals who make it up.

The right of 'first occupancy', though more real than the 'right of the strongest', becomes a genuine right only after the right of property has been established. All men have a natural right to what is necessary to them. But the positive act which establishes a man's claim to any particular item of property limits him to that and excludes him from all others. His share having been determined, he must confine himself to that, and no longer has any claim on the property of the community. That is why the right of 'first occupancy', however weak it be in a state of nature, is guaranteed to every man enjoying the status of citizen. Insofar as he benefits from this right, he withholds his claim, not so much from what is another's, as from what is not specifically his.

In order that the right of 'first occupancy' may be legalized, the following conditions must be present. (1) There must be no one already living on the land in question. (2) A man must occupy only so much of it as is necessary for his subsistence. (3) He must take possession of it, not by empty ceremony, but by virtue of his intention of work and to cultivate it, for that, in the absence of legal title, alone constitutes a claim which will be respected by others.

In effect, by according the right of 'first occupancy' to a man's needs and to his will to work, are we not stretching it as far as it will go? Should not some limits be set to this right? Has a man only to set foot on land belonging to the community to justify his claim to be its master? Just because he is strong enough, at one particular moment, to keep others off, can he demand that they shall never return? How can a man or a people take possession of vast territories, thereby excluding the rest of the world from their enjoyment, save by an act of criminal usurpation, since, as the result of such an act, the rest of humanity is deprived of the amenities of dwelling and subsistence which nature has provided for their common enjoyment? When Nuñez Balboa, landing upon a strip of coast, claimed the Southern Sea and the whole of South America as the property of the crown of Castille, was he thereby justified in dispossessing its former inhabitants, and in excluding from it all the other princes of the earth? Grant that, and there will be no end to such vain ceremonies. It would be open to His Catholic Majesty to claim from his council chamber possession of the whole universe, only excepting those portions of it already in the ownership of other princes.

One can understand how the lands of individuals, separate but contiguous, become public territory, and how the right of sovereignty, extending from men to the land they occupy, becomes at once real and personal—a fact which makes their owners more than ever dependent, and turns their very strength into a guarantee of their fidelity. This is an advantage which does not seem to have been considered by the monarchs of the ancient world, who, claiming to be no more than kings of the Persians, the Scythians, the Macedonians, seem to have regarded themselves rather as the rulers of men than as the masters of countries. Those of our day are cleverer, for they style themselves kings of France, of Spain, of England, and so forth. Thus, by controlling the land, they can be very sure of controlling its inhabitants.

The strange thing about this act of alienation is that, far from depriving its members of their property by accepting its surrender, the community actually establishes their claim to its legitimate ownership, and changes what was formerly mere usurpation into a right, by virtue of which they may enjoy possession. As owners they are trustees for the Commonwealth. Their rights are respected by their fellow citizens and are maintained by the united strength of the community against any outside attack. From ceding their property to the

state—and thus, to themselves—they derive nothing but advantage, since they have, so to speak, acquired all that they have surrendered. This paradox is easily explained once we realize the distinction between the rights exercised by the sovereign and by the owner over the same piece of property, as will be seen later.

It may so happen that a number of men begin to group themselves into a community before ever they own property at all, and that only later, when they have got possession of land sufficient to maintain them all, do they either enjoy it in common or parcel it between themselves in equal lots or in accordance with such scale of proportion as may be established by the sovereign. However this acquisition be made, the right exercised by each individual over his own particular share must always be subordinated to the overriding claim of the community as such. Otherwise there would be no strength in the social bond, nor any real power in the exercise of sovereignty.

I will conclude this chapter, and the present book, with a remark which should serve as basis for every social system: that, so far from destroying natural equality, the primitive compact substitutes for it a moral and legal equality which compensates for all those physical inequalities from which men suffer. However unequal they may be in bodily strength or in intellectual gifts, they become equal in the eyes of the law, and as a result of the compact into which they have entered.

BOOK II

I

That Sovereignty Is Inalienable

The first, and most important, consequence of the principles so far established is that only the general will can direct the powers of the state in such a way that the purpose for which it has been instituted, which is the good of all, will be achieved. For if the establishment of societies has been made necessary by the antagonism that exists between particular interests, it has been made possible by the conformity that exists between these same interests. The bond of society is what there is in common between these different interests, and if there were not some point in which all interests were identical, no society could exist. The bond of society is that identity of interests which all feel who compose it. In the absence of such an identity no society would be possible. Now, it is solely on the basis of this common interest that society must be governed.

I maintain, therefore, that sovereignty, being no more than the exercise of the general will, can never be alienated, and that the sovereign, who is a collective being only, can be represented by no one but himself. Power can be transmitted, but not will. And though, in fact, it is possible that the will of the individual may, on some point, accord with the general will, what is impossible is that any such agreement should be durable and constant. For the will of the individual tends naturally to privilege, the general will to equality. Still more impossible is it that there should be any guarantee of such a harmony of interests, even where it exists, since chance only, and not contrivance, is the foundation upon which it rests. It is certainly open to the sovereign to say—'What I wish at this moment agrees with what this or that individual wishes or says that he wishes': but he cannot say, 'What he may wish tomorrow will conform in every respect to my wish,' it being absurd to think that will can bind itself in respect of the future, and it being no part of the function of will to consent to any action contrary to the will of him who wills. If, therefore, the people undertake simply and

solely to obey, they, by that very act, dissolve the social bond, and so lose their character as a people. Once the master appears upon the scene, the sovereign vanishes, and the body politic suffers destruction.

This is not to say that orders issued by the rulers may not take on the semblance of the general will, so long as the sovereign, free by definition to oppose them, does not do so. In such cases, general silence may be held to imply the people's consent. This I shall explain more at length.

II

That Sovereignty Is Indivisible

For the same reason that sovereignty is inalienable, so, too, is it indivisible. For either the will is general or it is not. Either it is the will of the whole body of the people, or it is the will merely of one section. In the first case, this declared will is an act of sovereignty, and has the force of law. In the second, it is partial only, or, in other words, an act imposed by government; and then, the most that can be said of it is that it is a decree.

But our politicians, finding it impossible to divide the principle of sovereignty, nonetheless divide its objects. Act is separated from will, legislative power from executive; the right to levying taxes from the right of administering justice or declaring war; the administering of internal affairs from that of treating with foreign powers. Sometimes we find these various aspects of government intermingled, sometimes divided. Those responsible for such division make of the sovereign a fantastic creature of shreds and patches. It is as though a man were to be composed of different bodies, the one having eyes, another arms, a third feet, but none furnished with more than a single set of organs. It is said that the conjurors of Japan will cut a child in pieces in full view of the audience, and then, casting the fragments into the air, bring them to earth again all duly assembled into a living infant. Such, or almost such, are the tricks performed by our modern men of politics. The body of the Commonwealth is first dismembered with an adroitness which would do credit to a country fair, and then reassembled, no one knows how.

This error arises from a mistaken notion of the nature of sovereign authority, and from treating as separable parts what, in fact, are only different manifestations. For instance, it has become customary to consider the declaration of war and the making of peace as separate acts of sovereignty. But this is not so, since neither act is a law but only an application of the law, determining the special way in which the law shall be understood; as will be abundantly clear when the idea of law shall have been accurately defined.

If we follow up similarly the other divided functions of sovereignty, we shall see that wherever it appears to be separated that is only because we are viewing it wrongly, taking for parts of the sovereign power what, in reality, are all subordinated to it, implying a supreme act of will which such rights only exist to realize in fact.

It would be difficult to exaggerate the confusion which this lack of clear thinking has caused in the minds of those authors who have set themselves to define the different fields in which, on the basis of the general rules which they have laid down, the rights of kings and the rights of the people are separately valid. It must be obvious to any reader of the third and fourth chapters of Grotius's first book, how hopelessly that learned writer, and his translator Barbeyrac, become bogged down and tangled in their own sophisms, fearing to deduce too much or too little from their own premises, or to set at odds those

very interests which they have been at pains to conciliate. Grotius, living in France as a refugee, and out of love with his own country, was anxious to win the favour of Louis XIII to whom his book was dedicated. Consequently, he spared no pains to strip the people of all their rights, and expended much art in an attempt to transfer all of them to the king. In this he would have had the full sympathy of Barbeyrac, who dedicated his translation to George I, King of England. Unfortunately, however, as the result of the expulsion of James II (which he called his 'abdication') he found himself compelled to watch his words with the greatest care, twisting and shuffling in his efforts not to show William III in the light of a usurper. Had these two men based their work on true principles, all difficulties would have vanished, and their arguments would have been consistent. They would have found themselves, with wry faces, telling the truth and paying court only to the people. But the way of truth is not the high road to fortune: nor are embassies, professorships, and pensions in the people's gift.

III

Whether the General Will Can Err

It follows from what has been said above that the general will is always right and ever tends to the public advantage. But it does not follow that the deliberations of the people are always equally beyond question. It is ever the way of men to wish their own good, but they do not at all times see where that good lies. The people are never corrupted though often deceived, and it is only when they are deceived that they appear to will what is evil.

There is often considerable difference between the will of all and the general will. The latter is concerned only with the common interest, the former with interests that are partial, being itself but the sum of individual wills. But take from the expression of these separate wills the pluses and minuses—which cancel out, the sum of the differences is left, and that is the general will.

If the people, engaged in deliberation, were adequately informed, and if no means existed by which the citizens could communicate one with another, from the great number of small differences the general will would result, and the decisions reached would always be good. But when intriguing groups and partial associations are formed to the disadvantage of the whole, then the will of each of such groups is general only in respect of its own members, but partial in respect of the state. When such a situation arises it may be said that there are no longer as many votes as men, but only as many votes as there are groups. Differences of interest are fewer in number, and the result is less general. Finally, when one of these groups becomes so large as to swamp all the others, the result is not the sum of small differences, but one single difference. The general will does not then come into play at all, and the prevailing opinion has no more validity than that of an individual man.

If, then, the general will is to be truly expressed, it is essential that there be no subsidiary groups within the state, and that each citizen voice his own opinion and nothing but his own opinion. It was the magnificent achievement of Lycurgus to have established the only state of this kind ever seen. But where subsidiary groups do exist their numbers should be made as large as possible, and none should be more powerful than its fellows. This precaution was taken by Solon, Numa, and Servius. Only if it is present will it be possible to ascertain the general will, and to make sure that the people are not led into error.

IV

Of the Limits of the Sovereign Power

If the state or the city is nothing but a moral person the life of which consists in the union of its members, and if the most important of its concerns is the maintenance of its own being, then if follows that it must have at its disposition a power of compulsion covering the whole field of its operations in order that it may be in a position to shift and adjust each single part in a way that shall be most beneficial to the whole. As nature gives to each man complete power over his limbs, so, too, the social compact gives to the body politic complete power over its members: and it is this power, directed by the general will, which, as I have already pointed out, bears the name of sovereignty.

But we have to consider not only the state as a public person, but those individual persons, too, who compose it, and whose lives and liberties are, in nature, independent of it. It is important, therefore, that we carefully distinguish between the rights of the citizens and the rights of the sovereign, between the duties which the former owe as subjects, and the natural rights which, as men, they are entitled to enjoy.

It is agreed that what, as a result of the social compact, each man alienates of power, property, and liberty is only so much as concerns the well-being of the community. But, further, it must be admitted that the sovereign alone can determine how much, precisely, this is.

Such services as the citizen owes to the state must be rendered by him whenever the sovereign demands. But the sovereign cannot lay upon its subjects any burden not necessitated by the well-being of the community. It cannot even wish to do so, for in the realm of reason, as of nature, nothing is ever done without cause.

The undertakings which bind us to the Commonwealth are obligatory only because they are mutual: their nature being such that we cannot labour for others without, at the same time, labouring for ourselves. For how can the general will be always right, and how can all constantly will the happiness of each, if every single individual does not include himself in that word *each*, so that in voting for the general interest he may feel that he is voting for his own? Which goes to show that the equality of rights and the idea of justice which it produces derive from the preference which each man has for his own concerns—in other words, from human nature: that the general will, if it be deserving of its name, must be general, not in its origins only, but in its objects, applicable to all as well as operated *by* all, and that it loses its natural validity as soon as it is concerned to achieve a merely individual and limited end, since, in that case, we, pronouncing judgment on something outside ourselves, cease to be possessed of that true principle of equity which is our guide.

In fact, as soon as issue is joined on some *particular* point, on some *specific* right arising out of a situation which has not previously been regulated by some form of general agreement, we are in the realm of debate. The matter becomes a trial in which certain interested individuals are ranged against the public, but where there is no certainty about what law is applicable nor about who can rightly act as judge. It would be absurd in such a case to demand an *ad hoc* decision of the general will, since the general will would then be the decision of one of the parties only. To the other it would appear in the guise of a pronouncement made by some outside power, sectarian in its nature, tending to injustice in the particular instance, and subject to error. Thus, just as the will of the individual cannot represent the

general will, so, too, the general will changes its nature when called upon to pronounce upon a particular object. Insofar as it is general, it cannot judge of an individual person or an isolated fact. When, for instance, the people of Athens appointed or removed their leaders, according honours to one and penalties to another: when, in other words, using the machinery supplied by a multiplicity of specific decrees, they exercised, in a muddled sort of way, all the functions of government, they ceased, strictly speaking, to have any general will at all, and behaved not as sovereign so much as magistrate. This statement may seem to be at variance with generally accepted ideas. I ask only that I may be granted time in which to develop my own. What makes the will general is not the number of citizens concerned but the common interest by which they are united. For in the sort of community with which I am dealing, each citizen necessarily submits to the conditions which he imposes on his neighbours. Whence comes that admirable identity of interest and justice which give to the common deliberations of the people a complexion of equity. When, however, discussion turns on specific issues, this complexion vanishes, because there is no longer any common interest uniting and identifying the pronouncement of the judge with that of the interested party.

No matter by what way we return to our general principle, the conclusion must always be the same, to wit, that the social compact establishes between all the citizens of the state a degree of equality such that all undertake to observe the same obligations and to claim the same rights. Consequently, by the very nature of the pact, every act of sovereignty—that is to say, every authentic act of the general will—lays the same obligations and confers the same benefits on all. The sovereign knows only the nation as a whole and does not distinguish between the individuals who compose it.

What, then, is a true act of sovereignty? It is not a convention established between a superior and an inferior, but between the body politic and each of its members: a convention having the force of law because it is based upon the social contract: equitable, because it affects all alike: useful, because its sole object is the general good: firm, because it is backed by public force and the supreme power. So long as the subjects of a state observe only conventions of this kind, they are obeying not a single person, but the decision of their own wills. To ask what are the limits of the respective rights of sovereign and citizens is merely to ask to what extent the latter can enter into an undertaking with themselves, each in relation to all, and all in relation to each.

From which it becomes clear that the sovereign power, albeit absolute, sacrosanct, and inviolable, does not, and cannot, trespass beyond the limits laid down by general agreement, and that every man has full title to enjoy whatever of property and freedom is left to him by that agreement. The sovereign is never entitled to lay a heavier burden on any one of its subjects than on others, for, should it do so, the matter would at once become particular rather than general, and, consequently, the sovereign power would no longer be competent to deal with it.

These distinctions once admitted, it becomes abundantly clear that to say that the individual, by entering into the social contract, makes an act of renunciation is utterly false. So far from that being the case, his situation within the contract is definitely preferable to what it was before. Instead of giving anything away, he makes a profitable bargain, exchanging peril and uncertainty for security, natural independence for true liberty, the power of injuring others for his own safety, the strength

of his own right arm—which others might always overcome—for a right which corporate solidity renders invincible. The life which he devotes to the state is, by the state, continually protected, and, when he offers it in the state's defence, what else is he doing than giving back the very boon which he has received at its hands? What, in such circumstances, does he do that he has not done more often and more perilously in a state of nature when, inevitably involved in mortal combat, he defended at the risk of his life what served him to maintain it? All citizens, it is true, may, should the need arise, have to fight for their country, but no one of them has ever to fight singly for himself. Is it not preferable, in the interest of what makes for our security, to run some part of the risks which we should have to face in our own defence, were the boon of forming one of a society taken from us?. . . .

VII

Of the Legislator

In order to discover what social regulations are best suited to nations, there is needed a superior intelligence which can survey all the passions of mankind, though itself exposed to none: an intelligence having no contact with out nature, yet knowing it to the full: an intelligence, the well-being of which is independent of our own, yet willing to be concerned with it: which, finally, viewing the long perspectives of time, and preparing for itself a day of glory as yet far distant, will labour in one century to reap its reward in another. In short, only gods can give laws to men.

The same argument which Caligula applied in practice Plato used in theory when, in his dialogue of *The Statesman*, he sought to define the nature of the civil or 'royal' man. But if it be true that a great prince occurs but rarely, what shall be said of a great law-giver? The first has but to follow the rules laid down by the latter. The law-giver invents the machine, the prince merely operates it. 'When societies first come to birth,' says Montesquieu, 'it is the leaders who produce the institutions of the Republic. Later, it is the institutions which produce the leaders.'

Whoso would undertake to give institutions to a people must work with full consciousness that he has set himself to change, as it were, the very stuff of human nature; to transform each individual who, in isolation, is a complete but solitary whole, into a part of something greater than himself, from which, in a sense, he derives his life and his being; to substitute a communal and moral existence for the purely physical and independent life with which we are all of us endowed by nature. His task, in short, to take from a man his own proper powers, and to give him in exchange powers foreign to him as a person, which he can use only if he is helped by the rest of the community. The more complete the death and destruction of his natural powers, the greater and more durable will those be which he acquires, and the more solid and perfect will that community be of which he forms a part. So true is this that the citizen by himself is nothing, and can do nothing, save with the co-operation of his neighbours, and the power acquired by the whole is equal or superior to the sum of the powers possessed by its citizens regarded as natural men. When that result has been achieved, and only then, can we say that the art of legislation has reached the highest stage of perfection of which it is capable.

The legislator must, in every way, be an extraordinary figure in the state. He is so by reason of his genius, and no less so by that of his office. He is neither magistrate nor sovereign. His function is to constitute the state, yet in its constitution it has no part to play. It exists in isolation, and is superior to other functions, having nothing to do with the governance of men. For if it be true that he who commands men should not ordain laws, so, too, he who ordains laws should be no longer in a position to command men. Were it otherwise, the laws, mere ministers to his passions, would often do no more than perpetuate his acts of injustice, nor could he ever avoid the danger that his views as a man might detract from the sanctity of his work.

When Lycurgus gave laws to his country, he began by abdicating his royal powers. It was a custom obtaining in most of the Greek city-states, that the framing of their constitutions should be entrusted to foreigners. This practice has not seldom been copied in modern times by the republics of Italy, and was adopted by the state of Geneva, where it worked well. Rome, in her greatest age, saw all the crimes of tyranny revive within her frontiers, and was near to perishing, simply because she had united in the same hands legislative authority and sovereign power.

For all that, the Decemvirs never arrogated to themselves the power to establish any law on their own authority. 'Nothing of what we propose,' they said to the people, 'can become law without your consent. Romans, be yourselves the authors of those laws which are to ensure your happiness.'

Whoso codifies the laws of a community, therefore, has not, or should not have, any legislative right, a right that is incommunicable, and one of which the people, even should they wish to do so, cannot divest themselves. For, by reason of the social compact, the general will alone can constrain the individual citizen: nor is there any other way of making sure that the will of the individual is in conformity with the general will, save by submitting it to the free votes of the people. This I have said once already; but it is well that it should be repeated.

Two things, therefore, seemingly incompatible, are to be found within the operation of law-making—it is a task beyond the capabilities of mere humans to perform: for its execution we are offered an authority which is a thing of naught.

There is another difficulty, too, that demands attention. Those wise men who, in speaking to the vulgar herd, would use not its language but their own, will never be understood. Many thousands of ideas there are which cannot be translated into popular phraseology. Excessive generalizations and long-range views are equally beyond the comprehension of the average man, who, as a rule, approves only such schemes, in matters of government, as will redound to his personal advantage. He finds it difficult to see what benefit he is likely to derive from the ceaseless privations which good laws will impose upon him. For a young people to understand fully the pondered maxims of the statesman and to follow the rules of conduct which are essential to healthy community life, would be for the effect to precede the cause. For such a thing to happen, the social spirit which can be the product only of a country's institutions would have, in fact, to be present at their birth, and, even before the laws are operative, the citizen would have to be such as those same laws would make him. Since, then, the legislator can use neither force nor argument, he must, of necessity, have recourse to authority of a different kind which can lead without violence and persuade without convincing.

That is why, in all periods, the fathers of their country have been driven to seek the intervention of Heaven, attributing to the gods a wisdom that was really their own, in order that the people, subjected to the laws of the state no less than to those of nature, and recognizing in the creation of the city the same power at work as in that of its inhabitants, might freely obey and might bear with docility the yoke of public happiness. The legislator, by putting into the mouths of the immortals that sublime reasoning which is far beyond the reach of poor mankind, will, under the banner of divine authority, lead those to whom mere mortal prudence would ever be a stumbling-block. But it is not within the competence of every man to make the gods speak, nor to get himself believed when he claims to be their interpreter. The real miracle, and the one sufficient proof of the legislator's mission, is his own greatness of soul. Anyone can incise words on stone, bribe an oracle, claim some secret understanding with a high divinity, train a bird to whisper in his ear, or invent other ways, no less crude, for imposing on the people. He whose powers go no farther than that, may, if he be fortunate, hold the attention of a superstitious mob: but he will never found an empire, and his extravagant production will, in no long time, perish with him. Authority which has no true basis forms but a fragile bond. Only in wisdom can it find hope of permanence. The Jewish law still lives, and the law of the child of Ishmael which, for ten centuries, has regulated the conduct of half the world. They bear witness, even today, to the great men who gave them form. To the eyes of pride bred of philosophy or the blind spirit of party, they may seem no more than fortunate impostors, but true political wisdom will ever admire in their institutions the great and powerful genius which watches over the birth of civilizations destined to endure.

We should not, from all this, conclude, with Warburton, that politics and religion have, in the modern world, the self-same aim, but rather that, in the forming of nations, the one serves as the other's instrument. . . .

BOOK IV

I

That the General Will Is Indestructible

So long as a number of men assembled together regard themselves as forming a single body, they have but one will, which is concerned with their common preservation and with the well-being of all. When this is so, the springs of the state are vigorous and simple, its principles plain and clear-cut. It is not encumbered with confused or conflicting interests. The common good is everywhere plainly in evidence and needs only good sense to be perceived. Peace, unity, and equality are the foes of political subtlety. Upright and simple men are hard to deceive by the very reason of their simplicity. Lures and plausible sophistries have no effect upon them, nor are they even sufficiently subtle to become dupes. When one sees, in the happiest country in all the world, groups of peasants deciding the affairs of state beneath an oak tree, and behaving with a constancy of wisdom, can one help but despise the refinements of other nations which, at so great an expense of skill and mystification, make themselves at once illustrious and wretched?

A state thus governed has need of very few laws, and when it is found necessary to promulgate new ones, the necessity will be obvious to all. He who actually voices the proposal does but put into words what all have felt, and neither intrigue nor eloquence are needed to ensure the passing into law of what each has already determined to do so soon as he can be assured that his fellows will follow suit.

What sets theorists on the wrong tack is that, seeing only those states which have been badly constituted from the beginning, they are struck by the impossibility of applying such a system to *them*. The thought of all the follies which a clever knave with an insinuating tongue could persuade the people of Paris or of London to commit, makes them laugh. What they do not know is that Cromwell would have been put in irons by the people of Berne, and the Duc de Beaufort sent to hard labour by the Genevese.

But when the social bond begins to grow slack, and the state to become weaker; when the interests of individuals begin to make themselves felt, and lesser groups within the state to influence the state as a whole, then the common interest suffers a change for the worse and breeds opposition. No longer do men speak with a single voice, no longer is the general will the will of all. Contradictions appear, discussions arise, and even the best advice is not allowed to pass unchallenged.

Last stage of all, when the state, now near its ruin, lives on only in a vain and deceptive form, when the bond of society is broken in all men's hearts, when the vilest self-interest bears insolently the scared name of commonweal, then does the general will fall dumb. All, moved by motives unavowed, express their views as though such a thing as the state had never existed, and they were not citizens at all. In such circumstances, unjust decrees, aiming only at the satisfaction of private interests, can be passed under the guise of laws.

Does it follow from this that the general will is destroyed or corrupted? No; it remains constant, unalterable, and pure, but it becomes subordinated to other wills which encroach upon it. Each, separating his interest from the interest of all, sees that such separation cannot be complete, yet the part he plays in the general damage seems to him as nothing compared with the exclusive good which he seeks to appropriate. With the single exception of the particular private benefit at which he aims, he still desires the public good, realizing that it is likely to benefit him every whit as much as his neighbours. Even when he sells his vote for money, he does not extinguish the general will in himself, but merely eludes it. The fault that he commits is to change the form of the question, and to answer something which he was not asked. Thus, instead of saying, through the medium of his vote, 'This is of advantage to the state,' he says, 'It is to the advantage of this or that individual that such and such a proposition become law.' And so the law of public order in assemblies is not so much the maintenance of the general will, as the guarantee that it shall always be asked to express itself and shall always respond.

I might say much at this point on the simple right of voting in every act of sovereignty, a right of which nothing can deprive the citizen—and on that of speaking, proposing, dividing, and discussing: a right which the government is always very careful to leave only to its members: but this important matter would require a whole treatise to itself, and I cannot cover the whole ground in this one.

II

Of Voting

It is clear, from what has just been said, that the manner in which public affairs are conducted can give a pretty good indication of the state of a society's morale and general health. The greater the harmony when the citizens are assembled, the more predominant is the general will. But long debates, dissension, and uproar all point to the fact that private interests are in the ascendant and that the state as a whole has entered on a period of decline.

This seems less evident when two or more social orders are involved, as, in Rome, the patricians and the plebs, whose quarrels so often troubled the *comitia* even in the best days of the Republic. But this exception is more apparent than real. For, in such circumstances, there are, so to speak, because of a vice inherent in political bodies, two states in one. What is not true of the two together is true of each separately. Indeed, even in the most stormy times, the *plebiscita* of the Roman people, when the Senate did not interfere, were always passed quietly and by a large majority of votes. The citizens having but one interest, the people had but a single will.

At the other extremity of the scale unanimity returns; when, that is to say, the citizens, having fallen into servitude, have no longer either liberty or will. When that happens, fear and flattery transform votes into acclamations. Men no longer deliberate, they worship or they curse. In this base manner did the Senate express its views under the Emperors, sometimes with absurd precautions. Tacitus relates that, in the reign of Otho, the senators, in heaping execrations on Vitellius, were careful to make so great a din that, should he chance to become their master, he would not be able to tell what any one of them had said.

From these various considerations spring those general rules which should regulate the manner of counting votes and comparing opinions, according as whether the general will is more or less easily to be discerned, and the state more or less in a condition of decline.

There is one law only which, by its very nature, demands unanimous consent, and that is the social pact. For civil association is, of all acts, the most deliberately willed. Since every man is born free and his own master, none, under any pretext whatsoever, can enslave him without his consent. To decide that the son of a slave is born a slave is tantamount to saying that he is not born a man.

If, then, when the social pact is made, voices are raised in opposition, such opposition does not invalidate the contract, but merely excludes from it those who voice it, so that they become foreigners among the general body of the citizens. When the state is instituted, residence implies consent. To live in a country means to submit to its sovereignty.

In all matters other than this fundamental contract, a majority vote is always binding on all. This is a consequence of the contract itself. But, it may be asked, how can a man be free and yet constrained to conform to a will which is not his own? How comes it that the members of the opposition can be at the same time free and yet subject to laws which they have not voted?

My reply to this is that the question is wrongly put. The citizen consents to all the laws, even to those which have been passed in spite of him, even to those which will visit punishment upon him should he dare to violate any of them. The constant will of all the members of a state is the general will, and by virtue of it they are citizens and free men. When a law is proposed in the assembly of the people, what they are asked is not whether they approve or reject the proposal in question, but whether it is or is not in conformity will the general will, which is *their* will. It is on this point that the citizen expresses his opinion when he records his vote, and from the counting of the votes proceeds the declaration of the general will. When, therefore, a view which is at odds with my own wins the day, it proves only that I was deceived, and that what I took to be the general will was no such thing. Had my own opinion won, I should have done something quite other than

I wished to do, and in that case I should not have been free. True, this assumes that all the characteristics of the general will are still in the majority. When that ceases to be the case, no matter what side we are on, liberty has ceased to exist.

When I showed above how the wills of individuals come to be substituted for the general will in public deliberation, I made sufficiently clear what practical means existed for preventing this abuse. I shall have more to say on this point below. In regard to the proportional number of votes needed to declare this will, I have also stated the principles on which it can be determined. The difference of a single vote destroys equality: one voice raised in opposition makes unanimity impossible. But between unanimity and equality there are many unequal divisions, at each of which this number can be fixed as the state and the needs of the body politic may demand.

Two general rules may serve to regulate this proportion: one, that the more important and solemn the matters under discussion, the nearer to unanimity should the voting be: two, that the more it is necessary to settle the matter speedily, the less should be the difference permitted in balancing the votes for and against. Where a verdict must be obtained at a single sitting, a majority of one should be held to be sufficient. The first of these rules seems to be more suited to the passing of laws, the second to the transaction of business. Be that as it may, only a combination of them can give the best proportion for the determining of majorities.

Study Questions for the *Discourse on the Origin of Inequality*

1. What distinction in types of inequality does Rousseau make in the Exordium?
2. In what respect have social philosophers failed to understand the state of nature, according to Rousseau?
3. What characteristics distinguish human beings from other animals?
4. What is Rousseau's criticism of Hobbes's view of the state of nature?
5. What is the foundation of inequalities among humankind? What relationship does Rousseau see between inequality and the institution of private property?
6. Trace the origin of political society as Rousseau describes it. What reasons does Rousseau provide in favour of his account of the origin of governments?

Study Questions for *Of the Social Contract*

1. Explain Rousseau's claim that 'man is born free, and everywhere he is in chains.'
2. Why does Rousseau reject the idea that the strongest have the right to rule?
3. What is the essence of the social pact, according to Rousseau? What is the relationship among citizens, the sovereign, and the general will?
4. Rousseau notes that citizens who refuse to obey the general will should be 'forced to be free.' How should we interpret this paradoxical claim? Is Rousseau supportive of totalitarianism?
5. What benefits do human beings gain in transitioning from the state of nature to civil society? Describe Rousseau's distinction between the freedom we possess in the state of nature and the freedom we possess in civil society.
6. Describe Rousseau's ideal legislator. Why does Rousseau claim that a people as a whole, rather than a legislator, should create law?

Recommended Readings

Cassirer, Ernst, *The Question of Jean-Jacques Rousseau*, translated and edited by Peter Gay (Indiana University Press, 1963).

Damrosch, Leo, *Jean-Jacques Rousseau: Restless Genius* (Houghton Mifflin, 2005).

Gildin, Hilail, *Rousseau's Social Contract* (University of Chicago Press, 1982).

Masters, Roger, *The Political Philosophy of Rousseau* (Princeton University Press, 1968).

Melzer, Arthur, *The Natural Goodness of Man: The System of Rousseau's Thought* (University of Chicago Press, 1990).

Miller, James, *Rousseau: Dreamer of Democracy* (Yale University Press, 1984).

Okin, Susan Moller, *Women in Western Political Thought*, Part 3 (Princeton University Press, 1979).

Rousseau, Jean-Jacques, *Emile: Or, On Education*, introduction, translation and notes by Allan Bloom (Basic Books, 1979).

Schwartz, Joel, *The Sexual Politics of Jean-Jacques Rousseau* (University of Chicago Press, 1984).

Shklar, Judith, *Men and Citizens: A Study of Rousseau's Social Theory* (Cambridge University Press, 1969).

David Hume

David Hume (1711–1776) was born in Scotland to a family of lawyers and attended the University of Edinburgh as a young man. After studying law for approximately three years, he left the university without a degree and began a self-directed course of reading and studying at home. For most of his twenties, Hume laboured on his philosophical masterpiece, *A Treatise of Human Nature* (1739–40), which was published anonymously when Hume was only 28. Although the treatise was not a popular success, it did create a reputation for Hume as a skeptic and an atheist, which undermined his candidacy for academic positions as a professor of philosophy. Hume supported himself through positions as a tutor, a military secretary, and a librarian, while writing widely on philosophy and history. From 1752 to 1762, Hume published a six-volume history of England, which propelled him into literary fame in England and France. His major philosophical writings include an *Enquiry Concerning Human Understanding* (1748), *Dialogues Concerning Natural Religion* (published posthumously in 1779), and *Essays Moral and Political* (1741–42), which contains our selection, *Of the Original Contract*.

Until the time of his death, Hume's major philosophical writings did not receive the attention accorded his historical writings and political essays. He died unaware that his work in metaphysics, epistemology, and the philosophy of religion would have powerful impact on philosophical thought and establish him as a leading figure among modern philosophers. In time, Hume became known for his boldly skeptical and empirical approaches to a variety of philosophical problems, including the problem of personal identity, the existence of God, and the phenomena of causality and miraculous occurrences. In moral and political philosophy, Hume developed the first purely secular theory of moral obligation, emphasizing utility, liberty, and a natural moral sense. He influenced not only the classical utilitarian theorists Jeremy Bentham and John Stuart Mill but also Immanuel Kant, whom he awoke from his 'dogmatic slumbers'.

In social and political philosophy, Hume delves into the classical issues of liberty, authority, property, and justice, in addition to writing on economic theory and contract theory. His *Of the Original Contract* addresses the claim of modern social contract theorists that political authority is founded upon an original contract between citizens and governments. Appealing to the evidence of history and the observation of facts, Hume notes that generations of citizens have displayed knowledge of neither an original contract nor an inalienable natural right to private property. Present governments are often founded upon usurpation, unlawful succession, and conquest rather than upon any expressed or tacit consent of citizens. Nevertheless, Hume suggests, preserving a society requires a duty of civic allegiance to magistrates; the justification were always full of licence and disorder, notwithstanding the institutions and laws by which they were checked; how much more disorderly must they prove, where they form not the established constitution, but meet tumultuously on the dissolution of the ancient government, in order to give rise to a new one? How chimerical must it be to talk of a choice in such circumstances?

The Achæans enjoyed the freest and most perfect democracy of all antiquity; yet they employed force to oblige some cities to enter into their league, as we learn from Polybius.

Harry the IVth and Harry the VIIth of England, had really no title to the throne but a parliamentary election; yet they never would acknowledge it, lest they should thereby weaken, their authority. Strange, if the only real foundation of all authority be consent and promise?

It is in vain to say, that all governments are, or should be, at first, founded on popular consent, as much as the necessity of human affairs will admit. This favours entirely my pretension. I maintain, that human affairs will never admit of this consent, seldom of the appearance of it; but that conquest or usurpation, that is, in plain terms, force, by dissolving the ancient governments, is the origin of almost all the new ones which were ever established in the world. And that in the few cases where consent may seem to have taken place, it was commonly so irregular, so confined, or so much intermixed either with fraud or violence, that it cannot have any great authority.

My intention here is not to exclude the consent of the people from being one just foundation of government where it has place. It is surely the best and most sacred of any. I only pretend, that it has very seldom had place in any degree, and never almost in its full extent; and that, therefore, some other foundation of government must also be admitted.

Were all men possessed of so inflexible a regard to justice, that, of themselves, they would totally abstain from the properties of others; they had forever remained in a state of absolute liberty, without subjection to any magistrate or political society: but this is a state of perfection, of which human nature is justly deemed incapable. Again, were all men possessed of so perfect an understanding as always to know their own interests, no form of government had ever been submitted to but what was established on consent, and was fully canvassed by every member of the society: but this state of perfection is likewise much superior to human nature. Reason, history, and experience show us, that all political societies have had an origin much less accurate and regular; and were one to choose a period of time when the people's consent was the least regarded in public transactions, it would be precisely on the establishment of a new government. In a settled constitution their inclinations are often consulted; but during the fury of revolutions, conquests, and public convulsions, military force or political craft usually decides the controversy.

When a new government is established, by whatever means, the people are commonly dissatisfied with it, and pay obedience more from fear and necessity, than from any idea of allegiance or of moral obligation. The prince is watchful and jealous, and must carefully guard against every beginning or appearance of insurrection. Time, by degrees, removes all these difficulties, and accustoms the nation to regard, as their lawful or native princes, that family which at first they considered as usurpers or foreign conquerors. In order to found this opinion, they have no recourse to any notion of voluntary consent or promise, which, they know, never was, in this case, either expected or demanded. The original establishment was formed by violence, and submitted to from necessity. The subsequent administration is also supported by power, and acquiesced in by the people, not as a matter of choice, but of obligation. They imagine not that their consent gives their prince a title: but they willingly consent, because they think, that, from long possession, he has acquired a title, independent of their choice or inclination.

Should it be said, that, by living under the dominion of a prince which one might leave, every individual has given a *tacit* consent to his authority, and promised him obedience; it may be answered, that such an implied consent can only have place where a man imagines that the matter depends on his choice. But where he thinks (as all mankind do who are born under established governments) that, by his birth, he owes allegiance to a certain prince or certain form of government; it would be absurd to infer a consent or choice, which he expressly, in this case, renounces and disclaims.

Can we seriously say, that a poor peasant or artisan has a free choice to leave his country, when he knows no foreign language or manners, and lives, from day to day, by the small wages which he acquires? We may as well assert that a man, by remaining in a vessel, freely consents to the dominion of the master; though he was carried on board while asleep, and must leap into the ocean and perish, the moment he leaves her.

What if the prince forbid his subjects to quit his dominions; as in Tiberius's time, it was regarded as a crime in a Roman knight that he had attempted to fly to the Parthians, in order to escape the tyranny of that emperor? Or as the ancient Muscovites prohibited all travelling under pain of death? And did a prince observe, that many of his subjects were seized with the frenzy of migrating to foreign countries, he would, doubtless, with great reason and justice, restrain them, in order to prevent the depopulation of his own kingdom. Would he forfeit the allegiance of all his subjects by so wise and reasonable a law? Yet the freedom of their choice is surely, in that case, ravished from them.

A company of men, who should leave their native country, in order to people some uninhabited region, might dream of recovering their native freedom; but they would soon find, that their prince still laid claim to them, and called them his subjects, even in their new settlement. And in this he would but act conformably to the common ideas of mankind.

The truest *tacit* consent of this kind that is ever observed, is when a foreigner settles in any country, and is beforehand acquainted with the prince, and government, and laws, to which he must submit: yet is his allegiance, though more voluntary, much less expected or depended on, than that of a natural born subject. On the contrary, his native prince still asserts a claim to him. And if he punish not the renegade, when he seizes him in war with his new prince's commission; this clemency is not founded on the municipal law, which in all countries condemns the prisoner; but on the consent of princes, who have agreed to this indulgence, in order to prevent reprisals.

Did one generation of men go off the stage at once, and another succeed, as is the case with silkworms and butterflies, the new race, if they had sense enough to choose their government, which surely is never the case with men, might voluntarily, and by general consent, establish their own form of civil polity, without any regard to the laws or precedents which prevailed among their ancestors. But as human society is in perpetual flux, one man every hour going out of the world, another coming into it, it is necessary, in order to preserve stability in government, that the new brood should conform themselves to the established constitution, and nearly follow the path which their fathers, treading in the footsteps of theirs, had marked out to them. Some innovations must necessarily have place in every human institution; and it is happy where the enlightened genius of the age give these a direction to the side of reason, liberty, and justice: but violent innovations no individual is entitled to make: they are even dangerous to be attempted by the legislature: more ill than good is ever to be expected from them: and if history affords examples to the contrary, they are not to be drawn into precedent, and are only to be regarded as proofs, that the science of politics affords few rules, which will not admit of some exception, and which may not sometimes be controlled by fortune and accident. The violent innovations in the reign of Henry VIII proceeded from an imperious monarch, seconded by the appearance of legislative authority: those in the reign of Charles I were derived from faction and fanaticism; and both of them have proved happy in the issue. But even the former were long the source of many disorders, and still more dangers; and if the measures of allegiance were to be taken from the latter, a total anarchy must have place in human society, and a final period at once be put to every government.

Suppose that a usurper, after having banished his lawful prince and royal family, should establish his dominion for ten or a dozen years in any country, and should preserve so exact a discipline in his troops, and so regular a disposition in his garrisons that no insurrection had ever been raised, or even murmur heard against his administration: can it be asserted that the people, who in their hearts abhor his treason, have tacitly consented to his authority, and promised him allegiance, merely because, from necessity, they live under his dominion? Suppose again their native prince restored, by means of an army, which he levies in foreign countries: they receive him with joy and exultation, and show plainly with what reluctance they had submitted to any other yoke. I may now ask, upon what foundation the prince's title stands? Not on popular consent surely: for though the people willingly acquiesce in his authority, they never imagine that their consent made him sovereign. They consent; because they apprehend him to be already by birth, their lawful sovereign. And as to that tacit consent, which may now be inferred from their living under his dominion, this is no more than what they formerly gave to the tyrant and usurper.

When we assert, that all lawful government arises from the consent of the people, we certainly do them a great deal more honour than they deserve, or even expect and desire from us. After the Roman dominions became too unwieldy for the republic to govern them, the people over the whole known world were extremely grateful to Augustus for that authority which, by violence, he had established over them; and they showed an equal disposition to submit to the successor whom he left them by his last will and testament. It was afterwards their misfortune, that there never was, in one family, any long regular succession; but that their line of princes was continually broken, either by private assassinations or public rebellions. The *prætorian* bands, on the failure of every family, set up one emperor; the legions in the East a second; those in Germany, perhaps a third; and the sword alone could decide the controversy. The condition of the people in that mighty monarchy was to be lamented, not because the choice of the emperor was never left to them, for that was impracticable, but because they never fell under any succession of masters who might regularly follow each other. As to the violence, and wars, and bloodshed, occasioned by every new settlement, these were not blameable, because they were inevitable.

The house of Lancaster ruled in this island about 60 years; yet the partisans of the white rose seemed daily to multiply in England. The present establishment has taken place during a still longer period. Have all views of right in another family been utterly extinguished, even though scarce any man now alive had arrived at the years of discretion when it was expelled, or could have consented to its dominion, or have promised it allegiance?—a sufficient indication, surely, of the general sentiment of mankind on this head. For we blame not the partisans of the abdicated family merely on account of the long time during which they have preserved their imaginary loyalty. We blame them for adhering to a family which we affirm has been justly expelled, and which, from the moment the new settlement took place, had forfeited all title to authority.

But would we have a more regular, at least a more philosophical, refutation of this principle of an original contract, or popular consent, perhaps the following observations may suffice.

All *moral* duties may be divided into two kinds. The *first* are those to which men are impelled by a natural instinct or immediate propensity which operates on them, independent of all ideas of obligation, and of all views either to public or private utility. Of this nature are love of children, gratitude to benefactors, pity to the unfortunate. When we reflect on the advantage which results to society from such humane instincts, we pay them the just tribute of moral approbation and esteem: but the person actuated by them feels their power and influence antecedent to any such reflection.

The *second* kind of moral duties are such as are not supported by any original instinct of nature, but are performed entirely from a sense of obligation, when we consider the necessities of human society, and the impossibility of supporting it, if these duties were neglected. It is thus *justice*, or a regard to the property of others, and *fidelity*, or the observance of promises, become obligatory, and acquire an authority over mankind. For as it is evident that every man loves himself better than any other person, he is naturally impelled to extend his acquisitions as much as possible; and nothing can restrain him in this propensity but reflection and experience, by which he learns the pernicious effects of that licence, and the total dissolution of society which must ensue from it. His original inclination, therefore, or instinct, is here checked and restrained by a subsequent judgment or observation.

The case is precisely the same with the political or civil duty of *allegiance* as with the natural duties of justice and fidelity. Our primary instincts lead us either to indulge ourselves in unlimited freedom, or to seek dominion over others; and it is reflection only which engages us to sacrifice such strong passions to the interests of peace and public order. A small degree of experience and observation suffices to teach us, that society cannot possibly be maintained without the authority of magistrates, and that this authority must soon fall into contempt where exact obedience is not paid to it. The observation of these general and obvious interests is the source of all allegiance, and of that moral obligation which we attribute to it.

What necessity, therefore, is there to found the duty of *allegiance* or obedience to magistrates on that of *fidelity* or a regard to promises, and to suppose, that it is the consent of each individual which subjects him to government, when it appears that both allegiance and fidelity stand precisely on the same foundation, and are both submitted to by mankind, on account of the apparent interests and necessities of human society? We are bound to obey our sovereign, it is said, because we have given a tacit promise to that purpose. But why are we bound to observe our promise? It must here be asserted, that the commerce and intercourse of mankind, which are of such mighty advantage, can have no security where men pay no regard to their engagements. In like manner, may it be said that men could not live at all in society, at least in a civilized society, without laws, and magistrates, and judges, to prevent the encroachments of the strong upon the weak, of the violent upon the just and equitable. The obligation to allegiance being of like force and authority with the obligation to fidelity, we gain nothing by resolving the one into the other. The general interests or necessities of society are sufficient to establish both.

If the reason be asked of that obedience, which we are bound to pay to government, I readily answer, *Because society could not otherwise subsist*; and this answer is clear and intelligible to all mankind. Your answer is, *Because we should keep our word.* But besides, that nobody, till trained in a philosophical system, can either comprehend or relish this answer; besides this, I say, you find yourself embarrassed when it is asked, *Why we are bound to keep our word?* Nor can you give any answer but what would, immediately, without any circuit, have accounted for our obligation to allegiance.

But *to whom is allegiance due? And who is our lawful sovereign?* This question is often the most difficult of any, and liable to infinite discussions. When people are so happy that they can answer, *Our present sovereign, who inherits, in a direct line, from ancestors that have governed us for many ages,* this answer admits of no reply, even though historians, in tracing up to the remotest antiquity the origin of that royal family, may find, as commonly happens, that its first authority was derived from usurpation and violence. It is confessed that private justice, or the abstinence from the properties of others, is a most cardinal virtue. Yet reason tells us that there is no property in durable objects, such as lands or houses, when carefully examined in passing from hand to hand, but must, in some period, have been founded on fraud and injustice. The necessities of human society, neither in private nor public life, will allow of such an accurate inquiry; and there is no virtue or moral duty but what may, with facility, be refined away, if we indulge a false philosophy in sifting and scrutinizing it, by every captious rule of logic, in every light or position in which it may be placed.

The questions with regard to private property have filled infinite volumes of law and philosophy, if in both we add the commentators to the original text; and in the end, we may safely pronounce, that many of the rules there established are uncertain, ambiguous, and arbitrary. The like opinion may be formed with regard to the succession and rights of princes, and forms of government. Several cases no doubt occur, especially in the infancy of any constitution, which admit of no determination from the laws of justice and equity; and our historian Rapin pretends, that the controversy between Edward the Third and Philip de Valois was of this nature, and could be decided only by an appeal to Heaven, that is, by war and violence. . . .

We shall only observe, before we conclude, that though an appeal to general opinion may justly, in the speculative sciences of metaphysics, natural philosophy, or astronomy, be deemed unfair and inconclusive, yet in all questions with regard to morals, as well as criticism, there is really no other standard, by which any controversy can ever be decided. And nothing is a clearer proof, that a theory of this kind is erroneous, than to find, that it leads to paradoxes repugnant to the common sentiments of mankind, and to the practice and opinion of all nations and all ages. The doctrine, which founds all lawful government on an *original contract*, or consent of the people, is plainly of this kind; nor has the most noted of its partisans, in prosecution of it, scrupled to affirm, *that absolute monarchy is inconsistent with civil society, and so can be no form of civil government at all; and that the supreme power in a state cannot take from any man, by taxes and impositions, any part of his property, without his own consent or that of his representatives.* What authority any moral reasoning can have, which leads into opinions so wide of the general practice of mankind, in every place but this single kingdom, it is easy to determine.

The only passage I meet with in antiquity, where the obligation of obedience to government is ascribed to a promise, is in Plato's *Crito*; where Socrates refuses to escape from prison, because he had tacitly promised to obey the laws. Thus he builds a *Tory* consequence of passive obedience on a *Whig* foundation of the original contract.

New discoveries are not to be expected in these matters. If scarce any man, till very lately, ever imagined that government was founded on compact, it is certain that it cannot, in general, have any such foundation.

Study Questions for *Of the Original Contract*

1. At the beginning of *Of the Original Contract*, Hume notes his agreement with some of the basic premises of the modern social contract theorists. Which premises of the contract theorists does Hume accept?
2. Explain Hume's main criticisms of social contract theories. What does Hume say against the idea that an original contract has a morally binding force upon present generations? What does he say against the idea of tacit consent?
3. Explain the distinction Hume draws between natural moral duties and moral duties founded upon social communities. What is the foundation of civic obligation and the duty of allegiance to magistrates, for Hume?
4. Does Hume's final solution to the problem of civic obligation devolve into a Hobbesian argument for absolute political authority? Discuss.

Recommended Readings

Forbes, Duncan, *Hume's Philosophical Politics* (Cambridge University Press, 1975).

Hume, David, Essays *Moral, Political, and Literary*, edited by Eugene F. Miller (Liberty Classics, 1985).

Livingston, Donald, *Philosophical Melancholy and Delirium* (University of Chicago Press, 1998).

———— *Hume's Philosophy of Common Life* (University of Chicago Press, 1984).

MacIntyre, Alasdair, *Whose Justice? Which Rationality?* (University of Notre Dame Press, 1988).

Miller, David, *Philosophy and Ideology in Hume's Political Thought* (Clarendon Press, 1981).

Mossner, Ernest Campbell, *The Life of David Hume*, 2nd edn (Clarendon Press, 1980).

Smith, Norman Kemp, *The Philosophy of David Hume: A Critical Study of Its Origins and Central Doctrines* (Macmillan, 1964).

Stewart, John, *Opinion and Reform in Hume's Political Philosophy* (Princeton University Press, 1992).

Tweyman, Stanley, ed., *David Hume: Critical Assessments*, vol. 6: Politics, *Economics, Justice, Miscellaneous* (Routledge, 1995).

Whelan, Fredrick, *Order and Artifice in Hume's Political Thought* (Princeton University Press, 1985).

PART III

Nineteenth-Century Philosophers

John Stuart Mill and Harriet Taylor Mill

The British philosopher John Stuart Mill (1806–1873) was born the son of James Mill, who was a political philosopher and friend of the famous utilitarian Jeremy Bentham. James Mill and Jeremy Bentham sought to shape John Stuart Mill into an intellectual giant who would carry forward a utilitarian political agenda without the distractions of sentiment, religion, art, poetry, or speculative metaphysics. Mill learned Greek at the age of three, Latin by eight, and was competent in advanced mathematics, logic, and economics by the time he was a teenager. But at the age of 20, he suffered an intellectual and emotional breakdown resulting from his rigorous but sterile education. In recovering from his collapse, Mill turned to reading the romantic poetry of Wordsworth and Coleridge to cultivate experiences of emotions. As a mature thinker, he worked not only in ethical and political philosophy but also in logic, the philosophy of science, political economy, and religion. Throughout his life, he was an active social reformer dedicated to improving conditions for oppressed peoples; he defended the rights of women, poor and uneducated workers, colonial peoples, and political prisoners.

As a young man, Mill accepted the Benthamite ethical and political philosophy taught to him by his father and Bentham; he even led an organization of young utilitarian radicals dedicated to social progress as conceived by Bentham. Following his mental and emotional collapse at 20, he became convinced that a straightforward calculus of cost and benefit, or pain and pleasure, could not serve as an adequate framework for the human good. In *Utilitarianism* (1863), he argues that actions are right as they promote the greatest happiness or pleasure, where happiness is understood as requiring the development of distinctively human faculties, including the intellect, imagination, and capacities for feeling and moral sense. A person of intelligence would never consent to become a fool, nor would a person of good conscience consent to become selfish and base. The preferences of experienced judges, Mill reasoned, indicate the qualitative superiority of the higher pleasures. As he famously remarked in *Utilitarianism*, it is 'better to be Socrates dissatisfied than a pig satisfied.'

In *On Liberty* (1859), Mill observes that contemporary states and societies have gained an imbalance of power over individuals. In responding to this observation, he develops a utilitarian defence of the liberty of the individual: with greater freedom of expression, human beings could explore new forms of happiness, in like manner as they could reach new truths with greater freedom of opinion. Individual liberty should be restricted only when necessary to prevent harm to others; promoting the good of individuals—or preventing the harm they might inflict upon themselves—is not a sufficient justification for interfering with individual liberty. The principle of restricting individual liberty only to prevent harm to others—the harm principle—undermines a justification of paternalistic policies, which operate under the Platonic idea that ordinary citizens are often incapable of knowing their own good or of aligning their actions with knowledge of the good.

In writing *On Liberty* and other treatises, Mill worked in intellectual collaboration with his life-partner Harriet Taylor Mill (1807–1858), whom he met in 1830 not long after the crisis that produced his depression and subsequent emotional renewal. When the two met, Harriet Taylor was married to another man with whom she had three children, and the close relationship between Mill and Taylor, although platonic, was scandalous by Victorian standards. Harriet Taylor's husband died in 1849, and she and Mill married two years later, following the proper social period of mourning. In his *Autobiography* (1873) and in posthumously released letters to Taylor, Mill made clear that her influence on *On Liberty* was particularly strong, writing that Taylor deserved co-authorship of it, 'our best book,' for she had contributed several of the central ideas of the book, in addition to scrutinizing and revising the manuscript as a whole. In the dedication in *On Liberty*, Mill refers to Taylor as 'the inspirer, and in part the author of all that is best in my writings.' He was inconsolable when she died of tuberculosis in 1858.

Mill and Taylor each wrote political treatises on the emancipation of women. Taylor published *The Enfranchisement of Women* in 1851; Mill published *The Subjection of Women* in 1869, during his most prolific period at the end of his life. In nineteenth-century England, women were not only less educated than men—in part because they were barred from attending universities—but also possessed no legal rights to sue, own property, enter contracts, or obtain divorce. Any inheritance or earnings of a married woman belonged to her husband; indeed, her very body was the property of her husband. In *The Subjection of Women*, Mill argues that the legal subordination of women to men should be supplanted by a principle of complete political, social, and domestic equality. Harriet Taylor Mill makes a similar case for sexual equality in *The Enfranchisement of Women*, but unlike Mill, she focuses on addressing the objections that women are unfit for politics and that politics are unfit for women. Taylor placed more emphasis than Mill on the importance of women's participation in public life, arguing that the commonplace argument for an incommensurability between maternity and a public life is, in fact, merely a veiled suggestion that maternity be the only life resource of women.

On Liberty

I

Introductory

The subject of this Essay is not the so-called Liberty of the Will, so unfortunately opposed to the misnamed doctrine of Philosophical Necessity; but Civil, or Social Liberty: the nature and limits of the power which can be legitimately exercised by society over the individual. A question seldom stated, and hardly ever discussed, in general terms, but which profoundly influences the practical controversies of the age by its latent presence, and is likely soon to make itself recognized as the vital question of the future. It is so far from being new, that, in a certain sense, it has divided mankind, almost from the remotest ages; but in the stage of progress into which the more civilized portions of the species have now entered, it presents itself under new conditions, and requires a different and more fundamental treatment.

The struggle between Liberty and Authority is the most conspicuous feature in the portions of history with which we are earliest familiar, particularly in that of Greece, Rome, and England. But in old times this contest was between subjects, or some classes of subjects, and the Government. By liberty, was meant protection against the tyranny of the political rulers. The rulers were conceived (except in some of the popular governments of Greece) as in a necessarily antagonistic position to the people whom they ruled. They consisted of a governing One, or a governing tribe or caste, who derived their authority from inheritance or conquest, who, at all events, did not hold it at the pleasure of the governed, and whose supremacy men did not venture, perhaps did not desire, to contest, whatever precautions might be taken against its oppressive exercise. Their power was regarded as necessary, but also as highly dangerous; as a weapon which they would attempt to use against their subjects, no less than against external enemies. To prevent the weaker members of the community from being preyed upon by innumerable vultures, it was needful that there should be an animal of prey stronger than the rest, commissioned to keep them down. But as the king of the vultures would be no less bent upon preying on the flock than any of the minor harpies, it was indispensable to be in a perpetual attitude of defence against his beak and claws. The aim, therefore, of patriots was to set limits to the power which the ruler should be suffered to exercise over the community; and this limitation was what they meant by liberty. It was attempted in two ways. First, by obtaining a recognition of certain immunities, called political liberties or rights, which it was to be regarded as a breach of duty in the ruler to infringe, and which, if he did infringe, specific resistance, or general rebellion, was held to be justifiable. A second, and generally a later expedient, was the establishment of constitutional checks, by which the consent of the community, or of a body of some sort, supposed to represent its interests, was made a necessary condition to some of the more important acts of the governing power. To the first of these modes of limitation, the ruling power, in most European countries, was compelled, more or less, to submit. It was not so with the second; and, to attain this, or when already in some degree possessed, to attain it more completely, became everywhere the principal object of the lovers of liberty. And so long as mankind were content to combat one enemy by another, and to be ruled by a master, on condition of being guaranteed more or less efficaciously against his tyranny, they did not carry their aspirations beyond this point.

A time, however, came, in the progress of human affairs, when men ceased to think it a necessity of nature that their governors should be an independent power, opposed in interest to themselves. It appeared to them much better that the various magistrates of the State should be their tenants or delegates, revocable at their pleasure. In that way alone, it seemed, could they have complete security that the powers of government would never be abused to their disadvantage. By degrees this new demand for elective and temporary rulers became the prominent object of the exertions of the popular party, wherever any such party existed; and superseded, to a considerable extent, the previous efforts to limit the power of rulers. As the struggle proceeded for making the ruling power emanate from the periodical choice of the ruled, some persons began to think that too much importance had been attached to the limitation of the power itself. *That* (it might seem) was a resource against rulers whose interests were habitually opposed to those of the people. What was now wanted was, that the rulers should be identified with the people; that their interest and will should be the interest and will of the nation. The nation did not need to be protected against its own will. There was no fear of its tyrannizing over itself. Let the rulers be effectually responsible to it, promptly removable by it, and it could afford to trust them with power of which it could itself dictate the use to be made. Their power was but the nation's own power, concentrated, and in a form convenient for exercise. This mode of thought, or rather perhaps of feeling, was common among the last generation of European liberalism, in the Continental section of which it still apparently predominates. Those who admit any limit to what a government may do, except in the case of such governments as they think ought not to exist, stand out as brilliant exceptions among the political thinkers of the Continent. A similar tone of sentiment might by this time have been prevalent in our own country, if the circumstances which for a time encouraged it, had continued unaltered.

But, in political and philosophical theories, as well as in persons, success discloses faults and infirmities which failure might have concealed from observation. The notion, that the people have no need to limit their power over themselves, might seem axiomatic, when popular government was a thing only dreamed about, or read of as having existed at some distant period of the past. Neither was that notion necessarily disturbed by such temporary aberrations as those of the French Revolution, the worst of which were the work of a usurping few, and which, in any case, belonged, not to the permanent working of popular institutions, but to a sudden and convulsive outbreak against monarchical and aristocratic despotism. In time, however, a democratic republic came to occupy a large portion of the earth's surface, and made itself felt as one of the most powerful members of the community of nations; and elective and responsible government became subject to the observations and criticisms which wait upon a great existing fact. It was now perceived that such phrases as 'self-government', and 'the power of the people over themselves', do not express the true state of the case. The 'people' who exercise the power are not always the same people with those over whom it is exercised; and the 'self-government' spoken of is not the government of each by himself, but of each by all the rest. The will of the people, moreover, practically means the will of the most numerous or the most active *part* of the people; the majority, or those who succeed in making themselves accepted as the majority; the people, consequently, *may* desire to oppress a part of their number; and precautions are as much needed against this as against any other abuse of power. The limitation, therefore, of the power of government over individuals loses none of its importance when the holders of power are regularly accountable to the community, that is, to the strongest party therein. This view of things, recommending itself equally to the intelligence of thinkers and to the inclination of those important classes in European society to whose real or supposed interests democracy is adverse, has had no difficulty in establishing itself; and in political speculations 'the tyranny of the majority' is now generally included among the evils against which society requires to be on its guard.

Like other tyrannies, the tyranny of the majority was at first, and is still vulgarly, held in dread, chiefly as operating through the acts of the public authorities. But reflecting persons perceived that when society is itself the tyrant—society collectively, over the separate individuals who compose it—its means of tyrannizing are not restricted to the acts which it may do by the hands of its political functionaries. Society can and does execute its own mandates: and if it issues wrong mandates instead of right, or any mandates at all in things with which it ought not to meddle, it practises a social tyranny more formidable than many kinds of political oppression, since, though not usually upheld by such extreme penalties, it leaves fewer means of escape, penetrating much more deeply into the details of life, and enslaving the soul itself. Protection, therefore, against the tyranny of the magistrate is not enough: there needs protection also against the tyranny of the prevailing opinion and feeling; against the tendency of society to impose, by other means than civil penalties,

its own ideas and practices as rules of conduct on those who dissent from them; to fetter the development, and, if possible, prevent the formation, of any individuality not in harmony with its ways, and compel all characters to fashion themselves upon the model of its own. There is a limit to the legitimate interference of collective opinion with individual independence: and to find that limit, and maintain it against encroachment, is as indispensable to a good condition of human affairs, as protection against political despotism.

But though this proposition is not likely to be contested in general terms, the practical question, where to place the limit—how to make the fitting adjustment between individual independence and social control—is a subject on which nearly everything remains to be done. All that makes existence valuable to anyone, depends on the enforcement of restraints upon the actions of other people. Some rules of conduct, therefore, must be imposed, by law in the first place, and by opinion on many things which are not fit subjects for the operation of law. What these rules should be, is the principal question in human affairs; but if we except a few of the most obvious cases, it is one of those which least progress has been made in resolving. No two ages, and scarcely any two countries, have decided it alike; and the decision of one age or country is a wonder to another. . . .

The object of this Essay is to assert one very simple principle, as entitled to govern absolutely the dealings of society with the individual in the way of compulsion and control, whether the means used be physical force in the form of legal penalties, or the moral coercion of public opinion. That principle is, that the sale end for which mankind are warranted, individually or collectively, in interfering with the liberty of action of any of their number, is self-protection. That the only purpose for which power can be rightfully exercised over any member of a civilized community, against his will, is to prevent harm to others. His own good, either physical or moral, is not a sufficient warrant. He cannot rightfully be compelled to do or forbear because it will be better for him to do so, because it will make him happier, because, in the opinions of others, to do so would be wise, or even right. These are good reasons for remonstrating with him, or reasoning with him, or persuading him, or entreating him, but not for compelling him, or visiting him with any evil in case he do otherwise. To justify that, the conduct from which it is desired to deter him, must be calculated to produce evil to someone else. The only part of the conduct of anyone, for which he is amenable to society, is that which concerns others. In the part which merely concerns himself, his independence is, of right, absolute. Over himself, over his own body and mind, the individual is sovereign.

It is, perhaps, hardly necessary to say that this doctrine is meant to apply only to human beings in the maturity of their faculties. We are not speaking of children, or of young persons below the age which the law may fix as that of manhood or womanhood. Those who are still in a state to require being taken care of by others, must be protected against their own actions as well as against external injury. For the same reason, we may leave out of consideration those backward states of society in which the race itself may be considered as in its nonage. The early difficulties in the way of spontaneous progress are so great, that there is seldom any choice of means for overcoming them; and a ruler full of the spirit of improvement is warranted in the use of any expedients that will attain an end, perhaps otherwise unattainable. Despotism is a legitimate mode of government in dealing with barbarians, provided the end be their improvement, and the means justified by actually effecting that end. Liberty, as a principle, has no application to any state of things anterior to the time when mankind have become capable of being improved by free and equal discussion. Until then, there is nothing for them but implicit obedience to an Akbar or a Charlemagne, if they are so fortunate as to find one. But as soon as mankind have attained the capacity of being guided to their own improvement by conviction or persuasion (a period long since reached in all nations with whom we need here concern ourselves), compulsion, either in the direct form or in that of pains and penalties for non-compliance, is no longer admissible as a means to their own good, and justifiable only for the security of others.

It is proper to state that I forgo any advantage which could be derived to my argument from the idea of abstract right, as a thing independent of utility. I regard utility as the ultimate appeal on all ethical questions; but it must be utility in the largest sense, grounded on the permanent interests of man as a progressive being. Those interests, I contend, authorize the subjection of individual spontaneity to external control, only in respect to those actions of each, which concern the interest of other people. If anyone does an act hurtful to others, there is a prima facie case for punishing him, by law, or, where legal penalties are not safely applicable, by general disapprobation. There are also many positive acts for the benefit of others, which he may rightfully be compelled to perform; such as, to give evidence in a court of justice; to bear his fair share in the common defence, or in any other joint work necessary to the interest of the society of which he enjoys the protection; and to perform certain acts of individual beneficence, such as saving a fellow creature's life, or interposing to protect the defenceless against ill-usage, things which whenever it is obviously a man's duty to do, he may rightfully be made responsible to society for not doing. A person may cause evil to others not only by his actions but by his inaction, and in either case he is justly accountable to them for the injury. The latter case, it is true, requires a much more cautious exercise of compulsion than the former. To make anyone answerable for doing evil to others, is the rule; to make him answerable for not preventing evil, is, comparatively speaking, the exception. Yet there are many cases clear enough and grave enough to justify that exception. In all things which regard the external relations of the individual, he is *de jure* amenable to those whose interests are concerned, and if need be, to society as their protector. There are often good reasons for not holding him to the responsibility; but these reasons must arise from the special expediencies of the case: either because it is a kind of case in which he is on the whole likely to act better, when left to his own discretion, than when controlled in any way in which society have it in their power to control him; or because the attempt to exercise control would produce other evils, greater than those which it would prevent. When such reasons as these preclude the enforcement of responsibility, the conscience of the agent himself should step into the vacant judgment-seat, and protect those interests of others which have no external protection; judging himself all the more rigidly, because the case does not admit of his being made accountable to the judgment of his fellow creatures.

But there is a sphere of action in which society, as distinguished from the individual, has, if any, only an indirect interest; comprehending all that portion of a person's life and conduct which affects only himself, or if it also affects others, only with their free, voluntary, and undeceived consent and participation. When I say only himself, I mean directly, and in the first instance: for whatever affects himself, may affect others through himself; and the objection which may be grounded on this contingency will receive consideration in the sequel. This, then, is the appropriate region of human liberty. It comprises, first, the inward domain of consciousness; demanding liberty of conscience, in the most comprehensive sense; liberty of thought and feeling; absolute freedom of opinion and sentiment on all subjects, practical or speculative, scientific, moral, or theological. The liberty of expressing and publishing opinions may seem to fall under a different principle, since it belongs to that part of the conduct of an individual which concerns other people; but, being almost of as much importance as the liberty of thought itself, and resting in great part on the same reasons, is practically inseparable from it. Secondly, the principle requires liberty of tastes and pursuits; of framing the plan of our life to suit our own character; of doing as we like, subject to such consequences as may follow: without impediment from our fellow creatures, so long as what we do does not harm them, even though they should think our conduct foolish, perverse, or wrong. Thirdly, from this liberty of each individual, follows the liberty, within the same limits, of combination among individuals; freedom to unite, for any purpose not involving harm to others: the persons combining being supposed to be of full age, and not forced or deceived.

No society in which these liberties are not, on the whole, respected, is free, whatever may be its form of government; and none is completely free in which they do not exist absolute and unqualified. The only freedom which deserves the name, is that of pursuing our own good in our own way, so long as we do not attempt to deprive others of theirs, or impede their efforts to obtain it. Each is the proper guardian of his own health, whether bodily, or mental and spiritual. Mankind are greater gainers by suffering each other to live as seems good to themselves, than by compelling each to live as seems good to the rest.

Though this doctrine is anything but new, and, to some persons, may have the air of a truism, there is no doctrine which stands more directly opposed to the general tendency of existing opinion and practice. Society has expended fully as much effort in the attempt (according to its lights) to compel people to conform to its notions of personal, as of social excellence. The ancient commonwealths thought themselves entitled to practise, and the ancient philosophers countenanced, the regulation of every part of private conduct by public authority, on the ground that the State had a deep interest in the whole bodily and mental discipline of every one of its citizens; a mode of thinking which may have been admissible in small republics surrounded by powerful enemies, in constant peril of being subverted by foreign attack or internal commotion, and to which even a short interval of relaxed energy and self-command might so easily be fatal, that they could not afford to wait for the salutary permanent effects of freedom. In the modern world, the greater size of political communities, and, above all, the separation between spiritual and temporal authority (which placed the direction of men's consciences in other hands than those which controlled their worldly affairs), prevented so great an interference by law in the details of private life; but the engines of moral repression have been wielded more strenuously against divergence from the reigning opinion in self-regarding, than even in social matters; religion, the most powerful of the elements which have entered into the formation of moral feeling, having almost always been governed either by the ambition

of a hierarchy, seeking control over every department of human conduct, or by the spirit of Puritanism. . . .

II

Of the Liberty of Thought and Discussion

The time, it is to be hoped, is gone by, when any defence would be necessary of the 'liberty of the press' as one of the securities against corrupt or tyrannical government. No argument, we may suppose, can now be needed, against permitting a legislature or an executive, not identified in interest with the people, to prescribe opinions to them, and determine what doctrines or what arguments they shall be allowed to hear. This aspect of the question, besides, has been so often and so triumphantly enforced by preceding writers, that it needs not be specially insisted on in this place. Though the law of England, on the subject of the press, is as servile to this day as it was in the time of the Tudors, there is little danger of its being actually put in force against political discussion, except during some temporary panic, when fear of insurrection drives ministers and judges from their propriety; and, speaking generally, it is not, in constitutional countries, to be apprehended, that the government, whether completely responsible to the people or not, will often attempt to control the expression of opinion, except when in doing so it makes itself the organ of the general intolerance of the public. Let us suppose, therefore, that the government is entirely at one with the people, and never thinks of exerting any power of coercion unless in agreement with what it conceives to be their voice. But I deny the right of the people to exercise such coercion, either by themselves or by their government. The power itself is illegitimate.

The best government has no more title to it than the worst. It is as noxious, or more noxious, when exerted in accordance with public opinion, than when in opposition to it. If all mankind minus one, were of one opinion, and only one person were of the contrary opinion, mankind would be no more justified in silencing that one person, than he, if he had the power, would be justified in silencing mankind. Were an opinion a personal possession of no value except to the owner; if to be obstructed in the enjoyment of it were simply a private injury, it would make some difference whether the injury was inflicted only on a few persons or on many. But the peculiar evil of silencing the expression of an opinion is, that it is robbing the human race; posterity as well as the existing generation; those who dissent from the opinion, still more than those who hold it. If the opinion is right, they are deprived of the opportunity of exchanging error for truth: if wrong, they lose, what is almost as great a benefit, the clearer perception and livelier impression of truth, produced by its collision with error.

It is necessary to consider separately these two hypotheses, each of which has a distinct branch of the argument corresponding to it. We can never be sure that the opinion we are endeavouring to stifle is a false opinion; and if we were sure, stifling it would be an evil still.

First: the opinion which it is attempted to suppress by authority may possibly be true. Those who desire to suppress it, of course deny its truth; but they are not infallible. They have no authority to decide the question for all mankind, and exclude every other person from the means of judging. To refuse a hearing to an opinion, because they are sure that it is false, is to assume that *their* certainty is the same thing as *absolute* certainty. All silencing of discussion is an assumption of infallibility. Its condemnation may be allowed to rest on

this common argument, not the worse for being common. . . .

Let us now pass to the second division of the argument, and dismissing the supposition that any of the received opinions may be false, let us assume them to be true, and examine into the worth of the manner in which they are likely to be held, when their truth is not freely and openly canvassed. However unwillingly a person who has a strong opinion may admit the possibility that his opinion may be false, he ought to be moved by the consideration that however true it may be, if it is not fully, frequently, and fearlessly discussed, it will be held as a dead dogma, not a living truth.

There is a class of persons (happily not quite so numerous as formerly) who think it enough if a person assents undoubtingly to what they think true, though he has no knowledge whatever of the grounds of the opinion, and could not make a tenable defence of it against the most superficial objections. Such persons, if they can once get their creed taught from authority, naturally think that no good, and some harm, comes of its being allowed to be questioned. Where their influence prevails, they make it nearly impossible for the received opinion to be rejected wisely and considerately, though it may still be rejected rashly and ignorantly; for to shut out discussion entirely is seldom possible, and when it once gets in, beliefs not grounded on conviction are apt to give way before the slightest semblance of an argument. Waiving, however, this possibility—assuming that the true opinion abides in the mind, but abides as a prejudice, a belief independent of, and proof against, argument—this is not the way in which truth ought to be held by a rational being. This is not knowing the truth. Truth, thus held, is but one superstition the more, accidentally clinging to the words which enunciate a truth.

If the intellect and judgment of mankind ought to be cultivated, a thing which Protestants at least do not deny, on what can these faculties be more appropriately exercised by anyone, than on the things which concern him so much that it is considered necessary for him to hold opinions on them? If the cultivation of the understanding consists in one thing more than in another, it is surely in learning the grounds of one's own opinions. Whatever people believe, on subjects on which it is of the first importance to believe rightly, they ought to be able to defend against at least the common objections. But, someone may say, 'Let them be *taught* the grounds of their opinions. It does not follow that opinions must be merely parroted because they are never heard controverted. Persons who learn geometry do not simply commit the theorems to memory, but understand and learn likewise the demonstrations; and it would be absurd to say that they remain ignorant of the grounds of geometrical truths, because they never hear anyone deny, and attempt to disprove them.' Undoubtedly: and such teaching suffices on a subject like mathematics, where there is nothing at all to be said on the wrong side of the question. The peculiarity of the evidence of mathematical truths is, that all the argument is on one side. There are no objections, and no answers to objections. But on every subject on which difference of opinion is possible, the truth depends on a balance to the struck between two sets of conflicting reasons. Even in natural philosophy, there is always some other explanation possible of the same facts; some geocentric theory instead of heliocentric, some phlogiston instead of oxygen; and it has to be shown why that other theory cannot be the true one: and until this is shown, and until we know how it is shown, we do not understand the grounds of our opinion. But

when we turn to subjects infinitely more complicated, to morals, religion, politics, social relations, and the business of life, three-fourths of the arguments for every disputed opinion consist in dispelling the appearances which favour some opinion different from it. The greatest orator, save one, of antiquity, has left it on record that he always studied his adversary's case with as great, if not with still greater, intensity than even his own. What Cicero practised as the means of forensic success, requires to be imitated by all who study any subject in order to arrive at the truth. He who knows only his own side of the case, knows little of that. His reasons may be good, and no one may have been able to refute them. But if he is equally unable to refute the reasons on the opposite side; if he does not so much as know what they are, he has no ground for preferring either opinion. The rational position for him would be suspension of judgment, and unless he contents himself with that, he is either led by authority, or adopts, like the generality of the world, the side to which he feels most inclination. Nor is it enough, that he should hear the arguments of adversaries from his own teachers, presented as they state them, and accompanied by what they offer as refutations. That is not the way to do justice to the arguments, or bring them into real contact with his own mind. He must be able to hear them from persons who actually believe them; who defend them in earnest, and do their very utmost for them. He must know them in their most plausible and persuasive form; he must feel the whole force of the difficulty which the true view of the subject has to encounter and dispose of; else he will never really possess himself of the portion of truth which meets and removes that difficulty. Ninety-nine in a hundred of what are called educated men are in this condition; even of those who can argue fluently for their opinions. Their conclusion may be true, but it might be false for anything they know: they have never thrown themselves into the mental position of those who think differently from them, and considered what such persons may have to say; and consequently they do not, in any proper sense of the word, know the doctrine which they themselves profess. They do not know those parts of it which explain and justify the remainder; the considerations which show that a fact which seemingly conflicts with another is reconcilable with it, or that, of two apparently strong reasons, one and not the other ought to be preferred. All that part of the truth which turns the scale, and decides the judgment of a completely informed mind, they are strangers to; nor is it ever really known, but to those who have attended equally and impartially to both sides, and endeavoured to see the reasons of both in the strongest light. So essential is this discipline to a real understanding of moral and human subjects, that if opponents of all important truths do not exist, it is indispensable to imagine them, and supply them with the strongest arguments which the most skilful devil's advocate can conjure up.

To abate the force of these considerations, an enemy of free discussion may be supposed to say, that there is no necessity for mankind in general to know and understand all that can be said against or for their opinions by philosophers and theologians. That it is not needful for common men to be able to expose all the misstatements or fallacies of an ingenious opponent. That it is enough if there is always somebody capable of answering them, so that nothing likely to mislead uninstructed persons remains unrefuted. That simple minds, having been taught the obvious grounds of the truths inculcated on them, may trust to authority for the rest, and being aware

that they have neither knowledge nor talent to resolve every difficulty which can be raised, may repose in the assurance that all those which have been raised have been or can be answered, by those who are specially trained to the task.

Conceding to this view of the subject the utmost that can be claimed for it by those most easily satisfied with the amount of understanding of truth which ought to accompany the belief of it; even so, the argument for free discussion is no way weakened. For even this doctrine acknowledges that mankind ought to have a rational assurance that all objections have been satisfactorily answered; and how are they to be answered if that which requires to be answered is not spoken? or how can the answer be known to be satisfactory, if the objectors have no opportunity of showing that it is unsatisfactory? If not the public, at least the philosophers and theologians who are to resolve the difficulties, must make themselves familiar with those difficulties in their most puzzling form; and this cannot be accomplished unless they are freely stated, and placed in the most advantageous light which they admit of. . . .

If, however, the mischievous operation of the absence of free discussion, when the received opinions are true, were confined to leaving men ignorant of the grounds of those opinions, it might be thought that this, if an intellectual, is no moral evil, and does not affect the worth of the opinions, regarded in their influence on the character. The fact, however, is, that not only the grounds of the opinion are forgotten in the absence of discussion, but too often the meaning of the opinion itself. The words which convey it, cease to suggest ideas, or suggest only a small portion of those they were originally employed to communicate. Instead of a vivid conception and a living belief, there remain only a few phrases retained by rote; or, if any part, the shell and husk only of the meaning is retained, the finer essence being lost. The great chapter in human history which this fact occupies and fills, cannot be too earnestly studied and meditated on. . . .

To what an extent doctrines intrinsically fitted to make the deepest impression upon the mind may remain in it as dead beliefs, without being ever realized in the imagination, the feelings, or the understanding, is exemplified by the manner in which the majority of believers hold the doctrines of Christianity. By Christianity I here mean what is accounted such by all churches and sects—the maxims and precepts contained in the New Testament. These are considered sacred, and accepted as laws, by all professing Christians. Yet it is scarcely too much to say that not one Christian in a thousand guides or tests his individual conduct by reference to those laws. The standard to which he does refer it, is the custom of his nation, his class, or his religious profession. He has thus, on the one hand, a collection of ethical maxims, which he believes to have been vouchsafed to him by infallible wisdom as rules for his government; and on the other, a set of everyday judgments and practices, which go a certain length with some of those maxims, not so great a length with others, stand in direct opposition to some, and are, on the whole, a compromise between the Christian creed and the interests and suggestions of worldly life. To the first of these standards he gives his homage; to the other his real allegiance. . . .

It still remains to speak of one of the principal causes which make diversity of opinion advantageous, and will continue to do so until mankind shall have entered a stage of intellectual advancement which at present seems at an incalculable distance. We have hitherto considered only two possibilities: that the received opinion may be false, and some other opinion, consequently, true; or that, the received opinion being true, a conflict with the opposite error is essential to a clear apprehension and deep feeling of its truth. But there is a commoner case than either of these; when the conflicting doctrines, instead of being one true and the other false, share the truth between them; and the nonconforming opinion is needed to supply the remainder of the truth, of which the received doctrine embodies only a part. Popular opinions, on subjects not palpable to sense, are often true, but seldom or never the whole truth. They are a part of the truth; sometimes a greater, sometimes a smaller part, but exaggerated, distorted, and disjoined from the truths by which they ought to be accompanied and limited. Heretical opinions, on the other hand, are generally some of these suppressed and neglected truths, bursting the bonds which kept them down, and either seeking reconciliation with the truth contained in the common opinion, or fronting it as enemies, and setting themselves up, with similar exclusiveness, as the whole truth. The latter case is hitherto the most frequent, as, in the human mind, one-sidedness has always been the rule, and many-sidedness the exception. Hence, even in revolutions of opinion, one part of the truth usually sets while another rises. Even progress, which ought to superadd, for the most part only substitutes, one partial and incomplete truth for another; improvement consisting chiefly in this, that the new fragment of truth is more wanted, more adapted to the needs of the time, than that which it displaces. Such being the partial character of prevailing opinions, even when resting on a true foundation, every opinion which embodies somewhat of the portion of truth which the common opinion omits, ought to be considered precious, with whatever amount of error and confusion that truth may be blended. No sober judge of human affairs will feel bound to be indignant because those who force on our notice truths which we should otherwise have overlooked, overlook some of those which we see. Rather, he will think that so long as popular truth is one-sided, it is more desirable than otherwise that unpopular truth should have one-sided asserters too; such being usually the most energetic, and the most likely to compel reluctant attention to the fragment of wisdom which they proclaim as if it were the whole. . . .

We have now recognized the necessity to the mental well-being of mankind (on which all their other well-being depends) of freedom of opinion, and freedom of the expression of opinion, on four distinct grounds; which we will now briefly recapitulate.

First, if any opinion is compelled to silence, that opinion may, for aught we can certainly know, be true. To deny this is to assume our own infallibility:

Secondly, though the silenced opinion be an error, it may, and very commonly does, contain a portion of truth; and since the general or prevailing opinion on any subject is rarely or never the whole truth, it is only by the collision of adverse opinions that the remainder of the truth has any chance of being supplied.

Thirdly, even if the received opinion be not only true, but the whole truth; unless it is suffered to be, and actually is, vigorously and earnestly contested, it will, by most of those who receive it, be held in the manner of a prejudice, with little comprehension or feeling of its rational grounds. And not only this, but fourthly, the meaning of the doctrine itself will be in danger of being lost, or enfeebled, and deprived of its vital effect on the character and conduct: the dogma becoming a mere formal

profession, inefficacious for good, but cumbering the ground, and preventing the growth of any real and heartfelt conviction, from reason or personal experience. . . .

III

Of Individuality, as One of the Elements of Well-Being

Such being the reasons which make it imperative that human beings should be free to form opinions, and to express their opinions without reserve; and such the baneful consequences to the intellectual, and through that to the moral nature of man, unless this liberty is either conceded, or asserted in spite of prohibition; let us next examine whether the same reasons do not require that men should be free to act upon their opinions—to carry these out in their lives, without hindrance, either physical or moral, from their fellow men, so long as it is at their own risk and peril. This last proviso is of course indispensable. No one pretends that actions should be as free as opinions. On the contrary, even opinions lose their immunity, when the circumstances in which they are expressed are such as to constitute their expression a positive instigation to some mischievous act. An opinion that corn-dealers are starvers of the poor, or that private property is robbery, ought to be unmolested when simply circulated through the press, but may justly incur punishment when delivered orally to an excited mob assembled before the house of a corn-dealers, or when handed about among the same mob in the form of a placard. Acts, of whatever kind, which, without justifiable cause, do harm to others, may be, and in the more important cases absolutely require to be, controlled by the unfavourable sentiments, and, when needful, by the active interference of mankind. The liberty of the individual must be thus far limited; he must not make himself a nuisance to other people. But if he refrains from molesting others in what concerns them, and merely acts according to his own inclination and judgment in things which concern himself, the same reasons which show that opinion should be free, prove also that he should be allowed, without molestation, to carry his opinions into practice at his own cost. That mankind are not infallible; that their truths, for the most part, are only half-truths; that unity of opinion, unless resulting from the fullest and freest comparison of opposite opinions, is not desirable, and diversity not an evil, but a good, until mankind are much more capable than at present of recognizing all sides of the truth, are principles applicable to men's modes of action, not less than to their opinions. As it is useful that while mankind are imperfect there should be different opinions, so is it that there should be different experiments of living; that free scope should be given to varieties of character, short of injury to others; and that the worth of different modes of life should be proved practically, when anyone thinks fit to try them. It is desirable, in short, that in things which do not primarily concern others, individuality should assert itself. Where, not the person's own character, but the traditions or customs of other people are the rule of conduct, there is wanting one of the principal ingredients of human happiness, and quite the chief ingredient of individual and social progress.

In maintaining this principle, the greatest difficulty to be encountered does not lie in the appreciation of means towards an acknowledged end, but in the indifference of persons in general to the end itself. If it were felt that the free development of individuality is one of the leading essentials of well-being; that it is not only a co-ordinate element with all that is designated by the terms civilization, instruc-tion, education, culture, but is itself a necessary part and condition of all those things; there would be no danger that liberty should be undervalued, and the adjustment of the boundaries between it and social control would present no extraordinary difficulty. But the evil is, that individual spontaneity is hardly recognized by the common modes of thinking, as having any intrinsic worth, or deserving any regard on its own account. The majority, being satisfied with the ways of mankind as they now are (for it is they who make them what they are), cannot comprehend why those ways should not be good enough for everybody; and what is more, spontaneity forms no part of the ideal of the majority of moral and social reformers, but is rather looked on with jealousy, as a troublesome and perhaps rebellious obstruction to the general acceptance of what these reformers, in their own judgment, think would be best for mankind. Few persons, out of Germany, even comprehend the meaning of the doctrine which Wilhelm von Humboldt, so eminent both as a savant and as a politician, made the text of a treatise—that 'the end of man, or that which is prescribed by the eternal or immutable dictates of reason, and not suggested by vague and transient desires, is the highest and most harmonious development of his powers to a complete and consistent whole'; that, therefore, the object 'towards which every human being must ceaselessly direct his efforts, and on which especially those who design to influence their fellow men must ever keep their eyes, is the individuality of power and development'; that for this there are two requisites, 'freedom, and variety of situations'; and that from the union of these arise 'individual vigour and manifold diversity', which combine themselves in 'originality'. . . .

He who lets the world, or his own portion of it, choose his plan of life for him, has no need of any other faculty than the ape-like one of imitation. He who chooses his plan for himself, employs all his faculties. He must use observation to see, reasoning and judgment to foresee, activity to gather materials for decision, discrimination to decide, and when he has decided, firmness and self-control to hold to his deliberate decision. And these qualities he requires and exercises exactly in proportion as the part of his conduct which he determines according to his own judgment and feelings is a large one. It is possible that he might be guided in some good path, and kept out of harm's way, without any of these things. But what will be his comparative worth as a human being? It really is of importance, not only what men do, but also what manner of men they are that do it. Among the works of man, which human life is rightly employed in perfecting and beautifying, the first in importance surely is man himself. Supposing it were possible to get houses built, corn grown, battles fought, causes tried, and even churches erected and prayers said, by machinery—by automatons in human form—it would be a considerable loss to exchange for these automatons even the men and women who at present inhabit the more civilized parts of the world, and who assuredly are but starved specimens of what nature can and will produce. Human nature is not a machine to be built after a model, and set to do exactly the work prescribed for it, but a tree, which requires to grow and develop itself on all sides, according to the tendency of the inward forces which make it a living thing.

It will probably be conceded that it is desirable people should exercise their understandings, and that an intelligent following of custom, or even occasionally an intelligent deviation from custom, is better than a blind and simply mechanical adhesion to it. To a certain extent it is admitted, that our understanding should be our own: but there is not the same willingness to admit that our desires and impulses should be our own likewise; or that to possess impulses of our own, and of any strength, is anything but a peril and a snare. Yet desires and impulses are as much a part of a perfect human being, as beliefs and restraints: and strong impulses are only perilous when not properly balanced; when one set of aims and inclinations is developed into strength, while others, which ought to coexist with them, remain weak and inactive. It is not because men's desires are strong that they act ill; it is because their consciences are weak. There is no natural connection between strong impulses and a weak conscience. The natural connection is the other way. To say that one person's desires and feelings are stronger and more various than those of another, is merely to say that he has more of the raw material of human nature, and is therefore capable, perhaps of more evil, but certainly of more good. Strong impulses are but another name for energy. Energy may be turned to bad uses; but more good may always be made of an energetic nature, than of an indolent and impassive one. Those who have the most natural feeling, are always those whose cultivated feelings may be made the strongest. The same strong susceptibilities which make the personal impulses vivid and powerful, are also the source from whence are generated the most passionate love of virtue, and the sternest self-control. It is through the cultivation of these, that society both does its duty and protects its interests: not by rejecting the stuff of which heroes are made, because it knows not how to make them. A person whose desires and impulses are his own—are the expression of his own nature, as it has been developed and modified by his own culture—is said to have a character. One whose desires and impulses are not his own, has no character, no more than a steam-engine has a character. If, in addition to being his own, his impulses are strong, and are under the government of a strong will, he has an energetic character. Whoever thinks that individuality of desires and impulses should not be encouraged to unfold itself, must maintain that society has no need of strong natures—is not the better for containing many persons who have much character—and that a high general average of energy is not desirable.

In some early states of society, these forces might be, and were, too much ahead of the power which society then possessed of disciplining and controlling them. There has been a time when the element of spontaneity and individuality was in excess, and the social principle had a hard struggle with it. The difficulty then was, to induce men of strong bodies or minds to pay obedience to any rules which required them to control their impulses. To overcome this difficulty, law and discipline, like the Popes struggling against the Emperors, asserted a power over the whole man, claiming to control all his life in order to control his character—which society had not found any other sufficient means of binding. But society has now fairly got the better of individuality; and the danger which threatens human nature is not the excess, but the deficiency, of personal impulses and preferences. Things are vastly changed, since the passions of those who were strong by station or by personal endowment were in a state of habitual rebellion against laws and ordinances, and required to be rigorously chained up to enable the persons within their reach to enjoy any particle of security. In our times, from the highest class of society down to the lowest, everyone lives as under the eye of a hostile and dreaded censorship. Not only in what concerns others, but in what concerns only themselves, the individual or the family do not ask

themselves, What do I prefer? or, What would suit my character and disposition? or, What would allow the best and highest in me to have fair play, and enable it to grow and thrive? They ask themselves, What is suitable to my position? What is usually done by persons of my station and pecuniary circumstances? or (worse still), What is usually done by persons of a station and circumstances superior to mine? I do not mean that they choose what is customary, in preference to what suits their own inclination. It does not occur to them to have any inclination, except for what is customary. Thus the mind itself is bowed to the yoke: even in what people do for pleasure, conformity is the first thing thought of; they like in crowds; they exercise choice only among things commonly done: peculiarity of taste, eccentricity of conduct, are shunned equally with crimes: until by dint of not following their own nature, they have no nature to follow: their human capacities are withered and starved: they become incapable of any strong wishes or native pleasures, and are generally without either opinions or feelings of home growth, or properly their own. Now is this, or is it not, the desirable condition of human nature? . . .

IV

Of the Limits to the Authority of Society over the Individual

What, then, is the rightful limit to the sovereignty of the individual over himself? Where does the authority of society begin? How much of human life should be assigned to individuality, and how much to society?

Each will receive its proper share, if each has that which more particularly concerns it. To individuality should belong the part of life in which it is chiefly the individual that is interested; to society, the part which chiefly interests society.

Though society is not founded on a contract, and though no good purpose is answered by inventing a contract in order to deduce social obligations from it, everyone who receives the protection of society owes a return for the benefit, and the fact of living in society renders it indispensable that each should be bound to observe a certain line of conduct towards the rest. This conduct consists, first, in not injuring the interests of one another; or rather certain interests, which, either by express legal provision or by tacit understanding, ought to be considered as rights; and secondly, in each person's bearing his share (to be fixed on some equitable principle) of the labours and sacrifices incurred for defending the society or its members from injury and molestation. These conditions society is justified in enforcing at all costs to those who endeavour to withhold fulfilment. Nor is this all that society may do. The acts of an individual may be hurtful to others, or wanting in due consideration for their welfare, without going the length of violating any of their constituted rights. The offender may then be justly punished by opinion, though not by law. As soon as any part of a person's conduct affects prejudicially the interests of others, society has jurisdiction over it, and the question whether the general welfare will or will not be promoted by interfering with it, becomes open to discussion. But there is no room for entertaining any such question when a person's conduct affects the interests of no persons besides himself, or needs not affect them unless they like (all the persons concerned being of full age, and the ordinary amount of understanding). In all such cases there should be perfect freedom, legal and social, to do the action and stand the consequences.

It would be a great misunderstanding of this doctrine to suppose that it is one of selfish indifference, which pretends that human beings have no business with each other's conduct in life, and that they should not concern themselves about the well-doing or well-being of one another, unless their own interest is involved. Instead of any diminution, there is need of a great increase of disinterested exertion to promote the good of others. But disinterested benevolence can find other instruments to persuade people to their good, than whips and scourges, either of the literal or the metaphorical sort. I am the last person to undervalue the self-regarding virtues; they are only second in importance, if even second, to the social. It is equally the business of education to cultivate both. But even education works by conviction and persuasion as well as by compulsion, and it is by the former only that, when the period of education is past, the self-regarding virtues should be inculcated. Human beings owe to each other help to distinguish the better from the worse, and encouragement to choose the former and avoid the latter. They should be forever stimulating each other to increased exercise of their higher faculties, and increased direction of their feelings and aims towards wise instead of foolish, elevating instead of degrading, objects and contemplations. But neither one person, nor any number of persons, is warranted in saying to another human creature of ripe years, that he shall not do with his life for his own benefit what he chooses to do with it. He is the person most interested in his own well-being: the interest which any other person, except in cases of strong personal attachment, can have in it, is trifling, compared with that which he himself has; the interest which society has in him individually (except as to his conduct to others) is fractional, and altogether indirect: while, with respect to his own feelings and circumstances, the most ordinary man or woman has means of knowledge immeasurably surpassing those that can be possessed by anyone else. The interference of society to overrule his judgment and purposes in what only regards himself, must be grounded on general presumptions; which may be altogether wrong, and even if right, are as likely as not to be misapplied to individual cases, by persons no better acquainted with the circumstances of such cases than those are who look at them merely from without. In this department, therefore, of human affairs, individuality has its proper field of action. In the conduct of human beings towards one another, it is necessary that general rules should for the most part be observed, in order that people may know what they have to expect; but in each person's own concerns, his individual spontaneity is entitled to free exercise. Considerations to aid his judgment, exhortations to strengthen his will, may be offered to him, even obtruded on him, by others; but he himself is the final judge. All errors which he is likely to commit against advice and warning, are far outweighed by the evil of allowing others to constrain him to what they deem his good.

I do not mean that the feelings with which a person is regarded by others, ought not to be in any way affected by his self-regarding qualities or deficiencies. This is neither possible nor desirable. If he is eminent in any of the qualities which conduce to his own good, he is, so far, a proper object of admiration. He is so much the nearer to the ideal perfection of human nature. If he is grossly deficient in those qualities, a sentiment the opposite of admiration will follow. There is a degree of folly, and a degree of what may be called (though the phrase is not unobjectionable) lowness or depravation of taste, which, though it cannot justify doing harm to the person who manifests it, renders him necessarily and properly a subject of distaste, or, in extreme cases, even of contempt: a person could not have the opposite qualities in due strength without entertaining these feelings. Though doing no wrong to anyone, a person may so act as to compel us to judge him, and feel to him, as a fool, or as a being of an inferior order: and since this judgment and feeling are a fact which he would prefer to avoid, it is doing him a service to warn him of it beforehand, as of any other disagreeable consequence to which he exposes himself. It would be well, indeed, if this good office were much more freely rendered than the common notions of politeness at present permit, and if one person could honestly point out to another that he thinks him in fault, without being considered unmannerly or presuming. We have a right, also, in various ways, to act upon our unfavourable opinion of anyone, not to the oppression of his individuality, but in the exercise of ours. We are not bound, for example, to seek his society; we have a right to avoid it (though not to parade the avoidance), for we have a right to choose the society most acceptable to us. We have a right, and it may be our duty, to caution others against him, if we think his example or conversation likely to have a pernicious effect on those with whom he associates. We may give others a preference over him in optional good offices, except those which tend to his improvement. In these various modes a person may suffer very severe penalties at the hands of others, for faults which directly concern only himself; but he suffers these penalties only insofar as they are the natural, and, as it were, the spontaneous consequences of the faults themselves, not because they are purposely inflicted on him for the sake of punishment. A person who shows rashness, obstinacy, self-conceit—who cannot live within moderate means—who cannot restrain himself from hurtful indulgences—who pursues animal pleasures at the expense of those of feeling and intellect—must expect to be lowered in the opinion of others, and to have a less share of their favourable sentiments; but of this he has no right to complain, unless he has merited their favour by special excellence in his social relations, and has thus established a title to their good offices, which is not affected by his demerits towards himself.

What I contend for is, that the inconveniences which are strictly inseparable from the unfavourable judgment of others, are the only ones to which a person should ever be subjected for that portion of his conduct and character which concerns his own good, but which does not affect the interests of others in their relations with him. Acts injurious to others require a totally different treatment. Encroachment on their rights; infliction on them of any loss or damage not justified by his own rights; falsehood or duplicity in dealing with them; unfair or ungenerous use of advantages over them; even selfish abstinence from defending them against injury—these are fit objects of moral reprobation, and, in grave cases, of moral retribution and punishment. And not only these acts, but the dispositions which lead to them, are properly immoral, and fit subjects of disapprobation which may rise to abhorrence. Cruelty of disposition; malice and ill nature; that most anti-social and odious of all passions, envy; dissimulation and insincerity; irascibility on insufficient cause, and resentment disproportioned to the provocation; the love of domineering over others; the desire to engross more than one's share of advantages (the πλεονεξία of the Greeks); the pride which derives gratification from the abasement of others; the egotism which thinks self and its concerns more important than everything else, and decides all doubtful questions in its own favour—these are moral vices, and constitute a bad and odious moral character: unlike the self-regarding faults previously mentioned, which are not properly immoralities, and to whatever pitch they may be carried, do not constitute wickedness. They may be proofs of any amount of folly, or want of personal dignity and self-respect; but they are only a subject of moral reprobation when they involve a breach of duty to others, for whose sake the individual is bound to have care for himself. What are called duties to ourselves are not socially obligatory, unless circumstances render them at the same time duties to others. The term duty to oneself, when it means anything more than prudence, means self-respect or self-development; and for none of these is anyone accountable to his fellow creatures, because for none of them is it for the good of mankind that he be held accountable to them.

The distinction between the loss of consideration which a person may rightly incur by defect of prudence or of personal dignity, and the reprobation which is due to him for an offence against the rights of others, is not a merely nominal distinction. It makes a vast difference both in our feelings and in our conduct towards him, whether he displeases us in things in which we think we have a right to control him, or in things in which we know that we have not. If he displeases us, we may express our distaste, and we may stand aloof from a person as well as from a thing that displeases us; but we shall not therefore feel called on to make his life uncomfortable. We shall reflect that he already bears, or will bear, the whole penalty of his error; if he spoils his life by mismanagement, we shall not, for that reason, desire to spoil it still further: instead of wishing to punish him, we shall rather endeavour to alleviate his punishment, by showing him how he may avoid or cure the evils his conduct tends to bring upon him. He may be to us an object of pity, perhaps of dislike, but not of anger or resentment; we shall not treat him like an enemy of society: the worst we shall think ourselves justified in doing is leaving him to himself, if we do not interfere benevolently by showing interest or concern for him. It is far otherwise if he has infringed the rules necessary for the protection of his fellow creatures, individually or collectively. The evil consequences of his acts do not then fall on himself, but on others; and society, as the protector of all its members, must retaliate on him; must inflict pain on him for the express purpose of punishment, and must take care that it be sufficiently severe. In the one case, he is an offender at our bar, and we are called on not only to sit in judgment on him, but, in one shape or another, to execute our own sentence; in the other case, it is not our part to inflict any suffering on him, except what may incidentally follow from our using the same liberty in the regulation of our own affairs, which we allow to him in his.

The distinction here pointed out between the part of a person's life which concerns only himself, and that which concerns others, many persons will refuse to admit. How (it may be asked) can any part of the conduct of a member of society be a matter of indifference to the other members? No person is an entirely isolated being; it is impossible for a person to do anything seriously or permanently hurtful to himself, without mischief reaching at least to his near connections, and often far beyond them. If he injures his property, he does harm to those who directly or indirectly derived support from it, and usually diminishes, by a greater or less amount, the general resources of the community. If he deteriorates his bodily

or mental faculties, he not only brings evil upon all who depended on him for any portion of their happiness, but disqualifies himself for rendering the services which he owes to his fellow creatures generally; perhaps becomes a burthen on their affection or benevolence; and if such conduct were very frequent, hardly any offence that is committed would detract more from the general sum of good. Finally, if by his vices or follies a person does no direct harm to others, he is nevertheless (it may be said) injurious by his example; and ought to be compelled to control himself, for the sake of those whom the sight or knowledge of his conduct might corrupt or mislead.

And even (it will be added) if the consequences of misconduct could be confined to the vicious or thoughtless individual, ought society to abandon to their own guidance those who are manifestly unfit for it? If protection against themselves is confessedly due to children and persons under age, is not society equally bound to afford it to persons of mature years who are equally incapable of self-government? If gambling, or drunkenness, or incontinence, or idleness, or uncleanliness, are as injurious to happiness, and as great a hindrance to improvement, as many or most of the acts prohibited by law, why (it may be asked) should not law, so far as is consistent with practicability and social convenience, endeavour to repress these also? And as a supplement to the unavoidable imperfections of law, ought not opinion at least to organize a powerful police against these vices, and visit rigidly with social penalties those who are known to practise them? There is no question here (it may be said) about restricting individuality, or impeding the trial of new and original experiments in living. The only things it is sought to prevent are things which have been tried and condemned from the beginning of the world until now; things which experience has shown not to be useful or suitable to any person's individuality. There must be some length of time and amount of experience, after which a moral or prudential truth may be regarded as established: and it is merely desired to prevent generation after generation from falling over the same precipice which has been fatal to their predecessors.

I fully admit that the mischief which a person does to himself may seriously affect, both through their sympathies and their interests, those nearly connected with him, and in a minor degree, society at large. When, by conduct of this sort, a person is led to violate a distinct and assignable obligation to any other person or persons, the case is taken out of the self-regarding class, and becomes amenable to moral disapprobation in the proper sense of the term. If, for example, a man, through intemperance or extravagance, becomes unable to pay his debts, or, having undertaken the moral responsibility of a family, becomes from the same cause incapable of supporting or educating them, he is deservedly reprobated, and might be justly punished; but it is for the breach of duty to his family or creditors, not for the extravagance. If the resources which ought to have been devoted to them, had been diverted from them for the most prudent investment, the moral culpability would have been the same. George Barnwell murdered his uncle to get money for his mistress, but if he had done it to set himself up in business, he would equally have been hanged. Again, in the frequent case of a man who causes grief to his family by addiction to bad habits, he deserves reproach for his unkindness or ingratitude; but so he may for cultivating habits not in themselves vicious, if they are painful to those with whom he passes his life, or who from personal ties are dependent on him for their comfort. Whoever fails in the consideration generally due to the interests and feelings of others, not being compelled by some more imperative duty, or justified by allowable self-preference, is a subject of moral disapprobation for that failure, but not for the cause of it, nor for the errors, merely personal to himself, which may have remotely led to it. In like manner, when a person disables himself, by conduct purely self-regarding, from the performance of some definite duty incumbent on him to the public, he is guilty of a social offence. No person ought to be punished simply for being drunk; but a soldier or a policeman should be punished for being drunk on duty. Whenever, in short, there is a definite damage, or a definite risk of damage, either to an individual or to the public, the case is taken out of the province of liberty, and placed in that of morality or law.

But with regard to the merely contingent, or, as it may be called, constructive injury which a person causes to society, by conduct which neither violates any specific duty to the public, nor occasions perceptible hurt to any assignable individual except himself; the inconvenience is one which society can afford to bear, for the sake of the greater good of human freedom. If grown persons are to be punished for not taking proper care of themselves, I would rather it were for their own sake, than under pretence of preventing them from impairing their capacity of rendering to society benefits which society does not pretend it has a right to exact. But I cannot consent to argue the point as if society had no means of bringing its weaker members up to its ordinary standard of rational conduct, except waiting till they do something irrational, and then punishing them, legally or morally, for it. Society has had absolute power over them during all the early portion of their existence: it has had the whole period of childhood and nonage in which to try whether it could make them capable of rational conduct in life. The existing generation is master both of the training and the entire circumstances of the generation to come; it cannot indeed make them perfectly wise and good, because it is itself so lamentably deficient in goodness and wisdom; and its best efforts are not always, in individual cases, its most successful ones; but it is perfectly well able to make the rising generation, as a whole, as good as, and a little better than, itself. If society lets any considerable number of its members grow up mere children, incapable of being acted on by rational consideration of distant motives, society has itself to blame for the consequences. Armed not only with all the powers of education, but with the ascendancy which the authority of a received opinion always exercises over the minds who are least fitted to judge for themselves; and aided by the *natural* penalties which cannot be prevented from falling on those who incur the distaste or the contempt of those who know them; let not society pretend that it needs, besides all this, the power to issue commands and enforce obedience in the personal concerns of individuals, in which, on all principles of justice and policy, the decision ought to rest with those who are to abide the consequences. Nor is there anything which tends more to discredit and frustrate the better means of influencing conduct, than a resort to the worse. If there be among those whom it is attempted to coerce into prudence or temperance, any of the material of which vigorous and independent characters are made, they will infallibly rebel against the yoke. No such person will ever feel that others have a right to control him in his concerns, such as they have to prevent him from injuring them in theirs; and it easily comes to be considered a mark of spirit and courage to fly in the face of such usurped authority, and do with ostentation the exact opposite of what it enjoins; as in the fashion of grossness which succeeded, in the time of Charles II, to the fanatical moral intolerance of the Puritans. With respect to what is said of the necessity of protecting society from the bad example set to others by the vicious or the self-indulgent; it is true that bad example may have a pernicious effect, especially the example of doing wrong to others with impunity to the wrong-doer. But we are now speaking of conduct which, while it does no wrong to others, is supposed to do great harm to the agent himself: and I do not see how those who believe this, can think otherwise than that the example, on the whole, must be more salutary than hurtful, since, if it displays the misconduct, it displays also the painful or degrading consequences which, if the conduct is justly censured, must be supposed to be in all or most cases attendant on it.

But the strongest of all the arguments against the interference of the public with purely personal conduct, is that when it does interfere, the odds are that it interferes wrongly, and in the wrong place. On questions of social morality, of duty to others, the opinion of the public, that is, of an overruling majority, though often wrong, is likely to be still oftener right; because on such questions they are only required to judge of their own interests; of the manner in which some mode of conduct, if allowed to be practised, would affect themselves. But the opinion of a similar majority, imposed as a law on the minority, on questions of self-regarding conduct, is quite as likely to be wrong as right; for in these cases public opinion means, at the best, some people's opinion of what is good or bad for other people; while very often it does not even mean that; the public, with the most perfect indifference, passing over the pleasure or convenience of those whose conduct they censure, and considering only their own preference. There are many who consider as an injury to themselves any conduct which they have a distaste for, and resent it as an outrage to their feelings; as a religious bigot, when charged with disregarding the religious feelings of others, has been known to retort that they disregard his feelings, by persisting in their abominable worship or creed. But there is no parity between the feeling of a person for his own opinion, and the feeling of another who is offended at his holding it; no more than between the desire of a thief to take a purse, and the desire of the right owner to keep it. And a person's taste is as much his own peculiar concern as his opinion or his purse. It is easy for anyone to imagine an ideal public, which leaves the freedom and choice of individuals in all uncertain matters undisturbed, and only requires them to abstain from modes of conduct which universal experience has condemned. But where has there been seen a public which set any such limit to its censorship? or when does the public trouble itself about universal experience? In its interferences with personal conduct it is seldom thinking of anything but the enormity of acting or feeling differently from itself; and this standard of judgment, thinly disguised, is held up to mankind as the dictate of religion and philosophy, by nine-tenths of all moralists and speculative writers. These teach that things are right because they are right; because we feel them to be so. They tell us to search in our own minds and hearts for laws of conduct binding on ourselves and on all others. What can the poor public do but apply these instructions, and make their own personal feelings of good and evil, if they are tolerably unanimous in them, obligatory on all the world?

The Subjection of Women

The object of this essay is to explain, as clearly as I am able, the grounds of an opinion which I have held from the very earliest period when I had formed any opinions at all on social or political matters, and which, instead of being weakened or modified, has been constantly growing stronger by the progress of reflection and the experience of life: That the principle which regulates the existing social relations between the two sexes—the legal subordination of one sex to the other—is wrong in itself, and now one of the chief hindrances to human improvement; and that it ought to be replaced by a principle of perfect equality, admitting no power or privilege on the one side, nor disability on the other. . . .

The generality of a practice is in some cases a strong presumption that it is, or at all events once was, conducive to laudable ends. This is the case, when the practice was first adopted, or afterwards kept up, as a means to such ends, and was grounded on experience of the mode in which they could be most effectually attained. If the authority of men over women, when first established, had been the result of a conscientious comparison between different modes of constituting the government of society; if, after trying various other modes of social organization—the government of women over men, equality between the two, and such mixed and divided modes of government as might be invented—it had been decided, on the testimony of experience, that the mode in which women are wholly under the rule of men, having no share at all in public concerns, and each in private being under the legal obligation of obedience to the man with whom she has associated her destiny, was the arrangement most conducive to the happiness and well-being of both; its general adoption might then be fairly thought to be some evidence that, at the time when it was adopted, it was the best: though even then the considerations which recommended it may, like so many other primeval social facts of the greatest importance, have subsequently, in the course of ages, ceased to exist. But the state of the case is in every respect the reverse of this. In the first place, the opinion in favour of the present system, which entirely subordinates the weaker sex to the stronger, rests upon theory only; for there never has been trial made of any other: so that experience, in the sense in which it is vulgarly opposed to theory, cannot be pretended to have pronounced any verdict. And in the second place, the adoption of this system of inequality never was the result of deliberation, or forethought, or any social ideas, or any notion whatever of what conduced to the benefit of humanity or the good order of society. It arose simply from the fact that from the very earliest twilight of human society, every woman (owing to the value attached to her by men, combined with her inferiority in muscular strength) was found in a state of bondage to some man. Laws and systems of polity always begin by recognizing the relations they find already existing between individuals. They convert what was a mere physical fact into a legal right, give it the sanction of society, and principally aim at the substitution of public and organized means of asserting and protecting these rights, instead of the irregular and lawless conflict of physical strength. Those who had already been compelled to obedience became in this manner legally bound to it. Slavery, from being a mere affair of force between the master and the slave, became regularized and a matter of compact among the masters, who, binding themselves to one another for common protection, guaranteed

by their collective strength the private possessions of each, including his slaves. In early times, the great majority of the male sex were slaves, as well as the whole of the female. And many ages elapsed, some of them ages of high cultivation, before any thinker was bold enough to question the rightfulness, and the absolute social necessity, either of the one slavery or of the other. By degrees such thinkers did arise: and (the general progress of society assisting) the slavery of the male sex has, in all the countries of Christian Europe at least (though, in one of them, only within the last few years), been at length abolished, and that of the female sex has been gradually changed into a milder form of dependence. But this dependence, as it exists at present, is not an original institution, taking a fresh start from considerations of justice and social expediency—it is the primitive state of slavery lasting on, through successive mitigations and modifications occasioned by the same causes which have softened the general manners, and brought all human relations more under the control of justice and the influence of humanity. It has not lost the taint of its brutal origin. No presumption in its favour, therefore, can be drawn from the fact of its existence. The only such presumption which it could be supposed to have, must be grounded on its having lasted till now, when so many other things which came down from the same odious source have been done away with. And this, indeed, is what makes it strange to ordinary ears, to hear it asserted that the inequality of rights between men and women has no other source than the law of the strongest. . . .

Some will object, that a comparison cannot fairly be made between the government of the male sex and the forms of unjust power which I have adduced in illustration of it, since these are arbitrary, and the effect of mere usurpation, while it on the contrary is natural.

But was there ever any domination which did not appear natural to those who possessed it? There was a time when the division of mankind into two classes, a small one of masters and a numerous one of slaves, appeared, even to the most cultivated minds, to be a natural, and the only natural, condition of the human race. No less an intellect, and one which contributed no less to the progress of human thought, than Aristotle, held this opinion without doubt or misgiving; and rested it on the same premises on which the same assertion in regard to the dominion of men over women is usually based, namely that there are different natures among mankind, free natures, and slave natures: that the Greeks were of a free nature, the barbarian races of Thracians and Asiatics of a slave nature. But why need I go back to Aristotle? Did not the slave-owners of the Southern United States maintain the same doctrine, with all the fanaticism with which men cling to the theories that justify their passions and legitimate their personal interests? Did they not call heaven and earth to witness that the dominion of the white man over the black is natural, that the black race is by nature incapable of freedom, and marked out for slavery?—some even going so far as to say that the freedom of manual labourers is an unnatural order of things anywhere. Again, the theorists of absolute monarchy have always affirmed it to be the only natural form of government; issuing from the patriarchal, which was the primitive and spontaneous form of society, framed on the model of the paternal, which is anterior to society itself, and, as they contend, the most natural authority of all. Nay, for that matter, the law of force itself, to those who could not plead any other, has always seemed the most natural of all grounds for the exercise of authority. Conquering races hold it to be Nature's own dictate that the conquered should obey the conquerors, or, as they euphoniously paraphrase it, that the feebler and more unwarlike races should submit to the braver and manlier. The smallest acquaintance with human life in the Middle Ages shows how supremely natural the dominion of the feudal nobility over men of low condition appeared to the nobility themselves, and how unnatural the conception seemed, of a person of the inferior class claiming equality with them, or exercising authority over them. It hardly seemed less so to the class held in subjection. The emancipated serfs and burgesses, even in their most vigorous struggles, never made any pretension to a share of authority; they only demanded more or less of limitation to the power of tyrannizing over them. So true is it that unnatural generally means only uncustomary, and that everything which is usual appears natural. The subjection of women to men being a universal custom, any departure from it quite naturally appears unnatural. But how entirely, even in this case, the feeling is dependent on custom, appears by ample experience. Nothing so much astonishes the people of distant parts of the world, when they first learn anything about England, as to be told that it is under a queen: the thing seems to them so unnatural as to be almost incredible. To Englishmen this does not seem in the least degree unnatural, because they are used to it; but they do feel it unnatural that women should be soldiers or members of Parliament. In the feudal ages, on the contrary, war and politics were not thought unnatural to women, because not unusual; it seemed natural that women of the privileged classes should be of manly character, inferior in nothing but bodily strength to their husbands and fathers. The independence of women seemed rather less unnatural to Greeks than to other ancients, on account of the fabulous Amazons (whom they believed to be historical), and the partial example afforded by the Spartan women; who, thought no less subordinate by law than in other Greek states, were more free in fact, and being trained to bodily exercises in the same manner with men, gave ample proof that they were not naturally disqualified for them. There can be little doubt that Spartan experience suggested to Plato, among many other of his doctrines, that of the social and political equality of the two sexes.

But, it will be said, the rule of men over women differs from all these others in not being a rule of force: it is accepted voluntarily; women make no complaint, and are consenting parties to it. In the first place, a great number of women do not accept it. Ever since there have been women able to make their sentiments known by their writings (the only mode of publicity which society permits to them), an increasing number of them have recorded protests against their present social condition: and recently many thousands of them, headed by the most eminent women known to the public, have petitioned Parliament for their admission to the Parliamentary Suffrage. The claim of women to be educated as solidly, and in the same branches of knowledge, as men, is urged with growing intensity, and with a great prospect of success; while the demand for their admission into professions and occupations hitherto closed against them, becomes every year more urgent. Though there are not in this country, as there are in the United States, periodical Conventions and an organized party to agitate for the Rights of Women, there is a numerous and active Society organized and managed by women, for the more limited object of obtaining the political franchise. Nor is it only in our own country and in America that women are beginning to protest, more or less collectively, against the disabilities under which they labour. France, and Italy, and Switzerland, and Russia now

afford examples of the same thing. How many more women there are who silently cherish similar aspirations, no one can possibly know; but there are abundant tokens how many *would* cherish them, were they not so strenuously taught to repress them as contrary to the proprieties of their sex. It must be remembered, also, that no enslaved class ever asked for complete liberty at once. . . .

All causes, social and natural, combine to make it unlikely that women should be collectively rebellious to the power of men. They are so far in a position different from all other subject classes, that their masters require something more from them than actual service. Men do not want solely the obedience of women, they want their sentiments. All men, except the most brutish, desire to have, in the woman most nearly connected with them, not a forced slave but a willing one; not a slave merely, but a favourite. They have therefore put everything in practice to enslave their minds. The masters of all other slaves rely, for maintaining obedience, on fear; either fear of themselves, or religious fears. The masters of women wanted more than simple obedience, and they turned the whole force of education to effect their purpose. All women are brought up from the very earliest years in the belief that their ideal of character is the very opposite to that of men; not self-will, and government by self-control, but submission, and yielding to the control of others. All the moralities tell them that it is the duty of women, and all the current sentimentalities that it is their nature, to live for others; to make complete abnegation of themselves, and to have no life but in their affections. And by their affections are meant the only ones they are allowed to have—those to the men with whom they are connected, or to the children who constitute an additional and indefeasible tie between them and a man. When we put together three things—first, the natural attraction between opposite sexes; secondly, the wife's entire dependence on the husband, every privilege or pleasure she has being either his gift, or depending entirely on his will; and lastly, that the principal object of human pursuit, consideration, and all objects of social ambition, can in general be sought or obtained by her only through him—it would be a miracle if the object of being attractive to men had not become the polar star of feminine education and formation of character. And, this great means of influence over the minds of women having been acquired, an instinct of selfishness made man avail themselves of it to the utmost as a means of holding women in subjection, by representing to them meekness, submissiveness, and resignation of all individual will into the hands of a man, as an essential part of sexual attractiveness. Can it be doubted that any of the other yokes which mankind have succeeded in breaking, would have subsisted till now if the same means had existed, and had been as sedulously used, to bow down their minds to it? If it had been made the object of the life of every young plebeian to find personal favour in the eyes of some patrician, of every young serf with some seigneur; if domestication with him, and a share of his personal affections, had been held out as the prize which they all should look out for, the most gifted and aspiring being able to reckon on the most desirable prizes; and if, when this prize had been obtained, they had been shut out by a wall of brass from all interests not centring in him, all feelings and desires but those which he shared or inculcated; would not serfs and seigneurs, plebeians and patricians, have been as broadly distinguished at this day as men and women are? and would not all but a thinker here and there have believed the distinction to be a fundamental and unalterable fact in human nature?

The preceding considerations are amply sufficient to show that custom, however universal it may be, affords in this case no presumption, and ought not to create any prejudice, in favour of the arrangements which place women in social and political subjection to men. But I may go farther, and maintain that the course of history, and the tendencies of progressive human society, afford not only no presumption in favour of this system of inequality of rights, but a strong one against it; and that, so far as the whole course of human improvement up to this time, the whole stream of modern tendencies, warrants any inference on the subject, it is, that this relic of the past is discordant with the future, and must necessarily disappear.

For what is the peculiar character of the modern world—the difference which chiefly distinguishes modern institutions, modern social ideas, modern life itself, from those of times long past? It is, that human beings are no longer born to their place in life, and chained down by an inexorable bond to the place they are born to, but are free to employ their faculties, and such favourable chances as offer, to achieve the lot which may appear to them most desirable. Human society of old was constituted on a very different principle. All were born to a fixed social position, and were mostly kept in it by law, or interdicted from any means by which they could emerge from it. As some men are born white and others black, so some were born slaves and others freemen and citizens; some were born patricians, others plebeians; some were born feudal nobles, others commoners and *roturiers*. A slave or serf could never make himself free, nor, except by the will of his master, become so. In most European countries it was not till towards the close of the Middle Ages, and as a consequence of the growth of regal power, that commoners could be ennobled. Even among nobles, the eldest son was born the exclusive heir to the paternal possessions, and a long time elapsed before it was fully established that the father could disinherit him. Among the industrious classes, only those who were born members of a guild, or were admitted into it by its members, could lawfully practise their calling within its local limits; and nobody could practise any calling deemed important, in any but the legal manner—by processes authoritatively prescribed. Manufacturers have stood in the pillory for presuming to carry on their business by new and improved methods. In modern Europe, and most in those parts of it which have participated most largely in all other modern improvements, diametrically opposite doctrines now prevail. Law and government do not undertake to prescribe by whom any social or industrial operation shall or shall not be conducted, or what modes of conducting them shall be lawful. These things are left to the unfettered choice of individuals. Even the laws which required that workmen should serve an apprenticeship, have in this country been repealed: there being ample assurance that in all cases in which an apprenticeship is necessary, its necessity will suffice to enforce it. The old theory was, that the least possible should be left to the choice of the individual agent; that all he had to do should, as far as practicable, be laid down for him by superior wisdom. Left to himself he was sure to go wrong. The modern conviction, the fruit of a thousand years of experience, is, that things in which the individual is the person directly interested, never go right but as they are left to his own discretion; and that any regulation of them by authority, except to protect the rights of others, is sure to be mischievous. This conclusion, slowly arrived at, and not adopted until almost every possible application of the contrary theory had been made with disastrous result, now (in the industrial department) prevails universally in the most advanced countries, almost universally in all that have pretensions to any sort of advancement. It is not that all processes are supposed to be equally good, or all persons to be equally qualified for everything; but that freedom of individual choice is now known to be the only thing which procures the adoption of the best processes, and throws each operation into the hands of those who are best qualified for it. Nobody thinks it necessary to make a law that only a strong-armed man shall be a blacksmith. Freedom and competition suffice to make blacksmiths strong-armed men, because the weak-armed can earn more by engaging in occupations for which they are more fit. In consonance with this doctrine, it is felt to be an overstepping of the proper bounds of authority to fix beforehand, on some general presumption, that certain persons are not fit to do certain things. It is now thoroughly known and admitted that if some such presumptions exist, no such presumption is infallible. Even if it be well grounded in a majority of cases, which it is very likely not to be, there will be a minority of exceptional cases in which it does not hold: and in those it is both an injustice to the individuals, and a detriment to society, to place barriers in the way of their using their faculties for their own benefit and for that of others. In the cases, on the other hand, in which the unfitness is real, the ordinary motives of human conduct will on the whole suffice to prevent the incompetent person from making, or from persisting in, the attempt.

If this general principle of social and economical science is not true; if individuals, with such help as they can derive from the opinion of those who know them, are not better judges than the law and the government, of their own capabilities and vocation; the world cannot too soon abandon this principle, and return to the old system of regulations and disabilities. But if the principle is true, we ought to act as if we believed it, and not to ordain that to be born a girl instead of a boy, any more than to be born black instead of white, or a commoner instead of a nobleman, shall decide the person's position through all life—shall interdict people from all the more elevated social positions, and from all, except a few, respectable occupations. Even were we to admit the utmost that is ever pretended as to the superior fitness of men for all the functions now reserved to them, the same argument applies which forbids a legal qualification for members of Parliament. If only once in a dozen years the conditions of eligibility exclude a fit person, there is a real loss, while the exclusion of thousands of unfit persons is no gain; for if the constitution of the electoral body disposes them to choose unfit persons, there are always plenty of such persons to choose from. In all things of any difficulty and importance, those who can do them well are fewer than the need, even with the most unrestricted latitude of choice: and any limitation of the field of selection deprives society of some chances of being served by the competent, without ever saving it from the incompetent.

At present, in the more improved countries, the disabilities of women are the only case, save one, in which laws and institutions take persons at their birth, and ordain that they shall never in all their lives be allowed to compete for certain things. The one exception is that of royalty. Persons still are born to the throne; no one, not of the reigning family, can ever occupy it, and no one even of that family can, by any means but the course of hereditary succession, attain it. All other dignities and social advantages are open to the whole male sex: many indeed are only attainable by wealth, but wealth may be striven for by anyone, and is actually obtained by many men of the very

humblest origin. The difficulties, to the majority, are indeed insuperable without the aid of fortunate accidents; but no male human being is under any legal ban: neither law nor opinion superadd artificial obstacles to the natural ones. Royalty, as I have said, is excepted; but in this case everyone feels it to be an exception—an anomaly in the modern world, in marked opposition to its customs and principles, and to be justified only by extraordinary special expediencies, which though individuals and nations differ in estimating their weight, unquestionably do in fact exist. But in this exceptional case, in which a high social function is, for important reasons, bestowed on birth instead of being put up to competition, all free nations contrive to adhere in substance to the principle from which they nominally derogate; for they circumscribe this high function by conditions avowedly intended to prevent the person to whom it ostensibly belongs from really performing it; while the person by whom it is performed, the responsible minister, does obtain the post by a competition from which no full-grown citizen of the male sex is legally excluded. The disabilities, therefore, to which women are subject from the mere fact of their birth, are the solitary examples of the kind in modern legislation. In no instance except this, which comprehends half the human race, are the higher social functions closed against anyone by a fatality of birth which no exertions, and no change of circumstances, can overcome; for even religious disabilities (besides that in England and in Europe they have practically almost ceased to exist) do not close any career to the disqualified person in case of conversion.

The social subordination of women thus stands out an isolated fact in modern social institutions; a solitary breach of what has become their fundamental law; a single relic of an old world of thought and practice exploded in everything else, but retained in the one thing of most universal interest. . . .

Neither does it avail anything to say that the *nature* of the two sexes adapts them to their present functions and position, and renders these appropriate to them. Standing on the ground of common sense and the constitution of the human mind, I deny that anyone knows, or can know, the nature of the two sexes, as long as they have only been seen in their present relation to one another. If men had ever been found in society without women, or women without men, or if there had been a society of men and women in which the women were not under the control of the men, something might have been positively known about the mental and moral differences which may be inherent in the nature of each. What is now called the nature of women is an eminently artificial thing—the result of forced repression in some directions, unnatural stimulation in others. It may be asserted without scruple, that no other class of dependents have had their character so entirely distorted from its natural proportions by their relation with their masters; for, if conquered and slave races have been, in some respects, more forcibly repressed, whatever in them has not been crushed down by an iron heel has generally been let alone, and if left with any liberty of development, it has developed itself according to its own laws; but in the case of women, a hothouse and stove cultivation has always been carried on of some of the capabilities of their nature, for the benefit and pleasure of their masters. . . .

Hence, in regard to that most difficult question, what are the natural differences between the two sexes—a subject on which it is impossible in the present state of society to obtain complete and correct knowledge—while almost everybody dogmatizes upon it, almost all neglect and make light of the only means by which any partial insight can be obtained into it. This is, an analytic study of the most important department of psychology, the laws of the influence of circumstances on character. For, however great and apparently ineradicable the moral and intellectual differences between men and women might be, the evidence of their being natural differences could only be negative. Those only could be inferred to be natural which could not possibly be artificial—the residuum, after deducting every characteristic of either sex which can admit of being explained from education or external circumstances. The profoundest knowledge of the laws of the formation of character is indispensable to entitle anyone to affirm even that there is any difference, much more what the difference is, between the two sexes considered as moral and rational beings; and since no one, as yet, has that knowledge (for there is hardly any subject which, in proportion to its importance, has been so little studied), no one is thus far entitled to any positive opinion on the subject. Conjectures are all that can at present be made; conjectures more or less probable, according as more or less authorized by such knowledge as we yet have of the laws of psychology, as applied to the formation of character.

. . . Many a man thinks he perfectly understands women, because he has had amatory relations with several, perhaps with many of them. If he is a good observer, and his experience extends to quality as well as quantity, he may have learnt something of one narrow department of their nature—an important department, no doubt. But of all the rest of it, few persons are generally more ignorant, because there are few from whom it is so carefully hidden. The most favourable case which a man can generally have for studying the character of a woman, is that of his own wife: for the opportunities are greater, and the cases of complete sympathy not so unspeakably rare. And in fact, this is the source from which any knowledge worth having on the subject has, I believe, generally come. But most men have not had the opportunity of studying in this way more than a single case: accordingly one can, to an almost laughable degree, infer what a man's wife is like, from his opinions about women in general. To make even this one case yield any result, the woman must be worth knowing, and the man not only a competent judge, but of a character so sympathetic in itself, and so well adapted to hers, that he can either read her mind by sympathetic intuition, or has nothing in himself which makes her shy of disclosing it. . . .

One thing we may be certain of—that what is contrary to women's nature to do, they never will be made to do by simply giving their nature free play. The anxiety of mankind to interfere in behalf of nature, for fear lest nature should not succeed in effecting its purpose, is an altogether unnecessary solicitude. What women by nature cannot do, it is quite superfluous to forbid them from doing. What they can do, but not so well as the men who are their competitors, competition suffices to exclude them from; since nobody asks for protective duties and bounties in favour of women; it is only asked that the present bounties and protective duties in favour of men should be recalled. If women have a greater natural inclination for some things than for others, there is no need of laws or social inculcation to make the majority of them do the former in preference to the latter. Whatever women's services are most wanted for, the free play of competition will hold out the strongest inducements to them to undertake. And, as the words imply, they are most wanted for the things for which they are most fit; by the apportionment of which to them, the collective faculties of the two sexes can be applied on the whole with the greatest sum of valuable result.

The general opinion of men is supposed to be, that the natural vocation of a woman is that of a wife and mother. I say, is supposed to be, because, judging from acts—from the whole of the present constitution of society—one might infer that their opinion was the direct contrary. They might be supposed to think that the alleged natural vocation of women was of all things the most repugnant to their nature; insomuch that if they are free to do anything else—if any other means of living, or occupation of their time and faculties, is open, which has any chance of appearing desirable to them—there will not be enough of them who will be willing to accept the condition said to be natural to them. If this is the real opinion of men in general, it would be well that it should be spoken out. I should like to hear somebody openly enunciating the doctrine (it is already implied in much that it written on the subject)—'It is necessary to society that women should marry and produce children. They will not do so unless they are compelled. Therefore it is necessary to compel them.' The merits of the case would then be clearly defined. It would be exactly that of the slaveholders of South Carolina and Louisiana. 'It is necessary that cotton and sugar should be grown. White men cannot produce them. Negroes will not, for any wages which we choose to give. *Ergo* they must be compelled.' An illustration still closer to the point is that of impressment. Sailors must absolutely be had to defend the country. It often happens that they will not voluntarily enlist. Therefore there must be the power of forcing them. How often has this logic been used! and, but for one flaw in it, without doubt it would have been successful up to this day. But it is open to retort— First pay the sailors the honest value of their labour. When you have made it as well worth their while to serve you, as to work for other employers, you will have no more difficulty than others have in obtaining their services. To this there is no logical answer except 'I will not': and as people are now not only ashamed, but are not desirous, to rob the labourer of his hire, impressment is no longer advocated. Those who attempt to force women into marriage by closing all other doors against them, lay themselves open to a similar retort. If they mean what they say, their opinion must evidently be, that men do not render the married condition so desirable to women, as to induce them to accept it for its own recommendations. It is not a sign of one's thinking the boon one offers very attractive, when one allows only Hobson's choice, 'that or none'. And here, I believe, is the clue to the feelings of those men, who have a real antipathy to the equal freedom of women. I believe they are afraid, not lest women should be unwilling to marry, for I do not think that anyone in reality has that apprehension; but lest they should insist that marriage should be on equal conditions; lest all women of spirit and capacity should prefer doing almost anything else, not in their own eyes degrading, rather than marry, when marrying is giving themselves a master, and a master too of all their earthly possessions. And truly, if this consequence were necessarily incident to marriage, I think that the apprehension would be very well founded. I agree in thinking it probable that few women, capable of anything else, would, unless under an irresistible *entraînement,* rendering them for the time insensible to anything but itself, choose such a lot, when any other means were open to them of filling a conventionally honourable place in life: and if men are determined that the law of marriage shall be a law of despotism, they are quite right, in point of mere policy, in leaving to women only Hobson's choice. But, in that case, all that has been done in the modern world to relax the chain on the minds of women, has been a mistake. They never should have been allowed to receive a literary education. Women who read, much more women who write, are, in the existing constitution of things, a contradiction and a disturbing element: and it was wrong to bring women up with any acquirements but those of an odalisque, or of a domestic servant.

The Enfranchisement of Women

Most of our readers will probably learn from these pages for the first time, that there has arisen in the United States, and in the most civilized and enlightened portion of them, an organized agitation on a new question—new, not to thinkers, nor to anyone by whom the principles of free and popular government are felt as well as acknowledged, but new, and even unheard of, as a subject for public meetings and practical political action. This question is, the enfranchisement of women; their admission, in law and in fact, to equality in all rights, political, civil, and social, with the male citizens of the community.

It will add to the surprise with which many will receive this intelligence, that the agitation which has commenced is not a pleading by male writers and orators for women, those who are professedly to be benefited remaining either indifferent or ostensibly hostile: it is a political movement, practical in its objects, carried on in a form which denotes an intention to persevere. And it is a movement not merely *for* women, but *by* them. Its first public manifestation appears to have been a Convention of Women, held in the State of Ohio, in the spring of 1850. Of this meeting we have seen no report. On the 23rd and 24th of October last, a succession of public meetings was held at Worcester, in Massachusetts, under the name of a 'Women's Rights Convention', of which the president was a woman, and nearly all the chief speakers women; numerously reinforced, however, by men, among whom were some of the most distinguished leaders in the kindred cause of negro emancipation. A general and four special committees were nominated, for the purpose of carrying on the undertaking until the next annual meeting. . . .

That women have as good a claim as men have, in point of personal right, to the suffrage, or to a place in the jury-box, it would be difficult for anyone to deny. It cannot certainly be denied by the United States of America, as a people or as a community. Their democratic institutions rest avowedly on the inherent right of everyone to a voice in the government. Their Declaration of Independence, framed by the men who are still their great constitutional authorities—that document which has been from the first, and is now, the acknowledged basis of their polity, commences with this express statement:

> We hold these truths to be self-evident: that all men are created equal; that they are endowed by their Creator with certain inalienable rights; that among these are life, liberty, and the pursuit of happiness; that to secure these rights, governments are instituted among men, deriving their just powers from the consent of the governed.

We do not imagine that any American democrat will evade the force of these expressions by the dishonest or ignorant subterfuge, that 'men', in this memorable document, does not stand for human beings, but for one sex only; that 'life, liberty, and the pursuit of happiness' are 'inalienable rights' of only one moiety of the human species; and that 'the governed', whose consent is affirmed to be the only source of just power, are meant for that half of mankind only, who, in relation to the other, have hitherto assumed the character of *governors*. The contradiction between principle and practice cannot be explained away. A like dereliction of the fundamental maxims of their political creed has been committed by the Americans in the flagrant instance of the negroes; of this they are learning to recognize the turpitude. After a struggle which, by many of its incidents, deserves the name of heroic, the abolitionists are now so strong in numbers and in influence that they hold the balance of parties in the United States. It was fitting that the men whose names will remain associated with the extirpation, from the democratic soil of America, of the aristocracy of color, should be among the originators, for America and for the rest of the world, of the first collective protest against the aristocracy of sex; a distinction as accidental as that of colour, and fully as irrelevant to all questions of government.

Not only to the democracy of America, the claim of women to civil and political equality makes an irresistible appeal, but also to those radicals and chartists in the British islands, and democrats on the Continent, who claim what is called universal suffrage as an inherent right, unjustly and oppressively withheld from them. For with what truth or rationality could the suffrage be termed universal, while half the human species remain excluded from it? To declare that a voice in the government is the right of all, and demand it only for a part—the part, namely, to which the claimant himself belongs—is to renounce even the appearance of principle. The chartist who denies the suffrage women, is a chartist only because he is not a lord; he is one of those levellers who would level only down to themselves.

Even those who do not look upon a voice in the government as a matter of personal right, nor profess principles which require that it should be extended to all, have usually traditional maxims of political justice with which it is impossible to reconcile the exclusion of all women from the common rights of citizenship. It is an axiom of English freedom that taxation and representation should be co-extensive. Even under the laws which give the wife's property to the husband, there are many unmarried women who pay taxes. It is one of the fundamental doctrines of the British constitution, that all persons should be tried by their peers: yet women, whenever tried, are tried by male judges and a male jury. To foreigners the law accords the privilege of claiming that half the jury should be composed of themselves; not so to women. Apart from maxims of detail, which represent local and national rather than universal ideas; it is an acknowledged dictate of justice to make no degrading distinctions without necessity. In all things the presumption ought to be on the side of equality. A reason must be given why anything should be permitted to one person and interdicted to another. But when that which is interdicted includes nearly everything which those to whom it is permitted most prize, and to be deprived of which they feel to be most insulting; when not only political liberty but personal freedom of action is the prerogative of a caste; when even in the exercise of industry, almost all employments which task the higher faculties in an important field, which lead to distinction, riches, or even pecuniary independence, are fenced round as the exclusive domain of the predominant section, scarcely any doors being left open to the dependent class, except such as all who can enter elsewhere disdainfully pass by; the miserable expediencies which are advanced as excuses for so grossly partial a dispensation, would not be sufficient, even if they were real, to render it other than a flagrant injustice. While, far from being expedient, we are firmly convinced that the division of mankind into two castes, one born to rule over the other, is in this case, as in all cases, an unqualified mischief; a source of perversion and demoralization, both to the favoured class and to those at whose expense they are favoured; producing none of the good which it is the custom to ascribe to it, and forming a bar, almost insuperable while it lasts, to any really vital improvement, either in the character or in the social condition of the human race.

These propositions it is now our purpose to maintain. But before entering on them, we would endeavour to dispel the preliminary objections which, in the minds of persons to whom the subject is new, are apt to prevent a real and conscientious examination of it. The chief of these obstacles is that most formidable one, custom. Women never have had equal rights with men. The claim in their behalf, of the common rights of mankind, is looked upon as barred by universal practice. This strongest of prejudices, the prejudice against what is new and unknown, has, indeed, in an age of changes like the present, lost much of its force; if it had not, there would be little hope of prevailing against it. Over three-fourths of the habitable world, even at this day, the answer, 'it has always been so,' closes all discussion. But it is the boast of modern Europeans, and of their American kindred, that they know and do many things which their forefathers neither knew nor did; and it is perhaps the most unquestionable point of superiority in the present above former ages, that habit is not now the tyrant it formerly was over opinions and modes of action, and that the worship of custom is a declining idolatry. An uncustomary thought, on a subject which touches the greater interests of life, still startles when first presented; but if it can be kept before the mind until the impression of strangeness wears off, it obtains a hearing, and as rational a consideration as the intellect of the hearer is accustomed to bestow on any other subject.

In the present case, the prejudice of custom is doubtless on the unjust side. Great thinkers, indeed, at different times, from Plato to Condorcet, besides some of the most eminent names of the present age, have made emphatic protests in favour of the equality of women. And there have been voluntary societies, religious or secular, of which the Society of Friends is the most known, by whom that principle was recognized. But there has been no political community or nation in which, by law, and usage, women have not been in a state of political and civil inferiority. In the ancient world the same fact was alleged, with equal truth, in behalf of slavery. It might have been alleged in favour of the mitigated form of slavery, serfdom, all through the Middle Ages. It was urged against freedom of industry, freedom of conscience, freedom of the press; none of these liberties were thought compatible with a well-ordered state, until they had proved their possibility by actually existing as facts. That an institution or a practice is customary is no presumption of its goodness, when any other sufficient cause can be assigned for its existence. There is no difficulty in understanding why the subjection of women has been a custom. No other explanation is needed than physical force.

That those who were physically weaker should have been made legally inferior, is quite conformable to the mode in which the world has been governed. Until very lately, the rule of physical strength was the general law of human affairs. Throughout history, the nations, races, classes, which found themselves the strongest, either in muscles, in riches, or in military discipline, have conquered and held in subjection the rest. If, even in the most improved nations, the law of the sword is at last discountenanced as unworthy, it is only since the calumniated eighteenth century. Wars of conquest have only ceased since democratic revolutions began. The world is very young, and has but just begun to cast off injustice. It is only now getting rid of negro slavery. It is only now getting rid of monarchical despotism. It is only now getting rid of hereditary feudal nobility. It is only now getting rid of disabilities on the ground of religion. It is only beginning to treat any *men* as citizens, except the rich and a favoured portion of the middle class. Can we wonder that it has not yet done as much for women? As society was constituted until the last few generations, inequality was its very basis; association grounded on equal rights scarcely existed; to be equals was to be enemies; two persons could hardly co-operate in anything, or meet in any amicable relation, without the law's appointing that one of them should be the superior of the other. Mankind have outgrown this state, and all things now tend to substitute, as the general principle of human relations, a just equality, instead of the dominion of the strongest. But of all relations, that between men and women being the nearest and most intimate, and connected with the greatest number of strong emotions, was sure to be the last to throw off the old rules and receive the new: for in proportion to the strength of a feeling, is the tenacity with which it clings to the forms and circumstances with which it has even accidentally become associated.

When a prejudice, which has any hold on the feelings, finds itself reduced to the unpleasant necessity of assigning reasons, it thinks it has done enough when it has reasserted the very point in dispute, in phrases which appeal to the pre-existing feeling. Thus, many persons think they have sufficiently justified the restrictions on women's field of action, when they have said that the pursuits from which women are excluded are *unfeminine*, and that the *proper sphere* of women is not politics or publicity, but private and domestic life.

We deny the right of any portion of the species to decide for another portion, or any individual for another individual, what is and what is not their 'proper sphere'. The proper sphere for all human beings is the largest and highest which they are able to attain to. What this is, cannot be ascertained, without complete liberty of choice. The speakers at the Convention in America have therefore done wisely and right, in refusing to entertain the question of the peculiar aptitudes either of women or of men, or the limits within which this or that occupation may be supposed to be more adapted to the one or to the other. They justly maintain, that these questions can only be satisfactorily answered by perfect freedom. Let every occupation be open to all, without favour or discouragement to any, and employments will fall into the hands of those men or women who are found by experience to be most capable of worthily exercising them. There need be no fear that women will take out of the hands of men any occupation which men perform better than they. Each individual will prove his or her capacities, in the only way in which capacities can be proved—by trial; and the world will have the benefit of the best faculties of all its inhabitants. But to interfere beforehand by an arbitrary limit, and declare that whatever be the genius, talent, energy, or force of mind of an individual of a certain sex or class, those facilities shall not be exerted, or shall be exerted only in some few of the many

modes in which others are permitted to use theirs, is not only an injustice to the individual, and a detriment to society, which loses what it can ill spare, but is also the most effectual mode of providing that, in the sex or class so fettered, the qualities which are not permitted to be exercised shall not exist.

We shall follow the very proper example of the Convention, in not entering into the question of the alleged differences in physical or mental qualities between the sexes; not because we have nothing to say, but because we have too much; to discuss this one point tolerably would need all the space we have to bestow on the entire subject. But if those who assert that the 'proper sphere' for women is the domestic, mean by this that they have not shown themselves qualified for any other, the assertion evinces great ignorance of life and of history. Women have shown fitness for the highest social functions, exactly in proportion as they have been admitted to them. By a curious anomaly, though ineligible to even the lowest offices of state, they are in some countries admitted to the highest of all, the regal; and if there is any one function for which they have shown a decided vocation, it is that of reigning. Not to go back to ancient history, we look in vain for abler or firmer rulers than Elizabeth; than Isabella of Castile; than Maria Teresa; than Catherine of Russia; than Blanche, mother of Louis IX of France; than Jeanne d'Albret, mother of Henri Quatre. There are few kings on record who contended with more difficult circumstances, or overcame them more triumphantly, than these. Even in semi-barbarous Asia, princesses who have never been seen by men, other than those of their own family, or ever spoken with them unless from behind a curtain, have as regents, during the minority of their sons, exhibited many of the most brilliant examples of just and vigorous administration. In the Middle Ages, when the distance between the upper and lower ranks was greater than even between women and men, and the women of the privileged class, however subject to tyranny from the men of the same class, were at a less distance below them than anyone else was, and often in their absence represented them in their functions and authority—numbers of heroic chatelaines, like Jeanne de Montfort, or the great Countess of Derby as late even as the time of Charles I, distinguished themselves not only by their political but their military capacity. In the centuries immediately before and after the Reformation, ladies of royal houses, as diplomatists, as governors of provinces, or as the confidential advisers of kings, equalled the first statesmen of their time: and the treaty of Cambray, which gave peace to Europe, was negotiated in conferences where no other person was present, by the aunt of the Emperor Charles V, and the mother of Francis I.

Concerning the fitness, then, of women for politics, there can be no question: but the dispute is more likely to turn upon the fitness of politics for women. When the reasons alleged for excluding women from active life in all its higher departments, are stripped of their garb of declamatory phrases, and reduced to the simple expression of a meaning, they seem to be mainly three: the incompatibility of active life with maternity, and with the cares of a household; secondly, its alleged hardening effect on the character; and thirdly, the inexpediency of making an addition to the already excessive pressure of competition in every kind of professional or lucrative employment.

The first, the maternity argument, is usually laid most stress upon: although (it needs hardly be said) this reason, if it be one, can apply only to mothers. It is neither necessary nor just to make imperative on women that they shall be either mothers or nothing; or that if they have been mothers once, they shall be nothing else during the whole remainder of their lives. Neither women nor men need any law to exclude them from an occupation, if they have undertaken another which is incompatible with it. No one proposes to exclude the male sex from Parliament because a man may be a soldier or sailor in active service, or a merchant whose business requires all his time and energies. Nine-tenths of the occupations of men exclude them *de facto* from public life, as effectually as if they were excluded by law; but that is no reason for making laws to exclude even the nine-tenths, much less the remaining tenth. The reason of the case is the same for women as for men. There is no need to make provision by law that a woman shall not carry on the active details of a household, or of the education of children, and at the same time practise a profession or be elected to Parliament. Where incompatibility is real, it will take care of itself: but there is gross injustice in making the incompatibility a pretence for the exclusion of those in whose case it does not exist. And these, if they were free to choose, would be a very large proportion. The maternity argument deserts its supporters in the case of single women, a large and increasing class of the population; a fact which, it is not irrelevant to remark, by tending to diminish the excessive competition of numbers, is calculated to assist greatly the prosperity of all. There is no inherent reason or necessity that all women should voluntarily choose to devote their lives to one animal function and its consequences. Numbers of women are wives and mothers only because there is no other career open to them, no other occupation for their feelings or their activities. Every improvement in their education, and enlargement of their facilities—everything which renders them more qualified for any other mode of life, increases the number of those to whom it is an injury and an oppression to be denied the choice. To say that women must be excluded from active life because maternity disqualifies them for it, is in fact to say, that every other career should be forbidden them in order that maternity may be their only resource.

But secondly, it is urged, that to give the same freedom of occupation to women as to men, would be an injurious addition to the crowd of competitors, by whom the avenues to almost all kinds of employment are choked up, and its remuneration depressed. This argument, it is to be observed, does not reach the political question. It gives no excuse for withholding from women the rights of citizenship. The suffrage, the jury-box, admission to the legislature and to office, it does not touch. It bears only on the industrial branch of the subject. Allowing it, then, in an economical point of view, its full force; assuming that to lay open to women the employments now monopolized by men, would tend, like the breaking down of other monopolies, to lower the rate of remuneration in those employments; let us consider what is the amount of this evil consequence, and what the compensation for it. The worst ever asserted, much worse than is at all likely to be realized, is that if women competed with men, a man and a woman could not together earn more than is now earned by the man alone. Let us make this supposition, the most unfavourable supposition possible: the joint income of the two would be the same as before, while the woman would be raised from the position of a servant to that of a partner. Even if every woman, as matters now stand, had a claim on some man for support, how infinitely preferable is it that part of the income should be of the woman's earning, even if the aggregate sum were but little increased by it, rather than that she should be compelled to stand aside in order that men may be the sole earners, and the sole dispensers of what is earned. Even under the present laws respecting the property of

women, a woman who contributes materially to the support of the family, cannot be treated in the same contemptuously tyrannical manner as one who, however she may toil as a domestic drudge, is a dependent on the man for subsistence. As for the depression of wages by increase of competition, remedies will be found for it in time. Palliatives might be applied immediately; for instance, a more rigid exclusion of children from industrial employment, during the years in which they ought to be working only to strengthen their bodies and minds for after life. Children are necessarily dependent, and under the power of others; and their labour, being not for themselves but for the gain of their parents, is a proper subject for legislative regulation. With respect to the future, we neither believe that improvident multiplication, and the consequent excessive difficulty of gaining a subsistence, will always continue, nor that the division of mankind into capitalists and hired labourers, and the regulation of the reward of labourers mainly be demand and supply, will be forever, or even much longer, the rule of the world. But so long as competition is the general law of human life, it is tyranny to shut out one half of the competitors. All who have attained the age of self-government, have an equal claim to be permitted to sell whatever kind of useful labour they are capable of, for the price which it will bring.

The third objection to the admission of women to political or professional life, its alleged hardening tendency, belongs to an age now past, and is scarcely to be comprehended by people of the present time. There are still, however, persons who say that the world and its avocations render men selfish and unfeeling; that the struggles, rivalries, and collisions of business and of politics make them harsh and unamiable; that if half the species must unavoidably be given up to these things, it is the more necessary that the other half should be kept free from them; that to preserve women from the bad influences of the world, is the only chance of preventing men from being wholly given up to them.

There would have been plausibility in this argument when the world was still in the age of violence, when life was full of physical conflict, and every man had to redress his injuries or those of others, by the sword or by the strength of his arm. Women, like priests, by being exempted from such responsibilities, and from some part of the accompanying dangers, may have been enabled to exercise a beneficial influence. But in the present condition of human life, we do not know where those hardening influences are to be found, to which men are subject and from which women are at present exempt. Individuals now-a-days are seldom called upon to fight hand to hand, even with peaceful weapons; personal enmities and rivalries count for little in worldly transactions; the general pressure of circumstances, not the adverse will of individuals, is the obstacle men now have to make head against. That pressure, when excessive, breaks the spirit, and cramps and sours the feelings, but not less of women than of men, since they suffer certainly not less from its evils. There are still quarrels and dislikes, but the sources of them are changed. The feudal chief once found his bitterest enemy in his powerful neighbour, the minister or courtier in his rival for place: but opposition of interest in active life, as a cause of personal animosity, is out of date; the enmities of the present day arise not from great things but small, from

what people say of one another, more than from what they do; and if there are hatred, malice, and all uncharitableness, they are to be found among women fully as much as among men. In the present state of civilization, the notion of guarding women from the hardening influences of the world, could only be realized by secluding them from society altogether. The common duties of common life, as at present constituted, are incompatible with any other softness in women than weakness. Surely weak minds in weak bodies must ere long cease to be even supposed to be either attractive or amiable.

But, in truth, none of these arguments and considerations touch the foundations of the subject. The real question is, whether it is right and expedient that one-half of the human race should pass through life in a state of forced subordination to the other half. If the best state of human society is that of being divided into two parts, one consisting of persons with a will and a substantive existence, the other of humble companions to these persons, attached, each of them to one, for the purpose of bringing up *his* children, and making *his* home pleasant to him; if this is the place assigned to women, it is but kindness to educate them for this; to make them believe that the greatest good fortune which can befall them, is to be chosen by some man for this purpose; and that every other career which the world deems happy or honourable, is closed to them by the law, not of social institutions, but of nature and destiny.

Study Questions for *On Liberty*

1. How have human conceptions of 'liberty' and 'authority' evolved from antiquity to modernity, according to Mill? What is the 'simple principle' Mill defends throughout the essay? To whom does this principle not apply?
2. In chapter II, Mill argues for the complete liberty of thought, discussion, and expression of opinion. Outline Mill's argument. Why should the state refrain from suppressing opinions that are in fact false?
3. What are the social benefits of encouraging 'experiments of living' and the development of individuality?
4. In chapter IV, Mill notes that receiving the protections and benefits of society generates social obligations on the part of individual citizens. What are the social obligations of citizens?
5. How does Mill respond to the objection that 'no person is an entirely isolated being'? What should be the position of the state toward mischievous actions that harm others only by creating bad examples or diminishing social resources?
6. Throughout *On Liberty*, Mill argues against paternalistic policies that limit the liberty of individuals for the sake of their own good. What would Mill say about the legalization of drugs in contemporary societies? What might Mill say about placing controls upon pornographic publications and the pornography industry?

Study Questions for *The Subjection of Women* and *The Enfranchisement of Women*

1. Explain Mill's criticism of the common idea that the subordination of women to men is natural.
2. In addressing his opponents in chapter IV of *The Subjection of Women*, Mill describes several beneficial consequences of emancipating women. Briefly describe each of these benefits.
3. According to Taylor, why is women's suffrage an issue of particular importance to liberal democratic countries like the United States and England?
4. Taylor addresses three important objections against women's participation in the public sphere. List each of these objections and explain Taylor's response to each.
5. Compare and contrast Mill's *Subjection of Women* with *Taylor's Enfranchisement of Women*. What ideas do Mill and Taylor share? Where do the two differ on issues of sexual equality and female independence?

Recommended Readings

Annas, Julia, 'Mill and the Subjection of Women,' *Philosophy* 52 (1977): 179–94.

Berlin, Isaiah, 'John Stuart Mill and the Ends of Life' and 'Two Concepts of Liberty,' in *Four Essays on Liberty* (Oxford University Press, 1969).

Donner, Wendy, *The Liberal Self: John Stuart Mill's Moral and Political Philosophy* (Cornell University Press, 1991).

Gray, John, *Mill on Liberty: A Defence* (Routledge, 1983).

Held, Virginia, 'Justice and Harriet Taylor,' *The Nation*, 25 October 1971, 405–6.

Longino, Helen, 'Pornography, Freedom and Oppression: A Closer Look,' in *Take Back the Night*, edited by L. Lederer (William Morrow, 1980).

Morales, Maria, *Perfect Equality: John Stuart Mill on Well-Constituted Communities* (Rowman and Littlefield, 1996).

Ryan, Alan, *Mill* (Routledge, 1974).

Skorupski, John, *Why Read Mill Today?* (Routledge, 2006).

Szasz, Thomas, 'The Ethics of Addition,' in *Morality and Moral Controversies: Readings in Moral, Social and Political Philosophy*, 6th edn, edited by John Arthur (Prentice Hall, 2001).

Thomas, William, *J.S. Mill* (Oxford University Press, 1985).

Karl Marx and Fredrick Engels

Karl Marx (1818–1883) was born in Prussia to a large upper-middle-class Jewish family. At the behest of his father, he studied law at the University of Bonn, but Marx did not take well to the study of law and spent more time partying and writing poetry than studying law. His father soon transferred him to the University of Berlin, where he became engrossed in the study of philosophy and, in particular, in the work of the German philosopher G.F.W. Hegel. At 23, he earned a doctoral degree in philosophy for a dissertation on stoic and Epicurean philosophers. Although Marx hoped to occupy a university teaching post, he was unable to obtain such a position because of his known radical views on politics and religion. Instead, he worked as a journalist and newspaper editor, until increasing government censorship led him to resign his editorship in 1843. In that same year, Marx also married his childhood sweetheart, Jenny von Westphalen, and moved to Paris, where he edited a new journal, became more engrossed in communist theory, and met Friedrich Engels. Two years after moving to Paris, Marx was expelled from France—owing to the influence of the Prussian monarchy upon French officials—and he and Jenny moved to Brussels, England. Marx lived primarily in England for the remainder of his life, writing a hundred-volume opus of political philosophy and social criticism.

Marx and his family lived in poverty during the 1850s and 1860s, and the family lost three of their six children owing to illness and poverty. Marx typically worked ten hours a day studying economics and political theory in the British Museum, and he wrote at home long into the night. While living in England, he had no regular paid occupation but got by on whatever support Engels could provide.

Engels (1820–1895) was born into a wealthy Prussian family that owned and operated textile factories in Prussia and England. Until his retirement at 48, Engels helped to manage the financial affairs of his family's firm, and his first-hand observations of the conditions of factory workers, combined with his extensive reading of philosophy and political economy, made him a social critic of some influence. When only 25, he published a widely read critique of the industrial capitalism of nineteenth-century England, *The Condition of the Working Class in England* (1845). Engels also paid greater attention than Marx to the oppression of women, arguing famously in *The Origin of the Family, Private Property and the State* (1884) that the advent of the institution of private property marked the origin of the subordination of women.

Our first selection, 'Alienated Labour,' is an excerpt from the *Economic and Philosophical Manuscripts,* which Marx penned in 1844 shortly before beginning his lifelong collaboration with Engels. This excerpt contains Marx's idea that industrial capitalist societies transform labour—

a distinctively human activity with potential for individual self-expression and self-fulfilment—into a commodity sold by the worker and bought by an employer. The commoditization of labour, in turn, serves to alienate or estrange workers from the process of working, from the products of work, from themselves, and from other people.

Whereas the *Economic and Philosophical Manuscripts* were published only posthumously in 1932, *The Communist Manifesto* was published in 1848, when both Marx and Engels were young men. Its purpose was to unite oppressed workers of the world in revolution, and it set out to define the principles of the Communist League, a radical working-class organization that sought to overthrow proletariat rule in the nineteenth century. In the *Manifesto,* Marx and Engels discuss themes ranging from social inequalities to private property to the principles of a communist society. In a communist society, the institution of private property will be replaced with public control of the means of production, and the modern class division between bourgeois and proletariat will give way to a classless society in which all citizens can participate in productive work. In addition to answering several possible objections against the communist agenda, Marx and Engels set forward several key measures for implementation in a communist society. Notably, some of these measures—such as ending child labour, providing free public education for all young people, and instituting a graduated income tax system—were incorporated into capitalist economies in the twentieth century.

'Alienated Labour'

We started from the presuppositions of political economy. We accepted its vocabulary and its laws. We presupposed private property, the separation of labour, capital, and land, and likewise of wages, profit, and ground rent; also division of labour; competition; the concept of exchange value, etc. Using the very words of political economy we have demonstrated that the worker is degraded to the most miserable sort of commodity; that the misery of the workers is in inverse proportion to the power and size of his production; that the necessary result of competition is the accumulation of capital in a few hands, and thus a more terrible restoration of monopoly; and that finally the distinction between capitalist and landlord, and that between peasant and industrial workers disappears and the whole of society must fall apart into the two classes of the property owners and the propertyless workers.

Political economy starts with the fact of private property, it does not explain it to us. It conceives of the material process that private property goes through in reality in general abstract formulas which then have for it a value of laws. It does not understand these laws, i.e., it does not demonstrate how they arise from the nature of private property. Political economy does not afford us any explanation of the reason for the separation of labour and capital, of capital and land. When, for example, political economy defines the relationship of wages to profit from capital, the interest of the capitalist is the ultimate court of appeal, that is, it presupposes what should be its result. In the same way competition enters the argument everywhere. It is explained by exterior circumstances. But political economy tells us nothing about how far these exterior, apparently fortuitous circumstances are merely the expression of a necessary development. We have seen how it regards exchange itself as something fortuitous. The only wheels that political economy sets in motion are greed and war among the greedy, competition.

It is just because political economy has not grasped the connections in the movement that new contradictions have arisen in its doctrines, for example, between that of monopoly and that of competition, freedom of craft and corporations, division of landed property and large estates. For competition, free trade, and the division of landed property were only seen as fortuitous circumstances created by will and force, not developed and comprehended as necessary, inevitable, and natural results of monopoly, corporations, and feudal property.

So what we have to understand now is the essential connection of private property, selfishness, the separation of labour, capital, and landed property, of exchange and competition, etc.—the connection of all this alienation with the money system.

Let us not be like the political economist who, when he wishes to explain something, puts himself in an imaginary original state of affairs. Such an original state of affairs explains nothing. He simply pushes the question back into a grey and nebulous distance. He presupposes as a fact and an event what he ought to be deducing, namely the necessary connection between the two things, for example, between the division of labour and exchange. Similarly, the theologian explains the origin of evil through the fall, i.e., he presupposes as an historical fact what he should be explaining.

We start with a contemporary fact of political economy:

The worker becomes poorer the richer is his production, the more it increases in power and scope. The worker becomes a commodity that is all the cheaper the more commodities he creates. The depreciation of the human world progresses in direct proportion to the increase in value of the world of things. Labour does not only produce commodities; it produces itself and the labourer as a commodity and that to the extent to which it produces commodities in general.

What this fact expresses is merely this: the object that labour produces, its product, confronts it as an alien being, as a power independent of the producer. The product of labour is labour that has solidified itself into an object, made itself into a thing, the objectification of labour. The realization of labour is its objectification. In political economy this realization of labour appears as a loss of reality for the worker, objectification as a loss of the object or slavery to it, and appropriation as alienation, as externalization.

The realization of labour appears as a loss of reality to an extent that the worker loses his reality by dying of starvation. Objectification appears as a loss of the object to such an extent that the worker is robbed not only of the objects necessary for his life but also of the objects of his work. Indeed, labour itself becomes an object he can only have in his power with the greatest of efforts and at irregular intervals. The appropriation of the object appears as alienation to such an extent that the more objects the worker produces, the less he can possess and the more he falls under the domination of his product, capital.

All these consequences follow from the fact that the worker relates to the product of his labour as to an alien object. For it is evident from this presupposition that the more the worker externalizes himself in his work, the more powerful becomes the alien, objective world that he creates opposite himself, the poorer he becomes himself in his inner life, and the less he can call his own. It is just the same in religion. The more man puts into God, the less he retains in himself. The worker puts his life into the object and this means that it no longer belongs to him but to the object. So the greater this activity, the more the worker is without an object. What the product of his labour is, that he is not. So the greater this product the less he is himself. The externalization of the worker in his product implies not only that his labour becomes an object, an exterior existence, but also that it exists outside him, independent and alien, and becomes a self-sufficient power opposite him, that the life that he has lent to the object affronts him, hostile and alien.

Let us now deal in more detail with objectification, the production of the worker, and the alienation, the loss of the object, his product, which is involved in it.

The worker can create nothing without nature, the sensuous exterior world. It is the matter in which his labour realizes itself, in which it is active, out of which and through which it produces.

But as nature affords the means of life for labour in the sense that labour cannot live without objects on which it exercises itself, so it affords a means of life in the narrower sense, namely the means for the physical subsistence of the worker himself.

Thus the more the worker appropriates the exterior world of sensuous nature by his labour, the more he doubly deprives himself of the means of subsistence, firstly since the exterior sensuous world increasingly ceases to be an object belonging to his work, a means of subsistence for his labour; secondly, since it increasingly ceases to be a means of subsistence in the direct sense, a means for the physical subsistence of the worker.

Thus in these two ways the worker becomes a slave to his object: firstly he receives an object of labour, that is, he receives labour, and secondly, he receives the means of subsistence. Thus it is his object that permits him to exist first as a worker and secondly as a physical subject. The climax of this slavery is that only as a worker can he maintain himself as a physical subject and it is only as a physical subject that he is a worker.

(According to the laws of political economy the alienation of the worker in his object is expressed as follows: the more the worker produces the less he has to consume, the more values he creates the more valueless and worthless he becomes, the more formed the product the more deformed the worker, the more civilized the product the more barbaric the worker, the more powerful the work the more powerless becomes the worker, the more cultured the work the more philistine the worker becomes and more of a slave to nature.)

Political economy hides the alienation in the essence of labour by not considering the immediate relationship between the worker (labour) and production. Labour produces works of wonder for the rich, but nakedness for the worker. It produces palaces, but only hovels for the worker; it produces beauty, but cripples the worker; it replaces labour by machines, but throws a part of the workers back to a barbaric labour and turns the other part into machines. It produces culture, but also imbecility and cretinism for the worker.

The immediate relationship of labour to its products is the relationship of the worker to the objects of his production. The relationship of the man of means to the objects of production and to production itself is only a consequence of this first relationship. And it confirms it. We shall examine this other aspect later.

So when we ask the question: what relationship is essential to labour, we are asking about the relationship of the worker to production.

Up to now we have considered only one aspect of the alienation or externalization of the worker, his relationship to the products of his labour. But alienation shows itself not only in the result, but also in the act of production, inside productive activity itself. How would the worker be able to affront the product of his work as an alien being if he did not alienate himself in the act of production itself? For the product is merely the summary of the activity of production. So if the product of labour is externalization, production itself must be active externalization, the externalization of activity, the activity of externalization. The alienation of the object of labour is only the résumé of the alienation, the externalization in the activity of labour itself.

What does the externalization of labour consist of then?

Firstly, that labour is exterior to the worker, that is, it does not belong to his essence. Therefore he does not confirm himself in his work, he denies himself, feels miserable instead of happy, deploys no free physical and intellectual energy, but mortifies his body and ruins his mind. Thus the worker only feels a stranger. He is at home when he is not working and when he works he is not at home. His labour is therefore not voluntary but compulsory, forced labour. It is therefore not the satisfaction of a need but only a means to satisfy needs outside itself. How alien it really is is very evident from the fact that when there is no physical or other compulsion, labour is

avoided like the plague. External labour, labour in which man externalizes himself, is a labour of self-sacrifice and mortification. Finally, the external character of labour for the worker shows itself in the fact that it is not his own but someone else's, that it does not belong to him, that he does not belong to himself in his labour but to someone else. As in religion the human imagination's own activity, the activity of man's head and his heart, reacts independently on the individual as an alien activity of gods or devils, so the activity of the worker is not his own spontaneous activity. It belongs to another and is the loss of himself.

The result we arrive at then is that man (the worker) only feels himself freely active in his animal functions of eating, drinking, and procreating, at most also in his dwelling and dress, and feels himself an animal in his human functions.

Eating, drinking, procreating, etc. are indeed truly human functions. But in the abstraction that separates them from the other round of human activity and makes them into final and exclusive ends they become animal.

We have treated the act of alienation of practical human activity, labour, from two aspects. (1) The relationship of the worker to the product of his labour as an alien object that has power over him. This relationship is at the same time the relationship to the sensuous exterior world and to natural objects as to an alien and hostile world opposed to him. (2) The relationship of labour to the act of production inside labour. This relationship is the relationship of the worker to his own activity as something that is alien and does not belong to him; it is activity that is passivity, power that is weakness, procreation that is castration, the worker's own physical and intellectual energy, his personal life (for what is life except activity?) as an activity directed against himself, independent of him, and not belonging to him. It is self-alienation, as above it was the alienation of the object.

We now have to draw a third characteristic of alienated labour from the two previous ones.

Man is a species-being not only in that practically and theoretically he makes both his own and other species into his objects, but also, and this is only another way of putting the same thing, he relates to himself as to the present, living species, in that he relates to himself as to a universal and therefore free being.

Both with man and with animals the species-life consists physically in the fact that man (like animals) lives from inorganic nature, and the more universal man is than animals the more universal is the area of inorganic nature from which he lives. From the theoretical point of view, plants, animals, stones, air, light, etc. form part of human consciousness, partly as objects of natural science, partly as objects of art; they are his intellectual inorganic nature, his intellectual means of subsistence, which he must first prepare before he can enjoy and assimilate them. From the practical point of view, too, they form a part of human life and activity. Physically man lives solely from these products of nature, whether they appear as food, heating, clothing, habitation, etc. The universality of man appears in practice precisely in the universality that makes the whole of nature into his inorganic body in that it is both (i) his immediate means of subsistence and also (ii) the material object and tool of his vital activity. Nature is the inorganic body of a man, that is, insofar as it is not itself a human body. That man lives from nature means that nature is his body with which he must maintain a constant interchange so as not to die. That man's physical and intellectual life depends on nature merely means that nature depends on itself, for man is a part of nature.

While alienated labour alienates (1) nature from man, and (2) man from himself, his own active function, his vital activity, it also alienates the species from man; it turns his species-life into a means towards his individual life. Firstly it alienates species-life and individual life, and secondly in its abstraction it makes the latter into the aim of the former which is also conceived of in its abstract and alien form. For firstly, work, vital activity, and productive life itself appear to man only as a means to the satisfaction of a need, the need to preserve his physical existence. But productive life is species-life. It is life producing life. The whole character of a species, its generic character, is contained in its manner of vital activity, and free conscious activity is the species-characteristic of man. Life itself appears merely as a means to life.

The animal is immediately one with its vital activity. It is not distinct from it. They are identical. Man makes his vital activity itself into an object of his will and consciousness. He has a conscious vital activity. He is not immediately identical to any of his characterizations. Conscious vital activity differentiates man immediately from animal vital activity. It is this and this alone that makes man a species-being. He is only a conscious being, that is, his own life is an object to him, precisely because he is a species-being. This is the only reason for his activity being free activity. Alienated labour reverses the relationship so that, just because he is a conscious being, man makes his vital activity and essence a mere means to his existence.

The practical creation of an objective world, the working-over of inorganic nature, is the confirmation of man as a conscious species-being, that is, as a being that relates to the species as to himself and to himself as to the species. It is true that the animal, too, produces. It builds itself a nest, a dwelling, like the bee, the beaver, the ant, etc. But it only produces what it needs immediately for itself or its offspring; it produces one-sidedly, whereas man produces universally; it produces only under the pressure of immediate physical need, whereas man produces freely from physical need and only truly produces when he is thus free; it produces only itself, whereas man reproduces the whole of nature. Its product belongs immediately to its physical body, whereas man can freely separate himself from his product. The animal only fashions things according to the standards and needs of the species it belongs to, whereas man knows how to produce according to the measure of every species and knows everywhere how to apply its inherent standard to the object; thus man also fashions things according to the laws of beauty.

Thus it is in the working over of the objective world that man first really affirms himself as a species-being. This production is his active species-life. Through it nature appears as his work and his reality. The object of work is therefore the objectification of the species-life of man; for he duplicates himself not only intellectually, in his mind, but also actively in reality and thus can look at his image in a world he has created. Therefore when alienated labour tears from man the object of his production, it also tears from him his species-life, the real objectivity of his species, and turns the advantage he has over animals into a disadvantage in that his inorganic body, nature, is torn from him.

Similarly, in that alienated labour degrades man's own free activity to a means, it turns the species-life of man into a means for his physical existence.

Thus consciousness, which man derives from his species, changes itself through alienation so that species-life becomes a means for him.

Therefore alienated labour:

(3) makes the species-being of man, both nature and the intellectual faculties of his species, into a being that is alien to him, into a means for his individual existence. It alienates from man his own body, nature exterior to him, and his intellectual being, his human essence.

(4) An immediate consequence of man's alienation from the product of his work, his vital activity, and his species-being, is the alienation of man from man. When man is opposed to himself, it is another man that is opposed to him. What is valid for the relationship of a man to his work, of the product of his work and himself, is also valid for the relationship of man to other men and of their labour and the objects of their labour.

In general, the statement that man is alienated from his species-being means that one man is alienated from another as each of them is alienated from the human essence.

The alienation of man and in general of every relationship in which man stands to himself is first realized and expressed in the relationship with which man stands to other men.

Thus in the situation of alienated labour each man measures his relationship to other men by the relationship in which he finds himself placed as a worker.

We began with a fact of political economy, the alienation of the worker and his production. We have expressed this fact in conceptual terms: alienated, externalized labour. We have analysed this concept and thus analysed a purely economic fact.

Let us now see further how the concept of alienated, externalized labour must express and represent itself in reality.

If the product of work is alien to me, opposes me as an alien power, whom does it belong to then?

If my own activity does not belong to me and is an alien, forced activity, to whom does it belong then?

To another being than myself.

Who is this being?

The gods? Of course in the beginning of history the chief production, as for example, the building of temples, etc. in Egypt, India, and Mexico was both in the service of the gods and also belonged to them. But the gods alone were never the masters of the work. And nature just as little. And what a paradox it would be if, the more man mastered nature through his work and the more the miracles of the gods were rendered superfluous by the miracles of industry, the more man had to give up his pleasure in producing and the enjoyment in his product for the sake of these powers.

The alien being to whom the labour and the product of the labour belongs, whom the labour serves and who enjoys its product, can only be man himself. If the product of labour does not belong to the worker but stands over against him as an alien power, this is only possible in that it belongs to another man apart from the worker.

If his activity torments him it must be a joy and a pleasure to someone else. This alien power above man can be neither the gods nor nature, only man himself .

Consider further the above sentence that the relationship of man to himself first becomes objective and real to him through his relationship to other men. So if he relates to the product of his labour, his objectified labour, as to an object that is alien, hostile, powerful, and independent of him, this relationship implies that another man is the alien, hostile, powerful, and independent master of this object. If he relates to his own activity as to something unfree, it is a relationship to an activity that is under the domination, oppression, and yoke of another man.

Every self-alienation of man from himself and nature appears in the relationship in which he places himself and nature to other men distinct from himself. Therefore religious self-alienation necessarily appears in the relationship of layman to priest, or, because here we are dealing with a spiritual world, to a mediator, etc. In the practical, real world, the self-alienation can only appear through the practical, real relationship to other men. The means through which alienation makes progress are themselves practical. Through alienated labour, then, man creates not only his relationship to the object and act of production as to alien and hostile men; he creates too the relationship in which other men stand to his production and his product and the relationship in which he stands to these other men. Just as he turns his production into his own loss of reality and punishment and his own product into a loss, a product that does not belong to him, so he creates the domination of the man who does not produce over the production and the product. As he alienates his activity from himself, so he hands over to an alien person an activity that does not belong to him.

Up till now we have considered the relationship only from the side of the worker and we will later consider it from the side of the non-worker.

Thus through alienated, externalized labour the worker creates the relationship to this labour of a man who is alien to it and remains exterior to it. The relationship of the worker to his labour creates the relationship to it of the capitalist, or whatever else one wishes to call the master of the labour. Private property is thus the product, result, and necessary consequence of externalized labour, of the exterior relationship of the worker to nature and to himself.

Thus private property is the result of the analysis of the concept of externalized labour, i.e., externalized man, alienated work, alienated life, alienated man.

We have, of course, obtained the concept of externalized labour (externalized life) from political economy as the result of the movement of private property. But it is evident from the analysis of this concept that, although private property appears to be the ground and reason for externalized labour, it is rather a consequence of it, just as the gods are originally not the cause but the effect of the aberration of the human mind, although later this relationship reverses itself.

It is only in the final culmination of the development of private property that these hidden characteristics come once more to the fore, in that firstly it is the product of externalized labour and secondly it is the means through which labour externalizes itself, the realization of this externalization.

This development sheds light at the same time on several previously unresolved contradictions.

1. Political economy starts from labour as the veritable soul of production, and yet it attributes nothing to labour and everything to private property. Proudhon has drawn a conclusion from this contradiction that is favourable to labour and against private property. But we can see that this apparent contradiction is the contradiction of alienated labour with itself and that political economy has only expressed the laws of alienated labour.

We can therefore also see that wages and private property are identical: for wages, in which the product, the object of the labour, remunerates the labour itself, are just a necessary consequence of the alienation of labour. In the wage system the labour does not appear as the final aim but only as the servant of the wages. We will develop this later and for the moment only draw a few consequences.

An enforced raising of wages (quite apart from other difficulties, apart from the fact that, being an anomaly, it could only be maintained by force) would only mean a better payment of slaves and would not give this human meaning and worth either to the worker or to his labour.

Indeed, even the equality of wages that Proudhon demands only changes the relationship of the contemporary worker to his labour into that of all men to labour. Society is then conceived of as an abstract capitalist.

Wages are an immediate consequence of alienated labour and alienated labour is the immediate cause of private property. Thus the disappearance of one entails also the disappearance of the other.

2. It is a further consequence of the relationship of alienated labour to private property that the emancipation of society from private property, etc., from slavery, is expressed in its political form by the emancipation of the workers. This is not because only their emancipation is at stake but because general human emancipation is contained in their emancipation. It is contained within it because the whole of human slavery is involved in the relationship of the worker to his product and all slave relationships are only modifications and consequences of this relationship.

Just as we have discovered the concept of private property through an analysis of the concept of alienated, externalized labour, so all categories of political economy can be deduced with the help of these two factors. We shall recognize in each category of market, competition, capital, money, only a particular and developed expression of these first two fundamental elements.

However, before we consider this structure let us try to solve two problems:

1. To determine the general essence of private property as it appears as a result of

alienated labour in its relationship to truly human and social property.

2. We have taken the alienation and externalization of labour as a fact and analysed this fact. We now ask, how does man come to externalize, to alienate his labour? How is this alienation grounded in human development? We have already obtained much material for the solution of this problem, in that we have turned the question of the origin of private property into the question of the relationship of externalized labour to the development of human history. For when we speak of private property, we think we are dealing with something that is exterior to man. When we speak of labour, then we are dealing directly with man. This new formulation of the problem already implies its solution.

To take point 1, the general nature of private property and its relationship to truly human property.

Externalized labour has been broken down into two component parts that determine each other or are only different expressions of one and the same relationship. Appropriation appears as alienation, as externalization, and externalization as appropriation, and alienation as true enfranchisement. We have dealt with one aspect, alienated labour as regards the worker himself, that is, the relationship of externalized labour to itself. As a product and necessary result of this relationship we have discovered the property relationship of the non-worker to the worker and his labour.

As the material and summary expression of alienated labour, private property embraces both relationships, both that of the worker to his labour, the product of his labour and the non-worker, and that of the non-worker to the worker and the product of his labour.

We have already seen that for the worker who appropriates nature through his work, this appropriation appears as alienation, his own activity as activity for and of someone else, his vitality as sacrifice of his life, production of objects as their loss to an alien power, an alien man: let us now consider the relationship that this man, who is alien to labour and the worker, has to the worker, to labour and its object.

The first remark to make is that everything that appears in the case of the worker to be an activity of externalization, of alienation, appears in the case of the non-worker to be a state of externalization, of alienation.

Secondly, the real, practical behaviour of the worker in production and towards his product (as a state of mind) appears in the case of the non-worker opposed to him as theoretical behaviour. Thirdly, the non-worker does everything against the worker that the worker does against himself but he does not do against himself what he does against the worker.

Let us consider these three relationships in more detail. . . . [The manuscript breaks off unfinished here.]

The Communist Manifesto

A spectre is haunting Europe—the spectre of Communism. All the Powers of old Europe have entered into a holy alliance to exorcise this spectre: Pope and Tsar, Metternich and Guizot, French Radicals and German police-spies.

Where is the party in opposition that has not been decried as Communistic by its opponents in power? Where the Opposition that has not hurled back the branding reproach of Communism, against the more advanced opposition parties, as well as against its reactionary adversaries?

Two things result from this fact.

I. Communism is already acknowledged by all European Powers to be itself a Power.
II. It is high time that Communists should openly, in the face of the whole world, publish their views, their aims, their tendencies, and meet this nursery tale of the Spectre of Communism with a Manifesto of the party itself.

To this end, Communists of various nationalities have assembled in London, and sketched the following Manifesto, to be published in the English, French, German, Italian, Flemish, and Danish languages.

I

Bourgeois and Proletarians

The history of all hitherto existing society is the history of class struggles.

Freeman and slave, patrician and plebeian, lord and serf, guild-master and journeyman—in a word, oppressor and oppressed, stood in constant opposition to one another, carried on an uninterrupted, now hidden, now open fight, a fight that each time ended either in a revolutionary re-constitution of society at large or in the common ruin of the contending classes.

In the earlier epochs of history, we find almost everywhere a complicated arrangement of society into various orders, a manifold gradation of social rank. In ancient Rome, we have patricians, knights, plebeians, slaves; in the Middle Ages, feudal lords, vassals, guild-masters, journeymen, apprentices, serfs; in almost all of these classes, again, subordinate gradations.

The modern bourgeois society that has sprouted from the ruins of feudal society has not done away with class antagonisms. It has but established new classes, new conditions of oppression, new forms of struggle in place of the old ones.

Our epoch, the epoch of the bourgeoisie, possesses, however, this distinctive feature: it has simplified the class antagonisms. Society as a whole is more and more splitting up into two great hostile camps, into two great classes directly facing each other: Bourgeoisie and Proletariat.

From the serfs of the Middle Ages sprang the chartered burghers of the earliest towns. From these burgesses the first elements of the bourgeoisie were developed.

The discovery of America, the rounding of the Cape, opened up fresh ground for the rising bourgeoisie. The East Indian and Chinese markets, the colonization of America, trade with the colonies, the increase in the means of exchange and in commodities generally, gave to commerce, to navigation, to industry, an impulse never before known, and thereby, to the revolutionary element in the tottering feudal society, a rapid development.

The feudal system of industry, under which industrial production was monopolized by closed guilds, now no longer sufficed for the growing wants of the new markets. The manufacturing system took its place. The guild-masters were pushed on one side by the manufacturing middle class; division of labour between the different corporate guilds vanished in the face of division of labour in each single workshop.

Meantime the markets kept ever growing, the demand ever rising. Even manufacture no longer sufficed. Thereupon, steam and machinery revolutionized industrial production. The place of manufacture was taken by the giant, Modern Industry, the place of the industrial middle class, by industrial millionaires, the leaders of whole industrial armies, the modern bourgeois.

Modern industry has established the world-market, for which the discovery of America paved the way. This market has given an immense development to commerce, to navigation, to communication by land. This development has, in its turn, reacted on the extension of industry, and in proportion as industry, commerce, navigation, railways extended, in the same proportion the bourgeoisie developed, increased its capital, and pushed into the background every class handed down from the Middle Ages.

We see, therefore, how the modern bourgeoisie is itself the product of a long course of development, of a series of revolutions in the modes of production and of exchange.

Each step in the development of the bourgeoisie was accompanied by a corresponding political advance of that class. An oppressed class under the sway of the feudal nobility, an armed and self-governing association in the medieval commune; here independent urban republic (as in Italy and Germany), there taxable 'third estate' of the monarchy (as in

France), afterwards, in the period of manufacture proper, serving either the semi-feudal or the absolute monarchy as a counterpoise against the nobility, and, in fact, cornerstone of the great monarchies in general, the bourgeoisie has at last, since the establishment of Modern Industry and of the world-market, conquered for itself, in the modern representative State, exclusive political sway. The executive of the modern State is but a committee for managing the common affairs of the whole bourgeoisie.

The bourgeoisie, historically, has played a most revolutionary part.

The bourgeoisie, wherever it has got the upper hand, has put an end to all feudal, patriarchal, idyllic relations. It has pitilessly torn asunder the motley feudal ties that bound man to his 'natural superiors', and has left remaining no other nexus between man and man than naked self-interest, than callous 'cash payment'. It has drowned the most heavenly ecstasies of religious fervour, of chivalrous enthusiasm, of philistine sentimentalism, in the icy water of egotistical calculation. It has resolved personal worth into exchange value, and in place of the numberless indefeasible chartered freedoms, has set up that single, unconscionable freedom—Free Trade. In one word, for exploitation, veiled by religious and political illusions, it has substituted naked, shameless, direct, brutal exploitation.

The bourgeoisie has stripped of its halo every occupation hitherto honoured and looked up to with reverent awe. It has converted the physician, the lawyer, the priest, the poet, the man of science into its paid wage-labourers.

The bourgeoisie has torn away from the family its sentimental veil, and has reduced the family relation to a mere money relation.

The bourgeoisie has disclosed how it came to pass that the brutal display of vigour in the Middle Ages, which Reactionists so much admire, found its fitting complement in the most slothful indolence. It has been the first to show what man's activity can bring about. It has accomplished wonders far surpassing Egyptian pyramids, Roman aqueducts, and Gothic cathedrals; it has conducted expeditions that put in the shade all former Exoduses of nations and crusades.

The bourgeoisie cannot exist without constantly revolutionizing the instruments of production, and thereby the relations of production, and with them the whole relations of society. Conservation of the old modes of production in unaltered form, was, on the contrary, the first condition of existence for all earlier industrial classes. Constant revolutionizing of production, uninterrupted disturbance of all social conditions, everlasting uncertainty and agitation distinguish the bourgeois epoch from all earlier ones. All fixed, fast-frozen relations, with their train of ancient and venerable prejudices and opinions, are swept away, all new-formed ones become antiquated before they can ossify. All that is solid melts into air, all that is holy is profaned, and man is at last compelled to face with sober senses his real conditions of life and his relations with his kind.

The need of a constantly expanding market for its products chases the bourgeoisie over the whole surface of the globe. It must nestle everywhere, settle everywhere, establish connections everywhere.

The bourgeoisie has through its exploitation of the world-market given a cosmopolitan character to production and consumption in every country. To the great chagrin of Reactionists, it has drawn from under the feet of industry the national ground on which it stood. All old-established national industries have been destroyed or are daily being destroyed. They are dislodged by new industries, whose introduction becomes a life-and-death question for all civilized nations, by industries that no longer work up indigenous raw material, but raw material drawn from the remotest zones; industries whose products are consumed, not only at home, but in every quarter of the globe. In place of the old wants, satisfied by the productions of the country, we find new wants, requiring for their satisfaction the products of distant lands and climes. In place of the old local and national seclusion and self-sufficiency, we have intercourse in every direction, universal interdependence of nations. And as in material, so also in intellectual production. The intellectual creations of individual nations become common property. National one-sidedness and narrow-mindedness become more and more impossible, and from the numerous national and local literatures, there arises a world literature.

The bourgeoisie, by the rapid improvement of all instruments of production, by the immensely facilitated means of communication, draws all, even the most barbarian, nations into civilization. The cheap prices of its commodities are the heavy artillery with which it batters down all Chinese walls, with which it forces the barbarians' intensely obstinate hatred of foreigners to capitulate. It compels all nations, on pain of extinction, to adopt the bourgeois mode of production; it compels them to introduce what it calls civilization into their midst, i.e., to become bourgeois themselves. In one word, it creates a world after its own image.

The bourgeoisie has subjected the country to the rule of the towns. It has created enormous cities, has greatly increased the urban population as compared with the rural, and has thus rescued a considerable part of the population from the idiocy of rural life. Just as it has made the country dependent on the towns, so it has made barbarian and semi-barbarian countries dependent on the civilized ones, nations of peasants on nations of bourgeois, the East on the West.

The bourgeoisie keeps more and more doing away with the scattered state of the population, of the means of production, and of property. It has agglomerated population, centralized means of production, and has concentrated property in a few hands. The necessary consequence of this was political centralization. Independent or but loosely connected provinces, with separate interests, laws, governments, and systems of taxation, became lumped together into one nation, with one government, one code of laws, one national class-interest, one frontier, and one customs-tariff.

The bourgeoisie, during its rule of scarcely one hundred years, has created more massive and more colossal productive forces than have all preceding generations together. Subjection of Nature's forces to man, machinery, application of chemistry to industry and agriculture, steam-navigation, railways, electric telegraphs, clearing of whole continents for cultivation, canalization of rivers, whole populations conjured out of the ground—what earlier century had even a presentiment that such productive forces slumbered in the lap of social labour?

We see then that the means of production and of exchange, on whose foundation the bourgeoisie built itself up, were generated in feudal society. At a certain stage in the development of these means of production and of exchange, the conditions under which feudal society produced and exchanged, the feudal organization of agriculture and manufacturing industry, in one word, the feudal relations of property become no longer compatible with the already developed productive forces; they become so many fetters. They had to be burst asunder; they were burst asunder.

Into their place stepped free competition, accompanied by a social and political constitution adapted to it, and by the economical and political sway of the bourgeois class.

A similar movement is going on before our own eyes. Modern bourgeois society with its relations of production, of exchange and of property, a society that has conjured up such gigantic means of production and of exchange, is like the sorcerer, who is no longer able to control the powers of the nether world which he has called up by his spells. The history of industry and commerce for many a decade past is but the history of the revolt of modern productive forces against modern conditions of production, against the property relations that are the conditions for the existence of the bourgeoisie and of its rule. It is enough to mention the commercial crises that by their periodical return put on trial, each time more threateningly, the existence of the entire bourgeois society. In these crises a great part not only of the existing products, but also of the previously created productive forces, are periodically destroyed. In these crises there breaks out an epidemic that, in all earlier epochs, would have seemed an absurdity—the epidemic of over-production. Society suddenly finds itself put back into a state of momentary barbarism; it appears as if a famine, a universal war of devastation, has cut off the supply of every means of subsistence; industry and commerce seem to be destroyed; and why? Because there is too much civilization, too much means of subsistence, too much industry, too much commerce. The productive forces at the disposal of society no longer tend to further the development of the conditions of bourgeois property; on the contrary, they have become too powerful for these conditions, by which they are fettered, and so soon as they overcome these fetters, they bring disorder into the whole of bourgeois society, endanger the existence of bourgeois property. The conditions of bourgeois society are too narrow to comprise the wealth created by them. And how does the bourgeoisie get over these crises? On the one hand by enforced destruction of a mass of productive forces; on the other by the conquest of new markets, and by the more thorough exploitation of the old ones. That is to say, by paving the way for more extensive and more destructive crises, and by diminishing the means whereby crises are prevented.

The weapons with which the bourgeoisie felled feudalism to the ground are now turned against the bourgeoisie itself.

But not only has the bourgeoisie forged the weapons that bring death to itself; it has also called into existence the men who are to wield those weapons—the modern working class—the proletarians.

In proportion as the bourgeoisie, i.e., capital, is developed, in the same proportion is the proletariat, the modern working class, developed—a class of labourers, who live only so long as they find work, and who find work only so long as their labour increases capital. These labourers, who must sell themselves piecemeal, are a commodity, like every other article of commerce, and are consequently exposed to all the vicissitudes of competition, to all the fluctuations of the market.

Owing to the extensive use of machinery and to division of labour, the work of the proletarians has lost all individual character, and, consequently, all charm for the workman. He becomes an appendage of the machine, and it is only the most simple, most monotonous, and most easily acquired knack, that is required of him. Hence, the cost of production of a workman is restricted, almost entirely, to the means of subsistence that he requires for his maintenance, and for the propagation of his race. But the price of a commodity, and therefore also of labour, is equal to its cost of production. In proportion, therefore, as the repulsiveness of the work increases, the wage decreases. Nay more, in proportion as the use of machinery and division of labour increases, in the same proportion the burden of toil also increases, whether by prolongation of the working hours, by increase of the work exacted in a given time, or by increased speed of the machinery, etc.

Modern industry has converted the little workshop of the patriarchal master into the great factory of the industrial capitalist. Masses of labourers, crowded into the factory, are organized like soldiers. As privates of the industrial army they are placed under the command of a perfect hierarchy of officers and sergeants. Not only are they slaves of the bourgeois class, and of the bourgeois State; they are daily and hourly enslaved by the machine, by the overlooker, and, above all, by the individual bourgeois manufacturer himself. The more openly this despotism proclaims gain to be its end and aim, the more petty, the more hateful, and the more embittering it is.

The less the skill and exertion of strength implied in manual labour, in other words, the more modern industry becomes developed, the more is the labour of men superseded by that of women. Differences of age and sex have no longer any distinctive social validity for the working class. All are instruments of labour, more or less expensive to use, according to their age and sex.

No sooner is the exploitation of the labourer by the manufacturer, so far, at an end, and he receives his wages in cash, than he is set upon by the other portions of the bourgeoisie, the landlord, the shopkeeper, the pawnbroker, etc.

The lower strata of the middle class—the small tradespeople, shopkeepers, and retired tradesmen generally, the handicraftsmen and peasants—all these sink gradually into the proletariat, partly because their diminutive capital does not suffice for the scale on which Modern Industry is carried on, and is swamped in the competition with the large capitalists, partly because their specialized skill is rendered worthless by new methods of production. Thus the proletariat is recruited from all classes of the population.

The proletariat goes through various stages of development. With its birth begins its struggle with the bourgeoisie. At first the contest is carried on by individual labourers, then by the workpeople of a factory, then by the operatives of one trade, in one locality, against the individual bourgeois who directly exploits them. They direct their attacks not against the bourgeois conditions of production, but against the instruments of production themselves; they destroy imported wares that compete with their labour, they smash to pieces machinery, they set factories ablaze, they seek to restore by force the vanished status of the workman of the Middle Ages.

At this stage the labourers still form an incoherent mass scattered over the whole country, and broken up by their mutual competition. If anywhere they unite to form more compact bodies, this is not yet the consequence of their own active union, but of the union of the bourgeoisie, which class, in order to attain its own political ends, is compelled to set the whole proletariat in motion, and is moreover yet, for a time, able to do so. At this stage, therefore, the proletarians do not fight their enemies, but the enemies of their enemies, the remnants of absolute monarchy, the landowners, the non-industrial bourgeois, the petty bourgeoisie. Thus the whole historical movement is concentrated in the hands of the bourgeoisie; every victory so obtained is a victory for the bourgeoisie.

But with the development of industry the proletariat not only increases in number; it becomes concentrated in greater masses, its strength grows, and it feels that strength more. The various interests and conditions of life within the ranks of the proletariat are more and more equalized, in proportion as machinery obliterates all distinctions of labour, and nearly everywhere reduces wages to the same low level. The growing competition among the bourgeois, and the resulting commercial crises, make the wages of the workers ever more fluctuating. The unceasing improvement of machinery, ever more rapidly developing, makes their livelihood more and more precarious; the collisions between individual workmen and individual bourgeois take more and more the character of collisions between two classes. Thereupon the workers begin to form combinations (Trades' Unions) against the bourgeois; they club together in order to keep up the rate of wages; they found permanent associations in order to make provision beforehand for these occasional revolts. Here and there the contest breaks out into riots.

Now and then the workers are victorious, but only for a time. The real fruit of their battles lies, not in the immediate result, but in the ever-expanding union of the workers. This union is helped on by the improved means of communication that are created by modern industry and that place the workers of different localities in contact with one another. It was just this contact that was needed to centralize the numerous local struggles, all of the same character, into one national struggle between classes. But every class struggle is a political struggle. And that union, to attain which the burghers of the Middle Ages, with their miserable highways, required centuries, the modern proletarians, thanks to railways, achieve in a few years.

This organization of the proletarians into a class, and consequently into a political party, is continually being upset again by the competition between the workers themselves. But it ever rises up again, stronger, firmer, mightier. It compels legislative recognition of particular interests of the workers, by taking advantage of the divisions among the bourgeoisie itself. Thus the ten-hours' bill in England was carried.

Altogether, collisions between the classes of the old society further in many ways the course of development of the proletariat. The bourgeoisie finds itself involved in a constant battle. At first with the aristocracy; later on, with those portions of the bourgeoisie itself whose interests have become antagonistic to the progress of industry; at all times, with the bourgeoisie of foreign countries. In all these battles it sees itself compelled to appeal to the proletariat, to ask for its help, and thus to drag it into the political arena. The bourgeoisie itself, therefore, supplies the proletariat with its own elements of political and general education, in other words, it furnishes the proletariat with weapons for fighting the bourgeoisie.

Further, as we have already seen, entire sections of the ruling classes are, by the advance of industry, precipitated into the proletariat, or are at least threatened in their conditions of existence. These also supply the proletariat with fresh elements of enlightenment and progress.

Finally, in times when the class struggle nears the decisive hour, the process of dissolution going on within the ruling class, in fact within the whole range of old society, assumes such a violent, glaring character, that a small section of the ruling class cuts itself adrift, and joins the revolutionary class, the class that holds the future in its hands. Just as, therefore, at an earlier period, a section of the nobility went over to the bourgeoisie, so now a portion of the bourgeoisie goes over to the proletariat, and in particular, a portion of the bourgeois ideologists, who have raised themselves to the level of comprehending theoretically the historical movement as a whole.

Of all the classes that stand face to face with the bourgeoisie today, the proletariat alone is a really revolutionary class. The other classes decay and finally disappear in the face of Modern Industry; the proletariat is its special and essential product.

The lower middle class, the small manufacturer, the shopkeeper, the artisan, the peasant, all these fight against the bourgeoisie, to save from extinction their existence as fractions of the middle class. They are therefore not revolutionary, but conservative. Nay more, they are reactionary, for they try to roll back the wheel of history. If by chance they are revolutionary, they are so only in view of their impending transfer into the proletariat; they thus defend not their present, but their future interests, they desert their own standpoint to place themselves at that of the proletariat.

The 'dangerous class', the social scum, that passively rotting mass thrown off by the lowest layers of old society, may, here and there, be swept into the movement by a proletarian revolution; its conditions of life, however, prepare it far more for the part of a bribed tool of reactionary intrigue.

In the conditions of the proletariat, those of old society at large are already virtually swamped. The proletarian is without property; his relation to his wife and children has no longer anything in common with the bourgeois family relations; modern industrial labour, modern subjection to capital, the same in England as in France, in America as in Germany, has stripped him of every trace of national character. Law, morality, religion are to him so many bourgeois prejudices, behind which lurk in ambush just as many bourgeois interests.

All the preceding classes that got the upper hand sought to fortify their already acquired status by subjecting society at large to their conditions of appropriation. The proletarians cannot become masters of the productive forces of society, except by abolishing their own previous mode of appropriation, and thereby also every other previous mode of appropriation. They have nothing of their own to secure and to fortify; their mission is to destroy all previous securities for, and insurances of, individual property.

All previous historical movements were movements of minorities, or in the interests of minorities. The proletarian movement is the self-conscious, independent movement of the immense majority, in the interests of the immense majority. The proletariat, the lowest stratum of our present society, cannot stir, cannot raise itself up, without the whole superincumbent strata of official society being sprung into the air.

Though not in substance, yet in form, the struggle of the proletariat with the bourgeoisie is at first a national struggle. The proletariat of each country must, of course, first of all settle matters with its own bourgeoisie.

In depicting the most general phases of the development of the proletariat, we traced the more or less veiled civil war, raging within existing society, up to the point where that war breaks out into open revolution, and where the violent overthrow of the bourgeoisie lays the foundation for the sway of the proletariat.

Hitherto, every form of society has been based, as we have already seen, on the antagonism of oppressing and oppressed classes. But in order to oppress a class, certain conditions must be assured to it under which it can, at least, continue its slavish existence. The serf, in the period of serfdom, raised himself to membership in the commune, just as the petty bourgeois, under the yoke of feudal absolutism, managed to develop into a bourgeois. The modem labourer, on the contrary, instead of rising with the progress of industry, sinks deeper and deeper below the conditions of existence of his own class. He becomes a pauper, and pauperism develops more rapidly than population and wealth. And here it becomes evident, that the bourgeoisie is unfit any longer to be the ruling class in society, and to impose its conditions of existence upon society as an overriding law. It is unfit to rule because it is incompetent to assure an existence to its slave within his slavery, because it cannot help letting him sink into such a state that it has to feed him, instead of being fed by him. Society can no longer live under this bourgeoisie, in other words, its existence is no longer compatible with society.

The essential condition for the existence, and for the sway of the bourgeois class, is the formation and augmentation of capital; the condition for capital is wage-labour. Wage-labour rests exclusively on competition between the labourers. The advance of industry, whose involuntary promoter is the bourgeoisie, replaces the isolation of the labourers, due to competition, by their revolutionary combination, due to association. The development of Modern Industry, therefore, cuts from under its feet the very foundation on which the bourgeoisie produces and appropriates products. What the bourgeoisie, therefore, produces, above all, is its own grave-diggers. Its fall and the victory of the proletariat are equally inevitable.

II

Proletarians and Communists

In what relation do the Communists stand to the proletarians as a whole?

The Communists do not form a separate party opposed to other working-class parties.

They have no interests separate and apart from those of the proletariat as a whole.

They do not set up any sectarian principles of their own, by which to shape and mould the proletarian movement.

The Communists are distinguished from the other working-class parties by this only: 1. In the national struggles of the proletarians of the different countries, they point out and bring to the front the common interests of the entire proletariat, independently of all nationality. 2. In the various stages of development which the struggle of the working class against the bourgeoisie has to pass through, they always and everywhere represent the interests of the movement as a whole.

The Communists, therefore, are on the one hand, practically, the most advanced and resolute section of the working-class parties of every country, that section which pushes forward all others; on the other hand, theoretically, they have over the great mass of the proletariat the advantage of clearly understanding the line of march, the conditions, and the ultimate general results of the proletarian movement.

The immediate aim of the Communists is the same as that of all the other proletarian parties: formation of the proletariat into a class, overthrow of the bourgeois supremacy, conquest of political power by the proletariat.

The theoretical conclusions of the Communists are in no way based on ideas or principles that have been invented, or discovered, by this or that would-be universal reformer.

They merely express, in general terms, actual relations springing from an existing class struggle, from a historical movement going on under our very eyes. The abolition of existing property relations is not at all a distinctive feature of Communism.

All property relations in the past have continually been subject to historical change consequent upon the change in historical conditions.

The French Revolution, for example, abolished feudal property in favour of bourgeois property.

The distinguishing feature of Communism is not the abolition of property generally, but the abolition of bourgeois property. But modern bourgeois private property is the final and most complete expression of the system of producing and appropriating products that is based on class antagonisms, on the exploitation of many by the few.

In this sense, the theory of the Communists may be summed up in the single sentence: Abolition of private property.

We Communists have been reproached with the desire of abolishing the right of personally acquiring property as the fruit of a man's own labour, which property is alleged to be the groundwork of all personal freedom, activity, and independence.

Hard-won, self-acquired, self-earned property! Do you mean the property of the petty artisan and of the small peasant, a form of property that preceded the bourgeois form? There is no need to abolish that; the development of industry has to a great extent already destroyed it, and is still destroying it daily.

Or do you mean modern bourgeois private property?

But does wage-labour create any property for the labourer? Not a bit. It creates capital, i.e., that kind of property which exploits wage-labour, and which cannot increase except upon condition of begetting a new supply of wage-labour for fresh exploitation. Property, in its present form, is based on the antagonism of capital and wage-labour. Let us examine both sides of this antagonism.

To be a capitalist is to have not only a purely personal, but a social, status in production. Capital is a collective product, and only by the united action of many members, nay, in the last resort, only by the united action of all members of society, can it be set in motion.

Capital is, therefore, not a personal, it is a social power.

When, therefore, capital is converted into common property, into the property of all members of society, personal property is not thereby transformed into social property. It is only the social character of the property that is changed. It loses its class-character.

Let us now take wage-labour.

The average price of wage-labour is the minimum wage, i.e., that quantum of the means of subsistence which is absolutely requisite to keep the labourer in bare existence as a labourer. What, therefore, the wage-labourer appropriates by means of his labour merely suffices to prolong and reproduce a bare existence. We by no means intend to abolish this personal appropriation of the products of labour, an appropriation that is made for the maintenance and reproduction of human life, and that leaves no surplus wherewith to command the labour of others. All that we want to do away with is the miserable character of this appropriation, under which the labourer lives merely to increase capital, and is allowed to live only insofar as the interest of the ruling class requires it.

In bourgeois society, living labour is but a means to increase accumulated labour. In Communist society, accumulated labour is but a means to widen, to enrich, to promote the existence of the labourer.

In bourgeois society, therefore, the past dominates the present; in Communist society, the present dominates the past. In bourgeois society, capital is independent and has individuality, while the living person is dependent and has no individuality.

And the abolition of this state of things is called by the bourgeois abolition of individuality and freedom! And rightly so. The abolition of bourgeois individuality, bourgeois independence, and bourgeois freedom is undoubtedly aimed at.

By freedom is meant, under the present bourgeois conditions of production, free trade, free selling and buying.

But if selling and buying disappears, free selling and buying disappears also. This talk about free selling and buying, and all the other 'brave words' of our bourgeoisie about freedom in general, have a meaning, if any, only in contrast with restricted selling and buying, with the fettered traders of the Middle Ages, but have no meaning when opposed to the Communistic abolition of buying and selling, of the bourgeois conditions of production, and of the bourgeoisie itself.

You are horrified at our intending to do away with private property. But in your existing society, private property is already done away with for nine-tenths of the population; its existence for the few is solely due to its non-existence in the hands of those nine-tenths. You reproach us, therefore, with intending to do away with a form of property, the necessary condition for whose existence is the non-existence of any property for the immense majority of society.

In one word, you reproach us with intending to do away with your property. Precisely so; that is just what we intend.

From the moment when labour can no longer be converted into capital, money, or rent, into a social power capable of being monopolized, i.e., from the moment when individual property can no longer be transformed into bourgeois property, into capital, from that moment, you say, individuality vanishes.

You must, therefore, confess that by 'individual' you mean no other person than the bourgeois, than the middle-class owner of property. This person must, indeed, be swept out of the way, and made impossible.

Communism deprives no man of the power to appropriate the products of society;

all that it does is to deprive him of the power to subjugate the labour of others by means of such appropriation.

It has been objected that upon the abolition of private property all work will cease, and universal laziness will overtake us.

According to this, bourgeois society ought long ago to have gone to the dogs through sheer idleness; for those of its members who work acquire nothing, and those who acquire anything do not work. The whole of this objection is but another expression of the tautology: that there can no longer be any wage-labour when there is no longer any capital.

All objections urged against the Communistic mode of producing and appropriating material products have, in the same way, been urged against the Communistic modes of producing and appropriating intellectual products. Just as, to the bourgeois, the disappearance of class property is the disappearance of production itself, so the disappearance of class culture is to him identical with the disappearance of all culture.

That culture, the loss of which he laments, is, for the enormous majority, a mere training to act as a machine.

But don't wrangle with us so long as you apply, to our intended abolition of bourgeois property, the standard of your bourgeois notions of freedom, culture, law, etc. Your very ideas are but the outgrowth of the conditions of your bourgeois production and bourgeois property, just as your jurisprudence is but the will of your class made into a law for all, a will whose essential character and direction are determined by the economical conditions of existence of your class.

The selfish misconception that induces you to transform into eternal laws of nature and of reason the social forms springing from your present mode of production and form of property—historical relations that rise and disappear in the progress of production—this misconception you share with every ruling class that has preceded you. What you see clearly in the case of ancient property, what you admit in the case of feudal property, you are of course forbidden to admit in the case of your own bourgeois form of property.

Abolition of the family! Even the most radical flare up at this infamous proposal of the Communists.

On what foundation is the present family, the bourgeois family, based? On capital, on private gain. In its completely developed form this family exists only among the bourgeoisie. But this state of things finds its complement in the practical absence of the family among the proletarians, and in public prostitution.

The bourgeois family will vanish as a matter of course when its complement vanishes, and both will vanish with the vanishing of capital.

Do you charge us with wanting to stop the exploitation of children by their parents? To this crime we plead guilty.

But, you will say, we destroy the most hallowed of relations, when we replace home education by social.

And your education! Is not that also social, and determined by the social conditions under which you educate, by the intervention, direct or indirect, of society, by means of schools, etc.? The Communists have not invented the intervention of society in education; they do but seek to alter the character of that intervention, and to rescue education from the influence of the ruling class.

The bourgeois clap-trap about the family and education, about the hallowed co-relation of parent and child, becomes all the more disgusting, the more, by the action of Modern Industry, all family ties among the proletarians are torn asunder, and their children transformed into simple articles of commerce and instruments of labour.

But you Communists would introduce community of women, screams the whole bourgeoisie in chorus.

The bourgeois sees in his wife a mere instrument of production. He hears that the instruments of production are to be exploited in common, and, naturally, can come to no other conclusion than that the lot of being common to all will likewise fall to the women.

He has not even a suspicion that the real point aimed at is to do away with the status of women as mere instruments of production.

For the rest, nothing is more ridiculous than the virtuous indignation of our bourgeois at the community of women which, they pretend, is to be openly and officially established by the Communists. The Communists have no need to introduce community of women; it has existed almost from time immemorial.

Our bourgeois, not content with having the wives and daughters of their proletarians at their disposal, not to speak of common prostitutes, take the greatest pleasure in seducing each other's wives.

Bourgeois marriage is in reality a system of wives in common and thus, at the most, what the Communists might possibly be reproached with, is that they desire to introduce, in substitution for a hypocritically concealed, an openly legalized, community of women. For the rest, it is self-evident that the abolition of the present system of production must bring with it the abolition of the community of women springing from that system, i.e., of prostitution both public and private.

The Communists are further reproached with desiring to abolish countries and nationality.

The working men have no country. We cannot take from them what they have not got.

Since the proletariat must first of all acquire political supremacy, must rise to be the leading class of the nation, must constitute itself *the* nation, it is, so far, itself national, though not in the bourgeois sense of the word.

National differences and antagonisms between peoples are daily more and more vanishing, owing to the development of the bourgeoisie, to freedom of commerce, to the world-market, to uniformity in the mode of production and in the conditions of life corresponding thereto.

The supremacy of the proletariat will cause them to vanish still faster. United action, of the leading civilized countries at least, is one of the first conditions for the emancipation of the proletariat.

In proportion as the exploitation of one individual by another is put an end to, the exploitation of one nation by another will also be put an end to. In proportion as the antagonism between classes within the nation vanishes, the hostility of one nation to another will come to an end.

The charges against Communism made from a religious, a philosophical, and, generally, from an ideological standpoint are not deserving of serious examination.

Does it require deep intuition to comprehend that man's ideas, views, and conceptions, in one word, man's consciousness, changes with every change in the conditions of his material existence, in his social relation, and in his social life?

What else does the history of ideas prove, than that intellectual production changes its character in proportion as material production is changed? The ruling ideas of each age have ever been the ideas of its ruling class.

When people speak of ideas that revolutionize society, they do but express the fact that within the old society, the elements of a new one have been created, and that the dissolution of the old ideas keeps even pace with the dissolution of the old conditions of existence.

When the ancient world was in its last throes, the ancient religions were overcome by Christianity. When Christian ideas succumbed in the eighteenth century to rationalist ideas, feudal society fought its death battle with the then revolutionary bourgeoisie. The ideas of religious liberty and freedom of conscience merely gave expression to the sway of free competition within the domain of knowledge.

'Undoubtedly,' it will be said, 'religious, moral, philosophical, and juridical ideas have been modified in the course of historical development. But religion, morality, philosophy, political science, and law constantly survived this change.'

'There are, besides, eternal truths, such as Freedom, Justice, etc., that are common to all states of society. But Communism abolishes eternal truths, it abolishes all religion and all morality, instead of constituting them on a new basis; it therefore acts in contradiction to all past historical experience.'

What does this accusation reduce itself to? The history of all past society has consisted in the development of class antagonisms, antagonisms that assumed different forms at different epochs.

But whatever form they may have taken, one fact is common to all past ages, viz., the exploitation of one part of society by the other. No wonder, then, that the social consciousness of past ages, despite all the multiplicity and variety it displays, moves within certain common forms, or general ideas, which cannot completely vanish except with the total disappearance of class antagonisms.

The Communist revolution is the most radical rupture with traditional property relations; no wonder that its development involves the most radical rupture with traditional ideas.

But let us have done with the bourgeois objections to Communism.

We have seen above that the first step in the revolution by the working class is to raise the proletariat to the position of ruling class, to win the battle of democracy.

The proletariat will use its political supremacy to wrest, by degrees, all capital from the bourgeoisie, to centralize all instruments of production in the hands of the State, i.e., of the proletariat organized as the ruling class; and to increase the total of productive forces as rapidly as possible.

Of course, in the beginning this cannot be effected except by means of despotic inroads on the rights of property, and on the conditions of bourgeois production; by means of measures, therefore, which appear economically insufficient and untenable, but which, in the course of the movement, outstrip themselves, necessitate further inroads upon the old social order, and are unavoidable as a means of entirely revolutionizing the mode of production.

These measures will of course be different in different countries.

Nevertheless, in the most advanced countries, the following will be pretty generally applicable.

1. Abolition of property in land and application of all rents of land to public purposes.
2. A heavy progressive or graduated income tax.
3. Abolition of all right of inheritance.
4. Confiscation of the property of all emigrants and rebels.
5. Centralization of credit in the hands of the State, by means of a national bank

with State capital and an exclusive monopoly.

6. Centralization of the means of communication and transport in the hands of the State.

7. Extension of factories and instruments of production owned by the State; the bringing into cultivation of wastelands, and the improvement of the soil generally in accordance with a common plan.

8. Equal liability of all to labour. Establishment of industrial armies, especially for agriculture.

9. Combination of agriculture with manufacturing industries; gradual abolition of the distinction between town and country, by a more equable distribution of the population over the country.

10. Free education for all children in public schools. Abolition of children's factory labour in its present form. Combination of education with industrial production, etc., etc.

When, in the course of development, class distinctions have disappeared, and all production has been concentrated in the hands of associated individuals, the public power will lose its political character. Political power, properly so called, is merely the organized power of one class for oppressing another. If the proletariat during its contest with the bourgeoisie is compelled, by the force of circumstances, to organize itself as a class, if, by means of a revolution, it makes itself the ruling class, and, as such, sweeps away by force the old conditions of production, then it will, along with these conditions, have swept away the conditions for the existence of class antagonisms and of classes generally, and will thereby have abolished its own supremacy as a class.

In place of the old bourgeois society, with its classes and class antagonisms, we shall have an association, in which the free development of each is the condition for the free development of all.

Study Questions for 'Alienated Labour'

1. Marx begins his discussion of labour alienation by criticizing 'political economy'. What is political economy? What false assumptions befall the political economist, according to Marx?

2. Describe the four main facets of labour alienation discussed by Marx. Does Marx's discussion of labour alienation imply a theory of human nature?

3. Marx comments that placing an increasing value upon material things results in a devaluation of men and women themselves. Explain this comment in the context of Marx's theory of labour alienation.

Study Questions for *The Communist Manifesto*

1. Marx and Engels maintain that the history of humankind has been a history of class struggles. Describe the historical succession of class divisions discussed in section I of the *Manifesto*. How does the modern bourgeois continue to dominate and exploit the proletariat, according to Marx and Engels?
2. What are the distinguishing features of a communist society? In a communist society, would the state own the personal property of individuals?
3. How do Marx and Engels respond to the objections that (1) individuals possess a natural right to private property, and (2) eliminating private property would eliminate motivation for working?
4. In your view, does the twentieth-century collapse of anti-democratic communist states, such as the Soviet Union, disprove Marx's communist theory?

Recommended Readings

Avineri, Shlomo, *The Social and Political Thought of Karl Marx* (Cambridge University Press, 1970).

Berlin, Isaiah, *Karl Marx: His Life and Environment*, 4th edn (Oxford University Press, 1996).

Cohen, Gerald, *Karl Marx's Theory of History: A Defence*, 2nd edn (Oxford University Press, 2001).

Elster, Jon, *Making Sense of Marx* (Cambridge University Press, 1985).

McLellan, David, *Marxism after Marx: The Philosophy of Karl Marx*, 4th edn (Palgrave Macmillan, 2007).

Miller, Richard, *Analyzing Marx* (Princeton University Press, 1984).

Schumacher, E.F., 'Buddhist Economics,' in *Economics As If People Mattered* (Harper and Row, 1973).

Singer, Peter, *Marx: A Very Short Introduction* (Oxford University Press, 2000).

Roemer, John, *A General Theory of Exploitation and Class* (Harvard University Press, 1982).

Wolff, Jonathan, *Why Read Marx Today?* (Oxford University Press, 2002).

Wood, Alan, *Karl Marx* (Routledge & Kegan Paul, 1981).

PART IV

Twentieth-Century Philosophers

Hannah Arendt

Hannah Arendt (1906–1975) was born into a secular Jewish family and raised primarily in Königsberg, Germany. In 1924, she pursued an undergraduate degree at the University of Marburg, where she studied with the eminent German philosopher Martin Heidegger. Arendt and Heidegger had a romantic relationship that gave way in time to an intermittent lifelong friendship. Heidegger would later say that Arendt became his inspiration during his most productive period of work, during which he wrote *Being and Time* (1927); his philosophical methodology remained a lasting influence on her as well. Following her studies at Marburg, Arendt studied briefly with Edmund Husserl and completed her doctoral work at the University of Heidelberg under the supervision of Karl Jaspers, who became her lifelong friend and mentor.

A Jew living in Germany during Hitler's rise to power, Arendt worked to publicize the plight of Nazi victims and conducted research on anti-Semitic propaganda, for which she was arrested by the Gestapo. After managing a release from jail, Arendt fled Germany and lived in Paris for several years, during which time she worked with Jewish refugee organizations and associated with French existentialists, including Jean-Paul Sartre, Albert Camus, and Maurice Merleau-Ponty. In 1941, she emigrated to the United States and, in subsequent decades, occupied professorial positions at several American universities. Following the publication of her second book, *The Origins of Totalitarianism* (1951), Arendt gained prominence as a public intellectual whose work bore relevance to contemporary Cold War politics. In her next three book-length works, *The Human Condition* (1958), *Between Past and Future* (1961), and *On Revolution* (1968), she developed a political philosophy informed by the European phenomenological tradition. As a correspondent for the *New Yorker,* she covered the 1961 trial of Nazi bureaucrat Adolf Eichmann, later publishing her articles in *Eichmann in Jerusalem* (1963). From 1967 until the time of her death in 1975, she was a professor of political philosophy at the New School for Social Research in New York.

Writing from the perspective of a political refugee, Arendt argues that human rights are neither inalienable nor independent of states but vacuous outside of the particular political institutions that guarantee them. Her social and political philosophy as a whole treads across such themes as human rights, totalitarianism, conformism in mass societies, revolution, the nature of freedom, and the encroachment of economic concerns upon political spaces. Her principle work in political theory, *The Human Condition*, is an examination of politically relevant categories of human experience in which she aims to unearth the basic character of political action. Arendt distinguishes three categories of human activity—labour, work, and action—the last of which provides both a justification for social and political life and a non-utilitarian value for human civilization.

The Human Condition

Chapter I

The Human Condition

1 *Vita Activa* and the Human Condition

With the term *vita activa*, I propose to designate three fundamental human activities: labour, work, and action. They are fundamental because each corresponds to one of the basic conditions under which life on earth has been given to man.

Labour is the activity which corresponds to the biological process of the human body, whose spontaneous growth, metabolism, and eventual decay are bound to the vital necessities produced and fed into the life process by labour. The human condition of labour is life itself.

Work is the activity which corresponds to the unnaturalness of human existence, which is not imbedded in, and whose mortality is not compensated by, the species' ever-recurring life cycle. Work provides an 'artificial' world of things, distinctly different from all natural surroundings. Within its borders each individual life is housed, while this world itself is meant to outlast and transcend them all. The human condition of work is worldliness.

Action, the only activity that goes on directly between men without the intermediary of things or matter, corresponds to the human condition of plurality, to the fact that men, not Man, live on the earth and inhabit the world. While all aspects of the human condition are somehow related to politics, this plurality is specifically *the* condition—not only the *conditio sine qua non*, but the *conditio per quam*—of all political life. Thus the language of the Romans, perhaps the most political people we have known, used the words 'to live'

and 'to be among men' (*inter homines esse*) or 'to die' and 'to cease to be among men' (*inter homines esse desinere*) as synonyms. But in its most elementary form, the human condition of action is implicit even in Genesis ('Male and female created He *them*'), if we understand that this story of man's creation is distinguished in principle from the one according to which God originally created Man (*adam*), 'him' and not 'them', so that the multitude of human beings becomes the result of multiplication. Action would be an unnecessary luxury, a capricious interference with general laws of behaviour, if men were endlessly reproducible repetitions of the same model, whose nature or essence was the same for all and as predictable as the nature or essence of any other thing. Plurality is the condition of human action because we are all the same, that is, human, in such a way that nobody is ever the same as anyone else who ever lived, lives, or will live.

All three activities and their corresponding conditions are intimately connected with the most general condition of human existence: birth and death, natality and mortality. Labour assures not only individual survival, but the life of the species. Work and its product, the human artefact, bestow a measure of permanence and durability upon the futility of mortal life and the fleeting character of human time. Action, insofar as it engages in founding and preserving political bodies, creates the condition for remembrance, that is, for history. . . .

2 The Term *Vita Activa*

The term *vita activa* is loaded and overloaded with tradition. It is as old as (but not older than) our tradition of political thought. And this tradition, far from comprehending and conceptualizing all the political experiences of Western mankind, grew out of a specific historical constellation: the trial of Socrates and the conflict between the philosopher and the *polis*. It eliminated many experiences of an earlier past that were irrelevant to its immediate political purposes and proceeded until its end, in the work of Karl Marx, in a highly selective manner. The term itself, in medieval philosophy the standard translation of the Aristotelian *bios politikos*, already occurs in Augustine, where, as *vita negotiosa* or *actuosa*, it still reflects its original meaning: a life devoted to public-political matters.

Aristotle distinguished three ways of life (*bioi*) which men might choose in freedom, that is, in full independence of the necessities of life and the relationships they originated. This prerequisite of freedom ruled out all ways of life chiefly devoted to keeping one's self alive—not only labour, which was the way of life of the slave, who was coerced by the necessity to stay alive and by the rule of his master, but also the working life of the free craftsman and the acquisitive life of the merchant. In short, it excluded everybody who involuntarily or voluntarily, for his whole life or temporarily, had lost the free disposition of his movements and activities. The remaining three ways of life have in common that they were concerned with the 'beautiful', that is, with things neither necessary nor merely useful: the life of enjoying bodily pleasures in which the beautiful, as it is given, is consumed; the life devoted to the matters of the *polis*, in which excellence produces beautiful deeds; and the life of the philosopher devoted to inquiry into, and contemplation of, things eternal, whose everlasting beauty can neither be brought about through the producing interference of man nor be changed through his consumption of them.

The chief difference between the Aristotelian and the later medieval use of the term is that the *bios politikos* denoted explicitly only the realm of human affairs, stressing the action, *praxis*, needed to establish and sustain it. Neither labour nor work was considered to possess sufficient dignity to constitute a *bios* at all, an autonomous and authentically human way of life; since they served and produced what was necessary and useful, they could not be free, independent of human needs and wants. That the political way of life escaped this verdict is due to the Greek understanding of *polis* life, which to them denoted a very special and freely chosen form of political organization and by no means just any form of action necessary to keep men together in an orderly fashion. Not that the Greeks or Aristotle were ignorant of the fact that human life always demands some form of political organization and that ruling over subjects might constitute a distinct way of life; but the despot's way of life, because it was 'merely' a necessity, could not be considered free and had no relationship with the *bios politikos*.

Chapter II

The Public and the Private Realm

4 Man: A Social or a Political Animal

The *vita activa*, human life insofar as it is actively engaged in doing something, is always rooted in a world of men and of man-made things which it never leaves or altogether transcends. Things and men form the environment for each of man's activities, which would be pointless without such location; yet this environment, the world into which we are born, would not exist without the human activity which produced it, as in the case of fabricated things; which takes care of it, as in the case of cultivated land; or which established it through organization, as in the case of the body politic. No human life, not even the life of the hermit in nature's wilderness, is possible without a world which directly or indirectly testifies to the presence of other human beings.

All human activities are conditioned by the fact that men live together, but it is only action that cannot even be imagined outside the society of men. The activity of labour does not need the presence of others, though a being labouring in complete solitude would not be human but an *animal laborans* in the word's most literal significance. Man working and fabricating and building a world inhabited only by himself would still be a fabricator, though not *homo faber*: he would have lost his specifically human quality and, rather, be a god—not, to be sure, the Creator, but a divine demiurge as Plato described him in one of his myths. Action alone is the exclusive prerogative of man; neither a beast nor a god is capable of it, and only action is entirely dependent upon the constant presence of others. . . .

According to Greek thought, the human capacity for political organization is not only different from but stands in direct opposition to that natural association whose centre is the home (*oikia*) and the family. The rise of the city-state meant that man received 'besides his private life a sort of second life, his *bios politikos*. Now every citizen belongs to two orders of existence; and there is a sharp distinction in his life between what is his own (*idion*) and what is communal (*koinon*). It was not just an opinion or theory of Aristotle but a simple historical fact that the foundation of the *polis* was preceded by the destruction of all organized units resting on kinship, such as the *phratria* and the *phylē*. Of all the activities necessary and

present in human communities, only two were deemed to be political and to constitute what Aristotle called the *bios politikos*, namely action (*praxis*) and speech (*lexis*), out of which rises the realm of human affairs (*ta tōn anthrō pōn pragmata*, as Plato used to call it) from which everything merely necessary or useful is strictly excluded. . . .

What all Greek philosophers, no matter how opposed to *polis* life, took for granted is that freedom is exclusively located in the political realm, that necessity is primarily a pre-political phenomenon, characteristic of the private household organization, and that force and violence are justified in this sphere because they are the only means to master necessity—for instance, by ruling over slaves—and to become free. Because all human beings are subject to necessity, they are entitled to violence toward others; violence is the pre-political act of liberating oneself from the necessity of life for the freedom of world. This freedom is the essential condition of what the Greeks called felicity, *eudaimonia*, which was an objective status depending first of all upon wealth and health. To be poor or to be in ill health meant to be subject to physical necessity, and to be a slave meant to be subject, in addition, to man-made violence. This twofold and doubled 'unhappiness' of slavery is quite independent of the actual subjective well-being of the slave. Thus, a poor free man preferred the insecurity of a daily-changing labour market to regular assured work, which, because it restricted his freedom to do as he pleased every day, was already felt to be servitude (*douleia*), and even harsh, painful labour was preferred to the easy life of many household slaves. . . .

The *polis* was distinguished from the household in that it knew only 'equals', whereas the household was the centre of the strictest inequality. To be free meant both not to be subject to the necessity of life or to the command of another *and* not to be in command oneself. It meant neither to rule nor to be ruled. Thus within the realm of the household, freedom did not exist, for the household head, its ruler, was considered to be free only insofar as he had the power to leave the household and enter the political realm, where all were equals. To be sure, this equality of the political realm has very little in common with our concept of equality: it meant to live among and to have to deal only with one's peers, and it presupposed the existence of 'unequals' who, as a matter of fact, were always the majority of the population in a city-state. Equality, therefore, far from being connected with justice, as in modern times, was the very essence of freedom: to be free meant to be free from the inequality present in rulership and to move in a sphere where neither rule nor being ruled existed. . . .

[M]odern equality, based on the conformism inherent in society and possible only because behaviour has replaced action as the foremost mode of human relationship, is in every respect different from equality in antiquity, and notably in the Greek city-states. To belong to the few 'equals' (*homoioi*) meant to be permitted to live among one's peers; but the public realm itself, the *polis*, was permeated by a fiercely agonal spirit, where everybody had constantly to distinguish himself from all others, to show through unique deeds or achievements that he was the best of all (*aien aristeuein*). The public realm, in other words, was reserved for individuality; it was the only place where men could show who they really and inexchangeably were. It was for the sake of this chance, and out of love for a body politic that made it possible to them all, that each was more or less willing to share in the burden of jurisdiction, defence, and administration of public affairs. . . .

Chapter III

Labour

. . .

11 'The Labour of Our Body and the Work of Our Hands'

The distinction between labour and work which I propose is unusual. The phenomenal evidence in its favour is too striking to be ignored, and yet historically it is a fact that apart from a few scattered remarks, which moreover were never developed even in the theories of their authors, there is hardly anything in either the pre-modern tradition of political thought or in the large body of modern labour theories to support it. Against this scarcity of historical evidence, however, stands one very articulate and obstinate testimony, namely, the simple fact that every European language, ancient and modern, contains two etymologically unrelated words for what we have to come to think of as the same activity, and retains them in the face of their persistent synonymous usage.

Thus, Locke's distinction between working hands and a labouring body is somewhat reminiscent of the ancient Greek distinction between the *cheirotechnēs*, the craftsman, to whom the German *Handwerker* corresponds, and those who, like 'slaves and tame animals with their bodies minister to the necessities of life,' or in the Greek idiom, *tē sō mati ergazesthai*, work with their bodies (yet even here, labour and work are already treated as identical, since the word used is not *ponein* [labour] but *ergazesthai* [work]). Only in one respect, which, however, is linguistically the most important one, did ancient and modern usage of the two words as synonyms fail altogether, namely in the formation of a corresponding noun. Here again we find complete unanimity; the word 'labour', understood as a noun, never designates the finished product, the result of labouring, but remains a verbal noun to be classed with the gerund, whereas the product itself is invariably derived from the word for work, even when current usage has followed the actual modern development so closely that the verb form of the word 'work' has become rather obsolete.

The reason why this distinction should have been overlooked in ancient times and its significance remained unexplored seems obvious enough. Contempt for labouring, originally arising out of a passionate striving for freedom from necessity and a no less passionate impatience with every effort that left no trace, no monument, no great work worthy of remembrance, spread with the increasing demands of *polis* life upon the time of the citizens and its insistence on their abstention (*skholē*) from all but political activities, until it covered everything that demanded an effort. . . . It is only from the late fifth century onward that the *polis* began to classify occupations according to the amount of effort required, so that Aristotle called those occupations the meanest 'in which the body is most deteriorated.' Although he refused to admit *banausoi* to citizenship, he would have accepted shepherds and painters (but neither peasants nor sculptors).

. . . The opinion that labour and work were despised in antiquity because only slaves were engaged in them is a prejudice of modern historians. The ancients reasoned the other way around and felt it necessary to possess slaves because of the slavish nature of all occupations that served the needs for the maintenance of life. It was precisely on these grounds that the institution of slavery was defended and justified. To labour meant to be enslaved by necessity, and this enslavement was inherent in the conditions of human life. Because men were dominated by the necessities of life, they could win their freedom only through the domination of those whom they subjected to necessity by force. The slave's degradation was a blow of fate and a fate worse than death, because it carried with it a metamorphosis of man into something akin to a tame animal. A change in a slave's status, therefore, such as manumission by his master or a change in general political circumstance that elevated certain occupations to public relevance, automatically entailed a change in the slave's 'nature'.

The institution of slavery in antiquity, though not in later times, was not a device for cheap labour or an instrument of exploitation for profit but rather the attempt to exclude labour from the conditions of man's life. What men share with all other forms of animal life was not considered to be human. (This, incidentally, was also the reason for the much misunderstood Greek theory of the non-human nature of the slave. Aristotle, who argued this theory so explicitly, and then, on his deathbed, freed his slaves, may not have been so inconsistent as moderns are inclined to think. He denied not the slave's capacity to be human, but only the use of the word 'men' for members of the species man-kind as long as they are totally subject to necessity.) And it is true that the use of the word 'animal' in the concept of *animal laborans*, as distinguished from the very questionable use of the same word in the term *animal rationale*, is fully justified. The *animal laborans* is indeed only one, at best the highest, of the animal species which populate the earth.

It is not surprising that the distinction between labour and work was ignored in classical antiquity. The differentiation between the private household and the public political realm, between the household inmate who was a slave and the household head who was a citizen, between activities which should be hidden in privacy and those which were worth being seen, heard, and remembered, overshadowed and predetermined all other distinctions until only one criterion was left: is the greater amount of time and effort spent in private or in public? Is the occupation motivated by *cura private negotii* or *cura rei publicae*, care for private or for public business? With the rise of political theory, the philosophers overruled even these distinctions, which had at least distinguished between activities, by opposing contemplation to all kinds of activity alike. With them, even political activity was levelled to the rank of necessity, which henceforth became the common denominator of all articulations within the *vita activa*. Nor can we reasonably expect any help from Christian political thought, which accepted the philosophers' distinction, refined it, and, religion being for the many and philosophy only for the few, gave it general validity, binding for all men.

It is surprising at first glance, however, that the modern age—with its reversal of all traditions, the traditional rank of action and contemplation no less than the traditional hierarchy within the *vita activa* itself, with its glorification of labour as the source of all values and its elevation of the *animal laborans* to the position traditionally held by the *animal rationale*—should not have brought forth a single theory in which *animal laborans* and *homo faber*, 'the labour of our body and the work of our hands,' are clearly distinguished. Instead, we find first the distinction between productive and unproductive labour, then somewhat later the differentiation between skilled and unskilled work, and, finally, outranking both because seemingly of more elementary significance, the division of all activities into manual and intellectual labour. Of the three, however, only the distinction between productive and unproductive labour

goes to the heart of the matter, and it is no accident that the two greatest theorists in the field, Adam Smith and Karl Marx, based the whole structure of their argument upon it. The very reason for the elevation of labour in the modern age was its 'productivity', and the seemingly blasphemous notion of Marx that labour (and not God) created man or that labour (and not reason) distinguished man from the other animals was only the most radical and consistent formulation of something upon which the whole modern age was agreed.

Moreover, both Smith and Marx were in agreement with modern public opinion when they despised unproductive labour as parasitical, actually a kind of perversion of labour, as though nothing were worthy of this name which did not enrich the world. Marx certainly shared Smith's contempt for the 'menial servants' who like 'idle guests ... leave nothing behind them in return for their consumption.' Yet it was precisely these menial servants, these household inmates, *oiketai* or *familiares*, labouring for sheer subsistence and needed for effortless consumption rather than for production, whom all ages prior to the modern had in mind when they identified the labouring condition with slavery. What they left behind them in return for their consumption was nothing more or less than their masters' freedom or, in modern language, their masters' potential productivity.

In other words, the distinction between productive and unproductive labour contains, albeit in a prejudicial manner, the more fundamental distinction between labour and work. It is indeed the mark of all labouring that it leaves nothing behind, that the result of its effort is almost as quickly consumed as the effort is spent. And yet this effort, despite its futility, is born of a great urgency and motivated by a more powerful drive than anything else, because life itself depends upon it. The modern age in general and Karl Marx in particular, overwhelmed, as it were, by the unprecedented actual productivity of Western mankind, had an almost irresistible tendency to look upon all labour as work and to speak of the *animal laborans* in terms much more fitting for *homo faber*, hoping all the time that only one more step was needed to eliminate labour and necessity altogether.

No doubt the actual historical development that brought labour out of hiding and into the public realm, where it could be organized and 'divided', constituted a powerful argument in the development of these theories. Yet an even more significant fact in this respect, already sensed by the classical economists and clearly discovered and articulated by Karl Marx, is that the labouring activity itself, regardless of historical circumstances and independent of its location in the private or the public realm, possesses indeed a 'productivity' of its own, no matter how futile and non-durable its products may be. This productivity does not lie in any of labour's products but in the human 'power', whose strength is not exhausted when it has produced the means of its own subsistence and survival but is capable of producing a 'surplus', that is, more than is necessary for its own 'reproduction'. It is because not labour itself but the surplus of human 'labour *power*' (*Arbeits*kraft) explains labour's productivity that Marx's introduction of this term, as Engels rightly remarked, constituted the most original and revolutionary element of his whole system. Unlike the productivity of work, which adds new objects to the human artifice, the productivity of labour power produces objects only incidentally and is primarily concerned with the means of its own reproduction; since its power is not exhausted when its own reproduction has been secured, it can be used for the reproduction of more than one life process,

but it never 'produces' anything but life. Through violent oppression in a slave society or exploitation in the capitalist society of Marx's own time, it can be channelled in such a way that the labour of some suffices for the life of all.

From this purely social viewpoint, which is the viewpoint of the whole modern age but which received its most coherent and greatest expression in Marx's work, all labouring is 'productive', and the earlier distinction between the performance of 'menial tasks' that leave no trace and the production of things durable enough to be accumulated loses its validity. The social viewpoint is identical, as we saw before, with an interpretation that takes nothing into account but the life process of mankind, and within its frame of reference all things become objects of consumption. Within a completely 'socialized mankind', whose sole purpose would be the entertaining of the life process—and this is the unfortunately quite unutopian ideal that guides Marx's theories— the distinction between labour and work would have completely disappeared; all work would have become labour because all things would be understood, not in their worldly, objective quality, but as results of living labour power and functions of the life process.

It is interesting to note that the distinctions between skilled and unskilled and between intellectual and manual work play no role in either classical political economy or in Marx's work. Compared with the productivity of labour, they are indeed of secondary importance. Every activity requires a certain amount of skill, the activity of cleaning and cooking no less than the writing of a book or the building of a house. The distinction does not apply to different activities but notes only certain stages and qualities within each of them. It could acquire a certain importance through the modern division of labour, where tasks formerly assigned to the young and inexperienced were frozen into lifelong occupations. But this consequence of the division of labour, where one activity is divided into so many minute parts that each specialized performer needs but a minimum of skill, tends to abolish skilled labour altogether, as Marx rightly predicted. Its result is that what is bought and sold in the labour market is not individual skill but 'labour power', of which each living human being should possess approximately the same amount. Moreover, since unskilled work is a contradiction in terms, the distinction itself is valid only for the labouring activity, and the attempt to use it as a major frame of reference already indicates that the distinction between labour and work has been abandoned in favour of labour.

Quite different is the case of the more popular category of manual and intellectual work. Here, the underlying tie between the labourer of the hand and the labourer of the head is again the labouring process, in one case performed by the head, in the other by some other part of the body. Thinking, however, which is presumably the activity of the head, though it is in some way like labouring—also a process which probably comes to an end only with life itself—is even less 'productive' than labour; if labour leaves no permanent trace, thinking leaves nothing tangible at all. By itself, thinking never materializes into any objects. Whenever the intellectual worker wishes to manifest his thoughts, he must use his hands and acquire manual skills just like any other worker. In other words, thinking and working are two different activities which never quite coincide; the thinker who wants the world to know the 'content' of his thoughts must first of all stop thinking and remember his thoughts. Remembrance in this, as in all other cases, prepares the intangible and the futile for their eventual materialization; it is the

beginning of the work process, and like the craftsman's consideration of the model which will guide his work, its most immaterial stage. The work itself then always requires some material upon which it will be performed and which through fabrication, the activity of *homo faber*, will be transformed into a worldly object. The specific work quality of intellectual work is no less due to the 'work of our hands' than any other kind of work. . . .

The distinction between manual and intellectual work, though its origin can be traced back to the Middle Ages, is modern and has two quite different causes, both of which, however, are equally characteristic of the general climate of the modern age. Since under modern conditions every occupation had to prove its 'usefulness' for society at large, and since the usefulness of the intellectual occupations had become more than doubtful because of the modern glorification of labour, it was only natural that intellectuals, too, should desire to be counted among the working population. At the same time, however, and only in seeming contradiction to this development, the need and esteem of this society for certain 'intellectual' performances rose to a degree unprecedented in our history except in the centuries of the decline of the Roman Empire. It may be well to remember in this context that throughout ancient history the 'intellectual' services of the scribes, whether they served the needs of the public or the private realm, were performed by slaves and rated accordingly. Only the bureaucratization of the Roman Empire and the concomitant social and political rise of the emperors brought a re-evaluation of 'intellectual' services. Insofar as the intellectual is indeed not a 'worker'—who like all other workers, from the humblest craftsman to the greatest artist, is engaged in adding one more, if possible durable, thing to the human artifice—he resembles perhaps nobody so much as Adam Smith's 'menial servant', although his function is less to keep the life process intact and provide for its regeneration than to care for the upkeep of the various gigantic bureaucratic machines whose processes consume their services and devour their products as quickly and mercilessly as the biological life process itself.

Study Questions for *The Human Condition*

1. In chapter I, Arendt distinguishes three basic human activities: labour, work, and action. Describe each of these activities. How is each activity connected to a condition of human existence?
2. In discussing the term *vita activa* (the active life), Arendt notes that Aristotle distinguished freely chosen ways of life from ways of life driven by necessity. Why did the Greeks exclude labour and work from the active and free political life?
3. How did the Greeks distinguish the *polis* (the city-state) from the household? Why did the Greeks locate freedom exclusively in the political realm?
4. According to Arendt, the distinction between labour and work has been noted in scattered remarks of Western political philosophers and economic theorists but, until *The Human Condition*, has not been adequately appreciated or developed. How is the distinction between labour and work reminiscent of the Greek distinction between slaves and craftsmen?
5. How did Karl Marx develop the distinction between labour and work? What shortcoming does Arendt identify in Marx's account of labour?

Recommended Readings

Arendt, Hannah, *The Portable Hannah Arendt*, edited by Peter Baher (Penguin, 2000).

Benhabib, Seyla, *The Reluctant Modernism of Hannah Arendt*, new edn (Rowman and Littlefield, 2003).

Bernstein, Richard, *Hannah Arendt and the Jewish Question* (Polity Press, 1996).

Canovan, Margaret, *Hannah Arendt: A Reinterpretation of Her Political Thought* (Cambridge University Press, 1992).

Dietz, Mary, *Turning Operations: Feminism, Arendt and Politics* (Routledge, 2002).

Hinchman, Lewis, and Sandra Hinchman, eds, *Hannah Arendt: Critical Essays* (State University of New York Press, 1994).

Kristeva, Julia, *Hannah Arendt* (Columbia University Press, 2001).

Passerin d'Entrèves, Maurizio, *The Political Philosophy of Hannah Arendt* (Routledge, 1994).

Villa, Dana, ed., *Politics, Philosophy, Terror: Essays on the Thought of Hannah Arendt* (Princeton University Press, 1999).

Young-Bruehl, Elisabeth, *Hannah Arendt: For Love of the World*, 2nd edn (Yale University Press, 2004).

——— *Why Arendt Matters* (Yale University Press, 2006).

Jürgen Habermas

Jürgen Habermas (1929–) is a prominent German public intellectual and a leading philosopher of the Frankfurt School of critical theory. He was born in Düsseldorf, Germany, and came of age under the national socialist regime of the Nazi party. Following the Nuremburg trials and the publication of documentaries on the concentration camps, Habermas experienced a moral and political awakening with his contemporaries in the Hitler Youth in which, as he later remarked, 'all at once we saw we had been living in a politically criminal system.' As he comments in *Autonomy and Solidarity* (1992), this realization sparked his intellectual interest in politics and shaped some of the predominant themes of his work. In 1954, Habermas received a doctorate from the University of Bonn and subsequently continued studying philosophy and sociology under Max Horkheimer and Theodor Adorno at the Institute for Social Research in Frankfurt. He completed the *habilitation* (the European post-doctoral degree) in political science from the University of Marburg. Habermas has spent most of his professorial career at the universities of Heidelburg and Frankfurt and, during the 1970s, served as co-director of the Max Plank Institute in Starnberg. He is currently a permanent visiting professor of philosophy at Northwestern University.

Habermas's work reflects the influence of his mentors in the first generation of Frankfort School critical theorists. Frankfort School theorists—associated with the Institute for Social Research founded in Frankfurt in 1929—encompass a group of philosophers, sociologists, psychologists, and cultural critics who seek a renewal of Marxist social theory in the service of understanding contemporary social phenomena. The founding members of the Frankfort School, including Horkheimer and Adorno, favour critical theory over the Anglo-American philosophical tradition of empiricism and logical positivism. Whereas the latter 'traditional theory' contains the assumption that ideal theory mirrors a fixed and independent realm of facts, critical theorists view facts and theories as reciprocally self-determining within a historical process of human understanding. Critical theorists, including Habermas, seek to develop analyses of modern society that are self-reflective and capable of providing a normative foundation for social transformation.

Habermas's critical theory encompasses not only theories of democracy and morality but also theories of rationality, communication, socialization, and historical social evolution. In the tradition of the Frankfort School, his work is interdisciplinary and weaves together philosophical analyses with empirical understandings of the human sciences. One predominate recurring motif in his work is the central place of the public sphere in democratic theory. From his first published treatise, *The Structural Transformation of the Public Sphere* (1962), Habermas emphasizes that rational deliberation in the public sphere is a necessary precondition of a genuinely democratic state, for the legitimacy of democratic policies requires reasons that can withstand open and critical discussion among citizens. Habermas observes that bureaucratic and economic modes of communication have come to dominate mass media and modern society, thereby undermining true public discourse among citizens, but he remains optimistic that dominant technocratic modes of communication can be contained in favour of preserving spaces for rational public deliberation. In addition to his *Structural Transformation of the Public Sphere*, Habermas's principle works include *Theory and Practice* (1963), *Knowledge and Human Interests* (1968), his monumental *Theory of Communicative Action* (1981), *Between Facts and Norms* (1992), and *The Inclusion of the Other* (1996), from which our second selection is taken.

In our first selection, 'The Public Sphere' (1989), Habermas traces the historical development of the public sphere and discusses the relationship between the public sphere and the authority of the state. In contrast to Hannah Arendt, Habermas does not identify the ancient Greek city-state as the *locus classicus* of the public sphere but sees the latter eighteenth century as creating institutionally protected public discussions, which form the basis of the liberal model of the public sphere. In his view, the basic rights guaranteed to citizens in modern constitutions and charters generate a domain of private individuals who come together to form a public deliberative body. In our second selection, 'Three Normative Models of Democracy' (1999), Habermas distinguishes two classical ideals of democratic politics—the liberal and republican models—and introduces an original third model which he terms 'deliberative politics'. Deliberative politics integrates elements of both the liberal and republican models but includes a normative procedure for public deliberation and decision making centred around rational communication.

'The Public Sphere'

Concept

By 'public sphere' we mean first of all a domain of our social life in which such a thing as public opinion can be formed. Access to the public sphere is open in principle to all citizens. A portion of the public sphere is constituted in every conversation in which private persons come together to form a public. They are then acting neither as business or professional people conducting their private affairs, nor as legal consociates subject to the legal regulations of a state bureaucracy and obligated to obedience. Citizens act as a public when they deal with matters of general interest without being subject to coercion; thus with the guarantee that they may assemble and unite freely, and express and publicize their opinions freely. When the public is large, this kind of communication requires certain means of dissemination and influence; today, newspapers and periodicals, radio and television are the media of the public sphere. We speak of a political public sphere (as distinguished from a literary one, for instance) when the public discussions concern objects connected with the practice of the state. The coercive power of the state is the counterpart, as it were, of the political public sphere, but it is not a part of it. State power is, to be sure, considered 'public' power, but it owes the attribute of publicness to its task of caring for the public, that is, providing for the common good of all legal consociates. Only when the exercise of public authority has actually been subordinated to the requirement of democratic publicness does the political public sphere acquire an institutionalized influence on the government, by way of the legislative body. The term 'public opinion' refers to the functions of criticism and control of organized state authority that the public exercises informally, as well as formally during periodic elections. Regulations concerning the publicness (or publicity [*Publizität*] in its original meaning) of state-related activities, as, for instance, the public accessibility required of legal proceedings, are also connected with this function of public opinion. To the public sphere as a sphere mediating between state and society, a sphere in which the public as the vehicle of public opinion is formed, there corresponds the principle of publicness—the publicness that once had to win out against the secret politics of monarchs and that since then has permitted democratic control of state activity.

It is no accident that these concepts of the public sphere and public opinion were not formed until the eighteenth century. They derive their specific meaning from a concrete historical situation. It was then that one learned to distinguish between opinion and public opinion, or *opinion publique*. Whereas mere opinions (things taken for granted as part of a culture, normative convictions, collective prejudices, and judgments) seem to persist unchanged in their quasi-natural structure as a kind of sediment of history, public opinion, in terms of its very idea, can be formed only if a public that engages in rational discussion exists. Public discussions that are institutionally protected and that take, with critical intent, the exercise of political authority as their theme have not existed since time immemorial—they developed only in a specific phase of bourgeois society, and only by virtue of a specific constellation of interests could they be incorporated into the order of the bourgeois constitutional state.

History

It is not possible to demonstrate the existence of a public sphere in its own right, separate from the private sphere, in the European society of the High Middle Ages. At the same time, however, it is not a coincidence that the attributes of authority at that time were called 'public'. For a public representation of authority existed at that time. At all levels of the pyramid established by feudal law, the status of the feudal lord is neutral with respect to the categories 'public' and 'private'; but the person possessing that status represents it publicly; he displays himself, represents himself as the embodiment of a 'higher' power, in whatever degree. This concept of representation has survived into recent constitutional history. Even today the power of political authority on its highest level, however much it has become detached from its former basis, requires representation through the head of state. But such elements derive from a pre-bourgeois social structure. Representation in the sense of the bourgeois public sphere, as in 'representing' the nation or specific clients, has nothing to do with *representative publicness*, which inheres in the concrete existence of a lord. As long as the prince and the estates of his realm 'are' the land, rather than merely 'representing' it, they are capable of this kind of representation; they represent their authority 'before' the people rather than for the people.

The feudal powers (the church, the prince, and the nobility) to which this representative publicness adheres disintegrated in the course of a long process of polarization; by the end of the eighteenth century they had decomposed into private elements on the one side and public on the other. The position of the church changed in connection with the Reformation; the tie to divine authority that the church represented, that is, religion, became a private matter. Historically, what is called the freedom of religion safeguarded the first domain of private autonomy; the church itself continued its existence as one corporate body under public law among others. The corresponding polarization of princely power acquired visible form in the separation of the public budget from the private household property of the feudal lord. In the bureaucracy and the military (and in part also in the administration of justice), institutions of public power became autonomous vis-à-vis the privatized sphere of the princely court. In terms of the estates, finally, elements from the ruling groups developed into organs of public power, into parliament (and in part also into judicial organs); elements from the occupational status groups, insofar as they had become established in urban corporations and in certain differentiations within the estates of the land, developed into the sphere of bourgeois society, which would confront the state as a genuine domain of private autonomy.

Representative publicness gave way to the new sphere of 'public power' that came into being with the national and territorial states. Ongoing state activity (permanent administra-

tion, a standing army) had its counterpart in the permanence of relationships that had developed in the meantime with the stock market and the press, through traffic in goods and news. Public power became consolidated as something tangible confronting those who were subject to it and who at first found themselves only negatively defined by it. These are the 'private persons' who are excluded from public power because they hold no office. 'Public' no longer refers to the representative court of a person vested with authority; instead, it now refers to the competence-regulated activity of an apparatus furnished with a monopoly on the legitimate use of force. As those to whom this public power is addressed, private persons subsumed under the state form the public.

As a private domain, society, which has come to confront the state, as it were, is on the one hand clearly differentiated from public power; on the other hand, society becomes a matter of public interest insofar as with the rise of a market economy the reproduction of life extends beyond the confines of private domestic power. The *bourgeois public sphere* can be understood as the sphere of private persons assembled to form a public. They soon began to make use of the public sphere of informational newspapers, which was officially regulated, against the public power itself, using those papers, along with the morally and critically oriented weeklies, to engage in debate about the general rules governing relations in their own essentially privatized but publicly relevant sphere of commodity exchange and labour.

The Liberal Model of the Public Sphere

The medium in which this debate takes place —public discussion—is unique and without historical prototype. Previously the estates had negotiated contracts with their princes in which claims to power were defined on a case-by-case basis. As we know, this development followed a different course in England, where princely power was relativized through parliament, than on the Continent, where the estates were mediatized by the monarch. The 'third estate' then broke with this mode of equalizing power, for it could no longer establish itself as a ruling estate. Given a commercial economy, a division of authority accomplished through differentiation of the rights of those possessing feudal authority (liberties belonging to the estates) was no longer possible—the power under private law of disposition of capitalist property is non-political. The bourgeois are private persons; as such, they do not 'rule'. Thus their claims to power in opposition to public power are directed not against a concentration of authority that should be 'divided' but rather against the principle of established authority. The principle of control, namely publicness, that the bourgeois public opposes to the principle of established authority aims at a transformation of authority as such, not merely the exchange of one basis of legitimation for another.

In the first modern constitutions the sections listing basic rights provide an image of the liberal model of the public sphere: they guarantee society as a sphere of private autonomy; opposite it stands a public power limited to a few functions; between the two spheres, as it were, stands the domain of private persons who have come together to form a public and who, as citizens of the state, mediate the state with the needs of bourgeois society, in order, as the idea goes, to thus convert political authority to 'rational' authority in the medium of this public sphere. Under the presuppositions of a society based on the free exchange of commodities, it seemed that the general interest, which served as the criterion by which this kind of rationality was to be evaluated, would

be assured if the dealings of private persons in the marketplace were emancipated from social forces and their dealings in the public sphere were emancipated from political coercion.

The political daily press came to have an important role during this same period. In the second half of the eighteenth century, serious competition to the older form of news writing as the compiling of items of information arose in the form of literary journalism. Karl Bücher describes the main outlines of this development: 'From mere institutions for the publication of news, newspapers became the vehicles and guides of public opinion as well, weapons of party politics. The consequence of this for the internal organization of the newspaper enterprise was the insertion of a new function between the gathering of news and its publication: the editorial function. For the newspaper publisher, however, the significance of this development was that from a seller of new information he became a dealer in public opinion.' Publishers provided the commercial basis for the newspaper without, however, commercializing it as such. The press remained an institution of the public itself, operating to provide and intensify public discussion, no longer a mere organ for the conveyance of information, but not yet a medium of consumer culture.

This type of press can be observed especially in revolutionary periods, when papers associated with the tiniest political coalitions and groups spring up, as in Paris in 1789. In the Paris of 1848 every halfway prominent politician still formed his own club, and every other one founded his own *journal*: over 450 clubs and more than 200 papers came into being there between February and May alone. Until the permanent legalization of a public sphere that functioned politically, the appearance of a political newspaper was equivalent to engagement in the struggle for a zone of freedom for public opinion, for publicness as a principle. Not until the establishment of the bourgeois constitutional state was a press engaged in the public use of reason relieved of the pressure of ideological viewpoints. Since then it has been able to abandon its polemical stance and take advantage of the earning potential of commercial activity. The ground was cleared for this development from a press of viewpoints to a commercial press at about the same time in England, France, and the United States, during the 1830s. In the course of this transformation from the journalism of writers who were private persons to the consumer services of the mass media, the sphere of publicness was changed by an influx of private interests that achieved privileged representation within it.

The Public Sphere in Mass Welfare-State Democracies

The liberal model of the public sphere remains instructive in regard to the normative claim embodied in institutionalized requirements of publicness; but it is not applicable to actual relationships within a mass democracy that is industrially advanced and constituted as a social-welfare state. In part, the liberal model had always contained ideological aspects; in part, the social presuppositions to which those aspects were linked have undergone fundamental changes. Even the forms in which the public sphere was manifested, forms which made its idea seem to a certain extent obvious, began to change with the Chartist movement in England and the February Revolution in France. With the spread of the press and propaganda, the public expanded beyond the confines of the bourgeoisie. Along with its social exclusivity the public lost the cohesion given it by institutions of convivial social intercourse and by a relatively high standard of education.

Accordingly, conflicts which in the past were pushed off into the private sphere now enter the public sphere. Group needs, which cannot expect satisfaction from a self-regulating market, tend toward state regulation. The public sphere, which must now mediate these demands, becomes a field for competition among interests in the cruder form of forcible confrontation. Laws that have obviously originated under the 'pressure of the streets' can scarcely continue to be understood in terms of a consensus achieved by private persons in public discussion; they correspond, in more or less undisguised form, to compromises between conflicting private interests. Today it is social organizations that act in relation to the state in the political public sphere, whether through the mediation of political parties or directly, in interplay with public administration. With the interlocking of the public and private domains, not only do political agencies take over certain functions in the sphere of commodity exchange and social labour; societal powers also take over political functions. This leads to a kind of 'refeudalization' of the public sphere. Large-scale organizations strive for political compromises with the state and with one another, behind closed doors if possible; but at the same time they have to secure at least plebiscitarian approval from the mass of the population through the deployment of a staged form of publicity.

The political public sphere in the welfare state is characterized by a singular weakening of its critical functions. Whereas at one time publicness was intended to subject persons or things to the public use of reason and to make political decisions susceptible to revision before the tribunal of public opinion, today it has often enough already been enlisted in the aid of the secret policies of interest groups; in the form of 'publicity' it now acquires public prestige for persons or things and renders them capable of acclamation in a climate of non-public opinion. The term 'public relations' itself indicates how a public sphere that formerly emerged from the structure of society must now be produced circumstantially on a case-by-case basis. The central relationship of the public, political parties, and parliament is also affected by this change in function.

This existing trend toward the weakening of the public sphere, as a principle, is opposed, however, by a welfare-state transformation of the functioning of basic rights: the requirement of publicness is extended by state organs to all organizations acting in relation to the state. To the extent to which this becomes a reality, a no longer intact public of private persons acting as individuals would be replaced by a public of organized private persons. Under current circumstances, only the latter could participate effectively in a process of public communication using the channels of intra-party and intra-organizational public spheres, on the basis of a publicness enforced for the dealings of organizations with the state. It is in this process of public communication that the formation of political compromises would have to achieve legitimation. The idea of the public sphere itself, which signified a rationalization of authority in the medium of public discussions among private persons, and which has been preserved in mass welfare-state democracy, threatens to disintegrate with the structural transformation of the public sphere. Today it could be realized only on a different basis, as a rationalization of the exercise of social and political power under the mutual control of rival organizations committed to publicness in their internal structure as well as in their dealings with the state and with one another.

'Three Normative Models of Democracy'

I

The crucial difference between liberalism and republicanism consists in how the role of the democratic process is understood. According to the 'liberal' view, this process accomplishes the task of programming the state in the interest of society, where the state is conceived as an apparatus of public administration, and society is conceived as a system of market-structured interactions of private persons and their labour. Here politics (in the sense of the citizens' political will-formation) has the function of bundling together and bringing to bear private social interests against a state apparatus that specializes in the administrative employment of political power for collective goals.

On the republican view, politics is not exhausted by this mediating function but is constitutive for the socialization process as a whole. Politics is conceived as the reflexive form of substantial ethical life. It constitutes the medium in which the members of quasi-natural solidary communities become aware of their dependence on one another and, acting with full deliberation as citizens, further shape and develop existing relations of reciprocal recognition into an association of free and equal consociates under law. With this, the liberal architectonic of government and society undergoes an important change. In addition to the hierarchical regulatory apparatus of sovereign state authority and the decentralized regulatory mechanism of the market

—that is, besides administrative power and self-interest—*solidarity* appears as a third source of social integration.

This horizontal political will-formation aimed at mutual understanding or communicatively achieved consensus is even supposed to enjoy priority, both in a genetic and a normative sense. An autonomous basis in civil society independent of public administration and market-mediated private commerce is assumed as a precondition for the practice of civic self-determination. This basis prevents political communication from being swallowed up by the government apparatus or assimilated to market structures. Thus, on the republican conception, the political public sphere and its base, civil society, acquire a strategic significance. Together they are supposed to secure the integrative power and autonomy of the communicative practice of the citizens.[1] The uncoupling of political communication from the economy has as its counterpart a coupling of administrative power with the communicative power generated by political opinion- and will-formation.

These two competing conceptions of politics have different consequences.

(a) In the first place, their concepts of the citizen differ. According to the liberal view, the citizen's status is determined primarily by the individual rights he or she has vis-à-vis the state and other citizens. As bearers of individual rights citizens enjoy the protection of the government as long as they pursue their private interests within the boundaries drawn by legal statutes—and this includes protection against state interventions that violate the legal prohibition on government interference. Individual rights are negative rights that guarantee a domain of freedom of choice within which legal persons are freed from external compulsion. Political rights have the same structure: they afford citizens the opportunity to assert their private interests in such a way that, by means of elections, the composition of parliamentary bodies, and the formation of a government, these interests are finally aggregated into a political will that can affect the administration. In this way the citizens in their political role can determine whether governmental authority is exercised in the interest of the citizens as members of society.[2]

According to the republican view, the status of citizens is not determined by the model of negative liberties to which these citizens can lay claim as private persons. Rather, political rights—pre-eminently rights of political participation and communication—are positive liberties. They do not guarantee freedom from external compulsion, but guarantee instead the possibility of participating in a common practice, through which the citizens can first make themselves into what they want to be—politically responsible subjects of a community of free and equal citizens.[3] To this extent, the political process does not serve just to keep government activity under the surveillance of citizens who have already acquired a prior social autonomy through the exercise of their private rights and pre-political liberties. Nor does it act only as a hinge between state and society, for democratic governmental authority is by no means an original authority. Rather, this authority proceeds from the communicative power generated by the citizens' practice of self-legislation, and it is legitimated by the fact that it protects this practice by institutionalizing public freedom.[4] The state's raison d'être does not lie primarily in the protection of equal individual rights but in the guarantee of an inclusive process of opinion- and will-formation in which free and equal citizens reach an understanding on which goals and norms lie in the equal interest of all. In this way the republican citizen is credited with more than an exclusive concern with his or her private interests.

(b) The polemic against the classical concept of the legal person as bearer of individual rights reveals a controversy about the concept of law itself. Whereas on the liberal conception the point of a legal order is to make it possible to determine which individuals in each case are entitled to which rights, on the republican conception these 'subjective' rights owe their existence to an 'objective' legal order that both enables and guarantees the integrity of an autonomous life in common based on equality and mutual respect. On the one view, the legal order is conceived in terms of individual rights; on the other, their objective legal content is given priority.

To be sure, this conceptual dichotomy does not touch on the intersubjective content of rights that demand reciprocal respect for rights and duties in symmetrical relations of recognition. But the republican concept at least points in the direction of a concept of law that accords equal weight to both the integrity of the individual and the integrity of the community in which persons as both individuals and members can first accord one another reciprocal recognition. It ties the legitimacy of the laws to the democratic procedure by which they are generated and thereby preserves an internal connection between the citizens' practice of self-legislation and the impersonal sway of the law:

> For republicans, rights ultimately are nothing but determinations of prevailing political will, while for liberals, some rights are always grounded in a 'higher law' of transpolitical reason or revelation. . . . In a republican view, a community's objective, common good substantially consists in the success of its political endeavor to define, establish, effectuate, and sustain the set of rights (less tendentiously, laws) best suited to the conditions and *mores* of that community. Whereas in a contrasting liberal view, the higher-law rights provide the transactional structures and the curbs on power required so that pluralistic pursuit of diverse and conflicting interests may proceed as satisfactorily as possible.[5]

The right to vote, interpreted as a positive right, becomes the paradigm of rights as such, not only because it is constitutive for political self-determination, but because it shows how inclusion in a community of equals is connected with the individual right to make autonomous contributions and take personal positions on issues:

> [T]he claim is that we all take an interest in each others' enfranchisement because (i) our choice lies between hanging together and hanging separately; (ii) hanging together depends on reciprocal assurances to all of having one's vital interests heeded by others; and (iii) in the deeply pluralized conditions of contemporary American society, such assurances are not attainable through virtual representation, but only by maintaining at least the semblance of a politics in which everyone is conceded a voice.[6]

This structure, read off from the political rights of participation and communication, is extended to *all* rights via the legislative process constituted by political rights. Even the authorization guaranteed by private law to pursue private, freely chosen goals simultaneously imposes an obligation to respect the limits of strategic action which are agreed to be in the equal interest of all.

(c) The different ways of conceptualizing the role of citizen and the law express a deeper disagreement about the nature of the political process. On the liberal view, politics is essentially a struggle for positions that grant access to administrative power. The political process of opinion- and will-formation in the public sphere and in parliament is shaped by the competition of strategically acting collectives trying to maintain or acquire positions of power. Success is measured by the citizens' approval of persons and programs, as quantified by votes. In their choices at the polls, voters express their preferences. Their votes have the same structure as the choices of participants in a market, in that their decisions license access to positions of power that political parties fight over with a success-oriented attitude similar to that of players in the market. The input of votes and the output of power conform to the same pattern of strategic action.

According to the republican view, the political opinion- and will-formation in the public sphere and in parliament does not obey the structures of market processes but rather the obstinate structures of a public communication oriented to mutual understanding. For politics as the citizens' practice of self-determination, the paradigm is not the market but dialogue. From this perspective there is a structural difference between communicative power, which proceeds from political communication in the form of discursively generated majority decisions, and the administrative power possessed by the governmental apparatus. Even the parties that struggle over access to positions of governmental power must bend themselves to the deliberative style and the stubborn character of political discourse:

> Deliberation . . . refers to a certain attitude toward social cooperation, namely, that of openness to persuasion by reasons referring to the claims of others as well as one's own. The deliberative medium is a good faith exchange of views—including participants' reports of their own understanding

of their respective vital interests— . . . in which a vote, if any vote is taken, represents a pooling of judgments.[7]

Hence the conflict of opinions conducted in the political arena has legitimating force not just in the sense of an authorization to occupy positions of power; on the contrary, the ongoing political discourse also has binding force for the way in which political authority is exercised. Administrative power can only be exercised on the basis of policies and within the limits laid down by laws generated by the democratic process.

II

So much for the comparison between the two models of democracy that currently dominate the discussion between the so-called communitarians and liberals, above all in the US. The republican model has advantages and disadvantages. In my view it has the advantage that it preserves the radical democratic meaning of a society that organizes itself through the communicatively united citizens and does not trace collective goals back to 'deals' made between competing private interests. Its disadvantage, as I see it, is that it is too idealistic in that it makes the democratic process dependent on the virtues of citizens devoted to the public weal. For politics is not concerned in the first place with questions of ethical self-understanding. The mistake of the republican view consists in an ethical foreshortening of political discourse.

To be sure, ethical discourses aimed at achieving a collective self-understanding—discourses in which participants attempt to clarify how they understand themselves as members of a particular nation, as members of a community or a state, as inhabitants of a region, etc., which traditions they wish to cultivate, how they should treat each other, minorities, and marginal groups, in what sort of society they want to live—constitute an important part of politics. But under conditions of cultural and social pluralism, behind politically relevant goals there often lie interests and value-orientations that are by no means constitutive of the identity of the political community as a whole, that is, for the totality of an intersubjectively shared form of life. These interests and value-orientations, which conflict with one another within the same polity without any prospect of consensual resolution, need to be counterbalanced in a way that cannot be effected by ethical discourse, even though the results of this nondiscursive counterbalancing are subject to the proviso that they must not violate the basic values of a culture. The balancing of interests takes the form of reaching a compromise between parties who rely on their power and ability to sanction. Negotiations of this sort certainly presuppose a readiness to cooperate, that is, a willingness to abide by the rules and to arrive at results that are acceptable to all parties, though for different reasons. But compromise-formation is not conducted in the form of a rational discourse that neutralizes power and excludes strategic action. However, the fairness of compromises is measured by presuppositions and procedures which for their part are in need of rational, indeed normative, justification from the standpoint of justice. In contrast with ethical questions, questions of justice are not by their very nature tied to a particular collectivity. Politically enacted law, if it is to be legitimate, must be at least in harmony with moral principles that claim a general validity that extends beyond the limits of any concrete legal community.

The concept of deliberative politics acquires empirical relevance only when we take into account the multiplicity of forms of communication in which a common will is produced, that is, not just ethical self-clarification but also the balancing of interests and compromise, the purposive choice of means, moral justification, and legal consistency-testing. In this process the two types of politics which Michelman distinguishes in an ideal-typical fashion can interweave and complement one another in a rational manner. 'Dialogical' and 'instrumental' politics can *interpenetrate* in the medium of deliberation if the corresponding forms of communication are sufficiently institutionalized. Everything depends on the conditions of communication and the procedures that lend the institutionalized opinion- and will-formation their legitimating force. The third model of democracy, which I would like to propose, relies precisely on those conditions of communication under which the political process can be presumed to produce rational results because it operates deliberatively at all levels.

Making the proceduralist conception of deliberative politics the cornerstone of the theory of democracy results in differences both from the republican conception of the state as an ethical community and from the liberal conception of the state as the guardian of a market society. In comparing the three models, I take my orientation from that dimension of politics which has been our primary concern, namely, the democratic opinion- and will-formation that issue in popular elections and parliamentary decrees.

According to the liberal view, the democratic process takes place exclusively in the form of compromises between competing interests. Fairness is supposed to be guaranteed by rules of compromise-formation that regulate the general and equal right to vote, the representative composition of parliamentary bodies, their order of business, and so on. Such rules are ultimately justified in terms of liberal basic rights. According to the republican view, by contrast, democratic will-formation is supposed to take the form of an ethical discourse of self-understanding; here deliberation can rely for its content on a culturally established background consensus of the citizens, which is rejuvenated through the ritualistic re-enactment of a republican founding act. Discourse theory takes elements from both sides and integrates them into the concept of an ideal procedure for deliberation and decision-making. Weaving together negotiations and discourses of self-understanding and of justice, this democratic procedure grounds the presumption that under such conditions reasonable or fair results are obtained. According to this proceduralist view, practical reason withdraws from universal human rights or from the concrete ethical life of a specific community into the rules of discourse and forms of argumentation that derive their normative content from the validity-basis of action oriented to reaching understanding, and ultimately from the structure of linguistic communication.[8]

These descriptions of the structures of democratic process set the stage for different normative conceptualizations of state and society. The sole presupposition is a public administration of the kind that emerged in the early modern period together with the European state system and in functional interconnection with a capitalist economic system. According to the republican view, the citizens' political opinion- and will-formation forms the medium through which society constitutes itself as a political whole. Society is centred in the state; for in the citizens' practice of political self-determination the polity becomes conscious of itself as a totality and acts on itself via the collective will of the citizens. Democracy is synonymous with the political self-organization of society. This leads to a polemical understanding of politics as directed against the state apparatus. In Hannah Arendt's political writings one can see the thrust of republican arguments: in opposition to the civic privatism of a depoliticized population and in opposition to the acquisition of legitimation through entrenched parties, the political public sphere should be revitalized to the point where a regenerated citizenry can, in the forms of a decentralized self-governance, (once again) appropriate the governmental authority that has been usurped by a self-regulating bureaucracy.

According to the liberal view, this separation of the state apparatus from society cannot be eliminated but only bridged by the democratic process. However, the weak normative connotations of a regulated balancing of power and interests stands in need of constitutional channelling. The democratic will-formation of self-interested citizens, construed in minimalist terms, constitutes just one element within a constitution that disciplines governmental authority through normative constraints (such as basic rights, separation of powers, and legal regulation of the administration) and forces it, through competition between political parties, on the one hand, and between government and opposition, on the other, to take adequate account of competing interests and value orientations. This state-centred understanding of politics does not have to rely on the unrealistic assumption of a citizenry capable of acting collectively. Its focus is not so much the input of a rational political will-formation but the output of successful administrative accomplishments. The thrust of liberal arguments is directed against the disruptive potential of an administrative power that interferes with the independent social interactions of private persons. The liberal model hinges not on the democratic self-determination of deliberating citizens but on the legal institutionalization of an economic society that is supposed to guarantee an essentially non-political common good through the satisfaction of the private aspirations of productive citizens.

Discourse theory invests the democratic process with normative connotations stronger than those of the liberal model but weaker than those of the republican model. Once again, it takes elements from both sides and fits them together in a new way. In agreement with republicanism, it gives centre stage to the process of political opinion- and will-formation, but without understanding the constitution as something secondary; on the contrary, it conceives the basic principles of the constitutional state as a consistent answer to the question of how the demanding communicative presuppositions of a democratic opinion- and will-formation can be institutionalized. Discourse theory does not make the success of deliberative politics depend on a collectively acting citizenry but on the institutionalization of corresponding procedures. It no longer operates with the concept of a social whole centred in the state and conceived as a goal-oriented subject writ large. But neither does it localize the whole in a system of constitutional norms mechanically regulating the interplay of powers and interests in accordance with the market model. Discourse theory altogether jettisons the assumptions of the philosophy of consciousness, which invite us either to ascribe the citizens' practice of self-determination to one encompassing macro-subject or to apply the anonymous rule of law to competing individuals. The former approach represents the citizenry as a collective actor which reflects the whole and acts for its sake; on the latter, individual actors function as dependent variables in systemic processes that unfold blindly because no consciously executed collective decisions are possible over and above individual acts of choice (except in a purely metaphorical sense).

Discourse theory works instead with the *higher-level intersubjectivity* of communication processes that unfold in the institutionalized deliberations in parliamentary bodies, on the one hand, and in the informal networks of the public sphere, on the other. Both within and outside parliamentary bodies geared to decision-making, these subjectless modes of communication form arenas in which a more or less rational opinion- and will-formation concerning issues and problems affecting society as a whole can take place. Informal opinion-formation results in institutionalized election decisions and legislative decrees through which communicatively generated power is transformed into administratively utilizable power. As on the liberal model, the boundary between state and society is respected; but here civil society, which provides the social underpinning of autonomous publics, is as distinct from the economic system as it is from the public administration. This understanding of democracy leads to the normative demand for a new balance between the three resources of money, administrative power, and solidarity from which modern societies meet their need for integration and regulation. The normative implications are obvious: the integrative force of solidarity, which can no longer be drawn solely from sources of communicative action, should develop through widely expanded autonomous public spheres as well as through legally institutionalized procedures of democratic deliberation and decision-making and gain sufficient strength to hold its own against the other two social forces—money and administrative power.

III

This view has implications for how one should understand legitimation and popular sovereignty. On the liberal view, democratic will-formation has the exclusive function of *legitimating* the exercise of political power. The outcomes of elections license the assumption of governmental power, though the government must justify the use of power to the public and parliament. On the republican view, democratic will-formation has the significantly stronger function of *constituting* society as a political community and keeping the memory of this founding act alive with each new election. The government is not only empowered by the electorate's choice between teams of leaders to exercise a largely open mandate, but is also bound in a programmatic fashion to carry out certain policies. More a committee than an organ of the state, it is part of a self-governing political community rather than the head of a separate governmental apparatus. Discourse theory, by contrast, brings a third idea into play: the procedures and communicative presuppositions of democratic opinion- and will-formation function as the most important sluices for the discursive rationalization of the decisions of a government and an administration bound by law and statute. On this view, *rationalization* signifies more than mere legitimation but less than the constitution of political power. The power available to the administration changes its general character once it is bound to a process of democratic opinion- and will-formation that does not merely retrospectively monitor the exercise of political power but also programs it in a certain way. Notwithstanding this discursive rationalization, only the political system itself can 'act'. It is a subsystem specialized for collectively binding decisions, whereas the communicative structures of the public sphere comprise a far-flung network of sensors that respond to the pressure of society-wide problems and stimulate influential opinions. The public opinion which is worked up via democratic proce-

dures into communicative power cannot itself 'rule' but can only channel the use of administrative power in specific directions.

The concept of *popular sovereignty* stems from the republican appropriation and revaluation of the early modern notion of sovereignty originally associated with absolutist regimes. The state, which monopolizes the means of legitimate violence, is viewed as a concentration of power which can overwhelm all other temporal powers. Rousseau transposed this idea, which goes back to Bodin, to the will of the united people, fused it with the classical idea of the self-rule of free and equal citizens, and sublimated it into the modern concept of autonomy. Despite this normative sublimation, the concept of sovereignty remained bound to the notion of an embodiment in the (at first actually physically assembled) people. According to the republican view, the at least potentially assembled people are the bearers of a sovereignty that cannot in principle be delegated: in their capacity as sovereign, the people cannot let themselves be represented by others. Constitutional power is founded on the citizens' practice of self-determination, not on that of their representatives. Against this, liberalism offers the more realistic view that, in the constitutional state, the authority emanating from the people is exercised only 'by means of elections and voting and by specific legislative, executive, and judicial organs.'[9]

These two views exhaust the alternatives only on the dubious assumption that state and society must be conceived in terms of a whole and its parts, where the whole is constituted either by a sovereign citizenry or by a constitution. By contrast to the discourse theory of democracy corresponds the image of a *decentred* society, though with the political public sphere it sets apart an arena for the detection, identification, and interpretation of problems affecting society as a whole. If we abandon the conceptual framework of the philosophy of the subject, sovereignty need neither be concentrated in the people in a concretistic manner nor banished into the anonymous agencies established by the constitution. The 'self' of the self-organizing legal community disappears in the subjectless forms of communication that regulate the flow of discursive opinion- and will-formation whose fallible results enjoy the presumption of rationality. This is not to repudiate the intuition associated with the idea of popular sovereignty but rather to interpret it in intersubjective terms. Popular sovereignty, even though it has become anonymous, retreats into democratic procedures and the legal implementation of their demanding communicative presuppositions only to be able to make itself felt as communicatively generated power. Strictly speaking, this communicative power springs from the interactions between legally institutionalized will-formation and culturally mobilized publics. The latter for their part find a basis in the associations of a civil society distinct from the state and the economy alike.

The normative self-understanding of deliberative politics does indeed call for a discursive mode of socialization for the *legal community*; but this mode does not extend to the whole of the society in which the constitutionally established political system is *embedded*. Even on its own proceduralist self-understanding, deliberative politics remains a component of a complex society, which as a whole resists the normative approach of legal theory. In this regard, the discourse-theoretic reading of democracy connects with an objectifying sociological approach that regards the political system neither as the peak nor the centre, nor even as the structuring model of society, but as just *one* action system among others. Because it provides a kind of surety for

the solution of the social problems that threaten integration, politics must indeed be able to communicate, via the medium of law, with all of the other legitimately ordered spheres of action, however these may be structured and steered. But the political system remains dependent on other functional mechanisms, such as the revenue-production of the economic system, in more than just a trivial sense; on the contrary, deliberative politics, whether realized in the formal procedures of institutionalized opinion- and will-formation or only in the informal networks of the political public sphere, stands in an internal relation to the contexts of a rationalized lifeworld that meets it halfway. Deliberatively filtered political communications are especially dependent on the resources of the lifeworld—on a free and open political culture and an enlightened political socialization, and above all on the initiatives of opinion-shaping associations. These resources emerge and regenerate themselves spontaneously for the most part—at any rate, they can only with difficulty be subjected to political control.

Notes

1. Cf. H. Arendt, *On Revolution* (New York, 1965); *On Violence* (New York, 1970).
2. Cf. F.I. Michelman, 'Political Truth and the Rule of Law,' *Tel Aviv University Studies in Law 8* (1988): 283: 'The political society envisioned by bumper-sticker republicans is the society of private rights bearers, an association whose first principle is the protection of the lives, liberties, and estates of its individual members. In that society, the state is justified by the protection it gives to those prepolitical interests; the purpose of the constitution is to ensure that the state apparatus, the government, provides such protection for the people at large rather than serves the special interests of the governors or their

patrons; the function of citizenship is to operate the constitution and thereby to motivate the governors to act according to that protective purpose; and the value to you of your political franchise—your right to vote and speak, to have your views heard and counted—is the handle it gives you on influencing the system so that it will adequately heed and protect your particular, prepolitical rights and other interests.'

3. On the distinction between positive and negative freedom see Ch. Taylor, 'What Is Human Agency?' in *Human Agency and Language: Philosophical Papers 1* (Cambridge, 1985), 15–44.

4. Michelman, 'Political Truth and the Rule of Law,' 284: 'In [the] civic constitutional vision, political society is primarily the society not of rights bearers, but of citizens, an association whose first principle is the creation and provision of a public realm within which a people, together, argue and reason about the right terms of social coexistence, terms that they will set together and which they understand as comprising their common good. . . . Hence, the state is justified by its purpose of establishing and ordering the public sphere within which persons can achieve freedom in the sense of self-government by the exercise of reason in public dialogue.'

5. Michelman, 'Conceptions of Democracy in American Constitutional Argument: Voting Rights,' *Florida Law Review* 41 (1989): 446f. (hereafter 'Voting Rights').

6. Michelman, 'Voting Rights,' 484.

7. Michelman, 'Conceptions of Democracy in American Constitutional Argument: The Case of Pornography Regulation,' *Tennessee Law Review* 291 (1989): 293.

8. Cf. J. Habermas, 'Popular Sovereignty as Procedure,' in *Between Facts and Norms*, trans. W. Rehg (1996), 463–90.

9. Cf. *The Basic Law of the Federal Republic of Germany*, article 20, sec. 2.

Study Questions for 'The Public Sphere'

1. How does Habermas characterize the public sphere? What is the relationship between the public sphere and the authority of the state?

2. Habermas argues that institutionally protected public discussions have not always existed; they developed in the bourgeois society of eighteenth-century Europe. What historical transformations helped to generate the modern public sphere?

3. According to Habermas, how has the mass democracy of the welfare state eroded the normative ideal of the public sphere?

4. Compare Habermas's discussion of the public sphere with that of Hannah Arendt in *The Human Condition*. What Arendtian themes appear in Habermas's discussion of the public sphere? What differences can you identify between the two discussions?

Study Questions for 'Three Normative Models of Democracy'

1. Distinguish the liberal and republican models of politics discussed by Habermas. How do conceptions of citizenship, political rights, and law differ in these traditions?

2. What advantages and disadvantages does Habermas identify in the republican model of politics?
3. How does Habermas characterize his own model of deliberative politics? How does this model incorporate elements from the liberal and republican traditions? What new ideals does Habermas incorporate into the deliberative model?

Recommended Readings

Benhabib, Seyla, *Critique, Norm and Utopia: A Study of the Foundations of Critical Theory* (Columbia University Press, 1986).

Calhoun, Craig, ed., *Habermas and the Public Sphere* (MIT Press, 1992).

Crossley, Nick, and John Roberts, eds, *After Habermas: New Perspectives on the Public Sphere* (Blackwell, 2004).

Dews, Peter, ed., *Autonomy and Solidarity: Interviews with Jürgen Habermas* (Verso, 1992).

Finlayson, James, *Habermas: A Very Short Introduction* (Oxford University Press, 2005).

Fraser, Nancy, 'What's Critical about Critical Theory? The Case of Habermas and Gender,' in *Feminism as Critique: On the Politics of Gender*, edited by S. Benhabib and D. Cornell (University of Minnesota Press, 1987).

Johnson, Pauline, *Habermas: Rescuing the Public Sphere* (Routledge, 2006).

McCarthy, Thomas, *The Critical Theory of Jürgen Habermas* (MIT Press, 1978).

Meehan, Johanna, ed., *Feminists Read Habermas* (Routledge, 1995).

Mouffe, Chantal, *The Return of the Political* (Verso, 2005).

White, Steven, *The Recent Work of Jürgen Habermas: Reason, Justice and Modernity* (Cambridge University Press, 1989).

John Rawls

John Rawls (1921–2002) was born in Baltimore, Maryland, and educated at Princeton University. After completing his BA degree, Rawls enlisted in the United States army and served as an infantryman in the Pacific during World War II. He later commented that the conflict of the war deeply affected his life and his studies, promoting his interest in politics, political philosophy, and international justice. After obtaining a PhD in philosophy at Princeton, Rawls spent time at Oxford, Cornell, and MIT. He took a permanent appointment at Harvard University in 1962, where he taught until his retirement. Rawls spent approximately two decades formulating a theory of justice, which he called 'justice as fairness', and published the theory in *A Theory of Justice* in 1971. In the following decades, scholars published more than two thousand books and articles responding to Rawls's theory. His work has since become the cornerstone of contemporary political theory and has transformed the landscape of philosophical work on distributive justice and social institutions.

A modest individual, Rawls was surprised at the remarkable success of *A Theory of Justice*, and the attention his work received encouraged him to spend two additional decades defending and revising his theory of justice as fairness. His second book, *Political Liberalism*, examines the theory in the context of multicultural pluralism in liberal democracies. In his last book, *Justice as Fairness: A Restatement* (2001), Rawls defends the principles of justice developed in *A Theory of Justice* but employs new strategies in arguing for these principles. In this restatement, Rawls also moves away from his earlier suggestion that capitalist welfare states can support basic principles of justice, liberty, and equality. He instead makes a shift towards democratic socialism in maintaining that justice as fairness requires a 'property-owning democracy' in which all citizens have high levels of education.

In *A Theory of Justice*, Rawls appropriates the social contract tradition in reconciling a liberal commitment to individual rights and liberties with an egalitarian commitment to social and economic equality. In an original hypothetical position outside society—in which no one knows his or her particular natural talents, social class, sex, race, or conception of the good life—free and rational individuals would choose two primary principles of justice for the basic structure of society. The first principle of justice requires that all citizens have an equal share in an extensive scheme of liberties, rights, and obligations. The second principle requires that primary social goods, such as wealth, authority, and opportunity, be distributed equally, unless an unequal distribution works to the advantage of the least well-off members of society. 'It is not just,' Rawls maintains, 'that some should have less in order that others may prosper.' These basic principles of justice are termed the liberty principle and the difference principle, respectively.

A Theory of Justice

1. The Role of Justice

Justice is the first virtue of social institutions, as truth is of systems of thought. A theory however elegant and economical must be rejected or revised if it is untrue; likewise laws and institutions no matter how efficient and well-arranged must be reformed or abolished if they are unjust. Each person possesses an inviolability founded on justice that even the welfare of society as a whole cannot override. For this reason justice denies that the loss of freedom for some is made right by a greater good shared by others. It does not allow that the sacrifices imposed on a few are outweighed by the larger sum of advantages enjoyed by many. Therefore in a just society the liberties of equal citizenship are taken as settled; the rights secured by justice are not subject to political bargaining or to the calculus of social interests. The only thing that permits us to acquiesce in an erroneous theory is the lack of a better one; analogously, an injustice is tolerable only when it is necessary to avoid an even greater injustice. Being first virtues of human activities, truth and justice are uncompromising.

These propositions seem to express our intuitive conviction of the primacy of justice. No doubt they are expressed too strongly. In any event I wish to inquire whether these contentions or others similar to them are sound, and if so how they can be accounted for. To this end it is necessary to work out a theory of justice in the light of which these assertions can be interpreted and assessed. I shall begin by considering the role of the principles of justice. Let us assume, to fix ideas, that a society is a more or less self-sufficient association of persons who in their relations to one another recognize certain rules of conduct as binding and who for the most part act in accordance with them. Suppose further that these rules specify a system of cooperation designed to advance the good of those taking part in it. Then, although a society is a cooperative venture for mutual advantage, it is typically marked by a conflict as well as by an identity of interests. There is an identity of interests since social cooperation makes possible a better life for all than any would have if each were to live solely by his own efforts. There is a conflict of interests since persons are not indifferent as to how the greater benefits produced by their collaboration are distributed, for in order to pursue their ends they each prefer a larger to a lesser share. A set of principles is required for choosing among the various social arrangements which determine this division of advantages and for underwriting an agreement on the proper distributive shares. These principles are the principles of social justice: they provide a way of assigning rights and duties in the basic institutions of society and they define the appropriate distribution of the benefits and burdens of social cooperation.

Now let us say that a society is well-ordered when it is not only designed to advance the good of its members but when it is also effectively regulated by a public conception of justice. That is, it is a society in which (1) everyone accepts and knows that the others accept the same principles of justice, and (2) the basic social institutions generally satisfy and are generally known to satisfy these principles. In this case while men may put forth excessive demands on one another, they nevertheless acknowledge a common point of view from which their claims may be adjudicated. If men's inclination to self-interest makes their vigilance against one another necessary, their public sense of justice makes their secure association together possible. Among individuals with disparate aims and purposes a shared conception of justice establishes the bonds of civic friendship; the general desire for justice limits the pursuit of other ends. One may think of a public conception of justice as constituting the fundamental charter of a well-ordered human association.

Existing societies are of course seldom well-ordered in this sense, for what is just and unjust is usually in dispute. Men disagree about which principles should define the basic terms of their association. Yet we may still say, despite this disagreement, that they each have a conception of justice. That is, they understand the need for, and they are prepared to affirm, a characteristic set of principles for assigning basic rights and duties and for determining what they take to be the proper distribution of the benefits and burdens of social cooperation. Thus it seems natural to think of the concept of justice as distinct from the various conceptions of justice and as being specified by the role which these different sets of principles, these different conceptions, have in common.[1] Those who hold different conceptions of justice can, then, still agree that institutions are just when no arbitrary distinctions are made between persons in the assigning of basic rights and duties and when the rules determine a proper balance between competing claims to the advantages of social life. Men can agree to this description of just institutions since the notions of an arbitrary distinction and of a proper balance, which are included in the concept of justice, are left open for each to interpret according to the principles of justice that he accepts. These principles single out which similarities and differences among persons are relevant in determining rights and duties and they specify which division of advantages is appropriate. Clearly this distinc-

tion between the concept and the various conceptions of justice settles no important questions. It simply helps to identify the role of the principles of social justice.

Some measure of agreement in conceptions of justice is, however, not the only prerequisite for a viable human community. There are other fundamental social problems, in particular those of coordination, efficiency, and stability. Thus the plans of individuals need to be fitted together so that their activities are compatible with one another and they can all be carried through without anyone's legitimate expectations being severely disappointed. Moreover, the execution of these plans should lead to the achievement of social ends in ways that are efficient and consistent with justice. And finally, the scheme of social cooperation must be stable: it must be more or less regularly complied with and its basic rules willingly acted upon; and when infractions occur, stabilizing forces should exist that prevent further violations and tend to restore the arrangement. Now it is evident that these three problems are connected with that of justice. In the absence of a certain measure of agreement on what is just and unjust, it is clearly more difficult for individuals to coordinate their plans efficiently in order to insure that mutually beneficial arrangements are maintained. Distrust and resentment corrode the ties of civility, and suspicion and hostility tempt men to act in ways they would otherwise avoid. So while the distinctive role of conceptions of justice is to specify basic rights and duties and to determine the appropriate distributive shares, the way in which a conception does this is bound to affect the problems of efficiency, coordination, and stability. We cannot, in general, assess a conception of justice by its distributive role alone, however useful this role may be in identifying the concept of justice. We must take into account its wider connections; for even though justice has a certain priority, being the most important virtue of institutions, it is still true that, other things equal, one conception of justice is preferable to another when its broader consequences are more desirable.

2. The Subject of Justice

Many different kinds of things are said to be just and unjust: not only laws, institutions, and social systems, but also particular actions of many kinds, including decisions, judgments, and imputations. We also call the attitudes and dispositions of persons, and persons themselves, just and unjust. Our topic, however, is that of social justice. For us the primary subject of justice is the basic structure of society, or more exactly, the way in which the major social institutions distribute fundamental rights and duties and determine the division of advantages from social cooperation. By major institutions I understand the political constitution and the principal economic and social arrangements. Thus the legal protection of freedom of thought and liberty of conscience, competitive markets, private property in the means of production, and the monogamous family are examples of major social institutions. Taken together as one scheme, the major institutions define men's rights and duties and influence their life prospects, what they can expect to be and how well they can hope to do. The basic structure is the primary subject of justice because its effects are so profound and present from the start. The intuitive notion here is that this structure contains various social positions and that men born into different positions have different expectations of life determined, in part, by the political system as well as by economic and social circumstances. In this way the institutions of society favour certain starting places over others.

These are especially deep inequalities. Not only are they pervasive, but they affect men's initial chances in life; yet they cannot possibly be justified by an appeal to the notions of merit or desert. It is these inequalities, presumably inevitable in the basic structure of any society, to which the principles of social justice must in the first instance apply. These principles, then, regulate the choice of a political constitution and the main elements of the economic and social system. The justice of a social scheme depends essentially on how fundamental rights and duties are assigned and on the economic opportunities and social conditions in the various sectors of society.

The scope of our inquiry is limited in two ways. First of all, I am concerned with a special case of the problem of justice. I shall not consider the justice of institutions and social practices generally, nor except in passing the justice of the law of nations and of relations between states (§58). Therefore, if one supposes that the concept of justice applies whenever there is an allotment of something rationally regarded as advantageous or disadvantageous, then we are interested in only one instance of its application. There is no reason to suppose ahead of time that the principles satisfactory for the basic structure hold for all cases. These principles may not work for the rules and practices of private associations or for those of less comprehensive social groups. They may be irrelevant for the various informal conventions and customs of everyday life; they may not elucidate the justice, or perhaps better, the fairness of voluntary cooperative arrangements or procedures for making contractual agreements. The conditions for the law of nations may require different principles arrived at in a somewhat different way. I shall be satisfied if it is possible to formulate a reasonable conception of justice for the basic structure of society conceived for the time being as a closed system isolated from other societies. The significance of this special case is obvious and needs no explanation. It is natural to conjecture that once we have a sound theory for this case, the remaining problems of justice will prove more tractable in the light of it. With suitable modifications such a theory should provide the key for some of these other questions.

The other limitation on our discussion is that for the most part I examine the principles of justice that would regulate a well-ordered society. Everyone is presumed to act justly and to do his part in upholding just institutions. Though justice may be, as Hume remarked, the cautious, jealous virtue, we can still ask what a perfectly just society would be like.[2] Thus I consider primarily what I call strict compliance as opposed to partial compliance theory (§§25, 39). The latter studies the principles that govern how we are to deal with injustice. It comprises such topics as the theory of punishment, the doctrine of just war, and the justification of the various ways of opposing unjust regimes, ranging from civil disobedience and conscientious objection to militant resistance and revolution. Also included here are questions of compensatory justice and of weighing one form of institutional injustice against another. Obviously the problems of partial compliance theory are the pressing and urgent matters. These are the things that we are faced with in everyday life. The reason for beginning with ideal theory is that it provides, I believe, the only basis for the systematic grasp of these more pressing problems. The discussion of civil disobedience, for example, depends upon it (§§55–59). At least, I shall assume that a deeper understanding can be gained in no other way, and that the nature and aims of a perfectly just society is the fundamental part of the theory of justice.

Now admittedly the concept of the basic structure is somewhat vague. It is not always clear which institutions or features thereof should be included. But it would be premature to worry about this matter here. I shall proceed by discussing principles which do apply to what is certainly a part of the basic structure as intuitively understood; I shall then try to extend the application of these principles so that they cover what would appear to be the main elements of this structure. Perhaps these principles will turn out to be perfectly general, although this is unlikely. It is sufficient that they apply to the most important cases of social justice. The point to keep in mind is that a conception of justice for the basic structure is worth having for its own sake. It should not be dismissed because its principles are not everywhere satisfactory.

A conception of social justice, then, is to be regarded as providing in the first instance a standard whereby the distributive aspects of the basic structure of society are to be assessed. This standard, however, is not to be confused with the principles defining the other virtues, for the basic structure, and social arrangements generally, may be efficient or inefficient, liberal or illiberal, and many other things, as well as just or unjust. A complete conception defining principles for all the virtues of the basic structure, together with their respective weights when they conflict, is more than a conception of justice; it is a social ideal. The principles of justice are but a part, although perhaps the most important part, of such a conception. A social ideal in turn is connected with a conception of society, a vision of the way in which the aims and purposes of social cooperation are to be understood. The various conceptions of justice are the outgrowth of different notions of society against the background of opposing views of the natural necessities and opportunities of human life.

Fully to understand a conception of justice we must make explicit the conception of social cooperation from which it derives. But in doing this we should not lose sight of the special role of the principles of justice or of the primary subject to which they apply.

In these preliminary remarks I have distinguished the concept of justice as meaning a proper balance between competing claims from a conception of justice as a set of related principles for identifying the relevant considerations which determine this balance. I have also characterized justice as but one part of a social ideal, although the theory I shall propose no doubt extends its everyday sense. This theory is not offered as a description of ordinary meanings but as an account of certain distributive principles for the basic structure of society. I assume that any reasonably complete ethical theory must include principles for this fundamental problem and that these principles, whatever they are, constitute its doctrine of justice. The concept of justice I take to be defined, then, by the role of its principles in assigning rights and duties and in defining the appropriate division of social advantages. A conception of justice is an interpretation of this role.

Now this approach may not seem to tally with tradition. I believe, though, that it does. The more specific sense that Aristotle gives to justice, and from which the most familiar formulations derive, is that of refraining from *pleonexia*, that is, from gaining some advantage for oneself by seizing what belongs to another, his property, his reward, his office, and the like, or by denying a person that which is due to him, the fulfillment of a promise, the repayment of a debt, the showing of proper respect, and so on.[3] It is evident that this definition is framed to apply to actions, and persons are thought to be just insofar as they have, as one of the permanent elements of their character, a

steady and effective desire to act justly. Aristotle's definition clearly presupposes, however, an account of what properly belongs to a person and of what is due to him. Now such entitlements are, I believe, very often derived from social institutions and the legitimate expectations to which they give rise. There is no reason to think that Aristotle would disagree with this, and certainly he has a conception of social justice to account for these claims. The definition I adopt is designed to apply directly to the most important case, the justice of the basic structure. There is no conflict with the traditional notion.

3. The Main Idea of the Theory of Justice

My aim is to present a conception of justice which generalizes and carries to a higher level of abstraction the familiar theory of the social contract as found, say, in Locke, Rousseau, and Kant.[4] In order to do this we are not to think of the original contract as one to enter a particular society or to set up a particular form of government. Rather, the guiding idea is that the principles of justice for the basic structure of society are the object of the original agreement. They are the principles that free and rational persons concerned to further their own interests would accept in an initial position of equality as defining the fundamental terms of their association. These principles are to regulate all further agreements; they specify the kinds of social cooperation that can be entered into and the forms of government that can be established. This way of regarding the principles of justice I shall call justice as fairness.

Thus we are to imagine that those who engage in social cooperation choose together, in one joint act, the principles which are to assign basic rights and duties and to determine the division of social benefits. Men are to decide in advance how they are to regulate their claims against one another and what is to be the foundation charter of their society. Just as each person must decide by rational reflection what constitutes his good, that is, the system of ends which it is rational for him to pursue, so a group of persons must decide once and for all what is to count among them as just and unjust. The choice which rational men would make in this hypothetical situation of equal liberty, assuming for the present that this choice problem has a solution, determines the principles of justice.

In justice as fairness the original position of equality corresponds to the state of nature in the traditional theory of the social contract. This original position is not, of course, thought of as an actual historical state of affairs, much less as a primitive condition of culture. It is understood as a purely hypothetical situation characterized so as to lead to a certain conception of justice.[5] Among the essential features of this situation is that no one knows his place in society, his class position or social status, nor does any one know his fortune in the distribution of natural assets and abilities, his intelligence, strength, and the like. I shall even assume that the parties do not know their conceptions of the good or their special psychological propensities. The principles of justice are chosen behind a veil of ignorance. This ensures that no one is advantaged or disadvantaged in the choice of principles by the outcome of natural chance or the contingency of social circumstances. Since all are similarly situated and no one is able to design principles to favour his particular condition, the principles of justice are the result of a fair agreement or bargain. For given the circumstances of the original position, the symmetry of everyone's relations to each other, this initial situation is fair between individuals as moral persons, that is, as rational beings

with their own ends and capable, I shall assume, of a sense of justice. The original position is, one might say, the appropriate initial status quo, and thus the fundamental agreements reached in it are fair. This explains the propriety of the name 'justice as fairness': it conveys the idea that the principles of justice are agreed to in an initial situation that is fair. The name does not mean that the concepts of justice and fairness are the same, any more than the phrase 'poetry as metaphor' means that the concepts of poetry and metaphor are the same.

Justice as fairness begins, as I have said, with one of the most general of all choices which persons might make together, namely, with the choice of the first principles of a conception of justice which is to regulate all subsequent criticism and reform of institutions. Then, having chosen a conception of justice, we can suppose that they are to choose a constitution and a legislature to enact laws, and so on, all in accordance with the principles of justice initially agreed upon. Our social situation is just if it is such that by this sequence of hypothetical agreements we would have contracted into the general system of rules which defines it. Moreover, assuming that the original position does determine a set of principles (that is, that a particular conception of justice would be chosen), it will then be true that whenever social institutions satisfy these principles those engaged in them can say to one another that they are cooperating on terms to which they would agree if they were free and equal persons whose relations with respect to one another were fair. They could all view their arrangements as meeting the stipulations which they would acknowledge in an initial situation that embodies widely accepted and reasonable constraints on the choice of principles. The general recognition of this fact would provide the basis for a public acceptance of the corresponding principles of justice. No society can, of course, be a scheme of cooperation which men enter voluntarily in a literal sense; each person finds himself placed at birth in some particular position in some particular society, and the nature of this position materially affects his life prospects. Yet a society satisfying the principles of justice as fairness comes as close as a society can to being a voluntary scheme, for it meets the principles which free and equal persons would assent to under circumstances that are fair. In this sense its members are autonomous and the obligations they recognize self-imposed.

One feature of justice as fairness is to think of the parties in the initial situation as rational and mutually disinterested. This does not mean that the parties are egoists, that is, individuals with only certain kinds of interests, say in wealth, prestige, and domination. But they are conceived as not taking an interest in one another's interests. They are to presume that even their spiritual aims may be opposed, in the way that the aims of those of different religions may be opposed. Moreover, the concept of rationality must be interpreted as far as possible in the narrow sense, standard in economic theory, of taking the most effective means to given ends. I shall modify this concept to some extent, as explained later (§25), but one must try to avoid introducing into it any controversial ethical elements. The initial situation must be characterized by stipulations that are widely accepted.

In working out the conception of justice as fairness one main task clearly is to determine which principles of justice would be chosen in the original position. To do this we must describe this situation in some detail and formulate with care the problem of choice which it presents. These matters I shall take up in the immediately succeeding chapters. It may be observed, however, that once the principles of

justice are thought of as arising from an original agreement in a situation of equality, it is an open question whether the principle of utility would be acknowledged. Offhand it hardly seems likely that persons who view themselves as equals, entitled to press their claims upon one another, would agree to a principle which may require lesser life prospects for some simply for the sake of a greater sum of advantages enjoyed by others. Since each desires to protect his interests, his capacity to advance his conception of the good, no one has a reason to acquiesce in an enduring loss for himself in order to bring about a greater net balance of satisfaction. In the absence of strong and lasting benevolent impulses, a rational man would not accept a basic structure merely because it maximized the algebraic sum of advantages irrespective of its permanent effects on his own basic rights and interests. Thus it seems that the principle of utility is incompatible with the conception of social cooperation among equals for mutual advantage. It appears to be inconsistent with the idea of reciprocity implicit in the notion of a well-ordered society. Or, at any rate, so I shall argue.

I shall maintain instead that the persons in the initial situation would choose two rather different principles: the first requires equality in the assignment of basic rights and duties, while the second holds that social and economic inequalities, for example inequalities of wealth and authority, are just only if they result in compensating benefits for everyone, and in particular for the least advantaged members of society. These principles rule out justifying institutions on the grounds that the hardships of some are offset by a greater good in the aggregate. It may be expedient but it is not just that some should have less in order that others may prosper. But there is no injustice in the greater benefits earned by a few provided that the situation of persons not so fortunate is thereby improved. The intuitive idea is that since everyone's well-being depends upon a scheme of cooperation without which no one could have a satisfactory life, the division of advantages should be such as to draw forth the willing cooperation of everyone taking part in it, including those less well situated. The two principles mentioned seem to be a fair basis on which those better endowed, or more fortunate in their social position, neither of which we can be said to deserve, could expect the willing cooperation of others when some workable scheme is a necessary condition of the welfare of all.[6] Once we decide to look for a conception of justice that prevents the use of the accidents of natural endowment and the contingencies of social circumstance as counters in a quest for political and economic advantage, we are led to these principles. They express the result of leaving aside those aspects of the social world that seem arbitrary from a moral point of view.

The problem of the choice of principles, however, is extremely difficult. I do not expect the answer I shall suggest to be convincing to everyone. It is, therefore, worth noting from the outset that justice as fairness, like other contract views, consists of two parts: (1) an interpretation of the initial situation and of the problem of choice posed there, and (2) a set of principles which, it is argued, would be agreed to. One may accept the first part of the theory (or some variant thereof), but not the other, and conversely. The concept of the initial contractual situation may seem reasonable although the particular principles proposed are rejected. To be sure, I want to maintain that the most appropriate conception of this situation does lead to principles of justice contrary to utilitarianism and perfectionism, and therefore that the contract doctrine provides an alternative to these views. Still, one may

dispute this contention even though one grants that the contractarian method is a useful way of studying ethical theories and of setting forth their underlying assumptions.

Justice as fairness is an example of what I have called a contract theory. Now there may be an objection to the term 'contract' and related expressions, but I think it will serve reasonably well. Many words have misleading connotations which at first are likely to confuse. The terms 'utility' and 'utilitarianism' are surely no exception. They too have unfortunate suggestions which hostile critics have been willing to exploit; yet they are clear enough for those prepared to study utilitarian doctrine. The same should be true of the term 'contract' applied to moral theories. As I have mentioned, to understand it one has to keep in mind that it implies a certain level of abstraction. In particular, the content of the relevant agreement is not to enter a given society or to adopt a given form of government, but to accept certain moral principles. Moreover, the undertakings referred to are purely hypothetical: a contract view holds that certain principles would be accepted in a well-defined initial situation.

The merit of the contract terminology is that it conveys the idea that principles of justice may be conceived as principles that would be chosen by rational persons, and that in this way conceptions of justice may be explained and justified. The theory of justice is a part, perhaps the most significant part, of the theory of rational choice. Furthermore, principles of justice deal with conflicting claims upon the advantages won by social cooperation; they apply to the relations among several persons or groups. The word 'contract' suggests this plurality as well as the condition that the appropriate division of advantages must be in accordance with principles acceptable to all parties. The condition of publicity for principles of justice is also connoted by the contract phraseology. Thus, if these principles are the outcome of an agreement, citizens have a knowledge of the principles that others follow. It is characteristic of contract theories to stress the public nature of political principles. Finally there is the long tradition of the contract doctrine. Expressing the tie with this line of thought helps to define ideas and accords with natural piety. There are then several advantages in the use of the term 'contract'. With due precautions taken, it should not be misleading.

A final remark. Justice as fairness is not a complete contract theory. For it is clear that the contractarian idea can be extended to the choice of more or less an entire ethical system, that is, to a system including principles for all the virtues and not only for justice. Now for the most part I shall consider only principles of justice and others closely related to them; I make no attempt to discuss the virtues in a systematic way. Obviously if justice as fairness succeeds reasonably well, a next step would be to study the more general view suggested by the name 'rightness as fairness'. But even this wider theory fails to embrace all moral relationships, since it would seem to include only our relations with other persons and to leave out of account how we are to conduct ourselves toward animals and the rest of nature. I do not contend that the contract notion offers a way to approach these questions which are certainly of the first importance; and I shall have to put them aside. We must recognize the limited scope of justice as fairness and of the general type of view that it exemplifies. How far its conclusions must be revised once these other matters are understood cannot be decided in advance.

4. The Original Position and Justification

I have said that the original position is the appropriate initial status quo which insures that the fundamental agreements reached in it are fair. This fact yields the name 'justice as fairness'. It is clear, then, that I want to say that one conception of justice is more reasonable than another, or justifiable with respect to it, if rational persons in the initial situation would choose its principles over those of the other for the role of justice. Conceptions of justice are to be ranked by their acceptability to persons so circumstanced. Understood in this way the question of justification is settled by working out a problem of deliberation: we have to ascertain which principles it would be rational to adopt given the contractual situation. This connects the theory of justice with the theory of rational choice.

If this view of the problem of justification is to succeed, we must, of course, describe in some detail the nature of this choice problem. A problem of rational decision has a definite answer only if we know the beliefs and interests of the parties, their relations with respect to one another, the alternatives between which they are to choose, the procedure whereby they make up their minds, and so on. As the circumstances are presented in different ways, correspondingly different principles are accepted. The concept of the original position, as I shall refer to it, is that of the most philosophically favoured interpretation of this initial choice situation for the purposes of a theory of justice.

But how are we to decide what is the most favoured interpretation? I assume, for one thing, that there is a broad measure of agreement that principles of justice should be chosen under certain conditions. To justify a particular description of the initial situation one shows that it incorporates these commonly shared presumptions. One argues from widely accepted but weak premises to more specific conclusions. Each of the presumptions should by itself be natural and plausible; some of them may seem innocuous or even trivial. The aim of the contract approach is to establish that taken together they impose significant bounds on acceptable principles of justice. The ideal outcome would be that these conditions determine a unique set of principles; but I shall be satisfied if they suffice to rank the main traditional conceptions of social justice.

One should not be misled, then, by the somewhat unusual conditions which characterize the original position. The idea here is simply to make vivid to ourselves the restrictions that it seems reasonable to impose on arguments for principles of justice, and therefore on these principles themselves. Thus it seems reasonable and generally acceptable that no one should be advantaged or disadvantaged by natural fortune or social circumstances in the choice of principles. It also seems widely agreed that it should be impossible to tailor principles to the circumstances of one's own case. We should insure further that particular inclinations and aspirations, and persons' conceptions of their good do not affect the principles adopted. The aim is to rule out those principles that it would be rational to propose for acceptance, however little the chance of success, only if one knew certain things that are irrelevant from the standpoint of justice. For example, if a man knew that he was wealthy, he might find it rational to advance the principle that various taxes for welfare measures be counted unjust; if he knew that he was poor, he would most likely propose the contrary principle. To represent the desired restrictions one imagines a situation in which everyone is deprived of this sort of information. One excludes the knowledge of those contingencies which sets men at odds and allows them to be guided by their prejudices. In this manner the veil of ignorance is arrived at in a natural way. This concept should cause no difficulty if we keep in mind the constraints on arguments that it is meant to express. At any time we can enter the original position, so to speak, simply by following a certain procedure, namely, by arguing for principles of justice in accordance with these restrictions.

It seems reasonable to suppose that the parties in the original position are equal. That is, all have the same rights in the procedure for choosing principles; each can make proposals, submit reasons for their acceptance, and so on. Obviously the purpose of these conditions is to represent equality between human beings as moral persons, as creatures having a conception of their good and capable of a sense of justice. The basis of equality is taken to be similarity in these two respects. Systems of ends are not ranked in value; and each man is presumed to have the requisite ability to understand and to act upon whatever principles are adopted. Together with the veil of ignorance, these conditions define the principles of justice as those which rational persons concerned to advance their interests would consent to as equals when none are known to be advantaged or disadvantaged by social and natural contingencies.

There is, however, another side to justifying a particular description of the original position. This is to see if the principles which would be chosen match our considered convictions of justice or extend them in an acceptable way. We can note whether applying these principles would lead us to make the same judgments about the basic structure of society which we now make intuitively and in which we have the greatest confidence; or whether, in cases where our present judgments are in doubt and given with hesitation, these principles offer a resolution which we can affirm on reflection. There are questions which we feel sure must be answered in a certain way. For example, we are confident that religious intolerance and racial discrimination are unjust. We think that we have examined these things with care and have reached what we believe is an impartial judgment not likely to be distorted by an excessive attention to our own interests. These convictions are provisional fixed points which we presume any conception of justice must fit. But we have much less assurance as to what is the correct distribution of wealth and authority. Here we may be looking for a way to remove our doubts. We can check an interpretation of the initial situation, then, by the capacity of its principles to accommodate our firmest convictions and to provide guidance where guidance is needed.

In searching for the most favoured description of this situation we work from both ends. We begin by describing it so that it represents generally shared and preferably weak conditions. We then see if these conditions are strong enough to yield a significant set of principles. If not, we look for further premises equally reasonable. But if so, and these principles match our considered convictions of justice, then so far well and good. But presumably there will be discrepancies. In this case we have a choice. We can either modify the account of the initial situation or we can revise our existing judgments, for even the judgments we take provisionally as fixed points are liable to revision. By going back and forth, sometimes altering the conditions of the contractual circumstances, at others withdrawing our judgments and conforming them to principle, I assume that eventually we shall find a description of the initial situation that both expresses reasonable conditions and yields principles which match our considered judgments duly pruned and adjusted. This state of affairs I refer to as reflective equilibrium.[7] It is an equilibrium because at last our principles and judgments coincide; and it is reflective since we know to what principles our judgments conform and the premises of their derivation. At the moment everything is in order. But this equilibrium is not necessarily stable. It is liable to be upset by further examination of the conditions which should be imposed on the contractual situation and by particular cases which may lead us to revise our judgments. Yet for the time being we have done what we can to render coherent and to justify our convictions of social justice. We have reached a conception of the original position.

I shall not, of course, actually work through this process. Still, we may think of the interpretation of the original position that I shall present as the result of such a hypothetical course of reflection. It represents the attempt to accommodate within one scheme both reasonable philosophical conditions on principles as well as well as our considered judgments of justice. In arriving at the favoured interpretation of the initial situation there is no point at which an appeal is made to self-evidence in the traditional sense either of general conceptions or particular convictions. I do not claim for the principles of justice proposed that they are necessary truths or derivable from such truths. A conception of justice cannot be deduced from self-evident premises or conditions on principles; instead, its justification is a matter of the mutual support of many considerations, of everything fitting together into one coherent view.

A final comment. We shall want to say that certain principles of justice are justified because they would be agreed to in an initial situation of equality. I have emphasized that this original position is purely hypothetical.

It is natural to ask why, if this agreement is never actually entered into, we should take any interest in these principles, moral or otherwise. The answer is that the conditions embodied in the description of the original position are ones that we do in fact accept. Or if we do not, then perhaps we can be persuaded to do so by philosophical reflection. Each aspect of the contractual situation can be given supporting grounds. Thus what we shall do is to collect together into one conception a number of conditions on principles that we are ready upon due consideration to recognize as reasonable. These constraints express what we are prepared to regard as limits on fair terms of social cooperation. One way to look at the idea of the original position, therefore, is to see it as an expository device which sums up the meaning of these conditions and helps us to extract their consequences. On the other hand, this conception is also an intuitive notion that suggests its own elaboration, so that led on by it we are drawn to define more clearly the standpoint from which we can best interpret moral relationships. We need a conception that enables us to envision our objective from afar: the intuitive notion of the original position is to do this for us.[8] . . .

11. Two Principles of Justice

I shall now state in a provisional form the two principles of justice that I believe would be agreed to in the original position. The first formulation of these principles is tentative. As we go on I shall consider several formulations and approximate step by step the final statement to be given much later. I believe that doing this allows the exposition to proceed in a natural way.

The first statement of the two principles reads as follows.

First: each person is to have an equal right to the most extensive scheme of equal basic liberties compatible with a similar scheme of liberties for others.

Second: social and economic inequalities are to be arranged so that they are both (a) reasonably expected to be to everyone's advantage, and (b) attached to positions and offices open to all.

There are two ambiguous phrases in the second principle, namely 'everyone's advantage' and 'open to all'. Determining their sense more exactly will lead to a second formulation of the principle in §13. The final version of the two principles is given in §46; §39 considers the rendering of the first principle.

These principles primarily apply, as I have said, to the basic structure of society and govern the assignment of rights and duties and regulate the distribution of social and economic advantages. Their formulation presupposes that, for the purposes of a theory of justice, the social structure may be viewed as having two more or less distinct parts, the first principle applying to the one, the second principle to the other. Thus we distinguish between the aspects of the social system that define and secure the equal basic liberties and the aspects that specify and establish social and economic inequalities. Now it is essential to observe that the basic liberties are given by a list of such liberties. Important among these are political liberty (the right to vote and to hold public office) and freedom of speech and assembly; liberty of conscience and freedom of thought; freedom of the person, which includes freedom from psychological oppression and physical assault and dismemberment (integrity of the person); the right to hold personal property and freedom from arbitrary arrest and seizure as defined by the concept of the rule of law. These liberties are to be equal by the first principle.

The second principle applies, in the first approximation, to the distribution of income and wealth and to the design of organizations that make use of differences in authority and responsibility. While the distribution of wealth and income need not be equal, it must be to everyone's advantage, and at the same time, positions of authority and responsibility must be accessible to all. One applies the second principle by holding positions open, and then, subject to this constraint, arranges social and economic inequalities so that everyone benefits.

These principles are to be arranged in a serial order with the first principle prior to the second. This ordering means that infringements of the basic equal liberties protected by the first principle cannot be justified, or compensated for, by greater social and economic advantages. These liberties have a central range of application within which they can be limited and compromised only when they conflict with other basic liberties. Since they may be limited when they clash with one another, none of these liberties is absolute; but however they are adjusted to form one system, this system is to be the same for all. It is difficult, and perhaps impossible, to give a complete specification of these liberties independently from the particular circumstances—social, economic, and technological—of a given society. The hypothesis is that the general form of such a list could be devised with sufficient exactness to sustain this conception of justice. Of course, liberties not on the list, for example, the right to own certain kinds of property (e.g., means of production) and freedom of contract as understood by the doctrine of laissez-faire, are not basic; and so they are not protected by the priority of the first principle. Finally, in regard to

the second principle, the distribution of wealth and income, and positions of authority and responsibility, are to be consistent with both the basic liberties and equality of opportunity.

The two principles are rather specific in their content, and their acceptance rests on certain assumptions that I must eventually try to explain and justify. For the present, it should be observed that these principles are a special case of a more general conception of justice that can be expressed as follows.

All social values—liberty and opportunity, income and wealth, and the social bases of self-respect—are to be distributed equally unless an unequal distribution of any, or all, of these values is to everyone's advantage.

Injustice, then, is simply inequalities that are not to the benefit of all. Of course, this conception is extremely vague and requires interpretation.

As a first step, suppose that the basic structure of society distributes certain primary goods, that is, things that every rational man is presumed to want. These goods normally have a use whatever a person's rational plan of life. For simplicity, assume that the chief primary goods at the disposition of society are rights, liberties, and opportunities, and income and wealth. (Later on in Part Three the primary good of self-respect has a central place.) These are the social primary goods. Other primary goods such as health and vigour, intelligence and imagination, are natural goods; although their possession is influenced by the basic structure, they are not so directly under its control. Imagine, then, a hypothetical initial arrangement in which all the social primary goods are equally distributed: everyone has similar rights and duties, and income and wealth are evenly shared. This state of affairs provides a benchmark for judging improvements. If certain inequalities of wealth and differences in authority would make everyone better off than in this hypothetical starting situation, then they accord with the general conception.

Now it is possible, at least theoretically, that by giving up some of their fundamental liberties men are sufficiently compensated by the resulting social and economic gains. The general conception of justice imposes no restrictions on what sort of inequalities are permissible; it only requires that everyone's position be improved. We need not suppose anything so drastic as consenting to a condition of slavery. Imagine instead that people seem willing to forego certain political rights when the economic returns are significant. It is this kind of exchange which the two principles rule out; being arranged in serial order they do not permit exchanges between basic liberties and economic and social gains except under extenuating circumstances (§§26, 39).

For the most part, I shall leave aside the general conception of justice and examine instead the two principles in serial order. The advantage of this procedure is that from the first the matter of priorities is recognized and an effort made to find principles to deal with it. One is led to attend throughout to the conditions under which the absolute weight of liberty with respect to social and economic advantages, as defined by the lexical order of the two principles, would be reasonable. Offhand, this ranking appears extreme and too special a case to be of much interest; but there is more justification for it than would appear at first sight. Or at any rate, so I shall maintain (§82). Furthermore, the distinction between fundamental rights and liberties and economic and social benefits marks a difference among primary social goods that suggests an important division in the social system. Of course,

the distinctions drawn and the ordering proposed are at best only approximations. There are surely circumstances in which they fail. But it is essential to depict clearly the main lines of a reasonable conception of justice; and under many conditions anyway, the two principles in serial order may serve well enough.

The fact that the two principles apply to institutions has certain consequences. First of all, the rights and basic liberties referred to by these principles are those which are defined by the public rules of the basic structure. Whether men are free is determined by the rights and duties established by the major institutions of society. Liberty is a certain pattern of social forms. The first principle simply requires that certain sorts of rules, those defining basic liberties, apply to everyone equally and that they allow the most extensive liberty compatible with a like liberty for all. The only reason for circumscribing basic liberties and making them less extensive is that otherwise they would interfere with one another.

Further, when principles mention persons, or require that everyone gain from an inequality, the reference is to representative persons holding the various social positions, or offices established by the basic structure. Thus in applying the second principle I assume that it is possible to assign an expectation of well-being to representative individuals holding these positions. This expectation indicates their life prospects as viewed from their social station. In general, the expectations of representative persons depend upon the distribution of rights and duties throughout the basic structure. Expectations are connected: by raising the prospects of the representative man in one position we presumably increase or decrease the prospects of representative men in other positions. Since it applies to institutional forms, the second principle (or rather the first part of it) refers to the expectations of representative individuals. As I shall discuss below (§14), neither principle applies to distributions of particular goods to particular individuals who may be identified by their proper names. The situation where someone is considering how to allocate certain commodities to needy persons who are known to him is not within the scope of the principles. They are meant to regulate basic institutional arrangements. We must not assume that there is much similarity from the standpoint of justice between an administrative allotment of goods to specific persons and the appropriate design of society. Our common sense intuitions for the former may be a poor guide to the latter.

Now the second principle insists that each person benefit from permissible inequalities in the basic structure. This means that it must be reasonable for each relevant representative man defined by this structure, when he views it as a going concern, to prefer his prospects with the inequality to his prospects without it. One is not allowed to justify differences in income or in positions of authority and responsibility on the ground that the disadvantages of those in one position are outweighed by the greater advantages of those in another. Much less can infringements of liberty be counterbalanced in this way. It is obvious, however, that there are indefinitely many ways in which all may be advantaged when the initial arrangement of equality is taken as a benchmark. How then are we to choose among these possibilities? The principles must be specified so that they yield a determinate conclusion. I now turn to this problem. . . .

24. The Veil of Ignorance

The idea of the original position is to set up a fair procedure so that any principles agreed to will be just. The aim is to use the notion of pure procedural justice as a basis of theory. Somehow we must nullify the effects of specific contingencies which put men at odds and tempt them to exploit social and natural circumstances to their own advantage. Now in order to do this I assume that the parties are situated behind a veil of ignorance. They do not know how the various alternatives will affect their own particular case and they are obliged to evaluate principles solely on the basis of general considerations.[9]

It is assumed, then, that the parties do not know certain kinds of particular facts. First of all, no one knows his place in society, his class position or social status; nor does he know his fortune in the distribution of natural assets and abilities, his intelligence and strength, and the like. Nor, again, does anyone know his conception of the good, the particulars of his rational plan of life, or even the special features of his psychology such as his aversion to risk or liability to optimism or pessimism. More than this, I assume that the parties do not know the particular circumstances of their own society. That is, they do not know its economic or political situation, or the level of civilization and culture it has been able to achieve. The persons in the original position have no information as to which generation they belong. These broader restrictions on knowledge are appropriate in part because questions of social justice arise between generations as well as within them, for example, the question of the appropriate rate of capital saving and of the conservation of natural resources and the environment of nature. There is also, theoretically anyway, the question of a reasonable genetic policy. In these cases too, in order to carry through the idea of the original position, the parties must not know the contingencies that set them in opposition. They must choose principles the consequences of which they are prepared to live with whatever generation they turn out to belong to.

As far as possible, then, the only particular facts which the parties know is that their society is subject to the circumstances of justice and whatever this implies. It is taken for granted, however, that they know the general facts about human society. They understand political affairs and the principles of economic theory; they know the basis of social organization and the laws of human psychology. Indeed, the parties are presumed to know whatever general facts affect the choice of the principles of justice. There are no limitation on general information, that is, on general laws and theories, since conceptions of justice must be adjusted to the characteristics of the systems of social cooperation which they are to regulate, and there is no reason to rule out these facts. It is, for example, a consideration against a conception of justice that, in view of the laws of moral psychology, men would not acquire a desire to act upon it even when the institutions of their society satisfied it. For in this case there would be difficulty in securing the stability of social cooperation. An important feature of a conception of justice is that it should generate its own support. Its principles should be such that when they are embodied in the basic structure of society men tend to acquire the corresponding sense of justice and develop a desire to act in accordance with its principles. In this case a conception of justice is stable. This kind of general information is admissible in the original position.

The notion of the veil of ignorance raises several difficulties. Some may object that the exclusion of nearly all particular information makes it difficult to grasp what is meant by the original position. Thus it may be helpful to observe that one or more persons can at any time enter this position, or perhaps better, simulate the deliberations of this hypothetical situation, simply by reasoning in accordance with the appropriate restrictions. In arguing for a conception of justice we must be sure that it is among the permitted alternatives and satisfies the stipulated formal constraints. No considerations can be advanced in its favour unless they would be rational ones for us to urge were we to lack the kind of knowledge that is excluded. The evaluation of principles must proceed in terms of the general consequences of their public recognition and universal application, it being assumed that they will be complied with by everyone. To say that a certain conception of justice would be chosen in the original position is equivalent to saying that rational deliberation satisfying certain conditions and restrictions would reach a certain conclusion. If necessary, the argument to this result could be set out more formally. I shall, however, speak throughout in terms of the notion of the original position. It is more economical and suggestive, and brings out certain essential features that otherwise one might easily overlook.

These remarks show that the original position is not to be thought of as a general assembly which includes at one moment everyone who will live at some time; or, much less, as an assembly of everyone who could live at some time. It is not a gathering of all actual or possible persons. If we conceived of the original position in either of these ways, the conception would cease to be a natural guide to intuition and would lack a clear sense. In any case, the original position must be interpreted so that one can at any time adopt its perspective. It must make no difference when one takes up this viewpoint, or who does so: the restrictions must be such that the same principles are always chosen. The veil of ignorance is a key condition in meeting this requirement. It insures not only that the information available is relevant, but that it is at all times the same.

It may be protested that the condition of the veil of ignorance is irrational. Surely, some may object, principles should be chosen in the light of all the knowledge available. There are various replies to this contention. Here I shall sketch those which emphasize the simplifications that need to be made if one is to have any theory at all. (Those based on the Kantian interpretation of the original position are given later, §40). To begin with, it is clear that since the differences among the parties are unknown to them, and everyone is equally rational and similarly situated, each is convinced by the same arguments. Therefore, we can view the agreement in the original position from the standpoint of one person selected at random. If anyone after due reflection prefers a conception of justice to another, then they all do, and a unanimous agreement can be reached. We can, to make the circumstances more vivid, imagine that the parties are required to communicate with each other through a referee as intermediary, and that he is to announce which alternatives have been suggested and the reasons offered in their support. He forbids the attempt to form coalitions, and he informs the parties when they have come to an understanding. But such a referee is actually superfluous, assuming that the deliberations of the parties must be similar.

Thus there follows the very important consequence that the parties have no basis for bargaining in the usual sense. No one knows his situation in society nor his natural assets, and therefore no one is in a position to tailor principles to his advantage. We might imagine that one of the contractees threatens to hold out unless the others agree to principles favourable to him. But how does he know which principles are especially in his interests? The same holds for the formation of coalitions: if a group were to decide to band together to the disadvantage of the others, they would not know

how to favour themselves in the choice of principles. Even if they could get everyone to agree to their proposal, they would have no assurance that it was to their advantage, since they cannot identify themselves either by name or description. The one case where this conclusion fails is that of saving. Since the persons in the original position know that they are contemporaries (taking the present time of entry interpretation), they can favour their generation by refusing to make any sacrifices at all for their successors; they simply acknowledge the principle that no one has a duty to save for posterity. Previous generations have saved or they have not; there is nothing the parties can now do to affect that. So in this instance the veil of ignorance fails to secure the desired result. Therefore, to handle the question of justice between generations, I modify the motivation assumption and add a further constraint (§22). With these adjustments, no generation is able to formulate principles especially designed to advance its own cause and some significant limits on saving principles can be derived (§44). Whatever a person's temporal position, each is forced to choose for all.[10]

The restrictions on particular information in the original position are, then, of fundamental importance. Without them we would not be able to work out any definite theory of justice at all. We would have to be content with a vague formula stating that justice is what would be agreed to without being able to say much, if anything, about the substance of the agreement itself. The formal constraints of the concept of right, those applying to principles directly, are not sufficient for our purpose. The veil of ignorance makes possible a unanimous choice of a particular conception of justice. Without these limitations on knowledge the bargaining problem of the original position would be hopelessly complicated. Even if theoretically a solution were to exist, we would not, at present anyway, be able to determine it.

The notion of the veil of ignorance is implicit, I think, in Kant's ethics (§40). Nevertheless the problem of defining the knowledge of the parties and of characterizing the alternatives open to them has often been passed over, even by contract theories. Sometimes the situation definitive of moral deliberation is presented in such an indeterminate way that one cannot ascertain how it will turn out. Thus Perry's doctrine is essentially contractarian: he holds that social and personal integration must proceed by entirely different principles, the latter by rational prudence, the former by the concurrence of persons of good will. He would appear to reject utilitarianism on much the same grounds suggested earlier: namely, that it improperly extends the principle of choice for one person to choices facing society. The right course of action is characterized as that which best advances social aims as these would be formulated by reflective agreement, given that the parties have full knowledge of the circumstances and are moved by a benevolent concern for one another's interests. No effort is made, however, to specify in any precise way the possible outcomes of this sort of agreement. Indeed, without a far more elaborate account, no conclusions can be drawn.[11] I do not wish here to criticize others; rather, I want to explain the necessity for what may seem at times like so many irrelevant details.

Now the reasons for the veil of ignorance go beyond mere simplicity. We want to define the original position so that we get the desired solution. If a knowledge of particulars is allowed, then the outcome is biased by arbitrary contingencies. As already observed, to each according to his threat advantage is not a principle of justice. If the original position is to yield agreements that are just, the parties must be fairly situated and treated equally as moral persons. The arbitrariness of the world must be corrected for by adjusting the circumstances of the initial contractual situation. Moreover, if in choosing principles we required unanimity even when there is full information, only a few rather obvious cases could be decided. A conception of justice based on unanimity in these circumstances would indeed be weak and trivial. But once knowledge is excluded, the requirement of unanimity is not out of place and the fact that it can be satisfied is of great importance. It enables us to say of the preferred conception of justice that it represents a genuine reconciliation of interests.

A final comment. For the most part I shall suppose that the parties possess all general information. No general facts are closed to them. I do this mainly to avoid complications. Nevertheless a conception of justice is to be the public basis of the terms of social cooperation. Since common understanding necessitates certain bounds on the complexity of principles, there may likewise be limits on the use of theoretical knowledge in the original position. Now clearly it would be very difficult to classify and to grade the complexity of the various sorts of general facts. I shall make no attempt to do this. We do however recognize an intricate theoretical construction when we meet one. Thus it seems reasonable to say that other things equal one conception of justice is to be preferred to another when it is founded upon markedly simpler general facts, and its choice does not depend upon elaborate calculations in the light of a vast array of theoretically defined possibilities. It is desirable that the grounds for a public conception of justice should be evident to everyone when circumstances permit. This consideration favours, I believe, the two principles of justice over the criterion of utility. . . .

48. Legitimate Expectations and Moral Desert

There is a tendency for common sense to suppose that income and wealth, and the good things in life generally, should be distributed according to moral desert. Justice is happiness according to virtue. While it is recognized that this ideal can never be fully carried out, it is the appropriate conception of distributive justice, at least as a prima facie principle, and society should try to realize it as circumstances permit.[12] Now justice as fairness rejects this conception. Such a principle would not be chosen in the original position. There seems to be no way of defining the requisite criterion in that situation. Moreover, the notion of distribution according to virtue fails to distinguish between moral desert and legitimate expectations. Thus it is true that as persons and groups take part in just arrangements, they acquire claims on one another defined by the publicly recognized rules. Having done various things encouraged by the existing arrangements, they now have certain rights, and just distributive shares honour these claims. A just scheme, then, answers to what men are entitled to; it satisfies their legitimate expectations as founded upon social institutions. But what they are entitled to is not proportional to nor dependent upon their intrinsic worth. The principles of justice that regulate the basic structure and specify the duties and obligations of individuals do not mention moral desert, and there is no tendency for distributive shares to correspond to it.

This contention is borne out by the preceding account of common sense precepts and their role in pure procedural justice (§47). For examples, in determining wages a competitive economy gives weight to the precept of contribution. But as we have seen, the extent of one's contribution (estimated by one's marginal productivity) depends upon supply and demand. Surely a person's moral worth does not vary according to how many offer similar skills, or happen to want what he can produce. No one supposes that when someone's abilities are less in demand or have deteriorated (as in the case of singers) his moral deservingness undergoes a similar shift. All of this is perfectly obvious and has long been agreed to.[13] It simply reflects the fact noted before (§17) that it is one of the fixed points of our moral judgments that no one deserves his place in the distribution of natural assets any more than he deserves his initial starting place in society.

Moreover, none of the precepts of justice aims at rewarding virtue. The premiums earned by scarce natural talents, for example, are to cover the costs of training and to encourage the efforts of learning, as well as to direct ability to where it best furthers the common interest. The distributive shares that result do not correlate with moral worth, since the initial endowment of natural assets and the contingencies of their growth and nurture in early life are arbitrary from a moral point of view. The precept which seems intuitively to come closest to rewarding moral desert is that of distribution according to effort, or perhaps better, conscientious effort.[14] Once again, however, it seems clear that the effort a person is willing to make is influenced by his natural abilities and skills and the alternatives open to him. The better endowed are more likely, other things equal, to strive conscientiously, and there seems to be no way to discount for their greater good fortune. The idea of rewarding desert is impracticable. And certainly to the extent that the precept of need is emphasized, moral worth is ignored. Nor does the basic structure tend to balance the precepts of justice so as to achieve the requisite correspondence behind the scenes. It is regulated by the two principles of justice which define other aims entirely.

The same conclusion may be reached in another way. In the preceding remarks the notion of moral worth as distinct from a person's claims based upon his legitimate expectations has not been explained. Suppose, then, that we define this notion and show that it has no correlation with distributive shares. We have only to consider a well-ordered society, that is, a society in which institutions are just and this fact is publicly recognized. Its members also have a strong sense of justice, an effective desire to comply with the existing rules and to give one another that to which they are entitled. In this case we may assume that everyone is of equal moral worth. We have now defined this notion in terms of the sense of justice, the desire to act in accordance with the principles that would be chosen in the original position (§72). But it is evident that understood in this way, the equal moral worth of persons does not entail that distributive shares are equal. Each is to receive what the principles of justice say he is entitled to, and these do not require equality.

The essential point is that the concept of moral worth does not provide a first principle of distributive justice. This is because it cannot be introduced until after the principles of justice and of natural duty and obligation have been acknowledged. Once these principles are on hand, moral worth can be defined as having a sense of justice; and as I shall discuss later (§66), the virtues can be characterized as desires or tendencies to act upon the corresponding principles. Thus the concept of moral worth is secondary to those of right and justice, and it plays no role in the substantive definition of distributive shares. The case is analogous to the relation between the substantive rules of property and the law of robbery and theft. These offences and the demerits they entail presuppose the institution of property which is established for prior and independent social ends. For a society to organize itself with the aim of rewarding moral desert as a first principle would be like having the institution of property in order to punish thieves. The criterion to each according to his virtue would not, then, be chosen in the original position. Since the parties desire to advance their conceptions of the good, they have no reason for arranging their institutions so that distributive shares are determined by moral desert, even if they could find an antecedent standard for its definition.

In a well-ordered society individuals acquire claims to a share of the social product by doing certain things encouraged by the existing arrangements. The legitimate expectations that arise are the other side, so to speak, of the principle of fairness and the natural duty of justice. For in the way that one has a duty to uphold just arrangements, and an obligation to do one's part when one has accepted a position in them, so a person who has complied with the scheme and done his share has a right to be treated accordingly by others. They are bound to meet his legitimate expectations. Thus when just economic arrangements exist, the claims of individuals are properly settled by reference to the rules and precepts (with their respective weights) which these practices take as relevant. As we have seen, it is incorrect to say that just distributive shares reward individuals according to their moral worth. But what we can say is that, in the traditional phrase, a just scheme gives each person his due: that is, it allots to each what he is entitled to as defined by the scheme itself. The principles of justice for institutions and individuals establish that doing this is fair.

Now it should be noted that even though a person's claims are regulated by the existing rules, we can still make a distinction between being entitled to something and deserving it in a familiar although non-moral sense.[15]

To illustrate, after a game one often says that the losing side deserved to win. Here one does not mean that the victors are not entitled to claim the championship, or whatever spoils go to the winner. One means instead that the losing team displayed to a higher degree the skills and qualities that the game calls forth, and the exercise of which gives the sport its appeal. Therefore the losers truly deserved to win but lost out as a result of bad luck, or from other contingencies that caused the contest to miscarry. Similarly even the best economic arrangements will not always lead to the more preferred outcomes. The claims that individuals actually acquire inevitably deviate more or less widely from those that the scheme is designed to allow for. Some persons in favoured positions, for example, may not have to a higher degree than others the desired qualities and abilities. All this is evident enough. Its bearing here is that although we can indeed distinguish between the claims that existing arrangements require us to honour, given what individuals have done and how things have turned out, and the claims that would have resulted under more ideal circumstances, none of this implies that distributive shares should be in accordance with moral worth. Even when things happen in the best way, there is still no tendency for distribution and virtue to coincide.

No doubt some may still contend that distributive shares should match moral worth at least to the extent that this is feasible. They may believe that unless those who are better off have superior moral character, their having greater advantages is an affront to our sense of justice. Now this opinion may arise from thinking of distributive justice as somehow the opposite of retributive justice. It is true that in a reasonably well-ordered society those who are punished for violating just laws have normally done something wrong. This is because the purpose of the criminal law is to uphold basic natural duties, those which forbid us to injure other persons in their life and limb, or to deprive them of their liberty and property, and punishments are to serve this end. They are not simply a scheme of taxes and burdens designed to put a price on certain forms of conduct and in this way to guide men's conduct for mutual advantage. It would be far better if the acts proscribed by penal statutes were never done.[16] Thus a propensity to commit such acts is a mark of bad character, and in a just society legal punishments will only fall upon those who display these faults.

It is clear that the distribution of economic and social advantages is entirely different. These arrangements are not the converse, so to speak, of the criminal law, so that just as the one punishes certain offences, the other rewards moral worth.[17] The function of unequal distributive shares is to cover the costs of training and education, to attract individuals to places and associations where they are most needed from a social point of view, and so on. Assuming that everyone accepts the propriety of self- or group-interested motivation duly regulated by a sense of justice, each decides to do those things that best accord with his aims. Variations in wages and income and the perquisites of position are simply to influence these choices so that the end result accords with efficiency and justice. In a well-ordered society there would be no need for the penal law except insofar as the assurance problem made it necessary. The question of criminal justice belongs for the most part to partial compliance theory, whereas the account of distributive shares belongs to strict compliance theory and so to the consideration of the ideal scheme. To think of distributive and retributive justice as converses of one another is completely misleading and suggests a different justification for distributive shares than the one they in fact have.

Notes

1. Here I follow H.L.A. Hart, *The Concept of Law* (Oxford: Clarendon Press, 1961), 155–9.

2. *An Enquiry concerning the Principles of Morals*, sec. 3, pt 1, par. 3, ed. L.A. Selby-Bigge, 2nd edn (Oxford, 1902), 184.

3. *Nicomachean Ethics*, 1129b–1130b5. I have followed the interpretation of Gregory Vlastos, 'Justice and Happiness in *The Republic*,' in Plato: *A Collection of Critical Essays*, ed. Vlastos (Garden City, NY: Doubleday and Company, 1971), vol. 2, 70f. For a discussion of Aristotle on justice, see W.F.R. Hardie, *Aristotle's Ethical Theory* (Oxford: Clarendon Press, 1968), chap. 10.

4. As the text suggest, I shall regard Locke's *Second Treatise of Government*, Rousseau's *The Social Contract*, and Kant's ethical works beginning with *The Foundations of the Metaphysics of Morals* as definitive of the contract tradition. For all of its greatness, Hobbes's *Leviathan* raises special problems. A general historical survey is provided by J.W. Gough, *The Social Contract*, 2nd edn (Oxford: Clarendon Press, 1957), and Otto Gierke, *Natural Law and the Theory of Society*, translated and with an introduction by Ernest Barker (Cambridge: University Press, 1934). A presentation of the contract view as primarily an ethical theory is to be found in G.R. Grice, *The Grounds of Moral Judgment* (Cambridge: University Press, 1967). See also §19, note 30.

5. Kant is clear that the original agreement is hypothetical. See *The Metaphysics of Morals*, pt 1 (*Rechtslehre*), especially §§47, 52; and pt 2 of the essay 'Concerning the Common Saying: This May Be True in Theory but It Does Not Apply in Practice,' in *Kant's Political Writings*, ed. Hans Reiss and trans. H.B. Nisbet (Cambridge: University Press, 1970), 73–87. See Georges Vlachos, *La pensée politique de Kant* (Paris: Presses universitaires de France, 1962), 326–35; and J.G. Murphy, *Kant: The Philosophy of Right*

(London: Macmillan, 1970), 109–12, 133–6, for a further discussion.

6. For the formulation of this intuitive idea I am indebted to Allan Gibbard.

7. The process of mutual adjustment of principles and considered judgments is not peculiar to moral philosophy. See Nelson Goodman, *Fact, Fiction, and Forecast* (Cambridge, MA: Harvard University Press, 1955), 65–8, for parallel remarks concerning the justification of the principles of deductive and inductive inference.

8. Henri Poincaré remarks: 'Il nous faut une faculté qui nous fasse voir le but de loin, et, cette faculté, c'est l'intuition.' *La valeur de la science* (Paris: Flammarion, 1909), 27.

9. The veil of ignorance is so natural a condition that something like it must have occurred to many. The formulation in the text is implicit, I believe, in Kant's doctrine of the categorical imperative, both in the way this procedural criterion is defined and the use Kant makes of it. Thus when Kant tells us to test our maxim by considering what would be the case were it a universal law of nature, he must suppose that we do not know our place within this imagined system of nature. See, for example, his discussion of the topic of practical judgment in *The Critique of Practical Reason*, academy edition, vol. 5, 68–72. A similar restriction on information is found in J.C. Harsanyi, 'Cardinal Utility in Welfare Economics and in the Theory of Risk-Taking,' *Journal of Political Economy* 61 (1953). However, other aspects of Harsanyi's view are quite different, and he uses the restriction to develop a utilitarian theory. See the last paragraph of §27.

10. Rousseau, *The Social Contract*, bk 2, chap. 4, par. 5.

11. See R.B. Perry, *The General Theory of Value* (New York: Longmans, Green and Company, 1926), 674–82.

12. See, for example, W.D. Ross, *The Right and the Good* (Oxford: Clarendon Press, 1930), 21, 26–8, 35, 57f. Similarly, Leibniz in 'On the Ultimate Origin of Things' (1697) speaks of the law of justice which 'declares that each one [each individual] participate in the perfection of the universe and in a happiness of his own in proportion to his own virtue and to the good will he entertains toward the common good.' *Leibniz*, ed. P.P. Wiener (New York, Charles Scribner's Sons, 1951), 353.

13. See F.H. Knight, *The Ethics of Competition* (New York: Harper and Brothers, 1935), 54–7.

14. See ibid., 56n.

15. Here I borrow from Joel Feinberg, *Doing and Deserving* (Princeton: Princeton University Press, 1970), 64f.

16. See H.L.A. Hart, *The Concept of Law* (Oxford: Clarendon Press, 1961), 39; and Feinberg, *Doing and Deserving*, chap. 5.

17. On this point, see Feinberg, *Doing and Deserving*, 62, 69n.

Study Questions for *A Theory of Justice*

1. What role does justice play in social institutions, according to Rawls?
2. In section 3 of *A Theory of Justice*, how does Rawls distinguish the original position from the Archimedean point of social contract theories? In what way is Rawls's theory a contractarian theory?
3. Describe the Rawlsian original position and the veil of ignorance. What do the parties in the original position not know about themselves and their social positions?
4. Describe the two main principles of justice that Rawls develops in section 11. What particular liberties does he include in the first principle? What conditions does Rawls place upon social and economic inequalities in the second principle?
5. Rawls notes in section 48 that he rejects the commonsensical supposition that income, wealth, and other social goods should be distributed according to moral desert. Why does Rawls reject a correlation between distributive shares and moral worthiness?
6. Discuss one potential problem that you find with Rawls's theory of justice.

Recommended Readings

Barry, Brian, *Justice as Impartiality* (Oxford University Press, 1995).

Beitz, Charles, *Political Theory and International Relations*, 2nd edn (Princeton University Press, 1999).

Daniels, Norman, *Reading Rawls* (Stanford University Press, 1989).

Freeman, Samuel, *Justice and the Social Contract: Essays on Rawlsian Political Philosophy* (Oxford University Press, 2007).

Mandle, John, *What's Left of Liberalism? An Interpretation and Defense of Justice as Fairness* (Lexington Books, 2000).

Okin, Susan Moller, 'Forty Acres and a Mule for Women: Rawls and Feminism,' *Politics, Philosophy and Economics* 4, no. 2 (2005): 233–48.

Pogge, Thomas, *John Rawls: His Life and Theory* (Oxford University Press, 2007).

Rawls, John, *Justice as Fairness: A Restatement*, edited by Erin Kelley (Harvard University Press, 2001).

Sandel, Michael, *Liberalism and the Limits of Justice*, 2nd edn (Cambridge University Press, 1998).

John Hospers

John Hospers (1918–) was born in central Iowa and educated at the University of Iowa and Columbia University. He spent the majority of his career at the School of Philosophy at the University of Southern California, where he is now professor emeritus. Throughout his career, Hospers published prolifically in several areas of philosophy, including political philosophy, ethics, aesthetics, and epistemology. In epistemology, he is known for his arguments against skepticism and his distinction between strong and weak senses of knowing. His major books include *Libertarianism* (1971), *Understanding the Arts* (1982), *Law and the Market* (1985), *Human Conduct* (third edition, 1995), and *Introduction to Philosophical Analysis* (fourth edition, 2003). Owing in part to the influence of his monograph on the libertarian political movement, Hospers was nominated as the first Libertarian party candidate for the US presidency in 1971. When asked during radio program interviews 'What will you do for me if elected,' Hospers would reply, 'I will leave you alone to live your life as you choose.'

Relatively early in his career, Hospers met the Russian philosopher and novelist Ayn Rand, and the two became friends over a series of evenings of philosophical conversation. Hospers was impressed with her masterpiece *Atlas Shrugged* (1957), and his experience of reading the work while conversing with Rand revitalized his long-standing beliefs in libertarian economic and political principles. Although the friendship between Rand and Hospers ended at a meeting of the American Society for Aesthetics, when Rand did not take kindly to his public critique of her work, he was nevertheless lastingly influenced by her and remembered particularly her suggestion that 'the world is starving for good ideas.'

Libertarian political philosophers favour a minimal state and oppose government intrusion into the private lives of citizens. In 'What Libertarianism Is' (1974), Hospers defends libertarianism as the doctrine that individuals possess the right to live as they choose, except when such choices infringe on the equal right of others to live as they choose. In response to those who support public funding of the arts, for instance, Hospers argues that such subsidies are forms of legalized plunder and that lovers of the arts have no right to take a portion of other people's paycheques for the satisfaction of their desires. Likewise, Hospers opposes a state welfare system on the ground that no one should be a moral cannibal upon the lives and productive capacities of other people. In a libertarian framework, individuals possess a right to life, liberty, and property, but these rights are understood negatively rather than positively. If I have a right to life, you have an obligation to avoid harming me, but you do not have a positive obligation to help maintain my existence.

Role of Government

'What Libertarianism Is'

The political philosophy that is called libertarianism (from the Latin *libertas*, liberty) is the doctrine that every person is the owner of his own life, and that no one is the owner of anyone else's life; and that consequently every human being has the right to act in accordance with his own choices, unless those actions infringe on the equal liberty of other human beings to act in accordance with *their* choices. There are several other ways of stating the same libertarian thesis:

1. *No one is anyone else's master, and no one is anyone else's slave.* Since I am the one to decide how my life is to be conducted, just as you decide about yours, I have no right (even if I had the power) to make you my slave and be your master, nor have you the right to become the master by enslaving me. Slavery is *forced* servitude, and since no one owns the life of anyone else, no one has the right to enslave another. Political theories past and present have traditionally been concerned with who should be the master (usually the king, the dictator, or government bureaucracy) and who should be the slaves, and what the extent of the slavery should be. Libertarianism holds that no one has the right to use force to enslave the life of another, or any portion or aspect of that life.

2. *Other men's lives are not yours to dispose of.* I enjoy seeing operas; but operas are expensive to produce. Opera-lovers often say, 'The state (or the city, etc.) should subsidize opera, so that we can all see it. Also it would be for people's betterment, cultural benefit, etc.' But what they are advocating is nothing more or less than legalized plunder. They can't pay for the productions themselves, and yet they want to see opera, which involves a large number of people and their labour; so what they are saying in effect is, 'Get the money through legalized force. Take a little bit more out of every worker's paycheque every week to pay for the operas we want to see.' But I have no right to take by force from the workers' pockets to pay for what I want.

Perhaps it would be better if he *did* go to see opera—then I should try to convince him to go voluntarily. But to take the money from him forcibly, because in my opinion it would be good for *him*, is still seizure of his earnings, which is plunder.

Besides, if I have the right to force him to help pay for my pet projects, hasn't he equally the right to force me to help pay for his? Perhaps he in turn wants the government to subsidize rock-and-roll, or his new car, or a house in the country? If I have the right to milk him, why hasn't he the right to milk me? If I can be a moral cannibal, why can't he too?

We should beware of the inventors of utopias. They would remake the world according to their vision—with the lives and fruits of the labour of *other* human beings. Is it someone's utopian vision that others should build pyramids to beautify the landscape? Very well, then other men should provide the labour; and if he is in a position of political power, and he can't get men to do it voluntarily, then he must *compel* them to 'cooperate'—i.e., he must enslave them.

A hundred men might gain great pleasure from beating up or killing just one insignificant human being; but other men's lives are not theirs to dispose of. 'In order to achieve the worthy goals of the next five-year-plan, we must forcibly collectivize the peasants . . .'; but other men's lives are not theirs to dispose of. Do you want to occupy, rent-free, the mansion that another man has worked for 20 years to buy? But other men's lives are not yours to dispose of. Do you want operas so badly that everyone is forced to work harder to pay for their subsidization through taxes? But other men's lives are not yours to dispose of. Do you want to have free medical care at the expense of other people, whether they wish to provide it or not? But this would require them to work longer for you whether they want to or not, and other men's lives are not yours to dispose of. . . .

3. *No human being should be a nonvoluntary mortgage on the life of another.* I cannot claim your life, your work, or the products of your effort as mine. The fruit of one man's labour should not be fair game for every freeloader who comes along and demands it as his own. The orchard that has been carefully grown, nurtured, and harvested by its owner should not be ripe for the plucking for any bypasser who has a yen for the ripe fruit. The wealth that some men have produced should not be fair game for looting by government, to be used for whatever purposes its representatives determine, no matter what their motives in so doing may be. The theft of your money by a robber is not justified by the fact that he used it to help his injured mother.

It will already be evident that libertarian doctrine is embedded in a view of the rights of man. Each human being has the right to live his life as he chooses, compatibly with the equal right of all other human beings to live their lives as they choose.

All man's rights are implicit in the above statement. Each man has the right to life: any attempt by others to take it away from him, or even to injure him, violates this right, through the use of coercion against him. Each man has the right to liberty: to conduct his life in accordance with the alternatives open to him without coercive action by others. And every man

has the right to property: to work to sustain his life (and the lives of whichever others he chooses to sustain, such as his family) and to retain the fruits of his labour.

People often defend the rights of life and liberty but denigrate property rights, and yet the right to property is as basic as the other two; indeed, without property rights no other rights are possible. Depriving you of property is depriving you of the means by which you live. . . .

I have no right to decide how *you* should spend your time or your money. I can make that decision for myself, but not for you, my neighbour. I may deplore your choice of lifestyle, and I may talk with you about it provided you are willing to listen to me. But I have no right to use force to change it. Nor have I the right to decide how you should spend the money you have earned. I may appeal to you to give it to the Red Cross, and you may prefer to go to prizefights. But that is your decision, and however much I may chafe about it I do not have the right to interfere forcibly with it, for example by robbing you in order to use the money in accordance with *my* choices. (If I have the right to rob you, have you also the right to rob me?)

When I claim a right, I carve out a niche, as it were, in my life, saying in effect, 'This activity I must be able to perform without interference from others. For you and everyone else, this is off limits.' And so I put up a 'no trespassing' sign, which marks off the area of my right. Each individual's right is his 'no trespassing' sign in relation to me and others. I may not encroach upon his domain any more than he upon mine, without my consent. Every right entails a duty, true—but the duty is only that of *forbearance*—that is, of *refraining* from violating the other person's right. If you have a right to life, I have no right to take your life; if you have a right to the products of your labour (property), I have no right to take it from you without your consent. The non-violation of these rights will not guarantee you protection against natural catastrophes such as floods and earthquakes, but it will protect you against the aggressive activities *of other men.* And rights, after all, have to do with one's relations to other human beings, not with one's relations to physical nature.

Nor were these rights created by government; governments—some governments, obviously not all—*recognize* and *protect* the rights that individuals already have. Governments regularly forbid homicide and theft; and, at a more advanced stage, protect individuals against such things as libel and breach of contract. . . .

The *right to property* is the most misunderstood and unappreciated of human rights, and it is one most constantly violated by governments. 'Property' of course does not mean only real estate; it includes anything you can call your own—your clothing, your car, your jewellery, your books and papers.

The right of property is not the right to just *take* it from others, for this would interfere with *their* property rights. It is rather the right to work for it, to obtain non-coercively, the money or services which you can present in voluntary exchange.

The right to property is consistently underplayed by intellectuals today, sometimes even frowned upon, as if we should feel guilty for upholding such a right in view of all the poverty in the world. But the right to property is absolutely basic. It is your hedge against the future. It is your assurance that what you have worked to earn will still be there, and be yours, when you wish or need to use it, especially when you are too old to work any longer.

Government has always been the chief enemy of the right to property. The officials of government, wishing to increase their power,

and finding an increase of wealth an effective way to bring this about, seize some or all of what a person has earned—and since government has a monopoly of physical force within the geographical area of the nation, it has the power (but not the right) to do this. When this happens, of course, every citizen of that country is insecure: he knows that no matter how hard he works the government can swoop down on him at any time and confiscate his earning and possessions. A person sees his life savings wiped out in a moment when the tax-collectors descend to deprive him of the fruits of his work; or, an industry which has been 50 years in the making and cost millions of dollars and millions of hours of time and planning, is nationalized overnight. Or the government, via inflation, cheapens the currency, so that hard-won dollars aren't worth anything any more. The effect of such actions, of course, is that people lose hope and incentive; if no matter how hard they work the government agents can take it all away, why bother to work at all, for more than today's needs? Depriving people of property is *depriving them of the means by which they live*—the freedom of the individual citizen to do what he wishes with his own life and to plan for the future. Indeed, only if property rights are respected is there any point to planning for the future and working to achieve one's goals. *Property rights are what makes long-range planning possible*—the kind of planning which is a distinctively human endeavour, as opposed to the day-by-day activity of the lion who hunts, who depends on the supply of game tomorrow but has no real insurance against starvation in a day or a week. Without the right to property, the right to life itself amounts to little: how can you sustain your life if you cannot plan ahead? and how can you plan ahead if the fruits of your labour can at any moment be confiscated by government? . . .

Indeed, the right to property may well be considered second only to the right to life. Even the freedom of speech is limited by considerations of property. If a person visiting in your home behaves in a way undesired by you, you have every right to evict him; he can scream or agitate elsewhere if he wishes, but not in your home without your consent. Does a person have a right to shout obscenities in a cathedral? No, for the owners of the cathedral (presumably the Church) have not allowed others on their property for that purpose; one may go there to worship or to visit, but not just for any purpose one wishes. Their property right is prior to your or my wish to scream or expectorate or write graffiti on their building. Or, to take the stock example, does a person have a right to shout 'Fire!' falsely in a crowded theatre? No, for the theatre owner has permitted others to enter and use his property only for a specific purpose, that of seeing a film or watching a stage show. If a person heckles or otherwise disturbs other members of the audience, he can be thrown out. (In fact, he can be removed for any reason the owner chooses, provided his admission money is returned.) And if he shouts 'Fire!' when there is no fire, he may be endangering other lives by causing a panic or a stampede. The right to free speech doesn't give one the right to say anything anywhere; it is circumscribed by property rights.

Again, some people seem to assume that the right to free speech (including written speech) means that they can go to a newspaper publisher and demand that he print in his newspaper some propaganda or policy statement for their political party (or other group). But of course they have no right to the use of his newspaper. Ownership of the newspaper is the product of his labour, and he has a right to put into his newspaper whatever he wants, for whatever reason. If he excludes material which many readers would like to have in, perhaps they can find it in another newspaper or persuade him to print it himself (if there are enough of them, they will usually do just that). Perhaps they can even cause his newspaper to fail. But as long as he owns it, he has the right to put in it what he wishes; what would a property right be if he could not do this? They have no right to place their material in his newspaper without his consent—not for free, nor even for a fee. Perhaps other newspapers will include it, or perhaps they can start their own newspaper (in which case they have a right to put in it what they like). If not, an option open to them would be to mimeograph and distribute some handbills.

In exactly the same way, no one has a right to 'free television time' unless the owner of the television station consents to give it; it is his station, he has the property rights over it, and it is for him to decide how to dispose of his time. He may not decide wisely, but it is his right to decide as he wishes. If he makes enough unwise decisions, and courts enough unpopularity with the viewing public or the sponsors, he may have to go out of business; but as he is free to make his own decisions, so is he free to face their consequences. (If the government owns the television station, then government officials will make the decisions, and there is no guarantee of *their* superior wisdom. The difference is that when 'the government' owns the station, you are forced to help pay for its upkeep through your taxes, whether the bureaucrat in charge decides to give you television time or not.)

'But why have *individual* property rights? Why not have lands and houses owned by everybody together?' Yes, this involves no violation of individual rights, as long as everybody consents to this arrangement and no one is forced to join it. The parties to it may enjoy the communal living enough (at least for a time) to overcome certain inevitable problems: that some will work and some not, that some will achieve more in an hour than others can do in a day, and still they will all get the same income. The few who do the most will in the end consider themselves 'workhorses' who do the work of two or three or twelve, while the others will be 'freeloaders' on the efforts of these few. But as long as they can get out of the arrangement if they no longer like it, no violation of rights is involved. They got in voluntarily, and they can get out voluntarily; no one has used force.

'But why not say that everybody owns everything? That we *all* own everything there is?'

To some this may have a pleasant ring—but let us try to analyse what it means. If everybody owns everything, then everyone has an equal right to go everywhere, do what he pleases, take what he likes, destroy if he wishes, grow crops or burn them, trample them under, and so on. Consider what it would be like in practice. Suppose you have saved money to buy a house for yourself and your family. Now suppose that the principle, 'everybody owns everything,' becomes adopted. Well then, why shouldn't every itinerant hippie just come in and take over, sleeping in your beds and eating in your kitchen and not bothering to replace the food supply or clean up the mess? After all, it belongs to all of us, doesn't it? So we have just as much right to it as you, the buyer, have. What happens if we *all* want to sleep in the bedroom and there's not room for all of us? Is it the strongest who wins?

What would be the result? Since no one would be responsible for anything, the property would soon be destroyed, the food used up, the facilities non-functional. Beginning as a house that *one* family could use, it would end up as a house that *no one* could use. And if the principle continued to be adopted, no one

would build houses any more—or anything else. What for? They would only be occupied and used by others, without remuneration.

Suppose two men are cast ashore on an island, and they agree that each will cultivate half of it. The first man is industrious and grows crops and builds a shelter, making the most of the situation with which he is confronted. The second man, perhaps thinking that the warm days will last forever, lies in the sun, picks coconuts while they last, and does a minimum of work to sustain himself. At the time of harvest, the second man has nothing to harvest, nor does he assist the first man in his labours. But later when there is a dearth of food on the island, the second man comes to the first man and demands half of the harvest as his right. But of course he has no right to the product of the first man's labours. The first man may freely choose to give part of his harvest to the second out of charity rather than see him starve; but that is just what it is—charity, not the second man's right.

How can any of man's rights be violated? Ultimately, only by the use of force. I can make suggestions to you, I can reason with you, entreat you (if you are willing to listen), but I cannot *force* you without violating your rights; only by forcing you do I cut the cord between your free decisions and your actions. Voluntary relations between individuals involve no deprivation of rights, but murder, assault, and rape do, because in doing these things I make you the unwilling victim of my actions. A man beating his wife involves no violation of rights if she *wanted* to be beaten. *Force is behaviour that requires the unwilling involvement of other persons.*

Thus the use of force need not involve the use of physical violence. If I trespass on your property or dump garbage on it, I am violating your property rights, as indeed I am when I steal your watch; although this is not force in the sense of violence, it *is* a case of your being an unwilling victim of my action. Similarly, if you shout at me so that I cannot be heard when I try to speak, or blow a siren in my ear, or start a factory next door which pollutes my land, you are again violating my rights (to free speech, to property); I am, again, an unwilling victim of your actions. Similarly, if you steal a manuscript of mine and publish it as your own, you are confiscating a piece of my property and thus violating my right to keep what is the product of my labour. Of course, if I give you the manuscript with permission to sign your name to it and keep the proceeds, no violation of rights is involved—any more than if I give you permission to dump garbage on my yard.

According to libertarianism, the role of government should be limited to the retaliatory use of force against those who have initiated its use. It should not enter into any other areas, such as religion, social organization, and economics.

Government

Government is the most dangerous institution known to man. Throughout history it has violated the rights of men more than any individual or group of individuals could do: it has killed people, enslaved them, sent them to forced labour and concentration camps, and regularly robbed and pillaged them of the fruits of their expended labour. Unlike individual criminals, government has the power to arrest and try; unlike individual criminals, it can surround and encompass a person totally, dominating every aspect of one's life, so that one has no recourse from it but to leave the country (and in totalitarian nations even that is

prohibited). Government throughout history has a much sorrier record than any individual, even that of a ruthless mass murderer. The signs we see on bumper stickers are chillingly accurate: 'Beware: the Government is Armed and Dangerous.'

The only proper role of government, according to libertarians, is that of the protector of the citizen against aggression by other individuals. The government, of course, should never initiate aggression; its proper role is as the embodiment of the *retaliatory* use of force against anyone who initiates its use.

If each individual had constantly to defend himself against possible aggressors, he would have to spend a considerable portion of his life in target practice, karate exercises, and other means of self-defences, and even so he would probably be helpless against groups of individuals who might try to kill, maim, or rob him. He would have little time for cultivating those qualities which are essential to civilized life, nor would improvements in science, medicine, and the arts be likely to occur. The function of government is to take this responsibility off his shoulders: the government undertakes to defend him against aggressors and to punish them if they attack him. When the government is effective in doing this, it enables the citizen to go about his business unmolested and without constant fear for his life. To do this, of course, government must have physical power—the police, to protect the citizen from aggression within its borders, and the armed forces, to protect him from aggressors outside. Beyond that, the government should not intrude upon his life, either to run his business, or adjust his daily activities, or prescribe his personal moral code.

Government, then, undertakes to be the individual's protector; but historically governments have gone far beyond this function. Since they already have the physical power, they have not hesitated to use it for purposes far beyond that which was entrusted to them in the first place. Undertaking initially to protect its citizens against aggression, it has often itself become an aggressor—a far greater aggressor, indeed, than the criminals against whom it was supposed to protect its citizens. Governments have done what no private citizens can do: arrest and imprison individuals without a trial and send them to slave labour camps. Government must have power in order to be effective—and yet the very means by which alone it can be effective make it vulnerable to the abuse of power, leading to managing the lives of individuals and even inflicting terror upon them.

What then should be the function of government? In a word, the *protection of human rights.*

1. *The right to life:* libertarians support all such legislation as will protect human beings against the use of force by others, for example, laws against killing, attempted killing, maiming, beating, and all kinds of physical violence.

2. *The right to liberty:* there should be no laws compromising in any way freedom of speech, of the press, and of peaceable assembly. There should be no censorship of ideas, books, films, or of anything else by government.

3. *The right to property:* libertarians support legislation that protects the property rights of individuals against confiscation, nationalization, eminent domain, robbery, trespass, fraud and misrepresentation, patent and copyright, libel and slander.

Someone has violently assaulted you. Should he be legally liable? Of course. He has violated one of your rights. He has knowingly injured you, and since he has initiated aggression against you he should be made to expiate.

Someone has negligently left his bicycle on the sidewalk where you trip over it in the dark

and injure yourself. He didn't do it intentionally; he didn't mean you any harm. Should he be legally liable? Of course; he has, however unwittingly, injured you, and since the injury is caused by him and you are the victim, he should pay.

Someone across the street is unemployed. Should you be taxed extra to pay for his expenses? Not at all. You have not injured him, you are not responsible for the fact that he is unemployed (unless you are a senator or bureaucrat who agitated for further curtailing of business, which legislation passed, with the result that your neighbour was laid off by the curtailed business). You may voluntarily wish to help him out, or better still, try to get him a job to put him on his feet again; but since you have initiated no aggressive act against him, and neither purposely nor accidentally injured him in any way, you should not be legally penalized for the fact of his unemployment. (Actually, it is just such penalties that increase unemployment.)

One man, A, works hard for years and finally earns a high salary as a professional man. A second man, B, prefers not to work at all, and to spend wastefully what money he has (through inheritance), so that after a year or two he has nothing left. At the end of this time he has a long siege of illness and lots of medical bills to pay. He demands that the bills be paid by the government—that is, by the taxpayers of the land, including Mr A.

But of course B has no such right. He chose to lead his life in a certain way—that was his voluntary decision. One consequence of that choice is that he must depend on charity in case of later need. Mr A chose not to live that way. (And if everyone lived like Mr B, on whom would he depend in case of later need?) Each has a right to live in the way he pleases, but each must live with the consequences of his own decision (which, as always, fall primarily on himself). He cannot, in time of need, claim A's beneficence as his right.

If a house-guest of yours starts to carve his initials in your walls and break up your furniture, you have a right to evict him, and call the police if he makes trouble. If someone starts to destroy the machinery in a factory, the factory-owner is also entitled to evict him and call the police. In both cases, persons other than the owner are permitted on the property only under certain conditions, at the pleasure of the owner. If those conditions are violated, the owner is entitled to use force to set things straight. The case is exactly the same on a college or university campus: if a campus demonstrator starts breaking windows, occupying the president's office, and setting fire to a dean, the college authorities are certainly within their rights to evict him forcibly; one is permitted on the college grounds only under specific conditions, set by the administration: study, peaceful student activity, even political activity if those in charge choose to permit it. If they do not choose to permit peaceful political activity on campus, they may be unwise, since a campus is after all a place where all sides of every issue should get discussed, and the college that doesn't permit this may soon lose its reputation and its students. All the same, the college official who does not permit it is quite within his rights; the students do not own the campus, nor do the hired troublemakers imported from elsewhere. In the case of a privately owned college, the owners, or whoever they have delegated to administer it, have the right to make the decisions as to who shall be permitted on the campus and under what conditions. In the case of a state university or college, the ownership problem is more complex: one could say that the 'government' owns the campus or that 'the people' do since they are the taxpayers who support it; but in either case, the university administration has the delegated task of keeping order, and until they are removed by the state administration or the taxpayers, it is theirs to decide who shall be permitted on campus, and what non-academic activities will be permitted to their students on the premises.

Property rights can be violated by physical trespass, of course, or by anyone entering on your property for any reason without your consent. (If you *do* consent to having your neighbour dump garbage on your yard, there is no violation of your rights.) But the physical trespass of a person is only a special case of violation of property rights. Property rights can be violated by sound-waves, in the form of a loud noise, or the sounds of your neighbour's hi-fi set while you are trying to sleep. Such violations of property rights are of course the subject of action in the courts.

But there is another violation of property rights that has not thus far been honoured by the courts; this has to do with the effects of *pollution* of the atmosphere. . . .

What about automobiles, the chief polluters of the air? One can hardly sue every automobile owner. But one can sue the manufacturers of automobiles who do not install anti-smog devices on the cars which they distribute—and later (though this is more difficult), owners of individual automobiles if they discard the equipment or do not keep it functional.

The violation of rights does not apply only to air pollution. If someone with a factory upstream on a river pollutes the river, anyone living downstream from him, finding his water polluted, should be able to sue the owner of the factory. In this way the price of adding the anti-pollutant devices will be the owner's responsibility, and will probably be added to the cost of the products which the factory produces and thus spread around among all consumers, rather than the entire cost being borne by the users of the river in the form of polluted water, with the consequent impossibility of fishing, swimming, and so on. In each case, pollution would be stopped at the source rather than having its ill effects spread around to numerous members of the population.

What about property which you do not work to earn, but which you *inherit* from someone else? Do you have a right to that? You have no right to it until someone decides to give it to you. Consider the man who willed it to you: it was his, he had the right to use and dispose of it as *he* saw fit; and if he decided to give it to you, this is a windfall for you, but it was only the exercise of *his* right. Had the property been seized by the government at the man's death, or distributed among numerous other people designated by the government, it *would* have been a violation of his rights: for he, who worked to earn and sustain it, would not have been able to dispose of it according to his own judgment. If he doesn't have the right to determine who shall have it, who does?

What about the property status of your intellectual activity, such as inventions you may devise and books you write? These, of course, are your property also; they are the products of your mind; you worked at them, you created them. Prior to that, they did not exist. If you worked five years to write a book, and someone stole it and published it as his own, receiving royalties from its sales, he would have stolen your property just as surely as if he had robbed your home. The same is true if someone used and sold without your permission an invention which was the product of your labour and ingenuity.

The role of government with respect to this issue, at least most governments of the Western world, is a proper one: government protects the products of your labour from the moment they materialize. Copyright law protects your writings from piracy. In the United States, one's writings are protected for a period of 27 years, and another 27 if one applies for renewal of the copyright. In most other countries, they are protected for a period of 50 years after the author's death, permitting both himself and his surviving heirs to reap the fruits of his labour. After that they enter the 'public domain'—that is, anyone may reprint them without your or heirs' permission. Patent law protects your inventions for a limited period, which varies according to the type of invention. In no case are you forced to avail yourself of this protection; you need not apply for patent or copyright coverage if you do not wish to do so. But the protection of your intellectual property is there, in case you wish to use it.

What about the property status of the airwaves? Here the government's position is far more questionable. The government now claims ownership of the airwaves, leasing them to individuals and corporations. The government renews leases or refuses them depending on whether the programs satisfy authorities in the Federal Communications Commission. The official position is that 'we all own the airwaves'; but since only one party can broadcast on a certain frequency at a certain time without causing chaos, it is simply a fact of reality that 'everyone' cannot use it. In fact the government decides who shall use the airwaves, and one courts its displeasure only at the price of a revoked licence. One can write without government approval, but one cannot use the airwaves without the approval of government.

What policy should have been observed with regard to the airwaves? Much the same as the policy that was followed in the case of the Homestead Act, when the lands of the American West were opening up for settlement. There was a policy of 'first come, first served,' with the government parceling out a certain acreage for each individual who wanted to claim the land as his own. There was no charge for the land, but if a man had not used it and built a dwelling during the first two-year period, it was assumed that he was not home-steading and the land was given to the next man in line. The airwaves too could have been given out on a 'first come, first served' basis. The first man who used a given frequency would be its owner, and the government would protect him in the use of it against trespassers. If others wanted to use the same frequency, they would have to buy it from the first man, if he was willing to sell, or try to buy another, just as one now does with land.

Laws may be classified into three types: (1) laws protecting individuals against themselves, such as laws against fornication and other sexual behaviour, alcohol, and drugs; (2) laws protecting individuals against aggressions by other individuals, such as laws against murder, robbery, and fraud; (3) laws requiring people to help one another; for example, all laws which rob Peter to pay Paul, such as welfare.

Libertarians reject the first class of laws totally. Behaviour which harms no one else is strictly the individual's own affair. Thus, there should be no laws against becoming intoxicated, since whether or not to become intoxicated is the individual's own decision; but there should be laws against driving while intoxicated, since the drunken driver is a threat to every other motorist on the highway (drunken driving falls into type 2). Similarly, there should be no laws against drugs (except the prohibition of sale of drugs to minors) as long as the taking of these drugs poses no threat to anyone else. Drug addiction is a psychological problem to which no present solution exists. Most of the social harm caused by addicts, other than to themselves, is the result

of thefts which they perform in order to continue their habit—and then the *legal* crime is the theft, not the addiction. The actual cost of heroin is about 10 cents a shot; if it were legalized, the enormous traffic in illegal sale and purchase of it would stop, as well as the accompanying proselytization to get new addicts (to make more money for the pusher) and the thefts performed by addicts who often require 80 dollars a day just to keep up the habit. Addiction would not stop, but the crimes would: it is estimated that 75 per cent of the burglaries in New York City today are performed by addicts, and all these crimes could be wiped out at one stroke through the legalization of drugs. (Only when the taking of drugs could be shown to constitute a threat to *others*, should it be prohibited by law. It is only laws protecting people against *themselves* that libertarians oppose.)

Laws should be limited to the second class only: aggression by individuals against other individuals. These are laws whose function is to protect human beings against encroachment by others; and this, as we have seen, is (according to libertarianism) the sole function of government.

Libertarians also reject the third class of laws totally: no one should be forced by law to help others, not even to tell them the time of day if requested, and certainly not to give them a portion of one's weekly paycheque. Governments, in the guise of humanitarianism, have given to some by taking from others (charging a 'handling fee' in the process, which, because of the government's waste and inefficiency, sometimes is several hundred per cent). And in so doing they have decreased incentive, violated the rights of individuals, and lowered the standard of living of almost everyone.

All such laws constitute what libertarians call *moral cannibalism*. A cannibal in the physical sense is a person who lives off the flesh of other human beings. A *moral* cannibal is one who believes he has a right to live off the 'spirit' of other human beings—who believes that he has a moral claim on the productive capacity, time, and effort expended by others.

It has become fashionable to claim virtually everything that one needs or desires as one's *right*. Thus, many people claim that they have a right to a job, the right to free medical care, to free food and clothing, to a decent home, and so on. Now if one asks, apart from any specific context, whether it would be desirable if everyone had these things, one might well say yes. But there is a gimmick attached to each of them: *At whose expense?* Jobs, medical care, education, and so on, don't grow on trees. These are goods and services *produced only by men*. Who, then, is to provide them, and under what conditions?

If you have a right to a job, who is to supply it? Must an employer supply it even if he doesn't want to hire you? What if you are unemployable, or incurably lazy? (If you say 'the government must supply it,' does that mean that a job must be created for you which no employer needs done, and that you must be kept in it regardless of how much or little you work?) If the employer is forced to supply it at his expense even if he doesn't need you, then isn't *he* being enslaved to that extent? What ever happened to *his* right to conduct his life and his affairs in accordance with his choices?

If you have a right to free medical care, then, since medical care doesn't exist in nature as wild apples do, some people will have to supply it to you for free: that is, they will have to spend their time and money and energy taking care of you whether they want to or not. What ever happened to *their* right to conduct their lives as they see fit? Or do you have a right to violate theirs? Can there be a right to violate rights?

All those who demand this or that as a 'free service' are consciously or unconsciously evading the fact that there is in reality no such thing as free services. All man-made goods and services are the result of human expenditure of time and effort. There is no such thing as 'something for nothing' in this world. If you demand something free, you are demanding that other men give their time and effort to you without compensation. If they voluntarily choose to do this, there is no problem; but if you demand that they be *forced* to do it, you are interfering with their right not to do it if they so choose. 'Swimming in this pool ought to be free!' says the indignant passerby. What he means is that others should build a pool, others should provide the materials, and still others should run it and keep it in functioning order, so that *he* can use it without fee. But what right has he to the expenditure of *their* time and effort? To expect something 'for free' is to expect it *to be paid for by others* whether they choose to or not.

Many questions, particularly about economic matters, will be generated by the libertarian account of human rights and the role of government. Should government have no role in assisting the needy, in providing social security, in legislating minimum wages, in fixing prices and putting a ceiling on rents, in curbing monopolies, in erecting tariffs, in guaranteeing jobs, in managing the money supply? To these and all similar questions the libertarian answers with an unequivocal no.

'But then you'd let people go hungry!' comes the rejoinder. This, the libertarian insists, is precisely what would not happen; with the restrictions removed, the economy would flourish as never before. With the controls taken off business, existing enterprises would expand and new ones would spring into existence satisfying more and more consumer needs; millions more people would be gainfully employed instead of subsisting on welfare, and all kinds of research and production, released from the stranglehold of government, would proliferate, fulfilling man's needs and desires as never before. It has always been so whenever government has permitted men to be free traders on a free market. But *why* this is so, and how the free market is the best solution to all problems relating to the material aspect of man's life, is another and far longer story. It is told in detail in chapters 3 to 9 of my book, *Libertarianism*.

Study Questions for 'What Libertarianism Is'

1. How does Hospers define libertarianism? What is the primary role of government according to libertarians?
2. What does it mean to possess a right to life, liberty and property in a libertarian framework? Why is the right to property one of the most basic human rights, according to Hospers?
3. Describe Hospers's tri-fold classification of laws. Why do libertarians reject two of these three classes of laws?
4. Compare Hospers's libertarianism with the political philosophies of John Stuart Mill and John Locke. What concepts or principles does Hospers borrow from these thinkers? Where would Mill and Locke disagree with Hospers?
5. What are the strongest points made by Hospers? Are there any weaknesses in his arguments?

Recommended Readings

Arneson, Richard, 'Egalitarianism and the Undeserving Poor,' *Journal of Political Philosophy* 5 (December 1977): 327–50.

Cohen, Gerald A., *Self-Ownership, Freedom and Equality* (Cambridge University Press, 1995).

Machan, Tibor, and Douglas Rasmussen, eds, *Liberty for the 21st Century* (Rowman and Littlefield, 1995).

Miller, David, ed., *Liberty* (Oxford University Press, 1991).

Narveson, Jan, *The Libertarian Idea* (Broadview Press, 2001).

Nozick, Robert, *Anarchy, State and Utopia* (Basic Books, 1974).

Otsuka, Michael, *Libertarianism without Inequality* (Clarendon Press, 2003).

Vallentyne, Peter, and Hillel Steiner, eds, *Left Libertarianism and Its Critics: The Contemporary Debate* (Palgrave, 2000).

———— eds, *The Origins of Left Libertarianism: An Anthology of Historical Writings* (Palgrave, 2000).

Van Parijs, Philippe, *Real Freedom for All: What (If Anything) Can Justify Capitalism?* (Clarendon Press, 1995).

Carole Pateman

Carole Pateman was born in Sussex, England, and earned a PhD in political philosophy from Oxford University. She has held professorial appointments at the University of Sydney, Stanford University, Princeton University, and the University of California at Los Angeles, where she currently teaches in the Department of Political Science. Known for her work in democratic theory, political obligation, and feminist political philosophy, Pateman has served as president of the International Political Science Association and president of the Australasian Political Studies Association. Her books include *Participation and Democratic Theory* (1970), *The Problem of Political Obligation* (second edition, 1985), *Feminist Challenges* (1986), *The Sexual Contract* (1988), *The Disorder of Women* (1989), *Feminist Interpretations and Political Theory* (1991), and *Contract and Domination* (with Charles Mills, 2007).

In *The Sexual Contract*, Pateman develops a feminist critical analysis of social contract theory from Hobbes to Rawls, arguing that the social contract is a fraternal contract that rests upon the subordination of women to men. The classical social contract theorists offer differing conceptions of humanity in the state of nature, but each offers an account of human nature in which distinctively human characteristics are masculine characteristics. At the same time that classical theorists maintain men and women possess different natural attributes, they nevertheless subsume feminine beings under the genderless category of 'human being' and conflate 'individuals' with 'men'. Moreover, both classical and contemporary contract theorists direct attention to public civil society by maintaining an implicit (and sometimes explicit) contrast between a public sphere of freedom and equality among brothers and a private sphere of inequality among men, women, and children. Even in Rawls's *Theory of Justice*, the parties in the original position are heads of households or representatives deliberating on behalf of their wives.

The Sexual Contract

1

Contracting In

Telling stories of all kinds is the major way that human beings have endeavoured to make sense of themselves and their social world. The most famous and influential political story of modern times is found in the writings of the social contract theorists. The story, or conjectural history, tells how a new civil society and a new form of political right is created through an original contract. An explanation for the binding authority of the state and civil law, and for the legitimacy of modern civil government, is to be found by treating our society as if it had originated in a contract. The attraction of the idea of an original contract and of contract theory in a more general sense, a theory that claims that free social relations take a contractual form, is probably greater now than at any time since the seventeenth and eighteenth centuries when the classic writers told their tales. But today, invariably, only half the story is told. We hear an enormous amount about the *social* contract; a deep silence is maintained about the *sexual* contract.

The original contract is a sexual-social pact, but the story of the sexual contract has been repressed. Standard accounts of social contract theory do not discuss the whole story and contemporary contract theorists give no indication that half the agreement is missing. The story of the sexual contract is also about the genesis of political right, and explains why exercise of the right is legitimate—but this story is about political right as *patriarchal right* or sex-right, the power that men exercise over women. The missing half of the story tells how a specifically modern form of patriarchy is established. The new civil society created through the original contract is a patriarchal social order.

Social contract theory is conventionally presented as a story about freedom. One interpretation of the original contract is that the inhabitants of the state of nature exchange the insecurities of natural freedom for equal, civil freedom which is protected by the state. In civil society freedom is universal; all adults enjoy the same civil standing and can exercise their freedom by, as it were, replicating the original contract when, for example, they enter into the employment contract or the marriage contract. Another interpretation, which takes into account conjectural histories of the state of nature in the classic texts, is that freedom is won by sons who cast off their natural subjection to their fathers and replace paternal rule by civil government. Political right as paternal right is inconsistent with modern civil society. In this version of the story, civil society is created through the original contract after paternal rule—or patriarchy—is overthrown. The new civil order, therefore, appears to be anti-patriarchal or post-patriarchal. Civil society is created through contract so that contract and patriarchy appear to be irrevocably opposed.

These familiar readings of the classic stories fail to mention that a good deal more than freedom is at stake. Men's domination over women, and the right of men to enjoy equal sexual access to women, is at issue in the making of the original pact. The social contract is a story of freedom; the sexual contract is a story of subjection. The original contract constitutes both freedom and domination. Men's freedom and women's subjection are created through the original contract—and the character of civil freedom cannot be understood without the missing half of the story that reveals how men's patriarchal right over women is established through contract. Civil freedom is not universal. Civil freedom is a masculine attribute and depends upon patriarchal right. The sons overturn paternal rule not merely to gain their liberty but to secure women for themselves. Their success in this endeavour is chronicled in the story of the sexual contract. The original pact is a sexual as well as a social contract: it is sexual in the sense of patriarchal—that is, the contract establishes men's political right over women— and also sexual in the sense of establishing orderly access by men to women's bodies. The original contract creates what I shall call, following Adrienne Rich, 'the law of male sex-right'.[1] Contract is far from being opposed to patriarchy; contract is the means through which modern patriarchy is constituted.

One reason why political theorists so rarely notice that half the story of the original contract is missing, or that civil society is patriarchal, is that 'patriarchy' is usually interpreted patriarchally as paternal rule (the literal meaning of the term). So, for example, in the standard reading of the theoretical battle in the seventeenth century between the patriarchalists and social contract theorists, patriarchy is assumed to refer only to paternal right. Sir Robert Filmer claimed that political power was paternal power and that the procreative power of the father was the origin of political right. Locke and his fellow contract theorists insisted that paternal and political power were not the same and that contract was the genesis of political right. The contract theorists were victorious on this point; the standard interpretation is on firm ground—as far as it goes. Once more, a crucial portion of the story is missing. The true origin of political right is overlooked in this interpretation; no stories are told about its genesis (I attempt to remedy the omission in chapter 4). Political right originates in sexright or conjugal right. Paternal right is only one, and not the original, dimension of patriarchal power. A man's power as a father comes after he has exercised the patriarchal right of a man (a husband) over a woman (wife). The contract theorists had no wish to challenge the original patriarchal right in their onslaught on paternal right. Instead, they incorporated conjugal right into their theories and, in so doing, transformed the law of male sex-right into its modern contractual form. Patriarchy ceased to be paternal long ago. Modern civil society is not structured by kinship and the power of fathers; in the modern world, women are subordinated to men *as men*, or to men as a fraternity. The original contract takes place after the political defeat of the father and creates modern *fraternal patriarchy*.

Another reason for the omission of the story of the sexual contract is that conventional approaches to the classic texts, whether those of mainstream political theorists or their socialist critics, give a misleading picture of a distinctive feature of the civil society created through the original pact. Patriarchal civil society is divided into two spheres, but attention is directed to one sphere only. The story of the social contract is treated as an account of the creation of the public sphere of civil freedom. The other, private, sphere is not seen as politically relevant. Marriage and the marriage contract are, therefore, also deemed politically irrelevant. To ignore the marriage contract is to ignore half the original contract. In the classic texts, as I shall show in some detail, the sexual contract is displaced onto the marriage contract. The displacement creates a difficulty in retrieving and recounting the lost story. All too easily, the impression can be given that the sexual contract and the social contract are two separate, albeit related, contracts, and that the sexual contract concerns the private sphere.

Patriarchy then appears to have no relevance to the public world. On the contrary, patriarchal right extends throughout civil society. The employment contract and (what I shall call) the prostitution contract, both of which are entered into in the public, capitalist market, uphold men's right as firmly as the marriage contract. The two spheres of civil society are at once separate and inseparable. The public realm cannot be fully understood in the absence of the private sphere, and, similarly, the meaning of the original contract is misinterpreted without both, mutually dependent, halves of the story. Civil freedom depends on patriarchal right. . . .

The perception of civil society as a post-patriarchal social order also depends on the inherent ambiguity of the term 'civil society'. From one perspective, civil society is the contractual order that follows the pre-modern order of status, or the civil order of constitutional, limited government replaces political absolutism. From another perspective, civil society replaces the state of nature; and, yet again, 'civil' also refers to one of the spheres, the public sphere, of 'civil society'. Most advocates and opponents of contract theory trade on the ambiguity of 'civil'. 'Civil society' is distinguished from other forms of social order by the separation of the private from the public sphere; civil society is divided into two opposing realms, each with a distinctive and contrasting mode of association. Yet attention is focused on one sphere, which is treated as the only realm of political interest. Questions are rarely asked about the political significance of the existence of two spheres, or about how both spheres are brought into being. The origin of the public sphere is no mystery. The social contract brings the public world of civil law, civil freedom and equality, contract and the individual into being. What is the (conjectural) history of the origin of the private sphere?

To understand any classic theorist's picture of either the natural condition or the civil state, both must be considered together. 'Natural' and 'civil' are at once opposed to each other and mutually dependent. The two terms gain their meaning from their relationship to each other; what is 'natural' excludes what is 'civil' and vice versa. To draw attention to the mutual dependence of the state of nature/civil society does not explain why, after the original pact, the term 'civil' shifts and is used to refer not to the whole of 'civil society' but to one of its parts. To explain the shift, a double opposition and dependence between 'natural' and 'civil' must be taken into account. Once the original contract is entered into, the relevant dichotomy is between the private sphere and the civil, public sphere—a dichotomy that reflects the order of sexual difference in the natural condition, which is also a political difference. Women have no part in the original contract, but they are not left behind in the state of nature—that would defeat the purpose of the sexual contract! Women are incorporated into a sphere that both is and is not in civil society. The private sphere is part of civil society but is separated from the 'civil' sphere. The antinomy private/public is another expression of natural/civil and women/men. The private, womanly sphere (natural) and the public, masculine sphere (civil) are opposed but gain their meaning from each other, and the meaning of the civil freedom of public life is thrown into relief when counterposed to the natural subjection that characterizes the private realm (Locke misleads by presenting the contrast in patriarchal terms as between paternal and political power). What it means to be an 'individual', a maker of contracts and civilly free, is revealed by the subjection of women within the private sphere.

The private sphere is typically presupposed as a necessary, natural foundation for civil, i.e., public life, but treated as irrelevant to the concerns of political theorists and political activists. Since at least 1792 when Mary Wollstonecraft's *A Vindication of the Rights of Woman* appeared, feminists have persistently pointed to the complex interdependence between the two spheres, but, nearly two centuries later, 'civil' society is still usually treated as a realm that subsists independently. The origin of the private sphere thus remains shrouded in mystery. The mystery is deepened because discussions of social contract theory almost always pass directly from the eighteenth century to the present day and John Rawls's contemporary reformulation of the (social) contract story. Yet Sigmund Freud also (re) wrote more than one version of the story of the original contract. He is rarely mentioned, but perhaps there is good reason for the absence of Freud's name. Freud's stories make explicit that power over women and not only freedom is at issue before the original agreement is made, and he also makes clear that two realms are created through the original pact. In the classic texts (except for those of Hobbes) it can easily seem at first sight that there is no need to create the private sphere, since sexual relations between men and women, marriage and the family already exist in the state of nature. But the original contract brings 'civil society' into being, and the story of the sexual contract must be told in order to elucidate how the private realm (is held to be) established and why the separation from the public sphere is necessary. . . .

3

Contract, the Individual, and Slavery

Classic social contract theory and the broader argument that, ideally, all social relations should take a contractual form, derive from a revolutionary claim. The claim is that individuals are naturally free and equal to each other, or that individuals are born free and born equal. That such a notion can seem commonplace rather than revolutionary today is a tribute to the successful manner in which contract theorists have turned a subversive proposition into a defence of civil subjection. Contract theory is not the only example of a theoretical strategy that justifies subjection by presenting it as freedom, but contract theory is remarkable in reaching that conclusion from its particular starting-point. The doctrine of natural individual freedom and equality was revolutionary precisely because it swept away, in one fell swoop, all the grounds through which the subordination of some individuals, groups or categories of people to others had been justified; or, conversely, through which rule by one individual or group over others was justified. Contract theory was the emancipatory doctrine *par excellence*, promising that universal freedom was the principle of the modern era.

The assumption that individuals were born free and equal to each other meant that none of the old arguments for subordination could be accepted. Arguments that rulers and masters exercised their power through God's will had to be rejected; might or force could no longer be translated into political right; appeals to custom and tradition were no longer sufficient; nor were the various arguments from nature, whether they looked to the generative power of a father, or to superior birth, strength, ability, or rationality. All these familiar arguments became unacceptable because the doctrine of individual freedom and equality entailed that there was only one justification for subordination. A naturally free and equal individual must, necessarily, *agree* to be ruled by another. The creation of civil mastery and civil subordination must be voluntary; such relationships can be brought into being in one way only, through free agreement.

There are a variety of forms of free agreement but, for reasons which I shall explore below, contract has become paradigmatic of voluntary commitment.

When individuals must freely agree or contract to be governed, the corollary is that they may refuse to be bound. Since the seventeenth century, when doctrines of individual freedom and equality and of contract first became the basis for general theories of social life, conservatives of all kinds have feared that this possibility would become reality and that contract theory would therefore become destructive of social order. Children, servants, wives, peasants, workers, and subjects and citizens in the state would, it was feared, cease to obey their superiors if the bond between them came to be understood as merely conventional or contractual, and thus open to the whim and caprice of voluntary commitment. Conservatives had both cause to be alarmed and very little cause at all. The cause for alarm was that, in principle, it is hard to see why a free and equal individual should have sufficiently good reason to subordinate herself to another. Moreover, in practice, political movements have arisen over the past three centuries that have attempted to replace institutions structured by subordination with institutions constituted by free relationships. However, the anxiety was misplaced, not only because these political movements have rarely been successful, but because the alarm about contract theory was groundless. Rather than undermining subordination, contract theorists justified modern civil subjection.

The classic social contract theorists assumed that individual attributes and social conditions always made it reasonable for an individual to give an affirmative answer to the fundamental question whether a relationship of subordination should be created through contract. The point of the story of the social contract is that, in the state of nature, freedom is so insecure that it is reasonable for individuals to subordinate themselves to the civil law of the state, or, in Rousseau's version, to be subject to themselves collectively, in a participatory political association. The pictures of the state of nature and the stories of the social contract found in the classic texts vary widely, but despite their differences on many important issues, the classic contract theorists have a crucial feature in common. They all tell patriarchal stories.

Contract doctrine entails that there is only one, conventional, origin of political right, yet, except in Hobbes's theory where both sexes are pictured as naturally free and equal, the contract theorists also insist that men's right over women has a natural basis. Men alone have the attributes of free and equal 'individuals'. Relations of subordination between *men* must, if they are to be legitimate, originate in contract. Women are born into subjection. The classic writers were well aware of the significance of the assumptions of contract doctrine for the relation between the sexes. They could take nothing for granted when the premise of their arguments was potentially so subversive of all authority relations, including conjugal relations. The classic pictures of the state of nature take into account that human beings are sexually differentiated. Even in Hobbes's radically individualist version of the natural condition the sexes are distinguished. In contemporary discussions of the state of nature, however, this feature of human life is usually disregarded. The fact that 'individuals' are all of the same sex is never mentioned; attention is focused instead on different conceptions of the masculine 'individual'.

The naturally free and equal (masculine) individuals who people the pages of the social contract theorists are a disparate collection indeed. They cover the spectrum from

Rousseau's social beings to Hobbes's entities reduced to matter in motion, or, more recently, James Buchanan's reduction of individuals to preference and production functions; John Rawls manages to introduce both ends of the spectrum into his version of the contract story. Rousseau criticized his fellow social contract theorists for presenting individuals in the state of nature as lacking all social characteristics, and his criticism has been repeated many times. The attempt to set out the purely natural attributes of individuals is inevitably doomed to fail; all that *is* left if the attempt is consistent enough is a merely physiological, biological, or reasoning entity, not a human being. In order to make their natural beings recognizable, social contract theorists smuggle social characteristics into the natural condition, or their readers supply what is missing. The form of the state or political association that a theorist wishes to justify also influences the 'natural' characteristics that he gives to individuals; as Rawls stated recently, the aim of arguing from an original position, Rawls's equivalent to the state of nature, 'is to get the desired solution.'[2] What is not often recognized, however, is that the 'desired solution' includes the sexual contract and men's patriarchal right over women.

Despite disagreement over what counts as a 'natural' characteristic, features so designated are held to be common to all human beings. Yet almost all the classic writers held that natural capacities and attributes were sexually differentiated. Contemporary contract theorists implicitly follow their example, but this goes unnoticed because they subsume feminine beings under the apparently universal, sexually neuter category of the 'individual'. In the most recent rewriting of the social contract story sexual relations have dropped from view because sexually differentiated individuals have disappeared. In *A Theory of Justice*, the parties in the original position are purely reasoning entities. Rawls follows Kant on this point, and Kant's view of the original contract differs from that of the other classic contract theorists, although (as I shall indicate in chapter 6) in some other respects his arguments resemble theirs. Kant does not offer a story about the origins of political right or suggest that, even hypothetically, an original agreement was once made. Kant is not dealing in this kind of political fiction. For Kant, the original contract is 'merely an *idea* of reason',[3] an idea necessary for an understanding of actual political institutions. Similarly, Rawls writes in his most recent discussion that his own argument 'tries to draw solely upon basic intuitive ideas that are embedded in the political institutions of a constitutional democratic regime and the public traditions of their interpretation.' As an idea of reason, rather than a political fiction, the original contract helps 'us work out what we now think.'[4] If Rawls is to show how free and equal parties, suitably situated, would agree to principles that are (pretty near to) those implicit in existing institutions, the appropriate idea of reason is required. The problem about political right faced by the classic contract theorists has disappeared. Rawls's task is to find a picture of an original position that will confirm 'our' intuitions about existing institutions, which include patriarchal relations of subordination.

Rawls claims that his parties in their original position are completely ignorant of any 'particular facts' about themselves.[5] The parties are free citizens, and Rawls states that their freedom is a 'moral power to form, to revise, and rationally to pursue a conception of the good,' which involves a view of themselves as sources of valid claims and as responsible for their ends. If citizens change their idea of the good, this has no effect on their 'public identity', that is, their juridical standing as civil individuals or citizens. Rawls also states that the original position is a 'device of representation'.[6] But representation is hardly required. As reasoning entities (as Sandel has noticed), the parties are indistinguishable one from another. One party can 'represent' all the rest. In effect, there is only one individual in the original position behind Rawls's 'veil of ignorance'.[7] Rawls can, therefore, state that 'we can view the choice [contract] in the original position from the standpoint of one person selected at random.'[8]

Rawls's parties merely reason and make their choice—or the one party does this as the representative of them all—and so their bodies can be dispensed with. The representative is sexless. The disembodied party who makes the choice cannot know one vital 'particular fact', namely, its sex. Rawls's original position is a logical construction in the most complete sense; it is a realm of pure reason with nothing human in it—except that Rawls, of course, like Kant before him, inevitably introduces real, embodied male and female beings in the course of his argument. Before ignorance of 'particular facts' is postulated, Rawls has already claimed that parties have 'descendants' (for whom they are concerned), and Rawls states that he will generally view the parties as 'heads of families'.[9] He merely takes it for granted that he can, at one and the same time, postulate disembodied parties devoid of all substantive characteristics, and assume that sexual difference exists, sexual intercourse takes place, children are born and families formed. Rawls's participants in the original contract are, simultaneously, mere reasoning entities, and 'heads of families', or men who represent their wives.

Rawls's original position is a logical abstraction of such rigour that nothing happens there. In contrast, the various states of nature pictured by the classic social contract theorists are full of life. They portray the state of nature as a condition that extends over more than one generation. Men and women come together, engage in sexual relations, and women give birth. The circumstances under which they do so, whether conjugal relations exist and whether families are formed, depends on the extent to which the state of nature is portrayed as a social condition. I shall begin with Hobbes, the first contractarian, and his picture of the asocial war of all against all. Hobbes stands at one theoretical pole of contract doctrine and his radical individualism exerts a powerful attraction for contemporary contract theorists. However, several of Hobbes's most important arguments had to be rejected before modern patriarchal theory could be constructed.

For Hobbes, all political power was absolute power, and there was no difference between conquest and contract. Subsequent contract theorists drew a sharp distinction between free agreement and enforced submission and argued that civil political power was limited, constrained by the terms of the original contract, even though the state retained the power of life and death over citizens. Hobbes also saw all contractual relations, including sexual relations, as political, but a fundamental assumption of modern political theory is that sexual relations are not political. Hobbes was too revealing about the civil order to become a founding father of modern patriarchy. As I have already mentioned, Hobbes differs from the other classic contract theorists in his assumption that there is no natural mastery in the state of nature, not even of men over women; natural individual attributes and capacities are distributed irrespective of sex. There is no difference between men and women in their strength or prudence, and all individuals are isolated and mutually wary of each other. It follows that sexual relations can take place only under two circumstances;

either a man and woman mutually agree (contract) to have sexual intercourse, or a man, through some stratagem, is able to overpower a woman and take her by force, though she also has the capacity to retaliate and kill him.

Classic patriarchalism rested on the argument that political right originated naturally in fatherhood. Sons were born subject to their fathers, and political right was paternal right. Hobbes insists that all examples of political right are conventional and that, in the state of nature, political right is maternal not paternal. An infant, necessarily, has two parents ('as to the generation, God hath ordained to man a helper'),[10] but both parents cannot have dominion over the child because no one can obey two masters. In the natural condition the mother, not the father, has political right over the child; 'every woman that bears children, becomes both a *mother* and a *lord*.'[11] At birth, the infant is in the mother's power. She makes the decision whether to expose or to nourish the child. If she decides to 'breed him', the condition on which she does so is that, 'being grown to full age he become not her enemy';[12] that is to say, the infant must contract to obey her. The postulated agreement of the infant is one example of Hobbes's identification of enforced submission with voluntary agreement, one example of his assimilation of conquest and consent. Submission to overwhelming power in return for protection, whether the power is that of the conqueror's sword or the mother's power over her newly born infant, is always a valid sign of agreement for Hobbes: 'preservation of life being the end, for which one man becomes subject to another, every man [or infant] is supposed to promise obedience, to him [or her], in whose power it is to save, or destroy him.'[13] The mother's political right over her child thus originates in contract, and gives her the power of an absolute lord or monarch.

The mother's political power follows from the fact that in Hobbes's state of nature 'there are no matrimonial laws.'[14] Marriage does not exist because marriage is a long-term arrangement, and long-term sexual relationships, like other such relationships, are virtually impossible to establish and maintain in Hobbes's natural condition. His individuals are purely self-interested and, therefore, will always break an agreement, or refuse to play their part in a contract, if it appears in their interest to do so. To enter into a contract or to signify agreement to do so is to leave oneself open to betrayal. Hobbes's natural state suffers from an endemic problem of keeping contracts, of 'performing second'. The only contract that can be entered into safely is one in which agreement and performance take place at the same time. No problem arises if there is a simultaneous exchange of property, including property in the person, as in a single act of coitus. If a child is born as a consequence of the act, the birth occurs a long time later, so the child belongs to the mother. A woman can contract away her right over her child to the father, but there is no reason, given women's natural equality with men, why women should always do this, especially since there is no way of establishing paternity with any certainty. In the absence of matrimonial laws, as Hobbes notes, proof of fatherhood rests on the testimony of the mother. . . .

The 'natural' characteristics with which Hobbes endows his individuals mean that long-term relationships are very unlikely in his state of nature. However, Hobbes states in *Leviathan* that in the war of all against all 'there is no man who can hope by his own strength, or wit, to defend himself from destruction, without the help of confederates.'[15] But how can such a protective confederation be formed in the natural condition when there is an acute problem of keeping agreements? The answer is that confederations are formed by conquest, and, once formed, are called 'families'. Hobbes's 'family' is very peculiar and has nothing in common with the families in Filmer's pages, the family as found in the writings of the other classic social contract theorists, or as conventionally understood today. Consider Hobbes's definition of a 'family'. In *Leviathan* he states that a family 'consists of a man and his children; or of a man and his servants; or of a man, and his children, and servants together; wherein the father or master is the sovereign.'[16] In *De Cive* we find, '*a father* with his *sons* and *servants*, grown into a civil person by virtue of his paternal jurisdiction, is called a *family*.'[17] Only in *Elements of Law* does he write that 'the father or mother of the family is sovereign of the same.'[18] But the sovereign is very unlikely to be the mother, given Hobbes's references to 'man' and 'father' and the necessity of securing patriarchal right in civil society.

If one male individual manages to conquer another in the state of nature the conqueror will have obtained a servant. Hobbes assumes that no one would wilfully give up his life, so, with the conqueror's sword at his breast, the defeated man will make a (valid) contract to obey his victor. Hobbes defines dominion or political right acquired through force as 'the dominion of the master over his servant.'[19] Conqueror and conquered then constitute 'a little body politic, which consisteth of two persons, the one sovereign, which is called the *master*, or lord; the other subject, which is called the *servant*.'[20] Another way of putting the point is that the master and servant are a confederation against the rest, or, according to Hobbes's definition, they are a 'family'. Suppose, however, that a male individual manages to conquer a female individual. To protect her life she will enter into a contract of subjection—and so she, too, becomes the servant of a master, and a 'family' has again been formed,

held together by the 'paternal jurisdiction' of the master, which is to say, his sword, now turned into contract. Hobbes's language is misleading here; the jurisdiction of the master is not 'paternal' in the case of either servant. In an earlier discussion, together with Teresa Brennan, of the disappearance of the wife and mother in Hobbes's definition of the family, we rejected the idea that her status was that of a servant.[21] I now think that we were too hasty. If a man is able to defeat a woman in the state of nature and form a little body politic or a 'family', and if that 'family' is able to defend itself and grow, the conquered woman is subsumed under the status of 'servant'. All servants are subject to the political right of the master. The master is then also master of the woman servant's children; he is master of everything that his servant owns. A master's power over all the members of his 'family' is an absolute power.

In the state of nature, free and equal individuals can become subordinates through conquest—which Hobbes calls contract. But in the state of nature there are no 'wives'. Marriage, and thus husbands and wives, appear only in civil society where the civil law includes the law of matrimony. Hobbes assumes that, in civil society, the subjection of women to men is secured through contract; not an enforced 'contract' this time, but a marriage contract. Men have no need forcibly to overpower women when the civil law upholds their patriarchal political right through the marriage contract. Hobbes states that in civil society the husband has dominion 'because for the most part commonwealths have been erected by the fathers, not by the mothers of families.'[22] Or again, 'in all cities, . . . constituted of *fathers*, not *mothers*, governing their families, the domestical command belongs to the man; and such a contract, if it be made according to the civil laws, is called matrimony.'[23]

There are two implicit assumptions at work here. First, that husbands are civil masters because men ('fathers') have made the original social contract that brings civil law into being. The men who make the original pact ensure that patriarchal political right is secured in civil society. Second, there is only one way in which women, who have the same status as free and equal individuals in the state of nature as men, can be excluded from participation in the social contract. And they must be excluded if the contract is to be sealed; rational, free, and equal women would not agree to a pact that subordinated women to men in civil society. The assumption must necessarily be made that, by the time the social contract is made, all the women in the natural condition have been conquered by men and are now their subjects (servants). If any men have also been subjected and are in servitude, then they, too, will be excluded from the social contract. Only men who stand to each other as free and equal masters of 'families' will take part. . . .

Hobbes is unusual in his openness about the character and scope of political domination or political right in civil society. For Hobbes, the distinction between a civil individual or citizen and an individual in subjection to a master is not that the former is free and the latter bound; 'the subjection of them who institute a commonwealth themselves, is no less absolute, than the subjection of servants.' Rather, the difference is that those who subject themselves to Leviathan (the state) do so because they judge that there is good reason for their action, and so they live in 'a state of better hope' than servants. Their 'hope' arises from the fact that an individual 'coming in freely, calleth himself, though in subjection, a *freeman*,' and in civil society free men have 'the honour of equality of favour with other subjects,' and 'may expect employments of honor, rather than a servant.'[24] Or, as Hobbes puts

the point in another formulation, 'free subjects and sons of a family have above servants in every government and family where servants are; that they may both undergo the more honourable offices of the city or family.'[25] In civil society, Leviathan's sword upholds the civil laws that give individuals protection from forcible subjection, but individuals of their own volition can enter into contracts that constitute 'masters' and 'servants'. Or, more accurately, male individuals can.

In the natural state all women become servants, and all women are excluded from the original pact. That is to say, all women are also excluded from becoming civil individuals. No woman is a free subject. All are 'servants' of a peculiar kind in civil society, namely 'wives'. To be sure, women become wives by entering into a contract, and later I shall explore the puzzle of why beings who lack the status of (civil) individuals who can make contracts nonetheless are required to enter into the marriage contract. The relationship between a husband and wife differs from subjection between men, but it is important to emphasize that Hobbes insists that patriarchal subjection is also an example of *political* right. He stands alone in this. The other classic contract theorists all argue that conjugal right is not, or is not fully, political. . . .

The matter is more straightforward in the state of nature pictured by Locke. Women are excluded from the status of 'individual' in the natural condition. Locke assumes that marriage and the family exist in the natural state and he also argues that the attributes of individuals are sexually differentiated; only men naturally have the characteristics of free and equal beings. Women are naturally subordinate to men and the order of nature is reflected in the structure of conjugal relations. At first sight, however, Locke can appear to be a true anti-patriarchalist—Hinton claims that he 'countered the patriarchalist case almost too effectively'—and he has even been seen as an embryonic feminist.[26] Locke points out more than once that the Fifth Commandment does not refer only to the father of a family. A mother, too, exercises authority over children; the authority is parental not paternal. More strikingly, Locke suggests that a wife can own property in her own right, and he even introduces the possibility of divorce, of a dissoluble marriage contract. When 'Procreation and Education are secured and Inheritance taken care for,' then separation of husband and wife is a possibility; 'there being no necessity in the nature of the thing, nor to the ends of it, that it should always be for Life.' He goes on to say that the liberty that a wife has 'in many cases' to leave her husband illustrates that a husband does not have the power of an absolute monarch.[27]

In civil society, no one enjoys an *absolute* political right, unconstrained by the civil law. The question is not whether a husband is an absolute ruler, but whether he is a ruler at all, and, if he always has a limited (civil) right over his wife, how that comes about. Locke's answer is that conjugal power originates in nature. When arguing with Sir Robert Filmer about Adam and Eve, Locke disagrees about the character of Adam's power over Eve, not that his power exists. The battle is not over the legitimacy of a husband's conjugal right but over what to call it. Locke insists that Adam was not an absolute monarch, so that Eve's subjection was nothing more 'but that Subjection [wives] should ordinarily be in to their Husbands.' We know that wives should be subject, Locke writes, because 'generally the Laws of mankind and customs of Nations have ordered it so; *and there is, I grant, a Foundation in Nature for it.*'[28] The foundation in nature that ensures that the will of the husband and not that of the wife prevails is that the husband is 'the abler and the stronger'.[29] Women, that is to say, are not free

and equal 'individuals' but natural subjects. Once a man and a woman become husband and wife and decisions have to be made, the right to decide, or 'the last Determination, i.e., the Rule,' has to be placed with one or the other (even though Locke's argument against Filmer and Hobbes is designed to show why the rule of one man is incompatible with 'civil' life). Locke states that 'it naturally falls to the Man's share' to govern over their 'common Interest and Property', although a husband's writ runs no further than that.[30]

None of this disturbs Locke's picture of the state of nature as a condition 'wherein all the Power and Jurisdiction is reciprocal, . . . without Subordination or Subjection.' When he states that he will consider 'what State all Men are naturally in,' in order to arrive at a proper understanding of the character of (civil) political power, 'men' should be read literally.[31] The natural subjection of women, which entails their exclusion from the category of 'individual', is irrelevant to Locke's investigation. The subjection of women (wives) to men (husbands) is not an example of political domination and subordination. Locke has already made this clear, both in his argument with Filmer over Adam and Eve in the *First Treatise*, and in his opening statement in chapter I of the *Second Treatise* before he begins his discussion of the state of nature in chapter II. He writes that the power of a father, a master, a lord, and a husband are all different from that of a magistrate, who is a properly political ruler with the power of life and death over his subjects. In the *First Treatise*, Locke claims that Eve's subjection

can be no other Subjection than what every Wife owes her Husband . . . [Adam's] can be only a Conjugal Power, not Political, the Power that every Husband hath to order the things of private Concernment in his Family, as Proprietor of the Goods and Lands there, and to have his Will take place before that of his wife in all things of their common Concernment; but not a Political Power of Life and Death over her, much less over anybody else.[32]

Rousseau, who was critical of so much else in the theories of Hobbes, Pufendorf, and Locke, has no difficulty with their arguments about conjugal right. He maintains that civil order depends on the right of husbands over their wives, which, he argues, arises from nature, from the very different natural attributes of the sexes. Rousseau has much more to say than the other classic social contract theorists about what it is in women's natures that entails that they must be excluded from civil life. He elaborates at some length on the reasons why women 'never cease to be subjected either to a man or to the judgements of men,' and why a husband must be a 'master for the whole of life'.[33] . . .

Several puzzles, anomalies and contradictions, which I shall take up in subsequent chapters, arise from the theoretical manoeuvring of the classic social contract theorists on the question of conjugal right and natural freedom and equality. Perhaps the most obvious puzzle concerns the status of conjugal or sex-right; why, since Hobbes, has it so rarely been seen as an example of political power? In civil society all absolute power is illegitimate (uncivil), so the fact that a husband's right over his wife is not absolute is not sufficient to render his role non-political. On the other hand, a distinguishing feature of civil society is that only the government of the state is held to provide an example of political right. Civil subordination in other 'private' social arenas, whether the economy or the domestic sphere, where subordination is constituted through contract, is declared to be non-political.

There are other difficulties about the origin of conjugal right. The classic contract theorists' arguments about the state of nature contrive to exclude women from participation in the original contract. But what about the marriage contract? If women have been forcibly subjugated by men, or if they naturally lack the capacities of 'individuals', they *also* lack the standing and capacities necessary to enter into the original contract. Yet the social contract theorists insist that women are capable of entering, indeed, must enter, into one contract, namely the marriage contract. Contract theorists simultaneously deny and presuppose that women can make contracts. Nor does Locke, for example, explain why the marriage contract is necessary when women are declared to be naturally subject to men. There are other ways in which a union between a man and his natural subordinate could be established, but, instead, Locke holds that it is brought into being through contract, which is an agreement between two equals.

Nor do the puzzles end once the marriage contract is concluded. Most of the classic social contract theorists present marriage as a natural relationship that is carried over into civil society. Marriage is not unique in this respect, other contractual relations are held to exist in the natural condition. The curious feature of marriage is that it retains a natural status even in civil society. Once the original contract has been made and civil society has been brought into being, the state of nature is left behind and contract should create civil, not natural, relations. Certainly, the relation between employer and worker is seen as civil, as purely contractual or conventional. But marriage must necessarily differ from other contractual relations because an 'individual' and a natural subordinate enter into the contract, not two 'individuals'. Moreover, when the state of nature is left behind, the meaning of 'civil' society is not independently given, but depends upon the contrast with the 'private' sphere, in which marriage is the central relationship.

Notes

1. A. Rich, 'Compulsory Heterosexuality and Lesbian Existence,' *Signs* 5, no. 4 (1980): 645.
2. J. Rawls, *A Theory of Justice* (Cambridge, MA: Harvard University Press, 1971), 141.
3. I. Kant, *Political Writings*, ed. H. Reiss (Cambridge: Cambridge University Press, 1970), 79.
4. J. Rawls, 'Justice as Fairness: Political Not Metaphysical,' *Philosophy and Public Affairs* 14, no. 3 (1985): 225, 238.
5. Rawls, *Theory of Justice*, 137–8.
6. Rawls, 'Justice as Fairness,' 241, 236.
7. M. Sandel, *Liberalism and the Limits of Justice* (Cambridge: Cambridge University Press, 1982), 131.
8. Rawls, *Theory of Justice*, 139.
9. Ibid., 128.
10. T. Hobbes, 'Leviathan,' in *The English Works of Thomas Hobbes of Malmesbury* (hereafter *EW*) (T. Germany: Scientia Verlag Aalen, 1966), vol. 3, chap. 20, 186.
11. T. Hobbes, 'Philosophical Rudiments concerning Government and Society' (the English version of *De Cive*), EW, vol. 2, chap. 9, 116.
12. Ibid., chap. 9, 116.
13. Hobbes, 'Leviathan,' chap. 20, 188.
14. Ibid., 187.
15. Ibid., chap. 15, 133.
16. Ibid., chap. 20, 191.
17. Hobbes, 'Philosophical Rudiments,' chap. 9, 121.
18. Hobbes, 'De Corpore Politico,' chap. 4, 158.
19. Hobbes, 'Leviathan,' chap. 20, 189.
20. Hobbes, 'De Corpore Politico,' chap. 3, 149–50.
21. T. Brennan and C. Pateman, '" Mere Auxiliaries to the Commonwealth": Women and the Origins of Liberalism,' *Political Studies* 27, no. 2 (1979): 189–90. I was prompted to look at this again by J. Zvesper, 'Hobbes' Individualistic Analysis of the Family,' 'family' in the state of nature as like a 'family' in civil society, despite the absence of 'matrimonial laws'.
22. Hobbes, 'Leviathan,' chap. 15, 187.
23. Hobbes, 'Philosophical Rudiments,' chap. 9, 118.
24. Hobbes, 'De Corpore Politico,' chap. 4, 157–8.
25. Hobbes, 'Philosophical Rudiments,' chap. 9, 121.
26. Hinton, 'Husband, Fathers and Conquerors,' 66; and M.A. Butler, 'Early Liberal Roots of Feminism: John Locke and the Attack on Patriarchy,' *American Political Science Review* 72, 1 (1978): 135–50.
27. J. Locke, *Two Treatises of Government*, 2nd edn, ed. P. Laslett (Cambridge: Cambridge University Press, 1967), II, 183, II, 81–2.
28. Ibid., I, 47.
29. Ibid., II, 82.
30. Ibid.
31. Ibid., 4.
32. Ibid., I, 48.
33. J.-J. Rousseau, *Emile or on Education*, translated by A. Bloom (New York: Basic Books, 1979), 370, 404. In *The Problem of Political Obligation*, I argued that the form of Rousseau's original pact meant that it was not a 'contract'. Rousseau is, however, the leading theorist of the original sexual contract, which certainly is a contract. So, without implying that I have changed my mind about my previous interpretation (which is not the case), I shall refer to Rousseau here as a 'classic contract theorist'.

Study Questions for *The Sexual Contract*

1. According to Pateman, why is it important to study the writings of social contract theorists?
2. In chapter 3, Pateman discusses the revolutionary character of the contractarian doctrine of natural freedom and equality among human beings. How did this doctrine revolutionize political thought in the modern era? Why did conservatives fear that this doctrine would disrupt existing social orders?
3. How are problematic assumptions about gender manifested in the theories of Hobbes, Locke, Rousseau, and Rawls, according to Pateman? How do these theorists differ in their assumptions about men and women?
4. In your view, are the sexist assumptions identified by Pateman essential to the social and political philosophies of Hobbes, Locke, Rousseau, or Rawls?
5. Review the accounts of human nature (given in stories about human beings living in a state of nature) in the theories of Hobbes, Locke, and Rousseau. Are the hypothetical individuals in the state of nature in fact masculine beings?

Recommended Readings

Clark, Beverley, *Misogyny in the Western Philosophical Tradition* (Routledge, 1999).

Deutscher, Penelope, *Yielding Gender: Feminism, Deconstruction and the History of Philosophy* (Routledge, 1997).

Di Stefano, Christine, *Configurations of Masculinity: A Feminist Perspective on Modern Political Theory* (Cornell University Press, 1991).

Elshtain, Jean Bethke, *Public Man, Private Woman: Women in Social and Political Thought*, 2nd edn (Princeton University Press, 1993).

Held, Virginia, *Feminist Morality: Transforming Culture, Society and Politics* (University of Chicago Press, 1993).

Landes, Joan, *Feminism: The Public and the Private* (Oxford University Press, 1998).

Nussbaum, Martha C., 'Rawls and Feminism' in *The Cambridge Companion to Rawls*, edited by Samuel Freeman (Cambridge University Press, 2003).

Zack, Naomi, Laurie Shrage, and Crispin Sartwell, eds, *Race, Class, Gender and Sexuality* (Blackwell Publishers, 1998).

Charles Mills

Charles W. Mills earned his PhD in philosophy from the University of Toronto and is currently the John Evans Professor of Moral and Intellectual Philosophy at Northwestern University. He specializes in critical race theory, African-American philosophy, and social and political philosophy; within these areas, he works particularly on Marxist social theory and on issues pertaining to race, gender, and class. His first book, *The Racial Contract* (1997), won academic accolades for its groundbreaking critique of classical contractarian theory and mainstream political philosophy. In the past two decades, Mills has delivered over two hundred presentations and public addresses on race, class, and gender in philosophy. He is also author of *Blackness Visible: Essays on Philosophy and Race* (1998), *From Class to Race: Essays in White Marxism and Black Radicalism* (2003), *Contract and Domination* (with Carole Pateman, 2007), and *Radical Theory, Caribbean Reality: Race, Class and Social Domination* (2008).

In *The Racial Contract*, Mills offers both a model for understanding racial domination and a critical race analysis of social contract theorists from Hobbes to Kant. In the modern philosophical era, contractarian social and political philosophers have emphasized the values of equality, rights, and autonomy among all individuals at the same time that they implicitly or explicitly have excluded non-white peoples from moral and political personhood. The state of nature in classical contractarian theory, for example, is populated by non-white savages or 'idle Indians' who fail to demonstrate human industriousness and rationality in appropriating and transforming nature; the creation of a society from a state of savage wilderness and idle wasteland requires the intervention of white men. Mills argues further that although the terms of the social contract have now been formally extended to all peoples, the legacies of the racial contract remain largely ignored in contemporary mainstream political philosophy. In recent years, a minority of philosophers have begun to grapple seriously with racism, shifting away from abstract theories of justice towards developing anti-racist political-philosophical theory.

The Racial Contract

Introduction

White supremacy is the unnamed political system that has made the modern world what it is today. You will not find this term in introductory, or even advanced, texts in political theory. A standard undergraduate political philosophy course will start off with Plato and Aristotle, perhaps say something about Augustine, Aquinas, and Machiavelli, move on to Hobbes, Locke, Mill, and Marx, and then wind up with Rawls and Nozick. It will introduce you to notions of aristocracy, democracy, absolutism, liberalism, representative government, socialism, property-owning democracy, and libertarianism. But though it covers more than two thousand years of Western political thought and runs the ostensible gamut of political systems, there will be no mention of the basic political system that has shaped the world for the past several hundred years. And this omission is not accidental. Rather, it reflects the fact that standard textbooks and courses have for the most part been written and designed by whites, who take their racial privilege so much for granted that they do not even see it as *political*, as a form of domination. Ironically, the most important political system of recent global history—the system of domination by which white people have historically ruled over, and, in certain important ways, continue to rule over nonwhite people—is not seen as a political system at all. It is just taken for granted; it is the background against which other systems, which we *are* to see as political, are highlighted. This book is an attempt to redirect your vision, to make you see what, in a sense, has been there all along.

Philosophy has remained remarkably untouched by the debates over multiculturalism, canon reform, and ethnic diversity wracking the academy; both demographically and conceptually, it is one of the 'whitest' of the humanities. Blacks, for example, constitute only about 1 per cent of philosophers in North American universities—a hundred or so people out of more than ten thousand—and there are even fewer Latino, Asian-American, and Native American philosophers.[1] Surely this under-representation itself stands in need of an explanation, and in my opinion it can be traced in part to a conceptual array and a standard repertoire of concerns whose abstractness typically elides, rather than genuinely includes, the experience of racial minorities. Since (white) women have the demographic advantage of numbers, there are of course far more female philosophers in the profession than nonwhite philosophers (though still not proportionate to women's percentage of the population), and they have made far greater progress in developing alternative conceptualizations. Those African-American philosophers who do work in moral and political theory tend either to produce general work indistinguishable from that of their white peers or to focus on local issues (affirmative action, the black 'underclass') or historical figures (W.E.B. DuBois, Alain Locke) in a way that does not aggressively engage the broader debate.

What is needed is a global theoretical framework for situating discussions of race and white racism, and thereby challenging the assumptions of white political philosophy, which would correspond to feminist theorists' articulation of the centrality of gender, patriarchy, and sexism to traditional moral and political theory. What is needed, in other words, is a recognition that racism (or, as I will argue, global white supremacy) is *itself* a political system, a particular power structure of formal or informal rule, socio-economic privilege, and norms for the differential distribution of material wealth and opportunities, benefits and burdens, rights and duties. The notion of the Racial Contract is, I suggest, one possible way of making this connection with mainstream theory, since it uses the vocabulary and apparatus already developed for contractarianism to map this unacknowledged system.[2] Contract talk is, after all, the political lingua franca of our times.

We all understand the idea of a 'contract', an agreement between two or more people to do something. The 'social contract' just extends this idea. If we think of human beings as starting off in a 'state of nature', it suggests that they then *decide* to establish civil society and a government. What we have, then, is a theory that founds government on the popular consent of individuals taken as equals.[3]

But the peculiar contract to which I am referring, though based on the social contract tradition that has been central to Western political theory, is not a contract among everybody ('we the people') but among just the people who count, the people who really are people ('we the white people'). So it is a Racial Contract.

The social contract, whether in its original or in its contemporary version, constitutes a powerful set of lenses for looking at society and the government. But in its obfuscation of the ugly realities of group power and domination, it is, if unsupplemented, a profoundly misleading account of the way the modern world actually is and came to be. The 'Racial Contract' as a theory—I use quotation marks to indicate when I am talking about the theory of the Racial Contract, as against the Racial Contract itself—will explain that the Racial Contract is real, and that apparent racist violations of the terms of the social contract in fact *uphold* the terms of the Racial Contract.

The 'Racial Contract', then, is intended as a conceptual bridge between two areas now largely segregated from each other: on the one hand, the world of mainstream (i.e., white) ethics and political philosophy, preoccupied with discussions of justice and right in the (idealized) abstract, on the other hand, the world of Native American, African-American, and Third and Fourth World[4] political thought, historically focused on issues of conquest, imperialism, colonialism, white settlement, land rights, race and racism, slavery, Jim Crow, reparations, apartheid, cultural authenticity, national identity, *indigenismo*, Afrocentrism, etc. These issues hardly appear in mainstream political philosophy,[5] but they have been central to the political struggles of the majority of the world's population. Their absence from what is considered serious philosophy is a reflection not of their lack of seriousness but of the colour of the vast majority of Western academic philosophers (and perhaps *their* lack of seriousness).

The great virtue of traditional social contact theory was that it provided seemingly straightforward answers both to factual questions about the origins and workings of society and government and to normative questions about the justification of socio-economic structures and political institutions. Moreover, the 'contract' was very versatile, depending on how different theorists viewed the state of nature, human motivation, the rights and liberties people gave up or retained, the particular details of the agreement, and the resulting character of the government. In the modern Rawlsian version of the contract, this flexibility continues to be illustrated, since Rawls dispenses with the historical claims of classic contractarianism, and focuses instead on the justification of the basic structure of a 'well-ordered' society.[6]

From its 1650–1800 heyday as a grand quasi-anthropological account of the origins and development of society and the state, the contract has now become just a normative tool, a conceptual device to elicit our intuitions about justice.

But my usage is different. The 'Racial Contract' I employ is in a sense more in keeping with the spirit of the classic contractarians—Hobbes, Locke, and Rousseau.[7] I use it not merely normatively, to generate judgments about social justice and injustice, but descriptively, to *explain* the actual genesis of the society and the state, the way society is structured, the way the government functions, and people's moral psychology.[8] The most famous case in which the contract is used to explain a manifestly *non*-ideal society, what would be termed in current philosophical jargon a 'naturalized' account, is Rousseau's *Discourse on Inequality* (1755). Rousseau argues that technological development in the state of nature brings into existence a nascent society of growing divisions in wealth between rich and poor, which are then consolidated and made permanent by a deceitful 'social contract'.[9] Whereas the ideal contract explains how a just society would be formed, ruled by a moral government, and regulated by a defensible moral code, this *non*-ideal/naturalized contract explains how an unjust, *exploitative* society, ruled by an *oppressive* government, and regulated by an *immoral* code, comes into existence. If the ideal contract is to be endorsed and emulated, this non-ideal/naturalized contract is to be demystified and condemned. So the point of analysing the non-ideal contract is not to ratify it, but to use it to explain and expose the inequities of the actual non-ideal polity and to help us to see through the theories and moral justifications offered in defence of them. It gives us a kind of X-ray vision into the real internal logic of the socio-political system. Thus it does normative work for us not through its own values, which are detestable, but by enabling us to understand the polity's actual history and how these values and concepts have functioned to rationalize oppression, so as to reform them.

Carole Pateman's provocative 1988 feminist work, *The Sexual Contract*, is a good example of this approach (and the inspiration for my own book, though my use is somewhat different), which demonstrates how much descriptive/explanatory life there still is in the contract.[10] Pateman uses it naturalistically, as a way of modelling the internal dynamic of the non-ideal male-dominated societies that actually exist today. So this is, as indicated, a reversion to the original 'anthropological' approach in which the contract *is* intended to be historically explanatory. But the twist is, of course, that her purpose is now subversive: to excavate the hidden, unjust male covenant upon which the ostensibly gender-neutral social contract actually rests. By looking at Western society and its prevailing political and moral ideologies as if they were based on an unacknowledged 'Sexual Contract', Pateman offers a 'conjectural history' that reveals and exposes the normative logic that makes sense of the inconsistencies, circumlocutions, and evasions of the classic contract theorists and, correspondingly, the world of patriarchal domination their work has helped to rationalize.

My aim here is to adopt a non-ideal contract as a rhetorical trope and theoretical method for understanding the inner logic of *racial* domination and how it structures the polities of the West and elsewhere. The ideal 'social contract' has been a central concept of Western political theory for understanding and evaluating the social world. And concepts are crucial to cognition: cognitive scientists point out that they help us to categorize, learn, remember, infer, explain, problem-solve, generalize, analogize.[11] Correspondingly, the *lack* of appropriate concepts can hinder learning, interfere with memory, block inferences, obstruct explanation, and perpetuate problems. I am suggesting, then, that as a central concept the notion of a Racial Contract might be more revealing of the real character of the world we are living in, and the corresponding historical deficiencies of its normative theories and practices, than the raceless notions currently dominant in political theory.[12] Both at the primary level of an alternative conceptualization of the facts, and at the secondary (reflexive) level of a critical analysis of the orthodox theories themselves, the 'Racial Contract' enables us to engage with mainstream Western political theory to bring in race. Insofar as contractarianism is thought of as a useful way to do political philosophy, to theorize about how the polity was created and what values should guide our prescriptions for making it more just, it is obviously crucial to understand what the original and continuing 'contract' actually was and is, so that we can correct for it in constructing the ideal 'contract'. The 'Racial Contract' should therefore be enthusiastically welcomed by white contract theorists as well.

So this book can be thought of as resting on three simple claims: the existential claim—white supremacy, both local and global, exists and has existed for many years; the conceptual claim—white supremacy should be thought of as itself a political system; the methodological claim—as a political system, white supremacy can illuminatingly be theorized as being based on a 'contract' among whites, a Racial Contract.

Here, then, are ten theses on the Racial Contract, divided into three chapters.

Chapter 1

Overview

I will start with an overview of the Racial Contract, highlighting its differences from, as well as its similarities to, the classical and contemporary social contract. The Racial Contract is political, moral, and epistemological; the Racial Contract is real; and economically, in determining who gets what, the Racial Contract is an exploitation contract.

Thesis #1: The Racial Contract is political, moral, and epistemological.

The 'social contract' is actually several contracts in one. Contemporary contractarians usually distinguish, to begin with, between the *political* contract and the *moral* contract, before going on to make (subsidiary) distinctions within both. I contend, however, that the orthodox social contract also tacitly presupposes an 'epistemological' contract, and that for the Racial Contract it is crucial to make this explicit.

The political contract is an account of the origins of government and our political obligations to it. The subsidiary distinction sometimes made in the political contract is between the contract to establish *society* (thereby taking 'natural', pre-social individuals out of the state of nature and reconstructing and constituting them as members of a collective body), and the contract to establish the *state* (thereby transferring outright or delegating in a relationship of trust the rights and powers we have in the state of nature to a sovereign governing entity).[13] The moral contract, on the other hand, is the foundation of the moral code established for the society, by which the citizens are supposed to regulate their behaviour. The subsidiary distinction here is between two interpretations (to be discussed) of the relationship between the moral contract and state-of-nature morality. In modern versions of the contract, most notably Rawls's of course, the political contract largely vanishes, modern anthropology having long superseded the naive social origin histories of the classic contractarians. The focus is then almost exclusively on the moral contract. This is not conceived of as an actual historical event that took place on leaving the state of nature. Rather, the state of nature survives only in the attenuated form of what Rawls calls the 'original position', and the 'contract' is a purely hypothetical exercise (a thought experiment) in establishing what a just 'basic structure' would be, with a schedule of rights, duties, and liberties that shapes citizens' moral psychology, conceptions of the right, notions of self-respect, etc.[14]

Now the Racial Contract—and the 'Racial Contract' as a theory, that is, the distanced, critical examination of the Racial Contract—follows the classical model in being both socio-political and moral. It explains how society was created or crucially transformed, how the individuals in that society were reconstituted, how the state was established, and how a particular moral code and a certain moral psychology were brought into existence. (As I have emphasized, the 'Racial Contract' seeks to account for the way things are and how they came to be that way—the descriptive—as well as the way they should be—the normative—since indeed one of its complaints about white political philosophy is precisely its otherworldliness, its ignoring of basic political realities.) But the Racial Contract, as we will see, is also epistemological, prescribing norms for cognition to which its signatories must adhere. A preliminary characterization would run something like this:

The Racial Contract is that set of formal or informal agreements or meta-agreements (higher-level contracts about contracts, which set the limits of the contracts' validity) among the members of one subset of humans, henceforth designated by (shifting) 'racial' (phenotypical/genealogical/cultural) criteria W_1, W_2, W_3 . . . as 'white', and coextensive (making due allowance for gender differentiation) with the class of full persons, to categorize the remaining subset of humans as 'nonwhite', and of a different and inferior moral status, subpersons, so that they have a subordinate civil standing in the white or white-ruled polities the whites either already inhabit or establish or in transactions as aliens with these polities, and the moral and juridical rules normally regulating the behaviour of whites in their dealing with one another either do not apply at all in dealings with nonwhites or apply only in a qualified form (depending in part on changing historical circumstances and what particular variety of nonwhite is involved), but in any case the general purpose of the Contract is always the differential privileging of the whites as a group with respect to the nonwhites as a group, the exploitation of their bodies, land, and resources, and the denial of equal socioeconomic opportunities to them. All whites are beneficiaries of the Contract, though some whites are not signatories to it.[15]

It will be obvious, therefore, that the Racial Contract is not a contract to which the nonwhite subset of humans can be a genuinely consenting party (though, depending again on the circumstances, it may sometimes be politic to pretend that this is the case). Rather, it is a contract among those categorized as white over the nonwhites, who are thus the objects rather than the subjects of the agreement.

The logic of the classic social contract, political, moral, and epistemological, then undergoes a corresponding refraction, with shifts, accordingly, in the key terms and principles.

Politically, the contract to establish society and the government, thereby transforming abstract raceless 'men' from denizens of the state of nature into social creatures who are politically obligated to a neutral state, becomes the founding of a *racial polity*, whether white settler states (where pre-existing populations already are or can be made sparse) or what are sometimes called 'sojourner colonies', the establishment of a white presence and colonial rule over existing societies (which are somewhat more populous, or whose inhabitants are more resistant to being made sparse). In addition, the colonizing mother country is also changed by its relation to these new polities, so that its own citizens are altered.

In the social contract, the crucial human metamorphosis is from 'natural' man to 'civil/political' man, from the resident of the state of nature to the citizen of the created society. This change can be more or less extreme, depending on the theorist involved. For Rousseau it is a dramatic transformation, by which animal-like creatures of appetite and instinct become citizens bound by justice and self-prescribed laws. For Hobbes it is a somewhat more laid-back affair by which people who look out primarily for themselves learn to constrain their self-interest for their own good.[16] But in all cases the original 'state of nature' supposedly indicates the condition of *all* men, and the social metamorphosis affects them all in the same way.

In the Racial Contract, by contrast, the crucial metamorphosis is the preliminary conceptual partitioning and corresponding transformation of human populations into 'white' and 'nonwhite' men. The role played by the 'state of nature' then becomes radically different. In the white settler state, its role is not primarily to demarcate the (temporarily) pre-political state of 'all' men, but rather the permanently pre-political state, or, perhaps better, *non*-political state (insofar as 'pre-' suggests eventual internal movement toward), of nonwhite men. The establishment of society thus implies the denial that a society already existed; the creation of society *requires* the intervention of white men, who are thereby positioned as *already* socio-political beings. White men who are (definitionally) already part of society encounter nonwhites who are not, who are 'savage' residents of a state of nature characterized in terms of wildness, jungle, wasteland. These savages the white men bring partially into society as subordinate citizens or exclude on reservations or deny the existence of or exterminate. In the colonial case, admittedly pre-existing but (for one reason or another) deficient societies (decadent, stagnant, corrupt) are taken over and run for the 'benefit' of the nonwhite natives, who are deemed childlike, incapable of self-rule and handling their own affairs, and thus appropriately wards of the state. Here the natives are usually characterized as 'barbarians' rather than 'savages', their state of nature being somewhat farther away (though not, of course, as remote and lost in the past—if it ever existed in the first place—as the Europeans' state of nature). But in times of crisis the conceptual distance between the two, barbarian and savage, will tend to shrink or collapse, for this technical distinction within the nonwhite population is vastly less important than the *central* distinction between whites and nonwhites.

In both cases, then, though in different ways, the Racial Contract establishes a racial polity, a racial state, and a racial juridical system, where the status of whites and nonwhites is clearly demarcated, whether by law or custom. And the purpose of this state, by contrast with the neutral state of classic contractarianism, is, inter alia, specifically to maintain and reproduce this racial order, securing the privileges and advantages of the full white citizens and maintaining the subordination of nonwhites. Correspondingly, the 'consent' expected of the white citizens is in part conceptualized as a consent, whether explicit or tacit, to the racial order, to white supremacy, what could be called Whiteness. To the extent that those phenotypically/genealogically/culturally categorized as white fail to live up to the civic and political responsibilities of Whiteness, they are in dereliction of their duties as citizens. From the inception, then, race is in no way an 'afterthought', a 'deviation' from ostensibly raceless Western ideals, but rather a central shaping constituent of those ideals. . . .

Chapter 2

Details

Thesis #6: The Racial Contract underwrites the modern social contract and is continually being rewritten.

Radical feminists argue that the oppression of women is the oldest oppression. Racial oppression is much more recent. Whereas relations between the sexes necessarily go back to the origin of the species, an intimate and central relationship between Europe as a collective entity and non-Europe, 'white and nonwhite' races, is a phenomenon of the *modern* epoch. There is ongoing scholarly controversy over the existence and extent of racism in antiquity ('racism' as a complex of ideas, that is, as against a developed politico-economic system), with some writers, such as Frank Snowden, finding a period 'before color prejudice', in which blacks are obviously seen as equals, and others claiming that Greek and Roman bigotry

against blacks was there from the beginning.[17] But obviously, whatever the disagreement on this point, it would have to be agreed that the ideology of modern racism is far more theoretically developed than ancient or medieval prejudices and is linked (whatever one's view, idealist or materialist, of causal priority) to a system of European domination.

Nevertheless, this divergence does imply that different accounts of the Racial Contract are possible. The account I favour conceives the Racial Contract as creating not merely racial exploitation, but *race itself* as a group identity. In a contemporary vocabulary, the Racial Contract 'constructs' race. (For other accounts, for example more essentialist ones, racial self-identification would *precede* the drawing up of the Racial Contract.) 'White' people do not pre-exist but are brought into existence *as* 'whites' by the Racial Contract—hence the peculiar transformation of the human population that accompanies this contract. The white race is *invented*, and one becomes 'white by law'.[18]

In this framework, then, the golden age of contract theory (1650 to 1800) overlapped with the growth of a European capitalism whose development was stimulated by the voyages of exploration that increasingly gave the contract a *racial* subtext. The evolution of the modern version of the contract, characterized by an anti-patriarchalist Enlightenment liberalism, with its proclamation of the equal rights, autonomy, and freedom of all men, thus took place simultaneously with the massacre, expropriation, and subjection to hereditary slavery of men at least apparently human. This contradiction needs to be reconciled; it is reconciled through the Racial Contract, which essentially denies their personhood, and restricts the terms of the egalitarian social contract to whites. 'To invade and dispossess the people of an unoffending civilized country would violate morality and transgress the principles of international law,' writes Francis Jennings, 'but savages were exceptional. Being uncivilized by definition, they were outside the sanctions of both morality and law.'[19] The *Racial* Contract thus becomes the truth of the *social* contract.

There is some direct evidence of this link in the writings of the classic contract theorists themselves. That is, it is not merely a matter of hypothetical intellectual reconstruction on my part, arguing from silence that 'men' must have meant 'white men'. Already Hugo Grotius, whose early seventeenth-century work on natural law provided the crucial theoretical background for later contractarians, gives, as Robert Williams has pointed out, the ominous judgment that for 'barbarians', 'wild beasts rather than men, one may rightly say . . . that the most just war is against savage beasts, the next against men who are like beasts.'[20] But let us just focus on the four most important contract theorists: Hobbes, Locke, Rousseau, and Kant.[21]

Consider, to begin with, Hobbes's notoriously bestial state of nature, a state of war where life is 'nasty, brutish, and short'. On a superficial reading, it might seem that it is non-racial, equally applicable to everybody, but note what he says when considering the objection that 'there was never such a time, nor condition of warre as this.' He replies: 'I believe it was never generally so, over all the world: but there are many places, where they live so now,' his example being 'the savage people in many places of *America*.'[22] So a nonwhite people, indeed the very nonwhite people upon whose land his fellow-Europeans were then encroaching—and with whom Hobbes was involved through the Virginia Company—is his only real-life example of people in a state of nature. (And in fact, Richard Ashcraft has pointed out that the

phrasing and terminology of Hobbes's characterization may well have been derived directly from the writings of contemporaries about settlement in the Americas. The 'explorer' Walter Raleigh described a civil war as 'a state of War, which is the meer state of Nature of Men out of community, where all have an equal right to all things.' And two other authors of the time characterized the inhabitants of the Americas as 'people [who] lived like wild beasts, without religion, nor government, nor town, nor houses, without cultivating the land, nor clothing their bodies' and 'people living yet as the first men, without letters, without lawes, without Kings, without common wealthes, without arts . . . not civil by nature.')[23]

In the next paragraph, Hobbes goes on to argue that 'though there had never been any time, wherein particular men were in a condition of warre one against another,' there is 'in all times' a state of 'continuall jealousies' between kings and persons of sovereign authority. He presumably emphasizes this contention in order for the reader to imagine what would happen in the absence of a 'common Power to feare'.[24] But the text is confusing. How could it simultaneously be the case that 'there had never been' any such literal state-of-nature war, when in the previous paragraph he had just said that some people *were* living like that now? As a result of this ambiguity, Hobbes has been characterized as a literal contractarian by some commentators and as a hypothetical contractarian by others. But I think this minor mystery can be cleared up once we recognize that there is a tacit, incipiently racial logic in the text: the *literal* state of nature is reserved for a nonwhite people; for whites the state of nature is *hypothetical*. The conflict between whites is the conflict between those with *sovereigns*, that is, those who are already (and have always been) in society. From this conflict, one can extrapolate (gesturing at the racial abyss, so to speak) to what might happen in the absence of a ruling sovereign. But really we know that whites are too rational to allow this to happen to *them*. So the most notorious state of nature in the contractarian literature—the bestial war of all against all—is really a nonwhite figure, a racial object lesson for the more rational whites, whose superior grasp of natural law (here in its prudential rather than altruistic version) will enable them to take the necessary steps to avoid it and not to behave as 'savages'.

Hobbes has standardly been seen as an awkwardly transitional writer, caught between feudal absolutism and the rise of parliamentarianism, who uses the contract now classically associated with the emergence of liberalism to defend absolutism. But it might be argued that he is transitional in another way, in that in mid-seventeenth-century Britain the imperial project was not yet so fully developed that the intellectual apparatus of racial subordination had been completely elaborated. Hobbes remains enough of a racial egalitarian that, while singling out Native Americans for his real-life example, he suggests that without a sovereign *even Europeans* could descend to their state, and that the absolutist government appropriate for nonwhites could also be appropriate for whites.[25] The uproar that greeted his work can be seen as attributable at least in part to this moral/political suggestion. The spread of colonialism would consolidate an intellectual world in which this bestial state of nature would be reserved for nonwhite savages, to be despotically governed, while civil Europeans would enjoy the benefits of liberal parliamentarianism. *The Racial Contract began to rewrite the social contract.*

One can see this transition more clearly by the time of Locke, whose state of nature is normatively regulated by traditional (altruistic, non-prudential) natural law. It is a moralized state of nature in which private property and money exist, indeed a state of nature that is virtually civil. Whites can thus be literally in this state of nature (for a brief period, anyway) without its calling into question their innate qualities. Locke famously argues that God gave the world 'to the use of the Industrious and Rational,' which qualities were indicated by labour. So while industrious and rational Englishmen were toiling away at home, in America, by contrast, one found 'wild woods and uncultivated wast[e] . . . left to Nature' by the idle Indians.[26] Though whites share the state of nature for a time with nonwhites, then, their residence is necessarily briefer, since whites, by appropriating and adding value to this natural world, exhibit their superior rationality. So the mode of appropriation of Native Americans is no real mode of appropriation at all, yielding property rights that can be readily overridden (if they exist at all), and thereby rendering their territories normatively open for seizure once those who have long since *left* the state of nature (Europeans) encounter them. Locke's thesis was in fact to be the central pillar of the expropriation contract—'the principal philosophical delineation of the normative arguments supporting white civilization's conquest of America,' writes Williams[27] —and not merely in the United States but later in the other white settler states in Africa and the Pacific. Aboriginal economies did not improve the land and thus could be regarded as non-existent.

The practice, and arguably also the theory, of Locke played a role in the slavery contract also. In the *Second Treatise*, Locke defends slavery resulting from a just war, for example, a defensive war against aggression. But this would hardly be an accurate characterization of European raiding parties seeking African slaves, and in any case, in the same chapter

Locke explicitly opposes hereditary slavery and the enslavement of wives and children.[28] Yet Locke had earlier had investments in the slave-trading Royal African Company, and assisted in writing the slave constitution of Carolina. So one could argue that the Racial Contract manifests itself here in an astonishing inconsistency, which could, however, be simply resolved by the supposition that Locke saw blacks as inferior humans and thus as subject to a different set of normative rules.[29]

Rousseau's writings might seem to be something of an exception. After all, it is with his work that the notion of the 'noble savage' is associated (though the phrase is not actually his own). And in the *Discourse on Inequality*'s reconstruction of the origins of society, everybody is envisaged as having been in the state of nature (and thus to have been 'savage') at one time or another. But a careful reading of the text reveals, once again, crucial racial distinctions. The only natural savages cited are *nonwhite* savages, examples of European savages being restricted to reports of feral children raised by wolves and bears, child-rearing practices (we are told) comparable to those of Hottentots and Caribs.[30] (Europeans are so intrinsically civilized that it takes upbringing by animals to turn *them* into savages.) For Europe, savagery is in the dim distant past, since metallurgy and agriculture are the inventions leading to civilization, and it turns out that 'one of the best reasons why Europe, if not the earliest to be civilized, has been at least more continuously and better civilized than other parts of the world, is perhaps that it is at once the richest in iron and the most fertile in wheat.' By contrast: 'Both metallurgy and agriculture were unknown to the savages of America, who have always therefore remained savages.'[31] So even what might initially seem to be a more open environmental determinism, which would open the door to racial

egalitarianism rather than racial hierarchy, degenerates into massive historical amnesia and factual misrepresentation, driven by the presuppositions of the Racial Contract.

Moreover, to make the obvious point, even if some of Rousseau's nonwhite savages are 'noble', physically and psychologically healthier than the Europeans of the degraded and corrupt society produced by the real-life bogus contract, they are still *savages*. Leaving the state of nature, as Rousseau argues in *The Social Contract*, his later account of an ideal polity, is necessary for us to become fully human moral agents, beings capable of justice.[32] So the praise for nonwhite savages is a limited paternalistic praise, in no way to be taken to imply their equality, let alone superiority, to the civilized Europeans of the ideal polity. The underlying racial dichotomization and hierarchy of civilized and savage remains quite clear.

Textual silence also speaks loudly. In his critique of the darknesses of the French Enlightenment, political theorist Louis Sala-Molins points out the evasions in *The Social Contract*'s supposedly principled condemnation of *all* slavery: 'Rousseau, who resolutely condemned classical slavery, did not notice that the slave trade and the ordeal of Negroes in the Caribbean raised a philosophical problem. . . . I challenge anyone to find and show me the smallest little line where Rousseau condemns the kidnapping of Africans and their enslavement in the Antilles. It does not exist.' The indictment of ancient Greek and Roman slavery was one thing; the indictment of the contemporary enslavement of Africans was apparently another. Indeed the most famous contemporary codification and juridification of slavery was to be found precisely in the French *Code Noir*. Yet, as Sala-Molins emphasizes, the startling fact is that *Rousseau never mentions it in his writing*, focusing exclusively instead on the slavery of the ancient world: 'The Greek or Roman slave can serve as a term of comparison. . . . The Negro slave, the Negro, naturally a slave, does not fit the criteria of the comparable.'[33] In Susan Buck-Morss's summary: '[Rousseau] declared all men equal and saw private property as the source of inequality, but he never put two and two together to discuss French slavery for economic profit as central to arguments of both equality and property.'[34] So which 'men' was he really talking about?

Finally, Kant's version of the social contract is in a sense the best illustration of the grip of the Racial Contract on Europeans, since by this time the actual contract and the historical dimension of contractarianism had apparently vanished altogether. So here if anywhere, one would think—in this world of abstract persons, demarcated as such only by their rationality—race would have become irrelevant. But as Emmanuel Eze has demonstrated in great detail, this orthodox picture is radically misleading, and the nature of Kantian 'persons' and the Kantian 'contract' must really be rethought.[35] For it turns out that Kant, widely regarded as the most important moral theorist of the modern period, in a sense the father of modern moral theory, and—through the work of John Rawls and Jürgen Habermas—increasingly central to modern political philosophy as well, is *also* the father of the modern concept of race.[36] His 1775 essay 'The Different Races of Mankind' ('*Von den Verschiedenen Rassen der Menschen*') is a classic pro-hereditarian, anti-environmentalist statement of 'the immutability and permanence of race'. For him, comments George Mosse, 'racial makeup becomes an unchanging substance and the foundation of all physical appearance and human development, including intelligence.'[37] The famous modern theorist of personhood is also the foundational modern theorist of sub-personhood, though this distinction is, in what the suspicious might almost think a conspiracy to conceal embarrassing truths, far less well known.

As Eze points out, Kant taught anthropology and physical geography for 40 years, and his philosophical work really has to be read in conjunction with these lectures to understand how racialized his views on moral character were. His notorious comment in *Observations on the Feeling of the Beautiful and Sublime* is well-known to, and often cited by, black intellectuals: 'So fundamental is the difference between [the black and white] races of man . . . it appears to be as great in regard to mental capacities as in color' so that 'a clear proof that what [a Negro] said was stupid' was that 'this fellow was quite black from head to foot.'[38] The point of Eze's essay is that this remark is by no means isolated or a casual throwaway line that, though of course regrettable, has no broader implications. Rather, it comes out of a developed theory of race and corresponding intellectual ability and limitation. It only *seems* casual, unembedded in a larger theory, because white academic philosophy as an institution has had no interest in researching, pursuing the implications of, and making known to the world this dimension of Kant's work.

In fact, Kant demarcates and theorizes a colour-coded racial hierarchy of Europeans, Asians, Africans, and Native Americans, differentiated by their degree of innate *talent*. Eze explains: '"Talent" is that which, by "nature," guarantees for the "white," in Kant's racial rational and moral order, the highest position above all creatures, followed by the "yellow," the "black," and then the "red." Skin color for Kant is evidence of superior, inferior, or no "gift" of "talent," or the capacity to realize reason and rational-moral perfectibility through education. . . . It cannot, therefore, be argued that skin color for Kant was merely a physical characteristic. It is, rather, evidence of an unchanging and unchangeable moral quality.' Europeans, to no one's surprise I presume, have all the necessary talents to be morally self-educating; there is some hope for Asians, though they lack the ability to develop abstract concepts; the innately idle Africans can at least be educated as servants and slaves through the instruction of a split-bamboo cane (Kant gives some useful advice on how to beat Negroes efficiently); while the wretched Native Americans are just hopeless, and cannot be educated at all. So, in complete opposition to the image of his work that has come down to us and is standardly taught in introductory ethics courses, full personhood for Kant is actually dependent upon race. In Eze's summary, 'The black person, for example, can accordingly be denied full humanity since full and "true" humanity accrues only to the white European.'[39]

The recent furore about Paul de Man[40] and, decades earlier, Martin Heidegger, for their complicity with the Nazis, thus needs to be put into perspective. These are essentially bit players, minor leaguers. One needs to distinguish theory from actual practice, of course, and I'm not saying that Kant would have endorsed genocide. *But the embarrassing fact for the white West (which doubtless explains its concealment) is that their most important moral theorist of the past three hundred years is also the foundational theorist in the modern period of the division between* Herrenvolk *and* Untermenschen, *persons and sub-persons, upon which Nazi theory would later draw.* Modern moral theory and modern racial theory have the same father.

The Racial Contract, therefore, underwrites the social contract, is a visible or hidden operator that restricts and modifies the scope of its prescriptions. But since there is both synchronic and diachronic variation, there are many different versions or local instantiations of the Racial Contract, and they evolve over time, so that the effective force of the (nominal) social contract itself changes, and the kind of cognitive dissonance between the two alters. (This change has implications for the moral psychology of the white signatories and their characteristic patterns of insight and blindness.) The social contract is (in its original historical version) a specific discrete event that founds society, even if (through, e.g., Lockean theories of tacit consent) subsequent generations continue to ratify it on an ongoing basis. By contrast the Racial Contract is *continually being rewritten* to create different forms of the racial polity.

A global periodization, a timeline overview of the evolution of the Racial Contract, would highlight first of all the crucial division between the time before and the time after the institutionalization of global white supremacy. (Thus Janet Abu-Lughod's book about the thirteenth-century/fourteenth-century medieval world-system is titled *Before European Hegemony*.)[41] The time after would then be further subdivided into the period of formal, juridical white supremacy (the epoch of the European conquest, African slavery, and European colonialism, overt white racial self-identification, and the largely undisputed hegemony of racist theories) and the present period of de facto white supremacy, when whites' dominance is, for the most part, no longer constitutionally and juridically enshrined but rather a matter of social, political, cultural, and economic privilege based on the legacy of the conquest.

In the first period, the period of de jure white supremacy, the Racial Contract was explicit, the characteristic instantiations—the expropriation contract, the slave contract, the colonial contract—making it clear that whites were the privileged race and the egalitarian social contract applied only to them. (Cognitively, then, this period had the great virtue of social transparency: white supremacy was *openly* proclaimed. One didn't have to look for a *sub*text, because it was there in the text itself.) In the second period, on the other hand, the Racial Contract *has written itself out of formal existence*. The scope of the terms in the social contract has been formally extended to apply to everyone, so that 'persons' is no longer co-extensive with 'whites'. What characterizes this period (which is, of course, the present) is tension between continuing de facto white privilege and this *formal* extension of rights. The Racial Contract continues to manifest itself, of course, in unofficial local agreements of various kinds (restrictive covenants, employment discrimination contracts, political decisions about resource allocation, etc.). But even apart from these, a crucial manifestation is simply *the failure to ask certain questions*, taking for granted as a status quo and baseline the existing colour-coded configurations of wealth, poverty, property, and opportunities, the pretence that formal, juridical equality is sufficient to remedy inequities created on a foundation of several hundred years of racial privilege, and that challenging that foundation is a transgression of the terms of the social contract. (Though actually—in a sense—it *is*, insofar as the Racial Contract is the real meaning of the social contract.)

Globally, the Racial Contract effects a final paradoxical norming and racing of space, a *writing out* of the polity of certain spaces as conceptually and historically irrelevant to European and Euro-world development, so that these raced spaces are categorized as disjoined from the path of civilization (i.e., the European project). Fredric Jameson writes: 'Colonialism means that a significant structural segment of the economic system as a whole is now located elsewhere, beyond the metropolis, outside of the daily life and existential experience of the home country. . . . Such spatial disjunction has as its immediate consequence the inability to grasp the way the system functions as a whole.'[42] By the social contract's decision to remain in the space of the European nation-state, the connection between the development of this space's industry, culture, civilization and the material and cultural contributions of Afro-Asia and the Americas is denied, so it seems as if this space and its denizens are peculiarly rational and industrious, differentially endowed with qualities that have enabled them to dominate the world. One then speaks of the 'European miracle' in a way that conceives this once marginal region as sui generis, conceptually severing it from the web of spatial connections that made its development possible. *This* space actually comes to have the character it does because of the pumping exploitative causality established between it and those *other* conceptually invisible spaces. But by remaining within the boundaries of the European space of the abstract contract, it is valorized as unique, inimitable, autonomous. Other parts of the world then disappear from the white contractarian history, subsumed under the general category of risible non-European space, the 'Third World', where for reasons of local folly and geographical blight the inspiring model of the self-sufficient white social contract cannot be followed.

Nationally, within these racial polities, the Racial Contract manifests itself in white resistance to anything more than the *formal* extension of the terms of the abstract social contract (and often to that also). Whereas before it was denied that nonwhites *were* equal persons, it is now pretended that nonwhites *are* equal abstract persons who can be fully included in the polity merely by extending the scope of the moral operator, without any fundamental change in the arrangements that have resulted from the previous system of explicit de jure racial privilege. Sometimes the new forms taken by the Racial Contract are transparently exploitative, for example the 'Jim Crow' contract, whose claim of 'separate but equal' was patently ludicrous. But others—the job discrimination contract, the restrictive covenant—are harder to prove. Employment agencies use subterfuges of various kinds: 'In 1990, for example, two former employees of one of New York City's largest employment agencies divulged that discrimination was routinely practiced against black applicants, though concealed behind a number of code words. Clients who did not want to hire blacks would indicate their preference for applicants who were "All American." For its part the agency would signal that an applicant was black by reversing the initials of the placement counselor.'[43] Similarly, a study of how 'American apartheid' is maintained points out that whereas in the past realtors would have simply refused to sell to blacks, now blacks 'are met by a realtor with a smiling face who, through a series of ruses, lies, and deceptions, makes it hard for them to learn about, inspect, rent, or purchase homes in white neighborhoods. . . . Because the discrimination is latent, however, it is usually unobservable, even to the person experiencing it. One never knows for sure.'[44] Nonwhites will then find that race is, paradoxically, both everywhere and nowhere, structuring their lives but not formally recognized in political/moral theory. But in a racially structured polity, the only people who can find it psychologically possible to deny the centrality of race are those who are racially privileged, for whom race is invisible precisely because the world is structured around them, whiteness as the ground against which the figures of other races—those who, unlike us, are raced—appear. The fish does not see the water, and whites do not see the racial nature of a white polity because it is natural to them,

the element in which they move. As Toni Morrison points out, there are contexts in which claiming racelessness is itself a racial act.[45]

Contemporary debates between nonwhites and whites about the centrality or peripherality of race can thus be seen as attempts respectively to point out, and deny, the existence of the Racial Contract that underpins the social contract. The frustrating problem nonwhites have always had, and continue to have, with mainstream political theory is not with abstraction *itself* (after all, the 'Racial Contract' is itself an abstraction) but with an *idealizing* abstraction that abstracts away from the crucial realities of the racial polity.[46] The shift to the hypothetical, ideal contract encourages and facilitates this abstraction since the eminently *non*-ideal features of the real world are not part of the apparatus. There is then, in a sense, no conceptual point-of-entry to start talking about the fundamental way in which (as all nonwhites know) race structures one's life and affects one's life-chances.

The black law professor Patricia Williams complains about an ostensible neutrality that is really 'racism in drag', a system of 'racism as status quo' which is 'deep, angry, eradicated from view' but that continues to make people 'avoid the phantom as they did the substance,' 'defer[ring] to the unseen shape of things.'[47] The black philosophy professor Bill Lawson comments on the deficiencies of the conceptual apparatus of traditional liberalism, which has no room for the peculiar post-Emancipation status of blacks, simultaneously citizens and non-citizens.[48] The black philosopher of law Anita Allen remarks on the irony of standard American philosophy of law texts, which describe a universe in which 'all humans are paradigm rightsholders' and see no need to point out that the actual US record is somewhat different.[49] The retreat of mainstream normative moral and political theory into an 'ideal' theory that ignores race merely rescripts the Racial Contract as the invisible writing between the lines. So John Rawls, an American working in the late twentieth century, writes a book on justice widely credited with reviving postwar political philosophy in which not a single reference to American slavery and its legacy can be found, and Robert Nozick creates a theory of justice in holdings predicated on legitimate acquisition and transfer without more than two or three sentences acknowledging the utter divergence of US history from this ideal.[50]

The silence of mainstream moral and political philosophy on issues of race is a sign of the continuing power of the Contract over its signatories, an illusory colour blindness that actually entrenches white privilege. A genuine transcendence of its terms would require, as a preliminary, the acknowledgement of its past and present existence and the social, political, economic, psychological, and moral implications it has had both for its contractors and its victims. By treating the present as a somehow neutral baseline, with its given configuration of wealth, property, social standing, and psychological willingness to sacrifice, the idealized social contract renders permanent the legacy of the Racial Contract. The ever-deepening abyss between the First World and the Third World, where millions—largely nonwhite—die of starvation each year and many more hundreds of millions—also largely nonwhite—live in wretched poverty, is seen as unfortunate (calling, certainly, for the occasional charitable contribution) but unrelated to the history of trans-continental and intra-continental racial exploitation.

Finally, the Racial Contract evolves not merely by altering the relations between whites and nonwhites but by shifting the criteria for who counts as white and nonwhite. (So it is not merely that relations between the respective populations change but that the population boundaries themselves change also.) Thus—at least in my preferred account of the Racial Contract (again, other accounts are possible)—race is debiologized, making explicit its political foundation. *In a sense, the Racial Contract constructs its signatories as much as they construct it.* The overall trend is toward a limited expansion of the privileged human population through the 'whitening' of the previously excluded group in question, though there may be local reversals.

Notes

1. A 1994 report on American philosophy, 'Status and Future of the Profession,' revealed that 'only one department in 20 (28 of the 456 departments reporting) has any [tenure-track] African-American faculty, with slightly fewer having either Hispanic-American or Asian-American [tenure-track] faculty (17 departments in both cases). A mere seven departments have any [tenure-track] Native American faculty.' *Proceedings and Addresses of the American Philosophical Association* 70, no. 2 (1996): 137.

2. 'Contractarianism' is sometimes used in a more limited way to denote just the Hobbesian version of the contract, as against the Kantian version, which is then called 'contractualism'; see, for example, Stephen Darwall, ed., *Contractarianism/Contractualism* (Malden, MA: Blackwell, 2003). So to avoid confusion, I should just stipulate at the start that I will use *contractarianism* generally throughout to refer to social contract theory of all kinds.

3. For an overview, see, for example, Ernest Barker, Introduction to *Social Contract: Essays by Locke, Hume, and Rousseau,* ed. Barker (1947; reprint, Oxford: Oxford University Press, 1960); Michael Lessnoff, *Social Contract* (Atlantic Highlands, NJ: Humanities Press, 1986); Will Kymlicka, 'The Social Contract Tradition,' in *A Companion to*

Ethics, ed. Peter Singer (Cambridge, MA: Blackwell Reference, 1991), 186–96; Jean Hampton, 'Contract and Consent,' in *A Companion to Contemporary Political Philosophy*, ed. Robert E. Goodin and Philip Pettit (Cambridge, MA: Blackwell Reference, 1993), 379–93; David Boucher and Paul Kelly, 'The Social Contract and Its Critics: An Overview,' in *The Social Contract from Hobbes to Rawls*, ed. David Boucher and Paul Kelly (New York: Routledge, 1994), 1–34; Darwall, *Contractarianism/Contractualism*.

4. Indigenous peoples as a global group are sometimes referred to as the 'Fourth World'. See Roger Moody, ed., *The Indigenous Voice: Visions and Realities*, 2nd edn, rev. (Utrecht: International Books, 1993); orig. edn 1988.

5. For a praiseworthy exception, see Iris Marion Young, *Justice and the Politics of Difference* (Princeton, NJ: Princeton University Press, 1990). Young focuses explicitly on the implications for standard conceptions of justice of group subordination, including racial groups.

6. Credit for the revival of social contract theory, and indeed postwar political philosophy in general, is usually attributed to John Rawls, *A Theory of Justice*, rev. edn (Cambridge, MA: Harvard University Press, 1999); orig. edn 1971.

7. Thomas Hobbes, *Leviathan*, ed. Richard Tuck, rev. student edn (New York: Cambridge University Press, 1996); John Locke, *Two Treatises of Government*, ed. Peter Laslett, student edn (New York: Cambridge University Press, 1988); Jean-Jacques Rousseau, *Discourse on the Origins and Foundations of Inequality among Men*, trans. Maurice Cranston (New York: Penguin, 1984); Jean-Jacques Rousseau, *The Social Contract*, trans. Maurice Cranston (New York: Penguin, 1968). Immanuel Kant is of course also a classic contract theorist, but for him the contract is no more than 'an *idea* of reason'. See 'On the Common Saying: "This May Be True in Theory, but It Does Not Apply in Practice,"' in Kant, *Political Writings*, ed. Hans Reiss, 2nd edn (New York: Cambridge University Press, 1991), 79; orig. edn 1970.

8. In 'Contract and Consent,' 382, Jean Hampton reminds us that for the classic theorists, contract is intended 'simultaneously to describe the nature of political societies, and to prescribe a new and more defensible form for such societies.' In this essay, and also in 'The Contractarian Explanation of the State,' in *The Philosophy of the Human Sciences*, Midwest Studies in Philosophy, 15, ed. Peter A. French, Theodore E. Uehling, Jr, and Howard K. Wettstein (Notre Dame, IN: University of Notre Dame Press, 1990), 344–71, she argues explicitly for a revival of the old-fashioned, seemingly discredited 'contractarian explanation of the state'. Hampton points out that the imagery of 'contract' captures the essential point that 'authoritative political societies are human creations' (not divinely ordained or naturally determined) and '*conventionally* generated'. New (2007) postscript: I am utilizing this sense of 'explanation', which, it should be noted—a point on which I have been misunderstood by many critics—is not 'explanation' in the social-scientific sense, but (as should have been clear from the comparison with Rousseau) in the more abstract philosophical sense appropriate to social contract discourse.

9. Rousseau, *Discourse on Inequality*, pt 2.

10. Carole Pateman, *The Sexual Contract* (Stanford, CA: Stanford University Press, 1988). Pateman is generally dubious about all varieties of contract theory, but her specific critical focus in her book is really on what she calls 'contractarianism', by which she means Hobbesian/libertarian contract theory. See our exchange in chapter 1 of Carole Pateman and Charles W. Mills, *Contract and Domination* (Malden, MA: Polity Press, 2007). For me, it is not the case that a Racial Contract *had* to underpin the social contract, since I see this contract as a result of the particular conjunction of contingent cir-

cumstances in global history which led to European imperialism. And, as a corollary, I believe contract theory can be put to positive use once this hidden history is acknowledged: see my chapters in Pateman and Mills, *Contract and Domination*. For an example of the feminist use of Rawlsian contract theory, see Susan Moller Okin, *Justice, Gender, and the Family* (New York: Basic Books, 1989).

11. See, for example, Paul Thagard, *Conceptual Revolutions* (Princeton, NJ: Princeton University Press, 1992), 22.

12. See Hampton, 'Contract and Consent' and 'Contractarian Explanation.' Hampton's own focus is the liberal-democratic state, but obviously her strategy of employing 'contract' to conceptualize conventionally generated norms and practices is open to be adapted to the understanding of the *non*-liberal-democratic *racial* state, the difference being that 'the people' now become the white population.

13. Otto Gierke termed these respectively the *Gesellschaftsvertrag* and the *Herrschaftsvertrag*. For a discussion, see, for example, Barker, Introduction, *Social Contract*; and Lessnoff, *Social Contract*, chap. 3.

14. Rawls, *Theory of Justice*, part I.

15. In speaking generally of 'whites', I am not, of course, denying that there are gender relations of domination and subordination or, for that matter, class relations of domination and subordination within the white population. I am not claiming that race is the only axis of social oppression. But race is what I want to focus on; so in the absence of that chimerical entity, a unifying theory of race, class, and gender oppression, it seems to me that one has to make generalizations that it would be stylistically cumbersome to qualify at every point. So these should just be taken as read. Nevertheless, I do want to insist that my overall picture is roughly accurate, i.e., that whites *do* in general benefit from white supremacy (though gender and class differentiation mean, of course, that they do not benefit equally) and that historically white racial solidarity *has* overridden class and gender solidarity. Women, subordinate classes, and nonwhites may be oppressed in common, but it is not a common oppression: the structuring is so different that it has not led to any common front between them. Neither white women nor white workers have *as a group* (as against principled individuals) historically made common cause with nonwhites against colonialism, white settlement, slavery, imperialism, Jim Crow, apartheid. We all have multiple identities, and, to this extent, most of us are both privileged and disadvantaged by different systems of domination. But white racial identity has generally triumphed over all others; it *is* race that (transgender, transclass) has generally determined the social world and loyalties, the lifeworld, of whites—whether as citizens of the colonizing mother country, settlers, nonslaves, or beneficiaries of the 'colour bar' and the 'colour line'. There has been no comparable transracial 'workers'' world or transracial 'female' world: race is the identity around which whites have usually closed ranks. Nevertheless, as a concession, a semantic signal of this admitted gender privileging within the white population, by which white women's personhood is originally virtual, dependent on their having the appropriate relation (daughter, sister, wife) to the white male, I will sometimes deliberately use the non-gender-neutral 'men'. For some literature on these problematic intersections of identity, see, for example, Ruth Frankenberg, *White Women, Race Matters: The Social Construction of Whiteness* (Minneapolis, MN: University of Minnesota Press, 1993); Nupur Chaudhuri and Margaret Strobel, eds, *Western Women and Imperialism: Complicity and Resistance* (Bloomington, IN: Indiana University Press, 1992); Kum-Kum Bhavnani, ed., *Feminism and 'Race'* (New York: Oxford University Press, 2001); David R.

Roediger, *The Wages of Whiteness: Race and the Making of the American Working Class*, rev. edn (New York: Verso, 1999), orig. edn 1991.

16. Rousseau, *Social Contract*; Hobbes, *Leviathan*.

17. Frank M. Snowden, Jr, *Blacks in Antiquity: Ethiopians in the Greco-Roman Experience* (Cambridge, MA: Harvard University Press, 1970); Frank M. Snowden, Jr, *Before Color Prejudice: The Ancient View of Blacks* (Cambridge, MA: Harvard University Press, 1983).

18. Theodore W. Allen, *Racial Oppression and Social Control*, vol. 1 of *The Invention of the White Race* (New York: Verso, 1994); Ian F. Haney López, *White by Law: The Legal Construction of Race* (New York: New York University Press, 1996).

19. Francis Jennings, *The Invasion of America: Indians, Colonialism, and the Cant of Conquest* (New York: W.W. Norton, 1976), 60.

20. Hugo Grotius, *The Law of War and Peace*, trans. Francis W. Kelsey (Indianapolis, IN: Bobbs-Merrill, 1925), chap. 20, 'On Punishments,' of book 2, 506; quoted in Robert A. Williams Jr, 'The Algebra of Federal Indian Law: The Hard Trail of Decolonizing and Americanizing the White Man's Indian Jurisprudence,' *Wisconsin Law Review*, 1986, 250.

21. For the following, compare James Tully, *Strange Multiplicity: Constitutionalism in an Age of Diversity* (Cambridge: Cambridge University Press, 1995), esp. chap. 3, 'The Historical Formation of Modern Constitutionalism: The Empire of Uniformity,' 58–98. I thank Anthony Laden for bringing this book to my attention, which I only learned about when my own manuscript was on the verge of completion.

22. Hobbes, *Leviathan*, 89.

23. Quoted in Richard Ashcraft, 'Leviathan Triumphant: Thomas Hobbes and the Politics of Wild Men,' in *The Wild Man within: An Image in Western Thought from the Renaissance to Romanticism*, ed. Edward Dudley and Maximillian E. Novak (Pittsburgh, PA: University of Pittsburgh Press, 1972), 146–7. See also, more recently,

Barbara Hall, 'Race in Hobbes,' in *Race and Racism in Modern Philosophy*, ed. Andrew Valls (Ithaca, NY: Cornell University Press, 2005), 43–56.

24. Hobbes, *Leviathan*, 89–90.

25. Two hundred years later, by contrast, the British colonial enterprise, with the accompanying ontological dichotomization, was so well entrenched that John Stuart Mill experienced not the slightest qualm in asserting (in an essay now seen as a classic humanist defence of individualism and freedom) that the liberal harm principle 'is meant to apply only to human beings in the maturity of their faculties,' not to those 'backward states of society in which the race itself may be considered as in its nonage': 'Despotism is a legitimate mode of government in dealing with barbarians, provided the end be their improvement.' John Stuart Mill, *On Liberty and Other Writings*, ed. Stefan Collini (New York: Cambridge University Press, 1989), 13.

26. Locke, *Second Treatise*, chap. 5, 'Of Property.'

27. Robert A. Williams, Jr, 'Documents of Barbarism: The Contemporary Legacy of European Racism and Colonialism in the Narrative Traditions of Federal Indian Law,' *Arizona Law Review* 237 (1989), excerpted in *Critical Race Theory: The Cutting Edge*, ed. Richard Delgado (Philadelphia, PA: Temple University Press, 1995), 103.

28. Locke, *Second Treatise*, chap. 16, 'On Conquest.'

29. See, for example, Wayne Glausser's survey article, 'Three Approaches to Locke and the Slave Trade,' *Journal of the History of Ideas* 51, no. 2 (1990): 199–216, and, for more recent work, Robert Bernasconi and Anika Maaza Mann, 'The Contradictions of Racism: Locke, Slavery, and the *Two Treatises*,' in Valls, *Race and Racism in Modern Philosophy*, 89–107.

30. Rousseau, *Discourse on Inequality*, 83, 87, 90, 136, 140, 145 (nonwhite savages), 140 (European savages).

31. Rousseau, *Discourse on Inequality*, 116.

32. Rousseau, *Social Contract*, bk 1, chap. 8.

33. Louis Sala-Molins, *Dark Side of the Light: Slavery and the French Enlightenment*, trans. John Conteh-Morgan (Minneapolis, MN: University of Minnesota Press, 2006), 49, 73, 74. See also Louis Sala-Molins, *Le Code Noir, ou Le Calvaire de Canaan* (Paris: Presses universitaires de France, 1987).

34. Susan Buck-Morss, 'Hegel and Haiti,' *Critical Inquiry* 26, no. 4 (Summer 2000): 831.

35. Emmanuel Chukwudi Eze, 'The Color of Reason: The Idea of "Race" in Kant's Anthropology,' in *Postcolonial African Philosophy: A Critical Reader*, ed. Emmanuel Chukwudi Eze (Cambridge, MA: Blackwell, 1997), 103–40.

36. Eze cites the 1950 judgment of Earl Count that scholars often forget that 'Immanuel Kant produced the most profound raciological thought of the eighteenth century.' Earl W. Count, ed., *This Is Race: An Anthology Selected from the International Literature on the Races of Man* (New York: Henry Schuman, 1950), 704; quoted in Eze, 'Color of Reason,' 103. Compare the 1967 verdict of the German anthropologist Wilhelm Mühlmann that Kant is 'the founder of the modern concept of race', quoted in Leon Poliakov, 'Racism from the Enlightenment to the Age of Imperialism,' in *Racism and Colonialism*, ed. Robert Ross (The Hague: Leiden University Press, 1982), 59. See also, more recently, Robert Bernasconi, 'Who Invented the Concept of Race? Kant's Role in the Enlightenment Construction of Race,' in *Race*, ed. Bernasconi (Malden, MA: Blackwell, 2001), 11–36.

37. George L. Mosse, *Toward the Final Solution: A History of European Racism* (1978; reprint, Madison: University of Wisconsin Press, 1985), 30–1.

38. Immanuel Kant, *Observations on the Feeling of the Beautiful and Sublime*, trans. John T. Goldthwait (Berkeley: University of California Press, 1960), 111–13.

39. Eze, 'Color of Reason,' 119, 115–19, 121.

40. David Lehman, *Signs of the Times: Deconstruction and the Fall of Paul de Man* (New York: Poseidon Press, 1991).

41. Janet L. Abu-Lughod, *Before European Hegemony: The World System A.D. 1250–1350* (New York: Oxford University Press, 1989).

42. Fredric Jameson, 'Modernism and Imperialism,' in *Nationalism, Colonialism, and Literature*, ed. Seamus Deane (Minneapolis, MN: University of Minnesota Press, 1990), 50–1.

43. Stephen Steinberg, *Turning Back: The Retreat from Racial Justice in America* (Boston: Beacon Press, 1995), 152.

44. Douglas S. Massey and Nancy A. Denton, *American Apartheid: Segregation and the Making of the Underclass* (Cambridge, MA: Harvard University Press, 1993), 84, 97–8.

45. Toni Morrison, *Playing in the Dark: Whiteness and the Literary Imagination* (Cambridge, MA: Harvard University Press, 1992), 46.

46. See the discussion of 'idealizing' abstractions in Onora O'Neill, 'Justice, Gender, and International Boundaries,' in *The Quality of Life*, ed. Martha Nussbaum and Amartya Sen (Oxford: Clarendon Press, 1993), 303–23, and my elaboration on O'Neill, Mills, '"Ideal Theory" As Ideology,' *Hypatia: A Journal of Feminist Philosophy* 20, no. 3 (Summer 2005), 165–84.

47. Patricia J. Williams, *The Alchemy of Race and Rights* (Cambridge, MA: Harvard University Press, 1991), 116, 49.

48. Bill E. Lawson, 'Moral Discourse and Slavery,' in *Between Slavery and Freedom: Philosophy and American Slavery*, Howard McGary and Bill E. Lawson (Bloomington: Indiana University Press, 1992), 71–89.

49. Anita L. Allen, 'Legal Rights for Poor Blacks,' in *The Underclass Question*, ed. Bill E. Lawson (Philadelphia: Temple University Press, 1992), 117–39.

50. Rawls, *Theory of Justice*; Robert Nozick, *Anarchy, State, and Utopia* (New York: Basic Books, 1974).

Study Questions for *The Racial Contract*

1. In the introduction to *The Racial Contract*, Mills draws attention to the fact that contemporary political philosophers largely ignore the existence of white privilege and racist political structures. How does contemporary political philosophy reflect the concerns and interests of white academics, according to Mills? How is racism itself political?
2. What is the racial contract? What is the relationship between the racial contract and the social contract?
3. Describe the racial assumptions underlying the theories of Hobbes, Locke, Rousseau, and Kant (discussed by Mills in chapter 2). In your view, can the racial assumptions underlying these theories be expunged while leaving the theories intact? Would the theories be dramatically different without these assumptions?
4. Describe Mills's distinction between the past historical epoch of formal white supremacy and the present epoch of *de facto* white supremacy. What are the distinguishing characteristics of each epoch? How does the present epoch continue to manifest the original racial contract?

Recommended Readings

Appiah, Anthony, and Amy Gutmann, *Color Conscious: The Political Morality of Race* (Princeton University Press, 1996).

Babbitt, Susan, and Sue Campbell, eds, *Racism and Philosophy* (Cornell University Press, 1999).

Boxill, Bernard, ed., *Race and Racism* (Oxford University Press, 2000).

Mills, Charles, *Blackness Visible: Essays on Philosophy and Race* (Cornell University Press, 1998).

Pateman, Carole, and Charles Mills, *Contract and Domination* (Polity Pres, 2007).

Pittman, John, ed., *African-American Perspectives and Philosophical Traditions* (Routledge, 1997).

Sullivan, Shannon, and Nancy Tuana, eds, *Race and Epistemologies of Ignorance* (SUNY Press, 2007).

Taylor, Paul, *Race: A Philosophical Introduction* (Polity Press, 2004).

Valls, Andrew, ed., *Race and Racism in Modern Philosophy* (Cornell University Press, 2005).

West, Cornel, *Race Matters* (Vintage Books, 1993).

Yancy, George, ed., *What White Looks Like: African-American Philosophers on the Whiteness Question* (Routledge, 2004).

Michael Walzer

Michael Walzer (1935–) obtained his PhD in political science and history from Harvard University and is professor emeritus of the School of Social Sciences in the Institute for Advanced Study in Princeton, New Jersey. He served as a member of the institute faculty for 27 years, following an appointment as professor of government at Harvard University. He has published 27 books on political theory, social criticism, and moral philosophy, including *Just and Unjust Wars* (1977), *Spheres of Justice* (1983), *Pluralism, Justice and Equality* (1995), *On Toleration* (1997), *Arguing about War* (2004), and *Politics and Passion* (2005). He has also served as co-editor of the American political magazine *Dissent*, through which he has been an active social critic and commentator on US politics.

In our first selection, from *Spheres of Justice*, Walzer defends a pluralistic theory of distributive justice in which no single criterion of distribution should regulate all spheres of justice. Different spheres of social life—such as economic markets, educational institutions, the domains of love and friendship—operate with different conceptions of justice. A principle of need governs the distribution of basic material goods in social welfare systems; a principle of merit guides the distribution of accolades in higher education; and a principle of free exchange guides distributions of wealth in competitive economic markets. Walzer defends, as an overarching principle of justice, an ideal of 'complex equality', according to which political communities should maintain a separation among different spheres of justice so that inequalities in one sphere do not proliferate into other spheres and create pervasive social dominance. Even if an individual justly acquires a large amount of wealth, she should not be able to buy favouritism in the courts, political power, love, or friendship, or superior grades for herself or her children. (Some guys should not have all the luck, as Rod Stewart might say.) Our shared understandings of justice do not endorse a proliferation of inequalities across spheres of justice.

In contrast to John Rawls, Walzer argues that conceptions of justice should not be derived from a hypothetical Archimedean point (such as the original position), for justice is not a universal and unchanging ideal but a human construction varying across time and place. Citizens in Western liberal democracies often share pluralistic and egalitarian understandings of justice; however, other cultures embody different shared understandings of justice and social goods. Walzer accordingly eschews appeal to universal human goods or natural human rights throughout *Spheres of Justice*. In the latter part of our selection, Walzer looks at the social distribution of the negative good of hard work. Work that is harsh, unpleasant, or especially onerous (and often attached to other negative goods like sickness, poverty, danger, or degradation) is often performed by political outsiders, such as slaves or resident aliens, or alien insiders, such as women. Walzer suggests that in a just society all people should perform, at some point in their lives, a share of hard or dirty work so that fewer people would be subordinate members of the social and political community.

In 'Terrorism: A Critique of Excuses' (1988), Walzer turns his attention to a contemporary problem of international justice: understanding and responding to terrorism. He examines and rejects several possible excuses for terrorism, such as the excuse that terrorism is a last resort or an only resort for changing oppressive political structures. In his view, oppression is not a legitimate excuse for terrorism, but enemies of terrorism should do more than mount purely defensive strategies of resistance; they should also work to end conditions of oppression that serve as a rationale for terrorism in the first place. Both in his work on terrorism and in *Spheres of Justice*, Walzer develops political theories and principles that oppose oppressive practices, systematic inequalities, and forms of social domination.

Spheres of Justice

Preface

. . . The aim of political egalitarianism is a society free from domination. This is the lively hope named by the word *equality*: no more bowing and scraping, fawning and toadying; no more fearful trembling; no more high-and-mightiness; no more masters, no more slaves. It is not a hope for the elimination of differences; we don't all have to be the same or have the same amounts of the same things. Men and women are one another's equals (for all important moral and political purposes) when no one possesses or controls the means of domination. But the means of domination are differently constituted in different societies. Birth and blood, landed wealth, capital, education, divine grace, state power—all these have served at one time or another to enable some people to dominate others. Domination is always mediated by some set of social goods.

Though the experience is personal, nothing in the persons themselves determines its character. Hence, again, equality as we have dreamed of it does not require the repression of persons. We have to understand and control social goods; we do not have to stretch or shrink human beings.

My purpose in this book is to describe a society where no social good serves or can serve as a means of domination. I won't try to describe how we might go about creating such a society. The description is hard enough: egalitarianism without the Procrustean bed; a lively and open egalitarianism that matches not the literal meaning of the word but the richer furnishings of the vision; an egalitarianism that is consistent with liberty. At the same time, it's not my purpose to sketch a utopia located nowhere or a philosophical ideal applicable everywhere. A society of equals lies within our own reach. It is a practical possibility here and now, latent already, as I shall try to show, in our shared understandings of social goods. *Our shared understandings*: the vision is relevant to the social world in which it was developed; it is not relevant, or not necessarily, to all social worlds. It fits a certain conception of how human beings relate to one another and how they use the things they make to shape their relations.

My argument is radically particularist. I don't claim to have achieved any great distance from the social world in which I live. One way to begin the philosophical enterprise—perhaps the original way—is to walk out of the cave, leave the city, climb the mountain, fashion for oneself (what can never be fashioned for ordinary men and women) an objective and universal standpoint. Then one describes the terrain of everyday life from far away, so that it loses its particular contours and takes on a general shape. But I mean to stand in the cave, in the city, on the ground. Another way of doing philosophy is to interpret to one's fellow citizens the world of meanings that we share. Justice and equality can conceivably be worked out as philosophical artifacts, but a just or an egalitarian society cannot be. If such a society isn't already here—hidden, as it were, in our concepts and categories—we will never know it concretely or realize it in fact. . . .

1

Complex Equality

Pluralism

Distributive justice is a large idea. It draws the entire world of goods within the reach of philosophical reflection. Nothing can be omitted; no feature of our common life can escape scrutiny. Human society is a distributive community. That's not all it is, but it is importantly

that: we come together to share, divide, and exchange. We also come together to make the things that are shared, divided, and exchanged; but that very making—work itself—is distributed among us in a division of labour. My place in the economy, my standing in the political order, my reputation among my fellows, my material holdings: all these come to me from other men and women. It can be said that I have what I have rightly or wrongly, justly or unjustly; but given the range of distributions and the number of participants, such judgments are never easy.

The idea of distributive justice has as much to do with being and doing as with having, as much to do with production as with consumption, as much to do with identity and status as with land, capital, or personal possessions. Different political arrangements enforce, and different ideologies justify, different distributions of membership, power, honour, ritual eminence, divine grace, kinship and love, knowledge, wealth, physical security, work and leisure, rewards and punishments, and a host of goods more narrowly and materially conceived—food, shelter, clothing, transportation, medical care, commodities of every sort, and all the odd things (painting, rare books, postage stamps) that human beings collect. And this multiplicity of goods is matched by the multiplicity of distributive procedures, agents, and criteria. There are such things as simple distributive systems—slave galleys, monasteries, insane asylums, kindergartens (though each of these, looked at closely, might show unexpected complexities); but no full-fledged human society has ever avoided the multiplicity. We must study it all, the goods and the distributions, in many different times and places.

There is, however, no single point of access to this world of distributive arrangements and ideologies. There has never been a universal medium of exchange: Since the decline of the barter economy, money has been the most common medium. But the old maxim according to which there are some things that money can't buy is not only normatively but also factually true. What should and should not be up for sale is something men and women always have to decide and have decided in many different ways. Throughout history, the market has been one of the most important mechanisms for the distribution of social goods; but it has never been, it nowhere is today, a complete distributive system.

Similarly, there has never been either a single decision point from which all distributions are controlled or a single set of agents making decisions. No state power has ever been so pervasive as to regulate all the patterns of sharing, dividing, and exchanging out of which a society takes shape. Things slip away from the state's grasp; new patterns are worked out— familial networks, black markets, bureaucratic alliances, clandestine political and religious organizations. State officials can tax, conscript, allocate, regulate, appoint, reward, punish, but they cannot capture the full range of goods or substitute themselves for every other agent of distribution. Nor can anyone else do that: there are market coups and cornerings, but there has never been a fully successful distributive conspiracy.

And finally, there has never been a single criterion, or a single set of interconnected criteria, for all distributions. Desert, qualification, birth and blood, friendship, need, free exchange, political loyalty, democratic decision: each has had its place, along with many others, uneasily coexisting, invoked by competing groups, confused with one another.

In the matter of distributive justice, history displays a great variety of arrangements and ideologies. But the first impulse of the philosopher is to resist the displays of history, the world of appearances, and to search for some underlying unity: a short list of basic goods, quickly abstracted to a single good; a single distributive criterion or an interconnected set; and the philosopher himself standing, symbolically at least, at a single decision point. I shall argue that to search for unity is to misunderstand the subject matter of distributive justice. Nevertheless, in some sense the philosophical impulse is unavoidable. Even if we choose pluralism, as I shall do, that choice still requires a coherent defence. There must be principles that justify the choice and set limits to it, for pluralism does not require us to endorse every proposed distributive criteria or to accept every would-be agent. Conceivably, there is a single principle and a single legitimate kind of pluralism. But this would still be a pluralism that encompassed a wide range of distributions. By contrast, the deepest assumption of most of the philosophers who have written about justice, from Plato onward, is that there is one, and only one, distributive system that philosophy can rightly encompass.

Today this system is commonly described as the one that ideally rational men and women would choose if they were forced to choose impartially, knowing nothing of their own situation, barred from making particularist claims, confronting an abstract set of goods.[1] If these constraints on knowing and claiming are suitably shaped, and if the goods are suitably defined, it is probably true that a singular conclusion can be produced. Rational men and women, constrained this way or that, will choose one, and only one, distributive system. But the force of that singular conclusion is not easy to measure. It is surely doubtful that those same men and women, if they were transformed into ordinary people, with a firm sense of their own identity, with their own goods in their hands, caught up in everyday troubles, would reiterate their hypothetical choice or even recognize it as their own. The problem is not, most importantly, with the particularism of interest, which philosophers have always assumed they could safely—that is, uncontroversially—set aside. Ordinary people can do that too, for the sake, say, of the public interest. The greater problem is with the particularism of history, culture, and membership. Even if they are committed to impartiality, the question most likely to arise in the minds of the members of a political community is not, What would rational individuals choose under universalizing conditions of such-and-such a sort? But rather, What would individuals like us choose, who are situated as we are, who share a culture and are determined to go on sharing it? And this is a question that is readily transformed into, What choices have we already made in the course of our common life? What understandings do we (really) share?

Justice is a human construction, and it is doubtful that it can be made in only one way. At any rate, I shall begin by doubting, and more than doubting, this standard philosophical assumption. The questions posed by the theory of distributive justice admit of a range of answers, and there is room within the range for cultural diversity and political choice. It's not only a matter of implementing some singular principle or set of principles in different historical settings. No one would deny that there is a range of morally permissible implementations. I want to argue for more than this: that the principles of justice are themselves pluralistic in form; that different social goods ought to be distributed for different reasons, in accordance with different procedures, by different agents; and that all these differences derive from different understandings of the social goods themselves—the inevitable product of historical and cultural particularism.

A Theory of Goods

Theories of distributive justice focus on a social process commonly described as if it had this form:

People distribute goods to (other) people.

Here, 'distribute' means give, allocate, exchange, and so on, and the focus is on the individuals who stand at either end of these actions: not on producers and consumers, but on distributive agents and recipients of goods. We are as always interested in ourselves, but, in this case, in a special and limited version of ourselves, as people who give and take. What is our nature? What are our rights? What do we need, want, deserve? What are we entitled to? What would we accept under ideal conditions? Answers to these questions are turned into distributive principles, which are supposed to control the movement of goods. The goods, defined by abstraction, are taken to be movable in any direction.

But this is too simple an understanding of what actually happens, and it forces us too quickly to make large assertions about human nature and moral agency—assertions unlikely, ever, to command general agreement. I want to propose a more precise and complex description of the central process:

People conceive and create goods, which they then distribute among themselves.

Here, the conception and creation precede and control the distribution. Goods don't just appear in the hands of distributive agents who do with them as they like or give them out in accordance with some general principle.[2] Rather, goods with their meanings—because of their meanings—are the crucial medium of social relations; they come into people's minds before they come into their hands; distributions are patterned in accordance with shared conceptions of what the goods are and what they are for. Distributive agents are constrained by the goods they hold; one might almost say that goods distribute themselves among people.

> Things are in the saddle
> And ride mankind.[3]

But these are always particular things and particular groups of men and women. And, of course, we make the things—even the saddle. I don't want to deny the importance of human agency, only to shift our attention from distribution itself to conception and creation: the naming of the goods, and the giving of meaning, and the collective making. What we need to explain and limit the pluralism of distributive possibilities is a theory of goods. For our immediate purposes, that theory can be summed up in six propositions.

1. All the goods with which distributive justice is concerned are social goods. They are not and they cannot be idiosyncratically valued. I am not sure that there are any other kinds of goods; I mean to leave the question open. Some domestic objects are cherished for private and sentimental reasons, but only in cultures where sentiment regularly attaches to such objects. A beautiful sunset, the smell of new-mown hay, the excitement of an urban vista: these perhaps are privately valued goods, though they are also, and more obviously, the objects of cultural assessment. Even new inventions are not valued in accordance with the ideas of their inventors; they are subject to a wider process of conception and creation. God's goods, to be sure, are exempt from this rule—as in the first chapter of Genesis: 'and God saw every thing that He had made, and, behold, it was very good' (1:31). That evaluation doesn't require the agreement of mankind (who might be doubtful), or of a majority of

men and women, or of any group of men and women meeting under ideal conditions (though Adam and Eve in Eden would probably endorse it). But I can't think of any other exemptions. Goods in the world have shared meanings because conception and creation are social processes. For the same reason, goods have different meanings in different societies. The same 'thing' is valued for different reasons, or it is valued here and disvalued there. John Stuart Mill once complained that 'people like in crowds', but I know of no other way to like or to dislike social goods.[4] A solitary person could hardly understand the meaning of the goods or figure out the reasons for taking them as likable or dislikable. Once people like in crowds, it becomes possible for individuals to break away, pointing to latent or subversive meanings, aiming at alternative values—including the values, for example, of notoriety and eccentricity. An easy eccentricity has sometimes been one of the privileges of the aristocracy: it is a social good like any other.

2. Men and women take on concrete identities because of the way they conceive and create, and then possess and employ social goods. 'The line between what is me and mine,' wrote William James, 'is very hard to draw.'[5] Distributions cannot be understood as the acts of men and women who do not yet have particular goods in their minds or in their hands. In fact, people already stand in a relation to a set of goods; they have a history of transactions, not only with one another but also with the moral and material world in which they live. Without such a history, which begins at birth, they wouldn't be men and women in any recognizable sense, and they wouldn't have the first notion of how to go about the business of giving, allocating, and exchanging goods.

3. There is no single set of primary or basic goods conceivable across all moral and material worlds—or, any such set would have to be conceived in terms so abstract that they would be of little use in thinking about particular distributions. Even the range of necessities, if we take into account moral as well as physical necessities, is very wide, and the rank orderings are very different. A single necessary good, and one that is always necessary—food, for example—carries different meanings in different places. Bread is the staff of life, the body of Christ, the symbol of the Sabbath, the means of hospitality, and so on. Conceivably, there is a limited sense in which the first of these is primary, so that if there were 20 people in the world and just enough bread to feed the 20, the primacy of bread-as-staff-of-life would yield a sufficient distributive principle. But that is the only circumstance in which it would do so; and even there, we can't be sure. If the religious uses of bread were to conflict with its nutritional uses—if the gods demanded that bread be baked and burned rather than eaten—it is by no means clear which use would be primary. How, then, is bread to be incorporated into the universal list? The question is even harder to answer, the conventional answers less plausible, as we pass from necessities to opportunities, powers, reputations, and so on. These can be incorporated only if they are abstracted from every particular meaning—hence, for all practical purposes, rendered meaningless.

4. But it is the meaning of goods that determines their movement. Distributive criteria and arrangements are intrinsic not to the good-in-itself but to the social good. If we understand what it is, what it means to those for whom it is a good, we understand how, by whom, and for what reasons it ought to be distributed. All distributions are just or unjust relative to the social meanings of the goods at stake. This is in obvious ways a principle of legitimation, but it is also a critical principle.* When medieval Christians, for example, condemned the sin of simony, they were claiming that the meaning of a particular social good, ecclesiastical office, excluded its sale and purchase. Given the Christian understanding of office, it followed—I am inclined to say, it necessarily followed—that office holders should be chosen for their knowledge and piety and not for their wealth. There are presumably things that money can buy, but not this thing. Similarly, the words *prostitution* and *bribery*, like *simony*, describe the sale and purchase of goods that, given certain understandings of their meaning, ought never to be sold or purchased.

5. Social meanings are historical in character; and so distributions, and just and unjust distributions, change over time. To be sure, certain key goods have what we might think of as characteristic normative structures, reiterated across the lines (but not all the lines) of time and space. It is because of this reiteration that the British philosopher Bernard Williams

---

* Aren't social meanings, as Marx said, nothing other than 'the ideas of the ruling class', 'the dominant material relationships grasped as ideas'?[6] I don't think that they are ever only that or simply that, though the members of the ruling class and the intellectuals they patronize may well be in a position to exploit and distort social meanings in their own interests. When they do that, however, they are likely to encounter resistance, rooted (intellectually) in those same meanings. A people's culture is always a joint, even if it isn't an entirely cooperative, production; and it is always a complex production. The common understanding of particular goods incorporates principles, procedures, conceptions of agency, that the rulers would not choose if they were choosing *right now*—and so provides the terms of social criticism. The appeal to what I shall call 'internal' principles against the usurpations of powerful men and women is the ordinary form of critical discourse.

is able to argue that goods should always be distributed for 'relevant reasons'—where relevance seems to connect to essential rather than to social meanings.[7] The idea that offices, for example, should go to qualified candidates—though not the only idea that has been held about offices—is plainly visible in very different societies where simony and nepotism, under different names, have similarly been thought sinful or unjust. (But there has been a wide divergence of views about what sorts of position and place are properly called 'offices'.) Again, punishment has been widely understood as a negative good that ought to go to people who are judged to deserve it on the basis of a verdict, not of a political decision. (But what constitutes a verdict? Who is to deliver it? How, in short, is justice to be done to accused men and women? About these questions there has been significant disagreement.) These examples invite empirical investigation. There is no merely intuitive or speculative procedure for seizing upon relevant reasons.

6. When meanings are distinct, distributions must be autonomous. Every social good or set of goods constitutes, as it were, a distributive sphere within which only certain criteria and arrangements are appropriate. Money is inappropriate in the sphere of ecclesiastical office; it is an intrusion from another sphere. And piety should make for no advantage in the marketplace, as the marketplace has commonly been understood. Whatever can rightly be sold ought to be sold to pious men and women and also to profane, heretical, and sinful men and women (else no one would do much business). The market is open to all comers; the church is not. In no society, of course, are social meanings entirely distinct. What happens in one distributive sphere affects what happens in the others; we can

look, at most, for relative autonomy. But relative autonomy, like social meaning, is a critical principle—indeed, as I shall be arguing throughout this book, a radical principle. It is radical even though it doesn't point to a single standard against which all distributions are to be measured. There is no single standard. But there are standards (roughly knowable even when they are also controversial) for every social good and every distributive sphere in every particular society; and these standards are often violated, the goods usurped, the spheres invaded, by powerful men and women. . . .

Tyranny and Complex Equality

I want to argue that we should focus on the reduction of dominance—not, or not primarily, on the break-up or the constraint of monopoly. We should consider what it might mean to narrow the range within which particular goods are convertible and to vindicate the autonomy of distributive spheres. But this line of argument, though it is not uncommon historically, has never fully emerged in philosophical writing. Philosophers have tended to criticize (or to justify) existing or emerging monopolies of wealth, power, and education. Or, they have criticized (or justified) particular conversions—of wealth into education or of office into wealth. And all this, most often, in the name of some radically simplified distributive system. The critique of dominance will suggest instead a way of reshaping and then living with the actual complexity of distributions.

Imagine now a society in which different social goods are monopolistically held—as they are in fact and always will be, barring continual state intervention—but in which no particular good is generally convertible. As I go along, I shall try to define the precise limits on convertibility, but for now the general description will suffice. This is a complex egalitarian society. Though there will be many small inequalities, inequality will not be multiplied through the conversion process. Nor will it be summed across different goods, because the autonomy of distributions will tend to produce a variety of local monopolies, held by different groups of men and women. I don't want to claim that complex equality would necessarily be more stable than simple equality, but I am inclined to think that it would open the way for more diffused and particularized forms of social conflict. And the resistance to convertibility would be maintained, in large degree, by ordinary men and women within their own spheres of competence and control, without large-scale state action.

This is, I think, an attractive picture, but I have not yet explained just why it is attractive. The argument for complex equality begins from our understanding—I mean, our actual, concrete, positive, and particular understanding—of the various social goods. And then it moves on to an account of the way we relate to one another through those goods. Simple equality is a simple distributive condition, so that if I have 14 hats and you have 14 hats, we are equal. And it is all to the good if hats are dominant, for then our equality is extended through all the spheres of social life. On the view that I shall take here, however, we simply have the same number of hats, and it is unlikely that hats will be dominant for long. Equality is a complex relation of persons, mediated by the goods we make, share, and divide among ourselves; it is not an identity of possessions. It requires then, a diversity of distributive criteria that mirrors the diversity of social goods.

The argument for complex equality has been beautifully put by Pascal in one of his *Pensées*.

The nature of tyranny is to desire power over the whole world and outside its own sphere.

There are different companies—the strong, the handsome, the intelligent, the devout—and each man reigns in his own, not elsewhere. But sometimes they meet, and the strong and the handsome fight for mastery—foolishly, for their mastery is of different kinds. They misunderstand one another, and make the mistake of each aiming at universal dominion. Nothing can win this, not even strength, for it is powerless in the kingdom of the wise. . . .

Tyranny. The following statements, therefore, are false and tyrannical: 'Because I am handsome, so I should command respect.' 'I am strong, therefore men should love me. . . .' 'I am . . . et cetera.'

Tyranny is the wish to obtain by one means what can only be had by another. We owe different duties to different qualities: love is the proper response to charm, fear to strength, and belief to learning.[8]

Marx made a similar argument in his early manuscripts; perhaps he had this *pensée* in mind:

Let us assume man to be man, and his relation to the world to be a human one. Then love can only be exchanged for love, trust for trust, etc. If you wish to enjoy art you must be an artistically cultivated person; if you wish to influence other people, you must be a person who really has a stimulating and encouraging effect upon others. . . . If you love without evoking love in return, i.e., if you are not able, by the manifestation of yourself as a loving person, to make yourself a beloved person—then your love is impotent and a misfortune.[9]

These are not easy arguments, and most of my book is simply an exposition of their meaning. But here I shall attempt something more simple and schematic: a translation of the arguments into the terms I have already been using.

The first claim of Pascal and Marx is that personal qualities and social goods have their own spheres of operation, where they work their effects freely, spontaneously, and legitimately. There are ready or natural conversions that follow from, and are intuitively plausible because of, the social meaning of particular goods. The appeal is to our ordinary understanding and, at the same time, against our common acquiescence in illegitimate conversion patterns. Or, it is an appeal from our acquiescence to our resentment. There is something wrong, Pascal suggests, with the conversion of strength into belief. In political terms, Pascal means that no ruler can rightly command my opinions merely because of the power he wields. Nor can he, Marx adds, rightly claim to influence my actions: if a ruler wants to do that, he must be persuasive, helpful, encouraging, and so on. These arguments depend for their force on some shared understanding of knowledge, influence, and power. Social goods have social meanings, and we find our way to distributive justice through an interpretation of those meanings. We search for principles internal to each distributive sphere.

The second claim is that the disregard of these principles is tyranny. To convert one good into another, when there is no intrinsic connection between the two, is to invade the sphere where another company of men and women properly rules. Monopoly is not inappropriate within the spheres. There is nothing wrong, for example, with the grip that persuasive and helpful men and women (politicians) establish on political power. But the use of political power to gain access to other goods is a tyrannical use. Thus, an old description of tyranny is generalized: princes become tyrants, according to medieval writers, when they seize the property or invade the family of their subjects.[10] In political life—but more widely, too—the dominance of goods makes for the domination of people.

The regime of complex equality is the opposite of tyranny. It establishes a set of relationships such that domination is impossible. In formal terms, complex equality means that no citizen's standing in one sphere or with regard to one social good can be undercut by his standing in some other sphere, with regard to some other good. Thus, citizen X may be chosen over citizen Y for political office, and then the two of them will be unequal in the sphere of politics. But they will not be unequal generally so long as X's office gives him no advantages over Y in any other sphere—superior medical care, access to better schools for his children, entrepreneurial opportunities, and so on. So long as office is not a dominant good, is not generally convertible, office holders will stand, or at least can stand, in a relation of equality to the men and women they govern.

But what if dominance were eliminated, the autonomy of the spheres established—and the same people were successful in one sphere after another, triumphant in every company, piling up goods without the need for illegitimate conversions? This would certainly make for an inegalitarian society, but it would also suggest in the strongest way that a society of equals was not a lively possibility. I doubt that any egalitarian argument could survive in the face of such evidence. Here is a person whom we have freely chosen (without reference to his family ties or personal wealth) as our political representative. He is also a bold and inventive entrepreneur. When he was younger, he studied science, scored amazingly high grades in every exam, and made important discoveries. In war, he is surpassingly brave and wins the highest honours. Himself compassionate and compelling, he is loved by all who know him. Are there such people? Maybe so, but I have my doubts. We tell stories like the one I have just told, but the stories are fictions, the conversion of power or money or academic talent into legendary fame. In any case, there aren't enough such people to constitute a ruling class and dominate the rest of us. Nor can they be successful in every distributive sphere, for there are some spheres to which the idea of success doesn't pertain. Nor are their children likely, under conditions of complex equality, to inherit their success. By and large, the most accomplished politicians, entrepreneurs, scientists, soldiers, and lovers will be different people; and so long as the goods they possess don't bring other goods in train, we have no reason to fear their accomplishments.

The critique of dominance and domination points toward an open-ended distributive principle. *No social good x should be distributed to men and women who possess some other good y merely because they possess y and without regard to the meaning of x.* This is a principle that has probably been reiterated, at one time or another, for every y that has ever been dominant. But it has not often been stated in general terms. Pascal and Marx have suggested the application of the principle against all possible y's, and I shall attempt to work out that application. I shall be looking, then, not at the members of Pascal's companies—the strong or the weak, the handsome or the plain—but at the goods they share and divide. The purpose of the principle is to focus our attention; it doesn't determine the shares or the division. The principle directs us to study the meaning of social goods, to examine the different distributive spheres from the inside.

Three Distributive Principles

The theory that results is unlikely to be elegant. No account of the meaning of a social good, or of the boundaries of the sphere within which it legitimately operates, will be uncontroversial. Nor is there any neat procedure for generating or testing different accounts. At best, the arguments will be rough, reflecting the diverse and conflict-ridden character of the social life that we seek simultaneously to understand and to regulate—but not to regulate until we understand. I shall set aside, then, all claims made on behalf of any single distributive criterion, for no such criterion can possibly match the diversity of social goods. Three criteria, however, appear to meet the requirements of the open-ended principle and have often been defended as the beginning and end of distributive justice, so I must say something about each of them. Free exchange, desert, and need: all three have real force, but none of them has force across the range of distributions. They are part of the story, not the whole of it.

Free Exchange

Free exchange is obviously open-ended; it guarantees no particular distributive outcome. At no point in any exchange process plausibly called 'free' will it be possible to predict the particular division of social goods that will obtain at some later point.[11] (It may be possible, however, to predict the general structure of the division.) In theory at least, free exchange creates a market within which all goods are convertible into all other goods through the neutral medium of money. There are no dominant goods and no monopolies. Hence the successive divisions that obtain will directly reflect the social meanings of the goods that are divided. For each bargain, trade, sale, and purchase will have been agreed to voluntarily by men and women who know what that meaning is, who are indeed its makers. Every exchange is a revelation of social meaning. By definition, then, no *x* will ever fall into the hands of someone who possesses *y*, merely because he possesses *y* and without regard to what *x* actually means to some other member of society. The market is radically pluralistic in its operations and its outcomes, infinitely sensitive to the meanings that individuals attach to goods. What possible restraints can be imposed on free exchange, then, in the name of pluralism?

But everyday life in the market, the actual experience of free exchange, is very different from what the theory suggests. Money, supposedly the neutral medium, is in practice a dominant good, and it is monopolized by people who possess a special talent for bargaining and trading—the green thumb of bourgeois society. Then other people demand a redistribution of money and the establishment of the regime of simple equality, and the search begins for some way to sustain that regime. But even if we focus on the first untroubled moment of simple equality—free exchange on the basis of equal shares—we will still need to set limits on what can be exchanged for what. For free exchange leaves distributions entirely in the hands of individuals, and social meanings are not subject, or are not always subject, to the interpretative decisions of individual men and women.

Consider an easy example, the case of political power. We can conceive of political power as a set of goods of varying value, votes,

influence, offices, and so on. Any of these can be traded on the market and accumulated by individuals willing to sacrifice other goods. Even if the sacrifices are real, however, the result is a form of tyranny—petty tyranny, given the conditions of simple equality. Because I am willing to do without my hat, I shall vote twice; and you who value the vote less than you value my hat, will not vote at all. I suspect that the result is tyrannical even with regard to the two of us, who have reached a voluntary agreement. It is certainly tyrannical with regard to all the other citizens who must now submit to my disproportionate power. It is not the case that votes can't be bargained for; on one interpretation, that's what democratic politics is all about. And democratic politicians have certainly been known to buy votes, or to try to buy them, by promising public expenditures that benefit particular groups of voters. But this is done in public, with public funds, and subject to public approval. Private trading is ruled out by virtue of what politics, or democratic politics, is—that is, by virtue of what we did when we constituted the political community and of what we still think about what we did.

Free exchange is not a general criterion, but we will be able to specify the boundaries within which it operates only through a careful analysis of particular social goods. And having worked through such an analysis, we will come up at best with a philosophically authoritative set of boundaries and not necessarily with the set that ought to be politically authoritative. For money seeps across all boundaries—this is the primary form of illegal immigration; and just where one ought to try to stop it is a question of expediency as well as of principle. Failure to stop it at some reasonable point has consequences throughout the range of distributions, but consideration of these belongs in a later chapter.

Desert

Like free exchange, desert seems both open-ended and pluralistic. One might imagine a single neutral agency dispensing rewards and punishments, infinitely sensitive to all the forms of individual desert. Then the distributive process would indeed be centralized, but the results would still be unpredictable and various. There would be no dominant good. No *x* would ever be distributed without regard to its social meaning; for, without attention to what *x* is, it is conceptually impossible to say that *x* is deserved. All the different companies of men and women would receive their appropriate reward. How this would work in practice, however, is not easy to figure out. It might make sense to say of this charming man, for example, that he deserves to be loved. It makes no sense to say that he deserves to be loved by this (or any) particular woman. If he loves her while she remains impervious to his (real) charms, that is his misfortune. I doubt that we would want the situation corrected by some outside agency. The love of particular men and women, on our understanding of it, can only be distributed by themselves, and they are rarely guided in these matters by considerations of desert.

The case is exactly the same with influence. Here, let's say, is a woman widely thought to be stimulating and encouraging to others. Perhaps she deserves to be an influential member of our community. But she doesn't deserve that I be influenced by her or that I follow her lead. Nor would we want my followership, as it were, assigned to her by any agency capable of making such assignments. She may go to great lengths to stimulate and encourage me, and do all the things that are commonly called stimulating or encouraging. But if I (perversely) refuse to be stimulated or encouraged, I am not denying her anything that she deserves. The same argument holds by extension for

politicians and ordinary citizens. Citizens can't trade their votes for hats; they can't individually decide to cross the boundary that separates the sphere of politics from the marketplace. But within the sphere of politics, they do make individual decisions; and they are rarely guided, again, by considerations of desert. It's not clear that offices can be deserved—another issue that I must postpone; but even if they can be, it would violate our understanding of democratic politics were they simply distributed to deserving men and women by some central agency.

Similarly, however we draw the boundaries of the sphere within which free exchange operates, desert will play no role within those boundaries. I am skilful at bargaining and trading, let's say, and so accumulate a large number of beautiful pictures. If we assume, as painters mostly do, that pictures are appropriately traded in the market, then there is nothing wrong with my having the pictures. My title is legitimate. But it would be odd to say that I deserve to have them simply because I am good at bargaining and trading. Desert seems to require an especially close connection between particular goods and particular persons, whereas justice only sometimes requires a connection of that sort. Still, we might insist that only artistically cultivated people, who deserve to have pictures, should actually have them. It's not difficult to imagine a distributive mechanism. The state could buy all the pictures that were offered for sale (but artists would have to be licensed, so that there wouldn't be an endless number of pictures), evaluate them, and then distribute them to artistically cultivated men and women, the better pictures to the more cultivated. The state does something like this, sometimes, with regard to things that people need—medical care, for example—but not with regard to things that people deserve. There are practical difficulties here, but I suspect a deeper reason for this difference. Desert does not have the urgency of need, and it does not involve having (owning and consuming) in the same way. Hence, we are willing to tolerate the separation of owners of paintings and artistically cultivated people, or we are unwilling to require the kinds of interference in the market that would be necessary to end the separation. Of course, public provision is always possible alongside the market, and so we might argue that artistically cultivated people deserve not pictures but museums. Perhaps they do, but they don't deserve that the rest of us contribute money or appropriate public funds for the purchase of pictures and the construction of buildings. They will have to persuade us that art is worth the money; they will have to stimulate and encourage our own artistic cultivation. And if they fail to do that, their own love of art may well turn out to be 'impotent and a misfortune'.

Even if we were to assign the distribution of love, influence, offices, works of art, and so on, to some omnipotent arbiters of desert, how would we select them? How could anyone deserve such a position? Only God, who knows what secrets lurk in the hearts of men, would be able to make the necessary distributions. If human beings had to do the work, the distributive mechanism would be seized early on by some band of aristocrats (so they would call themselves) with a fixed conception of what is best and most deserving, and insensitive to the diverse excellences of their fellow citizens. And then desert would cease to be a pluralist criterion; we would find ourselves face to face with a new set (of an old sort) of tyrants. We do, of course, choose people as arbiters of desert—to serve on juries, for example, or to award prizes; it will be worth considering later what the prerogatives of a juror are. But it is important to stress here that he operates within a narrow range. Desert is a

strong claim, but it calls for difficult judgments; and only under very special conditions does it yield specific distributions.

Need

Finally, the criterion of need. 'To each according to his needs' is generally taken as the distributive half of Marx's famous maxim: we are to distribute the wealth of the community so as to meet the necessities of its members.[12] A plausible proposal, but a radically incomplete one. In fact, the first half of the maxim is also a distributive proposal, and it doesn't fit the rule of the second half. 'From each according to his ability' suggests that jobs should be distributed (or that men and women should be conscripted to work) on the basis of individual qualifications. But individuals don't in any obvious sense need the jobs for which they are qualified. Perhaps such jobs are scarce, and there are a large number of qualified candidates: which candidates need them most? If their material needs are already taken care of, perhaps they don't need to work at all. Or if, in some non-material sense, they all need to work, then that need won't distinguish among them, at least not to the naked eye. It would in any case be odd to ask a search committee looking, say, for a hospital director to make its choice on the basis of the needs of the candidates rather than on those of the staff and the patients of the hospital. But the latter set of needs, even if it isn't the subject of political disagreement, won't yield a single distributive decision.

Nor will need work for many other goods. Marx's maxim doesn't help at all with regard to the distribution of political power, honour and fame, sailboats, rare books, beautiful objects of every sort. These are not things that anyone, strictly speaking, needs. Even if we take a loose view and define the verb *to need* the way children do, as the strongest form of the verb *to want* we still won't have an adequate distributive criterion. The sorts of things that I have listed cannot be distributed equally to those with equal wants because some of them are generally, and some of them are necessarily, scarce, and some of them can't be possessed at all unless other people, for reasons of their own, agree on who is to possess them.

Need generates a particular distributive sphere, within which it is itself the appropriate distributive principle. In a poor society, a high proportion of social wealth will be drawn into this sphere. But given the great variety of goods that arises out of any common life, even when it is lived at a very low material level, other distributive criteria will always be operating alongside of need, and it will always be necessary to worry about the boundaries that mark them off from one another. Within its sphere, certainly, need meets the general distributive rule about *x* and *y*. Needed goods distributed to needy people in proportion to their neediness are obviously not dominated by any other goods. It's not having *y*, but only lacking *x* that is relevant. But we can now see, I think, that every criterion that has any force at all meets the general rule within its own sphere, and not elsewhere. This is the effect of the rule: different goods to different companies of men and women for different reasons and in accordance with different procedures. And to get all this right, or to get it roughly right, is to map out the entire social world. . . .

6

Hard Work

Equality and Hardness

It is not a question here of demanding or strenuous work. In that sense of the word, we can work hard in almost any office and at almost any job. I can work hard writing this book, and sometimes do. A task or a cause that seems to us worth the hard work it entails is clearly a good thing. For all our natural laziness, we go looking for it. But *hard* has another sense—as in 'hard winter' and 'hard heart'—where it means harsh, unpleasant, cruel, difficult to endure. Thus the account in Exodus of Israel's oppression, 'And the Egyptians embittered their lives with hard labour' (1:14). Here the word describes jobs that are like prison sentences, work that people don't look for and wouldn't choose if they had even minimally attractive alternatives. This kind of work is a negative good, and it commonly carries other negative goods in its train: poverty, insecurity, ill health, physical danger, dishonour, and degradation. And yet it is socially necessary work; it needs to be done, and that means that someone must be found to do it.

The conventional solution to this problem has the form of a simple equation: the negative good is matched by the negative status of the people into whose hands it is thrust. Hard work is distributed to degraded people. Citizens are set free; the work is imposed on slaves, resident aliens, 'guest workers'—outsiders all. Alternatively, the insiders who do the work are turned into 'inside' aliens, like the Indian untouchables or the American blacks after emancipation. In many societies, women have been the most important group of 'inside' aliens, doing the work that men disdained and freeing the men not only for more rewarding economic activities but also for citizenship and politics. Indeed, the household work that women traditionally have done—cooking, cleaning, caring for the sick and the old—makes up a substantial part of the hard work of the economy today, for which aliens are recruited (and women prominently among them).

The idea in all these cases is a cruel one: negative people for a negative good. The work should be done by men and women whose qualities it is presumed to fit. Because of their race or sex, or presumed intelligence, or social status, they deserve to do it, or they don't deserve not to do it, or they somehow qualify for it. It's not the work of citizens, free men, white men, and so on. But what sort of desert, what sort of qualification is this? It would be hard to say what the hard workers of this or any other society have done to deserve the danger and degradation their work commonly entails; or how they, and they alone, have qualified for it. What secrets have we learned about their moral character? When convicts do hard labour, we can at least argue that they deserve their punishment. But even they are not state slaves; their degradation is (most often) limited and temporary, and it is by no means clear that the most oppressive sorts of work should be assigned to them. And if not to them, surely to no one else. Indeed, if convicts are driven to hard labour, then ordinary men and women should probably be protected from it, so as to make it clear that they are not convicts and have never been found guilty by a jury of their peers. And if even convicts shouldn't be forced to endure the oppression (imprisonment being oppression enough), then it is *a fortiori* true that no one else should endure it.

Nor can it be imposed on outsiders. I have already argued that the people who do this sort of work are so closely tied into the everyday life of the political community that they can't rightly be denied membership. Hard work is a naturalization process, and it brings membership to those who endure the hardship. At the same time, there is something attractive about a community whose members resist hard work (and whose new members are naturalized into the resistance). They have a certain sense of themselves and their careers that rules out the acceptance of oppression; they refuse to be degraded and have the

strength to sustain the refusal. Neither the sense of self nor the personal strength are all that common in human history. They represent a significant achievement of modern democracy, closely connected to economic growth, certainly, but also to the success or the partial success of complex equality in the sphere of welfare. It is sometimes said to be an argument against the welfare state that its members are unwilling to take on certain sorts of jobs. But surely that is a sign of success. When we design a system of communal provision, one of our aims is to free people from the immediate constraints of physical need. So long as they are unfree, they are available for every sort of hard work, abased, as it were, by anticipation. Hungry, powerless, always insecure, they constitute 'the reserve army of the proletariat'. Once they have alternatives, they will rally and say No. Still, the work needs to be done. Who is to do it?

It is an old dream that no one will have to do it. We will solve the problem by abolishing the work, replacing men and women with machines wherever men and women find it unpleasant to be. Thus Oscar Wilde in his fine essay 'The Soul of Man under Socialism':

> All unintellectual labour, all monotonous, dull labour, all labour that deals with dreadful things and involves unpleasant conditions, must be done by machinery. Machinery must work for us in the coal mines and do all sanitary services, and be a stoker of steamers, and clean the streets, and run messages on wet days and do anything that is tedious and distressing.[13]

But that was always an unrealistic solution, for a great deal of hard work is required in the human services, where automation was never in prospect. Even where it was and still is in prospect, the invention and installation of the necessary machines is a much slower business than we once thought it would be. And machines as often replace people doing work they like to do as people doing 'tedious and distressing' work. Technology is not morally discriminating in its effects.

If we set automation aside, the most common egalitarian argument is that the work should be shared, rotated (like political offices) among the citizens. Everyone should do it—except convicts, of course, who now have to be excluded so as to make sure that the work carries no stigma. This is another example of simple equality. It has its beginning, I think, in the dangerous work of war. As we conscript young men for war, so, it's been said, we should conscript men and women generally for all those necessary jobs that are unlikely to attract volunteers. An army of citizens will replace the reserve army of the proletariat. This is an attractive proposal, and I shall want to give it its due. It can't be defended, however, across the range of hardness—not even across the range of danger. Hence I will have to consider more complex distributions. Negative goods have to be dispersed not only among individuals but also among distributive spheres. Some we can share in the same way that we share the costs of the welfare state; some, if market conditions are roughly egalitarian, we can buy and sell; some require political arguments and democratic decision-making. But all these forms have one thing in common: the distribution goes against the grain of the (negative) good. Except in the case of punishment, it just isn't possible to fit the distribution to the social meaning of the good, because there is no race or sex or caste and no conceivable set of individuals who can properly be singled out as society's hard workers. No one qualifies—there is no Pascalian company—and so all of us, in different ways and on different occasions, have to be available. . . .

Dirty Work

In principle, there is no such thing as intrinsically degrading work; degradation is a cultural phenomenon. It is probably true in practice, however, that a set of activities having to do with dirt, waste, and garbage has been the object of disdain and avoidance in just about every human society. (Fourier's children haven't yet learned the mores of their elders.) The precise list will vary from one time and place to another, but the set is more or less common. In India, for example, it includes the butchering of cows and the tanning of cowhide—jobs that have a rather different standing in Western cultures. But otherwise the characteristic occupations of the Indian untouchables suggest what we can think of as the third archetype of hard work: they are the scavengers and sweepers, the carriers of waste and night soil. No doubt the untouchables are peculiarly degraded, but it is difficult to believe that the work they do will ever be attractive or widely esteemed. Bernard Shaw was perfectly right to say that 'if all dustmen were dukes nobody would object to the dust,'[14] but it isn't easy to figure out how to produce such a happy arrangement. If all dustmen were dukes, they would find some new group, under another name, to do their dusting. Hence the question, in a society of equals, who will do the dirty work? has a special force. And the necessary answer is that, at least in some partial and symbolic sense, we will all have to do it. Then we will have an end to dukes, if not yet to dustmen. This is what Gandhi was getting at when he required his followers—himself, too—to clean the latrines of their ashram.[15] Here was a symbolic way of purging Hindu society of untouchability, but it also made a practical point: people should clean up their own dirt. Otherwise, the men and women who do it not only for themselves but for everyone else, too, will never be equal members of the political community.

What is required, then, is a kind of domestic *corvée*, not only in households—though it is especially important there—but also in communes, factories, offices, and schools. In all these places, we could hardly do better than to follow Walt Whitman's injunction (the poetry is weak but the argument right):

> For every man to see to it that he really do
>   something, for every woman too,
>
>   . . .
>
> To invent a little—something ingenious—to
>   aid the washing, cooking, cleaning,
>   And hold it no disgrace to take a hand
>   at them themselves.[16]

There would probably be less dirt to clean up if everyone knew in advance of making it that he couldn't leave the cleaning to someone else. But some people—patients in a hospital, for example—can't help but leave it to someone else, and certain sorts of cleaning are best organized on a large scale. Work of this sort might be done as part of a national service program. Indeed, war and waste seem the ideal subjects of national service: the first, because of the special risks involved; the second, because of the dishonour. Perhaps the work should be done by the young, not because they will enjoy it, but because it isn't without educational value. Perhaps each citizen should be allowed to choose when in the course of his life he will take his turn. But it is certainly appropriate that the cleaning of city streets, say, or of national parks should be the (part-time) work of the citizens.

It is not an appropriate goal for social policy, however, that all the dirty work that needs to be done should be shared among all the citizens. That would require an extraordinary degree of state control over everyone's life, and it would interfere radically with other kinds of work, some of it also necessary, some of it only useful. I have argued for a partial and symbolic sharing: the purpose is to break the link between dirty work and disrespect. In one sense, the break has already been accomplished, or substantially accomplished, through a long process of cultural transformation that begins with the early modern attack on feudal hierarchy. Before God, Puritan preachers taught, all human callings, all useful work, is equal.[17] Today we are likely to rank jobs as more or less desirable, not as more or less respectable. Most of us would deny that any socially useful work can be or should be debasing. And yet we still impose on hard-working fellow citizens patterns of behaviour, routines of distancing, that place them in a kind of pale: deferential movements, peremptory commands, refusals of recognition. When a garbage man feels stigmatized by the work he does, writes a contemporary sociologist, the stigma shows in his eyes. He enters 'into collusion with us to avoid contaminating us with his lowly self.' He looks away; and we do, too. 'Our eyes do not meet. He becomes a non-person.'[18] One way to break the collusion, and perhaps the best way, is to make sure that every citizen has a working knowledge of the working days of his hardest working fellows. Once that is done, it is possible to consider other mechanisms, including market mechanisms, for organizing the hard work of society.

So long as there is a reserve army, a class of degraded men and women driven by their poverty and their impoverished sense of their own value, the market will never be effective. Under such conditions, the hardest work is also the lowest paid, even though nobody wants to do it. But given a certain level of communal provision and a certain level of self-valuation, the work won't be done unless it is very well paid indeed (or unless the working conditions are very good). The citizens will find that if they want to hire their fellows as scavengers and sweepers, the rates will be high—much higher, in fact, than for more prestigious or pleasant work. This is a direct consequence of the fact that they are hiring *fellow* citizens. It is sometimes claimed that under conditions of genuine fellowship, no one would agree to be a scavenger or a sweeper. In that case, the work would have to be shared. But the claim is probably false. 'We are so accustomed,' as Shaw has written, 'to see dirty work done by dirty and poorly paid people that we have come to think that it is disgraceful to do it, and that unless a dirty and disgraced class existed, it would not be done at all.'[19] If sufficient money or leisure were offered, Shaw rightly insisted, people would come forward.

His own preference was for rewards that take the form of leisure or 'liberty'—which will always be, he argued, the strongest incentive and the best compensation for work that carries with it little intrinsic satisfaction:

In a picture gallery you will find a nicely dressed lady sitting at a table with nothing to do but to tell anyone who asks what is the price of any particular picture, and take an order for it if one is given. She has many pleasant chats with journalists and artists; and if she is bored she can read a novel. . . . But the gallery has to be scrubbed and dusted each day; and its windows have to be kept clean. It is clear that the lady's job is a much softer one than the charwoman's. To balance them you must either let them take their turns at the desk and at the scrubbing on alternate days or weeks; or else, as a first-class scrubber and duster and

cleaner might make a very bad business lady, and a very attractive business lady might make a very bad scrubber, you must let the charwoman go home and have the rest of the day to herself earlier than the lady at the desk.[20]

The contrast between the 'first-rate' charwoman and the 'very attractive' business lady nicely combines the prejudices of class and sex. If we set aside those prejudices, the periodic exchange of work is less difficult to imagine. The lady, after all, will have to share in the scrubbing, dusting, and cleaning at home (unless she has, as Shaw probably expected her to have, a charwoman there, too). And what is the charwoman to do with her leisure? Perhaps she will paint pictures or read books about art. But then, though the exchange is easy, it may well be resisted by the charwoman herself. One of the attractions of Shaw's proposal is that it establishes hard work as an opportunity for people who want to protect their time. So they will clean or scrub or collect garbage for the sake of their leisure, and avoid if they can any more engaging, competitive, or time-consuming employment. Under the right conditions, the market provides a kind of sanctuary from the pressures of the market. The price of the sanctuary is so many hours a day of hard work—for some people, at least, a price worth paying. . . .

There is no easy or elegant solution, and no fully satisfying solution, to the problem of hard work. Positive goods have, perhaps, their appropriate destination; negative goods do not. 'To escape facing this fact,' wrote Shaw, 'we may plead that some people have such very queer tastes that it is almost impossible to mention an occupation that you will not find somebody with a craze for. . . . The saying that God never made a job but he made a man or woman to do it is true up to a certain point.'21 But that plea doesn't take us very far. The truth is that hard work is unattractive work for most of the men and women who find themselves doing it. When they were growing up, they dreamed of doing something else. And as they age, the work gets more and more difficult. Thus, a 50-year-old garbage collector to Studs Terkel: 'the alleys are longer and the cans larger. Getting old.'22

We can share (and partially transform) hard work through some sort of national service; we can reward it with money or leisure; we can make it more rewarding by connecting it to other sorts of activity—political, managerial, and professional in character. We can conscript, rotate, cooperate, and compensate; we can reorganize the work and rectify its names. We can do all these things, but we will not have abolished hard work; nor will we have abolished the class of hard workers. The first kind of abolitionism is, as I have already argued, impossible; the second would merely double hardness with coercion. The measures that I have proposed are at best partial and incomplete. They have an end appropriate to a negative good: a distribution of hard work that doesn't corrupt the distributive spheres with which it overlaps, carrying poverty into the sphere of money, degradation into the sphere of honour, weakness and resignation into the sphere of power. To rule out negative dominance: that is the purpose of collective bargaining, cooperative management, professional conflict, the rectification of names—the politics of hard work. The outcomes of this politics are indeterminate, certain to be different in different times and places, conditioned by previously established hierarchies and social understandings. But they will also be conditioned by the solidarity, the skilfulness, and the energy of the workers themselves.

Notes

1. See John Rawls, *A Theory of Justice* (Cambridge, MA, 1971); Jürgen Habermas, *Legitimation Crisis*, trans. Thomas McCarthy (Boston, 1975), esp. 113; Bruce Ackerman, Social Justice in the Liberal State (New Haven, 1980).

2. Robert Nozick makes a similar argument in *Anarchy, State, and Utopia* (New York, 1974), 149–50, but with radically individualistic conclusions that seem to me to miss the social character of production.

3. Ralph Waldo Emerson, 'Ode,' in *The Complete Essays and Other Writings*, ed. Brooks Atkinson (New York, 1940), 770.

4. John Stuart Mill, 'On Liberty,' in *The Philosophy of John Stuart Mill*, ed. Marshall Cohen (New York, 1961), 255. For an anthropological account of liking and not liking social goods, see Mary Douglas and Baron Isherwood, *The World of Goods* (New York, 1979).

5. William James, quoted in C.R. Snyder and Howard Fromkin, *Uniqueness: The Human Pursuit of Difference* (New York, 1980), 108.

6. Karl Marx, *The German Ideology*, ed. R. Pascal (New York, 1947), 89.

7. Bernard Williams, *Problems of the Self: Philosophical Papers, 1956–1972* (Cambridge, UK, 1973), 230–49 ('The Idea of Equality'). This essay is one of the starting points of my own thinking about distributive justice. See also the critique of Williams's argument (and of an earlier essay of my own) in Amy Gutmann, *Liberal Equality* (Cambridge, UK, 1980), chap. 4.

8. Blaise Pascal, *The Pensées*, trans. J.M. Cohen (Hammondsworth, UK, 1961), 96 (no. 244).

9. Karl Marx, 'Economic and Philosophical Manuscripts,' in *Early Writings*, ed. T.B. Bottomore (London, 1963), 193–4. It is interesting to note an earlier echo of Pascal's argument in Adam Smith's *Theory of Moral Sentiments* (Edinburgh, 1813), vol. 1, 378–9; but Smith seems to have

believed that distributions in his own society actually conformed to this view of appropriateness—a mistake neither Pascal nor Marx ever made.

10. See the summary account in Jean Bodin, *Six Books of a Commonweale*, ed. Kenneth Douglas McRae (Cambridge, MA, 1962), 210–18.

11. Cf. Nozick on 'patterning', *Anarchy, State, and Utopia* [2], 155f.

12. Marx, 'Critique of the Gotha Program,' in Marx and Engels, *Selected Works* (Moscow, 1951), vol. 2, 23.

13. Oscar Wilde, 'The Soul of Man under Socialism,' reprinted in *The Artist As Critic: Critical Writings of Oscar Wilde*, ed. Richard Ellmann (New York, 1969), 269.

14. Bernard Shaw, *The Intelligent Woman's Guide to Socialism, Capitalism, Sovietism, and Fascism* (Hammondsworth, UK, 1937), 106.

15. Harold R. Isaacs, *India's Ex-Untouchables* (New York, 1974), 36–7.

16. Walt Whitman, 'Song of the Exposition,' in *Complete Poetry and Selected Prose*, ed. James E. Miller, Jr (Boston, 1959), 147.

17. See Michael Walzer, *The Revolution of the Saints: A Study in the Origin of Radical Politics* (Cambridge, MA, 1965), 214.

18. Stewart E. Perry, *San Francisco Scavengers: Dirty Work and the Pride of Ownership* (Berkeley, 1978), 7.

19. Shaw, *Woman's Guide* [11], 105.

20. Ibid., 109.

21. Ibid., 107.

22. Studs Terkel, *Working* (New York, 1975) [22], 153.

'Terrorism: A Critique of Excuses'

No one these days advocates terrorism, not even those who regularly practise it. The practice is indefensible now that it has been recognized, like rape and murder, as an attack upon the innocent. In a sense, indeed, terrorism is worse than rape and murder commonly are, for in the latter cases the victim has been chosen for a purpose; he or she is the direct object of attack, and the attack has some reason, however twisted or ugly it may be. The victims of a terrorist attack are third parties, innocent bystanders; there is no special reason for attacking them; anyone else within a large class of (unrelated) people will do as well. The attack is directed indiscriminately against the entire class. Terrorists are like killers on a rampage, except that their rampage is not just expressive of rage or madness; the rage is purposeful and programmatic. It aims at a general vulnerability: Kill these people in order to terrify those. A relatively small number of dead victims makes for a very large number of living and frightened hostages.

This, then, is the peculiar evil of terrorism—not only the killing of innocent people but also the intrusion of fear into everyday life, the violation of private purposes, the insecurity of public spaces, the endless coerciveness of precaution. A crime wave might, I suppose, produce similar effects, but no one plans a crime wave; it is the work of a thousand individual decision-makers, each one independent of the others, brought together only by the invisible hand. Terrorism is the work of visible hands; it is an organizational project, a strategic choice, a conspiracy to murder and intimidate . . . you and me. No wonder the conspirators have difficulty defending, in public, the strategy they have chosen.

The moral difficulty is the same, obviously, when the conspiracy is directed not against you and me but against them—Protestants, say, not Catholics; Israelis, not Italians or Germans; blacks, not whites. These 'limits' rarely hold for long; the logic of terrorism steadily expands the range of vulnerability. The more hostages they hold, the stronger the terrorists are. No one is safe once whole populations have been put at risk. Even if the risk were contained, however, the evil would be no different. So far as individual Protestants or Israelis or blacks are concerned, terrorism is random, degrading, and frightening. That is its hallmark, and that, again, is why it cannot be defended.

But when moral justification is ruled out, the way is opened for ideological excuse and apology. We live today in a political culture of excuses. This is far better than a political culture in which terrorism is openly defended and justified, for the excuse at least acknowledges the evil. But the improvement is precarious, hard won, and difficult to sustain. It is not the case, even in this better world, that terrorist organizations are without supporters. The support is indirect but by no means ineffective. It takes the form of apologetic descriptions and explanations, a litany of excuses that steadily undercuts our knowledge of the evil. Today that knowledge is insufficient unless it is supplemented and reinforced by a systematic critique of excuses. That is my purpose in this chapter. I take the principle for granted: that every act of terrorism is a wrongful act. The wrongfulness of the excuses, however, cannot be taken for granted; it has to be argued. The excuses themselves are familiar enough, the stuff of contemporary political debate. I shall state them in stereotypical form.

There is no need to attribute them to this or that writer, publicist, or commentator; my readers can make their own attributions.[1]

The Excuses for Terrorism

The most common excuse for terrorism is that it is a last resort, chosen only when all else fails. The image is of people who have literally run out of options. One by one, they have tried every legitimate form of political and military action, exhausted every possibility, failed everywhere, until no alternative remains but the evil of terrorism. They must be terrorists or do nothing at all. The easy response is to insist that, given this description of their case, they should do nothing at all; they have indeed exhausted their possibilities. But this response simply reaffirms the principle, ignores the excuse; this response does not attend to the terrorists' desperation. Whatever the cause to which they are committed, we have to recognize that, given the commitment, the one thing they cannot do is 'nothing at all'.

But the case is badly described. It is not so easy to reach the 'last resort'. To get there, one must indeed try everything (which is a lot of things) and not just once, as if a political party might organize a single demonstration, fail to win immediate victory, and claim that it was now justified in moving on to murder. Politics is an art of repetition. Activists and citizens learn from experience, that is, by doing the same thing over and over again. It is by no means clear when they run out of options, but even under conditions of oppression and war, citizens have a good run short of that. The same argument applies to state officials who claim that they have tried 'everything' and are now compelled to kill hostages or bomb peasant villages. Imagine such people called before a judicial tribunal and required to answer the question, What exactly did you try? Does anyone believe that they could come up with a plausible list? 'Last resort' has only a notional finality; the resort to terror is ideologically last, not last in an actual series of actions, just last for the sake of the excuse. In fact, most state officials and movement militants who recommend a policy of terrorism recommend it as a first resort; they are for it from the beginning, although they may not get their way at the beginning. If they are honest, then, they must make other excuses and give up the pretence of the last resort.

The second excuse is designed for national liberation movements struggling against established and powerful states. Now the claim is that nothing else is possible, that no other strategy is available except terrorism. This is different from the first excuse because it does not require would-be terrorists to run through all the available options. Or, the second excuse requires terrorists to run through all the options in their heads, not in the world; notional finality is enough. Movement strategists consider their options and conclude that they have no alternative to terrorism. They think that they do not have the political strength to try anything else, and thus they do not try anything else. Weakness is their excuse.

But two very different kinds of weakness are commonly confused here: the weakness of the movement vis-à-vis the opposing state and the movement's weakness vis-à-vis its own people. This second kind of weakness, the inability of the movement to mobilize the nation, makes terrorism the 'only' option because it effectively rules out all the others: non-violent resistance, general strikes, mass demonstrations, unconventional warfare, and so on.

These options are only rarely ruled out by the sheer power of the state, by the pervasiveness and intensity of oppression. Totalitarian states may be immune to non-violent or guerrilla resistance, but all the evidence suggests that they are also immune to terrorism. Or, more exactly, in totalitarian states, state terror dominates every other sort. Where terrorism is a possible strategy for the oppositional movement (in liberal and democratic states, most obviously), other strategies are also possible if the movement has some significant degree of popular support. In the absence of popular support, terrorism may indeed be the one available strategy, but it is hard to see how its evils can then be excused. For it is not weakness alone that makes the excuse, but the claim of the terrorists to represent the weak; and the particular form of weakness that makes terrorism the only option calls that claim into question.

One might avoid this difficulty with a stronger insistence on the actual effectiveness of terrorism. The third excuse is simply that terrorism works (and nothing else does); it achieves the ends of the oppressed even without their participation. 'When the act accuses, the result excuses.'[2] This is a consequentialist argument, and given a strict understanding of consequentialism, this argument amounts to a justification rather than an excuse. In practice, however, the argument is rarely pushed so far. More often, the argument begins with an acknowledgement of the terrorists' wrongdoing. Their hands are dirty, but we must make a kind of peace with them because they have acted effectively for the sake of people who could not act for themselves. But, in fact, have the terrorists' actions been effective? I doubt that terrorism has ever achieved national liberation—no nation that I know of owes its freedom to a campaign of random murder—although terrorism undoubtedly increases the power of the terrorists within the national liberation movement. Perhaps terrorism is also conducive to the survival and notoriety (the two go together) of the movement, which is now dominated by terrorists. But even if we were to grant some means-end relationship between terror and national liberation, the third excuse does not work unless it can meet the further requirements of a consequentialist argument. It must be possible to say that the desired end could not have been achieved through any other, less wrongful, means. The third excuse depends, then, on the success of the first or second, and neither of these look likely to be successful.

The fourth excuse avoids this crippling dependency. This excuse does not require the apologist to defend either of the improbable claims that terrorism is the last resort or that it is the only possible resort. The fourth excuse is simply that terrorism is the universal resort. All politics is (really) terrorism. The appearance of innocence and decency is always a piece of deception, more or less convincing in accordance with the relative power of the deceivers. The terrorist who does not bother with appearances is only doing openly what everyone else does secretly.

This argument has the same form as the maxim 'All's fair in love and war.' Love is always fraudulent, war is always brutal, and political action is always terrorist in character. Political action works (as Thomas Hobbes long ago argued) only by generating fear in innocent men and women. Terrorism is the politics of state officials and movement militants alike. This argument does not justify either the officials or the militants, but it does excuse them all. We hardly can be harsh with people who act the way everyone else acts. Only saints are likely to act differently, and sainthood in politics is supererogatory, a matter of grace, not obligation.

But this fourth excuse relies too heavily on our cynicism about political life, and cynicism only sometimes answers well to experience. In fact, legitimate states do not need to terrorize their citizens, and strongly based movements do not need to terrorize their opponents. Officials and militants who live, as it were, on the margins of legitimacy and strength sometimes choose terrorism and sometimes do not. Living in terror is not a universal experience. The world the terrorists create has its entrances and exits.

If we want to understand the choice of terror, the choice that forces the rest of us through the door, we have to imagine what in fact always occurs, although we often have no satisfactory record of the occurrence: A group of men and women, officials or militants, sits around a table and argues about whether or not to adopt a terrorist strategy. Later on, the litany of excuses obscures the argument. But at the time, around the table, it would have been no use for defenders of terrorism to say, 'Everybody does it,' because there they would be face to face with people proposing to do something else. Nor is it historically the case that the members of this last group, the opponents of terrorism, always lose the argument. They can win, however, and still not be able to prevent a terrorist campaign; the would-be terrorists (it does not take very many) can always split the movement and go their own way. Or, they can split the bureaucracy or the police or officer corps and act in the shadow of state power. Indeed, terrorism often has its origin in such splits. The first victims are the terrorists' former comrades or colleagues. What reason can we possibly have, then, for equating the two? If we value the politics of the men and women who oppose terrorism, we must reject the excuses of their murderers. Cynicism at such a time is unfair to the victims.

The fourth excuse can also take, often does take, a more restricted form. Oppression, rather than political rule more generally, is always terroristic in character, and thus, we must always excuse the opponents of oppression. When they choose terrorism, they are only reacting to someone else's previous choice, repaying in kind the treatment they have long received. Of course, their terrorism repeats the evil—innocent people are killed, who were never themselves oppressors—but repetition is not the same as initiation. The oppressors set the terms of the struggle. But if the struggle is fought on the oppressors' terms, then the oppressors are likely to win. Or, at least, oppression is likely to win, even if it takes on a new face. The whole point of a liberation movement or a popular mobilization is to change the terms. We have no reason to excuse the terrorism reactively adopted by opponents of oppression unless we are confident of the sincerity of their opposition, the seriousness of their commitment to a non-oppressive politics. But the choice of terrorism undermines that confidence.

We are often asked to distinguish the terrorism of the oppressed from the terrorism of the oppressors. What is it, however, that makes the difference? The message of the terrorist is the same in both cases: a denial of the people-hood and humanity of the groups among whom he or she finds victims. Terrorism anticipates, when it does not actually enforce, political domination. Does it matter if one dominated group is replaced by another? Imagine a slave revolt whose protagonists dream only of enslaving in their turn the children of their masters. The dream is understandable, but the fervent desire of the children that the revolt be repressed is equally understandable. In neither case does understanding make for excuse—not, at least, after a politics of universal freedom has become possible. Nor does an understanding of oppression excuse the terrorism of the oppressed, once we have grasped the meaning of 'liberation'.

These are the four general excuses for terror, and each of them fails. They depend upon statements about the world that are false,

historical arguments for which there is no evidence, moral claims that turn out to be hollow or dishonest. This is not to say that there might not be more particular excuses that have greater plausibility, extenuating circumstances in particular cases that we would feel compelled to recognize. As with murder, we can tell a story (like the story that Richard Wright tells in *Native Son*, for example) that might lead us, not to justify terrorism, but to excuse this or that individual terrorist. We can provide a personal history, a psychological study, of compassion destroyed by fear, moral reason by hatred and rage, social inhibition by unending violence—the product, an individual driven to kill or readily set on a killing course by his or her political leaders.[3] But the force of this story will not depend on any of the four general excuses, all of which grant what the storyteller will have to deny: that terrorism is the deliberate choice of rational men and women. Whether they conceive it to be one option among others or the only one available, they nevertheless argue and choose. Whether they are acting or reacting, they have made a decision. The human instruments they subsequently find to plant the bomb or shoot the gun may act under some psychological compulsion, but the men and women who choose terror as a policy act 'freely'. They could not act in any other way, or accept any other description of their action, and still pretend to be the leaders of the movement or the state. We ought never to excuse such leaders.

The Response to Terrorism

What follows from the critique of excuses? There is still a great deal of room for argument about the best way of responding to terrorism. Certainly, terrorists should be resisted, and it is not likely that a purely defensive resistance will ever be sufficient. In this sort of struggle, the offence is always ahead. The technology of terror is simple; the weapons are readily produced and easy to deliver. It is virtually impossible to protect people against random and indiscriminate attack. Thus, resistance will have to be supplemented by some combination of repression and retaliation. This is a dangerous business because repression and retaliation so often take terroristic forms and there are a host of apologists ready with excuses that sound remarkably like those of the terrorists themselves. It should be clear by now, however, that counterterrorism cannot be excused merely because it is reactive. Every new actor, terrorist or counterterrorist, claims to be reacting to someone else, standing in a circle and just passing the evil along. But the circle is ideological in character; in fact, every actor is a moral agent and makes an independent decision.

Therefore, repression and retaliation must not repeat the wrongs of terrorism, which is to say that repression and retaliation must be aimed systematically at the terrorists themselves, never at the people for whom the terrorists claim to be acting. That claim is in any case doubtful, even when it is honestly made. The people do not authorize the terrorists to act in their name. Only a tiny number actually participate in terrorist activities; they are far more likely to suffer than to benefit from the terrorist program. Even if they supported the program and hoped to benefit from it, however, they would still be immune from attack—exactly as civilians in time of war who support the war effort but are not themselves part of it are subject to the same immunity. Civilians may be put at risk by attacks on military targets, as by attacks on terrorist targets, but the risk must be kept to a minimum, even at some cost to the attackers. The refusal to make ordinary people into targets, whatever

their nationality or even their politics, is the only way to say no to terrorism. Every act of repression and retaliation has to be measured by this standard.

But what if the 'only way' to defeat the terrorists is to intimidate their actual or potential supporters? It is important to deny the premise of this question: that terrorism is a politics dependent on mass support. In fact, it is always the politics of an elite, whose members are dedicated and fanatical and more than ready to endure, or to watch others endure, the devastations of a counterterrorist campaign. Indeed, terrorists will welcome counterterrorism; it makes the terrorists' excuses more plausible and is sure to bring them, however many people are killed or wounded, however many are terrorized, the small number of recruits needed to sustain the terrorist activities.

Repression and retaliation are legitimate responses to terrorism only when they are constrained by the same moral principles that rule out terrorism itself. But there is an alternative response that seeks to avoid the violence that these two entail. The alternative is to address directly, ourselves, the oppression the terrorists claim to oppose. Oppression, they say, is the cause of terrorism. But that is merely one more excuse. The real cause of terrorism is the decision to launch a terrorist campaign, a decision made by that group of people sitting around a table whose deliberations I have already described. However, terrorists do exploit oppression, injustice, and human misery generally and look to these at least for their excuses. There can hardly be any doubt that oppression strengthens their hand. Is that a reason for us to come to the defence of the oppressed? It seems to me that we have our own reasons to do that, and do not need this one, or should not, to prod us into action. We might imitate those movement militants who argue against the adoption of a terrorist strategy—although not, as the terrorists say, because these militants are prepared to tolerate oppression. They already are opposed to oppression and now add to that opposition, perhaps for the same reasons, a refusal of terror. So should we have been opposed before, and we should now make the same addition.

But there is an argument, put with some insistence these days, that we should refuse to acknowledge any link at all between terrorism and oppression—as if any defence of oppressed men and women, once a terrorist campaign has been launched, would concede the effectiveness of the campaign. Or, at least, a defence of oppression would give terrorism the appearance of effectiveness and so increase the likelihood of terrorist campaigns in the future. Here we have the reverse side of the litany of excuses; we have turned over the record. First oppression is made into an excuse for terrorism, and then terrorism is made into an excuse for oppression. The first is the excuse of the far left; the second is the excuse of the neoconservative right.[4] I doubt that genuine conservatives would think it a good reason for defending the status quo that it is under terrorist attack; they would have independent reasons and would be prepared to defend the status quo against any attack. Similarly, those of us who think that the status quo urgently requires change have our own reasons for thinking so and need not be intimidated by terrorists or, for that matter, antiterrorists.

If one criticizes the first excuse, one should not neglect the second. But I need to state the second more precisely. It is not so much an excuse for oppression as an excuse for doing nothing (now) about oppression. The claim is that the campaign against terrorism has priority over every other political activity. If the people who take the lead in this campaign are the old oppressors, then we must make a kind of peace with them—temporarily, of course, until the terrorists have been beaten. This is a strategy that denies the possibility of a two-front war. So long as the men and women who pretend to lead the fight against oppression are terrorists, we can concede nothing to their demands. Nor can we oppose their opponents.

But why not? It is not likely in any case that terrorists would claim victory in the face of a serious effort to deal with the oppression of the people they claim to be defending. The effort would merely expose the hollowness of their claim, and the nearer it came to success, the more they would escalate their terrorism. They would still have to be defeated, for what they are after is not a solution to the problem but rather the power to impose their own solution. No decent end to the conflict in Ireland, say, or in Lebanon, or in the Middle East generally, is going to look like a victory for terrorism—if only because the different groups of terrorists are each committed, by the strategy they have adopted, to an indecent end.[5] By working for our own ends, we expose the indecency.

Oppression and Terrorism

It is worth considering at greater length the link between oppression and terror. To pretend that there is no link at all is to ignore the historical record, but the record is more complex than any of the excuses acknowledge. The first thing to be read out of it, however, is simple enough: Oppression is not so much the cause of terrorism as terrorism is one of the primary means of oppression. This was true in ancient times, as Aristotle recognized, and it is still true today. Tyrants rule by terrorizing their subjects; unjust and illegitimate regimes are upheld through a combination of carefully aimed and random violence.[6] If this method works in the state, there is no reason to think that it will not work, or that it does not work, in the liberation movement. Wherever we see terrorism, we should look for tyranny and oppression. Authoritarian states, especially in the moment of their founding, need a terrorist apparatus—secret police with unlimited power, secret prisons into which citizens disappear, death squads in unmarked cars. Even democracies may use terror, not against their own citizens, but at the margins, in their colonies, for example, where colonizers also are likely to rule tyrannically. Oppression is sometimes maintained by a steady and discriminate pressure, sometimes by intermittent and random violence—what we might think of as terrorist melodrama—designed to render the subject population fearful and passive.

This latter policy, especially if it seems successful, invites imitation by opponents of the state. But terrorism does not spread only when it is imitated. If it can be invented by state officials, it can also be invented by movement militants. Neither one need take lessons from the other; the circle has no single or necessary starting point. Wherever it starts, terrorism in the movement is tyrannical and oppressive in exactly the same way as is terrorism in the state. The terrorists aim to rule, and murder is their method. They have their own internal police, death squads, disappearances. They begin by killing or intimidating those comrades who stand in their way, and they proceed to do the same, if they can, among the people they claim to represent. If terrorists are successful, they rule tyrannically, and their people bear, without consent, the costs of the terrorists' rule. (If the terrorists are only partly successful, the costs to the people may be even greater: What they have to bear now is a war between rival terrorist gangs.) But terrorists cannot win the ultimate victory they seek without challenging the established regime or colonial power and the people it

claims to represent, and when terrorists do that, they themselves invite imitation. The regime may then respond with its own campaign of aimed and random violence. Terrorist tracks terrorist, each claiming the other as an excuse.

The same violence can also spread to countries where it has not yet been experienced; now terror is reproduced not through temporal succession but through ideological adaptation. State terrorists wage bloody wars against largely imaginary enemies: army colonels, say, hunting down the representatives of 'international communism'. Or movement terrorists wage bloody wars against enemies with whom, but for the ideology, they could readily negotiate and compromise: nationalist fanatics committed to a permanent irredentism. These wars, even if they are without precedents, are likely enough to become precedents, to start the circle of terror and counterterror, which is endlessly oppressive for the ordinary men and women whom the state calls its citizens and the movement its 'people'.

The only way to break out of the circle is to refuse to play the terrorist game. Terrorists in the state and the movement warn us, with equal vehemence, that any such refusal is a sign of softness and naiveté. The self-portrait of the terrorists is always the same. They are tough-minded and realistic; they know their enemies (or privately invent them for ideological purposes); and they are ready to do what must be done for victory. Why then do terrorists turn around and around in the same circle? It is true: Movement terrorists win support because they pretend to deal energetically and effectively with the brutality of the state. It also is true: State terrorists win support because they pretend to deal energetically and effectively with the brutality of the movement. Both feed on the fears of brutalized and oppressed people. But there is no way of overcoming brutality with terror. At most, the burden is shifted from these people to those; more likely, new burdens are added for everyone. Genuine liberation can come only through a politics that mobilizes the victims of brutality and takes careful aim at its agents, or by a politics that surrenders the hope of victory and domination and deliberately seeks a compromise settlement. In either case, once tyranny is repudiated, terrorism is no longer an option. For what lies behind all the excuses, of officials and militants alike, is the predilection for a tyrannical politics.

Notes

1. I cannot resist a few examples: Edward Said, 'The Terrorism Scam,' *The Nation*, 14 June 1986; and (more intelligent and circumspect) Richard Falk, 'Thinking about Terrorism,' *The Nation*, 28 June 1986.
2. Machiavelli, *The Discourses* I: ix. As yet, however, there have been no results that would constitute a Machiavellian excuse.
3. See, for example, Daniel Goleman, 'The Roots of Terrorism Are Found in Brutality of Shattered Childhood,' *New York Times*, 2 September 1986, Cl, 8. Goleman discusses the psychic and social history of particular terrorists, not the roots of terrorism.
4. The neoconservative position is represented, although not as explicitly as I have stated it here, in Benjamin Netanyahu, ed., *Terrorism: How the West Can Win* (New York: Farrar, Straus & Giroux, 1986).
5. The reason the terrorist strategy, however indecent in itself, cannot be instrumental to some decent political purpose is because any decent purpose must somehow accommodate the people against whom the terrorism is aimed, and what terrorism expresses is precisely the refusal of such an accommodation, the radical devaluing of the Other. See my argument in *Just and Unjust Wars* (New York: Basic Books, 1977), 197–206, especially 203.
6. Aristotle, *The Politics* 1313–1314a.

Study Questions for *Spheres of Justice*

1. How does Walzer characterize political egalitarianism? Do egalitarians recommend that all people possess the same amounts of social goods?
2. What problems does Walzer identify in Rawls's assumption that ideally rational individuals can discover a single correct theory of justice?
3. What sorts of goods does Walzer discuss in his account of distributive justice? How does Walzer support his claim that there does not exist a single set of primary or basic goods valued across all cultures?
4. Explain the ideals of complex equality and autonomy among spheres of justice. Why would an egalitarian favour these ideals?
5. What examples illustrate Walzer's principle that 'no social good x should be distributed to men and women who possess some other good y merely because they possess y and without regard to the meaning of y'?

6. Walzer rejects utopian visions of a world in which either everyone or no one performs hard or unpleasant work. Why does Walzer reject these classical egalitarian utopias? What solutions does Walzer himself suggest for the distribution of hard work?

Study Questions for 'Terrorism: A Critique of Excuses'

1. How does Walzer define terrorism? Why is terrorism morally worse than other kinds of attacks on innocent people, according to Walzer? Can you identify any problems with Walzer's characterization of terrorism?
2. Identify the four main excuses or justifications for terrorism discussed by Walzer. What reasons does Walzer provide for rejecting each of these possible excuses?
3. Why are purely defensive strategies of resistance to terrorism ineffective? Describe and evaluate the recommendations Walzer makes for responding to terrorism.
4. 'Terrorism: A Critique of Excuses' was originally published in 1988. Is Walzer's account of terrorism relevant to international terrorist attacks in the twenty-first century? Why or why not?

Recommended Readings

Anderson, Elizabeth, 'What Is the Point of Equality?' *Ethics* 109 (1999): 287–337.

Fullinwider, Robert, 'Understanding Terrorism,' in *Problems of International Justice*, edited by Steven Luper-Foy (Westview Press, 1988).

Holtug, Nils, and Kasper Lippert-Rasmussen, eds, *Egalitarianism: New Essays on the Nature and Value of Equality* (Oxford University Press, 2007).

Miller, David, *Principles of Social Justice* (Harvard University Press, 1999).

Miller, David, and Michael Walzer, eds, *Pluralism, Justice and Equality* (Oxford University Press, 1995).

Phillips, Anne, *Which Equalities Matter?* (Polity Press, 1999).

Primoratz, Igor, ed., *Terrorism: The Philosophical Issues* (Macmillan, 2004).

Sen, Amartya, *Inequality Reexamined* (Harvard University Press, 1992).

Young, Iris Marion, *Justice and the Politics of Difference* (Princeton University Press, 1990).

Susan Moller Okin

Susan Moller Okin (1946–2004) was born in Auckland, New Zealand, and earned MA and PhD degrees from Oxford University and Harvard University, respectively. At the time of her sudden and untimely death in 2004, she held a distinguished visiting professorship at Harvard University and was a member of the permanent faculty at Stanford University. She is known in the fields of philosophy and political science primarily for her feminist critical analyses of classical and contemporary political theories. Her first monograph, *Women in Western Political Thought* (1979), focuses on misogyny and patriarchy in classical political theory; her second book, *Justice, Gender, and the Family* (1989), examines the neglect of gender and the family in contemporary mainstream political philosophy. In the latter work, Okin argues not only that the family is an important subject of justice but also that justice within families requires remedying gendered inequalities in divisions of household labour and broader social imbalances of power between women and men.

Like Michael Walzer, Okin has a predominant concern with developing a theory of justice that supports social equity and undermines forms of oppression and dominance. In addition to critically analysing influential contemporary political philosophers from a feminist perspective, *Justice, Gender, and the Family* presents several suggestions for transforming workplace and family structures in order to support a society in which both men and women are free to participate fully in working, civic, or political life. As Okin writes, 'only when men participate equally in what have been principally women's realms of meeting the daily material and psychological needs of those close to them, and when women participate equally in what have been principally men's realms of larger scale production, government and artistic life, will members of both sexes be able to develop a more complete *human* personality than has hitherto been possible' (1989, 107).

In 'Is Multiculturalism Bad for Women?' Okin suggests that a tension exists between feminism and multiculturalism; the two are not similarly progressive political ideologies easily reconcilable with one another. Multicultural political philosophers often recommend preserving minority cultures through special group rights (see Will Kymlicka's *Multicultural Citizenship* in the next chapter), but these special group rights may condone or support cultural practices that are oppressive to women and girls. Okin argues that such customs as clitoridectomy, polygamy, and child marriage violate basic human rights and liberties recognized in Western liberal democracies and that cultural minorities living in liberal states should not be able to continue these practices by appealing to distinctive cultural traditions and special group rights. In the anthology *Is Multiculturalism Bad for Women?* (1999), 15 social and political theorists respond to Okin's essay on feminism and multiculturalism.

Justice, Gender, and the Family

1

Introduction: Justice and Gender

Almost every person in our society starts life in a family of some sort or other. Fewer of these families now fit the usual, though by no means universal, standard of previous generations, that is, wage-working father, homemaking mother, and children. More families these days are headed by a single parent; lesbian and gay parenting is no longer so rare; many children have two wage-working parents, and receive at least some of their early care outside the home. While its forms are varied, the family in which a child is raised, especially in the earliest years, is clearly a crucial place for early moral development and for the formation of our basic attitudes to others. It is, potentially, a place where we can *learn to be* just. It is especially important for the development of a sense of justice that grows from sharing the experiences of others and becoming aware of the points of view of others who are different in some respects from ourselves, but with whom we clearly have some interests in common. . . .

Most theorists of the past who stressed the importance of the family and its practices for the wider world of moral and political life by no means insisted on congruence between the structures or practices of the family and those of the outside world. Though concerned with moral development, they bifurcated public from private life to such an extent that they had no trouble reconciling inegalitarian, sometimes admittedly unjust, relations founded upon sentiment within the family with a more just, even egalitarian, social structure outside the family. Rousseau, Hegel, Tocqueville—all thought the family was centrally important for

the development of morality in citizens, but all defended the hierarchy of the marital structure while spurning such a degree of hierarchy in institutions and practices outside the household. Preferring instead to rely on love, altruism, and generosity as the basis for family relations, none of these theorists argued for *just* family structures as necessary for socializing children into citizenship in a just society.

The position that justice within the family is irrelevant to the development of just citizens was not plausible even when only men were citizens. John Stuart Mill, in *The Subjection of Women*, takes an impassioned stand against it. He argues that the inequality of women within the family is deeply subversive of justice in general in the wider social world, because it subverts the moral potential of men. Mill's first answer to the question, 'For whose good are all these changes in women's rights to be undertaken?' is: 'the advantage of having the most universal and pervading of all human relations regulated by justice instead of injustice.' Making marriage a relationship of equals, he argues, would transform this central part of daily life from 'a school of despotism' into 'a school of moral cultivation'.[1] He goes on to discuss, in the strongest of terms, the noxious effect of growing up in a family not regulated by justice. Consider, he says, 'the self-worship, the unjust self-preference' nourished in a boy growing up in a household in which 'by the mere fact of being born a male he is by right the superior of all and every one of an entire half of the human race.' Mill concludes that the example set by perpetuating a marital structure 'contradictory to the first principles of social justice' must have such 'a perverting influence' that it is hard even to imagine the good effects of changing it. All other attempts to educate people to respect and practise justice, Mill claims, will be superficial 'as long as the citadel of the enemy is not attacked.' Mill felt as much hope for what the family might be as he felt despair at what it was not. 'The family, justly constituted, would be the real school of the virtues of freedom,' primary among which was 'justice, . . . grounded as before on equal, but now also on sympathetic association.'[2] Mill both saw clearly and had the courage to address what so many other political philosophers either could not see, or saw and turned away from.

Despite the strength and fervour of his advocacy of women's rights, however, Mill's idea of a just family structure falls far short of that of many feminists even of his own time, including his wife, Harriet Taylor. In spite of the fact that Mill recognized both the empowering effect of earnings on one's position in the family and the limiting effect of domestic responsibility on women's opportunities, he balked at questioning the traditional division of labour between the sexes. For him, a woman's choice of marriage was parallel to a man's choice of a profession: unless and until she had fulfilled her obligations to her husband and children, she should not undertake anything else. But clearly, however equal the legal rights of husbands and wives, this position largely undermines Mill's own insistence upon the importance of marital equality for a just society. His acceptance of the traditional division of labour, without making any provision for wives who were thereby made economically dependent upon their husbands, largely undermines his insistence upon family justice as the necessary foundation for social justice.

Thus even those political theorists of the past who have perceived the family as an important school of moral development have rarely acknowledged the need for congruence between the family and the wider social order, which suggests that families themselves need to be just. Even when they have, as with Mill, they have been unwilling to push hard on the traditional division of labour within the family in the name of justice or equality.

Contemporary theorists of justice, with few exceptions, have paid little or no attention to the question of moral development—of how we are to *become* just. Most of them seem to think, to adapt slightly Hobbes's notable phrase, that just men spring like mushrooms from the earth.[3] Not surprisingly, then, it is far less often acknowledged in recent than in past theories that the family is important for moral development, and especially for instilling a sense of justice. As I have already noted, many theorists pay no attention at all to either the family or gender. In the rare case that the issue of justice within the family is given any sustained attention, the family is not viewed as a potential school of social justice.[4] In the rare case that a theorist pays any sustained attention to the development of a sense of justice or morality, little if any attention is likely to be paid to the family.[5] Even in the rare event that theorists pay considerable attention to the family *as* the first major locus of moral socialization, they do not refer to the fact that families are almost all still thoroughly gender-structured institutions.[6] . . .

In a just society, the structure and practices of families must give women the same opportunities as men to develop their capacities, to participate in political power and influence social choices, and to be economically secure. But in addition to this, families must be just because of the vast influence that they have on the moral development of children. The family is the primary institution of formative moral development. And the structure and practices of the family must parallel those of the larger society if the sense of justice is to be fostered and maintained. While many theorists of justice, both past and present, appear to have denied the importance of at least one of these factors, my own view is that both are absolutely crucial. A society that is committed to equal respect for all of its members, and to justice in social distributions of benefits and responsibilities, can neither neglect the family nor accept family structures and practices that violate these norms, as do current gender-based structures and practices. It is essential that children who are to develop into adults with a strong sense of justice and commitment to just institutions spend their earliest and most formative years in an environment in which they are loved and nurtured, *and* in which principles of justice are abided by and respected. What is a child of either sex to learn about fairness in the average household with two full-time working parents, where the mother does, at the very least, twice as much family work as the father? What is a child to learn about the value of nurturing and domestic work in a home with a traditional division of labour in which the father either subtly or not so subtly uses the fact that he is the wage earner to 'pull rank' on or to abuse his wife? What is a child to learn about responsibility for others in a family in which, after many years of arranging her life around the needs of her husband and children, a woman is faced with having to provide for herself and her children but is totally ill-equipped for the task by the life she agreed to lead, has led, and is expected to go on leading? . . .

8

Conclusion: Toward a Humanist Justice

The family is the linchpin of gender, reproducing it from one generation to the next. As we have seen, family life as typically practised in our society is not just, either to women or to children. Moreover, it is not conducive to the rearing of citizens with a strong sense of justice. In spite of all the rhetoric about equality between the sexes, the traditional or quasi-traditional division of family labour still prevails. Women are made vulnerable by constructing their lives around the expectation that they will be primary parents; they become more vulnerable within marriages in which they fulfill this expectation, whether or not they also work for wages; and they are most vulnerable in the event of separation or divorce, when they usually take over responsibility for children without adequate support from their ex-husbands. Since approximately half of all marriages end in divorce, about half of our children are likely to experience its dislocations, often made far more traumatic by the socio-economic consequences of both gender-structured marriage and divorce settlements that fail to take account of it. I have suggested that, for very important reasons, the family *needs* to be a just institution, and have shown that contemporary theories of justice neglect women and ignore gender. How can we address this injustice?

This is a complex question. It is particularly so because we place great value on our freedom to live different kinds of lives, there is no current consensus on many aspects of gender, and we have good reason to suspect that many of our beliefs about sexual difference and appropriate sex roles are heavily influenced by the very fact that we grew up in a gender-structured society. All of us have been affected, in our very psychological structures, by the fact of gender in our personal pasts, just as our society has been deeply affected by its strong influence in our collective past. Because of the lack of shared meanings about gender, it constitutes a particularly hard case for those who care deeply about both personal freedom and social justice. The way we divide the labour and responsibilities in our personal lives seems to be one of those things that people should be free to work out for themselves, but because of its vast repercussions it belongs clearly within the scope of things that must be governed by principles of justice. Which is to say, in the language of political and moral theory, that it belongs both to the sphere of 'the good' and to that of 'the right'.

I shall argue here that any just and fair solution to the urgent problem of women's and children's vulnerability must encourage and facilitate the equal sharing by men and women of paid and unpaid work, of productive and reproductive labour. We must work toward a future in which all will be likely to choose this mode of life. A just future would be one without gender. In its social structures and practices, one's sex would have no more relevance than one's eye colour or the length of one's toes. No assumptions would be made about 'male' and 'female' roles; childbearing would be so conceptually separated from child rearing and other family responsibilities that it would be a cause for surprise, and no little concern, if men and women were not equally responsible for domestic life or if children were to spend much more time with one parent than the other. It would be a future in which men and women participated in more or less equal numbers in every sphere of life, from infant care to different kinds of paid work to high-level politics. Thus it would no longer be the case that having no experience of raising children would be the practical prerequisite for attaining positions of the greatest social influence. Decisions about abortion and rape, about divorce settlements and sexual harassment, or about any other crucial social issues would not be made, as they often are now, by legislatures and benches of judges overwhelmingly populated by men whose power is in large part due to their advantaged position in the gender structure. If we are to be at all true to our democratic ideals, moving away from gender is essential. Obviously, the attainment of such a social world requires major changes in a multitude of institutions and social settings outside the home, as well as within it.

Such changes will not happen overnight. Moreover, any present solution to the vulnerability of women and children that is just and respects individual freedom must take into account that most people currently live in ways that are greatly affected by gender, and most still favour many aspects of current, gendered practices. Sociological studies confirm what most of us already infer from our own personal and professional acquaintances: there are no currently shared meanings in this country about the extent to which differences between the sexes are innate or environmental, about the appropriate roles of men and women, and about which family forms and divisions of labour are most beneficial for partners, parents, and children.[7] There are those, at one extreme, for whom the different roles of the two sexes, especially as parents, are deeply held tenets of religious belief. At the other end of the spectrum are those of us for whom the sooner all social differentiation between the sexes vanishes, the better it will be for all of us. And there are a thousand varieties of view in between. Public policies must respect people's views and choices. But they must do so only insofar as it can be ensured that these choices do not result, as they now do, in the vulnerability of women and children. Special protections must be built into our laws and public policies to ensure that, for those who choose it, the division of labour between the sexes does not result in injustice. In the face of these difficulties—balancing freedom and the effects of past choices against the needs of justice—I do not pretend to have arrived at any complete or fully satisfactory answers. But I shall attempt in this final chapter to suggest some social reforms, including changes in public policies and reforms of family law, that may help us work toward a solution to the injustices of gender.

Marriage has become an increasingly peculiar contract, a complex and ambiguous combination of anachronism and present-day reality. There is no longer the kind of agreement that once prevailed about what is expected of the parties to a marriage. Clearly, at least in the United States, it is no longer reasonable to assume that marriage will last a lifetime, since only half of current marriages are expected to. And yet, in spite of the increasing legal equality of men and women and the highly publicized figures about married women's increased participation in the labour force, many couples continue to adhere to more or less traditional patterns of role differentiation. As a recent article put it, women are 'out of the house but not out of the kitchen.'[8] Consequently, often working part-time or taking time out from wage work to care for family members, especially children, most wives are in a very different position from their husbands in their ability to be economically self-supporting. This is reflected, as we have seen, in power differentials between the sexes within the family. It means also, in the increasingly common event of divorce, usually by mutual agreement, that it is the mother who in 90 per cent of cases will have physical custody of the children. But whereas the greater need for money goes one way, the bulk of the earning power almost always goes the other. This is one of the most important causes of the feminization of poverty, which is affecting the life chances of ever larger numbers of children as well as their mothers. The division of labour within families has always adversely affected women, by making them economically dependent on men. Because of the increasing instability of marriage, its effects on children have now reached crisis proportions.

Some who are critical of the present structure and practices of marriage have suggested that men and women simply be made free to make their own agreements about family life, contracting with each other, much as business contracts are made.[9] But this takes insufficient account of the history of gender in our culture and our own psychologies, of the present substantive inequalities between the sexes, and, most important, of the well-being of the children who result from the relationship. As has long been recognized in the realm of labour relations, justice is by no means always enhanced by the maximization of freedom of contract, if the individuals involved are in unequal positions to start with. Some have even suggested that it is consistent with justice to leave spouses to work out their own divorce settlement.[10] By this time, however, the two people ending a marriage are likely to be far *more* unequal. Such a practice would be even more catastrophic for most women and children than is the present system. Wives in any but the rare cases in which they as individuals have remained their husbands' socioeconomic equals could hardly be expected to reach a just solution if left 'free' to 'bargain' the terms of financial support or child custody. What would they have to bargain *with*?

There are many directions that public policy can and should take in order to make relations between men and women more just. In discussing these, I shall look back to some of the contemporary ways of thinking about justice that I find most convincing. I draw particularly on Rawls's idea of the original position and Walzer's conception of the complex equality found in separate spheres of justice, between which I find no inconsistency. I also keep in mind critical legal theorists' critique of contract, and the related idea, suggested earlier, that rights to privacy that are to be valuable to all of us can be enjoyed only insofar as the sphere of life in which we enjoy them ensures the equality of its adult members and protects children. Let us begin by asking what kind of arrangements persons in a Rawlsian original position would agree to regarding marriage, parental and other domestic responsibilities, and divorce. What kinds of policies would they agree to for other aspects of social life, such as the workplace and schools, that affect men, women, and children and relations among them? And let us consider whether these arrangements would satisfy Walzer's separate spheres test—that inequalities in one sphere of life not be allowed to overflow into another. Will they foster equality within the sphere of family life? For the protection of the privacy of a domestic sphere in which inequality exists is the protection of the right of the strong to exploit and abuse the weak.

Let us first try to imagine ourselves, as far as possible, in the original position, knowing neither what our sex nor any other of our personal characteristics will be once the veil of ignorance is lifted.* Neither do we know our place in society or our particular conception of the good life. Particularly relevant in this context, of course, is our lack of knowledge of our beliefs about the characteristics of men

and women and our related convictions about the appropriate division of labour between the sexes. Thus the positions we represent must include a wide variety of beliefs on these matters. We may, once the veil of ignorance is lifted, find ourselves feminist men or feminist women whose conception of the good life includes the minimization of social differentiation between the sexes. Or we may find ourselves traditionalist men or women, whose conception of the good life, for religious or other reasons, is bound up in an adherence to the conventional division of labour between the sexes. The challenge is to arrive at and apply principles of justice having to do with the family and the division of labour between the sexes that can satisfy these vastly disparate points of view and the many that fall between.

There are some traditionalist positions so extreme that they ought not be admitted for consideration, since they violate such fundamentals as equal basic liberty and self-respect. We need not, and should not, that is to say, admit for consideration views based on the notion that women are inherently inferior beings whose function is to fulfill the needs of men. Such a view is no more admissible in the construction of just institutions for a modern pluralist society than is the view, however deeply held, that some are naturally slaves and others naturally and justifiably their masters. We need not, therefore, consider approaches to marriage that view it as an inherently and desirably hierarchical structure of dominance and subordination. Even if it were conceivable that a person who did not know whether he or she would turn out to be a man or a woman in the society being planned would subscribe

---

* I say 'so far as possible' because of the difficulties already pointed out in chapter 5. Given the deep effects of gender on our psychologies, it is probably more difficult for us, having grown up in a gender-structured society, to imagine not knowing our sex than anything else about ourselves. Nevertheless, this should not prevent us from trying.

to such views, they are not admissible. Even if there were no other reasons to refuse to admit such views, they must be excluded for the sake of children, for everyone in the original position has a high personal stake in the quality of childhood. Marriages of dominance and submission are bad for children as well as for their mothers, and the socio-economic outcome of divorce after such a marriage is very likely to damage their lives and seriously restrict their opportunities.

With this proviso, what social structures and public policies regarding relations between the sexes, and the family in particular, could we agree on in the original position? I think we would arrive at a basic model that would absolutely minimize gender. I shall first give an account of some of what this would consist in. We would also, however, build in carefully protective institutions for those who wished to follow gender-structured modes of life. These too I shall try to spell out in some detail.

Moving Away from Gender

First, public policies and laws should generally assume no social differentiation of the sexes. Shared parental responsibility for child care would be both assumed and facilitated. Few people outside of feminist circles seem willing to acknowledge that society does not have to choose between a system of female parenting that renders women and children seriously vulnerable and a system of total reliance on daycare provided outside the home. While high-quality daycare, subsidized so as to be equally available to all children, certainly constitutes an important part of the response that society should make in order to provide justice for women and children, it is only one part.[11] If we start out with the reasonable assumption that women and men are equally

parents of their children, and have equal responsibility for both the unpaid effort that goes into caring for them and their economic support, then we must rethink the demands of work life throughout the period in which a worker of either sex is a parent of a small child. We can no longer cling to the by now largely mythical assumption that every worker has 'someone else' at home to raise 'his' children.

The facilitation and encouragement of equally shared parenting would require substantial changes.[12] It would mean major changes in the workplace, all of which could be provided on an entirely (and not falsely) gender-neutral basis. Employers must be required by law not only completely to eradicate sex discrimination, including sexual harassment. They should also be required to make positive provision for the fact that most workers, for differing lengths of time in their working lives, are also parents, and are sometimes required to nurture other family members, such as their own aging parents. Because children are borne by women but can (and, I contend, should) be raised by both parents equally, policies relating to pregnancy and birth should be quite distinct from those relating to parenting. Pregnancy and childbirth, to whatever varying extent they require leave from work, should be regarded as temporarily disabling conditions like any others, and employers should be mandated to provide leave for all such conditions.[13] Of course, pregnancy and childbirth are far *more* than simply 'disabling conditions', but they should be treated as such for leave purposes, in part because their disabling effects vary from one woman to another. It seems unfair to mandate, say, eight or more weeks of leave for a condition that disables many women for less time and some for much longer, while *not* mandating leave for illnesses or other disabling conditions. Surely a society as rich as ours can afford to do both.

Parental leave during the post-birth months must be available to mothers and fathers on the same terms, to facilitate shared parenting; they might take sequential leaves or each might take half-time leave. All workers should have the right, without prejudice to their jobs, seniority, benefits, and so on, to work less than full-time during the first year of a child's life, and to work flexible or somewhat reduced hours at least until the child reaches the age of seven. Correspondingly greater flexibility of hours must be provided for the parents of a child with any health problem or disabling condition. The professions whose greatest demands (such as tenure in academia or the partnership hurdle in law) coincide with the peak period of child rearing must restructure their demands or provide considerable flexibility for those of their workers who are also participating parents. Large-scale employers should also be required to provide high-quality on-site daycare for children from infancy up to school age. And to ensure equal quality of daycare for all young children, *direct government subsidies* (not tax credits, which benefit the better-off) should make up the difference between the cost of high-quality daycare and what less well paid parents could reasonably be expected to pay.

There are a number of things that schools, too, must do to promote the minimization of gender. As Amy Gutmann has recently noted, in their present authority structures (84 per cent of elementary school teachers are female, while 99 per cent of school superintendents are male), 'schools do not simply reflect, they perpetuate the social reality of gender preferences when they educate children in a system in which men rule women and women rule children.' She argues that, since such sex stereotyping is 'a formidable obstacle' to chil-

dren's rational deliberation about the lives they wish to lead, sex should be regarded as a relevant qualification in the hiring of both teachers and administrators, until these proportions have become much more equal.[14]

An equally important role of our schools must be to ensure in the course of children's education that they become fully aware of the politics of gender. This does not only mean ensuring that women's experience and women's writing are included in the curriculum, although this in itself is undoubtedly important.[15] Its political significance has become obvious from the amount of protest that it has provoked. Children need also to be taught about the present inequalities, ambiguities, and uncertainties of marriage, the facts of workplace discrimination and segregation, and the likely consequences of making life choices based on assumptions about gender. They should be discouraged from thinking about their futures as *determined* by the sex to which they happen to belong. For many children, of course, personal experience has already 'brought home' the devastating effects of the traditional division of labour between the sexes. But they do not necessarily come away from this experience with positive ideas about how to structure their own future family lives differently. As Anita Shreve has recently suggested, 'the old home-economics courses that used to teach girls how to cook and sew might give way to the new home economics: teaching girls *and boys* how to combine working and parenting.'[16] Finally, schools should be required to provide high-quality after-school programs, where children can play safely, do their homework, or participate in creative activities.

The implementation of all these policies would significantly help parents to share the earning and the domestic responsibilities of their families, and children to grow up prepared for a future in which the significance of sex difference is greatly diminished. Men could participate equally in the nurturance of their children, from infancy and throughout childhood, with predictably great effects on themselves, their wives or partners, and their children. And women need not become vulnerable through economic dependence. In addition, such arrangements would alleviate the qualms many people have about the long hours that some children spend in daycare. If one parent of a preschooler worked, for example, from eight to four o'clock and the other from ten to six o'clock, a preschool child would be at daycare for only six hours (including nap time), and with each one or both of her or his parents the rest of the day. If each parent were able to work a six-hour day, or a four-day week, still less daycare would be needed. Moreover, on-site provision of daycare would enable mothers to continue to nurse, if they chose, beyond the time of their parental leave.[17]

The situation of single parents and their children is more complicated, but it seems that it too, for a number of reasons, would be much improved in a society in which sex difference was accorded an absolute minimum of social significance. Let us begin by looking at the situation of never-married mothers and their children. First, the occurrence of pregnancy among single teenagers, which is almost entirely unintended, would presumably be reduced if girls grew up more assertive and self-protective, and with less tendency to perceive their futures primarily in terms of motherhood. It could also be significantly reduced by the wide availability of sex education and contraception.[18] Second, the added weight of responsibility given to fatherhood in a gender-free society would surely give young men more incentive than they now have not to incur the results of careless sexual behaviour

until they were ready to take on the responsibilities of being parents. David Ellwood has outlined a policy for establishing the paternity of all children of single mothers at the time of birth, and for enforcing the requirement that their fathers contribute to their support throughout childhood, with provision for governmental backup support in cases where the father is unable to pay. These proposals seem eminently fair and sensible, although the minimum levels of support suggested ($1,500 to $2,000 per year) are inadequate, especially since the mother is presumed to be either taking care of the child herself or paying for daycare (which often costs far more than this) while she works.[19]

Third, never-married mothers would benefit greatly from a work structure that took parenthood seriously into account, as well as from the subsidization of high-quality daycare. Women who grew up with the expectation that their work lives would be as important a part of their futures as the work lives of men would be less likely to enter dead-ended, low-skilled occupations, and would be better able to cope economically with parenthood without marriage.

Most single parenthood results, however, not from single mothers giving birth, but from marital separation and divorce. And this too would be significantly altered in a society not structured along the lines of gender. Even if rates of divorce were to remain unchanged (which is impossible to predict), it seems inconceivable that separated and divorced fathers who had shared equally in the nurturance of their children from the outset would be as likely to neglect them, by not seeing them or not contributing to their support, as many do today. It seems reasonable to expect that children after divorce would still have two actively involved parents, and two working adults economically responsible for them.

Because these parents had shared equally the paid work and the family work, their incomes would be much more equal than those of most divorcing parents today. Even if they were quite equal, however, the parent without physical custody should be required to contribute to the child's support, *to the point where the standards of living of the two households were the same*. This would be very different from the situation of many children of divorced parents today, dependent for both their nurturance and their economic support solely on mothers whose wage work has been interrupted by primary parenting.

It is impossible to predict all the effects of moving toward a society without gender. Major current injustices to women and children would end. Men would experience both the joys and the responsibilities of far closer and more sustained contact with their children than many have today. Many immensely influential spheres of life—notably politics and the professional occupations—would for the first time be populated more or less equally by men and women, most of whom were also actively participating parents. This would be in great contrast to today, when most of those who rise to influential positions are either men who, if fathers, have minimal contact with their children, or women who have either forgone motherhood altogether or hired others as full-time caretakers for their children because of the demands of their careers. These are the people who make policy at the highest levels—policies not only *about* families and their welfare and about the education of children, but about the foreign policies, the wars and the weapons that will determine the future or the lack of future for all these families and children. Yet they are almost all people who gain the influence they do in part by never having had the day-to-day experience of nurturing a child. This is probably the most significant

aspect of our gendered division of labour, though the least possible to grasp. The effects of changing it could be momentous.

Protecting the Vulnerable

The pluralism of beliefs and modes of life is fundamental to our society, and the genderless society I have just outlined would certainly not be agreed upon by all as desirable. Thus when we think about constructing relations between the sexes that could be agreed upon in the original position, and are therefore just from all points of view, we must also design institutions and practices acceptable to those with more traditional beliefs about the characteristics of men and women, and the appropriate division of labour between them. It is essential, if men and women are to be allowed to so divide their labour, as they must be if we are to respect the current pluralism of beliefs, that society protect the vulnerable. Without such protection, the marriage contract seriously exacerbates the initial inequalities of those who entered into it, and too many women and children live perilously close to economic disaster and serious social dislocation; too many also live with violence or the continual threat of it. It should be noted here that the rights and obligations that the law would need to promote and mandate in order to protect the vulnerable need not—and should not—be designated in accordance with sex, but in terms of different functions or roles performed. There are only a minute percentage of 'househusbands' in this country, and a very small number of men whose work lives take second priority after their wives. But they can quite readily be protected by the same institutional structures that can protect traditional and quasi-traditional wives, so long as these are designed without reference to sex.

Gender-structured marriage, then, needs to be regarded as a currently necessary institution (because still chosen by some) but one that is socially problematic. It should be subjected to a number of legal requirements, at least when there are children.[20]* Most important, there is no need for the division of labour between the sexes to involve the economic dependence, either complete or partial, of one partner on the other. Such dependence can be avoided if both partners have *equal legal entitlement* to all earnings coming into the household. The clearest and simplest way of doing this would be to have employers make out wage cheques equally divided between the earner and the partner who provides all or most of his or her unpaid domestic services. In many cases, of course, this would not change the way couples actually manage their finances; it would simply codify what they already agree on—that the household income is rightly shared, because in a real sense jointly earned. Such couples recognize the fact that the wage-earning spouse is no more supporting the homemaking and child-rearing spouse than the latter is supporting the former; the form of support each offers the family is simply different. Such couples might well take both cheques, deposit them in a joint account, and really share the income, just as they now do with the earnings that come into the household.

In the case of some couples, however, altering the entitlement of spouses to the earned income of the household as I have suggested *would* make a significant difference. It would make a difference in cases where the earning or higher-earning partner now directly exploits this power, by refusing to make significant spending decisions jointly, by failing to share the income, or by psychologically or physically abusing the non-earning or low-earning partner, reinforced by the notion that she (almost always the wife) has little option but to put up with such abuse or to take herself and her children into a state of destitution. It would make a difference, too, in cases where the higher-earning partner indirectly exploits this earning power in order to perpetuate the existing division of labour in the family. In such instances considerable changes in the balance of power would be likely to result from the legal and societal recognition that the partner who does most of the domestic work of the family contributes to its well-being just as much, and therefore rightly *earns* just as much, as the partner who does most of the workplace work.

What I am suggesting is *not* that the wage-working partner pay the homemaking partner for services rendered. I do not mean to introduce the cash nexus into a personal relationship where it is inappropriate. I have simply suggested that since both partners in a traditional or quasi-traditional marriage work, there is no reason why only one of them should get paid, or why one should be paid far more than the other. The equal splitting of wages would constitute public recognition of the fact that the currently unpaid labour of families is just as important as the paid labour. If we do *not* believe this, then we should insist on the complete and equal sharing of both paid and unpaid labour, as occurs in the genderless model of marriage and parenting described earlier. It is only if we *do* believe it that society can justly allow couples to distribute the two types of labour so unevenly. But in such cases, given the enormous significance our society attaches to money and earnings, we should insist that the earnings be

---

* I see no reason why what I propose here should be restricted to couples who are legally married. It should apply equally to 'common law' relationships that produce children, and in which a division of labour is practised.

recognized as equally earned by the two persons. To call on Walzer's language, we should do this in order to help prevent the inequality of family members in the sphere of wage work to invade their domestic sphere.

It is also important to point out that this proposal does not constitute unwarranted invasion of privacy or any more state intervention into the life of families than currently exists. It would involve only the same kind of invasion of privacy as is now required by such things as registration of marriages and births, and the filing of tax returns declaring numbers and names of dependents. And it *seems* like intervention in families only because it would alter the existing relations of power within them. If a person's capacity to fulfill the terms of his or her work is dependent on having a spouse at home who raises the children and in other ways sustains that worker's day-to-day life, then it is no more interventionist to pay both equally for their contributions than only to pay one.

The same fundamental principle should apply to separation and divorce, to the extent that the division of labour has been practised within a marriage. Under current divorce laws, as we have seen, the terms of exit from marriage are disadvantageous for almost all women in traditional or quasi-traditional marriages. Regardless of the consensus that existed about the division of the family labour, these women lose most of the income that has supported them *and* the social status that attached to them because of their husband's income and employment, often at the same time as suddenly becoming single parents, and prospective wage workers for the first time in many years. This combination of prospects would seem to be enough to put most traditional wives off the idea of divorcing even if they had good cause to do so. In addition, since divorce in the great majority of states no longer requires the consent of both spouses, it seems likely that wives for whom divorce would spell economic and social catastrophe would be inhibited in voicing their dissatisfactions or needs within marriage. The terms of exit are very likely to affect the use and the power of voice in the ongoing relationship. At worst, these women may be rendered virtually defenceless in the face of physical or psychological abuse. This is not a system of marriage and divorce that could possibly be agreed to by persons in an original position in which they did not know whether they were to be male or female, traditionalist or not. It is a fraudulent contract, presented as beneficial to all but in fact to the benefit only of the more powerful.

For all these reasons, it seems essential that the terms of divorce be redrawn so as to reflect the gendered or non-gendered character of the marriage that is ending, to a far greater extent than they do now.[21] The legal system of a society that allows couples to divide the labour of families in a traditional or quasi-traditional manner *must* take responsibility for the vulnerable position in which marital breakdown places the partner who has completely or partially lost the capacity to be economically self-supporting. When such a marriage ends, it seems wholly reasonable to expect a person whose career has been largely unencumbered by domestic responsibilities to support financially the partner who undertook these responsibilities. This support, in the form of combined alimony and child support, should be far more substantial than the token levels often ordered by the courts now. *Both post-divorce households should enjoy the same standard of living.* Alimony should not end after a few years, as the (patronizingly named) 'rehabilitative alimony' of today does; it should continue for at least as long as the traditional division of labour in the marriage did and, in the case of short-term marriages that produced children, until the youngest child enters first grade and the custodial parent has a real chance of making his or her own living. After that point, child support should continue at a level that enables the children to enjoy a standard of living equal to that of the non-custodial parent. There can be no reason consistent with principles of justice that some should suffer economically vastly more than others from the break-up of a relationship whose asymmetric division of labour was mutually agreed on.

I have suggested two basic models of family rights and responsibilities, both of which are currently needed because this is a time of great transition for men and women and great disagreement about gender. Families in which roles and responsibilities are equally shared regardless of sex are far more in accord with principles of justice than are typical families today. So are families in which those who undertake more traditional domestic roles are protected from the risks they presently incur. In either case, justice as a whole will benefit from the changes. Of the two, however, I claim that the genderless family is more just, in the three important respects that I spelled out at the beginning of this book: it is more just to women; it is more conducive to equal opportunity both for women and for children of both sexes; and it creates a more favourable environment for the rearing of citizens of a just society. Thus, while protecting those whom gender now makes vulnerable, we must also put our best efforts into promoting the elimination of gender.

The increased justice to women that would result from moving away from gender is readily apparent. Standards for just social institutions could no longer take for granted and exclude from considerations of justice much of what women now do, since men would

share in it equally. Such central components of justice as what counts as productive labour, and what count as needs and deserts, would be greatly affected by this change. Standards of justice would become *humanist*, as they have never been before. One of the most important effects of this would be to change radically the situation of women as citizens. With egalitarian families, and with institutions such as workplaces and schools designed to accommodate the needs of parents and children, rather than being based as they now are on the traditional assumption that 'someone else' is at home, mothers would not be virtually excluded from positions of influence in politics and the workplace. They would be represented at every level in approximately equal numbers with men.

In a genderless society, children too would benefit. They would not suffer in the ways that they do now because of the injustices done to women. It is undeniable that the family in which each of us grows up has a deeply formative influence on us—on the kind of persons we want to be as well as the kind of persons we are.[22] This is one of the reasons why one *cannot* reasonably leave the family out of 'the basic structure of society', to which the principles of justice are to apply. Equality of opportunity to become what we want to be would be enhanced in two important ways by the development of families without gender and by the public policies necessary to support their development. First, the growing gap between the economic well-being of children in single-parent and those in two-parent families would be reduced. Children in single-parent families would benefit significantly if fathers were held equally responsible for supporting their children, whether married to their mothers or not; if more mothers had sustained labour force attachment; if high-quality daycare were subsidized; and if the workplace were designed to accommodate parenting. These children would be far less likely to spend their formative years in conditions of poverty, with one parent struggling to fulfill the functions of two. Their life chances would be significantly enhanced.

Second, children of both sexes in gender-free families would have (as some already have) much more opportunity for self-development free from sex-role expectations and sex-typed personalities than most do now. Girls and boys who grow up in highly traditional families, in which sex difference is regarded as a determinant of everything from roles, responsibilities, and privileges to acceptable dress, speech, and modes of behaviour, clearly have far less freedom to develop into whatever kind of person they want to be than do those who are raised without such constraints. It is too early for us to know a lot about the developmental outcomes and life choices of children who are equally parented by mothers and fathers, since the practice is still so recent and so rare. Persuasive theories such as Chodorow's, however, would lead us to expect much less differentiation between the sexes to result from truly shared parenting.[23] Even now, in most cases without men's equal fathering, both the daughters and the sons of wage-working mothers have been found to have a more positive view of women and less rigid views of sex roles; the daughters (like their mothers) tend to have greater self-esteem and a more positive view of themselves as workers, and the sons, to expect equality and shared roles in their own future marriages.[24] We might well expect that with mothers in the labour force *and* with fathers as equal parents, children's attitudes and psychologies will become even less correlated with their sex. In a very crucial sense, their opportunities to become the persons they want to be will be enlarged.

Finally, it seems undeniable that the enhancement of justice that accompanies the disappearance of gender will make the family a much better place for children to develop a sense of justice. We can no longer deny the importance of the fact that families are where we first learn, by example and by how we are treated, not only how people do relate to each other but also how they *should*. How would families not built on gender be better schools of moral development? First, the example of co-equal parents with shared roles, combining love with justice, would provide a far better example of human relations for children than the domination and dependence that often occur in traditional marriage. The fairness of the distribution of labour, the equal respect, and the *inter*dependence of his or her parents would surely be a powerful first example to a child in a family with equally shared roles. Second, as I have argued, having a sense of justice requires that we be able to empathize, to abstract from our own situation and to think about moral and political issues from the points of view of others. We cannot come to either just principles or just specific decisions by thinking, as it were, as if we were nobody, or thinking from nowhere; we must, therefore, learn to think from the point of view of others, including others who are different from ourselves.

To the extent that gender is de-emphasized in our nurturing practices, this capacity would seem to be enhanced, for two reasons. First, if female primary parenting leads, as it seems to, to less distinct ego boundaries and greater capacity for empathy in female children, and to a greater tendency to self-definition and abstraction in males, then might we not expect to find the two capacities better combined in children of both sexes who are reared by parents of both sexes? Second, the experience of *being* nurturers, throughout a

significant portion of our lives, also seems
likely to result in an increase in empathy, and
in the combination of personal moral capacities, fusing feelings with reason, that just
citizens need.[25]

Notes

1. John Stuart Mill, *The Subjection of Women* (1869),
   in Collected Works, ed. J.M. Robson (Toronto:
   University of Toronto Press, 1984), vol. 21, 324–
   95. At the time Mill wrote, women had no
   political rights and coverture deprived married
   women of most legal rights, too. He challenges
   all this in his essay.
2. Mill, *Subjection of Women*, 324–5, 394–5.
3. Hobbes writes of 'men . . . as if but even now
   sprung out of the earth . . . like mushrooms.'
   'Philosophical Rudiments concerning Government and Society,' in *The English Works of Thomas
   Hobbes*, ed. Sir William Molesworth (London:
   John Bohn, 1966), vol. 2, 109.
4. For example, Walzer, *Spheres of Justice* (New
   York: Basic Books, 1983), chap. 9, 'Kinship and
   Love.'
5. See Alan Gewirth, *Reason and Morality* (Chicago:
   University of Chicago Press, 1978). He discusses
   moral development from time to time, but places
   families within the broad category of 'voluntary
   associations' and does not discuss gender roles
   within them.
6. This is the case with both Rawls's *A Theory of
   Justice* (Cambridge: Harvard University Press,
   1971), discussed here and in chapter 5, and
   Phillips's sociologically oriented *Toward a Just
   Social Order* (Princeton: Princeton University
   Press, 1986), as discussed above.
7. See chap. 3, 67–8.
8. 'Women: Out of the House but Not out of the
   Kitchen, *New York Times*, 24 February 1988, A1,
   C10.
9. See, for example, Marjorie Maguire Schultz,
   'Contractual Ordering of Marriage: A New
   Model for State Policy,' *California Law Review*
   70, no. 2 (1982); Lenore Weitzman, *The
   Marriage Contract: Spouses, Lovers, and the Law*
   (New York: The Free Press, 1981), parts 3–4.
10. See, for example, David L. Kirp, Mark G. Yudof,
    and Marlene Strong Franks, *Gender Justice*
    (Chicago: University of Chicago Press, 1986),
    183–5. Robert H. Mnookin takes an only
    slightly less laissez-faire approach, in 'Divorce
    Bargaining: The Limits on Private Ordering,'
    University of Michigan Journal of Law Reform 18,
    no. 4 (1985).
11. It seems reasonable to conclude that the effects
    of daycare on children are probably just as vari-
    able as the effects of parenting—that is to say,
    very widely variable depending on the quality
    of the daycare and of the parenting. There is no
    doubt that good out-of-home daycare is expen-
    sive—approximately $100 per full-time week
    in 1987, even though child-care workers are
    now paid only about two-thirds as much per
    hour as other comparably educated women
    workers (Victor Fuchs, *Women's Quest for
    Economic Equality* [Cambridge: Harvard Uni-
    versity Press, 1988], 137–8). However, it is
    undoubtedly easier to control its quality than
    that of informal 'family daycare'. In my view,
    based in part on my experience of the excellent
    daycare centre that our children attended for a
    total of seven years, good-quality daycare must
    have small-scale 'home rooms' and a high staff-
    to-child ratio, and should pay staff better than
    most centres now do. For balanced studies of
    the effects of daycare on a poor population, see
    Sally Provence, Audrey Naylor, and June
    Patterson, *The Challenge of Daycare* (New
    Haven: Yale University Press, 1977); and, most
    recently, Lisbeth B. Schorr (with Daniel Schorr),
    *Within Our Reach—Breaking the Cycle of Dis-
    advantage* (New York: Anchor Press, Doubleday,
    1988), chap. 8.

12. Much of what I suggest here is not new; it has formed part of the feminist agenda for several decades, and I first made some of the suggestions I develop here in the concluding chapter of *Women in Western Political Thought* (Princeton: Princeton University Press, 1979). Three recent books that address some of the policies discussed here are Fuchs, *Women's Quest*, chap. 7; Philip Green, *Retrieving Democracy: In Search of Civic Equality* (Totowa, NJ: Rowman and Allanheld, 1985), 96–108; and Anita Shreve, *Remaking Motherhood: How Working Mothers Are Shaping Our Children's Future* (New York: Fawcett Columbine, 1987), 173–8. In Fuchs's chapter he carefully analyses the potential economic and social effects of alternative policies to improve women's economic status, and concludes that 'child-centred policies' such as parental leave and subsidized daycare are likely to have more of a positive impact on women's economic position than 'labour market policies' such as anti-discrimination, comparable pay for comparable worth, and affirmative action have had and are likely to have. Some potentially very effective policies, such as on-site daycare and flexible and/or reduced working hours for parents of young or 'special needs' children, seem to fall within both of his categories.

13. The dilemma faced by feminists in the recent California case *Guerra v. California Federal Savings and Loan Association*, 107 S. Ct. 683 (1987) was due to the fact that state law mandated leave for pregnancy and birth that it did not mandate for other disabling conditions. Thus to defend the law seemed to open up the dangers of discrimination that the earlier protection of women in the workplace had resulted in. (For a discussion of this general issue of equality versus difference, see, for example, Wendy W. Williams, 'The Equality Crisis: Some Reflections on Culture, Courts, and Feminism,' *Women's Rights Law Reporter* 7, no. 3 [1982].)

The Supreme Court upheld the California law on the grounds that it treated workers equally in terms of their rights to become parents.

14. Amy Gutmann, *Democratic Education* (Princeton: Princeton University Press, 1987), 112–15; quotation from 113–14. See also Elisabeth Hansot and David Tyack, 'Gender in American Public Schools: Thinking Institutionally,' *Signs* 13, no. 4 (1988).

15. A classic text on this subject is Dale Spender, ed., *Men's Studies Modified: The Impact of Feminism on the Academic Disciplines* (Oxford: Pergamon Press, 1981).

16. Shreve, *Remaking Motherhood*, 237.

17. Although 51 per cent of infants are breast-fed at birth, only 14 per cent are entirely breast-fed at six weeks of age. Cited from P. Leach, *Babyhood* (New York: Alfred A. Knopf, 1983), by Sylvia Ann Hewlett, in *A Lesser Life: The Myth of Women's Liberation in America* (New York: Morrow, 1986), 409 n34. Given this fact, it seems quite unjustified to argue that lactation *dictates* that mothers be the primary parents, even during infancy.

18. In Sweden, where the liberalization of abortion in the mid-1970s was accompanied by much expanded birth-control education and information and reduced-cost contraceptives, the rates of both teenage abortion and teenage birth decreased significantly. The Swedish teenage birth rate was by 1982 less than half what it had been in the 1970s. Mary Ann Glendon, *Abortion and Divorce in Western Law* (Cambridge: Harvard University Press, 1987), 23 and n65. Chapter 3 of Schorr's *Within Our Reach* gives an excellent account of programs in the United States that have proven effective in reducing early and unplanned pregnancies. Noting the strong correlation between emotional and economic deprivation and early pregnancy, she emphasizes the importance, if teenagers are to have the incentive not to become pregnant, of their believing that they have a real stake in

their own futures, and developing the aspirations and self-assertiveness that go along with this. As Victor Fuchs points out, approximately two-thirds of unmarried women who give birth are 20 or older (*Women's Quest*, p. 68). However, these women are somewhat more likely to have work skills and experience, and it seems likely that many live in informal 'common law marriage' heterosexual or lesbian partnerships, rather than being *in fact* single parents.

19. David Ellwood, *Poor Support: Poverty in the American Family* (New York: Basic Books, 1988), 163–74. He estimates that full-time daycare for each child can be bought for $3,000 per year, and half-time for $1,000. He acknowledges that these estimated costs are 'modest'. I think they are unrealistic, unless the care is being provided by a relative or close friend. Ellwood reports that, as of 1985, only 18 per cent of never-married fathers were ordered to pay child support, and only 11 per cent actually paid any (158).

20. Mary Ann Glendon has set out a 'children first' approach to divorce (Glendon, *Abortion and Divorce*, 94ff); here I extend the same idea to ongoing marriage, where the arrival of a child is most often the point at which the wife becomes economically dependent.

21. My suggestions for protecting traditional and quasi-traditional wives in the event of divorce are similar to those of Lenore Weitzman in *The Divorce Revolution: The Unexpected Social and Economic Consequences for Women and Children in America* (New York: The Free Press, 1985), chap. 11, and Mary Ann Glendon in *Abortion and Divorce*, chap. 2. Although they would usually in practice protect traditional wives, the laws should be gender-neutral so that they would equally protect divorcing men who had undertaken the primary functions of parenting and homemaking.

22. Here I paraphrase Rawls's wording in explaining why the basic structure of society is basic. 'The Basic Structure As Subject,' *American Philosophical Quarterly* 14, no. 2 (1977): 160.

23. See chap. 6 n58 in this volume.

24. Shreve, *Remaking Motherhood*, chaps 3–7.

25. See, for example, Sara Ruddick, 'Maternal Thinking,' *Feminist Studies* 6, no. 2 (1980); Diane Ehrensaft, 'When Women and Men Mother,' in *Mothering: Essays in Feminist Theory*, ed. Joyce Trebilcot (Totowa, NJ: Rowman and Allanheld, 1984); Judith Kegan Gardiner, 'Self Psychology as Feminist Theory,' *Signs* 12, no. 4 (1987), esp. 778–80.

'Is Multiculturalism Bad for Women?'

Until the past few decades, minority groups—immigrants as well as indigenous peoples—were typically expected to assimilate into majority cultures. This assimilationist expectation is now often considered oppressive, and many Western countries are seeking to devise new policies that are more responsive to persistent cultural differences. The appropriate policies vary with context: countries such as England, with established churches or state-supported religious education, find it difficult to resist demands to extend state support to minority religious schools; countries such as France, with traditions of strictly secular public education, struggle over whether the clothing required by minority religions may be worn in the public schools. But one issue recurs across all contexts, though it has gone virtually unnoticed in current debate: What should be done when the claims of minority cultures or religions clash with the norm of gender equality that is at least formally endorsed by liberal states (however much they continue to violate it in their practices)?

In the late 1980s, for example, a sharp public controversy erupted in France about whether Magrébin girls could attend school wearing the traditional Muslim head scarves regarded as proper attire for post-pubescent young women. Staunch defenders of secular education lined up with some feminists and far-right nationalists against the practice; much of the Old Left supported the multiculturalist demands for flexibility and respect for diversity, accusing opponents of racism or cultural imperialism. At the very same time, however, the public was virtually silent about a problem of vastly greater importance to many French Arab and African immigrant women: polygamy.

During the 1980s, the French government quietly permitted immigrant men to bring multiple wives into the country, to the point where an estimated 200,000 families in Paris are now polygamous. Any suspicion that official concern over head scarves was motivated by an impulse toward gender equality is belied by the easy adoption of a permissive policy on polygamy, despite the burdens this practice imposes on women and the warnings disseminated by women from the relevant cultures.[1] On this issue, no politically effective opposition galvanized. But once reporters finally got around to interviewing the wives, they discovered what the government could have learned years earlier: that the women affected by polygamy regarded it as an inescapable and barely tolerable institution in their African countries of origin, and an unbearable imposition in the French context. Overcrowded apartments and the lack of private space for each wife led to immense hostility, resentment,

even violence both among the wives and against each other's children.

In part because of the strain on the welfare system caused by families with 20 to 30 members, the French government has recently decided to recognize only one wife and to consider all the other marriages annulled. But what will happen to all the other wives and children? Having ignored women's views on polygamy for so long, the government now seems to be abdicating its responsibility for the vulnerability that its rash policy has inflicted on women and children.

The French accommodation of polygamy illustrates a deep and growing tension between feminism and multiculturalist concern for protecting cultural diversity. I think we—especially those of us who consider ourselves politically progressive and opposed to all forms of oppression—have been too quick to assume that feminism and multiculturalism are both good things which are easily reconciled. I shall argue instead that there is considerable likelihood of tension between them—more precisely, between feminism and a multiculturalist commitment to group rights for minority cultures.

A few words to explain the terms and focus of my argument. By *feminism*, I mean the belief that women should not be disadvantaged by their sex, that they should be recognized as having human dignity equal to that of men, and that they should have the opportunity to live as fulfilling and as freely chosen lives as men can. *Multiculturalism* is harder to pin down, but the particular aspect that concerns me here is the claim, made in the context of basically liberal democracies, that minority cultures or ways of life are not sufficiently protected by the practice of ensuring the individual rights of their members, and as a consequence these should also be protected through special *group* rights or privileges.

In the French case, for example, the right to contract polygamous marriages clearly constituted a group right not available to the rest of the population. In other cases, groups have claimed rights to govern themselves, to have guaranteed political representation, or to be exempt from certain generally applicable laws.

Demands for such group rights are growing—from indigenous native populations, minority ethnic or religious groups, and formerly colonized peoples (at least when the latter immigrate to the former colonial state). These groups, it is argued, have their own 'societal cultures' which—as Will Kymlicka, the foremost contemporary defender of cultural group rights, says—provide 'members with meaningful ways of life across the full range of human activities, including social, educational, religious, recreational, and economic life, encompassing both public and private spheres.'[2] Because societal cultures play so pervasive and fundamental a role in the lives of their members, and because such cultures are threatened with extinction, minority cultures should be protected by special rights. That, in essence, is the case for group rights.

Some proponents of group rights argue that even cultures that 'flout the rights of [their individual members] in a liberal society'[3] should be accorded group rights or privileges if their minority status endangers the culture's continued existence. Others do not claim that all minority cultural groups should have special rights, but rather that such groups—even illiberal ones that violate their individual members' rights, requiring them to conform to group beliefs or norms—have the right to be 'left alone' in a liberal society.[4] Both claims seem clearly inconsistent with the basic liberal value of individual freedom, which entails that group rights should not trump the individual rights of its members; thus I will not address the additional problems they present for feminists here.[5]

But some defenders of multiculturalism confine their defence of group rights largely to groups that are internally liberal.[6] Even with these restrictions, feminists—everyone, that is, who endorses the moral equality of men and women—should remain sceptical. So I will argue.

Gender and Culture

Most cultures are suffused with practices and ideologies concerning gender. Suppose, then, that a culture endorses and facilitates the control of men over women in various ways (even if informally, in the private sphere of domestic life). Suppose, too, that there are fairly clear disparities in power between the sexes, such that the more powerful, male members are those who are generally in a position to determine and articulate the group's beliefs, practices, and interests. Under such conditions, group rights are potentially, and in many cases actually, antifeminist. They substantially limit the capacities of women and girls of that culture to live with human dignity equal to that of men and boys, and to live as freely chosen lives as they can.

Advocates of group rights for minorities within liberal states have not adequately addressed this simple critique of group rights, for at least two reasons. First, they tend to treat cultural groups as monoliths—to pay more attention to differences between and among groups than to differences within them. Specifically, they accord little or no recognition to the fact that minority cultural groups, like the societies in which they exist (though to a greater or lesser extent), are themselves *gendered*, with substantial differences in power and advantage between men and women. Second, advocates of group rights pay little or no attention to the private sphere. Some of the most persuasive liberal defences of group rights urge that individuals need 'a culture of their own', and that only within such a culture can people develop a sense of self-esteem or self-respect, as well as the capacity to decide what kind of life is good for them. But such arguments typically neglect both the different roles that cultural groups impose on their members and the context in which persons' senses of themselves and their capacities are first formed *and* in which culture is first transmitted—the realm of domestic or family life.

When we correct for these deficiencies by paying attention to internal differences and to the private arena, two particularly important connections between culture and gender come into sharp relief, both of which underscore the force of this simple critique of group rights. First, the sphere of personal, sexual, and reproductive life functions as a central focus of most cultures, a dominant theme in cultural practices and rules. Religious or cultural groups often are particularly concerned with 'personal law'—the laws of marriage, divorce, child custody, division and control of family property, and inheritance.[7] As a rule, then, the defence of 'cultural practices' is likely to have much greater impact on the lives of women and girls than on those of men and boys, since far more of women's time and energy goes into preserving and maintaining the personal, familial, and reproductive side of life. Obviously, culture is not only about domestic arrangements, but they do provide a major focus of most contemporary cultures. Home is, after all, where much of culture is practised, preserved, and transmitted to the young. On the other hand, the distribution of responsibilities and power at home has a major impact on who can participate in and influence the more public parts of the cultural life, where rules and regulations about both public and private life are made. The more a culture requires or expects of women in the domestic sphere, the less opportunity they have of achieving equality with men in either sphere.

The second important connection between culture and gender is that most cultures have as one of their principal aims the control of women by men.[8] Consider, for example, the founding myths of Greek and Roman antiquity, and of Judaism, Christianity, and Islam: they are rife with attempts to justify the control and subordination of women. These myths consist of a combination of denials of women's role in reproduction; appropriations by men of the power to reproduce themselves; characterizations of women as overly emotional, untrustworthy, evil, or sexually dangerous; and refusals to acknowledge mothers' rights over the disposition of their children.[9] Think of Athena, sprung from the head of Zeus, and of Romulus and Remus, reared without a human mother. Or Adam, made by a male God, who then (at least according to one of the two biblical versions of the story) created Eve out of part of Adam. Consider Eve, whose weakness led Adam astray. Think of all those endless 'begats' in Genesis, where women's primary role in reproduction is completely ignored, or of the textual justifications for polygamy, once practised in Judaism, still practised in many parts of the Islamic world and (though illegally) by Mormons in some parts of the United States. Consider, too, the story of Abraham, a pivotal turning point in the development of monotheism.[10] God commands Abraham to sacrifice 'his' beloved son. Abraham prepares to do exactly what God asks of him, without even telling, much less asking, Isaac's mother, Sarah. Abraham's absolute obedience to God makes him the central, fundamental model of faith for all three religions.

Although the powerful drive to control women—and to blame and punish them for men's difficulty in controlling their own sexual impulses—has been softened considerably in the more progressive, reformed versions of

Judaism, Christianity, and Islam, it remains strong in their more orthodox or fundamentalist versions. Moreover, it is by no means confined to Western or monotheistic cultures. Many of the world's traditions and cultures, including those practised within formerly conquered or colonized nation-states—which certainly encompasses most of the peoples of Africa, the Middle East, Latin America, and Asia—are quite distinctly patriarchal. They too have elaborate patterns of socialization, rituals, matrimonial customs, and other cultural practices (including systems of property ownership and control of resources) aimed at bringing women's sexuality and reproductive capabilities under men's control. Many such practices make it virtually impossible for women to choose to live independently of men, to be celibate or lesbian, or to decide not to have children.

Those who practise some of the most controversial of such customs—clitoridectomy, polygamy, the marriage of children, or marriages that are otherwise coerced—sometimes explicitly defend them as necessary for controlling women and openly acknowledge that the customs persist at men's insistence. In an interview with *New York Times* reporter Celia Dugger, practitioners of clitoridectomy in Côte d'Ivoire and Togo explained that the practice 'helps insure a girl's virginity before marriage and fidelity afterward by reducing sex to a marital obligation.' As a female exciser said, '[a] woman's role in life is to care for her children, keep house and cook. If she has not been cut, [she] might think about her own sexual pleasure.'[11] In Egypt, where a law banning female genital cutting was recently overturned by a court, supporters of the practice say it 'curbs a girl's sexual appetite and makes her more marriageable.'[12] Moreover, in such societies, many women have no economically viable alternative to marriage.

In polygamous cultures, too, men readily acknowledge that the practice accords with their self-interest and is a means of controlling women. As a French immigrant from Mali said in a recent interview: 'When my wife is sick and I don't have another, who will care for me? . . . [O]ne wife on her own is trouble. When there are several, they are forced to be polite and well behaved. If they misbehave, you threaten that you'll take another wife.' Women apparently see polygamy very differently. French African immigrant women deny that they like polygamy and say that not only are they given 'no choice' in the matter, but their female forebears in Africa did not like it either.[13] As for child or otherwise coerced marriage: this practice is clearly a way not only of controlling who the girls or young women marry but also of ensuring that they are virgins at the time of marriage and, often, of enhancing the husband's power by creating a significant age difference between husbands and wives.

Consider, too, the practice—common in much of Latin America, rural Southeast Asia, and parts of West Africa—of pressuring or even requiring a rape victim to marry the rapist. In many such cultures—including 14 countries in Central and South America—rapists are legally exonerated if they marry or (in some cases) simply offer to marry their victims. Clearly, rape is not seen in these cultures primarily as a violent assault on the girl or woman herself but rather as a serious injury to her family and its honour. By marrying his victim, the rapist can help restore the family's honour and relieve it of a daughter who, as 'damaged goods', has become unmarriageable. In Peru, this barbaric law was amended for the worse in 1991: the co-defendants in a gang rape now are all exonerated if just one of them offers to marry the victim (feminists are fighting to get the law repealed). As a Peruvian taxi driver explained: 'Marriage is the right and proper thing to do after a rape. A raped woman is a used item. No one wants her. At least with this law the woman will get a husband.'[14] It is difficult to imagine a worse fate for a woman than being pressured into marrying the man who has raped her. But worse fates do exist in some cultures—notably in Pakistan and parts of the Arab Middle East, where women who bring rape charges quite frequently are charged themselves with the serious Muslim offence of *zina*, or sex outside of marriage. Law allows for the whipping or imprisonment of such women, and culture condones the killing or pressuring into suicide of a raped woman by relatives intent on restoring the family's honour.[15]

Thus many culturally based customs aim to control women and render them, especially sexually and reproductively, servile to men's desires and interests. Sometimes, moreover, 'culture' or 'traditions' are so closely linked with the control of women that they are virtually equated. In a recent news report about a small community of Orthodox Jews living in the mountains of Yemen, the elderly leader of this small polygamous sect is quoted as saying: 'We are Orthodox Jews, very keen on our traditions. If we go to Israel, we will lose hold over our daughters, our wives and our sisters.' One of his sons added, 'We are like Muslims, we do not allow our women to uncover their faces.'[16] Thus the servitude of women is presented as virtually synonymous with 'our traditions'. (Ironically, from a feminist point of view, the story was entitled 'Yemen's Small Jewish Community Thrives on Mixed Traditions.' Only blindness to sexual servitude can explain the title; it is inconceivable that the article would have carried such a title if it were about a community that practised any kind of slavery but sexual slavery.)

While virtually all of the world's cultures have distinctly patriarchal pasts, some—mostly, though by no means exclusively, Western liberal cultures—have departed far further from them than others. Western cultures, of course, still practise many forms of sex discrimination. They place far more importance on beauty, thinness, and youth in females and on intellectual accomplishment, skill, and strength in males. They expect women to perform for no economic reward far more than half of the unpaid work related to home and family, whether or not they also work for wages; partly as a consequence of this and partly because of workplace discrimination, women are far more likely than men to become poor. Girls and women are also subjected by men to a great deal of (illegal) violence, including sexual violence. But women in more liberal cultures are, at the same time, legally guaranteed many of the same freedoms and opportunities as men. In addition, most families in such cultures, with the exception of some religious fundamentalists, do not communicate to their daughters that they are of less value than boys, that their lives are to be confined to domesticity and service to men and children, and that their sexuality is of value only in marriage, in the service of men, and for reproductive ends. This situation, as we have seen, is quite different from that of women in many of the world's other cultures, including many of those from which immigrants to Europe and North America come.

Group Rights?

Most cultures are patriarchal, then, and many (though not all) of the cultural minorities that claim group rights are more patriarchal than the surrounding cultures. So it is no surprise that the cultural importance of maintaining control over women shouts out to us in the examples given in the literature on cultural diversity and group rights within liberal states. Yet, though it shouts out, it is seldom explicitly addressed.[17]

A paper by Sebastian Poulter about the legal rights and culture-based claims of various immigrant groups and Gypsies in contemporary Britain mentions the roles and status of women as 'one very clear example' of the 'clash of cultures'.[18] In it, Poulter discusses claims put forward by members of such groups for special legal treatment on account of their cultural differences. A few are non-gender-related claims; for example, a Muslim schoolteacher's being allowed to be absent part of Friday afternoons in order to pray, and Gypsy children's being subject to less stringent schooling requirements than others on account of their itinerant lifestyle. But the vast majority of the examples concern gender inequalities: child marriages, forced marriages, divorce systems biased against women, polygamy, and clitoridectomy. Almost all of the legal cases discussed by Poulter stemmed from women's or girls' claims that their individual rights were being truncated or violated by the practices of their own cultural groups. In a recent article by political philosopher Amy Gutmann, fully half her examples have to do with gender issues—polygamy, abortion, sexual harassment, clitoridectomy, and purdah.[19] This is quite typical in the literature on subnational multicultural issues. Moreover, the same linkage between culture and gender occurs in practice in the international arena, where women's human rights are often rejected by the leaders of countries or groups of countries as incompatible with their various cultures.[20]

Similarly, the overwhelming majority of 'cultural defences' that are increasingly being invoked in US criminal cases involving members of cultural minorities are connected with gender—in particular with male control over women and children.[21] Occasionally, cultural defences are cited in explanation of expectable violence among men or the ritual sacrifice of animals. Much more common, however, is the argument that, in the defendant's cultural group, women are not human beings of equal worth but rather subordinates whose primary (if not only) function is to serve men sexually and domestically. Indeed, the four types of cases in which cultural defences have been used most successfully are: (1) kidnap and rape by Hmong men who claim that their actions are part of their cultural practice of *zij poj niam*, or 'marriage by capture'; (2) wife-murder by immigrants from Asian and Middle Eastern countries whose wives have either committed adultery or treated their husbands in a servile way; (3) murder of children by Japanese or Chinese mothers who have also tried but failed to kill themselves, and who claim that because of their cultural backgrounds the shame of their husbands' infidelity drove them to the culturally condoned practice of mother-child suicide; and (4) in France—though not yet in the United States, in part because the practice was criminalized only in 1996—clitoridectomy. In a number of such cases, expert testimony about the accused's or defendant's cultural background has resulted in dropped or reduced charges, culturally based assessments of *mens rea*, or significantly reduced sentences. In a well-known recent case in the United States, an immigrant from rural Iraq married his two daughters, aged 13 and 14, to two of his friends, aged 28 and 34. Subsequently, when the older daughter ran away with her 20-year-old boyfriend, the father sought the help of the police in finding her. When they located her, they charged the father with child abuse and the two husbands and boyfriend with statutory rape. The Iraqis' defence is based in part on their cultural marriage practices.[22]

As the four examples show, the defendants are not always male, nor the victims always female. Both a Chinese immigrant man in New York who battered his wife to death for committing adultery and a Japanese immigrant woman in California who drowned her children and tried to drown herself because her husband's adultery had shamed the family relied on cultural defences to win reduced charges (from first-degree murder to second-degree murder or involuntary manslaughter). It might seem, then, that the cultural defence was biased toward the male in the first case and the female in the second. But though defendants of different sexes were cited, in both cases, the cultural message is similarly gender-biased: women (and children, in the second case) are ancillary to men and should bear the blame and the shame for any departure from monogamy. Whoever is guilty of the infidelity, the wife suffers: in the first case, by being brutally killed on account of her husband's rage at her shameful infidelity; in the second, by being so shamed and branded such a failure by his infidelity that she is driven to kill herself and her children. Again, the idea that girls and women are first and foremost sexual servants of men—that their virginity before marriage and fidelity within it are their pre-eminent virtues—emerges in many of the statements made in defence of cultural practices.

Western majority cultures, largely at the urging of feminists, have recently made substantial efforts to preclude or limit excuses for brutalizing women. Well within living memory, American men were routinely held less accountable for killing their wives if they explained their conduct as a crime of passion, driven as they were by jealousy and rage over the wife's infidelity. Also not long ago, female rape victims who did not have completely celibate pasts or who did not struggle—even when to do so meant endangering themselves—were routinely blamed for the attack. Things have now changed to some extent, and doubts about the turn toward cultural defences undoubtedly are prompted in part by a concern to preserve recent advances. Another concern is that such defences can distort perceptions of minority cultures by drawing excessive attention to negative aspects of them. But perhaps the primary concern is that, by failing to protect women and sometimes children of minority cultures from male and sometimes maternal violence, cultural defences violate women's and children's rights to equal protection of the laws.[23] When a woman from a more patriarchal culture comes to the United States (or some other Western, basically liberal, state), why should she be less protected from male violence than other women are? Many women from minority cultures have protested the double standard that is being applied on behalf of their aggressors.[24]

Liberal Defence

Despite all this evidence of cultural practices that control and subordinate women, none of the prominent defenders of multicultural group rights has adequately or even directly addressed the troubling connections between gender and culture or the conflicts that arise so commonly between feminism and multiculturalism. Will Kymlicka's discussion is, in this respect, representative.

Kymlicka's arguments for group rights are based on the rights of individuals and confine such privileges and protection to cultural groups that are internally liberal. Following John Rawls, Kymlicka emphasizes the fundamental importance of self-respect in a person's life. He argues that membership in a 'rich and secure cultural structure,'[25] with its own language and history, is essential both for the development of self-respect and for giving persons a context in which they can develop the capacity to make choices about how to lead their lives. Cultural minorities need special rights, then, because their cultures may otherwise be threatened with extinction, and cultural extinction would be likely to undermine the self-respect and freedom of group members. Special rights, in short, put minorities on an equal footing with the majority.

The value of freedom plays an important role in Kymlicka's argument. As a result, except in rare circumstances of cultural vulnerability, a group that claims special rights must govern itself by recognizably liberal principles, neither infringing on the basic liberties of its own members by placing internal restrictions on them nor discriminating among them on grounds of sex, race, or sexual preference.[26] This requirement is of great importance to a consistently liberal justification of group rights, because a 'closed' or discriminatory culture cannot provide the context for individual development that liberalism requires, and because otherwise collective rights might result in subcultures of oppression within and facilitated by liberal societies. As Kymlicka says, 'To inhibit people from questioning their inherited social roles can condemn them to unsatisfying, even oppressive lives.'[27]

As Kymlicka acknowledges, this requirement of internal liberalism rules out the justification of group rights for the 'many fundamentalists of all political and religious stripes who think that the best community is one in which all but their preferred religious, sexual, or aesthetic practices are outlawed.' For the promotion and support of *these* cultures undermines 'the very reason we had for being concerned with cultural membership—that it

allows for meaningful individual choice.'[28] But the examples I cited earlier suggest that far fewer minority cultures than Kymlicka seems to think will be able to claim group rights under his liberal justification. Though they may not impose their beliefs or practices on others, and though they may appear to respect the basic civil and political liberties of women and girls, many cultures do not, especially in the private sphere, treat them with anything like the same concern and respect with which men and boys are treated, or allow them to enjoy the same freedoms. Discrimination against and control of the freedom of females are practised, to a greater or lesser extent, by virtually all cultures, past and present, but especially by religious ones and those that look to the past—to ancient texts or revered traditions—for guidelines or rules about how to live in the contemporary world. Sometimes more patriarchal minority cultures exist in the midst of less patriarchal majority cultures; sometimes the reverse is true. In either case, the degree to which each culture is patriarchal and its willingness to become less so should be crucial factors in judgment about the justifications of group rights—once women's equality is taken seriously.

Clearly, Kymlicka regards cultures that discriminate overtly and formally against women —by denying them education or the right to vote or hold office—as not deserving special rights.[29] But sex discrimination is often far less overt. In many cultures, strict control of women is enforced in the private sphere by the authority of either actual or symbolic fathers, often acting through, or with the complicity of, the older women of the culture. In many cultures in which women's basic civil rights and liberties are formally assured, discrimination practised against women and girls within the household not only severely constrains their choices but also seriously threatens their well-being and even their lives.[30] And such sex discrimination—whether severe or more mild—often has very powerful *cultural* roots.

. Although Kymlicka rightly objects, then, to the granting of group rights to minority cultures that practise overt sex discrimination, his arguments for multiculturalism fail to register what he acknowledges elsewhere: that the subordination of women is often informal and private, and that virtually no culture in the world today, minority or majority, could pass his 'no sex discrimination' test if it were applied in the private sphere.[31] Those who defend group rights on liberal grounds need to address these very private, culturally reinforced kinds of discrimination. For surely self-respect and self-esteem require more than simple membership in a viable culture. Surely it is *not* enough for one to be able to 'question one's inherited social roles' and to have the capacity to make choices about the life one wants to lead, that one's culture be protected. At least as important to the development of self-respect and self-esteem is *our place within our culture*. And at least as pertinent to our capacity to question our social roles is *whether our culture instils in us and forces on us particular social roles*. To the extent that a girl's culture is patriarchal, in both these respects her healthy development is endangered.

Part of the Solution?

It is by no means clear, then, from a feminist point of view, that minority group rights are 'part of the solution'. They may well exacerbate the problem. In the case of a more patriarchal minority culture in the context of a less patriarchal majority culture, no argument can be made on the basis of self-respect or freedom that the female members of the culture have a clear interest in its preservation. Indeed, they *might* be much better off if the

culture into which they were born were either to become extinct (so that its members would become integrated into the less sexist surrounding culture) or, preferably, to be encouraged to alter itself so as to reinforce the equality of women—at least to the degree to which this value is upheld in the majority culture. Other considerations would, of course, need to be taken into account, such as whether the minority group speaks a language that requires protection, and whether the group suffers from prejudices such as racial discrimination. But it would take significant factors weighing in the other direction to counterbalance evidence that a culture severely constrains women's choices or otherwise undermines their well-being.

What some of the examples discussed above illustrate is how culturally endorsed practices that are oppressive to women can often remain hidden in the private or domestic sphere. In the Iraqi child marriage case mentioned above, if the father himself had not called in agents of the state, his daughters' plight might well not have become public. And when Congress in 1996 passed a law criminalizing clitoridectomy, a number of US doctors objected to the law on the basis that it concerned a private matter which, as one said, 'should be decided by a physician, the family, and the child.'[32] It can take more or less extraordinary circumstances for such abuses of girls or women to become public or for the state to be able to intervene protectively.

Thus it is clear that many instances of private-sphere discrimination against women on cultural grounds are never likely to emerge in public, where courts can enforce the women's rights and political theorists can label such practices as illiberal and therefore unjustified violations of women's physical or mental integrity. Establishing group rights to enable some minority cultures to preserve themselves may not be in the best interests of the girls and women of those cultures, even if it benefits the men.

Those who make liberal arguments for the rights of groups, then, must take special care to look at inequalities within those groups. It is especially important to consider inequalities between the sexes, since they are likely to be less public, and thus less easily discernible. Moreover, policies designed to respond to the needs and claims of cultural minority groups must take seriously the urgency of adequately representing less powerful members of such groups. Because attention to the rights of minority cultural groups, if it is to be consistent with the fundamentals of liberalism, must ultimately be aimed at furthering the well-being of the members of these groups, there can be no justification for assuming that the groups' self-proclaimed leaders—invariably composed mainly of their older and their male members—represent the interests of all of the groups' members. Unless women—and, more specifically, young women (since older women often are co-opted into reinforcing gender inequality)—are fully represented in negotiations about group rights, their interests may be harmed rather than promoted by the granting of such rights.

Notes

1. *International Herald Tribune*, 2 February 1996, News section.

2. Will Kymlicka, *Multicultural Citizenship: A Liberal Theory of Minority Rights* (Oxford: Oxford University Press, 1995), 89, 76. See also Kymlicka, *Liberalism, Community, and Culture* (Oxford: Clarendon Press, 1989). It should be noted that Kymlicka himself does not argue for extensive or permanent group rights for those who have voluntarily immigrated.

3. Avishai Margalit and Moshe Halbertal, 'Liberalism and the Right to Culture,' *Social Research* 61, no. 3 (Fall 1994): 491.

4. For example, Chandran Kukathas, 'Are There Any Cultural Rights?' *Political Theory* 20, no. 1 (1992): 105–39.

5. Okin, 'Feminism and Multiculturalism: Some Tensions,' *Ethics* 108, no. 4 (July 1998): 661–84.

6. For example, Kymlicka, *Liberalism, Community, and Culture and Multicultural Citizenship* (esp. chap. 8). Kymlicka does not apply his requirement that groups be internally liberal to those he terms 'national minorities', but I will not address that aspect of his theory here.

7. See, for example, Kirti Singh, 'Obstacles to Women's Rights in India,' in *Human Rights of Women: National and International Perspectives*, ed. Rebecca J. Cook (Philadelphia: University of Pennsylvania Press, 1994), 375–96, esp. 378–89.

8. I cannot discuss here the roots of this male preoccupation, except to say (following feminist theorists Dorothy Dinnerstein, Nancy Chodorow, Jessica Benjamin, and, before them, Jesuit anthropologist Walter Ong) that it seems to have a lot to do with female primary parenting. It is also clearly related to the uncertainty of paternity, which technology has now counteracted. If these issues are at the root of it, then the cultural preoccupation with controlling women is not an inevitable fact of human life but a contingent factor that feminists have a considerable interest in changing.

9. See, for example, Arvind Sharma, ed., *Women in World Religions* (Albany: SUNY Press, 1987); John Stratton Hawley, ed., *Fundamentalism and Gender* (Oxford: Oxford University Press, 1994).

10. See Carol Delaney, *Abraham on Trial: The Social Legacy of Biblical Myth* (Princeton: Princeton University Press, 1998). Note that in the Qur'anic version, it is not Isaac but Ishmael whom Abraham prepares to sacrifice.

11. *New York Times*, 26 June 1997, A9. The role that older women in such cultures play in perpetuating these practices is important but complex and cannot be addressed here.

12. *New York Times*, 26 June 1997, A9.

13. *International Herald Tribune*, 2 February 1996, News section.

14. *New York Times*, 12 March 1997, A8.

15. This practice is discussed in Henry S. Richardson, *Practical Reasoning about Final Ends* (Cambridge: Cambridge University Press, 1994), esp. 240–3, 262–3, 282–4.

16. *Agence France Presse*, 18 May 1997, International News section.

17. See, however, Bhikhu Parekh's 'Minority Practices and Principles of Toleration,' *International Migration Review* (April 1996): 251–84, in which he directly addresses and critiques a number of cultural practices that devalue the status of women.

18. Sebastian Poulter, 'Ethnic Minority Customs, English Law, and Human Rights,' *International and Comparative Law Quarterly* 36, no. 3 (1987): 589–615.

19. Amy Gutmann, 'The Challenge of Multiculturalism in Political Ethics,' *Philosophy and Public Affairs* 22, no. 3 (Summer 1993): 171–204.

20. Mahnaz Afkhami, ed., *Faith and Freedom: Women's Human Rights in the Muslim World* (Syracuse: Syracuse University Press, 1995); Valentine M. Moghadam, ed., *Identity, Politics and Women: Cultural Reassertions and Feminism in International Perspective* (Boulder, CO: Westview Press, 1994); Susan Moller Okin, 'Culture, Religion, and Female Identity Formation' (unpublished manuscript, 1997).

21. For one of the best and most recent accounts of this, and for legal citations for the cases mentioned below, see Doriane Lambelet Coleman, 'Individualizing Justice through Multiculturalism: The Liberals' Dilemma,' *Columbia Law Review* 96, no. 5 (1996): 1093–1167.

22. *New York Times*, 2 December 1996, A6.

23. See Coleman, 'Individualizing Justice through Multiculturalism.'

24. See, for example, Nilda Rimonte, 'A Question of Culture: Cultural Approval of Violence against Women in the Asian-Pacific Community and the Cultural Defense,' *Stanford Law Review* 43 (1991): 1311–26.

25. Kymlicka, *Liberalism, Community, and Culture*, 165.

26. Ibid., 168–72, 195–8.

27. Kymlicka, *Multicultural Citizenship*, 92.

28. Kymlicka, *Liberalism, Community, and Culture*, 171–2.

29. Kymlicka, *Multicultural Citizenship*, 153, 165.

30. See, for example, Amartya Sen, 'More Than One Hundred Million Women Are Missing,' *New York Review of Books*, 20 December 1990.

31. Will Kymlicka, *Contemporary Political Philosophy: An Introduction* (Oxford: Clarendon Press, 1990), 239–62.

32. *New York Times*, 12 October 1996, A6. Similar views were expressed on National Public Radio.

Study Questions for *Justice, Gender, and the Family*

1. According to Okin, why is the family an important subject for a theory of justice? What social transformations are necessary to bring about justice within families?

2. Okin notes that John Stuart Mill sets himself apart from other classical social theorists in arguing for justice within families and equality between the sexes. In what respect does Mill undermine his own arguments for gender equality, according to Okin?

3. Okin suggests that a just society 'would be one without gender.' What would a society without gender differentiation look like, according to Okin?
4. Okin notes that the Rawlsian original position provides a useful framework for thinking about social policies and gender equality. If you imagine yourself in Rawls's original position (without knowledge of your sex, your conception of the good life, or your beliefs about the characteristics of men and women), what principles of justice regarding gender and the family would you endorse?
5. According to Okin, what social transformations are necessary for bringing about justice between the sexes? Which of Okin's public policy recommendations appear most plausible or important? Are any of her recommendations problematic or ill-conceived, in your view?

Study Questions for 'Is Multiculturalism Bad for Women?'

1. Okin notes that until the late twentieth century, minority groups were often expected to assimilate into larger majority cultures, but this expectation is now considered oppressive. Why is the cultural expectation of assimilation oppressive?
2. What examples does Okin use in illustrating her claim that a tension exists between multiculturalism and feminism? Are these examples convincing?
3. How does Okin characterize multiculturalism? Why do multicultural political theorists recommend protecting minority cultures with special group rights?
4. Summarize the feminist critique of multiculturalist recommendations for special group rights for minority cultures. How does Okin critique Will Kymlicka's liberal defence of group rights?

Recommended Readings

Cohen, Joshua, Matthew Howard, and Martha Nussbaum, eds, *Is Multiculturalism Bad for Women?* (Princeton University Press, 1999).

Deveaux, Monique, *Gender and Justice in Multicultural Liberal States* (Oxford University Press, 2006).

McKinnon, Catharine, *Toward a Feminist Theory of the State* (Harvard University Press, 1989)

McLaughlin, Janice, *Feminist Social and Political Theory: Contemporary Debates and Dialogues* (Palgrave Macmillan, 2003).

Nussbaum, Martha, *Sex and Social Justice* (Oxford University Press, 1999).

Okin, Susan Moller, *Women in Western Political Thought* (Princeton University Press, 1979).

Phillips, Anne, ed., *Feminism and Politics* (Oxford University Press, 1998).

Sharma, Arvind, *Are Human Rights Western?* (Oxford University Press, 2006).

Charles Taylor

Charles Taylor (1931–) was born in Montreal, Quebec, and educated at McGill University and Oxford University. He held a distinguished professorship of moral and political philosophy at Oxford University before taking a professorship at McGill University, where he taught for several years. He is now professor emeritus at McGill and professor of law and philosophy at Northwestern University. A philosopher of diverse talents, Taylor publishes not only in social and political philosophy but also in religious moral theory, the philosophy of language, and the philosophy of Hegel. In 2007, he won the prestigious Templeton Prize—the most lucrative academic award in the world—in recognition of his work on secular and spiritual dimensions of human existence. His numerous books include *Hegel and Modern Society* (1979), *Sources of the Self* (1989), *The Ethics of Authenticity* (1992), *Philosophical Arguments* (1995), and *Varieties of Religion Today* (2002). In *Multiculturalism and 'The Politics of Recognition'* (1994), five leading political philosophers comment on Taylor's essay on the politics of recognition, our second selection in this chapter.

Within social and political philosophy, Taylor develops a communitarian critique of liberal political philosophies, but his interests also range beyond the liberal-communitarian debate and bring forward its complexity. His critique of political individualism is indebted to G.F.W. Hegel, on whom Taylor wrote two major books. In our first selection, 'Atomism' (1992), Taylor argues that political theorists who defend the priority of the individual over society, including some modern social contract theorists and their libertarian successors, rely upon an incoherent individualistic picture of human beings as socially atomistic, self-sufficient bearers of rights and freedoms. Liberal political theorists ascribe rights and freedoms to human beings in virtue of their specifically human capacities, such the capacity for free choice or free thought, but these very capacities emerge and develop only within a social community and a broader cultural, artistic, and intellectual civilization. Thus, Taylor argues, social belonging and cultural identity make more appropriate starting points for social and political theory than defences of individual rights and liberties.

In 'The Politics of Recognition,' Taylor examines nationalist, feminist, and multiculturalist political movements that link public recognition with personal identity. These political movements begin with the idea that recognition by others shapes the identity of an individual, and the identities of marginalized peoples suffer from a lack of public recognition or from misrecognition. Taylor traces the intellectual development of the politics of recognition, in part arguing that identity politics is born out of a historical shift from a pre-modern moral emphasis on honour to modern moral emphases on equality, dignity, and individual authenticity. The modern ideal of equal respect for all citizens has produced two competing modes of political theory: a politics of equal rights and entitlements and a politics of equal recognition of the differences and unique identities of individuals and cultural groups. Finally, Taylor suggests that political liberalism is not a neutral political backdrop for all cultures but an intellectual outgrowth of Western Christian civilization. The essay ends with a meditation on problems and paradoxes in multiculturalism.

'Atomism'

I would like to examine the issue of political atomism, or at least to try to clarify what this issue is. I want to say what I think atomist doctrines consist in, and to examine how the issue can be joined around them—this is, how they might be proved or disproved, or at least cogently argued for or against, and what in turn they may be used to prove.

The term 'atomism' is used loosely to characterize the doctrines of social-contract theory which arose in the seventeenth century and also successor doctrines which may not have made use of the notion of social contract but which inherited a vision of society as in some sense constituted by individuals for the fulfillment of ends which were primarily individual. Certain forms of utilitarianism are successor doctrines in this sense. The term is also applied to contemporary doctrines which hark back to social-contract theory, or which try to defend in some sense the priority of the individual and his rights over society, or which present a purely instrumental view of society.

Of course, any term loosely used in political discourse can be defined in a host of ways. And perhaps one should even leave out of philosophical discourse altogether those terms which tend to be branded as epithets of condemnation in the battle between different views. One might well argue that 'atomism' is one such, because it seems to be used almost exclusively by its enemies. Even extreme individualists like Nozick don't seem to warm to this term, but tend to prefer others, like 'individualism'.

Perhaps I am dealing with the wrong term. But there is a central issue in political theory which is eminently worth getting at under some description. And perhaps the best way of getting at it is this: what I am calling atomist doctrines underlie the seventeenth-century revolution in the terms of normative discourse, which we associate with the names of Hobbes and Locke.

These writers, and others who presented social-contract views, have left us a legacy of political thinking in which the notion of rights plays a central part in the justification of political structures and action. The central doctrine of this tradition is an affirmation of what we could call the primacy of rights.

Theories which assert the primacy of rights are those which take as the fundamental, or at least a fundamental, principle of their political theory the ascription of certain rights to individuals and which deny the same status to a principle of belonging or obligation, that is a principle which states our obligation as men to belong to or sustain society, or a society of a certain type, or to obey authority or an authority of a certain type. Primacy-of-right theories in other words accept a principle ascribing rights to men as binding unconditionally,[1] binding, that is, on men as such. But they do not accept as similarly unconditional a principle of belonging or obligation. Rather our obligation to belong to or sustain a society, or to obey its authorities, is seen as derivative, as laid on us conditionally, through our consent, or through its being to our advantage. The obligation to belong is derived in certain conditions from the more fundamental principle which ascribes rights.[2]

The paradigm of primacy-of-right theories is plainly that of Locke. But there are contemporary theories of this kind, one of the best known in recent years being that of Robert Nozick.[3] Nozick too makes the assertion of rights to individuals fundamental and then proceeds to discuss whether and in what conditions we can legitimately demand obedience to a state.

Primacy-of-right theories have been one of the formative influences on modern political consciousness. Thus arguments like that of Nozick have at least a surface plausibility for our contemporaries and sometimes considerably more. At the very least, opponents are brought up short, and have to ponder how to meet the claims of an argument which reaches conclusions about political obedience which lie far outside the common sense of our society; and this because the starting-point in individual rights has an undeniable *prima facie* force for us.

This is striking because it would not always have been so. In an earlier phase of Western civilization, of course, not to speak of other civilizations, these arguments would have seemed wildly eccentric and implausible. The very idea of starting an argument whose foundation was the rights of the individual would have been strange and puzzling—about as puzzling as if I were to start with the premise that the Queen rules by divine right. You might not dismiss what I said out of hand, but you would expect that I should at least have the sense to start with some less contentious premise and argue up to divine right, not take it as my starting-point.

Why do we even begin to find it reasonable to start a political theory with an assertion of individual rights and to give these primacy? I want to argue that the answer to this question lies in the hold on us of what I have called atomism. Atomism represents a view about human nature and the human condition which (among other things) makes a doctrine of the primacy of rights plausible; or, to put it negatively, it is a view in the absence of which this doctrine is suspect to the point of being virtually untenable.

How can we formulate this view? Perhaps the best way is to borrow the terms of the opposed thesis—the view that man is a social animal. One of the most influential formulations of this view is Aristotle's. He puts the point in terms of the notion of self-sufficiency (*autarkeia*). Man is a social animal, indeed a political animal, because he is not self-sufficient alone, and in an important sense is not self-sufficient outside a *polis*; Borrowing this term then, we could say that atomism affirms the self-sufficiency of man alone or, if you prefer, of the individual.

That the primacy-of-rights doctrine needs a background of this kind may appear evident to some; but it needs to be argued because it is vigorously denied by others. And generally proponents of the doctrine are among the most vigorous deniers. They will not generally admit that the assertion of rights is dependent on any particular view about the nature of man, especially one as difficult to formulate and make clear as this. And to make their political theory dependent on a thesis formulated in just this way seems to be adding insult to injury. For if atomism means that man is self-sufficient alone, then surely it is a very questionable thesis. . . .

The claim I am trying to make could be summed up in this way. (1) To ascribe the natural (not just legal) right of X to agent A is to affirm that A commands our respect, such that we are normally bound not to interfere with A's doing or enjoying of X. This means that to ascribe the right is far more than simply to issue the injunction: don't interfere with A's doing or enjoying X. The injunction can be issued, to self or others, without grounds, should we so choose. But to affirm the right is to say that a creature such as A lays a moral claim on us not to interfere. It thus also asserts something about A: A is such that this injunction is somehow inescapable.

(2) We may probe further and try to define what it is about A which makes the injunction inescapable. We can call this, whatever it is, A's essential property or properties, E. Then it is E (in our case, the essentially human capacities) which defines not only who are the bearers of rights but what they have rights to. A has a natural right to X, if doing or enjoying X is essentially part of manifesting E (e.g., if E is being a rational life-form, then A's have a natural right to life and also to the unimpeded development of rationality); or if X is a causally necessary condition of manifesting E (e.g., the ownership of property, which has been widely believed to be a necessary safeguard of life or freedom, or a living wage).

(3) The assertion of a natural right, while it lays on us the injunction to respect A in his doing or enjoying of X, cannot but have other moral consequences as well. For if A is such that this injunction is inescapable and he is such in virtue of E, then E is of great moral worth and ought to be fostered and developed in a host of appropriate ways, and not just not interfered with.

Hence asserting a right is more than issuing an injunction. It has an essential conceptual background, in some notion of the moral worth of certain properties or capacities, without which it would not make sense. Thus, for example, our position would be incomprehensible and incoherent if we ascribed rights to human beings in respect of the specifically human capacities (such as the right to one's own convictions or to the free choice of one's lifestyle or profession) while at the same time denying that these capacities ought to be developed, or if we thought it a matter of indifference whether they were realized or stifled in ourselves or others.

From this we can see that the answer to [the] question . . . why do we ascribe these rights to men and not to animals, rocks, or trees . . . is quite straightforward. It is because men and women are the beings who exhibit certain capacities which are worthy of respect. The fact that we ascribe rights to idiots, people in a coma, bad men who have irretrievably turned their back on the proper development of these capacities, and so on, does not show that the capacities are irrelevant. It shows only that we have a powerful sense that the status of being a creature defined by its potential for these capacities cannot be lost. This sense has been given a rational account in certain ways, such as, for instance, by the belief in an immortal soul. But it is interestingly enough shared even by those who have rejected all such traditional rationales. We sense that in the incurable psychotic there runs a current of human life, where the definition of 'human' may be uncertain but relates to the specifically human capacities; we sense that he has feelings that only a human being, a language-using animal, can have, that his dreams and fantasies are those which only a human can have. Pushed however deep, and however distorted, his humanity cannot be eradicated.

If we look at another extreme case, that of persons in a terminal but long-lasting coma, it would seem that the sense that many have that the life-support machines should be disconnected is based partly on the feeling that the patients themselves, should they *per impossible* be able to choose, would not want to continue, precisely because the range of human life has been shrunk here to zero.

How does the notion then arise that we can assert rights outside of a context of affirming the worth of certain capacities? The answer to this question will take us deep into the issue central to modern thought of the nature of the subject. We can give but a partial account here. There clearly are a wide number of different conceptions of the characteristically human capacities and thus differences too in what are recognized as rights. I will come back to this in another connection later.

But what is relevant for our purposes here is that there are some views of the properly human which give absolutely central importance to the freedom to choose one's own mode of life. Those who hold this ultra-liberal view are chary about allowing that the assertion of right involves any affirmation about realizing certain potentialities; for they fear that the affirming of any obligations will offer a pretext for the restriction of freedom. To say that we have a right to be free to choose our life-form must be to say that any choice is equally compatible with this principle of freedom and that no choices can be judged morally better or worse by this principle— although, of course, we might want to discriminate between them on the basis of other principles.

Thus if I have a right to do what I want with my property, then any disposition I choose is equally justifiable from the point of view of this principle: I may be judged uncharitable if I hoard it to myself and won't help those in need, or uncreative if I bury it in the ground and don't engage in interesting enterprises with it. But these latter criticisms arise from our accepting other moral standards, quite independent from the view that we have a right to do what we want with our own.

But this independence from a moral obligation of self-realization cannot be made good all around. All choices are equally valid; but they must be *choices*. The view that makes freedom of choice this absolute is one that exalts choice as a human capacity. It carries with it the demand that we become beings capable of choice, that we rise to the level of self-consciousness and autonomy where we can exercise choice, that we not remain enmired through fear, sloth, ignorance, or superstition in some code imposed by tradition, society, or fate which tells us how we should dispose of what belongs to us. Ultra-liberalism can only appear unconnected with any affirmation of worth and hence obligation of self-fulfilment, where people have come to accept the utterly facile moral psychology of traditional empiricism, according to which human agents possess the full capacity of choice as a given rather than as a potential which has to be developed.

If all this is valid, then the doctrine of the primacy of rights is not as independent as its proponents want to claim from considerations about human nature and the human social condition. For the doctrine could be undermined by arguments which succeeded in showing that men were not self-sufficient in the sense of the above argument—that is, that they could not develop their characteristically human potentialities outside of society or outside of certain kinds of society. The doctrine would in this sense be dependent on an atomist thesis, which affirms this kind of self-sufficiency.

The connection I want to establish here can be made following the earlier discussion of the background of rights. If we cannot ascribe natural rights without affirming the worth of certain human capacities, and if this affirmation has other normative consequences (i.e., that we should foster and nurture these capacities in ourselves and others), then any proof that these capacities can only develop in society or in a society of a certain kind is a proof that we ought to belong to or sustain society or this kind of society. But then, provided a social (i.e., an anti-atomist) thesis of the right kind can be true, an assertion of the primacy of rights is impossible; for to assert the rights in question is to affirm the capacities, and, granted the social thesis is true concerning these capacities, this commits us to an obligation to belong. This will be as fundamental as the assertion of rights, because it will be inseparable from it. So it would be incoherent to try to assert the rights, while denying the obligation or giving it the status of optional extra which we may or may not contract; this assertion is what the primary doctrine makes.

The normative incoherence becomes evident if we see what it would be to assert the primacy of rights in the face of such a social thesis. Let us accept, for the sake of this argument, the view that men cannot develop the fullness of moral autonomy—that is, the capacity to form independent moral convictions—outside a political culture sustained by institutions of political participation and guarantees of personal independence. In fact, I do not think this thesis is true as it stands, although I do believe that a much more complicated view, formed from this one by adding a number of significant reservations, is tenable. But, for the sake of simplicity, let us accept this thesis in order to see the logic of the arguments.

Now if we assert the right to one's own independent moral convictions, we cannot in the face of this social thesis go on to assert the primacy of rights, that is, claim that we are not under obligation 'by nature' to belong to and sustain a society of the relevant type. We could not, for instance, unreservedly assert our right in the face of, or at the expense of, such a society; in the event of conflict we should have to acknowledge that we were legitimately pulled both ways. For in undermining such a society we should be making the activity defended by the right assertion impossible of realization. But if we are justified in asserting the right, we cannot be justified in our undermining; for the same considerations which justify the first condemn the second.

In whatever way the conflict might arise it poses a moral dilemma for us. It may be that we have already been formed in this culture and that the demise of this mode of society will not deprive us of this capacity. But in asserting our rights to the point of destroying the society, we should be depriving all those who follow after us of the exercise of the same capacity. To believe that there is a right to independent moral convictions must be to believe that the exercise of the relevant capacity is a human good. But then it cannot be right, if no overriding considerations intervene, to act so as to make this good less available to others, even though in so doing I could not be said to be depriving them of their rights.

The incoherence of asserting primacy of rights is even clearer if we imagine another way in which the conflict could arise: that, in destroying the society, I would be undermining my own future ability to realize this capacity. For then, in defending my right, I should be condemning myself to what I should have to acknowledge as a truncated mode of life, in virtue of the same considerations that make me affirm the right. And this would be a paradoxical thing to defend as an affirmation of my rights—in the same way as it would be paradoxical for me to offer to defend you against those who menace your freedom by hiding you in my deep freeze. I would have to have misunderstood what freedom is all about; and similarly, in the above case, I should have lost my grasp of what affirming a right is.

We could put the point in another way. The affirmation of certain rights involves us in affirming the worth of certain capacities and thus in accepting certain standards by which a life may be judged full or truncated. We cannot then sensibly claim the morality of a truncated form of life for people on the ground of defending their rights. Would I be respecting your right to life if I agreed to leave you alive in a hospital bed, in an irreversible coma, hooked up to life-support machines? Or suppose I offered to use my new machine to erase totally your personality and memories and give you quite different ones? These questions are inescapably rhetorical. We cannot take them seriously as genuine questions because of the whole set of intuitions which surround our affirmation of the right to life. We assert this right because human life has a certain worth; but exactly wherein it has worth is negated by the appalling conditions I am offering you. That is why the offer is a sick joke, the lines of the mad scientist in a B movie.

It is the mad scientist's question, and not the question whether the person in the coma still enjoys rights, which should be decisive for the issue of whether asserting rights involves affirming the worth of certain capacities. For the latter question just probes the conditions of a right being valid; whereas the former shows us what it is to respect a right and hence what is really being asserted in a rights claim. It enables us to see what else we are committed to in asserting a right.

How would it do for the scientist to say, 'Well, I have respected his right to *life*, it is other rights (free movement, exercise of his profession, etc.) which I have violated'? For the separation in this context is absurd. True, we do sometimes enumerate these and other rights. But the right to life could never have been understood as excluding all these activities, as a right just to biological non-death in a coma. It is incomprehensible how anyone could assert a right to life meaning just this. 'Who calls that living?' would be the standard reaction. We could understand such an exiguous definition of life in the context of forensic medicine, for instance, but not in the affirmation of a right to life. And this is because the right-assertion is also an affirmation of worth, and this would be incomprehensible on behalf of this shadow of life.

If these arguments are valid, then the terms of the arguments are very different from what they are seen to be by most believers in the primacy of rights. Nozick, for instance, seems to feel that he can start from our intuitions that people have certain rights to dispose, say, of what they own so long as they harm no one else in doing so; and that we can build up (or fail to build up) a case for legitimate allegiance to certain forms of society and/or authority from this basis, by showing how they do not violate the rights. But he does not recognize that asserting rights itself involves acknowledging an obligation to belong. If the above considerations are valid, one cannot just baldly start with such an assertion of primacy. We would have to show that the relevant potentially mediating social theses are not valid; or, in other terms, we would have to defend a thesis of social atomism, that men are self-sufficient outside of society. We would have to establish the validity of arguing from the primacy of right.

But we can still try to resist this conclusion, in two ways. We can resist it first of all in asserting a certain schedule of rights. Suppose I make the basic right I assert that to life, on the grounds of sentience. This I understand in the broad sense that includes also other animals. Now sentience, as was said above, is not a capacity which can be realized or remain undeveloped; living things have it, and in dying they fail to have it; and there is an end to it. This is not to say that there are not conditions of severe impairment which constitute an infringement on sentient life, short of death. And clearly a right to life based on sentience would rule out accepting the mad scientist's offer just as much as any other conception of this right. But sentient life, while it can be impaired, is not a potential which we must develop and frequently fail to develop, as is the capacity to be a morally autonomous agent, or the capacity for self-determining freedom, or the capacity for the full realization of our talents.

But if we are not dealing with a capacity which can be underdeveloped in this sense, then there is no room for a thesis about the conditions of its development, whether social or otherwise. No social thesis is relevant. We are sentient beings whatever the social organization (or lack of it) of our existence; and if our basic right is to life, and the grounds of this right concern sentience (being capable of self-feeling, of desire and its satisfaction/frustration, of experiencing pain and pleasure), then surely we are beings of this kind in any society or none. In this regard we are surely self-sufficient.

I am not sure that even this is true—that is, that we really are self-sufficient even in regard to sentience. But it certainly is widely thought likely that we are. And therefore it is not surprising that the turn to theories of the primacy of rights goes along with an accentu-

ation of the right to life which stresses life as sentience. For Hobbes our attachment to life is our desire to go on being agents of desire. The connection is not hard to understand. Social theories require a conception of the properly human life which is such that we are not assured it by simply being alive, but it must be developed and it can fail to be developed; on this basis they can argue that society or a certain form of society is the essential condition of this development. But Hobbesian nominalism involves rejection utterly all such talk of forms or qualities of life which are properly human. Man is a being with desires, all of them on the same level. 'Whatsoever is the object of any man's desire . . . that is it which he for his part calleth good.'[4] At one stroke there is no further room for a social thesis; and at the same time the right to life is interpreted in terms of desire. To be alive now in the meaning of the act is to be an agent of desires.

So we can escape the whole argument about self-sufficiency, it would seem, by making our schedule of rights sparse enough. Primacy-of-rights talk tends to go with a tough-mindedness which dismisses discussion of the properly human life-form as empty and metaphysical. From within its philosophical position, it is impregnable; but this does not mean that it is not still open to objection.

For the impregnability is purchased at a high price. To affirm a right for man merely *qua* desiring being, or a being feeling pleasure and pain, is to restrict his rights to those of life, desire-fulfillment, and freedom and pain. Other widely claimed rights, like freedom, enter only as means to these basic ones. If one is a monster of (at least attempted) consistency, like Hobbes, then one will be willing to stick to this exiguous conception of rights regardless of the consequences. But even then the question will arise of what on this view is the value of human as against animal life; and of whether it really is not a violation of people's rights if we transform them, unknown to themselves, into child-like lotus-eaters, say, by injecting them with some drug.

In fact, most of those who want to affirm the primacy of rights are more interested in asserting the right of freedom, and moreover, in a sense which can only be attributed to humans, freedom to choose life plans, to dispose of possessions, to form one's own convictions and within reason act on them, and so on. But then we are dealing with capacities which do not simply belong to us in virtue of being alive—capacities which at least in some cases can fail to be properly developed; thus, the question of the proper conditions for their development arises.

We might query whether this is so with one of the freedoms mentioned above—that to dispose of one's own possessions. This is the right to property which has figured prominently with the right to life in the schedules put forwarded by defenders of primacy. Surely this right, while not something we can attribute to an animal, does not presuppose a capacity which could fail to be developed, at least for normal adults! We all are capable of possessing things, of knowing what we possess, and of deciding what we want to do with these possessions. This right does not seem to presuppose a capacity needing development, as does the right to profess independent convictions, for instance.

But those who assert this right almost always are affirming a capacity which we can fail to develop. And this becomes evident when we probe the reason for asserting this right. The standard answer, which comes to us from Locke, is that we need the right to property as an essential underpinning of life. But this is patently not true. Men have survived very well in communal societies all the way from paleolithic hunting clans through the Inca empire to contemporary China. And if one protests that the issue is not under what conditions one would not starve to death, but rather under what conditions one is independent enough of society not to be at its mercy for one's life, then the answer is that, if the whole point is being secure in my life, then I would be at less risk of death from agents of my own society in the contemporary Chinese commune than I would be in contemporary Chile. The property regime is hardly the only relevant variable.

But the real point is this: supposing a proponent of the right to property were to admit that the above was true—that the right to property does not as such secure life—would he change his mind? And the answer is, in the vast majority of cases, no. For what is at stake for him is not just life, but life in freedom. My life is safe in a Chinese commune, he might agree, but that is so only for so long as I keep quiet and do not profess heterodox opinions; otherwise the risks are very great. Private property is seen as essential, because it is thought to be an essential part of a life of genuine independence. But realizing a life of this form involves developing the capacity to act and choose in a genuinely independent way. And here the issue of whether a relevant social thesis is not valid can arise.

Hence this way of resisting the necessity of arguing for self-sufficiency (by scaling down one's schedules of rights to mere sentience or desire) is hardly likely to appeal to most proponents of primacy—once they understand the price they pay. For it involves sacrificing the central good of freedom, which it is their principal motive to safeguard.

There remains another way of avoiding the issue. A proponent of primacy could admit that the question arises of the conditions for the development of the relevant capacities; he could even agree that a human being entirely alone could not possibly develop them (this is pretty hard to contest: wolf-boys are not candidates for properly human freedoms), and yet argue that society in the relevant sense was not necessary.

Certainly humans need others in order to develop as full human beings, he would agree. We must all be nurtured by others as children. We can only flourish as adults in relationship with friends, mates, children, and so on. But all this has nothing to do with any obligations to belong to political society. The argument about the state of nature should never have been taken as applying to human beings alone in the wilderness. This is a Rousseauian gloss, but is clearly not the conception of the state of nature with Locke, for instance. Rather it is clear that men must live in families (however families are constituted); that they need families even to grow up human; and that they continue to need them to express an important part of their humanity.

But what obligations to belong does this put on them? It gives us obligations in regard to our parents. But these are obligations of gratitude, and are of a different kind; for when we are ready to discharge these obligations our parents are no longer essential conditions of our human development. The corresponding obligations are to our children, to give them what we have been given; and for the rest we owe a debt to those with whom we are linked in marriage, friendship, association, and the like. But all this is perfectly acceptable to a proponent of the primacy of rights. For all obligations to other adults are freely taken on in contracting marriage, friendships, and the like; there is no natural obligation to belong. The only involuntary associations are those between generations: our obligations to our parents and those to our children (if we can think of these as involuntary associations, since no one picks his children in the process

of natural generation). But these are obligations to specific people and do not necessarily involve continuing associations; and they are neither of them cases where the obligation arises in the way it does in the social thesis, that is that we must maintain the association as a condition of our continued development.

Hence we can accommodate whatever is valid in the social thesis without any danger to the primacy of rights. Family obligations and obligations of friendship can be kept separate from any obligations to belong.

I do not think that this argument will hold. But I cannot really undertake to refute it here, not just on the usual cowardly grounds of lack of space, but because we enter here precisely on the central issue of the human condition which divides atomism from social theories. And this issue concerning as it does the human condition cannot be settled in a knockdown argument. My aim in this paper was just to show that it is an issue, and therefore has to be addressed by proponents of primacy. For this purpose I would like to lay out some considerations to which I subscribe, but of which I can do no more than sketch an outline in these pages.

The kind of freedom valued by the protagonists of the primacy of rights, and indeed by many others of us as well, is a freedom by which men are capable of conceiving alternatives and arriving at a definition of what they really want, as well as discerning what commands their adherence or their allegiance. This kind of freedom is unavailable to one whose sympathies and horizons are so narrow that he can conceive only one way of life, for whom indeed the very notion of a way of life which is *his* as against everyone's has no sense. Nor is it available to one who is riveted by fear of the unknown to one familiar life-form, or who has been so formed in suspicion and hate of outsiders that he can never put himself in their place. Moreover, this capacity to conceive alternatives must not only be available for the less important choices of one's life. The greatest bigot or the narrowest xenophobe can ponder whether to have Dover sole or Wiener schnitzel for dinner. What is truly important is that one be able to exercise autonomy in the basic issues of life, in one's most important commitments.

Now, it is very dubious whether the developed capacity for this kind of autonomy can arise simply within the family. Of course, men may learn, and perhaps in part must learn, this from those close to them. But my question is whether this kind of capacity can develop within the compass of a single family. Surely it is something which only develops within an entire civilization. Think of the developments of art, philosophy, theology, science, of the evolving practices of politics and social organization, which have contributed to the historic birth of this aspiration to freedom, to making this ideal of autonomy a comprehensible goal men can aim at—something which is in their universe of potential aspiration (and it is not yet so for all men, and may never be).

But this civilization was not only necessary for the genesis of freedom. How could successive generations discover what it is to be an autonomous agent, to have one's own way of feeling, of acting, of expression, which cannot be simply derived from authoritative models? This is an identity, a way of understanding themselves, which men are not born with. They have to acquire it. And they do not in every society; nor do they all successfully come to terms with it in ours. But how can they acquire it unless it is implicit in at least some of their common practices, in the ways that they recognize and treat each other in their common life (for instance, in the acknowledgement of certain rights), or in the manner in which they deliberate with or address each other, or engage in economic exchange, or in some mode of public recognition of individuality and the worth of autonomy?

Thus we live in a world in which there is such a thing as public debate about moral and political questions and other basic issues. We constantly forget how remarkable that is, how it did not have to be so, and may one day no longer be so. What would happen to our capacity to be free agents if this debate should die away, or if the more specialized debate among intellectuals who attempt to define and clarify the alternatives facing us should also cease, or if the attempts to bring the culture of the past to life again as well as the drives to cultural innovation were to fall off? What would there be left to choose between? And if the atrophy went beyond a certain point, could we speak of choice at all? How long would we go on understanding what autonomous choice was? Again, what would happen if our legal culture were not constantly sustained by a contact with our traditions of the rule of law and a confrontation with our contemporary moral institutions? Would we have as sure a grasp of what the rule of law and the defence of rights required?

In other words, the free individual or autonomous moral agent can only achieve and maintain his identity in a certain type of culture, some of whose facets and activities I have briefly referred to. But these and others of the same significance do not come into existence spontaneously each successive instant. They are carried on in institutions and associations which require stability and continuity and frequently also support from society as a whole—almost always the moral support of being commonly recognized as important, but frequently also considerable material support. These bearers of our culture include museums, symphony orchestras, universities, laboratories, political parties, law courts, representative assemblies, newspapers, publishing houses, television stations, and so on. And I have to mention also the mundane elements of infrastructure without which we could not carry on these higher activities: buildings, railroads, sewage plants, power grids, and so on. Thus requirement of a living and varied culture is also the requirement of a complex and integrated society, which is willing and able to support all these institutions.[5]

I am arguing that the free individual of the West is only what he is by virtue of the whole society and civilization which brought him to be and which nourishes him; that our families can only form us up to this capacity and these aspirations because they are set in this civilization; and that a family alone outside of this context—the real old patriarchal family—was a quite different animal which never tended these horizons. And I want to claim finally that all this creates a significant obligation to belong for whoever would affirm the value of this freedom; this includes all those who want to assert rights either to this freedom or for its sake.

One could answer this by saying that the role of my civilization in forming me is a thing of the past; that, once adult, I have the capacity to be an autonomous being; and that I have no further obligation arising out of the exigencies of my development to sustain this civilization. I doubt whether this is in fact true; I doubt whether we could maintain our sense of ourselves as autonomous beings or whether even only a heroic few of us would succeed in doing so, if this liberal civilization of ours were to be thoroughly destroyed. I hope never to have to make the experiment. But even if we could, the considerations advanced a few pages back would be sufficient here: future generations will need this civilization to reach these aspirations; and if we affirm their worth,

we have an obligation to make them available to others. This obligation is only increased if we ourselves have benefited from this civilization and have been enabled to become free agents ourselves.

But then the proponent of primacy could answer by questioning what all this has to do with political authority, with the obligation to belong to a polity or to abide by the rules of a political society. Certainly, we could accept that we are only what we are in virtue of living in a civilization and hence in a large society, since a family or clan could not sustain this. But this does not mean that we must accept allegiance to a polity.

To this there are two responses. First, there is something persuasive about this objection in that it seems to hold out the alternative of an anarchist civilization—one where we have all the benefits of wide association and none of the pains of politics. And indeed, some libertarians come close to espousing an anarchist position and express sympathy for anarchism, as does Nozick. Now it is perfectly true that there is nothing in principle which excludes anarchism in the reflection that we owe our identity as free men to our civilization. But the point is that the commitment we recognize in affirming the worth of this freedom is a commitment to this civilization whatever are the conditions of its survival. If these can be assured in conditions of anarchy, that is very fortunate. But if they can only be assured under some form of representative government to which we all would have to give allegiance, then this is the society we ought to try to create and sustain and belong to. For this is by hypothesis the condition of what we have identified as a crucial human good, by the very fact of affirming this right. (I have, of course, taken as evident that this civilization could not be assured by some tyrannical form of government, because the civilization I am talking about is that which is the essential milieu for free agency.)

The crucial point here is this: since the free individual can only maintain his identity within a society/culture of a certain kind, he has to be concerned about the shape of this society/culture as a whole. He cannot, following the libertarian anarchist model that Nozick sketched,[6] be concerned purely with his individual choices and the associations formed from such choices to the neglect of the matrix in which such choices can be open or closed, rich or meagre. It is important to him that certain activities and institutions flourish in society. It is even of importance to him what the moral tone of the whole society is—shocking as it may be to libertarians to raise this issue— because freedom and individual diversity can only flourish in a society where there is a general recognition of their worth. They are threatened by the spread of bigotry, but also by other conceptions of life—for example, those which look on originality, innovation, and diversity as luxuries which society can ill afford given the need for efficiency, productivity, or growth, or those which in a host of other ways depreciate freedom.

Now, it is possible that a society and culture propitious for freedom might arise from the spontaneous association of anarchist communes. But it seems much more likely from the historical record that we need rather some species of political society. And if this is so then we must acknowledge an obligation to belong to this kind of society in affirming freedom. But there is more. If realizing our freedom partly depends on the society and culture in which we live, then we exercise a fuller freedom if we can help determine the shape of this society and culture. And this we can only do through instruments of common decision. This means that the political institutions in which we live may themselves be a crucial part

of what is necessary to realize our identity as free beings.

This is the second answer to the last objection. In fact, men's deliberating together about what will be binding on all of them is an essential part of the exercise of freedom. It is only in this way that they can come to grips with certain basic issues in a way which will actually have an effect in their lives. Those issues, which can only be effectively decided by society as a whole and which often set the boundary and framework for our lives, can indeed be discussed freely by politically irresponsible individuals wherever they have licence to do so. But they can only be truly *deliberated* about politically. A society in which such deliberation was public and involved everyone would realize a freedom not available anywhere else or in any other mode.

Thus, always granted that an anarchist society is not an available option, it is hard to see how one can affirm the worth of freedom in this sense of the exercise of autonomous deliberation and at the same time recognize no obligation to bring about and sustain a political order of this kind.

The argument has gone far enough to show how difficult it is to conclude here. This is because we are on a terrain in which our conception of freedom touches on the issue of the nature of the human subject, and the degree and manner in which this subject is a social one. To open this up is to open the issue of atomism, which is all I hoped to do in this paper. I wanted to show that there is an issue in the 'self-sufficiency' or not of man outside political society and that this issue cannot be side-stepped by those who argue from natural rights. This issue, as we can see, leads us very deep, and perhaps we can see some of the motivation of those who have waited to side-step it. It seems much easier and clearer to remain on the level of our intuitions about rights.

For we can now see more clearly what the issue about atomism is, and how uncommonly difficult it is. It concerns self-sufficiency, but not in the sense of the ability to survive north of Great Slave Lake. That is a question whether we can fulfill certain causal conditions for our continued existence. But the alleged social conditions for the full development of our human capacities are not causal in the same sense. They open another set of issues altogether: whether the condition for the full development of our capacities is not that we achieve a certain identity, which requires a certain conception of ourselves; and more fundamentally whether this identity is ever something we can attain on our own, or whether the crucial modes of self-understanding are not always created and sustained by the common expression and recognition they receive in the life of the society.

Thus the thesis just sketched about the social conditions of freedom is based on the notion, first, that developed freedom requires a certain understanding of self, one in which the aspirations to autonomy and self-direction become conceivable; and, second, that this self-understanding is not something we can sustain on our own, but that our identity is always partly defined in conversation with others or through the common understanding which underlies the practices of our society. The thesis is that the identity of the autonomous, self-determining individual requires a social matrix, one, for instance, which through a series of practices recognizes the right to autonomous decision and which calls for the individual having a voice in deliberation about public action.

This issue between the atomists and their opponents therefore goes deep; it touches the nature of freedom, and beyond this what it is to be a human subject; what is human identity, and how it is defined and sustained. It is not surprising therefore that the two sides talk past each other. For atomists the talk about identity and its conditions in social practice seems impossibly abstruse and speculative. They would rather found themselves on the clear and distinct intuition which we all share (all of us in this society, that is) about human rights.

For non-atomists, however, this very confidence in their starting-point is a kind of blindness, a delusion of self-sufficiency which prevents them from seeing that the free individual, the bearer of rights, can only assume this identity thanks to his relationship to a developed liberal civilization; that there is an absurdity in placing this subject in a state of nature where he could never attain this identity and hence never create by contract a society which respects it. Rather, the free individual who affirms himself as such *already* has an obligation to complete, restore, or sustain the society within which this identity is possible.

It is clear that we can only join this issue by opening up questions about the nature of man. But it is also clear that the two sides are not on the same footing in relationship to these questions. Atomists are more comfortable standing with the intuitions of common sense about the rights of individuals and are not at all keen to open these wider issues. And in this they derive support in those philosophical traditions which come to us from the seventeenth century and which started with the postulation of an extensionless subject, epistemologically a *tabula rasa* and politically a presuppositionless bearer of rights. It is not an accident that these epistemological and political doctrines are often found in the writings of the same founding figures.

But if this starting-point no longer appears to us self-evident, then we have to open up questions about the nature of the subject and the conditions of human agency. Among these is the issue about atomism. This is important for any theory of rights, but also for a great deal else besides. For the issue about atomism also underlies many of our discussions about obligation and the nature of freedom, as can already be sensed from the above. That is why it is useful to put it again on our agenda.

Notes

1. The words 'conditional/unconditional' may mislead, because there are certain theories of belonging, to use this term for them, which hold that our obligation to obey, or to belong to a particular society, may in certain circumstances be inoperative. For instance, medieval theories which justified tyrannicide still portrayed man as a social animal and were thus theories of belonging in the sense used here. But they allowed that in certain circumstances our obligation to obey that authority by which our society cohered was abrogated, and that when the ruler was a tyrant he might be killed. In this sense we could say that the obligation to obey was 'conditional'. But this is not the same as a theory of the primacy of right. For in theories of belonging it is clear that men *qua* men have an obligation to belong to and sustain society. There may be a restriction on what kind of society would fulfill the underlying goal, and from this a licence to break with perverted forms; but the obligation to belong itself was fundamental and unconditional; it held 'by nature'. In primacy-of-right theories the notion is that simply by nature we are under no obligation to belong whatever; we have first to contract such an obligation.

2. This may not be true of all doctrines which found a political theory on an affirmation of natural right. For the new doctrine of human rights which Professor Macpherson envisages in, for example, *Democratic Theory: Essays in Retrieval* (Oxford, 1973), 236, and which would free itself of 'the postulate of the inherent and permanent contentiousness of men,' would seem to involve an affirmation of individual rights which presuppose society, rather than merely setting the boundary conditions of its possible legitimacy.

3. R. Nosick, *Anarchy, State and Utopia* (Cambridge, MA, 1974).

4. T. Hobbes, *Leviathan*, pt 1, chap. 6.

5. This is what makes so paradoxical the position of someone like Robert Nozick. He presents (*Anarchy, State and Utopia*, particularly chap. 10) the model of an ideal society where within the framework of the minimal state individuals form or join only those associations which they desire and which will admit them. There is no requirement laid down concerning the overall pattern that will result from this. But can we really do without this? The aim of Nozick's utopian framework is to enable people to give expression to their real diversity. But what if the essential cultural activities which make a great diversity conceivable to people begin to falter? Or are we somehow guaranteed against this? Nozick does not discuss this; it is as though the conditions of a creative, diversifying freedom were given by nature. In this respect the standard utopian literature, which as Nozick says is concerned with the character of the ideal community and not just with a framework for any community, is more realistic. For it faces the question of what kind of community we need in order to be free men, and then goes on to assume that this is given non-coercively.

6. Ibid., chap. 10.

'The Politics of Recognition'

I

A number of strands in contemporary politics turn on the need, sometimes the demand, for *recognition*. The need, it can be argued, is one of the driving forces behind nationalist movements in politics. And the demand comes to the fore in a number of ways in today's politics, on behalf of minority or 'subaltern' groups, in some forms of feminism, and in what is today called the politics of 'multiculturalism'.

The demand for recognition in these latter cases is given urgency by the supposed links between recognition and identity, where this latter term designates something like a person's understanding of who they are, of their fundamental defining characteristics as a human being. The thesis is that our identity is partly shaped by recognition or its absence, often by the *mis*recognition of others, and so a person or group of people can suffer real damage, real distortion, if the people or society around them mirror back to them a confining or demeaning or contemptible picture of themselves. Nonrecognition or misrecognition can inflict harm, can be a form of oppression, imprisoning someone in a false, distorted, and reduced mode of being.

Thus some feminists have argued that women in patriarchal societies have been induced to adopt a depreciatory image of themselves. They have internalized a picture of their own inferiority, so that even when some of the objective obstacles to their advancement fall away, they may be incapable of taking advantage of the new opportunities. And beyond this, they are condemned to suffer the pain of low self-esteem. An analogous point has been made in relation to blacks: that white society has for generations projected a demeaning image of them, which some of them have been unable to resist adopting. Their own self-depreciation, on this view, becomes one of the most potent instruments of their own oppression. Their first task ought to be to purge themselves of this imposed and destructive identity. Recently, a similar point has been made in relation to indigenous and colonized people in general. It is held that since 1492 Europeans have projected an image of such people as somehow inferior, 'uncivilized', and through the force of conquest have often been able to impose this image on the conquered. The figure of Caliban has been held to epitomize this crushing portrait of contempt of New World aboriginals.

Within these perspectives, misrecognition shows not just a lack of due respect. It can inflict a grievous wound, saddling its victims with a crippling self-hatred. Due recognition is not just a courtesy we owe people. It is a vital human need.

In order to examine some of the issues that have arisen here, I'd like to take a step back, achieve a little distance, and look first at how this discourse of recognition and identity came to seem familiar, or at least readily understandable, to us. For it was not always so, and our ancestors of more than a couple of centuries ago would have stared at us uncomprehendingly if we had used these terms in their current sense. How did we get started on this?

Hegel comes to mind right off, with his famous dialectic of the master and the slave. This is an important stage, but we need to go a little farther back to see how this passage came to have the sense it did. What changed to make this kind of talk have sense for us?

We can distinguish two changes that together have made the modern preoccupation with identity and recognition inevitable. The first is the collapse of social hierarchies, which used to be the basis for honour. I am using *honour* in the ancient régime sense in which it is intrinsically linked to inequalities. For some to have honour in this sense, it is essential that not everyone have it. This is the sense in which Montesquieu uses it in his description of monarchy. Honour is intrinsically a matter of 'préférences'.[1] It is also the sense in which we use the term when we speak of honouring someone by giving her some public award, for example, the Order of Canada. Clearly, this award would be without worth if tomorrow we decided to give it to every adult Canadian.

As against this notion of honour, we have the modern notion of dignity, now used in a universalist and egalitarian sense, where we talk of the inherent 'dignity of human beings', or of citizen dignity. The underlying premise here is that everyone shares in it.[2] It is obvious that this concept of dignity is the only one compatible with a democratic society, and that it was inevitable that the old concept of honour was superseded. But this has also meant that the forms of equal recognition have been essential to democratic culture. For instance, that everyone be called 'Mr', 'Mrs', or 'Miss', rather than some people being called 'Lord' or 'Lady' and others simply by their surnames— or, even more demeaning, by their first names—has been thought essential in some democratic societies, such as the United States. More recently, for similar reasons, 'Mrs' and 'Miss' have been collapsed into 'Ms'. Democracy has ushered in a politics of equal recognition, which has taken various forms over the years, and has now returned in the form of demands for the equal status of cultures and of genders.

But the importance of recognition has been modified and intensified by the new understanding of individual identity that emerges at the end of the eighteenth century. We might speak of an *individualized* identity, one that is particular to me, and that I discover in myself. This notion arises along with an ideal, that of being true to myself and my own particular way of being. Following Lionel Trilling's usage in his brilliant study, I will speak of this as the ideal of 'authenticity'.[3] It will help to describe in what it consists and how it came about.

One way of describing its development is to see its starting point in the eighteenth-century notion that human beings are endowed with a moral sense, an intuitive feeling for what is right and wrong. The original point of this doctrine was to combat a rival view, that knowing right and wrong was a matter of calculating consequences, in particular, those concerned with divine reward and punishment. The idea was that understanding right and wrong was not a matter of dry calculation, but was anchored in our feelings.[4] Morality has, in a sense, a voice within.

The notion of authenticity develops out of a displacement of the moral accent in this idea. On the original view, the inner voice was important because it tells us what the right thing to do is. Being in touch with our moral feelings matters here, as a means to the end of acting rightly. What I'm calling the displacement of the moral accent comes about when being in touch with our feelings takes on independent and crucial moral significance. It comes to be something we have to attain if we are to be true and full human beings.

To see what is new here, we have to see the analogy to earlier moral views, where being in touch with some source—for example, God, or the Idea of the Good—was considered essential to full being. But now the source we have to connect with is deep within us. This fact is part of the massive subjective turn of modern culture, a new form of inwardness, in which we come to think of ourselves as beings with inner depths. At first, this idea that the source is within doesn't exclude our being related to God or the Ideas; it can be considered our proper way of relating to them. In a sense, it can be seen as just a continuation and intensification of the development inaugurated by Saint Augustine, who saw the road to God as passing through our own self-awareness. The first variants of this new view were theistic, or at least pantheistic.

The most important philosophical writer who helped to bring about this change was Jean-Jacques Rousseau. I think Rousseau is important not because he inaugurated the change; rather, I would argue that his great popularity comes in part from his articulating something that was in a sense already occurring in the culture. Rousseau frequently presents the issue of morality as that of our following a voice of nature within us. This voice is often drowned out by the passions that are induced by our dependence on others, the main one being *amour propre*, or pride. Our moral salvation comes from recovering authentic moral contact with ourselves. Rousseau even gives a name to the intimate contact with oneself, more fundamental than any moral view, that is a source of such joy and contentment: 'le sentiment de l'existence'.[5]

The ideal of authenticity becomes crucial owing to a development that occurs after Rousseau, which I associate with the name of Herder—once again, as its major early articulator, rather than its originator. Herder put forward the idea that each of us has an original way of being human: each person has his or her own 'measure'.[6] This idea has burrowed very deep into modern consciousness. It is a new idea. Before the late eighteenth century, no one thought that the differences between

human beings had this kind of moral significance. There is a certain way of being human that is *my* way. I am called upon to live my life in this way, and not in imitation of anyone else's life. But this notion gives a new importance to being true to myself. If I am not, I miss the point of my life; I miss what being human is for *me*.

This is the powerful moral ideal that has come down to us. It accords moral importance to a kind of contact with myself, with my own inner nature, which it sees as in danger of being lost, partly through the pressures toward outward conformity, but also because in taking an instrumental stance toward myself, I may have lost the capacity to listen to this inner voice. It greatly increases the importance of this self-contact by introducing the principle of originality: each of our voices has something unique to say. Not only should I not mould my life to the demands of external conformity; I can't even find the model by which to live outside myself. I can only find it within.[7]

Being true to myself means being true to my own originality, which is something only I can articulate and discover. In articulating it, I am also defining myself. I am realizing a potentiality that is properly my own. This is the background understanding to the modern ideal of authenticity, and to the goals of self-fulfillment and self-realization in which the ideal is usually couched. I should note here that Herder applied his conception of originality at two levels, not only to the individual person among other persons, but also to the culture-bearing people among other peoples. Just like individuals, a *Volk* should be true to itself, that is, its own culture. Germans shouldn't try to be derivative and (inevitably) second-rate Frenchmen, as Frederick the Great's patronage seemed to be encouraging them to do. The Slavic peoples had to find their own path. And European colonialism ought to be rolled back to give the peoples of what we now call the Third World their chance to be themselves unimpeded. We can recognize here the seminal idea of modern nationalism, in both benign and malignant forms.

This new ideal of authenticity was, like the idea of dignity, also in part an offshoot of the decline of hierarchical society. In those earlier societies, what we would now call identity was largely fixed by one's social position. That is, the background that explained what people recognized as important to themselves was to a great extent determined by their place in society, and whatever roles or activities attached to this position. The birth of a democratic society doesn't by itself do away with this phenomenon, because people can still define themselves by their social roles. What does decisively undermine this socially derived identification, however, is the ideal of authenticity itself. As this emerges, for instance, with Herder, it calls on me to discover my own original way of being. By definition, this way of being cannot be socially derived, but must be inwardly generated.

But in the nature of the case, there is no such thing as inward generation, monologically understood. In order to understand the close connection between identity and recognition, we have to take into account a crucial feature of the human condition that has been rendered almost invisible by the overwhelmingly monological bent of mainstream modern philosophy.

This crucial feature of human life is its fundamentally *dialogical* character. We become full human agents, capable of understanding ourselves, and hence of defining our identity, through our acquisition of rich human languages of expression. For my purposes here, I want to take *language* in a broad sense, covering not only the words we speak, but also other modes of expression whereby we define ourselves, including the 'languages' of art, of gesture, of love, and the like. But we learn these modes of expression through exchanges with others. People do not acquire the languages needed for self-definition on their own. Rather, we are introduced to them through interaction with others who matter to us—what George Herbert Mead called 'significant others'.[8] The genesis of the human mind is in this sense not monological, not something each person accomplishes on his or her own, but dialogical.

Moreover, this is not just a fact about *genesis*, which can be ignored later on. We don't just learn the languages in dialogue and then go on to use them for our own purposes. We are of course expected to develop our own opinions, outlook, stances toward things, and to a considerable degree through solitary reflection. But this is not how things work with important issues, like the definition of our identity. We define our identity always in dialogue with, sometimes in struggle against, the things our significant others want to see in us. Even after we outgrow some of these others—our parents, for instance—and they disappear from our lives, the conversation with them continues within us as long as we live.[9]

Thus, the contribution of significant others, even when it is provided at the beginning of our lives, continues indefinitely. Some people may still want to hold on to some form of the monological ideal. It is true that we can never liberate ourselves completely from those whose love and care shaped us early in life, but we should strive to define ourselves on our own to the fullest extent possible, coming as best we can to understand and thus get some control over the influence of our parents, and avoiding falling into any more such dependent relationships. We need relationships to fulfill, but not to define, ourselves.

The monological ideal seriously underestimates the place of the dialogical in human life. It wants to confine it as much as possible to the genesis. It forgets how our understanding of the good things in life can be transformed by our enjoying them in common with people we love; how some goods become accessible to us only through such common enjoyment. Because of this, it would take a great deal of effort, and probably many wrenching break-ups, to *prevent* our identity's being formed by the people we love. Consider what we mean by *identity*. It is who we are, 'where we're coming from.' As such it is the background against which our tastes and desires and opinions and aspirations make sense. If some of the things I value most are accessible to me only in relation to the person I love, then she becomes part of my identity.

To some people this might seem a limitation, from which one might aspire to free oneself. This is one way of understanding the impulse behind the life of the hermit or, to take a case more familiar to our culture, the solitary artist. But from another perspective, we might see even these lives as aspiring to a certain kind of dialogicality. In the case of the hermit, the interlocutor is God. In the case of the solitary artist, the work itself is addressed to a future audience, perhaps still to be created by the work. The very form of a work of art shows its character as *addressed*.[10] But however one feels about it, the making and sustaining of our identity, in the absence of a heroic effort to break out of ordinary existence, remains dialogical throughout our lives.

Thus my discovering my own identity doesn't mean that I work it out in isolation, but that I negotiate it through dialogue, partly overt, partly internal, with others. That is why the development of an ideal of inwardly generated identity gives a new importance to recognition. My own identity crucially depends on my dialogical relations with others.

Of course, the point is not that this dependence on others arose with the age of authenticity. A form of dependence was always there. The socially derived identity was by its very nature dependent on society. But in the earlier age recognition never arose as a problem. General recognition was built into the socially derived identity by virtue of the very fact that it was based on social categories that everyone took for granted. Yet inwardly derived, personal, original identity doesn't enjoy this recognition *a priori*. It has to win it through exchange, and the attempt can fail. What has come about with the modern age is not the need for recognition but the conditions in which the attempt to be recognized can fail. That is why the need is now acknowledged for the first time. In pre-modern times, people didn't speak of 'identity' and 'recognition'—not because people didn't have (what we call) identities, or because these didn't depend on recognition, but rather because these were then too unproblematic to be thematized as such.

It's not surprising that we can find some of the seminal ideas about citizen dignity and universal recognition, even if not in these specific terms, in Rousseau, whom I have wanted to identify as one of the points of origin of the modern discourse of authenticity. Rousseau is a sharp critic of hierarchical honour, of 'préférences'. In a significant passage of the *Discourse on Inequality*, he pinpoints a fateful moment when society takes a turn toward corruption and injustice, when people begin to desire preferential esteem.[11] By contrast, in republican society, where all can share equally in the light of public attention, he sees the source of health.[12] But the topic of recognition is given its most influential early treatment in Hegel.[13]

The importance of recognition is now universally acknowledged in one form or another; on an intimate plane, we are all aware of how identity can be formed or malformed through the course of our contact with significant others. On the social plane, we have a continuing politics of equal recognition. Both planes have been shaped by the growing ideal of authenticity, and recognition plays an essential role in the culture that has arisen around this ideal.

On the intimate level, we can see how much an original identity needs and is vulnerable to the recognition given or withheld by significant others. It is not surprising that in the culture of authenticity, relationships are seen as the key loci of self-discovery and self-affirmation. Love relationships are not just important because of the general emphasis in modern culture on the fulfillments of ordinary needs. They are also crucial because they are the crucibles of inwardly generated identity.

On the social plane, the understanding that identities are formed in open dialogue, unshaped by a predefined social script, has made the politics of equal recognition more central and stressful. It has, in fact, considerably raised the stakes. Equal recognition is not just the appropriate mode for a healthy democratic society. Its refusal can inflict damage on those who are denied it, according to a widespread modern view, as I indicated at the outset. The projection of an inferior or demeaning image on another can actually distort and oppress, to the extent that the image is internalized. Not only contemporary feminism but also race relations and discussions of multiculturalism are undergirded by the premise that the withholding of recognition can be a form of oppression. We may debate whether this factor has been exaggerated, but it is clear that the understanding of identity and authenticity has introduced a new dimension into the politics of equal recognition, which now operates with something like its own notion of authenticity, at least so far as the denunciation of other-induced distortions is concerned.

II

And so the discourse of recognition has become familiar to us, on two levels: First, in the intimate sphere, where we understand the formation of identity and the self as taking place in a continuing dialogue and struggle with significant others. And then in the public sphere, where a politics of equal recognition has come to play a bigger and bigger role. Certain feminist theories have tried to show the links between the two spheres.[14]

I want to concentrate here on the public sphere, and try to work out what a politics of equal recognition has meant and could mean.

In fact, it has come to mean two rather different things, connected, respectively, with the two major changes I have been describing. With the move from honour to dignity has come a politics of universalism, emphasizing the equal dignity of all citizens, and the content of this politics has been the equalization of rights and entitlements. What is to be avoided at all costs is the existence of 'first-class' and 'second-class' citizens. Naturally, the actual detailed measures justified by this principle have varied greatly, and have often been controversial. For some, equalization has affected only civil rights and voting rights; for others, it has extended into the socio-economic sphere. People who are systematically handicapped by poverty from making the most of their citizenship rights are deemed on this view to have been relegated to second-class status, necessitating remedial action through equalization. But through all the differences of interpretation, the principle of equal citizenship has come to be universally accepted. Every position, no matter how reactionary, is now defended under the colours of this principle. Its greatest, most recent victory was won by the civil rights movement of the 1960s in the

United States. It is worth noting that even the adversaries of extending voting rights to blacks in the southern states found some pretext consistent with universalism, such as 'tests' to be administered to would-be voters at the time of registration.

By contrast, the second change, the development of the modern notion of identity, has given rise to a politics of difference. There is, of course, a universalist basis to this as well, making for the overlap and confusion between the two. *Everyone* should be recognized for his or her unique identity. But recognition here means something else. With the politics of equal dignity, what is established is meant to be universally the same, an identical basket of rights and immunities; with the politics of difference, what we are asked to recognize is the unique identity of this individual or group, their distinctness from everyone else. The idea is that it is precisely this distinctness that has been ignored, glossed over, assimilated to a dominant or majority identity. And this assimilation is the cardinal sin against the ideal of authenticity.[15]

Now underlying the demand is a principle of universal equality. The politics of difference is full of denunciations of discrimination and refusals of second-class citizenship. This gives the principle of universal equality a point of entry within the politics of dignity. But once inside, as it were, its demands are hard to assimilate to that politics. For it asks that we give acknowledgement and status to something that is not universally shared. Or, otherwise put, we give due acknowledgement only to what is universally present—everyone has an identity—through recognizing what is peculiar to each. The universal demand powers an acknowledgement of specificity.

The politics of difference grows organically out of the politics of universal dignity through one of those shifts with which we are long familiar, where a new understanding of the human social condition imparts a radically new meaning to an old principle. Just as a view of human beings as conditioned by their socio-economic plight changed the understanding of second-class citizenship, so that this category came to include, for example, people in inherited poverty traps, so here the understanding of identity as formed in interchange, and as possibly so malformed, introduces a new form of second-class status into our purview. As in the present case, the socio-economic redefinition justified social programs that were highly controversial. For those who had not gone along with this changed definition of equal status, the various redistributive programs and special opportunities offered to certain populations seemed a form of undue favouritism.

Similar conflicts arise today around the politics of difference. Where the politics of universal dignity fought for forms of nondiscrimination that were quite 'blind' to the ways in which citizens differ, the politics of difference often redefines nondiscrimination as requiring that we make these distinctions the basis of differential treatment. So members of Aboriginal bands will get certain rights and powers not enjoyed by other Canadians, if the demands for Native self-government are finally agreed on, and certain minorities will get the right to exclude others in order to preserve their cultural integrity, and so on.

To proponents of the original politics of dignity, this can seem like a reversal, a betrayal, a simple negation of their cherished principle. Attempts are therefore made to mediate, to show how some of these measures meant to accommodate minorities can after all be justified on the original basis of dignity. These arguments can be successful up to a point. For instance, some of the (apparently) most fla-grant departures from 'difference-blindness' are reverse discrimination measures, affording people from previously unfavoured groups a competitive advantage for jobs or places in universities. This practice has been justified on the grounds that historical discrimination has created a pattern within which the unfavoured struggle at a disadvantage. Reverse discrimi-nation is defended as a temporary measure that will eventually level the playing field and allow the old 'blind' rules to come back into force in a way that doesn't disadvantage any-one. This argument seems cogent enough — wherever its factual basis is sound. But it won't justify some of the measures now urged on the grounds of difference, the goal of which is not to bring us back to an eventual 'difference-blind' social space but, on the contrary, to maintain and cherish distinctness, not just now but forever. After all, if we're concerned with identity, then what is more legitimate than one's aspiration that it never be lost?[16]

So even though one politics springs from the other, by one of those shifts in the defini-tion of key terms with which we're familiar, the two diverge quite seriously from each other. One basis for the divergence comes out even more clearly when we go beyond what each requires that we acknowledge—certain universal rights in one case, a particular iden-tity on the other—and look at the underlying intuitions of value.

The politics of equal dignity is based on the idea that all humans are equally worthy of respect. It is underpinned by a notion of what in human beings commands respect, however we may try to shy away from this 'metaphysical' background. For Kant, whose use of the term *dignity* was one of the earliest influential evocations of this idea, what com-manded respect in us was our status as rational agents, capable of directing our lives through principles.[17] Something like this has been the basis for our intuitions of equal dig-nity ever since, though the detailed definition of it may have changed.

Thus, what is picked out as of worth here is a *universal human potential*, a capacity that all humans share. This potential, rather than anything a person may have made of it, is what ensures that each person deserves respect. Indeed, our sense of the importance of poten-tiality reaches so far that we extend this pro-tection even to people who through some circumstance that has befallen them are inca-pable of realizing their potential in the normal way—handicapped people, or those in a coma, for instance.

In the case of the politics of difference, we might also say that a universal potential is at its basis, namely, the potential for forming and defining one's own identity, as an individual, and also as a culture. This potentiality must be respected equally in everyone. But at least in the intercultural context, a stronger demand has recently arisen: that one accord equal respect to actually evolved cultures. Critiques of European or white domination, to the effect that they have not only suppressed but failed to appreciate other cultures, consider these depreciatory judgments not only factually mis-taken but somehow morally wrong. When Saul Bellow is famously quoted as saying something like, 'When the Zulus produce a Tolstoy we will read him,'[18] this is taken as a quintessential statement of European arro-gance, not just because Bellow is allegedly being *de facto* insensitive to the value of Zulu culture, but frequently also because it is seen to reflect a denial in principle of human equal-ity. The possibility that the Zulus, while having the same potential for culture formation as anyone else, might nevertheless have come up with a culture that is less valuable than others is ruled out from the start. Even to entertain this possibility is to deny human equality. Bellow's error here, then, would not be a (possibly insensitive) particular mistake in evaluation, but a denial of a fundamental principle.

To the extent that this stronger reproach is in play, the demand for equal recognition extends beyond an acknowledgement of the equal value of all humans potentially, and comes to include the equal value of what they have made of this potential in fact. This creates a serious problem, as we shall see below.

These two modes of politics, then, both based on the notion of equal respect, come into conflict. For one, the principle of equal respect requires that we treat people in a difference-blind fashion. The fundamental intuition that humans command this respect focuses on what is the same in all. For the other, we have to recognize and even foster particularity. The reproach the first makes to the second is just that it violates the principle of nondiscrimination. The reproach the second makes to the first is that it negates identity by forcing people into a homogeneous mould that is untrue to them. This would be bad enough if the mould were itself neutral—nobody's mould in particular. But the complaint generally goes further. The claim is that the supposedly neutral set of difference-blind principles of the politics of equal dignity is in fact a reflection of one hegemonic culture. As it turns out, then, only the minority or suppressed cultures are being forced to take alien form. Consequently, the supposedly fair and difference-blind society is not only inhuman (because suppressing identities) but also, in a subtle and unconscious way, itself highly discriminatory.[19]

This last attack is the cruellest and most upsetting of all. The liberalism of equal dignity seems to have to assume that there are some universal, difference-blind principles. Even though we may not have defined them yet, the project of defining them remains alive and essential. Different theories may be put forward and contested—and a number have been proposed in our day[20]—but the shared assumption of the different theories is that one such theory is right.

The charge levelled by the most radical forms of the politics of difference is that 'blind' liberalisms are themselves the reflection of particular cultures. And the worrying thought is that this bias might not just be a contingent weakness of all hitherto proposed theories, that the very idea of such a liberalism may be a kind of pragmatic contradiction, a particularism masquerading as the universal.

I want now to try to move, gently and gingerly, into this nest of issues, glancing at some of the important stages in the emergence of these two kinds of politics in Western societies. I will first look at the politics of equal dignity. . . .

V

The politics of equal respect, then, at least in this more hospitable variant, can be cleared of the charge of homogenizing difference. But there is another way of formulating the charge that is harder to rebut. In this form, however, it perhaps ought not to be rebutted, or so I want to argue.

The charge I'm thinking of here is provoked by the claim sometimes made on behalf of 'difference-blind' liberalism that it can offer a neutral ground on which people of all cultures can meet and coexist. On this view, it is necessary to make a certain number of distinctions—between what is public and what is private, for instance, or between politics and religion—and only then can one relegate the contentious differences to a sphere that does not impinge on the political.

But a controversy like that over Salman Rushdie's *Satanic Verses* shows how wrong this view is. For mainstream Islam, there is no question of separating politics and religion the way we have come to expect in Western liberal society. Liberalism is not a possible meeting ground for all cultures, but is the political expression of one range of cultures, and quite incompatible with other ranges. Moreover, as many Muslims are well aware, Western liberalism is not so much an expression of the secular, post-religious outlook that happens to be popular among liberal *intellectuals* as a more organic outgrowth of Christianity—at least as seen from the alternative vantage point of Islam. The division of church and state goes back to the earliest days of Christian civilization. The early forms of the separation were very different from ours, but the basis was laid for modern developments. The very term *secular* was originally part of the Christian vocabulary.[21]

All this is to say that liberalism can't and shouldn't claim complete cultural neutrality. Liberalism is also a fighting creed. The hospitable variant I espouse, as well as the most rigid forms, has to draw the line. There will be variations when it comes to applying the schedule of rights, but not where incitement to assassination is concerned. But this should not be seen as a contradiction. Substantive distinctions of this kind are inescapable in politics, and at least the nonprocedural liberalism I was describing is fully ready to accept this.

But the controversy is nevertheless disturbing. It is so for the reason I mentioned above: that all societies are becoming increasingly multicultural, while at the same time becoming more porous. Indeed, these two developments go together. Their porousness means that they are more open to multinational migration; more of their members live the life of diaspora, whose centre is elsewhere. In these circumstances, there is something awkward about replying simply, 'This is how

we do things here.' This reply must be made in cases like the Rushdie controversy, where 'how we do things' covers issues such as the right to life and to freedom of speech. The awkwardness arises from the fact that there are substantial numbers of people who are citizens and also belong to the culture that calls into question our philosophical boundaries. The challenge is to deal with their sense of marginalization without compromising our basic political principles.

This brings us to the issue of multiculturalism as it is often debated today, which has a lot to do with the imposition of some cultures on others, and with the assumed superiority that powers this imposition. Western liberal societies are thought to be supremely guilty in this regard, partly because of their colonial past, and partly because of their marginalization of segments of their populations that stem from other cultures. It is in this context that the reply 'this is how we do things here' can seem crude and insensitive. Even if, in the nature of things, compromise is close to impossible here—one either forbids murder or allows it—the attitude presumed by the reply is seen as one of contempt. Often, in fact, this presumption is correct. Thus we arrive again at the issue of recognition.

Recognition of equal value was not what was at stake—at least in a strong sense—in the preceding section. There it was a question of whether cultural survival will be acknowledged as a legitimate goal, whether collective ends will be allowed as legitimate considerations in judicial review, or for other purposes of major social policy. The demand there was that we let cultures defend themselves, within reasonable bounds. But the further demand we are looking at here is that we all *recognize* the equal value of different cultures; that we not only let them survive, but acknowledge their *worth*.

What sense can be made of this demand? In a way, it has been operative in an unformulated state for some time. The politics of nationalism has been powered for well over a century in part by the sense that people have had of being despised or respected by others around them. Multinational societies can break up, in large part because of a lack of (perceived) recognition of the equal worth of one group by another. This is at present, I believe, the case in Canada—though my diagnosis will certainly be challenged by some. On the international scene, the tremendous sensitivity of certain supposedly closed societies to world opinion—as shown in their reactions to findings of, say, Amnesty International, or in their attempts through UNESCO to build a new world information order—attests to the importance of external recognition.

But all this is still *an sich*, not *für sich*, to use Hegelian jargon. The actors themselves are often the first to deny that they are moved by such considerations, and plead other factors, like inequality, exploitation, and injustice, as their motives. Very few Quebec independentists, for instance, can accept that what is mainly winning them their fight is a lack of recognition on the part of English Canada.

What is new, therefore, is that the demand for recognition is now explicit. And it has been made explicit, in the way I indicated above, by the spread of the idea that we are formed by recognition. We could say that, thanks to this idea, misrecognition has now graduated to the rank of a harm that can be hardheadedly enumerated along with the ones mentioned in the previous paragraph.

One of the key authors in this transition is undoubtedly the late Frantz Fanon, whose influential *Les Damnés de la Terre* (*The Wretched of the Earth*)[22] argued that the major weapon of the colonizers was the imposition of their image of the colonized on the subjugated people.

These latter, in order to be free, must first of all purge themselves of these depreciating self-images. Fanon recommended violence as the way to this freedom, matching the original violence of the alien imposition. Not all those who have drawn from Fanon have followed him in this, but the notion that there is a struggle for a changed self-image, which takes place both within the subjugated and against the dominator, has been very widely applied. The idea has become crucial to certain strands of feminism, and is also a very important element in the contemporary debate about multiculturalism.

The main locus of this debate is the world of education in a broad sense. One important focus is university humanities departments, where demands are made to alter, enlarge, or scrap the 'canon' of accredited authors on the grounds that the one presently favoured consists almost entirely of 'dead white males'. A greater place ought to be made for women, and for people of non-European races and cultures. A second focus is the secondary schools, where an attempt is being made, for instance, to develop Afrocentric curricula for pupils in mainly black schools.

The reason for these proposed changes is not, or not mainly, that all students may be missing something important through the exclusion of a certain gender or certain races or cultures, but rather that women and students from the excluded groups are given, either directly or by omission, a demeaning picture of themselves, as though all creativity and worth inhered in males of European provenance. Enlarging and changing the curriculum is therefore essential not so much in the name of a broader culture for everyone as in order to give due recognition to the hitherto excluded. The background premise of these demands is that recognition forges identity, particularly in its Fanonist application: dominant groups tend to entrench their hegemony by inculcating an image of inferiority in the subjugated. The struggle for freedom and equality must therefore pass through a revision of these images. Multicultural curricula are meant to help in this process of revision.

Although it is not often stated clearly, the logic behind some of these demands seems to depend upon a premise that we owe equal respect to all cultures. This emerges from the nature of the reproach made to the designers of traditional curricula. The claim is that the judgments of worth on which these latter were supposedly based were in fact corrupt, were marred by narrowness or insensitivity or, even worse, a desire to downgrade the excluded. The implication seems to be that absent these distorting factors, true judgments of value of different works would place all cultures more or less on the same footing. Of course, the attack could come from a more radical, neo-Nietzschean standpoint, which questions the very status of judgments of worth as such, but short of this extreme step (whose coherence I doubt), the presumption seems to be of equal worth.

I would like to maintain that there is something valid in this presumption, but that the presumption is by no means unproblematic, and involves something like an act of faith. As a presumption, the claim is that all human cultures that have animated whole societies over some considerable stretch of time have something important to say to all human beings. I have worded it in this way to exclude partial cultural milieux within a society, as well as short phases of a major culture. There is no reason to believe that, for instance, the different art forms of a given culture should all be of equal, or even of considerable, value; and every culture can go through phases of decadence.

But when I call this claim a 'presumption', I mean that it is a starting hypothesis with which we ought to approach the study of any other culture. The validity of the claim has to be demonstrated concretely in the actual study of the culture. Indeed, for a culture sufficiently different from our own, we may have only the foggiest idea *ex ante* of in what its valuable contribution might consist. Because, for a sufficiently different culture, the very understanding of what it is to be of worth will be strange and unfamiliar to us. To approach, say, a raga with the presumptions of value implicit in the well-tempered clavier would be forever to miss the point. What has to happen is what Gadamer has called a 'fusion of horizons'.[23] We learn to move in a broader horizon, within which what we have formerly taken for granted as the background to valuation can be situated as one possibility alongside the different background of the formerly unfamiliar culture. The 'fusion of horizons' operates through our developing new vocabularies of comparison, by means of which we can articulate these contrasts.[24] So that if and when we ultimately find substantive support for our initial presumption, it is on the basis of an understanding of what constitutes worth that we couldn't possibly have had at the beginning. We have reached the judgment partly through transforming our standards.

We might want to argue that we owe all cultures a presumption of this kind. I will explain later on what I think this claim might be based. From this point of view, withholding the presumption might be seen as the fruit merely of prejudice or of ill-will. It might even be tantamount to a denial of equal status. Something like this might lie behind the accusation levelled by supporters of multiculturalism against defenders of the traditional canon. Supposing that their reluctance to enlarge the canon comes from a mixture of prejudice and ill-will, the multiculturalists charge them with the arrogance of assuming their own superiority over formerly subject peoples.

This presumption would help explain why the demands of multiculturalism build on the already established principles of the politics of equal respect. If withholding the presumption is tantamount to a denial of equality, and if important consequences flow for people's identity from the absence of recognition, then a case can be made for insisting on the universalization of the presumption as a logical extension of the politics of dignity. Just as all must have equal civil rights, and equal voting rights, regardless of race or culture, so all should enjoy the presumption that their traditional culture has value. This extension, however logically it may seem to flow from the accepted norms of equal dignity, fits uneasily within them, as described in Section II, because it challenges the 'difference-blindness' that was central to them. Yet it does indeed seem to flow from them, albeit uneasily.

I am not sure about the validity of demanding this presumption as a right. But we can leave this issue aside, because the demand made seems to be much stronger. The claim seems to be that a proper respect for equality requires more than a presumption that further study will make us see things this way, but actual judgments of equal worth applied to the customs and creations of these different cultures. Such judgments seem to be implicit in the demand that certain works be included in the canon, and in the implication that these works have not been included earlier only because of prejudice or ill-will or the desire to dominate. (Of course, the demand for inclusion is *logically* separable from a claim of equal worth. The demand could be: Include these because they're ours, even though they may well be inferior. But this is not how the people making the demand talk.)

But there is something very wrong with the demand in this form. It makes sense to demand as a matter of right that we approach the study of certain cultures with a presumption of their value, as described above. But it can't make sense to demand as a matter of right that we come up with a final concluding judgment that their value is great, or equal to others'. That is, if the judgment of value is to register something independent of our own wills and desires, it cannot be dictated by a principle of ethics. On examination, either we will find something of great value in culture C, or we will not. But it makes no more sense to demand that we do so than it does to demand that we find the earth round or flat, the temperature of the air hot or cold.

I have stated this rather flatly, when as everyone knows there is a vigorous controversy over the 'objectivity' of judgments in this field, and whether there is a 'truth of the matter' here, as there seems to be in natural science, or indeed, whether even in natural science 'objectivity' is a mirage. I do not have space to address this here. I have discussed it somewhat elsewhere.[25] I don't have much sympathy for these forms of subjectivism, which I think are shot through with confusion. But there seems to be some special confusion in invoking them in this context. The moral and political thrust of the complaint concerns unjustified judgments of inferior status allegedly made of non-hegemonic cultures. But if those judgments are ultimately a question of the human will, then the issue of justification falls away. One doesn't, properly speaking, make judgments that can be right or wrong; one expresses liking or dislike, one endorses or rejects another culture. But then the complaint must shift to address the refusal to endorse, and the validity or invalidity of judgments here has nothing to do with it.

Then, however, the act of declaring another culture's creations to be of worth and the act of declaring oneself on their side, even if their creations aren't all that impressive, become indistinguishable. The difference is only in the packaging. Yet the first is normally understood as a genuine expression of respect, the second often as unsufferable patronizing. The supposed beneficiaries of the politics of recognition, the people who might actually benefit from acknowledgement, make a crucial distinction between the two acts. They know that they want respect, not condescension. Any theory that wipes out the distinction seems at least *prima facie* to be distorting crucial facets of the reality it purports to deal with.

In fact, subjectivist, half-baked neo-Nietzschean theories are quite often invoked in this debate. Deriving frequently from Foucault or Derrida, they claim that all judgments of worth are based on standards that are ultimately imposed by and further entrench structures of power. It should be clear why these theories proliferate here. A favourable judgment on demand is nonsense, unless some such theories are valid. Moreover, the giving of such a judgment on demand is an act of breathtaking condescension. No one can really mean it as a genuine act of respect. It is more in the nature of a pretend act of respect given on the insistence of its supposed beneficiary. Objectively, such an act involves contempt for the latter's intelligence. To be an object of such an act of respect demeans. The proponents of neo-Nietzschean theories hope to escape this whole nexus of hypocrisy by turning the entire issue into one of power and counterpower. Then the question is no more one of respect, but of taking sides, of solidarity. But this is hardly a satisfactory solution, because in taking sides they miss the driving force of this kind of politics, which is precisely the search for recognition and respect.

Moreover, even if one could demand it of them, the last thing one wants at this stage from Eurocentred intellectuals is positive judgments of the worth of cultures that they have

not intensively studied. For real judgments of worth suppose a fused horizon of standards, as we have seen; they suppose that we have been transformed by the study of the other, so that we are not simply judging by our original familiar standards. A favourable judgment made prematurely would be not only condescending but ethnocentric. It would praise the other for being like us.

Here is another severe problem with much of the politics of multiculturalism. The peremptory demand for favourable judgments of worth is paradoxically—perhaps one should say tragically—homogenizing. For it implies that we already have the standards to make such judgments. The standards we have, however, are those of North Atlantic civilization. And so the judgments implicitly and unconsciously will cram the others into our categories. For instance, we will think of their 'artists' as creating 'works', which we then can include in our canon. By implicitly invoking our standards to judge all civilizations and cultures, the politics of difference can end up making everyone the same.[26]

In this form, the demand for equal recognition is unacceptable. But the story doesn't simply end there. The enemies of multiculturalism in the American academy have perceived this weakness, and have used this as an excuse to turn their backs on the problem. But this won't do. A response like that attributed to Bellow which I quoted above, to the effect that we will be glad to read the Zulu Tolstoy when he comes along, shows the depths of ethnocentricity. First, there is the implicit assumption that excellence has to take forms familiar to us: the Zulus should produce a *Tolstoy*. Second, we are assuming that their contribution is yet to be made (*when* the Zulus produce a Tolstoy . . .). These two assumptions obviously go hand in hand. If they have to produce our kind of excellence, then obviously their only hope lies in the future. Roger Kimball puts it more crudely: 'The multiculturalists notwithstanding, the choice facing us today is not between a 'repressive' Western culture and a multicultural paradise, but between culture and barbarism. Civilization is not a gift, it is an achievement—a fragile achievement that needs constantly to be shored up and defended from besiegers inside and out.'[27]

There must be something midway between the inauthentic and homogenizing demand for recognition of equal worth, on the one hand, and the self-immurement within ethnocentric standards, on the other. There are other cultures, and we have to live together more and more, both on a world scale and commingled in each individual society.

What there is is the presumption of equal worth I described above: a stance we take in embarking on the study of the other. Perhaps we don't need to ask whether it's something that others can demand from us as a right. We might simply ask whether this is the way we ought to approach others.

Well, is it? How can this presumption be grounded? One ground that has been proposed is a religious one. Herder, for instance, had a view of divine providence, according to which all this variety of culture was not a mere accident but was meant to bring about a greater harmony. I can't rule out such a view. But merely on the human level, one could argue that it is reasonable to suppose that cultures that have provided the horizon of meaning for large numbers of human beings, of diverse characters and temperaments, over a long period of time—that have, in other words, articulated their sense of the good, the holy, the admirable—are almost certain to have something that deserves our admiration and respect, even if it is accompanied by much that we have to abhor and reject. Perhaps one could put it another way: it would take a

supreme arrogance to discount this possibility *a priori*.

There is perhaps after all a moral issue here. We only need a sense of our own limited part in the whole human story to accept the presumption. It is only arrogance, or some analogous moral failing, that can deprive us of this. But what the presumption requires of us is not peremptory and inauthentic judgments of equal value, but a willingness to be open to comparative cultural study of the kind that must displace our horizons in the resulting fusions. What it requires above all is an admission that we are very far away from that ultimate horizon from which the relative worth of different cultures might be evident. This would mean breaking with an illusion that still holds many 'multiculturalists'—as well as their most bitter opponents—in its grip.[28]

Notes

1. 'La nature de l'honneur est de demander des préférences et des distinctions . . .', Montesquieu, *De l'esprit des lois*, bk 3, chap. 7.
2. The significance of this move from 'honour' to 'dignity' is interestingly discussed by Peter Berger in his 'On the Obsolescence of the Concept of Honour,' in *Revisions: Changing Perspectives in Moral Philosophy,* ed. Stanley Hauerwas and Alasdair MacIntyre (Notre Dame, IN: University of Notre Dame Press, 1983), 172–81.
3. Lionel Trilling, *Sincerity and Authenticity* (New York: Norton, 1969).
4. I have discussed the development of this doctrine at greater length, at first in the work of Francis Hutcheson, drawing on the writings of the Earl of Shaftesbury, and its adversarial relation to Locke's theory in *Sources of the Self* (Cambridge, MA: Harvard University Press, 1989), chap. 15.

5. 'Le sentiment de l'existence dépouillé de toute autre affection est par lui-même un sentiment précieux de contentement et de paix qui suffiroit seul pour rendre cette existence chère et douce à qui sauroit écarter de soi toutes les impressions sensuelles et terrestres qui viennent sans cesse nous en distraire et en troubler ici bas la douceur. Mais la pluspart des hommes agités de passions continuelles connoissent peu cet état et ne l'ayant gouté qu'imparfaitement durant peu d'instans n'en conservent qu'une idée obscure et confuse qui ne leur en fait pas sentir le charme.' Jean-Jacques Rousseau, Les rêveries du promeneur solitaire, 'Cinquième promenade,' in Oeuvres complètes (Paris: Gallimard, 1959), 1:1047.

6. 'Jeder Mensch hat ein eigenes Maass, gleichsam eine eigne Stimmung aller seiner sinnlichen Gefühle zu einander.' Johann Gottlob Herder, Ideen, chap. 7, sec. 1, in Herders Sämtliche Werke, ed. Bernard Suphan (Berlin: Weidmann, 1877–1913), 13:291.

7. John Stuart Mill was influenced by this Romantic current of thought when he made something like the ideal of authenticity the basis for one of his most powerful arguments in On Liberty. See especially chapter 3, where he argues that we need something more than a capacity for 'apelike imitation': 'A person whose desires and impulses are his own—are the expression of his own nature, as it has been developed and modified by his own culture—is said to have a character.' 'If a person possesses any tolerable amount of common sense and experience, his own mode of laying out his existence is the best, not because it is the best in itself, but because it is his own mode.' John Stuart Mill, Three Essays (Oxford: Oxford University Press, 1975), 73, 74, 83.

8. George Herbert Mead, Mind, Self, and Society (Chicago: University of Chicago Press, 1934).

9. This inner dialogicality has been explored by M.M. Bakhtin and those who have drawn on his work. See, of Bakhtin, especially Problems of Dostoyevsky's Poetics, trans. Caryl Emerson (Minneapolis: University of Minnesota Press, 1984). See also Michael Holquist and Katerina Clark, Mikhail Bakhtin (Cambridge, MA: Harvard University Press, 1984); and James Wertsch, Voices of the Mind (Cambridge, MA: Harvard University Press, 1991).

10. See Bakhtin, 'The Problem of the Text in Linguistics, Philology and the Human Sciences,' in Speech Genres and Other Late Essays, ed. Caryl Emerson and Michael Holquist (Austin: University of Texas Press, 1986), 126, for this notion of a 'super-addressee', beyond our existing interlocutors.

11. Rousseau is describing the first assemblies: 'Chacun commença à regarder les autres et à vouloir être regardé soi-même, et l'estime publique eut un prix. Celui qui chantait ou dansait le mieux; le plus beau, le plus fort, le plus adroit ou le plus éloquent devint le plus considéré, et ce fut là le premier pas vers l'inégalité, et vers le vice en même temps.' Discours sur l'origine et les fondements de l'inégalité parmi les hommes (Paris: Granier-Flammarion, 1971), 210.

12. See, for example, the passage in the Considerations sur le gouvernement de Pologne where he describes the ancient public festival, in which all the people took part, in Du contrat social (Paris: Garnier, 1962), 345; and also the parallel passage in Lettre à D'Alembert sur les spectacles, in Du contrat social, 224–5. The crucial principle was that there should be no division between performers and spectators, but that all should be seen by all. 'Mais quels seront enfin les objets de ces spectacles? Qu'y montrera-t-on? Rien, si l'on veut. . . . Donnez les spectateurs en spectacles; rendez-les acteurs eux-mêmes; faites que chacun se voie et s'aime dans les autres, que tous en soient mieux unis.'

13. See Hegel, The Phenomenology of Spirit, trans. A.V. Miller (Oxford: Oxford University Press, 1977), chap. 4.

14. There are a number of strands that have linked these two levels, but perhaps special prominence

in recent years has been given to a psycho-analytically oriented feminism, which roots social inequalities in the early upbringing of men and women. See, for instance, Nancy Chodorow, *Feminism and Psychoanalytic Theory* (New Haven: Yale University Press, 1989); and Jessica Benjamin, *Bonds of Love: Psychoanalysis, Feminism and the Problem of Domination* (New York: Pantheon, 1988).

15. A prime example of this charge from a feminist perspective is Carol Gilligan's critique of Lawrence Kohlberg's theory of moral development, for presenting a view of human development that privileges only one facet of moral reasoning, precisely the one that tends to predominate in boys rather than girls. See Gilligan, *In a Different Voice* (Cambridge, MA: Harvard University Press, 1982).

16. Will Kymlicka, in his very interesting and tightly argued book *Liberalism, Community, and Culture* (Oxford: Clarendon Press, 1989), tries to argue for a kind of politics of difference, notably in relation to Aboriginal rights in Canada, but from a basis that is firmly within a theory of liberal neutrality. He wants to argue on the basis of certain cultural needs—minimally, the need for an integral and undamaged cultural language with which one can define and pursue his or her own conception of the good life. In certain circumstances, with disadvantaged populations, the integrity of the culture may require that we accord them more resources or rights than others. The argument is quite parallel to that made in relation to socio-economic inequalities that I mentioned above.

But where Kymlicka's interesting argument fails to recapture the actual demands made by the groups concerned—say Indian bands in Canada, or French-speaking Canadians—is with respect to their goal of survival. Kymlicka's reasoning is valid (perhaps) for *existing* people who find themselves trapped within a culture

under pressure, and can flourish within it or not at all. But it doesn't justify measures designed to ensure survival through indefinite future generations. For the populations concerned, however, that is what is at stake. We need only think of the historical resonance of 'la survivance' among French Canadians.

17. See Kant, *Grundlegung der Metaphysik der Sitten* (Berlin: Gruyter, 1968; reprint of the Berlin Academy edition), 434.

18. I have no idea whether this statement was actually made in this form by Saul Bellow, or by anyone else. I report it only because it captures a widespread attitude, which is, of course, why the story had currency in the first place.

19. One hears both kinds of reproach today. In the context of some modes of feminism and multiculturalism, the claim is the strong one, that the hegemonic culture discriminates. In the Soviet Union, however, alongside a similar reproach levelled at the hegemonic Great Russian culture, one also hears the complaint that Marxist-Leninist communism has been an alien imposition on all equally, even on Russia itself. The communist mould, on this view, has been truly nobody's. Solzhenitsyn has made this claim, but it is voiced by Russians of a great many different persuasions today, and has something to do with the extraordinary phenomenon of an empire that has broken apart through the quasi-secession of its metropolitan society.

20. See John Rawls, *A Theory of Justice* (Cambridge, MA: Harvard University Press, 1971); Ronald Dworkin, *Taking Rights Seriously* (London: Duckworth, 1977) and *A Matter of Principle* (Cambridge, MA: Harvard University Press, 1985); and Jürgen Habermas, *Theorie des kommunikativen Handelns* (Frankfurt: Suhrkamp, 1981).

21. The point is well argued in Larry Siedentop, 'Liberalism: The Christian Connection,' *Times Literary Supplement*, 24–30 March 1989, 308.

I have also discussed these issues in 'The Rushdie Controversy,' in *Public Culture* 2, no. 1 (Fall 1989), 118–22.

22. (Paris: Maspero, 1961).
23. *Wahrheit und Methode* (Tübingen: Mohr, 1975), 289–90.
24. I have discussed what is involved here at greater length in 'Comparison, History, Truth,' in *Myth and Philosophy*, ed. Frank Reynolds and David Tracy (Albany: State University of New York Press, 1990); and in 'Understanding and Ethnocentricity,' in *Philosophy and the Human Sciences* (Cambridge: Cambridge University Press, 1985).
25. See part 1 of *Sources of the Self*.
26. The same homogenizing assumptions underlie the negative reaction that many people have to claims to superiority in some definite respect on behalf of Western civilization, say in regard to

natural science. But it is absurd to cavil at such claims in principle. If all cultures have made a contribution of worth, it cannot be that these are identical, or even embody the same kind of worth. To expect this would be to vastly underestimate the differences. In the end, the presumption of worth imagines a universe in which different cultures complement each other with quite different kinds of contribution. This picture not only is compatible with, but demands judgments of, superiority-in-a-certain-respect.

27. 'Tenured Radicals,' *New Criterion*, January 1991, 13.
28. There is a very interesting critique of both extreme camps, from which I have borrowed in this discussion, in Benjamin Lee, 'Towards a Critical Internationalism' (forthcoming).

Study Questions for 'Atomism'

1. How does Taylor characterize the doctrine of atomism? Which social and political theories rest upon atomistic doctrines?
2. What problems does Taylor identify with social and political theories that defend the primacy of individual rights? List two distinct problems with these theories.
3. Explain Taylor's point regarding the social development of human capacitates. Does the social development of human capacities indeed present a problem for political theorists who assert the primacy of individual rights (like John Locke or John Hospers)?
4. Taylor comments that 'the free individual of the West is only what he is by virtue of the whole society and civilization which brought him to be and which nourishes him.' Do you agree that the cultural contextualization of freedom creates a social obligation of belonging?

Study Questions for 'The Politics of Recognition'

1. Describe the connection between recognition and identity presupposed in some contemporary forms of nationalist, feminist, and multiculturalist political movements.
2. What social and intellectual developments have shaped identity politics and the politics of recognition?
3. How does Taylor support his point that human beings define their identities in dialogue with others? What are the social and political ramifications of the dialogical character of the human condition?

4. Describe the differences between the 'politics of equal dignity' and the 'politics of difference'. How do these two modes of politics come into conflict?
5. Why is political liberalism not a neutral meeting ground for all cultures, according to Taylor? How does Taylor respond to the multiculturalist suggestion that Western intellectuals recognize the equal value of all cultures?

Recommended Readings

Abbey, Ruth, *Charles Taylor* (Princeton University Press, 2000).

———— ed., *Charles Taylor* (Cambridge University Press, 2004).

Appiah, Anthony, *The Ethics of Identity* (Princeton University Press, 2005).

Avineri, Shlomo, and Avner De-Shalit, eds, *Communitarianism and Individualism* (Oxford University Press, 1992).

Bell, Daniel, *Communitarianism and Its Critics* (Clarendon Press, 1993).

Buchanan, Alan, 'Assessing Communitarian Critiques of Liberalism,' *Ethics* 99 (1989): 852–82.

Gutmann, Amy, *Identity in Democracy* (Princeton University Press, 2003).

MacIntyre, Alasdair, *Whose Justice? Which Rationality?* (University of Notre Dame Press, 1988).

Sandel, Michael, *Liberalism and the Limits of Justice*, 2nd edn (Cambridge University Press, 1998).

Smith, Nicholas, 'Individual and Community,' in *Charles Taylor: Meaning, Morals and Modernity* (Polity Press, 2002).

Ricoeur, Paul, *Reflections on the Just* (University of Chicago Press, 2007).

Tully, James, ed., *Philosophy in an Age of Pluralism: The Philosophy of Charles Taylor in Question* (Cambridge University Press, 1994).

Will Kymlicka

Will Kymlicka is Canada Research Chair in Philosophy at Queen's University in Kingston, Ontario. He obtained a bachelor of arts in philosophy and politics from Queen's University and a doctorate in philosophy from Oxford University. He has held teaching positions and fellowships at universities in Canada, the United States, and Europe, including Central European University, the University of Toronto, and Princeton University. Author of five monographs and editor of several anthologies in political philosophy, Kymlicka is best known for his analyses of multiculturalism and his involvement with multicultural politics in Canada, which enshrines multiculturalism in its constitution. Kymlicka's monographs include *Liberalism, Community and Culture* (1989); *Multicultural Citizenship* (1995), from which our selection is taken; *Politics in the Vernacular* (2001); and *Contemporary Political Philosophy* (second edition, 2002). His work in political philosophy has been translated into 30 languages.

In *Multicultural Citizenship*, Kymlicka develops a liberal theory of minority rights in which justice for all citizens requires protecting ethnic and national minorities with group-differentiated rights. Language rights, self-government rights, and territorial rights help preserve the cultural particularity and political autonomy of indigenous peoples and national minorities, such as Quebecois and Puerto Ricans, who live within territories of larger nation-states. Similarly, rights against discrimination and rights to guaranteed political representation help protect ethnic, racial, and immigrant minorities from economic and political injustices. Kymlicka offers several points of defence for these and other forms of minority rights, including arguments based in the Canadian concept of political equality, in which 'the accommodation of differences is the essence of true equality.' Like John Stuart Mill, Kymlicka also suggests that cultural diversity provides a key context for the liberal value of freedom and for the development of individual conceptions of the good.

Multicultural Citizenship

Chapter 1

Introduction

The Issues

Most countries today are culturally diverse. According to recent estimates, the world's 184 independent states contain over 600 living language groups, and 5,000 ethnic groups. In very few countries can the citizens be said to share the same language, or belong to the same ethnonational group.

This diversity gives rise to a series of important and potentially divisive questions. Minorities and majorities increasingly clash over such issues as language rights, regional autonomy, political representation, education curriculum, land claims, immigration and naturalization policy, even national symbols, such as the choice of national anthem or public holidays. Finding morally defensible and politically viable answers to these issues is the greatest challenge facing democracies today. In Eastern Europe and the Third World, attempts to create liberal democratic institutions are being undermined by violent nationalist conflicts. In the West, volatile disputes over the rights of immigrants, indigenous peoples, and other cultural minorities are throwing into question many of the assumptions which have governed political life for decades. Since the end of the Cold War, ethnocultural conflicts have become the most common source of political violence in the world, and they show no sign of abating. . . .

The Western political tradition has been surprisingly silent on these issues. Most organized political communities throughout recorded history have been multiethnic, a testament to the ubiquity of both conquest and long-distance trade in human affairs. Yet most Western political theorists have operated with an idealized model of the *polis* in which fellow citizens share a common descent, language, and culture. Even when the theorists themselves lived in polyglot empires that governed numerous ethnic and linguistic groups, they have often written as if the culturally homogeneous city-states of Ancient Greece provided the essential or standard model of a political community.

To achieve this ideal of a homogeneous polity, governments throughout history have pursued a variety of policies regarding cultural minorities. Some minorities were physically eliminated, either by mass expulsion (what we now call 'ethnic cleansing') or by genocide. Other minorities were coercively assimilated, forced to adopt the language, religion, and customs of the majority. In yet other cases, minorities were treated as resident aliens, subjected to physical segregation and economic discrimination, and denied political rights.

Various efforts have been made historically to protect cultural minorities, and to regulate the potential conflicts between majority and minority cultures. Early in this century, bilateral treaties regulated the treatment of fellow nationals in other countries. For example, Germany agreed to accord certain rights and privileges to ethnic Poles residing within its borders, so long as Poland provided reciprocal rights to ethnic Germans in Poland. This treaty system was extended, and given a more multilateral basis, under the League of Nations.

However, these treaties were inadequate. For one thing, a minority was only ensured protection from discrimination and oppression if there was a 'kin state' nearby which took an

interest in it. Moreover, the treaties were desta-
bilizing, because where such kin states did
exist, they often used treaty provisions as
grounds for invading or intervening in weaker
countries. Thus Nazi Germany justified its
invasion of Poland and Czechoslovakia on the
grounds that these countries were violating the
treaty rights of ethnic Germans on their soil.

After World War II, it was clear that a different approach to minority rights was needed.
Many liberals hoped that the new emphasis on
'human rights' would resolve minority conflicts. Rather than protecting vulnerable
groups directly, through special rights for the
members of designated groups, cultural
minorities would be protected indirectly, by
guaranteeing basic civil and political rights to
all individuals regardless of group membership. Basic human rights such as freedom of
speech, association, and conscience, while
attributed to individuals, are typically exercised in community with others, and so provide protection for group life. Where these
individual rights are firmly protected, liberals
assumed, no further rights needed to be attributed to the members of specific ethnic or
national minorities:

> [T]he general tendency of the postwar
> movements for the promotion of human
> rights has been to subsume the problem of
> national minorities under the broader
> problem of ensuring basic individual rights
> to all human beings, without reference to
> membership in ethnic groups. The leading
> assumption has been that members of
> national minorities do not need, are not
> entitled to, or cannot be granted rights of a
> special character. The doctrine of human
> rights has been put forward as a substitute
> for the concept of minority rights, with the
> strong implication that minorities whose
> members enjoy individual equality of treat-
> ment cannot legitimately demand facilities
> for the maintenance of their ethnic partic-
> ularism. (Claude 1955, 211)

Guided by this philosophy, the United Nations
deleted all references to the rights of ethnic
and national minorities in its Universal Declaration of Human Rights.

The shift from group-specific minority
rights to universal human rights was embraced
by many liberals, partly because it seemed a
natural extension of the way religious minorities were protected. In the sixteenth century,
European states were being torn apart by conflict between Catholics and Protestants over
which religion should rule the land. These
conflicts were finally resolved, not by granting
special rights to particular religious minorities,
but by separating church and state, and
entrenching each's individual freedom of religion. Religious minorities are protected indirectly, by guaranteeing individual freedom of
worship, so that people can freely associate
with other co-religionists, without fear of state
discrimination or disapproval.

Many postwar liberals have thought that
religious tolerance based on the separation of
church and state provides a model for dealing
with ethnocultural differences as well. On this
view, ethnic identity, like religion, is something
which people should be free to express in their
private life, but which is not the concern of the
state. The state does not oppose the freedom of
people to express their particular cultural
attachments, but nor does it nurture such
expression—rather, to adapt Nathan Glazer's
phrase, it responds with 'benign neglect'
(Glazer 1975: 25; 1983: 124). The members
of ethnic and national groups are protected
against discrimination and prejudice, and they
are free to try to maintain whatever part of
their ethnic heritage or identity they wish,
consistent with the rights of others. But their

efforts are purely private, and it is not the place of public agencies to attach legal identities or disabilities to cultural membership or ethnic identity. This separation of state and ethnicity precludes any legal or governmental recognition of ethnic groups, or any use of ethnic criteria in the distribution of rights, resources, and duties.

Many liberals, particularly on the left, have made an exception in the case of affirmative action for disadvantaged racial groups. But in a sense this is the exception that proves the rule. Affirmative action is generally defended as a temporary measure which is needed to move more rapidly towards a 'colour-blind' society. It is intended to remedy years of discrimination, and thereby move us closer to the sort of society that would have existed had we observed the separation of state and ethnicity from the beginning. Thus the UN Convention on Racial Discrimination endorses affirmative action programs only where they have this temporary and remedial character. Far from abandoning the ideal of the separation of state and ethnicity, affirmative action is one method of trying to achieve that ideal.

Some liberals, particularly on the right, think it is counterproductive to pursue a 'colour-blind' society through policies that 'count by race'. Affirmative action, they argue, exacerbates the very problem it was intended to solve, by making people more conscious of group differences, and more resentful of other groups. This dispute amongst liberals over the need for remedial affirmative action programs is a familiar one in many liberal democracies.

But what most postwar liberals on both the right and left continue to reject is the idea of *permanent* differentiation in the rights or status of the members of certain groups. In particular, they reject the claim that group-specific rights are needed to accommodate enduring cultural differences, rather than remedy his-torical discrimination. As we will see in subsequent chapters, postwar liberals around the world have repeatedly opposed the idea that specific ethnic or national groups should be given a permanent political identity or constitutional status.

However, it has become increasingly clear that minority rights cannot be subsumed under the category of human rights. Traditional human rights standards are simply unable to resolve some of the most important and controversial questions relating to cultural minorities: which languages should be recognized in the parliaments, bureaucracies, and courts? Should each ethnic or national group have publicly funded education in its mother tongue? Should internal boundaries (legislative districts, provinces, states) be drawn so that cultural minorities form a majority within a local region? Should governmental powers be devolved from the central level to more local or regional levels controlled by particular minorities, particularly on culturally sensitive issues of immigration, communication, and education? Should political offices be distributed in accordance with a principle of national or ethnic proportionality? Should the traditional homelands of indigenous peoples be reserved for their benefit, and so protected from encroachment by settlers and resource developers? What are the responsibilities of minorities to integrate? What degree of cultural integration can be required of immigrants and refugees before they acquire citizenship?

The problem is not that traditional human rights doctrines give us the wrong answer to these questions. It is rather that they often give no answer at all. The right to free speech does not tell us what an appropriate language policy is; the right to vote does not tell us how political boundaries should be drawn, or how powers should be distributed between levels of government; the right to mobility does not tell us what an appropriate immigration and naturalization policy is. These questions have been left to the usual process of majoritarian decision-making within each state. The result, I will argue, has been to render cultural minorities vulnerable to significant injustice at the hands of the majority, and to exacerbate ethnocultural conflict.

To resolve these questions fairly, we need to supplement traditional human rights principles with a theory of minority rights. The necessity for such a theory has become painfully clear in Eastern Europe and the former Soviet Union. Disputes over local autonomy, the drawing of boundaries, language rights, and naturalization policy have engulfed much of the region in violent conflict. There is little hope that stable peace will be restored, or that basic human rights will be respected, until these minority rights issues are resolved.

It is not surprising, therefore, that minority rights have returned to prominence in international relations. For example, the Conference on Security and Co-operation in Europe (CSCE) adopted a declaration on the Rights of National Minorities in 1991, and established a High Commissioner on National Minorities in 1993. The United Nations has been debating both a Declaration on the Rights of Persons Belonging to National or Ethnic, Religious and Linguistic Minorities (1993), and a Draft Universal Declaration on Indigenous Rights (1988). The Council of Europe adopted a declaration on minority language rights in 1992 (the European Charter for Regional or Minority Languages). Other examples could be given.

However, these declarations remain controversial. Some were adopted hastily, to help prevent the escalation of conflict in Eastern Europe. As a result, they are quite vague, and often seem motivated more by the need to appease belligerent minorities than by any

clear sense of what justice requires. Both the underlying justification for these rights, and their limits, remain unclear.

I believe it is legitimate, and indeed unavoidable, to supplement traditional human rights with minority rights. A comprehensive theory of justice in a multicultural state will include both universal rights, assigned to individuals regardless of group membership, and certain group-differentiated rights or 'special status' for minority cultures.

Recognizing minority rights has obvious dangers. The language of minority rights has been used and abused not only by the Nazis, but also by apologists for racial segregation and apartheid. It has also been used by intolerant and belligerent nationalists and fundamentalists throughout the world to justify the domination of people outside their group, and the suppression of dissenters within the group. A liberal theory of minority rights, therefore, must explain how minority rights coexist with human rights, and how minority rights are limited by principles of individual liberty, democracy, and social justice. . . .

Chapter 2

The Politics of Multiculturalism

. . .

Three Forms of Group-Differentiated Rights

Virtually all liberal democracies are either multinational or polyethnic, or both. The 'challenge of multiculturalism' is to accommodate these national and ethnic differences in a stable and morally defensible way (Gutmann 1993). In this section, I will discuss some of the most important ways in which democracies have responded to the demands of national minorities and ethnic groups.

In all liberal democracies, one of the major mechanisms for accommodating cultural differences is the protection of the civil and political rights of individuals. It is impossible to overstate the importance of freedom of association, religion, speech, mobility, and political organization for protecting group difference. These rights enable individuals to form and maintain the various groups and associations which constitute civil society, to adapt these groups to changing circumstances, and to promote their views and interests to the wider population. The protection afforded by these common rights of citizenship is sufficient for many of the legitimate forms of diversity in society.

Various critics of liberalism—including some Marxists, communitarians, and feminists—have argued that the liberal focus on individual rights reflects an atomistic, materialistic, instrumental, or conflictual view of human relationships. I believe that this criticism is profoundly mistaken, and that individual rights can be and typically are used to sustain a wide range of social relationships. Indeed, the most basic liberal right—freedom of conscience—is primarily valuable for the protection it gives to intrinsically social (and non-instrumental) activities.

However, it is increasingly accepted in many countries that some forms of cultural difference can only be accommodated through special legal or constitutional measures, above and beyond the common rights of citizenship. Some forms of group difference can only be accommodated if their members have certain group-specific rights—what Iris Young calls 'differentiated citizenship' (I. Young 1989: 258).

For example, a recent government publication in Canada noted that:

In the Canadian experience, it has not been enough to protect only universal individual rights. Here, the Constitution and ordinary laws also protect other rights accorded to individuals as members of certain communities. This accommodation of both types of rights makes our constitution unique and reflects the Canadian value of equality that accommodates difference. The fact that community rights exist alongside individual rights goes to the very heart of what Canada is all about. (Government of Canada 1991, 3)

It is quite misleading to say that Canada is unique in combining universal individual rights and group-specific 'community rights'. Such a combination exists in many other federal systems in Europe, Asia, and Africa. As I noted earlier, even the constitution of the United States, which is often seen as a paradigm of individualism, allows for various group-specific rights, including the special status of American Indians and Puerto Ricans.

It is these special group-specific measures for accommodating national and ethnic differences that I will focus on. There are at least three forms of group-specific rights: (1) self-government rights; (2) polyethnic rights; and (3) special representation rights. . . .

1. *Self-government rights.* In most multination states, the component nations are inclined to demand some form of political autonomy or territorial jurisdiction, so as to ensure the full and free development of their cultures and the best interests of their people. At the extreme, nations may wish to secede, if they think their self-determination is impossible within the larger state.

The right of national groups to self-determination is given (limited) recognition in international law. According to the United Nations' Charter, 'all peoples have the right to self-determination.' However, the UN has not defined 'peoples', and it has generally applied the principle of self-determination only to overseas colonies, not internal national minorities, even when the latter were subject to the same sort of colonization and conquest as the former. This limitation on self-determination to overseas colonies (known as the 'saltwater thesis') is widely seen as arbitrary, and many national minorities insist that they too are 'peoples' or 'nations', and, as such, have the right of self-determination. They demand certain powers of self-government which they say were not relinquished by their (often involuntary) incorporation into a larger state.

One mechanism for recognizing claims to self-government is federalism, which divides powers between the central government and regional subunits (provinces/states/cantons). Where national minorities are regionally concentrated, the boundaries of federal subunits can be drawn so that the national minority forms a majority in one of the subunits. Under these circumstances, federalism can provide extensive self-government for a national minority, guaranteeing its ability to make decisions in certain areas without being outvoted by the larger society.

For example, under the federal division of powers in Canada, the province of Quebec (which is 80 per cent francophone) has extensive jurisdiction over issues that are crucial to the survival of the French culture, including control over education, language, culture, as well as significant input into immigration policy. The other nine provinces also have these powers, but the major impetus behind the existing division of powers, and indeed behind the entire federal system, is the need to accommodate the Québécois. At the time of Confederation, most English Canadian leaders were in favour of a unitary state, like Britain, and agreed to a federal system primarily to accommodate French Canadians.

One difficulty in a federal system is maintaining the balance between centralization and decentralization. While most Quebecers want an even more decentralized division of powers, most English Canadians favour a stronger central government. One of the challenges facing Canada, therefore, is finding an acceptable form of 'asymmetrical federalism' which grants Quebec powers not given to other provinces. Other federal states face a similar problem.

Federalism is often used to accommodate national diversity, and so some commentators include the rights and powers attached to federal units amongst the 'collective rights' of national minorities (e.g., F. Morton 1985: 77; Van Dyke 1982: 24–31). Of course, many federal systems arose for reasons quite unrelated to cultural diversity. Federalism is often simply a form of administrative decentralization (as in Germany), or the result of historical accidents of colonization (as in Australia). There is no inherent connection between federalism and cultural diversity. But federalism is one common strategy of accommodating national minorities. It is not surprising that countries which are 'a federation of peoples' should also form a political federation.

In the United States, however, a deliberate decision was made not to use federalism to accommodate the self-government rights of national minorities. It would have been quite possible in the nineteenth century to create states dominated by the Navaho, for example, or by Chicanos, Puerto Ricans, and native Hawaiians. At the time these groups were incorporated into the United States, they formed majorities in their homelands. However, a deliberate decision was made not to accept any territory as a state unless these national groups were outnumbered. In some cases, this was achieved by drawing boundaries so that Indian tribes or Hispanic groups were outnumbered (Florida). In other cases, it was achieved by delaying statehood until anglophone settlers swamped the older inhabitants (e.g., Hawaii; the southwest). In cases where the national minority was not likely to be outnumbered, a new type of non-federal political unit was created, such as the 'commonwealth' of Puerto Rico or the 'protectorate' of Guam. As a result, none of the 50 states can be seen as ensuring self-government for a national minority, the way that Quebec ensures self-government for the Québécois. Self-government is instead achieved through political institutions located inside existing states (e.g., Indian reservations), or entirely outside the federal system (e.g., Puerto Rico, Guam). This has tended to make national minorities in the United States more vulnerable, since their self-government powers do not have the same constitutional protection as states' rights. On the other hand, it has provided greater flexibility in redefining those powers so as to suit the needs and interests of each minority. It is much easier to negotiate new self-government provisions for the Navaho or Puerto Ricans than to modify the powers of individual states.

Federalism can only serve as a mechanism for self-government if the national minority forms a majority in one of the federal subunits as the Québécois do in Quebec. This is not true of most indigenous peoples in North America, who are fewer in number and whose communities are often dispersed across state/provincial lines. Moreover, with few exceptions (such as the Navaho), no redrawing of the boundaries of these federal subunits would create a state, province, or territory with an indigenous majority. It would have been possible to create a state or province dominated by an Indian tribe in the nineteenth century, but, given the massive influx of settlers since then, it is now virtually inconceivable.

One exception concerns the Inuit in the north of Canada, who wish to divide the Northwest Territories into two, so that they will form the majority in the eastern half (to be called 'Nunavut'). This redrawing of federal boundaries is seen as essential to the implementation of the Inuit's right of self-government, and has recently been approved by the federal government.

For the other indigenous peoples in North America, however, self-government has been primarily tied to the system of reserved lands (known as tribal 'reservations' in the United States, and band 'reserves' in Canada). Substantial powers have been devolved from the federal government to the tribal/band councils which govern each reserve. Indian tribes/bands have been acquiring increasing control over health, education, family law, policing, criminal justice, and resource development. They are becoming, in effect, a third order of government, with a collection of powers that is carved out of both federal and state/provincial jurisdictions. However, the administrative difficulties are daunting. Indian tribes/bands differ enormously in the sorts of powers they desire. Moreover, they are territorially located within existing states/provinces, and must co-ordinate their self-government with state/provincial agencies. The exact scope and mechanisms of indigenous self-government in Canada and the United States therefore remain unclear.

Similar systems of self-government exist, or are being sought, by many other indigenous peoples. A recent international declaration regarding the rights of indigenous peoples emphasizes the importance of political self-government. In many parts of the world, however, the hope for political powers is almost utopian, and the more immediate goal is simply to secure the existing land base from further erosion by settlers and resource developers. Indeed, a recent study showed that the single largest cause of ethnic conflict in the world today is the struggle by indigenous peoples for the protection of their land rights.

Self-government claims, then, typically take the form of devolving political power to a political unit substantially controlled by the members of the national minority, and substantially corresponding to their historical homeland or territory. It is important to note that these claims are not seen as a temporary measure, nor as a remedy for a form of oppression that we might (and ought) someday to eliminate. On the contrary, these rights are often described as 'inherent', and so permanent (which is one reason why national minorities seek to have them entrenched in the constitution).

2. *Polyethnic rights.* As I noted earlier, immigrant groups in the last 30 years have successfully challenged the 'Anglo-conformity' model which assumed that they should abandon all aspects of their ethnic heritage and assimilate to existing cultural norms and customs. At first, this challenge simply took the form of demanding the right freely to express their particularity without fear of prejudice or discrimination in the mainstream society. It was the demand, as Walzer put it, that 'politics be separated from nationality—as it was already separated from religion' (Walzer 1982: 6–11).

But the demands of ethnic groups have expanded in important directions. It became clear that positive steps were required to root out discrimination and prejudice, particularly against visible minorities. For this reason, anti-racism policies are considered part of the 'multiculturalism' policy in Canada and Australia, as are changes to the education curriculum to recognize the history and contribution of minorities. However, these policies are primarily directed at ensuring the effective exercise of the common rights of citizenship, and so do not really qualify as group-differentiated citizenship rights.

Some ethnic groups and religious minorities have also demanded various forms of public funding of their cultural practices. This includes the funding of ethnic associations, magazines, and festivals. Given that most liberal states provide funding to the arts and museums, so as to preserve the richness and diversity of our cultural resources, funding for ethnic studies and ethnic associations can be seen as falling under this heading. Indeed, some people defend this funding simply as a way of ensuring that ethnic groups are not discriminated against in state funding of art and culture. Some people believe that public funding agencies have traditionally been biased in favour of European-derived forms of cultural expression, and programs targeted at ethnic groups remedy this bias. . . .

Perhaps the most controversial demand of ethnic groups is for exemptions from laws and regulations that disadvantage them, given their religious practices. For example, Jews and Muslims in Britain have sought exemption from Sunday closing or animal-slaughtering legislation; Sikh men in Canada have sought exemption from motorcycle helmet laws and from the official dress-codes of police forces, so that they can wear their turban; Orthodox Jews in the United States have sought the right to wear the yarmulka during military service; and Muslim girls in France have sought exemption from school dress-codes so that they can wear the *chador*.

These group-specific measures—which I call 'polyethnic rights'—are intended to help ethnic groups and religious minorities express their cultural particularity and pride without it hampering their success in the economic and political institutions of the dominant society. Like self-government rights, these polyethnic rights are not seen as temporary, because the cultural differences they protect are not something we seek to eliminate. . . .

3. *Special representation rights*. While the traditional concern of national minorities and ethnic groups has been with either self-government or polyethnic rights, there has been increasing interest by these groups, as well as other non-ethnic social groups, in the idea of special representation rights.

Throughout the Western democracies, there is increasing concern that the political process is 'unrepresentative', in the sense that it fails to reflect the diversity of the population. Legislatures in most of these countries are dominated by middle-class, able-bodied, white men. A more representative process, it is said, would include members of ethnic and racial minorities, women, the poor, the disabled, etc. The under-representation of historically disadvantaged groups is a general phenomenon. In the United States and Canada, women, racial minorities, and indigenous peoples all have under one-third of the seats they would have based on their demographic weight. People with disabilities and the economically disadvantaged are also significantly under-represented.

One way to reform the process is to make political parties more inclusive, by reducing the barriers which inhibit women, ethnic minorities, or the poor from becoming party candidates or party leaders; another way is to adopt some form of proportional representation, which has historically been associated with greater inclusiveness of candidates.

However, there is increasing interest in the idea that a certain number of seats in the legislature should be reserved for the members of disadvantaged or marginalized groups. During the debate in Canada over the Charlottetown Accord, for example, a number of recommendations were made for the guaranteed representation of women, ethnic minorities, official language minorities, and Aboriginals.

Group representation rights are often defended as a response to some systemic disadvantage or barrier in the political process which makes it impossible for the group's views and interests to be effectively represented. Insofar as these rights are seen as a response to oppression or systemic disadvantage, they are most plausibly seen as a temporary measure on the way to a society where the need for special representation no longer exists—a form of political 'affirmative action'. Society should seek to remove the oppression and disadvantage, thereby eliminating the need for these rights.

However, the issue of special representation rights for groups is complicated, because special representation is sometimes defended, not on grounds of oppression, but as a corollary of self-government. A minority's right to self-government would be severely weakened if some external body could unilaterally revise or revoke its powers, without consulting the minority or securing its consent. Hence it would seem to be a corollary of self-government that the national minority be guaranteed representation on any body which can interpret or modify its powers of self-government (e.g., the Supreme Court). Since the claims of self-government are seen as inherent and permanent, so too are the guarantees of representation which flow from it (unlike guarantees grounded on oppression).

This is just a brief sketch of three mechanisms used to accommodate cultural differences. . . . Virtually every modern democracy employs one or more of these mechanisms. Obviously, these three kinds of rights can overlap, in the sense that some groups can claim more than one kind of right. For example, indigenous groups may demand both special representation in the central government, in virtue of their disadvantaged position, and various powers of self-government, in virtue of their status as a 'people' or 'nation'. But these rights need not go together. An oppressed group, like the disabled, may seek special representation, but have no basis for claiming either self-government or polyethnic rights. Conversely, an economically successful immigrant group may seek polyethnic rights, but have no basis for claiming either special representation or self-government, etc. . . . .

Chapter 6

Justice and Minority Rights

. . .

1. The Equality Argument

Many defenders of group-specific rights for ethnic and national minorities insist that they are needed to ensure that all citizens are treated with genuine equality. On this view, 'the accommodation of differences is the essence of true equality,' and group-specific rights are needed to accommodate our differences. I think this argument is correct, within certain limits.

Proponents of 'benign neglect' will respond that individual rights already allow for the accommodation of differences, and that true equality requires equal rights for each individual regardless of race or ethnicity. As I noted, . . . this assumption that liberal equality precludes group-specific rights is relatively recent, and arose in part as an (over-)generalization of the racial desegregation movement in the United States. It has some superficial plausibility. In many cases, claims for group-specific rights are simply an attempt by one group to dominate and oppress another.

But some minority rights eliminate, rather than create, inequalities. Some groups are unfairly disadvantaged in the cultural marketplace, and political recognition and support rectify this disadvantage. I will start with the case of national minorities. The viability of their societal cultures may be undermined by economic and political decisions made by the majority. They could be outbid or outvoted on resources and policies that are crucial to the survival of their societal cultures. The members of majority cultures do not face this problem. Given the importance of cultural membership, this is a significant inequality which, if not addressed, becomes a serious injustice.

Group-differentiated rights—such as territorial autonomy, veto powers, guaranteed representation in central institutions, land claims, and language rights—can help rectify this disadvantage, by alleviating the vulnerability of minority cultures to majority decisions. These external protections ensure that members of the minority have the same opportunity to live and work in their own culture as members of the majority.

. . . [T]hese rights may impose restrictions on the members of the larger society, by making it more costly for them to move into the territory of the minority (e.g., longer residency requirements, fewer government services in their language), or by giving minority members priority in the use of certain land and resources (e.g., indigenous hunting and fishing rights). But the sacrifice required of nonmembers by the existence of these rights is far less than the sacrifice members would face in the absence of such rights.

Where these rights are recognized, members of the majority who choose to enter the minority's homeland may have to forgo certain benefits they are accustomed to. This is a burden. But without such rights, the members of many minority cultures face the loss of their culture, a loss which we cannot reasonably ask people to accept.

Any plausible theory of justice should recognize the fairness of these external protections for national minorities. They are clearly justified, I believe, within a liberal egalitarian theory, such as Rawls's and Dworkin's, which emphasizes the importance of rectifying unchosen inequalities. Indeed inequalities in cultural membership are just the sort which Rawls says we should be concerned about, since their effects are 'profound and pervasive and present from birth' (Rawls 1971: 96; cf. Dworkin 1981).

This equality-based argument will only endorse special rights for national minorities if there actually is a disadvantage with respect to cultural membership, and if the rights actually serve to rectify the disadvantage. Hence the legitimate scope of these rights will vary with the circumstances. In North America, indigenous groups are more vulnerable to majority decisions than the Québécois or Puerto Ricans, and so their external protections will be more extensive. For example, restrictions on the sale of land which are necessary in the context of indigenous peoples are not necessary, and hence not justified, in the case of Quebec or Puerto Rico.

At some point, demands for increased powers or resources will not be necessary to ensure the same opportunity to live and work in one's culture. Instead, they will simply be attempts to gain benefits denied to others, to have more resources to pursue one's way of life than others have. This was clearly the case with apartheid, where whites constituting under 20 per cent of the population controlled 87 per cent of the land mass of the country, and monopolized all the important levers of state power.

One could imagine a point where the amount of land reserved for indigenous peoples would not be necessary to provide reasonable external protections, but rather would simply provide unequal opportunities to them. Justice would then require that the holdings of indigenous peoples be subject to the same redistributive taxation as the wealth of other advantaged groups, so as to assist the less well-off in society. In the real world, of course, most indigenous peoples are struggling to maintain the bare minimum of land needed to sustain the viability of their communities. But it is possible that their land holdings could exceed what justice allows.

The legitimacy of certain measures may also depend on their timing. For example, many people have suggested that a new South African constitution should grant a veto power over certain important decisions to some or all of the major national groups. This sort of veto power is a familiar feature of various 'consociational democracies' in Europe, and, as I discuss in the next chapter, under certain circumstances it can promote justice. But it would probably be unjust to give privileged groups a veto power before there has been a dramatic redistribution of wealth and opportunities (Adam 1979: 295). A veto power can promote justice if it helps protect a minority from unjust policies that favour the majority; but it is an obstacle to justice if it allows a privileged group the leverage to maintain its unjust advantages.

So the ideal of 'benign neglect' is not in fact benign. It ignores the fact that the members of a national minority face a disadvantage which the members of the majority do not face. In any event, the idea that the government could be neutral with respect to ethnic and national groups is patently false. As I noted in chapter 5, one of the most important determinants of whether a culture survives is whether its language is the language of government—i.e., the language of public schooling, courts, legislatures, welfare agencies, health services, etc. When the government decides the language of public schooling, it is providing what is probably the most important form of support needed by societal cultures, since it guarantees the passing on of the language and its associated traditions and conventions to the next generation. Refusing to provide public schooling in a minority language, by contrast, is almost inevitably condemning that language to ever-increasing marginalization.

The government therefore cannot avoid deciding which societal cultures will be supported. And if it supports the majority culture, by using the majority's language in schools and public agencies, it cannot refuse official recognition to minority languages on the ground that this violates 'the separation of state and ethnicity'. This shows that the analogy between religion and culture is mistaken. As I noted earlier, many liberals say that just as the state should not recognize, endorse, or support any particular church, so it should not recognize, endorse, or support any particular cultural group or identity. . . . But the analogy does not work. It is quite possible for a state not to have an established church. But the state cannot help but give at least partial establishment to a culture when it decides which language is to be used in public schooling, or in the provision of state services. The state can (and should) replace religious oaths in courts with secular oaths, but it cannot replace the use of English in courts with no language. . . .

One could argue that decisions about the language of schooling and public services should be determined, not by officially recognizing the existence of various groups, but simply by allowing each political subunit to make its own language policy on a democratic basis. If a national minority forms a majority in the relevant unit, they can decide to have their mother tongue adopted as an official language in that unit. But this is because they are a local majority, not because the state has officially recognized them as a 'nation'.

This is sometimes said to be the American approach to language rights, since there is no constitutional definition of language rights in the United States. But in fact the American government has historically tried to make sure that such 'local' decisions are always made by political units that have an anglophone majority. As discussed in chapter 2, decisions about state borders, or about when to admit territories as states, have been explicitly made with the aim of ensuring that there will be an anglophone majority. States in the American southwest and Hawaii were only offered statehood when the national minorities residing in those areas were outnumbered by settlers and immigrants. And some people oppose offering statehood to Puerto Rico precisely on the grounds that it will never have an anglophone majority (Rubinstein 1993; Glazer 1983: 280). . . .

The whole idea of 'benign neglect' is incoherent, and reflects a shallow understanding of the relationship between states and nations. In the areas of official languages, political boundaries, and the division of powers, there is no way to avoid supporting this or that societal culture, or deciding which groups will form a majority in political units that control culture-affecting decisions regarding language, education, and immigration.

So the real question is, what is a fair way to recognize languages, draw boundaries, and distribute powers? And the answer, I think, is that we should aim at ensuring that all national groups have the opportunity to maintain themselves as a distinct culture, if they so choose. This ensures that the good of cultural membership is equally protected for the members of all national groups. In a democratic society, the majority nation will always have its language and societal culture supported, and will have the legislative power to protect its interests in culture-affecting decisions. The question is whether fairness requires that the same benefits and opportunities should be given to national minorities. The answer, I think, is clearly yes.

Hence group-differentiated self-government rights compensate for unequal circumstances which put the members of minority cultures at a systemic disadvantage in the cultural marketplace, regardless of their personal choices in life. This is one of many areas in which true equality requires not identical treatment, but rather differential treatment in order to accommodate differential needs.

This does not mean that we should entirely reject the idea of the cultural marketplace. Once the societal cultures of national groups are protected, through language rights and territorial autonomy, then the cultural marketplace does have an important role to play in determining the character of the culture. Decisions about which particular aspects of one's culture are worth maintaining and developing should be left to the choices of individual members. For the state to intervene at this point to support particular options or customs within the culture, while penalizing or discouraging others, would run the risk of unfairly subsidizing some people's choices (Kymlicka 1989). But that is not the aim or effect of many rights for national minorities, which are instead concerned with external protections. . . .

Let me now turn to polyethnic rights for ethnic groups. I believe there is an equality-based argument for these rights as well, which also invokes the impossibility of separating state from ethnicity, but in a different way. I argued . . . that the context of choice for immi-

grants, unlike national minorities, primarily involves equal access to the mainstream culture(s). Having uprooted themselves from their old culture, they are expected to become members of the national societies which already exist in their new country. Hence promoting the good of cultural membership for immigrants is primarily a matter of enabling integration, by providing language training and fighting patterns of discrimination and prejudice. Generally speaking, this is more a matter of rigorously enforcing the common rights of citizenship than providing group-differentiated rights. Insofar as common rights of citizenship in fact create equal access to mainstream culture, then equality with respect to cultural membership is achieved.

But even here equality does justify some group-specific rights. Consider the case of public holidays. Some people object to legislation that exempts Jews and Muslims from Sunday closing legislation, on the ground that this violates the separation of state and ethnicity. But almost any decision on public holidays will do so. In the major immigration countries, public holidays currently reflect the needs of Christians. Hence government offices are closed on Sunday, and on the major religious holidays (Easter, Christmas). This need not be seen as a deliberate decision to promote Christianity and discriminate against other faiths (although this was undoubtedly part of the original motivation). Decisions about government holidays were made when there was far less religious diversity, and people just took it for granted that the government workweek should accommodate Christian beliefs about days of rest and religious celebration.

But these decisions can be a significant disadvantage to the members of other religious faiths. And having established a workweek that favours Christians, one can hardly object to exemptions for Muslims or Jews on the ground that they violate the separation of state and ethnicity. These groups are simply asking that their religious needs be taken into consideration in the same way that the needs of Christians have always been taken into account. Public holidays are another significant embarrassment for the 'benign neglect' view, and it is interesting to note how rarely they are discussed in contemporary liberal theory.

Similar issues arise regarding government uniforms. Some people object to the idea that Sikhs or Orthodox Jews should be exempted from requirements regarding headgear in the police or military. But here again it is important to recognize how the existing rules about government uniforms have been adopted to suit Christians. For example, existing dress-codes do not prohibit the wearing of wedding rings, which are an important religious symbol for many Christians (and Jews). And it is virtually inconceivable that designers of government dress-codes would have ever considered designing a uniform that prevented people from wearing wedding rings, unless this was strictly necessary for the job. Again, this should not be seen as a deliberate attempt to promote Christianity. It simply would have been taken for granted that uniforms should not unnecessarily conflict with Christian religious beliefs. Having adopted dress-codes that meet Christian needs, one can hardly object to exemptions for Sikhs and Orthodox Jews on the ground that they violate 'benign neglect'.

One can multiply the examples. For example, many state symbols such as flags, anthems, and mottoes reflect a particular ethnic or religious background ('In God We Trust'). The demand by ethnic groups for some symbolic affirmation of the value of polyethnicity (e.g., in government declarations and documents) is simply a demand that their identity be given the same recognition as the original Anglo-Saxon settlers.

It may be possible to avoid some of these issues by redesigning public holidays, uniforms, and state symbols. It is relatively easy to replace religious oaths with secular ones, and so we should. It would be more difficult, but perhaps not impossible, to replace existing public holidays and workweeks with more 'neutral' schedules for schools and government offices.

But there is no way to have a complete 'separation of state and ethnicity'. In various ways, the ideal of 'benign neglect' is a myth. Government decisions on languages, internal boundaries, public holidays, and state symbols unavoidably involve recognizing, accommodating, and supporting the needs and identities of particular ethnic and national groups. Nor is there any reason to regret this fact. There is no reason to regret the existence of official languages and public holidays, and no one gains by creating unnecessary conflicts between government regulations and religious beliefs. The only question is how to ensure that these unavoidable forms of support for particular ethnic and national groups are provided fairly—that is, how to ensure that they do not privilege some groups and disadvantage others. Insofar as existing policies support the language, culture, and identity of dominant nations and ethnic groups, there is an argument of equality for ensuring that some attempts are made to provide similar support for minority groups, through self-government and polyethnic rights.

2. The Role of Historical Agreements

A second argument in defence of group-differentiated rights for national minorities is that they are the result of historical agreements, such as the treaty rights of indigenous peoples, or the agreement by which two or more peoples agreed to federate.

There are a variety of such agreements in Western democracies, although their provisions have often been ignored or repudiated. For example, the American government has unilaterally abrogated certain treaties with Indian tribes, and the Canadian government proposed in 1969 to extinguish all of its Indian treaties. The language rights guaranteed to Chicanos in the American southwest under the 1848 Treaty of Guadalupe Hidalgo were rescinded by the anglophone settlers as soon as they formed a majority. The language and land rights guaranteed to the Métis under the Manitoba Act of 1870 suffered the same fate in Canada. Yet many treaties and historical agreements between national groups continue to be recognized, and some have considerable legal force. For example, the 1840 Treaty of Waitangi signed by Maori chiefs and British colonists in New Zealand, declared a 'simple nullity' in 1877, has re-emerged as a central legal and political document (Sharp 1990).

The importance of honouring historical agreements is emphasized by proponents of group-differentiated rights, but has had little success convincing opponents. Those people who think that group-differentiated rights are unfair have not been appeased by pointing to agreements that were made by previous generations in different circumstances, often undemocratically and in conditions of substantial inequality in bargaining power. Surely some historical agreements are out of date, while others are patently unfair, signed under duress or ignorance. Why should not governments do what principles of equality require now, rather than what outdated and often unprincipled agreements require?

One answer is to reconsider an underlying assumption of the equality argument. The equality argument assumes that the state must treat its citizens with equal respect. But there is the prior question of determining which citizens should be governed by which states. For example, how did the American government acquire the legitimate authority to govern Puerto Rico or the Navaho? And how did the Canadian government acquire legitimate authority over the Québécois and the Métis? . . .

This historical argument may justify the same rights as the equality argument. Many of the group-differentiated rights which are the result of historical agreements can be seen as providing the sort of protection required by the equality argument. For example, the right to local autonomy for Indian tribes/bands could be justified on the equality argument, if it helps the larger state show equal concern for the members of Indian communities. Autonomy is also justified on the historical argument, insofar as Indian peoples never gave the federal government jurisdiction over certain issues.

Indeed, it is likely that the equality and historical arguments will yield similar policies. If local autonomy is required to ensure that members of a minority are not disadvantaged, then it is likely that the minority would have demanded autonomy as part of the terms of federation (had the negotiations been fair).

The negotiations between English and French regarding the terms of federation in Canada provide a clear example of this. The Québécois realized that if they agreed to enter the Canadian state in 1867, they would become a permanent minority in the country, and so could be outvoted on decisions made at the federal level. They therefore faced the question whether they should remain outside Confederation, maintaining their status as a separate colony within the British Empire, and hoping one day to become a separate country with a francophone majority.

Québécois leaders agreed to join Canada, even though they would be a minority in the federal parliament. But in return they insisted that jurisdiction over language and education be guaranteed to the provinces, not the federal government. This was 'the non-negotiable condition in return for which they were prepared to concede the principle of representation by population' in the new parliament, a principle that 'would institutionalize their minority position' within the new country (J. Smith 1993: 75). In deciding whether to accept the terms of federation, therefore, Québécois leaders were explicitly concerned about equality—that is, how to ensure that they would not be disadvantaged in the new country. Since they had considerable bargaining power in the negotiations, they were able to ensure their equality in the agreement, through guarantees of language rights and provincial autonomy.

While the equality and historical arguments often lead to the same result, they are nonetheless quite distinct. On the historical argument, the question is not how should the state treat 'its' minorities, but rather what are the terms under which two or more peoples decided to become partners? The question is not how should the state act fairly in governing its minorities, but what are the limits to the state's right to govern them? . . .

One difficulty with historical agreements is that they are often hard to interpret. For example, the Canadian government claims Quebec's 'right to be different' was implicitly recognized in the original Confederation agreement (Government of Canada 1991: p. vi). But others deny this, and insist that Confederation was a union of provinces, not a compact between two cultures. Similar disputes arise over the interpretation of some Indian treaties. Moreover, some Indian tribes did not sign treaties, or signed them under duress. It seems arbitrary and unfair that some groups signed historical agreements while others, through no fault of their own, did not.

Where historical agreements are absent or disputed, groups are likely to appeal to the equality argument. Indian tribes/bands which have clear treaty rights often rest their claim for group-differentiated status on historical agreement; groups who did not sign treaties are more likely to appeal to the equality argument. It is often quite arbitrary whether a particular group happened to sign a particular agreement. However, the equality argument can help those groups which, for whatever reason, lack historical rights.

. . . Since historical agreements must always be interpreted, and inevitably need to be updated and revised, we must be able to ground the historical agreements in a deeper theory of justice. The historical and equality arguments must work together.

3. The Value of Cultural Diversity

A third defence of group-differentiated rights for national minorities appeals to the value of cultural diversity. As I have discussed, liberals extol the virtue of having a diversity of lifestyles within a culture, so presumably they also endorse the additional diversity which comes from having two or more cultures in the same country. Surely intercultural diversity contributes to the richness of people's lives, as well as intra-cultural diversity (Schwartz 1986, chap. 1).

This argument is attractive to many people because it avoids relying solely on the interests of group members, and instead focuses on how the larger society also benefits from group-differentiated rights. As Richard Falk puts it, 'societal diversity enhances the quality of life, by enriching our experience, expanding cultural resources.' Hence protecting minority cultures 'is increasingly recognized to be an expression of overall enlightened self-interest' (Falk 1988: 23). Whereas the first two arguments appeal to the *obligations* of the majority, this third argument appeals to the *interests* of the majority, and defends rights in terms of self-interest, not justice.

Cultural diversity is said to be valuable, both in the quasi-aesthetic sense that it creates a more interesting world, and because other cultures contain alternative models of social organization that may be useful in adapting to new circumstances. This latter point is often made with respect to indigenous peoples, whose traditional lifestyles provide a model of a sustainable relationship to the environment. As Western attitudes towards nature are increasingly recognized to be unsustainable and self-destructive, indigenous peoples 'may provide models, inspiration, guidance in the essential work of world order redesign' (Falk 1988, 23; cf. Clay 1989, 233; O'Brien 1987, 358).

There is some truth in this argument about the value of cultural diversity. Nonetheless, I think it is a mistake to put much weight on it as a defence of national rights. First, one of the basic reasons for valuing intra-cultural diversity has less application to intercultural diversity. The value of diversity within a culture is that it creates more options for each individual, and expands her range of choices. But protecting national minorities does not expand the range of choices open to members of the majority in the same way. . . . [C]hoosing to leave one's culture is qualitatively different from choosing to move around within one's culture. The former is a difficult and painful prospect for most people, and very few people in the mainstream choose to assimilate into a minority culture. Indeed, measures to protect national minorities may actually reduce diversity within the majority culture, compared with a situation where minorities, unable to maintain their own societal culture, are forced to integrate and add their distinc-

tive contribution to the diversity of the mainstream culture. Having two or more cultures within a state does expand choices for each individual, but only to a limited degree, and it would be implausible to make this the primary justification for minority rights.

There are other aesthetic and educational benefits from cultural diversity, apart from the value of expanding individual choice. But it is not clear that any of these values by themselves can justify minority rights. One problem is that the benefits of diversity to the majority are spread thinly and widely, whereas the costs for particular members of the majority are sometimes quite high. Everyone may benefit, in a diffuse way, from having flourishing minority cultures in Quebec and Puerto Rico. But some members of the majority culture are asked to pay a significant price so that others can gain this diffuse benefit. For example, unilingual anglophones residing in Quebec or Puerto Rico are unlikely to get government employment or publicly funded education in English—benefits which they would take for granted elsewhere. Similarly, non-Indians residing on Indian lands may be discriminated against in terms of their access to natural resources, or their right to vote in local elections. It is not clear that the diffuse benefits of diversity for society as a whole justify imposing these sorts of sacrifices on particular people. It seems to me that these sacrifices are only consistent with justice if they are needed, not to promote benefits to the members of the majority, but to prevent even greater sacrifices to the members of the national minority.

Moreover, there are many ways of promoting diversity, and it seems likely that protecting national minorities involves more cost to the majority than other possible ways. For example, a society could arguably gain more diversity at less cost by increasing immigration from a variety of countries than by protecting national minorities. The diversity argument cannot explain why we have an obligation to sustain the particular sort of diversity created by the presence of a viable, self-governing national minority.

There is one further problem with the diversity argument. Let us say that the aesthetic or educational value of diversity does justify imposing certain costs on people in the majority culture. Why then does the value of diversity not also justify imposing a duty on the members of the minority to maintain their traditional culture? If the benefits of cultural diversity to the larger society can justify restricting individual liberties or opportunities, why does it matter whether these restrictions are imposed on people inside or outside the group? I noted earlier that a liberal theory of minority rights can accept external protections, but not internal restrictions. It is difficult to see how the diversity argument can make this distinction. Because it appeals to the interests of the larger society, it cannot explain why minorities should be able to decide for themselves whether or how to maintain their culture.

So it seems to me that the diversity argument is insufficient, by itself, to justify the rights of national minorities. Protecting national minorities does provide benefits to the majority, and these are worth pointing out. But these diffuse benefits are better seen as a desirable by-product of national rights, rather than their primary justification. To date, most majority cultures have not seen it in their 'enlightened self-interest' to maintain minority cultures. No doubt this is due in part to ethnocentric prejudice, but we must recognize the powerful interests that majority nations often have in rejecting self-government rights for national minorities—e.g., increased access to the minority's land and resources, increased

individual mobility, political stability, etc. It is unlikely that majorities will accept national rights solely on the basis of self-interest, without some belief that they have an obligation of justice to accept them. Conversely, it is unlikely that majorities will accept their obligations of justice towards national minorities without a belief that they gain something in the process. The diversity argument works best, therefore, when it is combined with arguments of justice.

The diversity argument is more plausible as a defence of polyethnic rights for ethnic groups. Unlike national self-government, these rights do contribute directly to diversity within the majority culture. Moreover, they do not involve the same sort of restrictions on the mobility or economic opportunities of the majority. Indeed, certain polyethnic policies can be seen as natural extensions of state policies regarding the funding of the arts, museums, educational television, etc. Yet here again the problem arises that there are many ways of promoting diversity. Teaching children to be bilingual promotes diversity, but this cannot explain why we should teach immigrant languages in particular. Hence the diversity argument supplements, but cannot replace, justice arguments based on equality or historical agreement. . . .

5. Conclusion

In the last two chapters, I have tried to show that liberals can and should accept a wide range of group-differentiated rights for national minorities and ethnic groups, without sacrificing their core commitments to individual freedom and social equality.

. It may be useful briefly to summarize my argument. I have tried to show how freedom of choice is dependent on social practices, cultural meanings, and a shared language.

Our capacity to form and revise a conception of the good is intimately tied to our membership in a societal culture, since the context of individual choice is the range of options passed down to us by our culture. Deciding how to lead our lives is, in the first instance, a matter of exploring the possibilities made available by our culture.

However, minority cultures in multination states may need protection from the economic or political decisions of the majority culture if they are to provide this context for their members. For example, they may need self-governing powers or veto rights over certain decisions regarding language and culture, and may need to limit the mobility of migrants or immigrants into their homelands.

While these group-differentiated rights for national minorities may seem discriminatory at first glance, since they allocate individual rights and political powers differentially on the basis of group membership, they are in fact consistent with liberal principles of equality. They are indeed required by the view, defended by Rawls and Dworkin, that justice requires removing or compensating for undeserved or 'morally arbitrary' disadvantages, particularly if these are 'profound and pervasive and present from birth' (Rawls 1971, 96). Were it not for these group-differentiated rights, the members of minority cultures would not have the same ability to live and work in their own language and culture that the members of majority cultures take for granted. This, I argued, can be seen as just as profound and morally arbitrary a disadvantage as the inequalities in race and class that liberals more standardly worry about.

This equality-based argument for group-differentiated rights for national minorities is further strengthened by appeals to historical agreements and the value of cultural diversity. And it is confirmed by the way that liberals implicitly invoke cultural membership to defend existing state borders and restrictions on citizenship. I have also argued that poly-ethnic rights for ethnic groups can be justified in terms of promoting equality and cultural diversity within the mainstream culture.

These claims are by no means uncontroversial, and there are many places where they could be challenged. One could deny that cultural meanings are dependent on a societal culture, or that individuals are closely tied to their own particular societal culture. One could also deny that minority cultures are vulnerable to the decisions of the larger society; or that this vulnerability constitutes an injustice; or that historical agreements have any moral weight; or that cultural diversity is worth promoting.

Yet I think each of these claims is plausible. Anyone who disputes them would be required to provide some alternative account of what makes meaningful choices available to people, or what justice requires in terms of language rights, public holidays, political boundaries, and the division of powers. Moreover, one would also have to offer an alternative account of the justification for restricting citizenship to the members of a particular group, rather than making it available to anyone who desires it. It is not enough to simply assert that a liberal state should respond to ethnic and national differences with benign neglect. That is an incoherent position that avoids addressing the inevitable connections between state and culture.

The idea that group-differentiated rights for national and ethnic groups can and should be accepted by liberals is hardly a radical suggestion. In fact, many multination liberal democracies already accept such an obligation, and provide public schooling and government services in the language of national minorities. Many have also adopted some form of federalism, so that national minorities will form a majority in one of the federal units (states, provinces, or cantons). And many polyethnic liberal states have adopted various forms of polyethnic policies and group-specific rights or exemptions for immigrant groups. Like Jay Sigler, I believe that providing a liberal defence of minority rights 'does not create a mandate for vast change. It merely ratifies and explains changes that have taken place in the absence of theory' (Sigler 1983: 196).

Selected Bibliography

Claude, Inis (1955), *National Minorities: An International Problem* (Cambridge, MA: Harvard University Press).

Clay, Jason (1989), 'Epilogue: The Ethnic Future of Nations,' *Third World Quarterly* 11/4: 223–33.

Dworkin, Ronald (1981), 'What Is Equality? Part II: Equality of Resources,' *Philosophy and Public Affairs* 10/4: 283–345.

Falk, Richard (1988), 'The Rights of Peoples (in Particular Indigenous Peoples),' in James Crawford, ed., *The Rights of Peoples* (Oxford: Oxford University Press), 17–37.

Glazer, Nathan (1975), *Affirmative Discrimination: Ethnic Inequality and Public Policy* (New York: Basic Books).

——— (1983), *Ethnic Dilemmas: 1964–1982* (Cambridge, MA: Harvard University Press).

Government of Canada (1991), *Shaping Canada's Future Together: Proposals* (Ottawa: Supply and Services).

Gutmann, Amy (1993), 'The Challenge of Multiculturalism to Political Ethics,' *Philosophy and Public Affairs* 22/3: 171–206.

Kymlicka, Will (1989), 'Liberal Individualism and Liberal Neutrality,' *Ethics* 99/4: 883–905.

Morton, F.L. (1985), 'Group Rights versus Individual Rights in the Charter: The Special Cases of Natives and the Québécois,' in N. Nevitte and A. Kornberg, eds, *Minorities and the Canadian State* (Oakville: Mosaic Press), 71–85.

O'Brien, Sharon (1987), 'Cultural Rights in the United States: A Conflict of Values,' *Law and Inequality Journal* 5: 267–358.

Rawls, John (1971), *A Theory of Justice* (London: Oxford University Press).

Rubinstein, Alvin (1993), 'Is Statehood for Puerto Rico in the National Interest?' *In Depth: A Journal for Values and Public Policy*, Spring, 87–99.

Schwartz, Brian (1986), *First Principles, Second Thoughts: Aboriginal Peoples, Constitutional Reform and Canadian Statecraft* (Montreal: Institute for Research on Public Policy).

Sharp, Andrew (1990), *Justice and the Maori: Maori Claims in New Zealand Political Argument in the 1980s* (Auckland: Oxford University Press).

Sigler, Jay (1983), *Minority Rights: A Comparative Analysis* (Westport, CT: Greenwood).

Smith, Jennifer (1993), 'Canadian Confederation and the Influence of American Federalism,' in Marian McKenna, ed., *The Canadian and American Constitutions in Comparative Perspective* (Calgary: University of Calgary Press), 65–85.

Van Dyke, Vernon (1982), 'Collective Entities and Moral Rights: Problems in Liberal-Democratic Thought,' *Journal of Politics* 44: 21–40.

Walzer, Michael (1982), 'Pluralism in Political Perspective,' in *The Politics of Ethnicity*, edited by M. Walzer (Cambridge, MA: Harvard University Press), 1–28.

Young, Iris Marion (1989), 'Polity and Group Difference: A Critique of the Ideal of Universal Citizenship,' *Ethics* 99/2: 250–74.

Study Questions for *Multicultural Citizenship*

1. Why is the subject of cultural diversity important, according to Kymlicka? What social and political issues surround debates about cultural diversity?
2. What approaches and policies have governments historically used to accommodate cultural diversity? What questions concerning cultural minorities are left unresolved by traditional human rights doctrines?
3. What three forms of group-specific rights does Kymlicka discuss? Provide examples of each type of group-specific right.
4. Kymlicka notes that federalist policies can help national minorities retain the right of self-governance. How does Kymlicka define federalism? What are some possible difficulties with federalist policies?
5. Describe the equality argument for minority rights. How does Kymlicka respond to proponents of 'benign neglect', who think political equality requires equal rights for all people regardless of race or ethnicity?
6. What role do historical agreements play in Kymlicka's defence of group-specific rights? Why is an appeal to the value of cultural diversity insufficient as a defence of minority rights?

Recommended Readings

Banting, Keith, and Will Kymlicka, eds, *Multiculturalism and the Welfare State: Recognition and Redistribution in Contemporary Democracies* (Oxford University Press, 2006).

Benhabib, Seyla, *Claims of Culture: Equality and Diversity in the Global Era* (Princeton University Press, 2002).

Barry, Brian, *Culture and Equality: An Egalitarian Critique of Multiculturalism* (Harvard University Press, 2001).

Gracia, Jorge, *Surviving Race, Ethnicity and Nationality* (Roman and Littlefield, 2005).

Kymlicka, Will, *Politics in the Vernacular: Nationalism, Multiculturalism and Citizenship* (Oxford University Press, 2001).

Parekh, Bhikhu, *Rethinking Multiculturalism: Cultural Diversity and Political Theory*, 2nd edn (Harvard University Press, 2006).

Phillips, Anne, *Multiculturalism without Culture* (Princeton University Press, 2007).

Young, Iris Marion, *Inclusion and Democracy* (Oxford University Press, 2000).

Credits